THE STRUGGLE FOR

Sovereignty

Seventeenth-Century
English Political Tracts

VOLUME I

Edited and with an Introduction by
Joyce Lee Malcolm

LIBERTY FUND
Indianapolis

Library of Congress Cataloging-in-Publication Data
The struggle for sovereignty: seventeenth-century English political tracts/
edited and with an introduction by Joyce Lee Malcolm.

    p.   cm.

    Includes bibliographical references and index.

    ISBN 0-86597-187-0 (2-vol. set: hardcover).—ISBN 0-86597-189-7 (2-vol. set: pbk.).—ISBN 0-86597-152-8 (vol. 1: hardcover).—ISBN 0-86597-153-6 (vol. 1: pbk.).—ISBN 0-86597-186-2 (vol. 2: hardcover).—ISBN 0-86597-188-9 (vol. 2: pbk.).

    1. Great Britain—Politics and government—1603–1714. 2. Political science—Great Britain—History—17th century. 3. Civil rights—Great Britain—History—17th century. 1. Malcolm, Joyce Lee.

JN191.S77   1999
323.5′0941′09032—DC21   97-28248

99 00 01 02 03 C 5 4 3 2 1

99 00 01 02 03 P 5 4 3 2 1

Liberty Fund, Inc.
8335 Allison Pointe Trail, Suite 300
Indianapolis, Indiana 46250-1684

TO *Geoffrey Elton* AND *John Kenyon*

Contents

Battle Joined 1640–1648

Uncharted Waters

Law and Conscience During the Confusions and Revolutions of Government

The "After Game"

VOLUME 2

Preface

May you live in interesting times, an old curse goes. The seventeenth century in England was nothing if not an interesting time. But unlike most turbulent centuries, it was no dark age. Quite the contrary, it was an era of great intellectual achievement. This was especially true in the realm of political thought, for at the core of England's traumatic upheavals lay a fundamental intellectual controversy over the source and nature of political sovereignty. It was an intricate subject of the utmost importance that touched virtually every aspect of the relationship between the individual and the state. The source of sovereignty was no simple matter in a kingdom that boasted it possessed an "absolute" monarch presiding over a limited monarchy—a mixed government nicely balanced between power and liberty. Contradictory political and religious assumptions undergirded the English constitution. Most of the time Englishmen juggled these underlying inconsistent beliefs with remarkable equanimity. Indeed, their political system was capable of great flexibility. But flexibility and accommodation vanished when exalted pretensions for royal power clashed with the jealously guarded rights and privileges of the Parliament and with claims for the supremacy of the law. Upon the outcome of this confrontation over sovereignty would hang the form of English government and the rights of its people.

Happily the debate over sovereignty took place in print as scholars, statesmen, lawyers, clergymen, government propagandists, and other concerned individuals snatched their pens, racked their brains, and wrote. The preferred form was the essay published as a pamphlet or tract—a format that ideally suited the urgency of the controversy. Tracts could be quickly composed and speedily printed. Thousands appeared. Often a provocative tract would inspire several published replies, followed by the original author's response. Issues and arguments evolved in counterpoint with political events, sometimes provoking them, sometimes responding, sometimes justifying, sometimes—as in the case of Charles I's famous "Answer to the Nineteen Propositions"—becoming a part of the shifting situation. The result was a literature unprecedented in volume and of immense influence upon English and American constitutional thought and practice.

Many of the most valuable and influential of these tracts have long been out of print. The aim of *The Struggle for Sovereignty* is to publish a selection of the best and most important examples of this rich political literature. The hope is that bringing these essays to a larger audience will broaden general knowledge of seventeenth-century political thought. Certainly these tracts illustrate the debt subsequent generations owe to the political writers of that era. They also provide a more reliable context for an assessment of the thought of Locke, Milton, Hobbes, and Filmer. The tracts in these volumes span the entire century and set out the key elements of the constitutional debate as it unfolded. Volume 1 begins just prior to the reign of James I and concludes at the eve of the restoration of monarchy in 1660. Volume 2 resumes with the restoration of the monarchy and concludes with issues provoked by the Glorious Revolution. Within each volume tracts have been arranged in chronological order and divided into broad, thematic groups.

Compiling this collection has been a daunting task, and a word is in order about the criteria that governed the choice of tracts. Rather than presenting a sample of eloquent political writing, I focused on the issues under discussion. Therefore my first priority has been to select those tracts that not only best present the arguments on a subject but also do so cogently and concisely. For example, while Henry

Parker wrote other excellent and influential essays, his "Case of Ship-mony" was selected because it best illustrates the grave constitutional consequences that many of his contemporaries saw in the imposition of what they regarded as an illegal tax. For the same reason I included tracts that present a range of viewpoints. Here I am only too aware of a major omission—the works of the Levellers. This is not because the Levellers' views were unimportant but because limitations of space persuaded me to exclude pieces already available in print. Since Leveller works are especially well preserved, it seemed preferable to rescue important works that are not. Hence I have reprinted key tracts not readily available or at least not available in complete form.

Choice of candidates for inclusion was more seriously limited by the early decision to reprint works in their entirety rather than excerpts from them. The obvious advantages to this method are that readers are not dependent on anyone's prior judgment about which portions of an essay are significant and therefore can see the work whole. This decision, however, meant that longer tracts had to be excluded. Those familiar with the political essays of the seventeenth century know that many tracts were long—some attaining book length. Thus these two volumes include fewer tracts than could otherwise have been the case, and many excellent works could not be considered. Tracts that are reprinted, however, are entire, with two minor exceptions. In volume 1 only the second chapter of Heylyn's "A Briefe and Moderate Answer" was reprinted. But this chapter was responding to a particular sermon of Henry Burton's and is thus complete in itself. In volume 2 only the first five chapters of "The Arraignment of Co-Ordinate-Power" have been printed. These five chapters are quite independent of the last chapters, which are both narrowly technical and lengthy. It seemed better to reprint only the first chapters of this useful essay than omit the whole.

Other points. Where possible I have included one tract replying to another, thus allowing readers to sample the give-and-take of a debate as it occurred. For example, the exchange between Henry Ferne and Charles Herle over whether, in Ferne's words, "Subjects may take Arms and resist? and whether that case be now?" is a famous debate between two of the best minds on the royalist and parliamentarian sides, respectively.

Operating under these constraints, I have endeavored to present the work of as many authors as possible. For this reason I rarely include more than one tract by a writer. The glaring exception occurs in volume 2 where readers will find three tracts by Anthony Ashley Cooper, the Earl of Shaftesbury. Shaftesbury has been allotted more space than others because few tracts dealing with pressing constitutional issues were published in the 1670s and because his essays are excellent. It is no accident that both exceptions to my guidelines occur in volume 2. Strict censorship was imposed during the Restoration and this fact, together with the more muted debate generally, meant that there were periods when few tracts unfavorable to the authorities were published. This is not the place to provide an essay on censorship during the seventeenth century. Suffice it to say that during this time spells of prolific publishing and little effective control of the press alternated with periods when strict censorship drove critics of the government either to silence or to anonymous publication and subterfuge. Several of the tracts in *The Struggle for Sovereignty* are anonymous. Where the authorship of a tract is in doubt, I have followed the attribution of the *Wing Short Title Catalogue*.

The contemporary market for tracts was so brisk that many essays went into several editions. Where this is the case I have preferred the first edition when it was available. Subsequent editions often contain responses to critics of the first edition. They are, therefore, longer—a disadvantage from my point of view. For the same reason the arguments in later editions tend to be more dilute with new passages inserted into the original text. Political tracts appeared in a variety of formats. I have included a mix of the most popular styles of the genre —formal dialogues, sermons, published speeches, familiar letters.

It has been a great luxury to be able to publish two volumes. Even so, after severely winnowing the hundreds of tracts I read to a manageable number, my initial selection would have created two books, each of which was fully double the present length. In short, the choice has not been an easy one. I am acutely mindful of the many excellent works that could not be included. Nevertheless, I hope the reader will find that closer acquaintance with the thought and wit of these particular authors will be time well spent and will find their tracts to be of interest, insight, and value. For myself, I have found them often brilliant, invariably thought-provoking, sometimes exasperating, always fresh, and frequently delightful.

EDITORIAL APPROACH

Fashions in editorial approach, as in all else, change. Earlier in this century editors thought nothing of silently altering early works, changing even the language itself. The trend is now moving in the direction of producing something very close to a facsimile of an original text. I have taken a middle road. Because the goal is to make these works accessible, even to those unfamiliar with seventeenth-century English literature, some sensitive modernizing has been done. Occurrences of blackletter type have not been reproduced and spellings that might confuse have been changed (a decision I am confident the writers of the seventeenth century would approve). In addition, the spelling of proper names within individual tracts has been made consistent, unusual punctuation has been brought up-to-date, and with a few exceptions, contractions not now in use have been spelled out. Because tracts often were published in haste, they frequently contained misprints. Such typographical mistakes have been corrected. Seventeenth-century printers capitalized some words in titles because the words began a new line or for other reasons of design. The titles of the tracts contained in these volumes retain their original spellings and punctuation; except on the title pages, capitalization in the tract titles follows modern convention.

In several instances, the Greek script was illegible in the original. I have indicated the missing text in those cases with three ellipsis points enclosed by brackets. A few tracts contained prefaces that, for reasons of space, I have not reprinted, although I have noted in the relevant headnotes any dedications these included. Marginalia have also been omitted. Marginal notes usually were confined to the notation of references, and these tend to be listed in barely legible, severely abbreviated, form. The practice of using marginalia was especially common and the list of references especially lengthy in published sermons. I hope these omissions will not detract from readers' appreciation of the text, and I urge those readers with particular interest in the prefaces or the marginalia to consult the original pamphlets.

Apart from these exceptions, the text has been painstakingly reproduced. The language has been faithfully preserved, as have the capitalization and italics of the originals. All departures from twentieth-century norms stand as a continual reminder that one is dealing with another era.

The introductions and editorial footnotes are designed to aid readers unfamiliar with the political thought of seventeenth-century England. A grasp of the historical and philosophical background, in all its bewildering complexity, with all its contradictions, subtleties, and shifts, is critical to a sensible reading of these works. True, the conceptions with which the authors wrestled are profound, the political dilemmas eternal, but they were men of their century facing urgent contemporary problems. To miss that is to mistake their meaning.

Acknowledgments

I should like to thank all those who have generously assisted in and encouraged this ambitious undertaking. The Huntington Library awarded me a Fletcher Jones Foundation fellowship, which permitted the use of their splendid collection of seventeenth-century pamphlets, and the Earhart Foundation followed with a generous fellowship research grant. Bentley College awarded me a Bentley Institute Fellowship, which provided both funds and time to carry out the work.

Many scholars and friends read and commented on the selection of tracts and the introductory essays. In particular I would like to thank Quentin Skinner for his continuing encouragement throughout this project; John Morrill, David Wootton, and Donald Lutz for reviewing the lists of tracts and making valuable comments on the introductions; and Mark Goldie for his thoughts on the Restoration tracts. Many thanks as well to Derek Hirst for recommending Goodwin's "Right and Might Well Mett"; to Tim Harris for drawing my attention to "Captain Thorogood His Opinion of the Point of Succession"; to John Morrill for urging the inclusion of Algernon Sidney's splendid scaffold speech; and to Quentin Skinner for recommending the work of William Sherlock. I should also like to express my gratitude to Sir Geoffrey Elton and John Kenyon, good friends who are sorely missed, and to whom this collection is dedicated.

A special acknowledgment must go to Kim Cretors who valiantly undertook the formidable challenge of deciphering all these idiosyncratic texts and putting them on computer. My research assistants were a splendid help. I should like especially to thank Jeff Strong and Jacqueline Allard for their ingenuity in tracking down elusive references.

My family, as always, has been patient beyond belief or fairness. Living with a historian is never easy, especially a talkative one pre-occupied with constitutional issues. The flaws that remain in the work, and I fear they are many, are my own.

Introduction

> Whose rights are to predominate in the State, the rights of the ruler or those
> of the people, the rights of the governed or those of government? It is this
> vexed question which produces tension in the structure of constitutional
> monarchy—a tension which may only make itself felt on exceptional occa-
> sions, but then shakes the whole edifice to the point of collapse.
> —Fritz Kern, *Kingship and Law in the Middle Ages*

Seventeenth-century Englishmen were thoroughly confused about
sovereignty, knew they were, but found the ambiguity tolerable. "To
demand which estate may challenge this power of final determination of fundamental controversies arising betwixt them," Philip
Hunton wrote in 1643, "is to demand which of them shall be absolute
... if the nondecision be tolerable, it must remain undecided."[1] Unfortunately in 1643 war between the king and Parliament had made
nondecision increasingly impracticable. In that case Hunton advised
"every person ... [to] ... aid that part which in his best reason and
judgement stands for the publike good." It was not a choice anyone
had wished to make. At the beginning of the seventeenth century
Englishmen prided themselves on their government's nice balance
between liberty and authority. It was this balance they hoped they
had restored as the century closed. But in the years between, the
scales tipped one way and then another as dissension, civil war, revolution, restoration, dissension, and revolution followed one another
in giddy and unprecedented procession goaded by, and in turn setting
in motion, probing of virtually every aspect of the relationship be-

---

1. Philip Hunton, "A Treatise of Monarchy" (1643), 69, 73.

tween the individual and the state.[2] Central to these events and this relationship were rival claims for sovereignty. Claims were advanced for the sovereignty of nearly every component of English government—for the sovereignty of the king alone, for the king in Parliament, for the two houses of Parliament and the House of Commons alone, for the sovereignty of the law and that of the people.

If the scope of the controversy was unprecedented, so was the opportunity for debate. For the first time in their history Englishmen had the opportunity for political argument on a grand scale, and for the first time they were in a position to choose between political visions. Happily the shifting, intense, and at times profound debate on sovereignty was published, largely in the form of hastily written tracts printed in unprecedented quantities.[3] Thanks to the "swarming number of pamphleteers" stricken with what a correspondent of Lord Conway diagnosed as "a powerful disease, this writing," we can read for ourselves the political theories and analyses of scores of the best minds of that talented, turbulent, and pivotal age.[4] The literature they left has been of the greatest consequence for succeeding generations across the entire political spectrum.

There are a variety of compelling justifications for a collection of these essays. The most general was touched upon by the royalist Bishop Brian Duppa in 1656 when he praised Photius, whose an-

2. Some historians and philosophers argue that, as Wedgwood wrote, "Theory and doctrine are more often the explanation of actions already envisaged or performed than their initial inspiration." See C. V. Wedgwood, *The King's War: 1641–1647* (London, 1966), 11. I believe that the preaching of a particular theory can, of itself, provoke.

3. More than twenty-two thousand pamphlets, speeches, sermons, and issues of newspapers were published between 1640 and 1661. Perez Zagorin, in his *Rebels and Rulers, 1500–1600* (Cambridge, 1982), 149, points out that the sum of publications issued during the "revolutionary period" probably exceeded "the entire output of the English press since the beginning of printing in England in 1475."

4. See "Thomas Scot's Account of His Actions as Intelligencer During the Commonwealth," *English Historical Review*, ed. C. H. Firth (1897), 12:121; and Sir Theodore Turquet de Mayerne to Lord Conway, 8 October 1651, Marjorie H. Nicholson, ed., *Conway Letters* (London, 1930), 21.

thology *Bibliotheca* included the names and works of many classical authors "which else had utterly perished" and heartily wished "there wer found som to imitate him; for besides preserving the memory, both of greater and more especially lesser tracts and treatises (which ar commonly lost like pinns and needles, and never recovered again), there might be great use made of it, both in the exercising of every man's own judgement, and giving an edge to the judgement of others."[5] It is hoped this collection of seventeenth-century tracts might be of similar "great use." Issues of sovereignty are chronic, and the struggles of seventeenth-century men to achieve liberty with order speak to us still. Moreover, while much study has been lavished upon those few seventeenth-century theorists later centuries have deemed original and important, the works of other excellent thinkers, such as Henry Ferne, Francis Rous, and Gilbert Burnet, now nearly as lost as Duppa's "pinns and needles," were frequently more typical of their age and more influential during it, and furnish an intellectual context in which a Hobbes and a Locke can be better understood and more justly evaluated.

Beyond such a general purpose is the historian's purpose. As Bernard Bailyn wrote of the pamphlets of the American Revolution, these tracts "reveal not merely positions taken but the reasons why positions were taken; they reveal motive and understanding: the assumptions, beliefs, and ideas—the articulated world view—that lay behind the manifest events of the time."[6]

Lastly, many seventeenth-century historians now question the assumption that clashing constitutional theories played a prominent role in the civil war. They rightly stress the political concepts most Englishmen shared, but some have gone on to marginalize and be-

5. See Sir Gyles Isham, ed., *The Correspondence of Bishop Brian Duppa and Sir Justinian Isham, 1650–1660*, Northants. Rec. Soc., vol. 17 (Lamport, 1951), 117.
6. Bernard Bailyn, *The Ideological Origins of the American Revolution* (Cambridge, Mass., 1967), vi.

little the importance and the quality of the political theories so passionately argued prior to, and during, the civil war era.[7] Indeed, one scholar maintained that "from the time religious and ecclesiastical splits seriously damaged parliamentary unity to the time when that unity was, after a fashion, restored at dreadful cost, constitutional thought was suspended."[8] The political treatises of the Restoration period have suffered less belittlement only because until recently they have not been the subject of serious consideration.[9] In both instances

7. Conrad Russell, for example, a leader among revisionists, takes issue with the notion that "these divergent theories had something to do with the causes of the Civil War." Russell finds the political thought of little worth. He writes that the parliamentary arguments and what he terms "the makeshift and almost ramshackle manner in which they were put together to meet circumstances as they arose" suggests "that the body of ideas about how the country should be governed were not really the central element in the cause for which they fought: they were, like their medieval predecessors, ad hoc ideas constructed out of any materials ready to hand, to serve the immediate purpose of clipping the wings of a king with whom they simply could not cope." See Conrad Russell, *The Causes of the English Civil War* (Oxford, 1990; rpt., 1991), 145, 160 (page citations are to the reprint edition). Michael Seymour, in his dissertation on government propaganda during the Interregnum, ignores the content of progovernment tracts because of their "intellectual poverty" and decides "intellectual justifications" on behalf of the government "are best catagorised by reference to the relationship of their authors to the government, rather than by their content." See Seymour, "Pro-Government Propaganda in Interregnum England, 1649–1660" (Ph.D. diss., Cambridge University), 53. On the other hand, see J. P. Sommerville, *Politics and Ideology in England, 1603–1640* (London, 1986). Sommerville deals only with the period leading up to the civil war but reasserts the importance of the ideological divisions that developed prior to it. Margaret Judson in her classic work, *The Crisis of the Constitution: An Essay in Constitutional and Political Thought in England, 1603–1645* (New Brunswick, N.J., 1949), 8–9, finds a "meagerness" of political thought in the political thinking of men participating in the controversy between king and Parliament before the civil war but argues that beginning in 1642 "there began an outpouring of political thought more extensive and more profound than England had ever experienced before."

8. M. J. Mendle, "Politics and Political Thought, 1640–42," in *The Origins of the English Civil War*, ed. Conrad Russell (London, 1973), 233.

9. Excellent work on the treatises of the Restoration has been done in recent years. See, for example, Mark Goldie, "The Roots of True Whiggism, 1688–94," *History of Political Thought* (summer, June 1980): 195–236, and "The Revolution of 1689 and the Structure of Political Argument: An Essay and an Annotated Bibliography of Pamphlets on the Allegiance Controversy," *Bulletin of Research in the Humanities* (winter 1980): 473–564; John Kenyon, "The Revolution of 1688: Resistance and Contract," in *Historical Perspectives: Studies in English Thought and Society*, ed. Neil McKendrick (London, 1974), and *Revolution Principles: The Politics of Party* (Cambridge, 1977); and Tim Harris, *London Crowds in the Reign of Charles II: Propaganda and Politics from the Restoration Until the Exclusion Crisis* (Cambridge, 1987).

exposure to the published tracts of influential, if lesser known, authors provides an opportunity for a larger audience to evaluate their quality and significance and hopefully arrive at a richer understanding of the century's political thought and conflicts.

When I first traveled to Great Britain I was cautioned, "Just because you speak the same language, don't think you understand each other." That advice is just as sound for the time traveler determined to fathom the tangled intellectual milieu of seventeenth-century Englishmen. In addition to the need to understand a battery of then commonly accepted political notions, it is important to be aware that the vocabulary central to the debate over sovereignty—words such as "sovereign" and "absolute"—had meanings so various and shifting that the protagonists themselves were often confused. This brief introduction can do no more than point out the major landmarks and landmines of that philosophical universe. The fascinating implications and nuances of the discussion will be left to the authors themselves.

Let us begin with those political understandings Englishmen shared, for their inherent contradictions were at the root of the trouble.[10] We will then consider the various claims for supremacy. The English king was head of both church and state. His political position was ancient, his role as supreme head of the Church of England less than a century old when James I came to the throne in 1603. This double role had great potential to ensure a secure and powerful monarchy but also generated inconsistent constitutional expectations.

10. Corinne Weston distinguishes the doctrine of the ancient constitution and the political theory of order espoused by James I and finds, "Although it appeared at times as if the two sets of ideas coexisted harmoniously even within the mind of a Coke or a Pym, these were nonetheless incompatible." Weston, "England: Ancient Constitution and Common Law," in *The Cambridge History of Political Thought*, ed. J. H. Burns and Mark Goldie (Cambridge, 1991), 394–95.

The glory of the constitution was regarded by many as its balance and reciprocity: balance between the king's prerogatives and people's liberties and between the king's duty to his subjects and their obedience to him. This last was viewed as a kind of contract in which the king was bound to maintain the customs and liberties of his subjects by his coronation oath while his subjects were bound to him by oaths of loyalty and supremacy.[11] Thus, while the English government was a hereditary monarchy—then considered the most stable form of polity—it was no simple monarchy since the king's powers were limited by the laws and customs of the realm and, in the critical areas of legislation and direct taxation, were shared with Parliament. Parliament comprised the monarch and representatives of the three estates of the realm—the lords spiritual and the lords temporal who sat in the House of Lords, and the townsmen and gentry whose represen-

11. For detailed information on a variety of the topics discussed in this introduction, see such fine classic studies as Margaret Judson, *The Crisis of the Constitution* and *From Tradition to Political Reality* (Hamden, Conn., 1980), and J. G. A. Pocock, *The Ancient Constitution and the Feudal Law: A Study of English Historical Thought in the Seventeenth Century: A Reissue with a Retrospect* (Cambridge, 1987). There are many excellent recent studies. See, for example, J. H. Burns and Mark Goldie, eds., *The Cambridge History of Political Thought: 1450–1700*; John Kenyon, *The Stuart Constitution: 1603–1688*, 2d ed. (Cambridge, 1986); J. P. Sommerville, *Politics and Ideology in England: 1603–1640*; Michael Mendle, *Dangerous Positions: Mixed Government, the Estates of the Realm, and the Making of the Answer to the XIX Propositions* (Alabama, 1985); John Morrill, *The Nature of the English Revolution* (London, 1993), and John Morrill, Paul Slack, and Daniel Woolf, eds., *Public Duty and Private Conscience in Seventeenth-Century England: Essays Presented to G. E. Aylmer* (Oxford, 1993); Quentin Skinner, *The Foundations of Modern Political Thought* (Cambridge, 1978), especially vol. 2, chap. 9; Skinner, "History and Ideology in the English Revolution," *Historical Journal* 8, no. 1 (1965): 151–78; Corinne Weston, *English Constitutional Theory and the House of Lords, 1556–1832* (New York, 1965), and Corinne Weston and Janelle Greenberg, *Subjects and Sovereigns; The Grand Controversy over Legal Sovereignty in Stuart England* (Cambridge, 1981); David Wootton, ed., *Divine Right and Democracy* (London, 1986), introduction; Wootton, "From Rebellion to Revolution: The Crisis of the Winter of 1642/3 and the Origins of Civil War Radicalism," *English Historical Review* (1990): 654–69; the essays by Jess Stoddart Flemion, in Clyve Jones and David Lewis Jones, eds., *Peers, Politics, and Power: The House of Lords, 1603–1911* (London, 1986); Richard Tuck, *Philosophy and Government, 1572–1651* (Cambridge, 1993); and J. G. A. Pocock, ed., with Gordon Schochet and Lois Schwoerer, *The Varieties of British Political Thought, 1500–1800* (Cambridge, 1993).

tatives sat in the House of Commons.[12] This gave credibility to the belief of Englishmen that their government was a judicious mixture of monarchy, aristocracy, and democracy possessing the advantages and avoiding the weaknesses of each.[13] Although the concepts of the contract theory and mixed government imbedded in these notions, with their implication that the king might be held to account by his people, were prudently silenced in the immediate aftermath of the 1605 Gunpowder Plot, both theories resurfaced in the late 1630s.[14]

The king's relationship with Parliament was complex. It shared his legislative and fiscal authority, and the king in Parliament was regarded as English government at its most potent. But Parliament was, in many respects, a creature of the Crown. The king decided when it should be summoned and when dissolved, and no bill could become law without his consent.[15] Moreover, he had numerous opportunities to manipulate the membership of the Commons, while in the House of Lords the spiritual lords—the bishops—were royal appointees and the ranks of lay peers could be supplemented at his pleasure.[16] Then too enforcement of parliamentary statutes was left to

12. There had been important exceptions to strict hereditary monarchy in English history, but the form of government was still hereditary monarchy. On the issue of the succession, see Howard Nenner, *The Right to Be King: The Succession to the Crown of England, 1603–1714* (Chapel Hill, N.C., 1995).

13. See Mendle, *Dangerous Positions*, 2–3.

14. See Wootton, *Divine Right and Democracy*, 30.

15. Parliament met in 1601, had five sessions between 1604–10, met again in 1614, 1621, 1624, 1625, 1626, 1628–29, and twice in 1640.

16. After 1625, for example, when churchmen who favored the views of Charles and Laud filled most of the posts, Flemion found "the clerical block formed the most secure source of royalist votes left in the upper house—more loyal than the Privy Council itself." Moreover, thirty-five "politically active" bishops averaged 84 percent attendance, 20 percent above the average lay attendance. See Jess Stoddart Flemion, "The Nature of Opposition in the House of Lords in the Early Seventeenth Century: A Revaluation," in *Peers, Politics, and Power*, ed. Jones and Jones, 16, n. 34. During the debate on the Petition of Right in 1628 Charles created four new peers to bolster his side. See Flemion, "The Struggle for the Petition of Right in the House of Lords: The Study of an Opposition Party Victory," in *Peers, Politics, and Power*, 33, 33 n. 8.

the king and his courts, and the right to dispense with or suspend a law was part of his prerogative.[17] Nonetheless, Parliament was the highest court in the realm because it alone was able to legislate and, so it contended, best able to interpret the law. It also served as a council to the king. In it "the whole body of the realm, and every particular member thereof, either in person or by representation (upon their own free elections) . . . [were] by the laws of the realm deemed to be personally present."[18] Englishmen regarded Parliament as necessary to the maintenance of their ancient rights.

These rights and customs were continually evolving, but their gist was believed to be immemorial, not the gift of any monarch, undisturbed even by the Norman conquest.[19] The key rights had been laid down in Magna Carta, the Great Charter of 1215, reconfirmed by English monarchs no less than thirty-two times.[20] The famed legal scholars, Henry de Bracton and Sir John Fortescue, stressed the legal constraints on English kingship. Bracton defined the English monarch as not subject to any man but under God and the law. Fortescue saw the royal office as "dominium politicum et regale" not "dominium regale," that is constitutional, rather than absolute, monarchy.[21] James I boasted monarchy was the "supremest thing upon earth," but conceded he was "King by the common law of the

---

17. There was great frustration, for instance, about the failure of the Stuarts to enforce the laws against Catholics with any vigor.

18. This description is from The Succession Act, 1 Jac. 1, c. 1, cited by Kenyon, *Stuart Constitution*, 21.

19. This dichotomy between an immemorial law and a continually developing one is discussed in detail by Glenn Burgess, *The Politics of the Ancient Constitution: An Introduction to English Political Thought, 1603–1642* (London, 1992). The conquest theory was extremely important in the seventeenth-century debate. A conquered people were believed to have no rights that their conqueror was bound to respect. For further reading on this issue, see Pocock, *Ancient Constitution and the Feudal Law*; and Skinner, "History and Ideology in the English Revolution," 151–78.

20. Weston, "England: Ancient Constitution and Common Law," 379.

21. See Sir John Fortescue, *The Governance of England*, ed. C. Plummer (Oxford, 1885), 109ff.

land."[22] James added that a king governing a settled kingdom "leaves to be a king, and degenerates into a tyrant, as soon as he leaves off to rule according to his laws."[23]

The boundary between the king's prerogative powers and the people's customs and liberties was set by common law and statute law and patrolled by the judges. Judges were sworn to do equal right to rich and poor and to ignore even the king's orders in reaching their decisions. Yet judges were appointed by the Crown and under Charles I served at pleasure, rather than during good behavior.[24] This was why John Selden, the famous jurist, found the king's oath "not security enough for our Property for he swears to Govern according to Law; now the Judges they interpret the Law, and what Judges can be made to do we know."[25] But skeptics aside, the courts were regarded as key to the maintenance of English liberties, and an English monarch employed the courts for blatant political advantage at his peril.

Law was not the only sanction for royal authority. Like all supreme magistrates, the king was believed to hold his power from God and to be ultimately answerable to God. He was described as absolute despite the constraints on his powers, because as head of both church

22. James I, Speech to Parliament, 21 March 1610, in Kenyon, *Stuart Constitution*, 12. And see John Cowell, *The Interpreter; or Book containing the Signification of Words*, 1st ed., 1607 (London, 1637); especially definitions of king, parliament, prerogative, and subsidy. These were not changed in the second edition.

23. Kenyon, *The Stuart Constitution*, 12.

24. Charles I changed the description of the judges' patents. The clause *Quam diu se bene gesserit*, during good behavior, was left out, and a new clause, *durante bene placito*, during the pleasure of the grantor, was inserted. This was complained of in clause 38 of the Grand Remonstrance as meant "the better to hold a rod over them." See S. R. Gardiner, *The Constitutional Documents of the Puritan Revolution: 1625–1660*, 3d ed., rev. (Oxford, 1968), 213.

25. John Selden, *The Table Talk of John Selden*, ed. S. W. Singer, 3d ed. (London, 1860), 177. Charles deepened such doubts when he warned that to the judges "only under me belongs the interpretation of laws." Charles I, Speech at Prorogation of Parliament, 26 June 1628, in W. J. Jones, *Politics and the Bench: The Judges and the Origins of the English Civil War* (London, 1971), 75.

and state he was not accountable to any outside potentate. The meshing of religion and politics in the early modern era had a significant theoretical and constitutional impact. The king's position in the state church meant any alienation from that church could affect his subjects' loyalty to him. After the pope excommunicated Henry VIII, English Catholics were freed from their oaths of obedience. They were urged to work toward the conversion or overthrow of the Protestant monarch. On the other side of the Christian spectrum, English Presbyterians and Independents desired a more independent, more radical, English church. The Church of England saw itself as a vital prop of the Crown. Its leading clergy were royal appointees. When the Stuart kings began to embrace absolutist notions, clerics who exalted monarchy and preached absolute obedience to the king were promoted. Dissenters of both the Catholic right and the Calvinist left, on the other hand, found it necessary to seek religious and philosophical justification for their religious opposition and, *in extremis*, for political resistance as well.[26]

In ordinary times, the flexibility in the constitution and relative moderation of the church kept government and community in tolerable harmony. But the system had no sure way to prevent a monarch intent upon becoming absolute from doing so, or any remedy for a king who, as James I put it, "leaves to be a king, and degenerates into a tyrant." It was a dilemma that would haunt the men and women of the 1640s, 1650s, 1660s, and 1680s and force the issue of sovereignty to the fore. Scripture was an uncertain guide. It admonished men to "render unto Caesar the Things that are Caesar's and unto God the Things that are God's," but not what to do when Caesar's commands

26. While the king was supreme head of the Church of England and could shape its practice and personnel, Parliament claimed a share in religious policies. It had passed the great acts of the English Reformation, in particular the Act of Supremacy, and while its later influence often amounted to little more than fretting at royal appointments and liturgical changes, only Parliament could create penalties for religious offenses touching life, limb, or property.

opposed God's. Different Protestant denominations had different answers. English Puritans had inherited a Calvinist "ideological armory" that permitted defense against a godless monarch if it were led by magistrates.[27] Of course, if the king behaved like a tyrant, it could be argued he was no longer king. His subjects were then released from their oaths of loyalty, and religious teachings on obedience did not apply. Resistance was not rebellion. This position, royalists would repeatedly point out, resembled the Catholic notion that a monarch could be deposed by the pope and his subjects released from their obedience.

The Church of England, as befitted an established church, took a different stance. Given both its own remarkable origins under Henry VIII and associated threats to the Crown, one of its emphatic teachings was the necessity for obedience. It was a teaching with profound constitutional resonance, drummed as it was into the ears of thousands of English men and women in numberless Sunday sermons. Looking back the emphasis on political obedience seems excessive. The homily "against Disobedience and willful Rebellion" is not only the longest homily in the Book of Homilies used as the basis for sermons but more than double the length of any other. This is in addition to a separate homily, the "Exhortation to Obedience."[28] Neither gave more than passing reference to obedience to parents and superiors; both concentrated almost exclusively on obedience to the

27. See, for example, Zagorin, *Rebels and Rulers, 1500–1660*; and Skinner, *Foundations of Modern Political Thought*, vol. 2, pt. 3.

28. *Sermons or Homilies Appointed to Be Read in Churches in the Time of Queen Elizabeth of Famous Memory*, first published in 1562 (London, 1830 [?]). The *Book of Homilies* was first published in 1547, and the homily on obedience dates from that time. Under Queen Mary two new homilies were added—one on the authority of Peter, the second on the fathers and the papacy. Both rebutted the antipapal arguments of the 1547 homily on obedience. These were removed under Elizabeth I. The *Homily against Disobedience and Wilful Rebellion*, however, was first published in 1570 in response to the anti-Protestant Northern Revolt in the winter of 1569 and the papal bull of February 1570, which excommunicated and deposed Elizabeth. See Ronald B. Bond, ed., *Certain Sermons or Homilies (1547) and A Homily against Disobedience and Wilful Rebellion* (Toronto, 1987), 40–44.

Crown. Without kings, rulers, and judges, the clergy taught, "no man shall ride or go by the highway unrobbed, no man shall sleep in his own house or bed unkilled, no man shall keep his wife, children, and possessions in quietness, all things shall be common."[29] The homily goes on to insist that the power and authority of kings are the ordinances "not of man, but of God." Christians were not to raise their hands against their rulers or even to think evil of them. While the Elizabethan text was intended to counter the pope's claimed power to depose kings, the language was drawn, and presumably meant, more broadly.[30] The Fifth Commandment was understood to enjoin obedience to one's political, as well as biological, parent.

The homily on disobedience and rebellion raised the issue of what subjects should do if faced with a wicked ruler. The answer was emphatic:

> What shall subjects do then? shall they obey valiant, stout, wise, and good princes, and contemn, disobey, and rebel against children being their princes, or against undiscreet and evil governors? God forbid: for first, what a perilous thing were it to commit unto the subjects the judgment, which prince is wise and godly, and his government good, and which is otherwise; as though the foot must judge of the head: an enterprise very heinous, and must needs breed rebellion. . . . If therefore all subjects that mislike of their prince should rebel, no realm should ever be without rebellion.[31]

The homily on obedience explained that if the king or magistrates gave orders contrary to Christian teachings "*we must rather obey God than man,*" but added "in that case we may not in any wise withstand violently, or rebel against rulers, or make any insurrection, sedition, or tumults . . . against the anointed of the Lord, or any of his officers;

29. *Sermons or Homilies*, 115.
30. Ibid., 116, 654.
31. Ibid., 609.

but we must in such case patiently suffer all wrongs and injuries, referring the judgment of our cause only to God."[32] Saints Peter and
Paul were cited as proof that kings were to be obeyed "although they
abuse their power" for "whosoever withstandeth, shall get to themselves damnation; for whosoever withstandeth, withstandeth the ordinance of God."[33]

The homily on "disobedience and rebellion" claimed Lucifer as the
"first author and founder of rebellion."[34] Congregations were reminded of the biblical admonition "rebellion is as the sin of witch-
craft," a violation of all ten commandments. Rather than resist
godless and wicked rulers Christians were to rely upon tears, prayers,
and, if need be, suffer martyrdom. One of James I's chaplains, John
Rawlinson, neatly distinguished kings from tyrants: "a *King* makes
the law his will, because he wills that which the law wills. But a *tyrant*
makes his will a law, because what he wills, he will have to be law."[35]
Nevertheless Rawlinson insisted, if the king were "the very worst that
may be, a tyrant; one that will make the law an out-law; yet shall it
not be lawfull for any mortall man vindictively to meddle with
him."[36] Scripture, as interpreted by the Anglican hierarchy, cared
nothing for the ancient constitution, the law, or Magna Carta. Englishmen were enjoined to follow the example of the early Christian
martyrs, not King John's barons.

---

32. Ibid., 122–23.

33. Ibid., 118–19, 606. St. Paul, Romans 13.1 is the foundation of much of the teaching and
worth quoting at length: "Let every soul be subject unto the higher powers, for there is no
power but of God, and the powers that be are ordained of God. Whosoever therefore resisteth
the power, resisteth the ordinance of God; and they that resist shall receive to themselves
damnation. . . . Wherefore ye must be subject, not because of wrath only, but also for conscience' sake. . . . Give every man therefore his due; tribute to whom tribute belongeth; custom to whom custom is due; fear to whom fear belongeth; honour to whom ye owe honour."

34. *Sermons or Homilies*, 606.

35. John Rawlinson, "Vivat Rex. A Sermon Preached at Paul's Crosse on the day of his
Majesties happie inauguration, March 24, 1614" (Oxford, 1619), 7.

36. Rawlinson, "Vivat Rex," 7.

English law was scarcely more helpful. The chief legal guidance was the antique maxim "the king can do no wrong." This was ordinarily understood to mean that if the king gave illegal commands they were not to be obeyed, and ministers who carried them out, though not the king himself, would be subject to punishment.[37] But in the course of the century's quarrels that tenet would be given a variety of interpretations. Royal apologists saw it as proof the king was above the law. His opponents read the tenet as evidence that since a king could do no wrong any king who behaved in an illegal manner was, as James I conceded, no longer king. In any case Charles, rather unwisely, argued that because he could do no wrong, neither could those who acted on his behalf.[38] Some jurists, on the other hand, read it to mean that the king's illegal commands were void on their face and should be ignored. The law had no procedure to hold the king himself accountable. This was not the case for rebellious lords, commons, judges, or bishops. A rebellious parliament could be dissolved by the king. It was only containment of royal power for which there was no accepted remedy.

THE VOCABULARY OF SOVEREIGNTY

Even without the king, Parliament, people, or lawyers seeking to enhance their share of power, the English ideal of a balanced government was beset with problems. The interpretations sixteenth-century Continental philosophers had given to "absolute" and "sovereign," terms Englishmen were accustomed to applying to their kings, were

37. John Pym, the opposition leader, reminded Parliament in 1641: "It is a great Prerogative to the King and a great honour attributed to him in a Maxime of our Law, that he can doe no wrong, he is the fountain of Justice, and if there be any injustice in the execution of his Commands, the Law casts it upon the Ministers, and frees the King." John Pym, "A Declaration of Grievances...." (London, 1641), 2. This definition is a paraphrase of that used by Hugo Grotius, *On the Law of War and Peace*, Book 1, chap. 2, vii. Also see Joyce L. Malcolm, "Doing No Wrong: Law, Liberty, and the Constraint of Kings," *Journal of British Studies*, forthcoming.
38. Wootton, *Divine Right and Democracy*, 30–31.

sufficiently influential in England to set political nerves jangling.[39] If the definition of sovereign was that power whose actions were not subject to the legal control of another and could not be rendered void by the operation of another human will, it was unclear just who or what was England's sovereign. If the king was sovereign then he could not be subject to Parliament or the law. The king in Parliament came closer to the definition, but Parliament only met intermittently and in important respects answered to the higher authority of the law. Statutes approved by the king in Parliament were regularly modified by the justices in the royal courts and could even be found to be against law and therefore void.

Popular understanding of the English constitution was also challenged by the influential sixteenth-century French philosopher Jean Bodin. In his classic study *The Six Books of the Commonwealth*, Bodin insisted sovereignty must be not only absolute—"not limited either in power, or in function, or in length of time"—but indivisible.[40] "To combine monarchy with democracy and with aristocracy," as the English claimed to do, was in Bodin's estimation "impossible and contradictory, and cannot even be imagined."[41] He specifically considered the English Parliament but found: "The entire sovereignty belongs undivided to the kings of England and that the Estates are only witnesses. . . . The sovereignty of the monarchy is in no way altered by the presence of the Estates."[42] To Bodin "the main point of

39. The struggles between kings and their people and between church and state in sixteenth-century Europe produced a body of literature exalting absolutism on the one hand and arguing for resistance to it on the other. See, for example, Skinner, *Foundations of Modern Political Thought*, vol. 2, "The Age of Reformation"; J. N. Figgis, *Political Thought from Gerson to Grotius: 1414–1625* (rpt., New York, 1960). The following definition is a paraphrase of that used by Hugo Grotius, *On the Law of War and Peace*, Book 1, chap. 2, vii.

40. This work first appeared in 1576 and was translated into English in 1606.

41. Jean Bodin, *The Six Books of the Commonwealth*, Book 1, chap. 8, in *On Sovereignty*, ed. and trans. Julian H. Franklin (Cambridge, 1992), 2; Book 2, chap. 1, 92. Bodin was adamant that "there is not now, and never was, a state compounded of aristocracy and democracy, much less of the three forms of state." Bodin, Book 1, chap. 8, 23.

42. Ibid.

sovereign majesty and absolute power consists of giving the law to subjects in general without their consent."[43]

Consider an incident that occurred over the use of the word "sovereign." When the Petition of Right was being drafted in 1628, the Lords moved to add a paragraph expressing "due regard to leave entire that sovereign Power, wherewith your Majesty is trusted for the protection, safety, and happiness of your people." Many in the Commons voiced their dismay. "What is 'sovereign power'?" John Alford asked. "Bodin says it is that that is free from any condition.... Let us give that to the King that the law gives him, and no more." John Pym continued, "I know not what it is.... I know how to add 'sovereign' to his person, but not to his power." The great jurist, Sir Edward Coke, pleaded that the Lords' proposal would "overthrow all our petition.... I know the prerogative is part of the law, but 'sovereign power' is no parliament word in my opinion. It weakens Magna Carta and all other statutes, for they are absolute without any saving of sovereign power.... We must not admit of it; and to qualify it, it is impossible."[44] The Lords capitulated, and the offending language was rejected. The Petition of Right opened with dutiful reference to "our Sovereign Lord the King," and men continued to refer to "sovereignty in a king," but Coke and his colleagues had thwarted legal recognition of such sovereign power.

Or take "absolute." The Speaker of the Commons welcomed James to his first English parliament by proclaiming that they had "exchanged our exquisite Queen for an absolute King." But when James "desired and commanded, as an absolute King, that there might be a conference between the House and the judges," members

---

43. Ibid., 23.
44. This debate took place on 20 May 1648. See Robert C. Johnson, Mary Frear Keeler, Maija Jansson Cole, and William B. Bidwell, eds., *Common Debates: 1628* (New Haven, 1977), 3:494–95.

were alarmed by his use of the term "absolute."[45] James may have been misunderstood, perhaps "all he was asserting was his rightful authority as a monarch whose claim to the English throne was beyond challenge," the customary meaning of "absolute." But apparently members did not see it that way.[46] They were wise to be cautious for James intermittently pressed for absolutist powers, and there were those who argued that Charles I possessed the more potent meanings Europeans were giving these customary terms. It was presumably in response to this threat that Coke had already begun to make exalted claims for the antiquity and supremacy of the law.

THE SOVEREIGNTY OF THE KING

The contention that English monarchs were absolute within their realm may have begun as a defense of royal religious supremacy, vis-à-vis the pope, but by the early seventeenth century it had become a flirtation with a more complete absolutism known as the divine right of kings. While there was general agreement that all who ruled did so by divine right, what was novel and controversial in the divine right thesis were the powers attributed to that right, an exclusive, unlimited, irresistible sovereignty.[47] J. N. Figgis found its complete form included the following propositions:

    1. *Monarchy is a divinely ordained institution.*

45. Cited by Roger Lockyer, *The Early Stuarts: A Political History of England, 1603–1642* (London, 1989), 159.
46. Ibid.
47. Conrad Russell takes issue with Johann Sommerville over the importance of this theory as a source of dissension. Russell is quite right that the basic proposition that the source of royal power was divine was not controversial, only the powers attributed to the divine right monarch were. Sommerville is correct that the full-blown theory was a serious source of controversy and unable to be reconciled to the ancient constitution. See Russell, *Origins*, 146–49, and "Divine Rights in the Early Seventeenth Century," in *Public Duty and Private Conscience*, ed. Morrill, Slack, and Woolf, 101–20; Russell, *The Causes of the English Civil War*, 65–68, 145–49; and Sommerville, *Politics and Ideology in England*, 3–4; chap. 1.

2. *Hereditary right is indefeasible.* The succession to monarchy is regulated by the law of primogeniture. The right acquired by birth cannot be forfeited through any acts of usurpation, of however long continuance, by any incapacity in the heir, or by any act of deposition.

3. *Kings are accountable to God alone.* Monarchy is pure, the sovereignty being entirely vested in the king whose power is incapable of legal limitation. All law is a mere concession of his will, and all constitutional forms and assemblies exist entirely at his pleasure. He cannot limit or divide or alienate the sovereignty, so as in any way to prejudice the right of his successor to its complete exercise. A mixed or limited monarchy is a contradiction in terms.

4. *Non-resistance and passive obedience are enjoined by God.* Under any circumstances resistance to a king is a sin, and ensures damnation. Whenever the king issues a command directly contrary to God's law, God is to be obeyed rather than man, but the example of the primitive Christians is to be followed and all penalties attached to the breach of the law are to be patiently endured.[48]

Echoes of these views appear in the published works of clerical, legal, and lay supporters of James I and Charles I and in their own royal pronouncements. All argue from Scripture and the law of nature that absolute monarchy is *the* divinely ordained form of government, many pointing to instances in Scripture of kings created by God. Adam is transposed into the first king as well as the father of mankind. Monarchy is depicted as the most natural, stable, and perfect form of government, even though the power of kings cannot be limited and subjects might be abused. Because England is a monar-

---

48. See John Neville Figgis, ed., *The Divine Right of Kings* (London, 1965), 5–6.

chy its king, by definition, is absolute and necessarily above the law and Parliament, answerable only to God. History is employed to demonstrate that England's kings are more ancient than parliaments. Both the common law and the people's rights exist by his grace. That is, no right is a *right*, all are mere gifts of the Crown. Because the king is God's agent there can be no active resistance to him or to his officials, merely a passive resistance in extreme cases. Clerical authors tended to subscribe to a more extreme form of absolutism, but all royalist writers espoused variations on Figgis's divine right monarchy.

Examples of such texts abound in the years leading up to the civil war. To take a notorious example, Roger Maynwaring, one of Charles's chaplains, claimed in a fit of zealous sermonizing reprinted below that kings were above all, "inferiour to none, to no *man*, to no *multitudes* of men, to no *Angell*, to no *order of Angels*."[49] According to Maynwaring that meant that "all the significations of a *Royall pleasure*, are, and ought to be, to all *Loyall subiects*, in the nature and force of a *Command*."[50] Subjects must either obey the king's sovereign will —"which gives a binding force to all his *Royall Edicts*"—even if "flatly against the Law of God," or suffer patiently.[51] Maynwaring's sermon was published by royal command and so outraged public opinion that when Parliament next met, Maynwaring was charged with an intention to destroy it, sentenced to the Fleet, and fined £1,000. Charles agreed to suppress the offending tract but a month later rewarded Maynwaring with the first of a series of preferments that culminated in the bishopric of St. Davids.

In another notable case John Cowell, in his legal dictionary *Interpreter*, described the king as "above the Law by his absolute power..."

---

49. Roger Maynwaring, "Religion and Alegiance: In Two Sermons Preached Before the Kings Maiestie," reprinted below, 59.

50. Ibid., 63.

51. Ibid., 64.

and though for the better and equall course in making Lawes, hee doe admit the three Estates, that is, Lords Spirituall, Lords Temporall, and the Commons unto Councell: yet this . . . is not of constraint, but of his owne benignitie, or by reason of his promise made upon oath, at the time of his coronation."[52] Cowell wrote of Parliament: "And of these two one must needes bee true, that either the King is above the Parliament, that is, the positive lawes of his kingdome, or else that hee is not an absolute King."[53]

On the sensitive issue of "subsidie," or tax, Cowell observed: "Some hold opinion, that this Subsidie is granted by the Subject to the Prince, in recompense or consideration, that whereas the Prince of his absolute power, might make Lawes of himselfe, hee doth of favour admit the consent of his Subjects therein. . . ."[54]

These definitions provoked such furor that James I agreed to condemn the book, but in 1637 Charles allowed it to be reissued. James and Charles apparently shared Cowell's opinions. In 1621, when in defiance of James's injunction that they not "meddle henceforth with any thing concerning our government or deep matters of state," the Commons claimed a right to do so, James retorted: "we cannot allow of the style, calling it your *antient and undoubted right and inheritance*; but could rather have wished that ye had said, That your privileges were derived from the grace and permission of our ancestors and us, for most of them grow from precedents, which shows rather a toleration than inheritance."[55]

Whether James did not "appreciate or even understand" the English constitution, or simply did not accept it, he was realist enough

---

52. Cowell, *Interpreter*, definition of King.
53. Ibid., definition of Parliament.
54. Ibid., definition of Subsidy.
55. James I, dated 10 December 1621 in answer to the petition of the House of Commons of 9 December 1621, in John Rushworth, *Historical Collections of Private Passages of State, Weighty Matters of Law, Remarkable Proceedings in Five Parliaments: 1618–29* (London: 1659–1701), 1:46.

to modify his behavior in the face of widespread anger.[56] But popular nerves were so frayed by 1625 when Charles's first Parliament met, that a worried member cautioned, "We are the last monarchy in Christendom that retain our original rights and constitutions. Let us not perish now!"[57]

Charles pressed his agenda with more daring and obstinacy than his father. While he wrote no books on kingship, he made his feelings plain in his declarations, appointments, and the publication of tracts that advocated divine right. For example, Charles warned the parliament of 1626: "Parliaments are altogether in my power for their calling, sitting, and dissolution; therefore as I find the fruits of them good or evil, they are to continue or not to be."[58] He informed the parliament of 1628 that common danger was the cause of its meeting, supply the end, and unless every man there did his duty other means would be used to obtain the needed funds. "Take not this as a threatening," he added, "for I scorn to threaten any but my equals."[59] At the prorogation of that tense session the king chaffed, "I owe an account of my actions to none but to God alone."[60] It was the parliament of 1628 that, in an act of desperation, attempted to defend

56. C. H. McIlwain, *The Political Works of James I* (New York, 1965), xxxvi. Conrad Russell has argued that James's views of divine right monarchy were traditional and that he saw the king's role as divinely ordained but limited. See Russell, "Divine Rights in the Early Seventeenth Century," 115–20. Also see Jenny Wormold, "James VI and I, *Basilikon Doron* and *The Trew Law of Free Monarchies*: The Scottish Context and the English Translation," 36–54, and Paul Christianson, "Royal and Parliamentary Voices on the Ancient Constitution, c. 1604–1621," in *The Mental World of the Jacobean Court*, ed. Linda Levy Peck (Cambridge, 1991), 71–98.

57. Sir Robert Phelips, cited in Catherine Drinker Bowen, *The Lion and the Throne: The Life and Times of Sir Edward Coke* (Boston, 1956), 470.

58. S. R. Gardiner, *Constitutional Documents of the Puritan Revolution*, 6.

59. Cited in *Lion and the Throne*, 481. For an excellent essay on Charles's relationship with the Parliament of 1628, see Richard Cust, "Charles I and the Parliament of 1628," *Trans. Royal Historical Society*, 6th ser., 2 (1992): 25–50.

60. Gardiner, *Constitutional Documents of the Puritan Revolution*, 73. The "Declaration Shewing the Causes of the late Dissolution" in 1629 begins: "Howsoever princes are not bound to give account of their actions, but to God alone; yet for the satisfaction of the minds and

English liberties with passage of the Petition of Right. Charles reluctantly agreed to the petition but vowed not to call another parliament until his subjects came to "a better understanding of us," and he
made it an offense to repeat rumors about a parliament being summoned.[61]

In the absence of parliaments, Charles raised monies by resorting
to his emergency powers. This use of emergency powers when there
was no emergency was considered "legal tyranny."[62] The king admitted as much in 1642 when he referred to his government of the 1630s
as "departing too much from the known rule of law, to an arbitrary
power."[63] His stratagems led to a highly publicized series of legal
challenges. The king's position was upheld in each case, but it proved
a pyrrhic victory for the Crown and a disaster for the bench.[64] Henry
Parker's vigorous denunciation of the verdict in the shipmoney case,
reprinted below, eloquently presents the grave constitutional ramifi-
cations contemporaries saw. Edward Hyde, an attorney and future
royalist, was one of many who found Charles's politicization of royal
judges unprecedented, and more alarming than any particular verdict: "it is very observable that, in the wisdom of former times, when
the prerogative went highest . . . never any court of law, very seldom

affections of our loving subjects, we have thought good to set down thus much by way of declaration. . . . "

61. See Richard Cust, "Charles I and the Parliament of 1628," *Trans. Royal Historical Society*, 6th ser., 2 (1992): 45.

62. See Morrill, *The Nature of the English Revolution*, 289–91; John Guy, "The Origins of
the Petition of Right," *Historical Journal* 25 (1982): 289–312; John Reeve, *Charles I and the Making of the Personal Rule* (Cambridge, 1989), 32–33; John Reeve, "Arguments in King's Bench in
1629 Concerning the Imprisonment of Members of the House of Commons," *Journal British
Studies* 25 (1986); and Richard Cust, *The Forced Loan and English Politics* (London, 1988), 39–82.

63. See "His Majesties Declaration to all his loving subjects," 12 August 1642, cited by Morrill, "Charles I and Tyranny," 294. A variety of means were used by Charles to raise funds. Medieval dues were resurrected, customs duties collected without parliamentary approval, and
shipmoney was extended to inland counties. The Crown imprisoned large numbers of men
who refused to pay "forced" loans.

64. For a quick review of these cases, see Kenyon, *Stuart Constitution*, 74–110. And see
below, Henry Parker, "The Case of Shipmony Briefly Discoursed" (London, 1640).

any judge, or lawyer of reputation, was called upon to assist in an act of power; the Crown well knowing the moment of keeping those the objects of reverence and veneration with the people...."[65] But "in the business of the shipmoney and in many other cases in the Star-chamber and at Council-board," Hyde observed, "there were many impertinencies, incongruities, and insolencies, in the speeches and orations of the judges, much more offensive and much more scandalous than the judgments and sentences themselves."[66] These cases that drew the royal judges to the forefront of the struggle for sovereignty, not on behalf of the law but of the Crown, cost them their reputation as guardians of the people's rights.

Charles took shelter under the ancient constitution in 1642 in his Answer to Parliament's Nineteen Propositions. The ancient constitution provided monarchs special powers to cope with extraordinary occasions, as the Earl of Strafford pleaded in his defense before the House of Lords: "The prerogative must be used, as God doth his omnipotency at extraordinary occasions; the laws . . . must have place at all other times, and yet there must be a prerogative if there must be extraordinary occasions."[67] As for individual liberties, Strafford added, "I have and shall ever aim at a fair but a bounded liberty, remembering always that I am a freeman, but a subject; that I have a right, but under a monarch."

Had the king's aim been to preserve his traditional powers, upholding the ancient constitution was perhaps the most compelling approach. But nearly all pamphleteers advocating royal sovereignty steered clear of references to English legal and constitutional traditions.[68] A notable exception was their fondness for the legal tenet,

---

65. Edward, Earl of Clarendon, in *The History of the Rebellion and Civil Wars in England*, ed. W. Dunn Macray (Oxford, 1888; rpt. 1969), 1:88.

66. Clarendon, *History*, 1:89.

67. See Kenyon, *Stuart Constitution*, 194.

68. See Joyce Lee Malcolm, *Caesar's Due: Loyalty and King Charles, 1642–1646* (London, 1983), 131–40.

"The king can do no wrong," which they interpreted to mean that
the king was above the law.[69]

The promise of unchecked power made absolutist arguments al-
luring for kings. But in addition to the hostility the arguments
aroused and their indifference to legality, they contained dangerous
liabilities. Unwavering obedience to a ruler meant that any ruler, even
a usurper, must be obeyed. The English crown had been won by the
sword more than once, most recently by Henry Tudor in 1485, but in
such instances legitimacy, continuity, and order were stressed to win
over the population, not insistence upon absolute obedience.

The argument that since kingship was older than Parliament, that
that institution and the people's liberties were mere gifts from kings,
also had its hazards. It harked back to William the Conqueror. Conquerors were believed to have absolute power over those they conquered. Hence, the claim of right from William jeopardized all the
rights of Englishmen. Pym pointed out the danger when he presented the House of Commons' indictment for treason against the
Earl of Strafford. To Pym's mind Strafford's justification for his harsh
treatment of the Irish—"They were a conquered Nation"—had
"more mischiefe in it than the thing it selfe":

> They were a Conquered Nation. There cannot be a word more
> pregnant, and fruitfull in Treason, than that word is: There are
> few Nations in the world that have not been conquered; and no
> doubt but the Conquerour may give what Lawes he please to
> those that are conquered ... England hath been conquered, and
> Wales hath been conquered, and by this reason will be in little
> better case then Ireland.[70]

---

69. This interpretation is at odds with a broad range of commentary on that phrase. See
Malcolm, "Doing No Wrong," forthcoming.

70. John Pym, "The Speech or Declaration of *John Pym*, Esquire: After the Recapitulation or Summing Up of the Charge of *High-Treason, Against* Thomas, Earle of Strafford"
(London, 1641), reprinted below, 132.

Any subsequent conqueror would automatically fall heir to such power. How then could the rightful king regain his throne? Pym also noted that if a king rules as a conqueror the people are restored to the right of the conquered, to recover their liberty if they can.

After a conquest a distinction often arose between the king "de facto" and the king "de jure." Henry VII's De facto Act of 1495, which held those loyal to the king "for the time being" blameless from later charges of treason, was cited in the 1660s by individuals accused of complicity with the Interregnum governments. In sum, extreme absolutist arguments were weapons to be employed with caution. They tended to backfire.

THE SOVEREIGNTY OF LAW

In the early years of the seventeenth century, as claims that monarchs were above the law gained currency, a rival view—of a law more ancient than any king, a law that defined kingship—also gained ground. Its advocates saw England's vast accretion of customs, principles, and rules as the collective wisdom of its people. Pym reminded the Lords, "Your Honours, your Lives, your Liberties and Estates are all in the keeping of the Law."[71] The proper execution of the laws, the royalist Sir Roger Twysden claimed, was the "greatest (earthly) blessing of Englishmen."[72]

The preeminent champion of the law was the brilliant and combative Sir Edward Coke, whose extraordinary career spanned three reigns.[73] As an attorney Coke was a strenuous defender of the

---

71. Ibid.

72. [Sir Roger Twysden], "The Commoners Liberty: or, The Englishman's Birth-Right" (London, 1648), 1.

73. Coke served as solicitor-general, recorder of London, speaker of the House of Commons, and attorney-general under Queen Elizabeth; as James I's chief justice of the court of Common Pleas, privy councillor, and chief justice of the court of King's Bench; and lived to play a significant part in the early parliaments of Charles I.

Crown, as a judge a daring defender of the law, as parliamentarian a staunch defender of the rights of Parliament. His famous reports of Elizabethan and Jacobean cases began to appear in 1600 and by 1615 had run to eleven volumes.[74] Like Cowell's *Interpreter*, Coke's *Reports* had a constitutional thrust. Lord Chancellor Ellesmere accused Coke of dishonest reporting and of having "purposely laboured to derogate much from the rights of the Church and dignity of church-men, and to disesteem and weaken the power of the king in the ancient use of his prerogative."[75] Whether Coke's *Reports* did "purposely" derogate the rights of church and Crown, they had that impact.

Both the prefaces to Coke's *Reports* and the cases he included are noteworthy. The prefaces constitute a magnificent tribute to the common law. Coke found "no Learning so excellent both for Prince and Subject, as Knowledge of Laws; and no Knowledge of any Laws (I speak of human) so necessary for all Estates . . . as the common Laws of England."[76] He refuted the claim that English monarchy was more ancient than the people's rights. True, the English had been conquered, but Coke argued "the several Conquerors and Governors" of the realm, "Romans, Saxons, Danes, or Normans," found English laws so excellent they chose not to alter them.[77] The law courts and the High Court of Parliament Coke considered "a part of the frame of the common laws."[78] He even found ancient statutes

---

74. We are told Coke was so respected that during these years no other reports appeared "as it became all the rest of the lawyers to be silent whilst their oracle was speaking." See *Modern Reports, or Select Cases Adjudged in the Courts of King's Bench, Chancery, Common Pleas, and Exchequer, since the Restoration of Charles II*, vol. 5, viii.

75. Cited by Kenyon, *Stuart Constitution*, 86.

76. Edward Coke, Preface, The Second Part of the *Reports* (London, 1602), reprinted below, 6.

77. See below, Coke, Preface, The Second Part of the *Reports*; and see prefaces to *Eighth Report* and *Ninth Report*.

78. Coke, *Reports*, Preface, *Ninth Report*, xxv.

that mandated frequent meetings of Parliament.[79] Parliament's champions leapt upon the finding that Parliament was not the creation of any monarch.[80]

The contents of Coke's *Reports* also had constitutional significance. Some cases he includes fix the jurisdiction of clerical and common law courts, generally to the benefit of common law, and decide questions of royal prerogative. "Prohibitions del Roy" takes up the prickly issue of whether the king of England can interpret law himself and whether he is bound by the law. Here Coke falls back on Bracton's pronouncement that the king is under no man, but under God and the law.[81] When Coke discussed cases where precedents for greater royal powers were cited, he countered with a preeminent claim of right from Magna Carta and the comments of ancient legal authorities.

Yet while the lavish praise for common law helped to elevate the High Court of Parliament and circumscribe the powers of the Crown, the main thrust was for the sovereignty of law itself. As Francis Bacon explained: "In the Laws we have a native interest, it is our birth-right and our inheritance . . . under a Law we must live, and under a known law, and not under an arbitrary law is our happiness that we do live."[82] Legal experts held any action of the Crown or Parliament that was against law—that is natural, fundamental law—void. This was the usual understanding of the phrase "the king can do no wrong."[83] Statute law enacted by Parliament was also held to be

79. Coke claimed a statute of King Alfred called for Parliament to meet twice a year at London and found evidence it even met once during the reign of William the Conqueror. Coke, Preface, *Ninth Report*, xi–xii, xviii.

80. Coke, Preface, *Ninth Report*, xi.

81. See below, Coke, "Prohibitions del Roy," 5 Jac. 1 (1607), in Coke's *Reports*, vol. 6, part 12, 18.

82. See James Spedding, ed., *Life and Letters of Francis Bacon* (London, 1861–74), 6:15, 18, 19.

83. A tract attributed to Sir Roger L'Estrange, reprinted below, explains:
Certain it is that our King in his personall capacity, made no Laws, so neither did he, by himself, execute or interpret any: No Judge took notice of his single Command, to

merely declarative of common law and if found to be at odds with it was also "void in the act." As Coke explains in a famous passage in Bonham's Case: "in many cases the common law will control acts of Parliament and some times adjudge them to be utterly void; For when an Act of Parliament is against common right and reason, or repugnant, or impossible to be performed, the common law will control it and adjudge such Act to be void."[84]

This "sovereign law" was not written statute, or common usage, or even Magna Carta but the law of equity and right reason. The test of right reason was its harmony with the law of nature or natural law. Unfortunately, the vagueness of natural law made it a slippery standard to apply. Those who argued for the sovereignty of kings often based this thesis on the supposed preference for monarchy in nature. But those who defended the many against the tyranny of an individual ruler argued that the most basic law of nature was a right to self-defense.

Statesmen, clergymen, and pamphleteers could debate the meaning and application of natural and common law, but the law was interpreted by learned judges. This was the Achilles heel in the theory of the law as sovereign. The judges, royal appointees, were thrust into *the* pivotal role. Charles altered judges' patents so they no longer sat

---

justifie any Trespass; no, not so much, as the breaking of an Hedge; his Power limited by his Justice, he was (equally with the meanest of his Subjects) concerned in that honest Maxime, *We may do just so much and no more, than we have right to do*; And it was most properly said, *He could do no wrong*; because if it were wrong, he did it not, he could not do it; It was void in the act, punishable in his agent.
[Sir Roger L'Estrange], "A *Plea* for Limited Monarchy," 503. For a good account of natural law, see Richard Tuck, *Natural Rights Theories: Their Origin and Development* (Cambridge, 1979).
84. Coke, *Reports*, vol. 4, part 8, 118a. And see volume 2, Anonymous, "Vox Populi: Or the People's Claim to Their Parliaments Sitting," 659, where the author explains: "The Statute Laws are Acts of Parliament which are (or ought to be) only Declaratory of the Common Law, which as you have heard is founded upon right Reason and Scripture; for we are told, that if anything is enacted contrary thereto, it is void and null. . . ."

during good behavior but at the pleasure of the grantor, "the better," the Grand Remonstrance charged, "to hold a rod over them."[85]

Most Stuart judges seemed anxious to avoid the constitutional spotlight. S. R. Gardiner finds "tacit renunciation by the Judges of that high authority which the Commons thrust upon them in 1628."[86] "They refused to be arbitrators between the King and the nation," he argued. "They accepted the position which Bacon had assigned them, of lions beneath the throne, upon whom was imposed the duty of guarding the throne from attack."[87] The result was, as W. J. Jones found, that the judges in the reign of Charles I submissively legitimated the king's use of obsolete customs and fees until "in the end, judicial approval and political absurdity walked hand in hand."[88] All this notwithstanding, the claim for the supremacy of law was an attractive one that found its way into numerous arguments for the limitation of royal power, sometimes also of parliamentary power, occasionally of both.

THE SOVEREIGNTY OF PARLIAMENT

Parliament is often portrayed as the aggressor in the struggle for sovereignty. Its prewar pronouncements have been variously characterized as the high road to civil war, unwarranted aggression, or, if

---

85. See note 24 above. And see Grand Remonstrance, clause 38. Kenyon believes the significance of this change has been overstated. See Kenyon, *Stuart Constitution*, 74–75. In a speech to his judges in Star Chamber James had pointed out: "As kings borrow their power from God, so judges from kings; and as kings are to account to God, so judges unto God and kings." "Encroach not upon the prerogative of the Crown," he warned. "If there fall out a question that concerns my prerogative or mystery of state, deal not with it till you consult with the king or his council. . . . That which concerns the mystery of the king's power is not lawful to be disputed." Kenyon, *Stuart Constitution*, 84–85.

86. S. R. Gardiner, *A History of England, 1628–1637* (London, 1877), 1:153.

87. Ibid.

88. Jones, *Politics and the Bench*, 89.

defensive, then "neurotically defensive." The king had regarded Parliament's defense of its privileges and the people's liberties, even its committee system, as an attack upon monarchy itself.[89] And it has been argued recently that it was Parliament's first assertion of sovereignty in 1642 that brought the country to the "constitutional impasse" that led to war.[90] But this is to overlook the fact that Parliament's initial reactions were defensive and only shifted to the offense gradually and *in extremis*.[91] James's pretensions had frightened his first parliament into drafting the "Form of Apology and Satisfaction" to remind him their "privileges and liberties" were their "right and due inheritance, no less than our very lands and goods," that "this High Court of Parliament . . . gives laws to other courts, but from other courts receives neither laws nor orders."[92] The king was God's lieutenant, but the Commons claimed to speak for his people whose voice "in the things of their knowledge, is said to be as the voice of God."[93] In 1604, however, this voice spoke in a whisper.

Parliament was less reticent about its claim to be the highest court. "Such matters as for difficulty are not fit for the Judges, or through eminent delay are not despatched by the Judges," Edward Hyde told

89. In Charles I's "Declaration Shewing the Causes of the Late Dissolution," 10 March 1629, the king argued: "In these innovations (which we will never permit again) they pretended indeed our service, but their drift was to break, by this means through all respects and ligaments of government, and to erect an universal over-swaying power to themselves, which belongs only to us, and not to them." Reprinted in Gardiner, *Constitutional Documents*, 95. Also see Cust, "Charles I and the Parliament of 1628," 40.

90. Michael Mendle, "Parliamentary Sovereignty: A Very English Absolutism," in *Political Discourse in Early Modern Britain*, ed. Nicholas Phillipson and Quentin Skinner (Cambridge, 1993), 97.

91. Kenyon sets out these three interpretations in *Stuart Constitution*, 25.

92. See Kenyon, *Stuart Constitution*, 29–35. Kenyon believes the view that "The Apology" was the first of the series of great constitutional protests that led directly to 1641 is exaggerated. Where it was once thought aggressive he finds it can be equally regarded as "neurotically defensive" (Kenyon, 25). "The Apology" was drafted by a committee of Parliament but never approved by the full body. It does seem to reflect the views of many members, albeit many found it imprudent for Parliament to approve it. See G. R. Elton, "A High Road to Civil War?" in *Studies in Tudor and Stuart Politics and Government* (Cambridge, 1974), 2:164–82.

93. Kenyon, *Stuart Constitution*, 35.

the Commons, "shall be determined in Parliament."[94] Some polemicists had begun to portray the king as the people's servant, Parliament their representative.[95] But Parliament's own constitutional pronouncements—the Protestation of 1621 and Petition of Right of 1628—bear out its contention that it was defending the ancient constitution. Even after it began to encroach upon royal prerogatives with passage of the Grand Remonstrance, the Militia Ordinance, and the Nineteen Propositions, Parliament stuck to its conservative rhetoric.[96] Throughout the year prior to war, it avoided branding Charles a tyrant or even asserting that he had behaved in an arbitrary manner.[97] The drafters of the Grand Remonstrance removed the words "tyranny" and "arbitrary" from their long and otherwise belligerent text.[98] Not until 6 June 1642 when they needed to justify passage of the Militia Ordinance without royal consent did the two Houses claim supreme authority.

> The High Court of parliament is not only a court of judicature, enabled by the laws to adjudge and determine the rights and liberties of the kingdom, against such patents and grants of his Majesty as are prejudicial thereunto. . . . it is likewise a council, to provide for the necessities, prevent the imminent dangers,

94. Edward Hyde, "Speech at a conference," cited by A. D. T. Cromartie, "The Printing of Parliamentary Speeches November 1640–July 1642," *Historical Journal* 33, 1 (1990), 34.

95. William Pierrepont, in a speech in July 1641, placed the source of power there: "Unlimited power must be in some to make and repeal laws to fit the dispositions of times and persons. Nature placeth this in common consent only, and where all cannot conveniently meet, instructeth them to give their consents to some they know or believe so well of as to be bound to what they agree on. His Majesty, your Lordships, and the Commons are thus met in Parliament, and so long as we are often reduced to this main foundation our King and we shall prosper." Pierrepont, 6 July 1641, from Rushworth, *Historical Collections*, 2:601–5.

96. A careful reading of the key parliamentary documents in question bears out the view that Parliament continued to be defensive. For copies of the parliamentary documents in question, see Kenyon, *Stuart Constitution*, 29–35, 42–43, 68–71.

97. John Morrill, "Charles I, Tyranny, and the English Civil War," in *The Nature of the English Revolution*, 292–94.

98. Morrill outlines the latest evidence that Charles had, in fact, behaved in a manner that he labels legal tyranny. See "Charles I, Tyranny, and the English Civil War," 289–91.

and preserve the public peace and safety of the kingdom, and to declare the king's pleasure in those things are requisite thereunto; and what they do herein hath the stamp of royal authority, although his Majesty, seduced by evil counsel, do in his own person oppose or interrupt the same.[99]

Within the month Henry Parker, Parliament's leading theorist, had resolutely insisted upon the sovereignty of the Lords and Commons in his provocative reply to the king's Answer to the Nineteen Propositions, "Observations upon some of his Majesties late Answers and Expresses."[100]

The ground had been prepared for the notion Parliament could act without, or in opposition to, the king by a shift in the way his parliamentary role was understood. He had been considered the head of Parliament. Its three estates were the lords spiritual, the lords temporal, and the commons. When the classical division of governments into monarchy, aristocracy, and democracy was reintroduced into England in the mid-sixteenth century, English government began to be viewed as a mixture of all three.[101] In 1591 William Lambarde, a

99. The declaration laid the foundation for this claim as follows:

The question is not, whether it belong to the king or no, to restrain such force, but, if the king shall refuse to discharge that duty and trust, whether there is not a power in the two Houses to provide for the safety of the parliament and peace of the kingdom, which is the end for which the ordinance concerning the militia was made, and being agreeable to the scope and purpose of the law, cannot in reason be adjudged to be contrary to it....

It is acknowledged that the king is the fountain of justice and protection, but the acts of justice and protection are not exercised in his own person, nor depend upon his pleasure, but by his courts, and by his ministers, who must do their duty therein, though the king in his own person should forbid them; and therefore if judgments should be given by them against the king's will and personal command, yet are they the king's judgments.

See Kenyon, *Stuart Constitution*, 226.

100. See Henry Parker, "Observations upon some of his Majesties late Answers and Expresses" (London, [2 July] 1642); Judson, *The Crisis of the Constitution*, 425–26, 435; and Judson, *From Tradition to Political Reality*, 11, 43. See also Michael Mendle, "Parliamentary Sovereignty," 116–18.

101. Michael Mendle attacks Weston's analysis of the three coordinate estates as too narrow in approach. I have drawn the information about the introduction of the classical analysis

renowned legal antiquary, redefined the three estates of Parliament to correspond with the three types of government. The king, in this analysis, was one of the estates, the others being the House of Lords and the House of Commons. By implication the two houses "were equal partners in lawmaking with the king," the clergy were no longer a separate estate.[102] Lambarde's definition had gained acceptance by 1640 and was officially, if reluctantly, endorsed by Charles in 1642 in his Answer to Parliament's Nineteen Propositions.[103] Charles did not write his Answer, however, and probably disagreed with this part of it for, as Pocock reminds us, he died "affirming other principles."[104]

Charles's acceptance of the monarchy as one of three estates of Parliament had grave repercussions. It strengthened the view that the king in parliament, not the king alone, was sovereign. It reduced the king to one of three apparent equals, and accepted elimination of the bishops as a distinct estate. Moreover, the concept of three forms of government introduced a republican component into English political theory. And since each form was supposed to possess "an inherent tendency to degeneration," the king's power was per se imperfect, not the earthly representative of divine power.[105] All this had the effect of reducing the king to an estate of his own realm.

---

of the three forms of government from Mendle, *Dangerous Positions*, 2–3. Also see Markku Peltonen, *Classical Humanism and Republicanism in English Political Thought, 1570–1640* (Cambridge, 1995).

102. Weston, "England: Ancient Constitution and Common Law," 393–94. Lambarde endorsed the concept of an immemorial parliament and even an immemorial house of commons and recognized the share of the two houses in lawmaking.

103. Corinne Weston has studied this alteration extensively and attributed great moment to it. See Weston, *English Constitutional Theory and the House of Lords*. But see Mendle, *Dangerous Positions*, where he takes issue with Weston's interpretation.

104. Lucius Cary, Viscount Falkland, and John Colepeper are believed to have written the king's Answer. Weston, *English Constitutional Theory*, 26–28. For Pocock's comments, see J. G. A. Pocock, ed., *The Political Works of James Harrington* (Cambridge, 1977), 19–20.

105. In the view of Englishmen "only the wisdom of the ancestors had succeeded 'as far as humane prudence can contrive,' in combining it with the aristocratic and democratic powers which were its equals." See Pocock, *Ancient Constitution and the Feudal Law*, 309.

WAR FOOTING

The civil war seemed to Englishmen an unnatural war, a war without an enemy.[106] They felt distraught at what appeared then, and has appeared since, as an inexorable march to war. In the months before the battle of Edgehill Englishmen from across the realm pleaded for compromise in a great avalanche of petitions to the king and Parliament.[107] All to no avail.

As the tracts in this volume illustrate, the focus of the quarrel shifted along with political events. Until 1641 the central issue was whether the king was sovereign with unlimited power or accountable to the law and his subjects. Once the king had left London, debate turned to whether the two houses of Parliament could function without a king, and whether the severely reduced numbers of MPs still sitting at Westminster constituted a true parliament. And leading up to and after the outbreak of war there was understandable concern about what circumstances, if any, justified resistance to the monarch. In order to wage war both king and Parliament had to assert their right to govern alone. This was more difficult for Parliament, which claimed to be governing in the name of king and Parliament while fighting against Charles Stuart. Even if the king's role was seen as merely coordinate, he was essential to the regular functioning of Parliament. It could not legislate without him. Worse, opposition to him, even by MPs, bore the stigma of rebellion. Parliament and its advocates tried various ways of getting around these difficulties. The two houses repeated to the point of absurdity the old saw that the king was an innocent misled by evil councilors. When

---

106. Comments that the civil war was an unnatural war abound in the literature and personal documents of the period. Sir William Waller, one of the most successful parliamentarian officers, referred to it as a war without an enemy in a letter to his old friend and royalist officer Sir Ralph Hopton. See Richard Ollard, *This War Without an Enemy: A History of the English Civil Wars* (London, 1976), 85.

107. See, for example, Malcolm, *Caesar's Due*, 21–22.

this proved no longer tenable they began to distinguish between the king and his office. The ancient laws of Edward the Confessor appeared to support this distinction: "The king, because he is the vicar of the highest king, is appointed for this purpose, to rule the earthly kingdom, and the Lord's people, and, above all things, to reverence his holy church . . . which unless he do, the name of a king agreeth not unto him, but he loseth the name of a king."[108] Parliament insisted it fought in defense of the ancient constitution, against the person of Charles Stuart. Its battle flags bore the slogan, "For King and Parliament," while the royalist slogan was simply "For the King." The distinction between the king and his office—the theory of the king's "two bodies"—evoked Catholic and Calvinist justifications of resistance to a godless ruler. Royalists pounced upon such arguments as "papist." Yet, the distinction between kings and tyrants had considerable theoretical foundation and served Parliament's supporters well.[109] More practical, Parliament rediscovered the concept of the "ordinance" as an alternative to a statute, a decree that could be used in time of emergency in the absence of the king.[110] *Salus populi*, the safety of the realm, was acknowledged as the highest law. With that in mind Parliament argued it was forced to act to save itself and the country.

Almost certainly most Englishmen and most of those taking sides in the civil war wanted a compromise. Indeed, in the Solemn League and Covenant of 1643, Parliament's agreement with the Scots, it had declared this one of its principal aims. In token, as John Kenyon points out, it was not until June 1644 that MPs who had sided with the king were formally expelled and new elections held for their

---

108. See Weston, "England: Ancient Constitution and Common Law," 386.

109. See Janelle Greenberg, "Our Grand Maxim of State, 'The King Can Do No Wrong,'" *History of Political Thought* 12 (summer 1991): esp. 217–18, 220.

110. On the introduction of the ordinance in these circumstances, see Mendle, "Parliamentary Sovereignty," 112–14.

seats.[111] But once fighting had started, whenever compromise seemed possible the radical elements on both sides became more vocal, obstinate, and extreme.[112] David Wootton finds this true during the winter of 1642/43 when there was fear the longing for a settlement might lead Parliament to give in to the king. Indeed, Wootton dates the origins of the transition "from rebellion to revolution" to that period. The debates throughout that winter foreshadowed many of the arguments that would be used in 1646 by the Levellers.[113]

On the royalist side tracts published on the king's behalf were controlled tightly by the Crown.[114] Most abandoned the moderate tone of his Answer to the Nineteen Propositions and reverted to harping upon his divine right and the sin of rebellion. They even echoed Charles's claim that his opponents only pretended to fight for English laws and liberties but actually sought personal power.

Argument became more intense after the surrender of Charles in 1646. The long and fruitless negotiations between him and his victorious parliament led to general frustration, in particular among members of the New Model Army, who feared all they had fought for would be lost. The army's proposals for future government and the rise of the Leveller party dominated the pamphlet conversation of 1646 and 1647. The Levellers' program, extreme for the time, demanded social reform, religious toleration, a wider franchise, and abolition of the monarchy and House of Lords. The importance of the Levellers to contemporary politics and theory has been over-emphasized because of our respect for their opinions. Their chief

111. Kenyon, *Stuart Constitution*, 243.

112. See David Wootton, "From Rebellion to Revolution: The Crisis of the Winter of 1642/3 and the Origins of Civil War Radicalism," *English Historical Review* (July 1990): 654–69.

113. Ibid., 656. On the Levellers, see, for example, G. E. Aylmer, *The Levellers in the English Revolution* (London, 1975), and William Haller and G. Davies, *The Leveller Tracts: 1647–1653* (New York, 1944).

114. See Malcolm, *Caesar's Due*, 124–48.

contemporary impact was on the men of the New Model Army. Nonetheless their arguments highlight the parameters of the political and social thought of that era.

The stalemate caused by Charles's refusal to surrender his powers and Parliament's inability to trust him was shattered in 1648 when a series of uprisings known as the second civil war broke out. As far as the New Model Army was concerned, this was final proof of the king's intransigence and duplicity. Once they had restored order, the army took matters into their own hands, seizing the king and, in December 1648, purging the more moderate members from Parliament. Pride's Purge fractured what unity remained within the victorious party and alienated a large segment of the English population. The pretence that members still sitting in Parliament (derisively known as the Rump) were representative of the English people, or still a parliament became far more difficult to sustain. A vigorous argument was advanced by John Goodwin in a tract published 2 January 1649 that the true representative of the people was the parliamentary army, not the Rump Parliament.[115] It was incumbent upon the army to act in the public interest. Two days later, on 4 January 1649, the Rump claimed sovereignty for itself. Its proclamation explained that "the people are, under God, the original of all just power," and the Commons of England, "in parliament assembled," as representatives of the people "have the supreme power in this nation."[116] It announced whatever the House of Commons "declared for law" had the force of law "although the consent and concurrence of king, or House of Peers, be not had thereunto."

If this were not provocative enough, the decision to put the king on trial led to a spate of passionate tracts that labored over the issue

---

115. See below, John Goodwin, "Right and Might Well Mett" (London, 1649), 307–58.
116. See Kenyon, *Stuart Constitution*, 292.

of whether the king was above the law, where sovereignty lay, and what action it was appropriate to take. One of these, the anonymous tract "The Peoples Right Briefly Asserted"[117] published two weeks before Charles's execution, argued that the people had the right to depose a tyrant.

Charles's execution on 30 January 1649 followed by the abolition of the monarchy and the House of Lords was a watershed. Not only those who supported the Crown during the civil war, but thousands who supported Parliament were distressed by a turn of events so contrary to their hopes. Gone was the ancient constitution. Gone the Church of England. Gone the familiar landmarks. The central question was whether the radical parliamentarians governing the realm constituted a legitimate authority or were usurpers. If they were usurpers were they entitled to obedience? The Rump's declaration in March, "Expressing the Grounds of Their Late Proceedings, and of Setling the Present Government in the Way of a Free State," is reprinted below. It asserted that the foundation of government was an agreement of the people, an agreement Charles had violated by his tyrannical behavior. He had therefore forfeited his right to the crown. But the Rump's own advocates quickly switched to the simpler and starker argument that the war had been an appeal to the judgment of God, and God had decided in favor of Parliament. In fact Charles had been charged at his trial with attempting to thwart the decision of God by stirring up further war against his subjects.

Since God had ordained the new government, it was the subject's duty to obey. Ironically, the debate after January 1649 found royalists and Anglican clergy, who had advocated absolute obedience even to a tyrant, arguing for a right to resist, while parliamentarian pamphleteers defended obedience to the government in power, whatever

---

117. This tract is reprinted below, 359–68.

its legitimacy. Over time, they claimed, that obedience bestowed legitimacy.[118]

When the Rump tried to ensure obedience through the imposition of the Engagement oath in 1650, the oath itself became the focus of intense controversy.[119] It required adults "to be true and faithful to the Commonwealth of England as it is now established, without a king or House of Lords." The ensuing argument raised fundamental questions of allegiance and duty. The new oath was designed to give as little offense as possible. Still it seemed in direct opposition to the traditional oath of allegiance to the king, which posed a special problem for royalists. It was just as difficult to square with the Solemn League and Covenant of 1643 dear to Presbyterians. This last required subjects to pledge, among other things, "to preserve and defend the king's Majesty's person and authority" with "no thoughts or intentions to diminish his Majesty's just power and greatness."[120] Debate also focused on the binding power of oaths, the appropriate object to which allegiance was due, and the proper behavior of law-abiding men.

The language of the Engagement Oath ensured that the spotlight would be turned on the commonwealth, the community itself, as an object of loyalty, and the primacy of its needs over any specific form of government or particular governors. The Rump's defenders sensibly focused on the welfare of the people, their safety and immediate interest, and on concern for the peace and quiet of the realm. This

118. For information on the debates of this period, see John M. Wallace, "The Engagement Controversy, 1649–1652: An Annotated List of Pamphlets," *Bulletin of the New York Public Library* 68 (1964): 384–405; and Pocock, *Ancient Constitution*, 327.

119. An Act for Subscribing the Engagement, 2 January 1649, reprinted in Kenyon, *Stuart Constitution*, 307–8.

120. "A solemn league and covenant for the reformation and defence of religion, the honour and happiness of the King, and the peace and safety of the three kingdoms of England, Scotland and Ireland," reprinted in Kenyon, *Stuart Constitution*, 239–42. This oath was taken by the Westminster Assembly and House of Commons, 25 September 1643.

argument, that the welfare of the people, *salus populi*, was necessarily more important than the welfare of a single individual had undergirded both royalist and parliamentarian arguments from the outset. The royalists claimed rebellion could not be tolerated because it caused the greatest disruption to the common weal. Supporters of Parliament believed the welfare of the community must be placed before that of monarchical will. Resistance became legitimate when the people were forced to defend themselves from the machinations of their king.

The most famous of those weighing in with a critical approach to the engagement controversy was Thomas Hobbes. Hobbes had fled to the Continent before the civil war but later joined the royalists in exile. *Leviathan* was published in 1651 at the height of the debate. It offended the royalists and led to Hobbes's sudden return to England, where it met with a somewhat better reception. Hobbes credits *Leviathan*, with its insistence upon obedience to the government that can offer protection, with persuading many hundreds of royalist gentlemen to submit to the new regime. This is doubtful as his amoral tone shocked rather than persuaded both royalists and parliamentarians. His views on obedience, however, were in line with those of less cynical authors writing at the time.[121]

Most members of Parliament and their supporters did not wish to claim the right of conquest. Instead, they based their right to govern the realm on their claim to represent the people, then enthusiastically claimed for the people the origins of power and even supreme power. But they generally agreed that the people's power had been transferred to their representatives in Parliament and stated, or implied, that there it must remain. In 1641 William Pierrepont claimed

---

121. See, for example, Rous, "The Lawfulnes of Obeying the Present Government," and Lawson, "Conscience Puzzel'd About Subscribing the New Engagement," reprinted below, 393–404, 435–44, as well as Anthony Ascham, "Of the Confusions and Revolutions of Governments" (London, November 1649). And see Skinner, "History and Ideology in the English Revolution."

the supremacy of the three estates lay in Parliament as the people's representatives: "Unlimited power must be in some to make and repeal laws to fit the dispositions of times and persons. Nature placeth this in common consent only, and where all cannot conveniently meet, instructeth them to give their consents to some they know or believe so well of as to be bound to what they agree on."[122] Even those who argued that the people held the king to account, hesitated to give the people similar control of Parliament. Once representatives had been selected the power was theirs. Charles Herle, a supporter of Parliament writing in 1642, asked whether if neither the king nor Parliament should discharge their trust "the people might rise and make resistance against both." He answered that this was a position "which no man (I know) maintaines."[123] Instead Herle finds, "the Parliament's, is the people's owne consent, which once passed they cannot revoke . . . no power can be imployed but what is reserved, and the people have reserved no power in themselves from themselves in Parliament."[124]

The anonymous author of "The Peoples Right Briefly Asserted," published on the eve of the king's trial, came to the same conclusion by a slightly different route. He linked the people with Parliament and, quoting Bartolus, stated that a king may commit treason for which he can be deposed and punished "by that Lord against whom he hath offended, which is the People and those who represent them."[125] He argues that "the Law is more powerful than the King . . . But the whole Body of the people are more powerful than the Law, as being the parent of it."[126] The people never gave away all their

122. William Pierrepont speaking against Sir Robert Berkeley, 6 July 1641, reprinted in Jones, *Politics and the Bench*, 211.
123. [Charles Herle], "A Fuller Answer to a Treatise Written by Doctor *Ferne*, reprinted below, 255.
124. Ibid.
125. "The Peoples Right Briefly Asserted" (London, 1649), reprinted below, 364.
126. Ibid.

power, even in hereditary monarchy. However, in his view what they reserved was "their supream Power of making Election, when need required."[127] He concludes, the Parliament, "if they had a lawful power to proceed in this War," have power to dispose of their victory "as they shall think best for the future security of the whole people, whom they represent."[128] This is advocating parliamentary sovereignty on the basis that the people had irrevocably transferred their sovereignty to their representatives.

A case was made for the sovereignty of the people in a powerful tract by William Ball published in 1646. Ball argues that a free people such as the English may bestow what he calls their "power extensive" on a king or a parliament but not their "primitive, or intensive power." Nor did they cease to be free "notwithstanding their long Lease of Trust."[129] The final freedom "to dispose, or determine themselves... they never part, or parted withall; for at what time soever they should do it, they cease to be... a free People, or a People which are freely under a Law by common consent."[130] Thus he argued that the English people "never gave, or voluntarily asserted, that their Kings, or Parliaments, or Both, should have an absolute Domineering, or Arbitrary power over them, but only a Discresive, or Legall Authority intended ever for their good in generall."[131] If need be they were entitled to defend themselves against both king and Parliament. He granted that Parliament was the highest "Court extensive" but found "the People in generall... are the highest, or greatest Power Intensive, in that they are the efficient, and finall cause under God, of the Parliament."[132]

127. Ibid., 362.
128. Ibid., 368.
129. William Ball, "*Constitutio Liberi Populi.* Or, the Rule of a Free-Born People" (London, 1646), reprinted below, 296.
130. Ibid., 287–88.
131. Ibid., 290.
132. Ibid., 294.

The republican experiment also produced an outpouring of new ideas about the ideal arrangements for English government. Among the most notable were those of James Harrington, whose *Commonwealth of Oceana* appeared in 1656.[133] Other supporters of a parliamentary system, both defenders and critics of the Interregnum governments, took to their pens. Isaac Pennington Jr., son of the famous London alderman, considered deeply how government might be restructured to protect popular liberties and produced a highly original tract recommending the separation of powers, the separation of church and state, and other notions that foreshadowed ideas John Locke would later champion.[134]

Throughout the Interregnum much was done in the name of the people, but popular sovereignty was never permitted. In fact during the Interregnum the sovereignty of Parliament was never tested for the Rump, and protectorate parliaments were not representative and were too unpopular to hold a traditional general election to correct that defect. Nor were the ideas proposed for a more perfect republic put into practice. The Rump and the Protectorate of Oliver Cromwell did produce governments that were sovereign, but without a solid, theoretical basis for that sovereignty, merely, dare it be said, the rights of a conqueror. Nevertheless notions of sovereignty continued to be debated and old ideas championed despite the contemporary political reality. The disintegration into political confusion and arrival in London of George Monck and his army provoked the frantic publication of pamphlets recommending various courses for the future. Their authors pleaded, argued, and cajoled in a desperate effort to persuade Monck and later the members of the Convention. Among these pamphlets was Sir Roger L'Estrange's nostalgic "*Plea*

133. Harrington's best-known work is *Oceana* (1656), but between 1656 and 1660 he also wrote a series of tracts defending his views. See J. G. A. Pocock, ed., *The Political Works of James Harrington* (Cambridge, 1977).

134. See Isaac Pennington Jr., "The Right, Liberty and Safety of the People Briefly Asserted" (London, 1651), reprinted below, 445–89.

for Limited Monarchy, As It Was Established in This Nation Before the Late War." On the other side John Milton, in what was probably his most passionate essay, "The Readie & Easie Way to Establish a Free Commonwealth," pleaded for the preservation of a republic, rather than "the perpetual bowings and cringings of an abject people" under monarchy.[135] But all Milton's eloquence was unavailing. At the last, when the realm seemed about to collapse into anarchy, the appeal of the ancient constitution, fraught with weaknesses, complexity, and no clear sovereign, proved irresistible as the basis for English government.

135. See these tracts, reprinted below.

Chronology

1603	Accession of James I (King James VI of Scotland).
1604	Hampton Court Conference.
1605	Gunpowder Plot.
1618	Outbreak of Thirty Years War.
1625	Death of James I; accession of Charles I.
1627	Five Knights' Case.
1628	Parliament meets. Petition of Right.
1629	England begins eleven-year period without a parliament.
1633	Appointment of Archbishop Laud.
1634	First levy of ship money.
1637	King wins Ship Money Case, 7 judges for, 5 against.
1638	Scottish National Covenant.
1639	First Bishops' War.
1640	Short Parliament meets in April. Long Parliament meets in November.
1641	Uprising in Ireland, massacre of Protestants.
1642	Outbreak of civil war.
1643	Solemn League and Covenant. Scots enter war in England.
1645	New Model Army created.
1646	Charles surrenders.
1647	Charles captured by army. Army debates at Putney.
1648	Second civil war. Pride's Purge.
1649	Charles tried and executed. Monarchy and House of Lords abolished. England declared a commonwealth.

1650   Engagement Oath required. Charles II and Scots defeated
        at Dunbar.
1651   Charles II and Scots defeated at Worcester. Charles flees to
        France.
1653   Cromwell expels the Rump Parliament. Instrument of
        Government drawn up. Cromwell becomes Lord Protec-
        tor.
1654   First Protectorate Parliament.
1655   Penruddock's uprising.
1656   Rule of Major Generals. Second Protectorate Parliament.
1657   Cromwell refuses crown.
1658   Cromwell dies. Richard Cromwell becomes Protector.
1659   Richard Cromwell resigns. Rump Parliament recalled.
        George Monck marches with army to London.
1660   Long Parliament recalled. Convention Parliament sum-
        moned. Charles II invited back. Monarchy restored. Trial
        of regicides.
1661   Cavalier parliament meets. Passage Militia Act, Corpora-
        tion Act.
1662   Passage Uniformity Act. Trial of Sir Henry Vane.
1670   Secret Treaty between Charles II and Louis XIV.
1672   Charles issues Declaration of Indulgence.
1673   Test Act.
1678   Second Test Act.
1680   Exclusion Bill introduced.
1683   Rye House Plot. Trial of William Lord Russell, Algernon
        Sidney. Oxford decrees condemn all resistance.
1685   Charles II dies. Accession of James II.
1687   James II issues Declaration of Indulgence.
1688   Seven Bishops Trial. Arrival of William of Orange. Glori-
        ous Revolution.
1689   Convention Parliament meets. Bill of Rights. Accession of
        William and Mary.

Under God
and the Law

Sir Edward Coke, 1552–1634

The Second PART of the

REPORTS

OF

EDWARD COKE,

Her Majesty's ATTORNEY-GENERAL,

OF

Divers Matters in Law, with great and mature Consideration
resolv'd and adjudg'd, which were never resolv'd or adjudg'd
before; and the Reasons and Causes thereof; during the Reign
of the most Illustrious and Renowned Queen *ELIZABETH,*
the Fountain of all JUSTICE, and the LIFE of the LAW.

With REFERENCES to all the BOOKS of the *COMMON
LAW,* as well Ancient as Modern.

Videte quod non mihi soli laboravi, sed omnibus exquirentibus scientiam.
ECCLESIASTICUS, CAP. 24.
*Lex est commune praeceptum, virorum prudentium consultum, delictorum quae sponte
vel ignorantia contrahuntur, communis reipublicae sponsio.*
PAPIAN, LIB. I. *Definit'.*
Lex dicitur a ligando, quia obligat; vel dicitur a legendo, quia publice legatur.
ISIODORUS.
*Cum dico legem, a me dici nihil aliud intelligi volo quam imperium; sine quo domus ulla,
nec civitas, nec gens, nec hominum universum genus stare, nec rerum natura omnis,
nec ipse mundus potest.* CIC. LIB. I. de Legibus.

Thomas Wight. 1602.

*T*he feisty and brilliant Sir Edward Coke was probably the greatest champion of the common law. His extraordinary career spanned three reigns: he served as speaker of the House of Commons and later as attorney-general under Queen Elizabeth; as chief justice of the common pleas and chief justice of the King's Bench under James I; and was an outspoken member of Parliament under James and Charles I. His role in a series of cases that limited the powers of the king and church courts led to his dismissal from the bench in 1616. Coke remained active in Parliament, leading the effort for passage of the Protestation of 1621 and the Petition of Right in 1628.

Coke's renowned Reports of cases he heard argued during the reigns of Elizabeth and James began to appear in 1600 and ran to thirteen volumes, the last two published by Parliament after his *death. They are the most famous reports ever written on the common law and appeared in numerous editions, abridgments, and translations. The prefaces were in Latin and English, the main texts in Norman French with the pleadings in Latin. In the prefaces Coke laid out his defense of the antiquity and superiority of the common law and the high court of parliament as well as the independence of the judiciary. He exalted claims to individual liberties derived from a constitution more ancient than Magna Carta and laid a basis for both the British and American legal systems. Notwithstanding attacks on the accuracy of his versions of cases, his impact was enormous. The preface to the second volume of* Reports, *reprinted here, first appeared in 1602 while Coke was attorney-general. The original title page was entirely in Latin.*

To the learned Reader.

There are (sayth *Euripides*) three vertues worthe our meditation; To honour God, our Parents who begat us, καὶ νόμους τε κοινοὺς Ἑλλάδος and these Common Lawes of Greece. The like doe I say to thee (Gentle Reader), next to thy dutie and pietie to God, and his annointed thy gracious Soveraigne, and thy honour to thy Parentes, yeeld due reverence and obedience to the Common Lawes of England: for all Lawes (I speake of human) these are most equall and most certaine, of greatest antiquitie, and least delay, and most beneficiall and easie to be observed; As if the module of a Preface would permit, I could defende against any man that is not malicious without understanding, and make manifest to any of judgement and indifferency, by proofes pregnant and demonstrative, and by Recordes and Testimonies luculent and irrefragable: *Sed sunt quidam fastidiosi, qui nescio quo malo affectu oderunt Artes antequam pernoverunt.* There is no Jewell in the world comparable to learning; No learning so excellent both for Prince and Subject as knowledge of Lawes; and no knowledge of any Lawes, (I speake of human) so necessarie for all estates, and for all causes, concerning goodes, landes, or life, the common Lawes of England. If the beautie of other Countries be faded and wasted with bloudie warres, thank God for the admirable peace wherein this Realme hath long flourished under the due administration of these Lawes. If thou readest of the tyranny of other Nations, wherein powerfull will and pleasure standes for Law & Reason, and where upon conceit of mislike, men are suddenly poisoned, or otherwise murthered, and never called to aunswere; Praise God for the Justice of thy gracious Soveraigne, who (to the worlde's admiration), governeth her people by God's goodnesse in peace and prosperity by these Lawes, and punisheth not the greatest offendor, no, though his offence be *crimen laese Majestatis,* Treason against her sacred person, but by the just and equall proceedings of Law.

If in other kingdomes, the Lawes seeme to governe: But the Judges had rather misconstrue the Law, and doe injustice, than Displease the King's humour, whereof the Poet speaketh; *Ad libitum Regis, sonuit sententia Legis:* Blesse God for *Queene Elizabeth,* whose continuall charge to her Justices agreeable with her auncient Lawes, is, that for no commaundement under the great or privie Seale, writtes or letters, common right be disturbed or delayed.[1] And if any such commaundement (upon untrue surmises) should come, that the Justices of her Lawes should not therefore cease to doe right in any point.[2] And this agreeth with the auncient Law of England, declared by the great Charter, and spoken in the person of the king; *Nulli vendemus, nulli negabimus, aut differemus Justiciam vel Rectum.*[3]

If the auncient Lawes of this noble Island had not excelled all others, it could not be but some of the severall Conquerors, and Governors thereof; That is to say, the Romanes, Saxons, Danes, or Normans, and specially the Romanes, who (as they justly may) doe boast of their Civill Lawes, would (as every of them might) have altered or changed the same.

For thy comfort and incouragement, cast thine eye upon the Sages of the Law, that have been before thee, and never shalt thou finde

1. 2 Edw. III, cap. 8, Statute of Northampton, 1328. This section reads "That it shall not be commanded by the great Seal nor the little Seal to disturb or delay common Right; and though such Commandments do come, the Justices shall not therefore leave to do right in any point." See *Statutes of the Realm,* vol. 1, 259.

2. 20 Edw. III, cap. 1, 1346, Ordinance for the Justices. In Section 1 the king proclaims that all his justices have been commanded "That they shall from henceforth do equal Law and Execution of right to all our Subjects, rich and poor, without having regard to any Person, and without omitting to do right for any Letters or Commandment which may come to them from Us, or from any other, or by any other cause." See *Statutes of the Realm,* vol. 1, 303.

20 Edw. III, cap. 2, 1346. Here the king states that in the same manner in which he commanded the justices to do right, "We have ordained in the right of the Barons of the Exchequer. ... That they shall do right and reason to all our Subjects great and small; and that they shall deliver the People reasonably and without delay of the Business which they have to do before them, without undue tarrying as hath been done in times past."

3. Magna Carta, cap. 29. "To no one will we sell, to no one will we deny or delay right or justice."

any that hath excelled in the knowledge of these Lawes, but hath sucked from the breasts of that divine knowledge, honesty, gravity, and integrity, and by the goodnes of God hath obtained, a greater blessing and ornament than any other profession, to their familie and posteritie. As by the page following, taking some for many you may perceive; for it is an undoubted truth, *That the just shall flourish as the Palme tree, and spread abroad as the Cedars of Libanus.*

Their example and thy profession doe require thy imitation: for hetherto I never saw any man of a loose and lawles life, attaine to any sound and perfect knowledge of the said lawes. And on the other side, I never saw any man of excellent judgement in these Lawes, but was withall (being taught by such a Master) honest, faithfull, and vertuous.

If you observe any diversities of oppinions amongest the professors of the Lawes, contende you (as it behoveth) to be learned in your profession, and you shall finde, that it is *Hominis vitium, non professionis.* And to say the trueth, the greatest questions arrise not upon any of the Rules of the Common Law, but sometimes uppon Conveyances and Instruments made by men unlearned; Many times upon Willes intricately, absurdly, and repugnantly set downe, by Parsons, Scriveners, and such other Imperites.[4] And oftentimes upon Actes of Parliament, overladen with provisoes, and additions, and many times on a sudden penned or corrected by men of none or verie little judgement in Law.

If men would take sound advise and counsell in making of their Conveyances, Assurances, Instruments, and Willes: And Councellors would take paines to be rightly and truely informed of the true state of their Client's case, so as their advise and counsel might be apt & agreeable to their Client's estate: And if Acts of Parliament were after the olde fashion penned, and by such only as perfectly

4. Unskillful ones.

knew what the Common Law was before the making of any Act of
Parliament concerning that matter, as also how farre forth former
Statutes had provided remedie for former mischiefes and defects discovered by experience; Then should verie few questions in Law arise,
and the learned should not so often and so much perplexe their
heades, to make attonement and peace by construction of Law betweene insensible and disagreeing wordes, sentences, and Provisoes,
as they now doe.

In all my time, I have not knowen two questions made of the right
of Discents, of Escheates by the common Lawe &c. so certaine and
sure the Rules thereof be: Happy were Artes if their professors would
contende, and have a conscience to be learned in them, and if none
but the learned would take upon them to give judgement of them.

Your kind and favorable acceptation (gentle Reader) of my former
Edition, hath caused me to publish these few cases in performance of
my former promise, & I wish to you all no lesse profit in reading of
them, than I perswade myselfe to have reaped in observing of them.
This only of the learned I desire.

Perlege, sed si quid novisti rectius istis,
Candidus imperti; si non hiis utere mecum.

Sir Edward Coke 1552–1634

The Twelfth part of the

REPORTS
OF SIR
EDWARD COKE, Kt.
OF
Divers Resolutions and Judgments given upon solemn
Arguments, and with great Deliberation and Conference with
the Learned J U D G E S in Cases of

LAW,
The most of them very Famous, being of the K I N G S
especiall Reference, from the

COUNCIL TABLE,
Concerning the *Prerogative;* As for the digging of
Salt-peter, Forfeitures, Forrests, Proclamations, *&c.* And the Ju-
risdictions of the Admiralty, Common Pleas, Star-Chamber, High Com-
mission, Court of Wards, Chancery, *&c.* And Expositions and Resolutions
concerning Authorities, both Ecclesiasticall and Civill, within this Realme.
Also the Formes and Proceedings of Parliaments, both in
ENGLAND, & *IRELAND;*
With an Exposition of *Poynings* LAW.

Non est leges condendi authoritas; ubi non est obediendi necessitas, & é converso.

*With Alphabeticall Tables, wherein may be found the Principall Matters
contained in this Book.*

LONDON,
Printed for *Henry Twyford* and *Thomas Dring*, and are to be
sold in *Vine-Court* Middle Temple, and at the *George* in *Fleet-street,*
neer *Cliffords-Inne,* 1658.

*P*rohibitions del Roy," printed in part 12 of Coke's celebrated Reports, is one of the most cited of all Coke's cases and of clear importance to the issue of sovereignty. King James had raised the question of the king's right to decide cases in the court of King's Bench. This pretension, Coke informs us, he tactfully denied, pointing out that while the law was based upon reason and his majesty was well endowed with that commodity, cases were not to be decided by natural reason "but by the artificial reason and judgment of Law"—an art that required many years to master. James then cautioned that this being so the king would be under the Law "which was Treason to affirm." Coke deftly handled this crucial point in a famous response. He quoted the great medieval jurist Henry Bracton's pronouncement that the king was under no man, but he was under God and the law.

Writs of prohibition had been used to remove cases from ecclesias-

tical and admiralty courts to the common law courts on the ground the former courts lacked proper jurisdiction to try them. Coke had angered the church by repeatedly using writs of prohibition against ecclesiastical courts. A prohibition del roy denies the king's jurisdiction.

This case occurred in 1607 while Coke was James's chief justice of the common pleas but was not published until 1656. The edition used here is that of 1658. The manuscript version of the twelfth part of the reports in which it appeared was among Coke's papers seized by Charles I in 1634 upon Coke's death. Seven years later, on the petition of the House of Commons, Charles returned the manuscripts to Coke's heir, Sir Robert Coke. Coke's planned twelfth volume of Reports *was published during the Protectorate. The mistakes in several of the legal citations are doubtless due to the fact that the work was published by those less painstaking than the author.*

Michaelmas Term. 5 James I
Prohibitions del Roy.

Note, upon Sunday, the tenth of *November,* in this same Terme, the King, upon complaint made to him by *Bancroft* Arch-bishop of *Canterbury,* concerning Prohibitions, the King was informed, that when Question was made of what matters the Ecclesiasticall Judges have Cognizance, either upon the Exposition of the Statutes concerning Tiths, or any other thing Ecclesiasticall, or upon the Statute 1. Eliz.[1] concerning the high Commission, or in any other case in which there is not expresse Authority in Law, the King himselfe may decide it in his Royall person; and that the Judges are but the Delegates of the King, and that the King may take what causes he shall please to determine, from the determination of the Judges, and may determine them himselfe. And the Archbishop said, that this was cleer in Divinity, that such Authority belongs to the King by the Word of God in the Scripture. To which it was answered by me, in the presence, and with the cleer consent of all the Justices of *England* and Barons of the Exchequer, that the King in his own person cannot adjudge any case, either criminall, as Treason, Felony, *&c.* or betwixt party and party, concerning his Inheritance, Chattels, or Goods, *&c.* but this ought to be determined and adjudged in some Court of Justice, according to the Law and Custome of England, and alwayes Judgements are given, *Ideo consideratum est per Curiam,* so that the Court gives the Judgement. And the King hath his Court, *viz.* in the upper House of Parliament, in which he with his Lords is the supreame Judge over all other Judges; For if Error be in the Common Pleas,

---

1. Eliz. cap. 1, 1558/59, An Act Restoring to the Crown the Ancient Jurisdiction over the State Ecclesiastical and Spiritual, and Abolishing All Foreign Power Repugnant to the Same. This act created the powerful Court of High Commission, an ecclesiastical court with jurisdiction over the ecclesiastical state and persons as well as issues of heresies, schisms, contempts, and enormities. See *Statutes of the Realm,* vol. 4, part 1, 350–55.

that may be reversed in the King's Bench: And if the Court of King's Bench erre, that may be reversed in the upper house of Parliament, by the King, with the assent of the Lords Spirituall and Temporall, without the Commons: And in this respect the King is called the Chief Justice, 20 H. 7.7.2.[2] by Brudnell:[3] And it appears in our Books, that the King may sit in the Star-Chamber, but this was to consult with the Justices, upon certain Questions proposed to them, and not in *Judicio;* So in the King's Bench he may sit, but the Court gives the Judgment. And it is commonly said in our Books, that the King is alwayes present in Court in the Judgement of Law; and upon this he cannot be non-suit:[4] But the Judgements are alwayes given *Per Curiam;* and the Judges are sworn to execute Justice according to Law and custome of *England.* And it appeares by the Act of Parliament, of *2 Ed. 3. cap. 9.*[5] *2. Ed. 3. cap. 1.*[6] That neither by the great Seale, nor by the little Seale, Justice shall be delayed; *ergo,* the King cannot take any cause out of any of his Courts, and give Judgment upon it himselfe, but in his owne cause he may stay it, as it doth appeare, H.4.8.[7] And the Judges informed the King, that no King after the conquest assumed to himselfe to give any Judgment in any cause

2. This citation is incorrect and probably should read 19 Hen. VII, cap. 7, 1503–4. This statute declares that corporations shall not make or enforce any ordinances without the approbation of the chancellor, nor may any corporations restrain suits in the King's courts. See *Statutes of the Realm,* vol. 2, 652–53.

3. Robert Brudenell was an important justice of the late fifteenth and early sixteenth centuries serving as chief justice from 1521 to 1531. Here Coke also cites 2.R.3.9.21. This citation is incorrect as no statutes were passed after the first year of Richard III. This should probably be 1 Ric. III, cap. 9, An Act touchinge the Marchaunts of Italy, 1483–84. See *Statutes of the Realm,* vol. 2, 489–93, and 490, n. 8.

4. "Non-suit" is the name of a judgment against a party in a legal proceeding who has failed to appear to prosecute his action or failed to prove his case.

5. This citation ought to be to 2. Edw. III, Statute of Northampton, cap. 8, 1328, which states that "it shall not be commanded by the great Seal nor the little Seal to disturb or delay common Right; and though such Commandments do come, the Justices shall not therefore leave to do right in any point." See *Statutes of the Realm,* vol. 1, 259.

6. 2 Edw. III, Statute of Northampton, cap. 1, 1328, confirms that Magna Carta and the Charter of the Forest shall be observed in all points. See *Statutes of the Realm,* vol. 1, 257.

7. This appears to be an inaccurate citation as there were no laws passed in 17 Henry VI.

whatsoever, which concerned the administration of Justice within
this Realme, but these were solely determined in the Courts of Justice.[8] And the King cannot arrest any man, as the Book is in 1 H.7.4.[9]
for the party cannot have remedy against the King, so if the King give
any Judgment, what remedy can the party have, *vide 39 Ed. 3.14.*[10]
One who had a Judgment reversed before the Councill of State: it
was held utterly void, for that it was not a place where Judgment may
be reversed, *vide 1.H.7.4* Hussey chiefe Justice,[11] who was Attorney to
Ed. 4. reports, that Sir John Markham chief Justice said to King Edward 4 That the King cannot arrest a man for suspition of Treason or
Felony, as other of his Leiges may; for that if it be a wrong to the
party grieved, he can have no remedy. And it was greatly marvelled
that the Arch-bishop durst informe the King, that such absolute
power and authority as is aforesaid, belonged to the King by the
Word of God, *vide 4.H.4.cap.22*[12] which being translated into Latine,
the effect is, *Judicia in Curia Regis reddita non annihilentur, sed stet
judicium in suo robore quousq; per judicium Curiae Regis tanquam er-*

8. 1 Edw. 3, cap. 14, None shall commit Maintenance. This statute states, "Because the
King desireth that common Right be administered to all Persons, as well Poor as Rich; he commandeth and defendeth, That none of his Counsellors, nor of his House, nor none other of
his Ministers, nor no great Man of the Realm by himself, nor by other, by sending of Letters,
nor otherwise, nor none other in this Land, great nor small, shall take upon them to maintain
Quarels nor Parties in the Country, to the Let and Disturbance of the Common Law." See
Statutes at Large, vol. 1, 195.

9. 1. Hen. VII, cap. 4, 1485, An Act for Bishops to Punish Priests and Other Religious Men
for Dishonest Life gives bishops the authority to imprison priests for incontinency.

10. This citation is inaccurate as there are no statutes between the thirty-eighth and the
forty-second years of Edward III. However, 37 Edw. III, cap. 18, makes the point discussed.
See *Statutes of the Realm,* vol. 1, 382.

11. Sir William Hussey or Huse was chief justice of the King's Bench under Henry VII
from 1481 until his death in 1495. He successfully protested against the practice of the Crown
consulting with judges.

12. 4. Hen. IV, cap. 22, 1402, repeats the statute 25 Edw. III, st. 6, cap. 3, which states that
the king's appointments to benefices will be repealed and annulled if the title is found to be
unjust or the benefice already filled. In the latter instance the incumbent is entitled to due
process.

roneum, &c. vide West, 2 cap. 5.[13] *vide le Stat. de Marbridge. cap 1.*[14] *Provisum est, concordatum, & concessum, quod tam majores quam minores justitiam habeant & recipiant in Curia Domini Regis, & vide le Stat. de Mag. Charta. cap. 29.,*[15] *25 Ed. 3. cap. 5.*[16] None may be taken by petition or suggestion made to our Lord the King or his Councill, unless by Judgement. And *43 Ed. 3. cap. 3.*[17] no man shall be put to answer without presentment before the Justices, matter of Record, or by due Processe, or by Writ Originall, according to the Ancient Law of the Land: And if anything be done against it, it shall be void in Law and held for Error, *vide 28 Ed. 3. cap. 3.,*[18] *37 Ed. 3. cap. 18.,*[19]

13. 13 Edw. I, Statute of Westminster, sec. cap. 5, 1285, concerns writs for the recovery of an advowson of a church, apparently necessary because of competing claims to present. Judgments in these cases were to remain in force until reversed and remedies to cover particular circumstances are laid out.

14. 52 Hen. III, The Statute of Marlborough, cap. 1, 1267, entitles all persons to receive justice from the king's courts. Those who take revenge themselves shall be punished. See *Statutes of the Realm*, vol. 1, 19.

15. Magna Carta, 1225, cap. 29, the version commonly referred to in the seventeenth century, is the famous linchpin of the great charter. It combines cap. 39 of the 1215 version with cap. 40, the two together usually counted as cap. 29. It reads, "No free man shall be taken or imprisoned, or disseised of any freehold of his or of his liberties or free customs, or outlawed or exiled or in any way ruined, nor will we go or send against him, except by lawful judgment of his peers or by the law of the land. To no one will we sell, to no one will we deny or delay, right or justice."

16. 25 Edw. III, stat. 5, cap. 4, 1351–52, states that no one shall be taken "by Petition or Suggestion made to our Lord the King, or to his Council" without lawful presentment, or disenfranchised but by "the Course of the Law." If anything is done to the contrary "it shall be redressed and holden for none." See *Statutes of the Realm*, vol. 1, 321.

17. 43 Edw. III, cap. 3, 1369, was designed to prevent extortions by the king's butler and his lieutenants who had been taking the goods of merchants for the king's use, in particular wine.

18. 28 Edw. III, cap. 3, 1354, None shall be condemned without due Process of Law. This chapter specifically protects every man "of what Estate or Condition that he be." See *Statutes of the Realm*, vol. 1, 345.

19. 37 Edw. III, cap. 18, 1363. The act states that men have made suggestions to the king that, contrary to Magna Carta, certain individuals be imprisoned and dispossessed without due process of law. All those that make such suggestions are henceforth to be taken before the "Chancellor, Treasurer, and his Grand Council," must find surety to pursue their suggestion and, if it be found evil, incur the same pain "the other should have had if he were attainted." See *Statutes of the Realm*, vol. 1, 382.

vide 17 R. 2. ex rotulis Parliamenti in Turri act 10.[20] A controversie of Land between parties was heard by the King, and sentence given, which was repealed, for this, that it did belong to the common Law. Then the King said, that he thought the Law was founded upon reason, and that he and others had reason, as well as the Judges: To which it was answered by me, that true it was, that God had endowed his Majesty with excellent Science and great endowments of nature, but his Majesty was not learned in the Lawes of his Realm of *England,* and causes which concerne the life, or inheritance, or goods, or fortunes of his Subjects; they are not to be decided by naturall reason, but by the artificiall reason and judgment of Law, which Law is an art which requires long study and experience, before that a man can attain to the cognizance of it; And that the Law was the golden metwand and measure to try the Causes of the Subjects; and which protected his Majesty in safety and peace: With which the King was greatly offended, and said, that then he should be under the Law, which was Treason to affirm, as he said; To which I said, that *Bracton* saith, *Quod Rex non debet esse sub homine, sed sub Deo & Lege.*[21]

---

20. 17 Ric. II. c. 10, 1393–94, Two Lawyers shall be Commissioners of Goal Delivery. See *Statutes of the Realm,* vol. 2, 90.
21. That the King was under no man, but under God and the Law.

Sovereignty in the King Alone

William Goodwin, d. 1610

A

SERMON

PREACHED BEFORE
THE KINGS MOST
EXCELLENT MAIES-
TIE At Woodstocke,
Avg. 28. 1614.

BY

William Goodwin, *Deane of Christ's Church and Vice-Chancellor of the Vniversity of Oxon.*

Published by Commandement.

AT OXFORD,

Printed by Joseph Barnes. 1614

*W*illiam Goodwin delivered the sermon published here in his capacity as chaplain to James I toward the end of his long and successful career in the Church of England. Goodwin had held a variety of benefices in Yorkshire and London before arriving in Oxfordshire. In 1611 he was made dean of Christ Church college in Oxford and in 1614, when he preached this sermon before the king at Woodstock, he had just been made vice chancellor of Oxford University.

Goodwin's sermon contains the emphasis, usual for the time, upon the independence of the English king from the power of the pope. However, Goodwin goes on to stress that the king was also exempt from the power of the law. Dutiful subjects, he assured worshippers, *were bound to obey the king even if he became a tyrant. These teachings obviously pleased James who ordered the sermon to be published. On the other hand, it was bound to irritate many politically active gentlemen. Only four years before, Parliament had been so incensed by the absolutist opinions expressed by John Cowell in* The Interpreter, *a law dictionary, that it took the unusual step of censuring the book. At that time James had prudently rescinded approval for the book's publication. His command that Goodwin's sermon be published would suggest that James's action in Cowell's case was only a strategic retreat, but that he was quite prepared to broadcast notions similar to Cowell's when opportunity presented itself. This sermon appears to be Goodwin's only publication and appeared in only one edition.*

See! I have this day set thee up, over Nations & Kingdomes, to plucke up, to roote out, to destroy, to overthrow, to build, and to plant.

It is not my purpose to extoll the Dignity, or discourse of the Duety of a *Prophet*, in the presence of a King. The wordes of my Text, I confesse, naturally exact it; yet may it seeme unseasonable, in this Royall Presence, in this place, especially in these times. Miserable, & wretched times! in which the chiefe and principall, the essentiall and fundamentall points of Religion, and Christianity, which should breed Peace in our Consciences, and bring Salvation to our Soules, are almost growne harsh and out of fashion, stale, and out of request. Looke into the many Bookes and volumes, which in these later yeares, have proceeded from our *English Fugitives*, and *Romish adversaries;* in some, you shall finde the Name of Christ seldome mentioned; in many, no one point of Religion handled; in most, if any be handled, it is but *obiter*, and *in transitu*,[1] by the way, and superficially, to farce and stuffe out the volume; the maine scope, & drift of all, hath beene, to advance the *Miter* above the *Crowne*, and to erect the *Monster* of the more than Transcendent Superioritie of the Sea and Church of *Rome*. Insomuch that we are now forced to spend our times & studies, our paines and watchings, our Books and writings, our discourses and preachings, yea our very Spirits and Lives, in upholding the Thrones, in sustaining the Scepters, in setling the Crownes, nay in vindicating the Lives, the Estates, and Dignities of Sacred and Anointed Kings, from the unjust and bloody Assasinations of Romish and Antichristian Tyranny.[2]

Our chiefe, nay our only Religion, in these days consists not in the Faith of that one only *Christ*, that one only deare & beloved *Sonne of*

1. Offhand; in passing.
2. The Gunpowder Plot in 1605, the work of a group of fanatical Catholics, was discovered just in time to prevent the explosion meant to kill James I and the members of both houses of Parliament.

that Living God: but in a servile and slavish Submission and Prostitution to the Sea, and Pope of Rome. You knowe whose resolution it is, *Quicquid profiteatur, Catholicus non est, qui est, à Romani Pontificis obedientiâ, alienus.*[3] Professe what you will professe, understand the Scriptures never so exactly, imbrace the Gospell never so sincerely, beleeve all the Articles of Faith never so stedfastly, professe the Truth never so constantly, practice the workes of Charitie never so devoutly, suffer, & shed your Blood, & lay downe your Lives for Christ never so patiently; I adde, Invocate all the Saints in Heaven, adore the Fleshly Body of Christ in the Sacrament, mutter your Confession, performe your Penance, buy your Absolution, purchase Pardons, & Indulgences; All this, and more, is not sufficient, to constitute a *Catholike.* One thing remaines, you must cast down your *Crownes* at the Feet of that *Man of sin,* you must leave your Kingdomes to bee disposed, at his pleasure; otherwise you have no part in the true Church, you can expect no portion in God's kingdome. If he *Thunder,* the Earth must *Shake,* the *Foundations of the world* must be *moved,* the Thrones of Kings must totter, their scepters must fall out of their hands, their Crownes must be torne from their Heads, All must be cast at his Feet. If you demand *(Quo warranto?)* by what warrant, and Commission, He claimes it? The words of my Text, *See! this day have I set thee up, &c.* they are his warrant, they are his Commission. A weake warrant, of so unjust usurpation! as I trust I shall make manifest, if first you will give mee leave briefly to unfold the words themselves.

The words in their *proper* and naturall, in their literall & *Principall* sense, are appropriated to Christ Jesus, the Prince of Prophets, who hath *Excellentiam Potestatis.* Personally they are directed to Jeremy; who was *Propheta constitutus, antequàm natus,* ordained a Prophet of God, before he was borne, the Sonne of Man. In a *subordinate,* and

3. Whatever he may profess, he is not a Catholic who is estranged from obedience to the Roman pontiff.

qualified sense, they may be applied to *all* the *Prophets*, all the *Apostles*, all the *Ministers* of the Gospell; who have *delegatam Potestatem*. All *Similiter*, but not *Aequaliter*, with like, but not with equall power, being *set over Nations and Kingdomes, &c.* Christ, in that high *Preeminence*, and superexcellency of *all power*, which was *given* him *of his Father, both in Heaven and in Earth: Jeremy*, by *extraordinary* calling and vocation from Heaven: the rest, by *subordinate* and delegate Commission, being *sent of Christ*, as *He was sent of his Father*, & having the word of *Reconciliation* committed unto them.

In the wordes I observe, first, their *Commission; I have set thee up.* Secondly, the *Extent*, and latitude of their *jurisdiction; above Nations, above Kingdomes.* Thirdly, their *Worke;* and that is twofold, *ad Destructionem: ad Aedificationem, to plucke up, to root out, &c. to plant, and to build.* In other things, *Facilius est destruere, quàm astruere*; yet where Sinne is the subject wee worke upon, it is so incorporate into the nature of man, that it is farre greater difficultie, *to pluck up*, and *root out*, than *to plant;* and to *destroy*, & *overthrow*, than to *build.* Therefore the Spirit of God mentioneth *quatuor Tristia: duo Laeta; foure Destroying*, but only *two Edifying* Metaphors. Lastly, I observe, that the true and only *End* of *plucking up*, and *rooting out*, is *planting;* the *End* of *overthrowing*, and *destroying*, is *Building.*

The *Commission* is *Authenticall*, rooted in Heaven and grounded upon God's Ordination. The *Extent* & latitude, is *large* and ample: no Estate, no Dignitie, no Throne, no Crowne, no Scepter, no Diadem exempt from it. The *worke* is *powerfull* on both sides. I had almost said *Omnipotent;* for, *Habet quandam Omnipotentiam, non ex Spiritu nostro, sed ex Spiritu, qui est in Spirita nostro;* The word of God, in the mouth of his basest servants, hath in it a kinde of Omnipotencie, not by any vertue that is in them, but by the power of that Spirit that worketh in them. The *End* is full of *Grace*, and of *Favour.*

First, I meet with a note of observation, set (as it were) in the very Front, and Forehead of my Text, [*Vide*] [*See*] to this end, that, *Qui*

Manus ad Clavum, & Oculos, ad Caelum, He which sits at the Sterne, either of Civil, or Ecclesiasticall governement, whether He sit on the Throne, or in the Chaire, His eye must ever be fixed in Heaven, upon the Pole by which his course must be guided, & conducted. For both in Kingdome, and in Church, *Christus in Imo, Christus in Summo;* Christ is the roote, Christ is the roofe; Christ is the beginning, Christ is the ending, Christ is A, Christ is Θ; Christ is the foundation, Christ is the perfection of all. The Prosperitie, & Peace, the Abundance and Wealth, the Honour and Dignitie, the Stabilitie and Perpetuitie of all, stands upon his Favour, and is upheld by his Blessing. It is He, that must blesse us here, it is He that must crowne us hereafter. [*See*] we enjoy the Blessing, let Him have the Glory. From Him we have our Constitution and Commission, *Ego constitui, I have set thee up:* otherwise, Τίς πρὸς ταῦτα ἱκανος; who is sufficient for these things? What are our earthen vessels, to hold that inestimable and heavenly Treasure? What our uncleane Hands, to breake, and distribute that heavenly Manna? What our leaden and drossy pipes, to receave, or convey that water of life? Τίς πρὸς ταῦτα ἱκανος; Who is sufficient for these things? *No man takes this Honour to himselfe, but he which is called of God, as was Aaron? The excellencie of this power it is not of Men,* but it is *of God.*

Before I formed thee in the wombe, I knew thee, before thou camest out the wombe, I sanctified thee; there is *Electio ad salutem: I have ordained thee to be a Prophet,* and *See! this day I have set thee up, &c.* there is *Electio ad Munus;* chosen to salvation before eternity, called to the Office of a Prophet this Day. These do not always concurre in one subject; but where they meet, a thousand thousand Blessings accompany that constitution, & a thousand thousand times blessed is he, that is chosen of God both to save himselfe, and to save others.

Dei Agricultura estis, Dei Aedificium estis; you are God's husbandry, you are God's building. *Ager, Mundus: Aedificium, Fideles;* the world is his Field, the Faithfull are his Building. *Ager non est Agricolae, sed*

Patris familiûs, Aedificium non est Architecti, sed Domini: the field is not the Husbandman's but the owner's, the building is not the workeman's, but the Lord's. In this Husbandry there is not a fit labourer, that is not sent of God into his Harvest, *Mat.9.* In this Building there is not a meete workeman, which is not inspired from Heaven, as was *Aholiah* and *Bezaleel, Exod. 31.* He which buildes and he which plants, hee which plucks up, and hee which rootes out is nothing, but Hee which gives the Blessing and encrease, Hee is all in all. *Rusticani Sudoris Schemate quodam, labor spiritualis expressus est;* The worke of a Prophet is illustrated by resemblance with the toile of an Husbandman, and the whole comparison is meerely Tropicall, Figurative, & Metaphoricall. *Nulla est excusatio carnaliter interpretanti, in huius modi loquutionibus Tropicis:* It is an absurditie beyond absurditie, to make literall interpretation of Figurative and Metaphoricall Speeches. Nay it is an Impietie beyond Impietie, to change the elegant resemblances, which the Spirit of God useth in the Scripture, to Actuall and Reall, and bloody Executions of unjust and usurped Tyranny. Certainely God never sent forth his Prophets, as Incendiaries, & Assasinates, with Fire and Sword, with Poison & Gunpowder, *to pluck up, to root out, to destroy, to overthrow.* He sent them that the world might be saved, but not ruinated by them.

The rule is generall, *Quicquid in Scripturis Sacris asperum, savŭ, crudele sonat, & commendatur à Sanctis faĉtum, aut inbetur ut facient, non ad literă, sed ad cupiditatis Regnum, & vincendos anime Hostes intelligitur esse scriptum.* Whatsoever in the Scriptures is commanded or commended in the Saints, and favoreth of violence, asperitie, crueltie, it is not Literally, but Figuratively to be understood and executed.

If you demand, *Qui Vectes? quae Ferramenta?* with what tooles, and with what Engins He performes so glorious a worke? They are set in the words next before my Text, *Behold, I have put my word in thy mouth;* a word sharper than a two-edged Sword, which enters and divides, and woundes, and kills; but, *Culpas non Homines;* it kills Sinne, but it saves men. To this worke he hath set apart *Esay,* and *Jeremy,* not *Zenacherib,* not *Nabuchadnezar,* not *Antiochia; Peter & Paule,* not *Herod* and *Nero; Augustine, Ambrose,* & the *Holy Fathers,* not *Domitian,* and *Julian,* bloody Emperors; *Luther, Calvin,* & many worthies in his Church, not *Hildebrand, Julius, Boniface, Pius, Sixtus,* & the rest of that rabble. Those *pluckt up, & rooted out Gladiouris,* with the Sword of their Lippes; these *destroy, overthrow,* murder, massacre, *Ore Gladii,* with the dint and edge of the Sword. Thus, *Imperiale fit Papale, Spirituale fit Temporale;* the Imperiall right is made Papall, and the Spirituall Ministery is changed into open & professed Tyranny. But *Quis constituit?* whence have they their *Ordination?* from whom can they challenge their *Commission?*

They are *set up, Super Nationes & Regna,* above Nations, above Kingdomes. An ample & a *large Jurisdiction!* but *Ministerium impositum est, non Dominum datum;* I see a dutie and a charge laid upon us, which we must exercise, I see no Soveraigntie, no Dominion given unto us that we should execute. *Qui ad Episcopatum vocatur, ad Servitutem vocatur, non ad Dominium Ecclesiae;* he that is called to the office of a Prophet, is called to serve, and minister, not to rule and domineere in the Church. I read, that *their Sound,* I find not, that their Sword, *should go through the world.* It is true, there is no Privilege, there is no Exemption, there is no Throne, there is no Crowne, there is no Scepter, there is no Diadem, that is not subject to this glorious Ministration. Wee may not feare the faces of mortall men. *Saule* must heare of his witchcrafts, *David* of his adultery, *Ahab* of *Naboth's* vineyard, *Herod* of his brother *Philip's* wife; *Israel* must heare of her Sinnes, *Judah* of her Transgressions, *Samaria* of her Idolatries, *Jerusalem* of her Abominations. And where we could beare rule, and domineere, and offer force, and use violence, and beat downe sin, and cry out against iniquitie, till their eares tingle, & their Hearts tremble in the midst of their Bowels, we doe nothing but our duties. For this cause are wee *set over Nations, over Kingdomes*. Herein is our true honour, herein our true Preeminence. Which hath caused the ancient and holy Fathers so often to extoll the dignitie of their Ministery, and sometimes, not to compare only, but to preferre it before and above the highest earthly Soveraigntie. *Imperium ipsi quoque gerimus, addo etiam praestantius ac perfectius; vos enim, potestati mea meisque subselliis Lex Christi Subiecit:*[4] spoken in the presence, and to the person of an Emperour. We also have our authoritie, & that more perfect, and more glorious than your Soveraigntie; for even your majestie hath the law of Christ subjected to our Pulpit. It is to our Pulpit, not to our Tribunal; where wee may reprove, not chastise, reprehend, not punish, depresse, not depose: to us your Soules, to you our Bodies are committed; into our Handes the Keyes, into your Handes the Sworde is delivered; wee must denounce, you must execute, God's Judgements; wee can shut out of Heaven, you may *root out* of the earth. God hath *set* his servants *over Nations, & Kingdomes*, as He set Jonas over *Niniveh, ut eversi in malo aedificarentur in Bono;* that their sinnes might be pluckt up, & rooted out, their estate established, the sentence denounced against them reversed, their Ruine & Destruction prevented, their Pardon and Peace procured. God hath not set them, as he set *Salmanazar, Zenacherib, Nabuchadnezar,* over *Israel* and *Judah,* as his whips and scourges, or rather as his Sword & Executioners; ut *Aedificati in malo e, verterentur in toto,* that when their sinnes were ripe, they should draw the line of emptinesse over them, and chaine their Kings, and fetter their Nobles, and ruinate their estates, and dispose of their kingdomes. We may, nay we must, denounce God's judgements, but the sword, which must execute them, Hee hath put into another's Hand. If our Saviour demaunde *Quis me Judicem?* Who hath made me a Judge over you? and would not end a Controversie, that was brought unto Him: may not

4. We also hold a dominion, I add, more outstanding and more perfect than he (the emperor); for the law of Christ subjected you to my power and to my seat of authority.

we lawfully aske, *Quis vos Principes?* who hath made you Princes? nay more than Princes? to dispose of the estates, of all, yea Lawfull, Anointed, and Soveraigne Princes?

Their *work* is to *pluck up* and to *root out,* to *destroy,* to *overthrow.* True! but, *Disce sarculo opus esse, non sceptro, ut facias opus Prophetae:* See, a Sheepehooke, not a Scepter, a weeding hooke, not a Sword, is the Instrument that fits the Hand, and agrees with the worke of a Prophet. *Cum audis Regna & Nationes, noli Carnaliter intelligere, sed cogita Animas Regnatas à Peccato; delicta, cogita, quae evellenda & suffo-dienda, à sermonibus Dei:* When you heare of *Nations* and of *King-domes,* and of *plucking up* and *rooting out,* dreame not of earthly kingdoms; but remember, Satan hath a kingdome within you, and *sinne* hath gotten Dominion over you; follow, pursue, kill, mortifie these enimies, *pluck up, root out, destroy, overthrow* this *Kingdome.* This is a true Prophetical, Evangelicall work, which cannot be desti-tute, either of a Blessing here, or a reward hereafter. There was a time, wherein God promised, and in his due time Hee performed it; *Men shall turne their swordes into scythes, and their Speares into Mat-tockes, and there shall none hurt nor destroy in all the mountaine of my Holynesse.* There was never time wherein Satan practised it not, in these our times hee hath effected it; men have turned their scythes into Swords, & their Mattockes into Speares, and with *Julius* the sec-ond, their Miters, into Helmets, and the Keyes of *Peter,* into the Sword of *Paule.* There is now nothing, but Blood & Slaughter, but Stabbings and Poisonings, and fire, and Gunpowder, but Deposing & Ruinating. And *ubique Religio praetenditur, ubi omnia, & Humana et Divina violantur,* and when all the Lawes both of God and Man are violated, Religion Must cover all, & the Censure of the Church must warrant all. We have seene with our Eyes, the most woful and disastrous effects and fruits of this Doctrine the sunne ever looked upon. You cannot but remember them, I take no pleasure to repeate them. God hath set Bounds and limits, unto all Authority; the Au-

thority of the Church is confined, to the Courts of Conscience, not
extended, to the Courtes of Justice. The *worke* of a *Prophet* is appropriated to the *rooting out* of sin, not improved to the ruinating of
Kingdomes. And this is the end and perfection of all, so to *plucke up*
and *roote out,* that we *plant,* so to *destroy* & *overthrow,* that we *build.*

This is indeed the Proper and Naturall worke of God's Ministers,
to *plucke up,* and to *roote out,* is Accidentall and forced upon them, to
plant and to *build,* is Essentiall to their Office, & affected by them.
That is their Hope, and their Joy and their Crowne of rejoicing, in
the Day of the *Lord* Jesus. *Suprema lex salus Ecclesiae;* The fundamentall Law of the Church and the most glorious worke of the sacred
Ministery never reached to the Bodies, or Goods, or Lives of Men,
but ever was accomplished in the salvation of the soules of men. It is
the observation of *Chrysostom, Saepè solet Scriptura uti verbis malis in
re bona;* the spirit of God in the Scriptures, often useth sharpe, dis-
pleasing, and destructive phrases, where yet it intends to produce
Blessed, Gracious, and vital effects. *Ignis, Gladius, verba mala sunt;*
Fire, Sword, are words cloathed with Terror, and usually Instruments
of Death. But the Fire that came downe from Heaven, & sate on the
apostles, *illuminat, non incendit,* enlightens, scortches not, inflames,
burnes not, purges, but consumes not. The sword, which God hath
put into the Hands, into the Mouthes rather, of his *Prophets, vomi-
cam incidere potest,* may launce and open the impostumation, which
hath beene long breeding in us, cuts, but hurts not, heales, but endangers not. God authorizing his servants to wound, but for that
they might heale againe, to kill, but for that they might quicken
againe, to *plucke up* and *roote out,* but so that they might *plant* againe,
to *destroy,* and *overthrow,* but so that they might *build* againe.

Of the *plucking up* and *rooting out* of our Adversaries the world
hath had long and wofull experience, the Turks, and Infidels have
made their advantage, the Church hath felt the smart, and all Chris-

tendome to this day groanes under the weight & burden of it. If you seeke for their *Plantings* and *Buildings,* you must saile to the *Indies,* and search into remote, barbarous, and unknowne Lands; it may be in the passage you may heare, of fruitfull *Plantations* & of glorious *Buildings,* and of strange Miracles, and of wonderfull conversions; but in the end, you shall find, and see, their Plantations have beene watered with Blood, the Foundations of their Buildings laid in Blood, in the Blood of innumerable thousands, of poore and naked Innocents; themselves being witnesses against themselves, and their owne *Jesuites* deploring and detesting their more than inhumane & Devillish Cruelty.

Thus have I posted over the words of my Text, that you may perceive we detract nothing from the authoritie of a Prophet. His *constitution* is from God. We exempt no man from their lawfull *jurisdiction;* they are *Set up, Super Nationes, Super Regna,* above Nations, above Kingdomes. Wee acknowledge their *worke* powerfull, to *plucke up, root out, &c.* but, *In Criminibus, non in possessionibus Potestas ista,* this power is excercised in extirpation of sinnes, not in extermination of Kingdomes; &, *Linguâ, non Manu, Ore, non Gladio, Precibus, non Armis;* It must be executed with our Tongues, not with our Hands, with our Words, not with our Swordes, with our Prayers, not with our weapons. Lastly, we yeeld double, and treble honour to those, which *so roote out,* that still they may *plant,* which *so destroy,* that yet they may still *build up.*

O how easily, & how amply could I here discourse of the Kingdome of Christ Jesus! of his many victories, and his glorious Triumphs! all achieved, *Non aliis Armis quam clangente Evangelii Buccinâ, sonante Apostolorum Doctrinâ,* with no other weapons, but by the sound of his Gospell, and the foolishnesse of the preaching of his Apostles. Thus, thus hath it pleased him to raze downe the walls of *Jericho!* Thus, thus hath hee built up the walls of his Beloved

Jerusalem! Thus hath he planted his faith, overcome the world, subdued Nations, conquered Kingdomes, and spread his Dominion from Sea to Sea, and from the River unto the ends of the world!

If I have but touched, where I should have enlarged, and have digressed from the Observations my Text naturally affordeth; that which the *Apostle* useth as his just Apologie, *Vos coegistis*, you have enforced me; I trust with your Favours it may bee accepted as a faire excuse, *Illi coegerunt*, our Adversaries have compelled me. For it is not easie, nay it is impossible, for a true man, always to keep the King's highway, especially if he be driven to follow *Hue and Cry* after Theeves and Murderers. I am now in this pursuit; I find God to be dishonoured, his Scriptures adulterated, the peace of his Church disturbed, the soules of men bewitched, our estate endangered, tyranny usurped: if I cannot yeeld remedy, I cannot but give warning. It is not now a question disputed, but a case resolved, if the Prince fall from God, the people must fall from him, they may, nay they must resist & take Armes; *Principes iam inauguratos & consecratos Regnique potitos deturbare possunt, imò debent & tenentur facire, si vires suppetant, idque in extremo animarum periculo, ac discrimine.* And if these resolutions bee growne into practises & executions, so that we cannot live amongst these men without danger, surely they should not live amongst us in such jollity, in such security. *Caput iniquitatis tenet ista iniquitas;* this is an abomination above all abominations. Religion must cover all and these very words of my Text must warrant all! *By this and such like, Catholike men are warranted, that they be no Traitors, nor hold positions treasonable, false and undutiful, in answering, or beleeving that for heresie, and such like notorious wickedness, a Prince otherwise lawfull and anointed, may be excommunicated, forsaken, resisted, by warrant of holie Churches' judgment, and censure.*

I omit the writings of private men, though their bookes are full of it; I find it in their *Lawes*, in their *Bulls*, in their *Publike & authenticall Instruments*, the monster of their more than supreame Supremacy,

all their unheard-of usurpation, and tyranny over Princes, Kingdomes, the estate and lives of lawfull and annointed Kings, grounded
upon this Tropicall, Figurative, and Metaphoricall foundation! *See, I
have this day set thee up, &c.* In their well known and often mentioned
Canon, *Unam sanctam; Ecclesiastica potestas Terrenam habet instituere,
& Judicare: sic verificatur Vaticinium Hieremiae; Ecce, ego constitui.* In
the *Bull* of *Paulus tertius* against Henry the 8. *Praecipuum super omnes
Reges universae Terrae, cunctosque populos, obtinentes Principatum,
juxta Hieremiae vaticiniū, Ecce ego constitui te, &c. Regem Henricum
Regno privamus, &c. Having obtained chiefe principality, over all the
Kings of the whole earth, and over all nations, according to the prophecy
of Jeremy,* See, this day I have set thee up, &c. *We depose King* Henry
*of this kingdome, and him and all his favourers doe Wee smite with the
sword of accursing, excommunication, & eternall damnation; his subjects
we absolve from their Oath of Allegiance, and all subjection to their King,
and besides we exhort and require them to take Armes, and in all hostile
maner to pursue them.* By the way it is not unworthy the observation;
that in the next immediately following chapter there is *Institutio &
confirmatio Societatis nominis Jesu,* that they might have new & pesti-
lent instruments, to uphold their new challenge and prodigious Practise. In the *Bull* of *Pius quintus,* against Q. Elizabeth, of famous and
ever blessed memory; *Regnans in excelsis, unum Romanum Pontificem
super omnes Gentes & omnia Regna Principem constituit, qui evellat,
destruat, disperdat, dissipet, &c. He that raigneth in the highest Heavens,
hath constituted the one only Pope of Rome, a Prince over all nations, and
all kingdomes, to plucke up, to root out, &c. Armed by his authority, who
hath placed us in this supreame Throne of Justice, we deprive* Elizabeth
*of her pretended right to the Kingdome, and of all Soveraignty, Dignity,
and Preeminence, and discharge her Nobles and Subjects from their oath
of Allegiance, and obedience due unto Her.*

Heare you not the *Beast* in the Revelation, *Loquentem magnalia,*
speaking *great things,* and uttering *Blasphemies* against *God,* and

against *Heaven?* challenging *power over Kindreds, and Tongues, and Nations?* Let them *whose names are not written in the book of life worship him.* The *French* have prooved that these are but *Bruta Fulmina,* Brutish Thunderbolts; the *Venetians,* that this is but *Ignis fatuus,* a false fire; God hath proved unto *us,* that they are *Blessings,* and not curses: for where they have cursed most, he hath blest most. Blessed be his name for ever, and for ever!

I cannot prosecute every particular; I would draw all unto an head, & yeeld unto the Church, whatsoever she may justly challenge, & suppose (that which they can never prove, wee may never grant) that all authority of this Church is in the See, and the Pope of Rome: yet can it never be stretched or tentered, to the discharging of subjects from their Allegeance, or deposing of Princes, from their Dignities. I will not deny, but that these words, *to plucke up, to roote out, to build, and to plant,* may bee parralell, to *binding* and *loosing* in the Gospell; and that by these and such like the Church may lawfully challenge *Authority,* yea *over Nations and Kingdomes,* to *foretell,* and *threaten,* and *denounce* God's judgments. But God hath made a *Distinction,* betwixt the *Sword* and the *Keyes,* and hath set a separation betwixt the *Prince,* and the *Priest.* Insomuch that the Prince cannot snatch the Keyes, out of the hand of the Priest, without open sacriledge: the Priest may not wrest the sword, out of the hand of the Prince, without manifest impiety and unjust usurpation. Therefore my *Conclusion* is, that,

> The sentence of Excommunication, (suppose) it bee justly deserved, suppose it be lawfully denounced, (which I suppose, but grant not), yet hath it not that Power and Effect, to discharge subjects of their Duety and Allegiance, or to depose Princes of their Estate and Dignities.

And here we must *observe;* first, that wee suppose Darknesse to be Light, and Falsehood to be Truth, and Usurpation to be Justice, and Tyranny to bee Equity; for all this, and much more than this, they must suppose, which suppose the *Excommunications* of the Pope, to be *Just* and *Lawfull.* Secondly, that I speake of *Lawfull* and *Annointed* Kings, I meddle not with *Intruders* and *Usurpers.* Thirdly, that wee deny not, but *Princes* by *Heresie,* by *Idolatry,* by *Apostacy,* by other Notorious *Crimes,* may deserve to be *Censured:* and in this case, we may & must *tell* them, that these *Sinnes* are *Pernicious* to their *Soules,* and *Perillous* to their *Estates;* yet is it God alone, and no man on the Earth, that can make them *Forfeitures* of their *Kingdomes.* Fourthly, that we exempt not Kings, from the just censure and reprehension of the Church. Wee honour the *Courage* and *resolution* of *Ambrose,* wee admire the moderation & submission of *Theodosius:* though we doubt whether we may imitate the one, or expect the other; but we abhor the partiality of the *Pope,* who will *exempt himselfe,* where he *subjects Princes. Nauarrus* enquires, *Quis possit excommunicaris?* and resolves, he must be *Homo, Mortalis, Baptizatus, habens superiorem:* and therefore amongst others, there are exempt, *Locusta, Infidelis, Daemon, Papa;* a *Locust* or noisome beast, hee is not Man; an *Infidell* he is not *Baptized;* the *Devil,* he is not *mortal;* the *Pope,* though an *Heretique, He falls into the hands of God, he is not subject to any human Power.* See how fitly he hath matched, & ranked his *priviledged quaternion;* I malice not their combination, I dispute not of their *Exemption:* but suppose all, and more than all, against which I can yet take infinite, and just exceptions, I still hold my *Conclusion.* My *proofes* I reduce to foure heads; 1. The *Prerogative Royall* of a King, 2. The *Duty indispensable* of a Subject; 3. The *Continuall Practise* of the Church; 4. The *Nature, Effects, Limitations,* and *End* of *Excommunication.*

The very name of a *Lawfull* and *Anointed* King is sacred, his *Authoritie* soveraigne, his *Person* inviolable. *Major erit, quam cui possit Censura nocere. Everie Soule* must be *Subject unto Him,* though he be an Evangelist, though an Apostle, though a Prophet, not Obedient only, but subject: yea and that *Paul* a blessed Apostle, to *Nero* a Monster of Men, and a bloody persecutor. No man may stir an Hand or a Foot without him: if he bid save, they save, if hee bid kill they kill, *ipse solutus Legibus,* himselfe exempted from his lawes, nor from the *Direction,* and Observance of them, but from the *Punishment* and penalty of them; ἁμαρτήσας οὐ κολάζεται.[5] It is a speech, and an act worthiest an *Emperour,* to oblige and binde himselfe to his lawes: it is a speech & practice unfitting the authority of any earthly power to say, if hee transgresse I will chastice him. It was once the language of the Church. *Wee adore the Emperour as a man, next unto God, and inferiour to none but him alone.* It was once the stile of the Pope, *Ego indignus Maiestatis vestra Famulus,* I the unworthy servant of your Majestie. It was once & is still, the prerogative of a King, *Nullis vocatur ad poenam Legibus; tutus imperii potestate:* There is no Tribunall, to which he may be cited; no law by which he may be punished. He is secured by the preeminence of his Soveraignety. *Who can lay his hand upon God's annointed, and be innocent? Who can? No man, Because God hath planted him above all men, and hath given no man authority to punish Him; God alone will take vengeance on his sinnes. Therfore David, when Saul hunted after his innocent soul, as after a prey, yet could appeale neither to judge, nor to High Priest, but to God alone, let God be judge between thee and betweene me. David,* when he confessed his sinne, forgot not his *Preeminence; To thee, Thee only have I sinned. I have sinned;* An ingenuous confession which obtained a gracious pardon; *The Lord hath put away thy sin. To thee,* a necessary exaggeration, no man sees, or truly sorrowes for the heinousnes of his sin, without a true apprehension of that glorious Majesty, which he hath offended in sinning. But *To thee, Thee only;* in his lowest submission to God, remembring his high Preeminence above men. I doubt not but *David* sinned against *Bethsabee,* and that a grievous and an uncleane sinne; against *Uriah,* and that a bloody, and a crying sinne,

---

5. Having transgressed he is not punished.

against the *Child of adulterie,* and that a deadly, and a killing sin, against his *kingdome,* & that a ruinating, and demolishing sin; against his owne soule, and that a fearefull and a pernicious sinne. *In istos peccauit; Deo soli Peccauit: against* all those he sinned, but *To* God only. *They* might *complaine* and *Accuse and Testifie* against him; but *God alone,* was to *Judge,* to *Condemne,* to *Punish* him; *Tibi peccaui, longè aliud est quam in te Peccaui: we sinne against them whom wee wrong by sinning; wee sin to him, who can remit or punish, who can pardon or bee Revenged for our wrong, Rex erat, ita ut nullius subiacere Iudicio;* he was a King, therefore *To God only,* he sinned before whose Tribunall only hee was to appeare, and from whose mouth only, hee was to receive his judgement.

What then? Do we exempt Kings from the observation of the Lawes of God? No, wee binde them rather with a double bond, *Qua Reges, Qua homines;* as they are *Men,* & have *soules* to be saved, as they are Kings, and have *Thrones* to be *established.* And herein are wee *set over* them, *to plucke up and to roote out,* to reprove, to correct, to proclaime to the terror of their soules, though not to the losse of their Kingdomes. *Eò terribilius puniendi, quò possunt peccare liberius:* the greater their *Exemption* here, the more fearefull their *Judgement* hereafter; the ampler their *Priviledge* here, the more intolerable their *Plagues* hereafter. They may escape the hands of Men: if they continue in their sinnes; they shall not escape the hands of God neither alive nor dead. But the *Laws* of *God,* of *Nature,* of *Nations,* of the *Church,* of *free Monarchies,* the *Lawes Imperiall,* all *Priviledge* and *Exempt* them; they cannot be deposed by the sentence, they may not bee *deprived* by the force of any *Mortall Man.* Therefore suppose in some causes they might be *Excommunicated,* which I yeeld not, in any; yet in no case hath Excommunication that force, to *depose* them. *Reges sunt,* They are Kings.

They are Kings, we are *Subjects,* bound in a bond, & obligation, which exceeds all other Bonds, & cancels all other obligations. A *Son*

unto his *Father,* a *Wife* unto her *husband, a Servant* unto his *Master,*
an *Homager* unto his *Lord,* an *Inferiour* to his *Superiour, Nature, Sense,
Reason, Humanitie, Christianitie, Divinitie* binds them to *Obedience,*
with a Bond which cannot bee broken: but the Bond of Allegiance to
our King containes them all, exceeds them all. Is Hee not a *Father,* an
Husband, a *Master,* a *Lord,* nay as God unto his subjects? Was not
Moses, Aaron's God, a God to the High Priest, and to the Father of
the Priesthood. No warrant can I then find from Heaven; no dispensation upon the Earth, that can justifie, or excuse the least *Disobedience.* It may bee that a prince is injurious to his Subjects: *Omnis
illegitima defensio Filii adversus Patrem;* Is he worthy the name of a
Sonne, that will enter an action of Trespasse against his *Father?* It
may be his yoke is heavy, and his loines burdenous; *Ferendo & pa-
tiendo, lenienda Iniuria est;* Patience, and toleration, is the best leni-
tive, and the readiest remedie. It may be he is irreligious and would
draw others after him: *Religio defendenda est moriendo, non occidendo,
patientiâ, non Savitiâ, non scelere, sed Fide;* Religion is to be maintained, by dying ourselves for it, not by murdering others for it, by
patience, not by fury, by loyalty, not by rebellion. It may bee hee is a
Tyrannt and bloody: but *Inde Imperator, undè homo antequàm Imperator, inde potestas unde Spiritus,* He made him a *King,* which made
him a Man; and he receaved his authoritie from him, from whom he
receaved his breath. *Saviat, Laniet, Nubecula est, citò transibit.* Let
him rage, kill, Massacre, hee is but a storme, sent of God to chastise
his children, expect but God's leasure, he will soone vanish, and God
will send a calme againe: as he speakes in *Tacitus; Nŏ est nostrum aes-
timare quem supra ceteros, & quibus de causis extollas; nobis obsequis glo-
ria relicta est.* God sets up whom pleases him; our Vertue, our Dutie,
our Glory consists in our Obedience, not for feare only, but for conscience, not [. . .], to our gratious Lords, but even [. . .], those whom
hee hath set to be whippes & scourges over us. Are wee then bound

to obey them in all things? and to say, as the *Israelites* did to *Joshuah*, *All that thou commandest we will doe?* No; for there may be a time, wherein wee must say rather with the Apostles; *It is better to obey God, than to obey Men.* And if there be an opposition between the will of God, and the commandement of the King then we must crave pardon; *Da veniam Imperator, Tu Carcerem, Ille Gehennam.* But in all cases, yea of profest *Heresie*, yea of open *Idolatry*, yea of manifest *Apostasie*, our *tongues* are *bound*, we may not *speak* evil of them; our very *thoughts bound*, we may not *conspire* against them; our *hands bound*, we may not so much as *lift up* our little finger against them. In all cases, *Erubescit Ecclesia, Filios fieri Castigatores Parentum;* The Church hath ever shamed to make the Sonnes correctors of their Parents: and *Gladium dare, in manus Filii ad trucidandum Patrem, membri ad concidendum corpus, Nefas est, & insanura;* to put a sword into the hand of a Sonne to kill his Father; of a member to wound his own head, or stab into his own heart, it is more than impietie, more than madnesse. *The Sonne unto the Father, the Wife unto the Husband, the Servant unto his Master, the Monke unto his Abbot; the Priest unto his Bishop is bound to performe due and canonical obedience, notwithstanding any sentence of excommunication.* Are all these bound, and may subjects be discharged? God hath directly commanded *Obedience*, and subjection; therefore no man directly or indirectly, absolutely or respectively, by temporal jurisdiction, or in *Ordine ad Spiritualia*, as a Pope, or as a Prince, can justifie the least disobedience, or warrant so much as a thought of rebellion: no dispensation can discharge the Subject, no sentence can depose a lawfull and an anointed King. God, which is the God *of order*, & not of confusion, *foresaw in his wisdome, that it were better for the estates of Kingdomes,* & lesse injurious to his Church, *if the insolency of a wicked King, were sometimes tolerated without controll, than that the estate of his chiefe deputy, and Lieutenant upon the earth should be subjected to change and alteration, to deprivation, or deposing, at the pleasure and partialitie* either of Priest, or *of People*. The one may be the cause of many disorders, the other must needes bee the Mother of perpetuall confusion.

In the *Practice of the Church*, wee have *Confitentes Reos*, the evidence and confession of our Adversaries. For they which confesse it was not done in the *Primitive* times, *quia deerant vires Temporales; and that the Emperours Constantine, Valens, Julian, and others might have beene by the Bishops Excommunicated, and deposed, and all their people released from their obedience; if the Church or Catholikes, had had competent forces to have resisted.* I say, they which yeeld reason why it was not done, evidently acknowledge it was not done.

Looke into the estate of the *Jewes*, and times of the *Prophets;* looke into the days of Christ, and of his *Apostles;* looke into the days of our *Fathers*, and *Primitive* times: you shall finde many open *Idolaters;* bloody *Persecutors*, backsliding *Apostataes*, many branded with the marke of *Jeroboam, which* sinned, & *made Israel to sinne;* yet not one dispossessed of his inheritance, or deprived from his kingdome.

There is a particle in my Text, to which, if to any our Adversaries may lay just claime, and that is *Hodiè this Day:* for their unjust *challenge* of *Supremacie*, and Domination over Princes, is *Nupera, Novitia, Hodierna;* it is New, it is Late, and in Comparison it is but a *Day* old. I am sure *Ab Initio non fuit sic;* from the beginning it was not so; nay long after the beginning it was not so. *Primus Hildebrandus; Hildebrand*[6] was the first that ever practised it, and that *Novello Schismate*, making a new *Rent* betwixt the Church, and the *Empire. Lego, relego, nusquam inuenio quenquam ante hunc Regno privatum*, I read, and read againe, but I never find any in any age, before Henry the 4th, deposed from his estate and deprived of his *Empire*. Henry the first Patient, *Hildebrand* the first Agent; a man abhorred of all the

---

6. Hildebrand, Pope Gregory VII (1073–1085), proclaimed extensive rights for the papacy including the right to depose monarchs. He got into a famous test of wills with Henry IV when he excommunicated that Holy Roman Emperor.

world, renowned by *Cardinall Allen,* as a notable *good man, and learned, who suffered whatsoever he did suffer for meere justice, in that he did Godly, Honourably, and by the Duety of his Pastorship whatsoever he did against the Emperour.*

Now began the *New, Popish, Antichristian* world, to come to his Height before which time, there was never Flatterer so shamefull, as to yeeld, never Pope so impudently audacious as to challenge this transcendent *Authority over* Princes. Which enforced *Abulensis* to distinguish betwixt Kings of *former,* and Kings of *later* times; *Non est simile de Regibus illis, et Regibus nostris,* the Kings then, the Kings now are not alike; *Rex tum praeerat sacerdotibus, & poterat Occidere, à fortiori privare Dignitatibus, & Officiis;* the King was then above the *Priest,* and might take his *Life* from him, much more *depose* him from his *Office* and Dignity. But that was in the *olde* world; & *Franciscus Romulus (quem Bellarminses benè & novit & amat* whom *Bellarmine* both knows and loves); (*Bellarmine*[7] himselfe being the *Author* of that *Booke,* as neere Kin to *Him,* as to *Tortus*) puts a difference betwixt the *Popes,* in *Primitive* times, and in *our Dayes.* They were fitted *ad subeundum martyrium,* these now made *ad Coercendos Principes;* They to suffer *martyrdome,* these to raise *Rebellions;* They taught *Patience,* these practise *violence;* They professed *subjection,* these move *seditions;* They quenched the blood of Tyrants with their *Innocent Blood;* the bloodthirstinesse of these cannot be swaged, but with the *Sacred Blood* of *God's Anointed.* All this is [*Hodie*] *This Day!* Lamentable it is, that ever the sunne shined, or gave light unto *this Day.* Before Christ, & a thousand yeeres after Christ, *Nec usut, nec exemplum, nec mentio,* there was neither Practice, nor *Precedent* nor challenge, nor *mention,* of this *Tyranny.* The Possessions and *Inheritance* of *Private* men, the

7. Cardinal Roberto Francesco Romolo Bellarmine, a sixteenth-century Jesuit theologian, was author of *Disputationes de Controversiis Christianae Fidei adversus hujus temporis Haereticos,* an uncompromising defense of Catholic doctrine. Among other things he maintained the pope's right to depose rulers.

Crownes & Thrones of Princes, were then accounted of another Nature. They held them not of the Church, they could not be deprived of them by the Church. The Church could not *bestow* on her dearest Children by any *Blessing;* the Church could not then, therefore cannot now, *deprive* her greatest enimies of them by any *Curse, Sentence, Censure, Excommunication.* The *Prophets* never claimed it; our *Savior* never gave it; the *Apostles* never received it; the *Holie Fathers* never heard of it: shall we thinke them carelesse of their lawfull Authority? Nay rather, we conclude, that they, which challendge to be their *Successors,* are *Usurpers* of New, unheard of, and unjust Tyranny.

It is true that the *sentence of Excommunication* hath ever beene, and ever should be, accounted a fearefull and terrible sentence, a grievous and intolerable Punishment; by some called *Virga ferrea,* a Rod of Iron, by some *Mucro Spiritualis* a spiritual sword, by many *Fulmen Ecclesiasticum,* the Churche's Thunderbolt; which shakes the Consciences, affrights the Spirits, dauntes the Hearts, & leaves behinde it a Terror in the Souls of Men. In the definition of their *Greater Excommunication,* which I finde in their Law, I finde these circumstances. 1. The *Judge,* and that is the Church, or some Authorized by the Church. 2. The *Nature;* it is a *Censure Ecclesiasticall.* 3. The *Cause, Consumacy* in some open notorious *mortall sinne.* 4. The *Proceeding* must be *Canonicall;* the *Delinquents* openly *called,* and have their *just defence.* 5. The *Effect, separation* from the *Prayers,* from the *Sacraments,* from the *Society* of the *Faithfull.* Lastly, the *End,* that he may be ashamed, being ashamed, he may convert, converting, *repent,* repenting, he may *be saved.* Here is all *Spirituall, Judge, Nature, Cause, Proceeding, Effect, End,* All *Spirituall.* Here is *Exclusion* from *Spirituall Comforts;* here is no *violence* to their *Persons,* no prejudice to their *Estates. In Ecclesia Disciplina visibilis Gladius cessaturus;* in the Discipline of the Church, there is no use of the *visible* and material s*word:* for we are *set up,* to watch over your soules, another beares the *sword, Evaginandum nutu sacerdotis,* to be unsheathed at the Becke of the

Priest; as *Bernard* speakes, and *Allen* urges, but *Nuta(i) Rogatü; Nondum mandant, Praelati Domino Regi, sed supplicant, sive Rogant;* at the becke, that is at the Petition, of the Prelates; for in this Case the Prelates commaunde not our Lord the King, but they supplicate, and make Request unto him. It is the confession of their owne Law, it is the ground of their *Significavit; Ecclesia non habet ultra, quod faciat,* the *Authority* of the Church is *ended,* when the *sentence* of excommunication is *pronounced.* The Church can proceede no further, then, *Tradatur Curiae seculari; Brachium seculare in vocandum;* the Secular Power must bee implored; the Authority of the Prince must be assistant. It is true, that the Law alleadges: *Mille exempla sunt, & Constitutiones,* there are many Examples and Constitutions, wherein it is evident, that they which contain the censure of the Church, have beene *Banished, Proscribed, Imprisoned,* but *per Publicas Potestates,* by Publique, and Temporall Authority of Princes, *per Potestates (i) Principes.*

And here, as in handling all causes of this nature, we must *distinguish* betwixt the *jurisdiction* which the Church may claime by *Commission* from Christ, and that which the Church hath receaved by *Donation,* and *Indulgence* of Princes; betwixt that which appertaines to *Excommunication properly,* & in its owne nature, and the *Penalties* that have beene inflicted upon the contemners of that sentence, by the Laws and favour of the highest Magistrate. For hereof the *Church* of *Rome* makes no small advantage, when whatsoever shee hath receaved by the *bountie* of *Princes,* whatsoever she hath gained, by subtiltie, or by violence, by the keyes of *Peter,* or sword of *Paul,* she now claimes all, as due unto her, *Jure Divino;* & she bindes all, *ex salute Animarum;* as if she possessed all immediatly by God's *ordinance,* which shee, by her inordinate pride, ambition, and tyranny hath usurped. I finde in the Schoole, that the nature of Excommunication is *Purgativa respectu Ecclesiae,* Purgative in respect of the Church, it purges here from impious and wicked men; *Praeservativa respectu fidelium*, preservative in respect of the members of the Church, who are by that meanes freed from danger of infection; *Sanative respectu delinquentis*, of an healing and curing qualitie to the delinquent: in no case doe I find that it is *Privativa*, or *Destructiva*, that it shakes the Thrones or endangers the Crownes of delinquent Princes.

The *Effects* of *excommunication*, which the Canonists gather out of the Scriptures, are these; *Have no company with him*, 2. Tim. 3. *With such an one eate not*, I. Cor. 5. *Receave him not to house, neither bid him God speed*, 2. Io. 10. *Let him be delivered to Satan*, I. Cor. 5. *Let him be unto thee, as an Heathen, & a Publican*, Mat. 18. In *Summa Angelica*, I finde 21 *Effects* specified, yet no *Deposing*, no *Depriving* our voluntary *Company*, but not our necessarie *Dutie*, our familiar *Salutations*, but not our publike *subjection* is forbidden. Some benefits belong unto us, as wee are *Men*, some as wee are *Christians:* conceive that a man is deprived of all those blessings, which Christianitie, Religion, Faith, Baptisme, the Church, the Word, the Prayers, the Societie of the Saints can bring unto him, yet his House, his Treasure, his Palace, his Crowne, his Estate, his Regalitie is still in safetie. Looke what hee *gaines* by his *incorporation* into the Church, what hee *looses* by his *Excommunication* out of the Church: but what by nature, by birthright, by just inheritance, by lawfull succession hath descended unto him, of that no Censure of the Church can deprive him. The Church cannot make him a King; once anointed of God, the Church cannot make him no King.

In the Law the rigor of these *Effects* is many ways qualified, and at least *dispensed* with, if not utterly extinguished. If our *Commodity* draw us, if the *Law* bind us, if our *Estate* & condition require it, if *Ignorance* privilege us, if *Necessitie* enforce us; *Excommunication* cannot discharge us: wee may *eate*, wee may *company*, we may *converse*, we must obey. The estate of a Subject hath all these dependances upon his Soveraigne, therefore no warrant for disobedience.

Per Excommunicationem Charitas non tollitur; By Excommunication Charity is not excluded: we may *Activè* and *Passivè* performe to him, or receave from him any worke of Charitie. *Praeceptum Ecclesiae pro charitate institutum contra charitatem militare non potest;* the commandement of the Church which consists in love may not warre against itselfe, and abandon Love. *By excommunication, a man ceases not to be a man, neither doth hee loose his libertie;* Hee retaines all abilitie, wherewith he is naturally furnished, and may doe all things which are agreeable to the Lawes of Nature, Lawes of Nations, Lawes Imperiall. If we may performe the workes of *Charitie,* wee must performe the duties of *Obedience;* if hee loose not his *Liberty,* certainely he looses not his *Soveraigntie:* if wee may doe what the Lawes of nature and men allow, wee must doe what the Lawes of God command; (that is) whosoever curse, we must blesse, & honour, and obey, and serve, and hazard goods, and venture Lives, and spend the last droppe of our dearest blood for the protection of our King, whom God hath set over us.

Lastly, *Excommunicatio Medicinalis est non Mortalis, Disciplinans, non Eradicans;* the *End* is to cure, not to kill, to correct, not to destroy. *Non enim perdendos sed corrigendos curandosque suscepimus;* whatsoever authority the Church hath receaved, it is for *edification,* it is not for *destruction.* If wee refuse their *Society,* it is that they may be ashamed: if we be forced to *deliver them to Satan,* it is that they may be saved in the day of the *Lord Jesus. The weapons of our warfare are not carnall,* yet are they *mighty to cast downe everything that exalts itselfe against God. Bellum cum vitiis, non cū Hominibus;* our warefare it is with sinne, it is not with men: and this is *Bellum* ἄσπονδον, a warre that admits no truce, no cessation. It is not enough to cut, or to lop here, but we must *plucke up,* and *root out,* & not leave a sprig, least it take roote and spring up againe: these *children of Edom* must bee *dashed in peeces,* these *tares rooted out,* and extirpated, the Kingdome, the Dominion of Satan utterly *overthrowne,* and ruinated, not a stone left on a stone, nor head, nor taile, nor stalke nor bud remaining. And

this is *Ministerium omni imperio gloriosius;* a service more glorious
than a Kingdome: *Kings* themselves never happy, but when they submit their Crownes to this Ministery. It is reported of a *Turkish* Emperour, when he saw a Christian murdered, because he would not
deny his Faith, and turn *Turke,* with his owne hands he slew the
malefactor, cast him out on a dunghill, & cryed out with indignation; *Is this the way to spred the faith of Mahomet?* Is it not a shame
that should be perpetrated amongst Christians, which is abhorred
and detested amongst Turkes and Infidels? Shall they not, through
you, rise up in judgement, and condemn the murders, the massacres,
the Assassinations of these days? Is this the way to promote the
Gospell of *Christ Jesus?* It is the note of S. *Austin, in fact is Prophetarum, intuere quomodò intelligenda sunt verba Prophetarum.* Hee indeed applies them to another matter, but they have their truth, and
use in this also. Will you understand the meaning of the words of the
Prophets? try them by the deeds of the Prophets. Did *Jeremie plucke
up,* or *root out,* did he *destroy,* or *overthrow* estate, Kingdom, Prince,
or privat person? He lived & threatened their ruine, that he might
have extirpated their sinne: hee lived, and saw their ruine, and therefore saw them *rooted out* by the sword of the enemy, because hee, and
God's Prophets could not prevaile to *root out* their iniquity. One example for all. *Saul* was *excommunicated,* not *in Foro Fori,* but *in Foro
Poli;* not at the Tribunal of a mortall man, but by the doome and sentence of God himselfe. God did not only cast him out of his *Church,*
and reprobate him out of the number of his elect; but in expresse
termes hee rent his Kingdome from him, and gave it to another man.
David was anointed *King* by the speciall command of *God,* and by
the hand of God's Prophet. In this case might *David* resist where
God had rejected? Or might he depose him whom God had repro-
bated?

   Nay even in this case, standing under the heavy sentence of *divine
excommunication, who can lay his hand upon God's Annointed, and be*

innocent? When he had cut off but the lappe of his Garment, his heart smote him; *The Lord keepe me, from doing that thing unto my Master, the Lord's Anointed, to lay mine hand upon him, for He is the Anointed of the Lord. As the Lord liveth, either the Lord shall smite Him, or his Day shall come to Die, or He shall descend into Battaile and perish. The Lord keepe me from laying mine hand uppon the Lord's Anointed. Propter unctionem & honoravit viuum, & vindicavit Mortuum.* He was still His *master,* he was still the *Lord's Anointed,* therefore hee still *Honoured* him living, and revenged him dead. In the hand of any earthly man, there may bee *Clavis Errans;*[8] not so, in the hand of God. And is he still a King, whom God hath rejected? And is he no King, whom that *man of sinne* hath excommunicated? I collect all. The *Prerogative* of a lawfull and *Annointed King,* is *Sacred,* and Inviolable; The *Duty* of a *Subject* is a strong obligation, & indispensable. The practice of the Church hath ever been *Obedience* unto Blood, not Rebellion or trechery to effusion of blood; The *nature of excommunication* is *spirituall,* not temporall; the *Effect, Losse* of *Heavenly comforts,* not of earthly kingdomes. The *Limitations* allow, nay require and exact *Fidelity,* in Naturall subjects; the *End* is *charitable; Repentance, & restitutio in integrum.*[9] Repentance is late, if once *Murdered;* Restitution impossible, if once *deposed.* Therefore,

> *Hath not the Sentence of Excommunication, suppose it be justly deserved: suppose it be lawfully denounced: I speake by supposition, not by concession: the force and Effect to discharge subjects of their Allegiance, or to depose Lawfull and Annointed Kings from their estate and Dignitie.*

Why then should a *Kingdome* so long instructed, so well grounded in *Religion,* totter, & stagger, as it were affrighted, & amazed at the

---

8. *Clavis:* power of the keys is the power of judgment as in the sacrament of penance or reconciliation. *Clavis errans:* there may be one who errs in the power of the key, that is on the human side of the equation. The reference is to the Petrine commission, Matt. 16: 18–19.

9. Complete restitution.

sound of this *brutish* and counterfeit *thunderbolt?* at the slashing of this *Ignis fatuus?*[10] Why do they live amongst us, why say I, live? *Viuunt & in Senatum veniunt.*[11] They live & flourish, & we lodge them in our bosomes; who hold it *religion,* nay *merit,* nay *supereroga-tion,* & the speediest and the directest *way to heaven,* to passe through a *Field* and a *Sea of Bloud,* of *Sacred* and *Innocent* Bloud, to that *Glorious,* & undefiled *Inheritance?* What can you expect of them, but that they should be, not *Prickes* in your *eyes,* and *Thornes* in your *Sides,* as God spake and *Israel* experienced in the *Cananites;* but *Swords* in your sides, and *Pistols* in your bosomes, and *Poison* in your Cups, and *Gunpowder* in your Vaults? *Parricida moritur, Parricidium vivit;*[12] some of the Traitours have their Reward, and are dead; but whilest there is a *Devil* in *Hell,* a *Pope* in *Rome,* Murders, Mas-sacrings, Treasons, shall never die. I have one Comfort; I know *Heaven* is above *Hell,* God above *Satan,* and we live under his *Pro-tection,* (I would we lived Religiously, in his *feare!*) whose eyes are ever open to *descry* their conspiracies, and his Hand ever Potent, to *over-throw* their *Machinations.* I never was, I never will be a perswader to the least *Cruelty:* only remember, there may be *Crudelis misericordia,* a mercy more cruell than cruelty itselfe. I resolve with *Augustine, Savire nolomus, e dormire nolumus:* I would not perswade to *Cruelty,* but I would gladly rowse you from *Security;* and with the same Fa-ther; Nec obtentu *Diligentia sauiamus, nec nomine Patientiae tor-pescemus;* I hate that *Diligence* that leades to *Cruelty,* I cannot endure that *Patience,* that endes in *Stupidity.*

But whilst I am pleading against their unjust *Tyranny,* I may not be altogether forgetfull of the performance of mine owne *Duety.* For, *See! this Day,* I am *set up, above Nations, and above Kingdomes, &c.* and *a Necessity is laid upon me, & wo is unto me,* if I labour not, *to*

---

10. Insipid fire.
11. They live on and come to the Senate.
12. The parricide dies; the act of parricide lives on.

plucke up, to roote out, &c, that *roote of bitterness,* which hath beene the true cause of the *plucking up* & extirpation, the *rooting out* & extermination of all estates and Kingdomes that ever flowrished, and are come to ruine: I meane *Irreligion* and *Impiety.* It is a generall, and a true observation, *Imperium & Religio pariter defecerunt;*[13] there never yet arose any storme, to the ruine, of any Estate and Kingdome, but it sensibly grew from those vapors, which ascended from backwardness, or coldness, from contempt or indifferencie in Religion. It is as true *ubi Procella, ibi Peccatŭ;* where there is a storme that endangereth the ship, surely *Jonas* is there, or the sinne of *Jonas,* or a worse than *Jonas,* or a more prodigious *sinne* than his sinne. I see many *Executioners* of God's just Judgements, *Fire, Sword, Pestilence, Famine.* The *Fire* never consumed, but *sinne* blew the *Coles,* & inflamed it. The *Sword,* never prevailed, but *Sinne* set an *Edge* on it. *Pestilence* never infected, but *Sinne* spread the *Contagion* of it. God never sent *cleanesse of Teeth,* but *sinne* made the *Heavens* as *Brasse,* and the *Earth* as *Iron,* and the *fields* as the *Heath,* and the fat *Pastures,* as the *Desert.* God indeed is the *Judge* of all; but *Sinne* is the *Cause* of all.

And therefore, *Qui vultis Deum Imperatori Propitium, estote, Religiosi in Deum;* As many as beare good will to *zion,* and pray for the *Peace* and *Prosperity* of their Soveraigne, let them grow and encrease in Grace, in Faith, in Religion, in Piety, in Zeale, in Sanctitie, in the knowledge, and in the love of our *Lord* Jesus Christ; that God may be pleased, and we may be blessed. *Plucke up, Roote out, Destroy, Overthrow,* Irreligion, Neutrality, Superstition, Indifferencie, Sinne, Impiety. God will *pluck up,* & *roote out* your enimies, God will *Build,* and *Plant,* and Protect, & Establish, & Blesse, your Estate, your Soveraigne, your Peace, your Prosperity.

Even so Blesse us, *Gracious Father,* that wee may serve thee. Let thine and our enimies consume like a Snaile that melteth, and like

13. Empire and religion have failed at the same time.

the untimely fruit of a woman that never saw the sun. But let the King live, & Raigne, and let his Throne be established, and his Days be multiplied, his Posterity be Blessed, and let there not want one of this Royalle seede, to sit on the Throne of this Kingdome, untill the coming of *Christ Jesus*. And let the Heart of everyone wither in the middest of his Bowels, and let their Tongues cleave to the Roofes of their Mouthes forever, that without *Aequivocation*, heartily, and un-fainedly, will not say, Amen.

FINIS.

Roger Maynwaring, 1590–1653

RELIGION
AND
ALEGIANCE:
IN TWO SERMONS
Preached before the KINGS
MAIESTIE:

The one on the fourth of Iuly, *Anno* 1627.
AT OATLANDS.
The other on the 29. *of* Iuly *the same yeere,*
AT ALDERTON.

By ROGER MAYNWARING *Doctor*
in Diuinitie, one of his Majesties Chaplaines
in Ordinarie: and then, in his Month
of Attendance.

By His MAIESTIES Speciall Command.

LONDON,
Printed by *I. H.* for RICHARD BADGER.
1 6 2 7.

*R*oger Maynwaring was to become notorious for the extreme divine right opinions set forth in the two sermons that composed his sole, printed work. A year after receiving his doctoral degree from Oxford, Maynwaring was appointed chaplain in ordinary to Charles I. In this capacity, in July 1627, he preached two sermons before the king, one on 4 July on religion, the other on 29 July on allegiance. The first of these is reprinted here. In it Maynwaring argues that Englishmen are bound, on pain of damnation, to pay all taxes and loans demanded by the king regardless of whether Parliament had given its consent. A month later the two sermons were published, apparently at the command of the king but the order was later attributed to the influence of Archbishop Laud.

When Parliament met in 1628 outraged members of the House of Commons drew up formal charges against Maynwaring accusing him of meaning to destroy Parliament. They sentenced him to prison during the pleasure of the house, fined him £1,000, and suspended him from his offices for three years. Contrite and frightened, Maynwaring appeared before the Commons to plead repentance. He was sent to the

Fleet prison for the duration of the Parliament. At the members' insistence, Charles also issued a proclamation "for the calling in and suppressing" of the two offending sermons.

Charles did not hide his sympathy for Maynwaring and his divine right views however. A month after Maynwaring was sentenced the king presented the offender to the living of Stanford Rivers, Essex. During the 1630s further royal preferments were showered upon Maynwaring, culminating in 1635 with his consecration to the bishopric of St. David's.

When the Short Parliament met in March 1640, despite the press of other business, angry members of the Lords, where Maynwaring was now entitled to sit, promptly took up the issue of this last appointment and succeeded in depriving him of his vote. New charges were prepared against him, this time for popish innovations. When the Long Parliament met, members imprisoned Maynwaring, removing all his preferments. He died in 1653.

The volume in which Maynwaring's two sermons appeared was published in two editions in 1627 and reprinted in 1667 and 1709.

The First Sermon, Preached before the Kings Majestie at *Oatlands*, on the fourth day of *July*, 1627.

ECCLESIASTES 8.2.

I counsell thee, *to keepe the Kings commandement, and that in regard of the oath of God.*

Unity is the foundation of all *difference* and *Distinction; Distinction* the mother of *Multitude; Multitude* and number inferre *Relation;* which is the knot and confederation of things different, by reason of some Respect they beare unto each other. These *Relations* and Respects challenge Duties correspondent; according as they stand in distance or deerenesse, afarre off, or neere conjoined.

Of all *Relations,* the first and most originall is that betweene the *Creator,* and the *Creature;* whereby that which is made depends upon the Maker thereof, both in *Constitution* and *Preservation:* for which, the *Creature* doth ever owe to the *Creator,* the actuall & perpetuall performance of that, which, to its *Nature* is most agreeable: which duty is called *Naturall.* And sometimes also is the *Creature* bound to submit in those things, that are quite and cleane against the naturall, both inclination, and operation thereof; if the *Creator's* pleasure be so to command it: which dutifull submission is called by the *Divines,* an *Obedientiall capacity,* in that which is made, by all meanes to doe homage to him that made it of meere nothing.

The next, is that betweene *Husband* and *Spouse;* a *respect,* which even *Ethnick Antiquity* called and accounted *Sacred:* the foule violation of which *sacred Bed* and bond of *Matrimony,* was ever counted hainous; and justly recompenced with *that wound and dishonour,* that *could never bee blotted out.*

Upon this, followed *that* third *bond* of reference which is betweene *Parents,* and *Children;* where, if dutifull *obedience* be not performed by them that received, to them that gave their being; the malediction is

56

no lesse than this, that *their light shall be put out in obscure darkenesse, the Ravens of the valleyes to picke out their eyes, and the young Eagles to eate them up.*

In the fourth place, did likewise accrew that necessary dependance of the *Servant* on his *Lord;* God having so ordained, *that the eyes of Servants should looke unto the hand of their Masters; and the eyes of the Hand-maid, unto the hand of her Mistresse.*

From all which forenamed *Respects*, there did arise that most *high, sacred,* and *transcendent Relation,* which naturally growes betweene *The Lord's Anointed,* and their loyall *Subjects:* to, and over whom, their lawfull *Soveraignes* are no lesse than *Fathers, Lords, Kings,* and *Gods* on earth.

Now, as the Duties comporting with all these severall *Relations,* if they shall be answerably done, are the cause of all the prosperity, happinesse, and felicity which doth befall them in their severall stations: so is it, in the world, the only cause of all tranquillity, peace, and order; and those things, which *distinction, number,* and *disparitie* of *Condition* have made *Different,* it most effectually reduceth to *Union:* that, as of *One* there arose *many,* so, by this means, doe *Multitudes* become to bee made *One* againe. Which happy *Reunion, Nature* doth by all meanes much affect: but the effecting thereof is the maine and most gratious worke of *Religion.* Which the wisdome of *Salomon* well seeing, and the *Spirit* that was in him well searching into, hee sends forth the sententious dictates of his divine and Royall wisdome, fenced with no lesse reason, than the fortresse of *Religion;* in these words following: *I counsel thee, to keepe the King's commandement, and that in regard of the oath of God.*

This is *God's* Text, and the *King's:* and for the sake of all *Kings* was it written. And as the *King* is the sacred & supreme Head of *two Bodies,* the one *Spirituall,* the other *Secular:* so, this high and royall Text containes in it two parts correspondent: The one *Civill,* which is a *Counsell of State,* or a politique caution; *I counsell thee to keepe the*

King's commandement: the other *Spirituall,* which is a *devout* or *religious reason; And that in regard of the oath of God.* The *First* part is founded upon the *Second;* the *Second* is the ground of the *First: Religion* the stay of *Politie;* which, if it be truly taught, devoutly followed, & sincerely practiced, is the roote of all virtues; the foundation of all well-ordered Commonweales; and the well-head, from whence, all, even temporall felicity doth flow. The zeale, and fervor of which *Religion,* if at any time it fall into a wane or declination, contempt or derision, portends evermore, the Ruine and desolation of that *State* and *Kingdome,* where, the service and worship of him *who sits in heaven,* is set at naught: and fills the world with terrible examples of *God's* revenging Justice, and most irefull indignation.

Now, in the first part, doe lie these particulars.

1. First, there is *Rex,* a *King.*

2. Secondly, *Mandatum Regis,* the *Commandement of a King.*

3. Then, *Custodia Mandati, the Keeping* of, and *obedience* to this Commandement.

4. After this, *Consilium, Counsell* to pursue, and practise this obedience.

And lastly, the *Counsellor,* who gives this most divine and Royall Counsell; which is no lesse than *Salomon:* who (as wee all know) was,

1. A *King,* and the Sonne of a *King.*

2. A *King,* and the wisest of all *Kings.*

3. A *King,* and a *Preaching King.*

4. A *King,* and a very Faire (if not the Fairest and clearest) *Type* of him, who was *the King of Kings,* and *Lord of Lords.*

To ingeminate againe, the parts of the Text: 1. *Rex,* a King: and what is higher (in heaven or earth) than a King? God only excepted, who is *excelso excelsior: higher than the highest.* 2. *Mandatum Regis:* and what is stronger than it? For ver. 4. *Sermo eius potestate plenus.* 3. Obedience to this Commandement: and what more rightfull, just, and equall with men? what with God more acceptable? 4. Counsell, to follow this: what more needfull, wise, or gratious? 5. And all this from such a Counsellor, than which, none ever greater, but he alone, of whom it was said, *Ecce plus quàm Salomon, hîc: Behold, a greater than Salomon, is here.*

A King: This is the *Suppositum,* or *Person* on whose behalfe this *Counsell* is given: and it is a *Rule* of that *Science,* whose Maximes are priviledged from errour; that, *Actiones sunt suppositorum; Individualls challenge all activity* as *peculiar unto them.* Now, all things that worke, and have any operation, must (of necessity) worke by some *Power,* or ability which is in them. All *Power* is either such as is *Created,* and *derived* from some higher Cause, or such, as is *Uncreated,* and *Independent.* Of this last kinde, is that *Power* which is in God alone; who is *selfe-able* in all things, and most puissant of himself, and from, and by no other. All *Powers* created are of God; *no power, unlesse it bee given from above.* And *all powers,* that are of this sort, *are ordained of God.* Among all the *Powers* that be ordained of God, the *Regall* is most *high, strong* and *large:* Kings above all, inferiour to none, to no *man,* to no *multitudes* of men, to no *Angell,* to no *order* of *Angels.* For though in *Nature, Order,* and *Place,* the *Angels* be superiour to men: yet, to *Powers* and persons *Royall,* they are not, in regard of any dependence that *Princes* have of them. Their *Power* then the *highest.* No *Power,* in the world, or in the *Hierarchy* of the *Church,* can lay restraint upon these supreames; therefore theirs the *strongest.* And the *largest* it is, for that no parts within their *Dominions,* no persons under their *Jurisdictions* (be they never so great) can be priviledged from their *Power;* nor bee exempted from their care, bee they never so meane. To this *Power,* the highest and greatest Peere must stoope, and cast downe his Coronet, at the footstoole of his *Soveraigne.* The poorest creature, which lieth by the wall, or goes by the highwayside, is not without sundry and sensible tokens of that *sweet* and *Royall care,* and *providence;* which extendeth itselfe to the lowest of his *Subjects.* The way, they passe by, is the *King's* highway.

The *Lawes*, which make provision for their reliefe, take their binding force from the *Supreame* will of their *Liege-Lord*. The bread, that feedes their hungry soules, the poore ragges, which hide their nakedness, all are the fruit and superfluity of that happie plenty and abundance caused by a *wise* and *peaceable* government. Whereas, if we should come to heare *the dreadfull and confused noyse of warre, and to see those garments rolled in blood, if plough-shares should bee turned into swords, and sythes into speares;* then Famine *of bread,* and *cleanesse of teeth,* and dearth of all good things, would bee the just and most deserved punishment, of all, both their, and our sinnes.

Now, to this *high, large,* and most *constraining Power* of *Kings*, not only *Nature*, but even *God* himselfe gives from heaven, most full and ample Testimonie: and that this Power is not meerely *human*, but *Superhuman*, and indeed no lesse than a *Power Divine*. Though *Majesty* (saith *Herodotus*) be *shrouded under Mortality, yet is it endowed with such a Power from above, as beares no small resemblance with the Deity.* For if it were of men, or if that *Power* which is dispersed in *Communities* and *multitudes*, were collected and settled in the *King;* then might this Power be thought *human*, and to rise from men. But, because God would have men to conceive quite otherwise of *Regal Soveraignty;* therefore himselfe pronounceth this of them, who weare *Crownes* on their heads, sit upon *Thrones*, and with *Scepters* in their hands rule Nations; *I said yee are Gods.*

That sublime *Power* therefore which resides in earthly *Potentates*, is not a *Derivation*, or *Collection* of human power scattered among many, and gathered into one head, but a *participation* of God's owne *Omnipotency*, which hee never did communicate to any *multitudes* of men in the world, but, *only*, and *immediately*, to his owne Vicegerents. And, that is his meaning when he saith, *By me Kings raigne; Kings* they are, by my immediate constitution; and by *me* also, doe they Rule, and exercise their so high and large Authoritie.

This therefore may be well conceived to be the cause, wherefore

God doth pleade in *Scripture,* and that so *mainely,* not only for the *Soveraignty,* but also for the *Security* of his *Anointed; I said yee are Gods:* and *he* saith it in no secret, but standing in *Synagoga Deorum;* for so the Psalme begins, as if he would have all the world take knowledge of what he said. Then, *Per me Reges regnant.* After that, *Nolite tangere Christos meos.* And lastly, *Curse not the King; Ne detrahas Regi* (sayes the Vulgar) *Traduce not, detract not from the King.* Put all together, 1. *I said yee are Gods.* 2. By *me Kings raigne.* 3. *Touch not mine Anointed.* 4. *And speake not amisse of the King, no not in thy secret thought.* And take we these sentences asunder againe, thus:

1. *I said yee are Gods:* there's their sublime and independent *Soveraigntie.*

2. *Per me Reges regnant:* there's their unresistable *Authority.*

3. *Nolite tangere Christos meos:* there's their *sacred* and *anointed Majestie,* with the *security* of their royall *State,* and *persons.*

4. *In cogitatione tuâ, Regi ne detrahas: speake not ill of the King, in thy thought:* there's the tendering, and preserving of their great and precious *Names* from obloquie; and the safety, and indemnity of their *Royall fame* and *glorie.*

To put then, an end to this first point: Royalty is an Honour, wherein, Kings are stated *immediately* from God. *Fathers* they are, & who gave *Fathers* Authority over their Families, but hee alone, from whom all the *Fatherhood in heaven and earth is named?* The *power* of *Princes* then, is both *Naturall,* and *Divine,* not from any consent or allowance of men. And hee that gaine-says this, *transgreditur terminos quos posuêrunt Patres, saith Antonine.* Not therefore, in any *consent* of Men, not in *Grace,* not in any *Municipall Law,* or *Locall custome,* not in any law *Nationall,* nor yet in the law of *Nations,* which, consent of men, and tract of time, hath made forcible; not finally, in the *Pope,* or any *People* is *Regall preheminencie* founded; for *Adam* had *Dominion* setled in him, before ever there was either *Pope,* or *People.* Neither *Popes* nor *Populous Multitudes* have any right to give, or take, in this case. So *that Royalty* is a Prehemencie wherein *Monarches* are invested, *immediately* from God; For *by him doe they raigne.* And likewise *Sacred* to *God* himselfe; *For hee who toucheth* them, *toucheth the apple of God's owne eye:* and therefore, *Touch not mine anointed.*

Supreame also it is, and *Independent* upon any *Man, Men,* or *Angels;* and for this saith he; *They are Gods:* whose glorious and dreadfull *Names,* must not bee medled with by any wicked *tongues,* or *pennes,* nor mingled with any lewd perverse or depraving *thoughts;* and for this, *Curse not the King in thy thought.*

And yet notwithstanding this; they are to bee sustained, and supplied by the hands and helpes of men; for *the King himselfe is served by the field; & Reddite quae Caesaris, Caesari: Render as due,* not give as *arbitrary,* for, *for this cause pay wee tribute,* saith the great *Apostle. God* alone it is, who hath set *Crownes* on their heads, put *scepters,* yea and revenging *swords* into their hands, setled them in their *thrones;* for this, doe their *Royalties* render to *God* (as a due debt) that great *Care, Paines,* and *Providence* which they sustaine in the ruling over, and preserving of their people in wealth, peace, and godlinesse: and for this, doe the people render, *as due,* to them againe, by *naturall* and *originall Justice, tribute, to whom tribute, custome, to whom custome appertaineth.*

The second point was, *Mandatum Regis;* the *Commandement of the King.* Now, a *Mandate* or Commaund is a signification of his will, who hath power to send it forth. Five severall *Intimations* of the will are observed by the *Divines.* 1. Either, when a man doth undertake the transacting, and doing of anything himselfe, and that is cleere intimation of his will, by reason that *all actions rise from the will:* whose proper sway is, to set on worke all the power of the soule, and parts of the body. Or 2. when some *Counsell* is given for ought to be dispatched, by which the *Will* and *Pleasure* of him who gives the *Counsell,* is signified; and that which is counselled, is shewne possible to be done, and that, in reason, it ought not to be left undone. 3. The

Permitting also of anything to be done, where there is power to hinder it, is a cleere intimation (at least), of a kinde of resolution, to have it done. But 4. the *Resolute* and *Mandatory forbidding,* Or 5. *commanding* of anything, is the most undoubted and expresse declaration of his will, who hath *Power* and *Jurisdiction,* so to derive his pleasure.

Now then, a *Commandement* is an act descending from three most eminent faculties of the human soule. First, from the *Understanding,* finding out by exact discourse, advice, and counsell, what is to be done, by which *extensions* of reason, the Intellectual part drawes to practise. Secondly, from the *Judgement,* decreeing and resolving what is the meetest to bee done, amongst many particulars. And lastly, from the *Imperiall* sway of the *Will,* which fastens a *Command* on all other powers, to doe their parts, for the dispatch of such designes, as *Reason* hath found out, and *Judgement* thought meete or necessary to be done.

To draw then towards some conclusion of the point in hand; All the *significations* of a *Royall pleasure,* are, and ought to be, to all *Loyall Subjects,* in the nature, and force of a *Command.* As well, for that none may, nor can search into the high discourse, and deepe *Counsells* of *Kings;* seeing *their hearts are so deepe,* by reason of their distance from common men, even as the heavens are in respect of the earth. Therefore said he, who was wise in heart, and deepe in Counsell, *The heavens for height, and the earth for depth, and the heart of a King is unsearchable.* As also, for that none may dare to call in question the *Judgement of a King,* because, the heart of *a King is in the hand of God, and hee turneth it which way hee pleaseth.* Who then may question that, which, God doth proclaime from heaven to bee in his hands, and at his guidance? And for his Soveraigne *will* (which gives a binding force, to all his *Royall Edicts,* concluded out of the Reasons of *State,* and depth of *Counsell)* who may dare *resist* it, without incurable waste and breach of *Conscience?* seeing the *Apostle* speakes under termes of so great terrour; that he who *resists* commits a sinne done with an high hand, *for he resists the ordinance of God:* and so contracts an hainous guilt, and incurres likewise the *heaviest punishment:* for, to his owne soule doth he receive Damnation.

Nay, though any *King* in the world should command flatly against the Law of God, yet were his *Power* no otherwise at all, to be resisted, but, for the not doing of *His will,* in that which is cleerely unlawfull, to indure with patience, whatsoever penalty *His pleasure* should inflict upon them, who in this case would desire rather to obey God than Man. By which patient and meeke suffering of their *Soveraigne's* pleasure, they should become glorious *Martyrs:* whereas, by resisting of *His will,* they should forever endure the paine, and staine of odious Traitors, and impious Malefactors.

But, on the other side; if any *King* shall *command* that, which stands not in any opposition to the originall Lawes of *God, Nature, Nations,* and the *Gospell;* (though it be not correspondent in every circumstance, to Lawes Nationall, and Municipall) no Subject may, without hazard of his own Damnation, in rebelling against God, *question,* or *disobey* the will and pleasure of his *Soveraigne.* For, as a *Father* of the Countrey, hee commands what his pleasure is, out of *counsell* and *judgement.* As a *King* of Subjects, he injoines it. As a *Lord* over God's inheritance, hee exacts it. As a *Supreame head* of the body, he adviseth it. As a *Defendour* of the *Faith,* hee requires it as their homage. As a *Protectour* of their persons, lives, and states, he deserves it. And as the *Soveraigne procurer* of all the happinesse, peace, and welfare, which they enjoy, who are under him, hee doth most *justly* claime it at their hands. *To Kings* therefore, in all these respects, nothing can be denied (without manifest and sinfull violation of Law and Conscience) that may answer their *Royall state* and *Excellency:* that may further the supply of their Urgent Necessities: that may be for the security of their Royall persons (whose lives are worth millions of others): that may serve for the Protection of their Kingdomes, Territories, and Dominions: that may enable them to yeeld Reliefe, aide, and succour to their deere & Royall Confederates & Allies: or that may be for the defence, and Propagation of that sacred and precious Truth; the publique profession whereof, *They* doe maintaine by their Lawes, and Prerogatives Royall.

The third *point* is *Obedience. Obedience* is a *willing* and *Understanding* act of an *Inferiour,* done at the command, and to the honour of a *Superiour. Reasonable* then, and *Willing,* must it be. *Violenced-duties, forced* and *extorted actions,* are not within the compasse of true *Obedience. Voluntary* service is that which pleaseth *God* and *Man.* And so well doth this suit with the nature of *God,* (to whom all things ought to yeeld most willing obedience) that hee pronounceth it *better than sacrifice, and to hearken, better than the fat of Rammes.*

Every will therefore, and *Inclination* that is in the Creature, is charged with the dutie of *Obedience* toward the *Maker* of it. To this end, *God* hath planted a double Capacity, and possibility in the Creature, to submit to his pleasure. The one is *Naturall,* by which, the Creature, in all its actions, that follow, and flow from its forme, doth actually and perpetually serve the *Creatour:* as the *Heavens,* in moving; the *Earth,* in standing still; the *Fire,* in burning; the *Air,* and *Water,* in refreshing, cooling, and flowing.

The other capacity, is called *Obedientiall:* whereby the Creature is ever ready to doe that which is contrary to its owne *Nature;* if the Maker's pleasure bee to command it so. And with this *Obedience,* did the *Earth* fearefully shrinke, and fall asunder, to swallow up those Rebells against *God,* and the *King;* so to give them a sudden and ready passage into *hell,* by a direct and streight *diameter.* Thus, did the *waters* stand on heapes, and leave the Channell dry, that *God's people might finde a marvelous way, and his enemies a strange death.* Thus, did *stones* yeeld to be lifted up against their nature, into the air, that they might fall backe, and recoile with greater violence; to bruise and braine the enemies of his people. Thus, did the *Fire* of the

Babilonian-Furnace refresh the three *Children.* And thus, in fine, did
the *Sunne stand still* in *Gibeon, and the Moone,* in *the Valley of Aialon;*
to give the longer *light,* and lesser *heate* to them, who fought for *him,*
that made both *Sunne* and *Moone.*

Now, this *Power* which God hath over, & this kinde of Subjection
which he receives from the Creature, is a *priviledge,* and *prerogative,*
which God hath reserved only to himselfe; and not communicated, at
any time, to any *King,* or *Caesar,* to have, or to receive *Regularly:* but
only, by way of *Impetration,* and extraordinary *Dispensation,* for dispatch of some miraculous worke, as it was in *Moses,* and *Josuah.*

All the *Obedience* therefore, that Man can challenge from man, is,
in part, *Naturall;* as agreeable and convenient to their inclinations:
and, in part, *Morall,* in as much as it is *Free* and *Willing.* And this, of
right, may every *Superiour* exact of his *Inferiour,* as a due debt. And
every *Inferiour* must yeeld it unto his lawfull *Superiour,* for the same
reason. *Children,* to *Parents,* in discipline, and Domesticalls: *Servants,*
to their *Lords,* in their respective and obliged duties: *Souldiers,* to their
Commanders, in Martiall affaires, and feates of Armes: *People,* to their
Pastours, in Conscientious-duties and matters of Salvation: Subjects,
to their lawfull *Soveraignes,* in the high Concernements, of State and
Policie. And *This* is that *Obedience,* wherewith we are all charged in
this Text, by the *Word* of *God,* and *Wisdome* of *Salomon.*

To draw then toward an end of this third point: We may observe,
that, in the *Text,* there is a double, nay a treble *Majestie:* The *Divine
Majestie* of him, who is the *Living God, and everlasting King;* The
Majestie of *King Salomon,* that gives the *Counsell;* And the *Majestie* of
all *Kings,* on whose behalfe this *Counsell* is given. And, did we well
consider the *King,* that gives the *Counsell;* and the *King,* that is now
to receive the *Obedience;* and the *King,* for whose sake it is to be given;
and the *Reason,* why: *In regard of the oath of God:* it were reason sufficient, without any more adoe, to perswade all *Rationall-men,* to accept of this *Counsell.*

But, there be Pretenders of *Conscience,* against *Obedience;* of *Religion,* against *Allegiance;* of *Human* Lawes, against *Divine;* of *Positive,* against *Naturall;* and so, of *Man's* Wisdome, against the will and wisdome of *God;* and of their owne *Counsells,* against the *Counsell* of *Salomon.* These men (no doubt) may bee wise in their generation; but wiser than *Salomon* no man can thinke them: nor (as I hope) doe they thinke themselves so, for if they did, of such there were little hope. Some there were, in the days of *Justin Martyr,* who were so strongly conceited of their owne wayes, as to thinke *themselves* wiser than the *Scriptures.* Upon them, and the like, Saint *Augustine,* (against the *Donatists*), lets fall this sentence, as an *heavy beame to bruise their hairy scalps: They* (saith he) *who preferre their owne desires of contention, before divine and human testimonies; deserve, that, neither their words should be ever held for Lawes, nor their deeds taken for Precedents.* Now therefore, *Salomon's* wisdome is great, and his *Counsell* deepe, and able to perswade; and, if these men's wisdome be from above, as *Salomon's* was, it is no doubt perswadeable. And, if I wisht it were, and that they would be perswaded, (as some have beene) I would propound unto their view, a few short *Considerations,* which, (if they would please well, and seriously to weigh them) might (with facility) remove, as well, all their *Speculative,* as, *Practique* errours.

First, if they would please to consider, that, though such *Assemblies,* as are the *Highest,* and *greatest Representations* of a *Kingdome,* be most *Sacred* and *honourable,* and *necessary* also for those ends to which they were at first instituted: yet know we must, that, ordained they were not to this end, to contribute any *Right* to *Kings,* whereby to challenge *Tributary aides* and *Subsidiary* helpes;[1] but for the more equall *Imposing,* and more easie *Exacting* of that, which, unto *Kings* doth appertaine, by *Naturall* and *Originall Law,* and *Justice;* as their

---

1. The "*Tributary* aides and *Subsidiary* helpes" in question are probably the forced loans levied in 1626. These loans differed from earlier forced loans because all subsidy payers were assessed. They seemed to constitute taxation without parliamentary approval.

proper *Inheritance* annexed to their *Imperiall Crownes*, from their very births. And therefore, if, by a *Magistrate*, that is Supreame; if, upon *Necessity*, extreame and urgent; such Subsidiary helpes be required: a *Proportion* being held respectively to the abilities of the Persons charged, and the *Summe, or Quantity* so required, surmount not (too *remarkeably*) the use and charge for which it was levied; very hard would it be for any man in the world, that should not accordingly satisfie such demaunds; to defend his Conscience, from that heavy prejudice of *resisting the Ordinance of God*, and *receiving* to himselfe *Damnation:* though every of those Circumstances be not observed, which by the Municipall Lawes is required.

Secondly, if they would consider the *Importunities*, that often may be; the urgent and pressing *Necessities* of State, that cannot stay (without certaine and apparent danger) for the *Motion*, and *Revolution* of so great and vast a body, as such *Assemblies* are; nor yet abide those long and pawsing *Deliberations*, when they are assembled; nor stand upon the answering of those jealous and *overwary* cautions, and objections made by some, who (wedded over-much to the love of *Epidemicall* and *Popular* errours) are bent to crosse the Just and lawfull designes of their wise and gratious *Soveraignes:* and that, under the plausible shewes of singular liberty, and freedome; which, if their Consciences might speake, would appeare nothing more than the satisfying either of private humours, passions, or purposes.

In the third place; if they would well weigh the *Importance, weight,* and *moment* of the present affaires; for which such helpes are required.

1. It is for the honour of his *Sacred Majestie;* and to enable *him* to do that which he hath promised in the *word* of a *King:* that is, to give supplie to those Warres, which, the *Resolutions* of his owne *Subjects* represented in the high Court of *Parliament*, caused him to undertake; and that, with the highest *Protestations*, and fullest *Assurances*

from *them,* to yeeld *him* all those *Subsidiarie* helpes that way, which, the *Power,* or *Love* of Subjects, could possibly reach unto.

2. It is for the *Security* of his Royall State and Person, which ought ever to be most deare and tender unto us: his *Life* being worth Millions of ours.

3. It is for the *Safety* and *Protection* of his *Majestie's Kingdomes, Territories,* and *Dominions.*

4. It is for the *Reliefe,* and *Succour* of his Royall and Confederate *Uncle* the *King* of *Denmarke;* who, in a Cause that much neerer concernes us, than it doth himselfe, hath hazarded his life, Crowne, and Kingdome; as they well know.

5. It is also, for the *Securing,* and *Preserving* of all our *Lives, Goods* and *States,* and the *Preventing* of Forreigne Invasions, by bitter and subtile enemies of ours, both intended, and projected.

6. And lastly: It is for the *Defence,* and *Propagation* of that *Sacred* and *Precious Truth,* which we all professe to follow, protest our Interest in, and resolve to die for; if need require, and occasion bee offered.

Fourthly, if they would Consider, what *Treasures* of wealth are dispended within this Realme, upon purposes of infinite less importance: Nay, to *lewd & vile* uses, much is spent and with wonderfull alacrity quite cast away: what within, and what without the body; upon backe, and belly, upon fingers, and feete, Rings and Roses, rioting, and drunkennesse, in chambering, and wantonnesse, in pride, and vanity, in lust, and luxury, in strife, and envie; So that, if *God* come to claime his *Tenth,* or the *King* his *Tribute,* the *Devill* is gone away with all. So that, we cannot say, as Saint *Augustine* yet sometimes said, *Quod non accipit Christus, tollit fiscus:* but where the Devill hath devoured all, there, *God* and the *King,* doe loose their right. *Mundus totus in maligno positus.*

Fifthly, if they would consider, what *Advantage* this their *Recu-*

sancy in *Temporalls* gives to the common *Adversarie:* who, for disobedience in *Spiritualls,* hath hitherto alone inherited that *Name.*
For, that, which we ourselves condemne in them, blame them for so
doing, and professe to hate that *Religion,* that teacheth them so to
doe; that is, to refuse *Subjection* unto *Princes,* in *Spiritualls:* The same
(if not worse) some of our owne side now (if ours they be) dare to
practise. For, in *Temporalls* they submit to his *Majestie;* though he be
no Defendour, but a Suppressour of their *Religion.* Of their *Lives,*
and *States,* indeed, his *Majestie* is a most gratious *Protector;* but of
their *Religion* not so. Of our *Lives, States, Faith,* and *Religion,* is his
Sacred Majestie a most gratious *Defendour,* by his *Lawes,* and *Prerogative Royall;* and in his owne *Person,* a most glorious *Example* of zealous and active Devotion. Therefore, *wee* must needs bee argued of
lesse *Conscience,* and more ingratitude, both to God, and the *King;* if
in *Temporall* things we obey not. *They,* in *Spiritualls,* deny *Subjection,*
wherein they may perhaps frame unto themselves some reasons of
probabilitie, that their offence is not so hainous. If *we,* in *Temporalls,*
shall bee *Refractary,* what colour of reason can possibly we finde out,
to make our defence withall, without the utter shaming of ourselves,
and laying a *staine* (that cannot easily be washed out) upon that *Religion,* which his *Majestie* doth so gratiously maintaine, and ourselves
Professe?

And last of all, (to conclude) if they would consider and know, that
hee who doth not, upon the former reasons and Considerations,
yeeld all willing *Obedience* to this *Counsell* of grace; and observe the
Command of his *Soveraigne; as Salomon* here adviseth: is so farre from
being a good *man,* or a good *Christian,* or a good *Subject,* that he is
not worthy to be reputed amongst the *Reasonables;* but such as the
Apostle calls *absurd and unreasonable men.* And, if they shall now at
length thinke upon this *Transcendent* dutie, to doe it with all *Obedience,* and *Alacritie;* to *God,* shall they doe that, which, to him, will be
most acceptable: to his *Anointed,* shall they give great content, in the

performance of that promise, we all made to his *Majestie*, by way of *Representation*, in that high and honourable Court of *Parliament:* to their deere and *Native Countrie*, shall they doe that, which, by *Nature* they are bound to doe: to *themselves*, shall they doe well, yea, their owne *soules* shall they reward with good, and their *Consciences* with perpetuall Peace. *Amen*.

Et sic, liberavi animam meam.

FINIS.

Peter Heylyn, 1600–1662

A Briefe and
Moderate
ANSWER,
TO
The seditious and scandalous Chal-
lenges of *Henry Burton*, late of
Friday-Streete;

In the two *sermons*, by him preached on the
fifth of *November.* 1636. And in the
Apologie prefixt before them.

BY
P E T E R H E Y L Y N.
1. P E T. 2.13,14.
Submit your selves to every ordinance of man for the Lords sake,
whether it be to the King as supreame: or unto Governors, as unto
them which are sent by him, for the punishment of evill doers, and
for the praise of them that doe well.

L O N D O N :
Printed by *Ric. Hodgkinsonne;* and are to be sold by *Daniel*
Frere, dwelling in *little-Brittan,* at the signe of the
red-Bull. Anno Domini 1637.

*P*eter Heylyn was an Oxford-trained clergyman. From the late 1620s he devoted his talents to promoting divine right monarchy and attacking Puritan beliefs. His efforts quickly brought him to the attention of William Laud and won him a variety of posts. In 1633 he assisted the Court in its case against the pugnacious and outspoken Presbyterian William Prynne. Three years later he obliged the king by writing a history of the sabbath that attacked Puritan scruples. And in 1640 Heylyn was credited with persuading the Convocation of the Church of England to endorse seventeen new canons that specifically asserted the divine right of kings.

With the outbreak of civil war Heylyn escaped to Oxford, where he was employed as editor of the royalist newspaper Mercurius Aulicus. He would live to serve as subdean at Westminster at the coronation of Charles II. Heylyn was described by contemporaries as an acrimonious controversialist, "a bluster-master," "very conceited and pragmatical."

Heylyn's pen was at the service of the Crown and episcopal establishment in "Briefe and Moderate Answer," a not-so-brief tract of some 194 pages published in 1637. It appeared in a single edition. His *purpose was to challenge the religious and political beliefs of the Puritan Henry Burton, a man as outspoken as Heylyn himself. From his London pulpit Burton is said to have conducted "aggressive warfare" against episcopal practices. He was just as insistent that there must be limitations on royal power.*

Undeterred by a citation in 1626 for his attack on Archbishop Laud, or by his imprisonment in 1629 for attacking bishops in "Babel no Bethel," Burton denounced bishops again in November 1636, this time in two sermons published under the title "For God and the King." He was hauled before the Star Chamber the following year for seditious libel and, along with two other prominent dissenters, Bastwick and Prynne, was brutally punished with deprivation, degradation, fine, pillory, the clipping of his ears, and imprisonment. The release of the three men was one of the first official acts of the Long Parliament.

Chapter two of Heylyn's lengthy reply to Burton is reprinted here. This chapter is a response to Burton's "For God and the King," itself 166 pages long. Heylyn's refutation does double duty as it provides the modern reader with a healthy dose of Burton's arguments as well as a biting refutation of them by a vigorous proponent of divine right.

Chap. II.
The Kings authority restrained, and the obedience of the subject
limited within narrow bounds, by H. B. with the removall of those
bounds.

The title of the sermon scanned, and the whole divided. H. B. offended
with the unlimited power of kings, the bounds by him prescribed to the
power of kings, both dangerous and doubtfull. The power of kings how
amplified by Jewes, Christians, Heathens. *What the King cannot doe,*
and what power is not in him, by Mass. Burton's *doctrine. The* Positive
Lawes *of the* Realme *conferre no power upon the King, nor confirme*
none to him. The whole obedience of the subject restrained by H. B. *to the*
Lawes *of the Realme; and grounded on the mutuall stipulation betweene*
King and people. The dangerous sequells of that doctrine.

A Pravis ad praecipitia. Wee are on the declining hand, out of the
Hall into the Kitchin, from an Apologie that was full of weakenesse,
unto a Sermon or rather a Pasquill farre more full of wickednesse:
yet were we guided either by the Text or Title, we might perswade
ourselves there were no such matter, nothing but piety and zeale, and
whatsoever a faire shew can promise. But for the Title Sir (I hope
you know your owne words in your doughtie dialogue betweene
A. and B.) *you know the proverbe, Fronti rara fides, the fowlest causes*
may have the fairest pretences. For whereas you entitle it, for God and
the King, you doe therein as Rebells doe most commonly in their insurrections: pretend the safety of the King, and preservation of Religion, when as they doe intend to destroy them both. The civill warre
in France, raised by the Duke of Burgundy and Berry against Lewis
the eleventh, was christened by the specious name of *Le bien Public,*
for the Common-wealth; but there was nothing lesse intended than
the common good. And when the Jewes cryed *Templum Domini,*
Templum Domini, they did but as you doe, abuse the people, and
colour their ambition, or their malice, choose you which you will,

with a shew of zeale. So that your Title may be likened very fitly, to those Apothecaries' boxes which *Lactantius* speakes of, *quorum tituli remedium habent, pixides venenum,* poysons within, and medecines writ upon the Paper. So for your Text, we will repeat that too, that men may see the better how you doe abuse it. *My sonne feare thou the Lord, and the King, and meddle not with them that are given to change; For their calamity shall arise suddenly, and who knoweth the ruine of them both, Prov.* 24.21,22. A Text indeed well chosen but not well applied. For had you looked upon yourselfe and the Text together, and followed the direction which is therein given you, you had not so long hunted after *innovations,* as for these many yeares it is knowne you have; and so might possibly have escaped that calamitie which is now like to fall upon you. But it's the nature of your humour, as of some diseases, to turne all things unto the nourishment of the part that is ill affected. Meane while you make the Scriptures but a *nose of wax,* as Pighius once prophanly called it; by wresting it maliciously to serve your turnes; and so confirme the vulgar Papists in contempt of that, which were it not for you, and such as you, they might more easily bee induced both to heare and reverence. Now for the method of your *Sermon* (I meane to call it so no more) though you observe no method in it, but wander up and downe in repetitions and *tautologies,* as your custome is: I must thus dispose it. The passages therein, either of scandall or sedition, I shall reduce especially unto these two heads: those which reflect upon the King's most excellent Majestie, and those which strike directly against the Bishops. That which reflects upon the King, either relates to his authoritie, or his actions. That which doth strike against the Bishops is to be considered as it is referred either unto their place, or to their persons, or finally to their proceedings: and these proceedings are againe to bee considered, either in reference to their Courts, and behaviour there, or to their government of and in the Church, and carriage in that weighty office, wherein you charge them with eight kinds of innovations, most of the generall kinds being subdivided into several branches. For a conclusion of the whole, I shall present unto yourselfe, by way of Corollarie, or resultancie out of all the premisses, how farre you are or may prove guilty of sedition, for that Pulpit pasquill of yours: and so commend you to repentance, and the grace of God. In ripping up whereof, as I shall keepe myselfe especially to your Pulpit-Pasquill: so if I meete with any *variae lectiones,* in your *Apologie,* or *Epistles,* or the *Newes from Ipswich,* or your addresses to the Lords of the Privie Councell, and my Lords the Judges, I shall use them also either for explication or for application. Such your extravagancies, as cannot easily be reduced to the former heads, I either shall passe over, or but touch in *transitu.* This is the order I shall use.

First for the King, you may remember what I told you was the *Puritan tenet,* that Kings are but the Ministers of the Commonwealth, and that they have no more authority than what is given them by the people. This though you doe not say expresly, and *in terminis,* yet you come very neare it, to a *tantamont:* finding great fault with that unlimited power which some give to kings, and as also with that absolute obedience which is exacted of the subject. One of your doctrines is, that *all our obedience to Kings and Princes and other superiors must be regulated by our obedience to God.* Your reason is, *because the King is God's Minister and Vice-regent, and commands as from God, so for God, and in God.* Your doctrine and your reason, might become a right honest man. But whats your use?

Your first use is, for reprehension or refutation of those that so advance man's ordinances and commandements, as though they be contrary to God's Law, and the fundamentall lawes of the state, yet so presse men to the obedience of them as they hold them for no better than rebells, and to deserve to be hanged drawne and quartered that refuse to obey them, pag. 77. So pag. 88. a second sort come here to be reproved, that on the other side separate the feare of the King from the feare of the Lord:

and those are such as attribute to Kings such an unlimited power, as if he were God Almightie himselfe; so as hereby they would seeme to ascribe that omnipotency to the King which the *Pope* assumes, and his parasites ascribe to his holinesse. So pag. 89. Thus these men crying up, and exacting universall absolute obedience to man, they doe hereby cast the feare of God, and so his Throne, downe to the ground.

Finally you reckon it amongst the *Innovations* wherewith you charge the *Prelats* in point of *doctrine,* that they "have laboured to make a change in the doctrine of *obedience to Superiours,* setting man so in God's throne, that all obedience to man must be absolute without regard to God and *conscience,* whose only rule is the word of God," pag. 126. In all which passages, however you pretend the word of God, the fundamentall Lawes of state, and conscience: yet clearly you expresse your disaffection unto the soveraignty of Princes, and in effect leave them no greater power than every private man shall thinke fit to give them. Besides there is a tacite implication also, that the King exercises an unlimited power, which cannot possibly consist with the subject's conscience, the fundamentall lawes of the Kingdome, or the word of God. It had beene very well done of you to have told the people, what were the fundamentall lawes of State, which were so carefully to be preserved; within what bounds and limits the authority of Kings is to be confined, and to have given them a more speciall knowledge of the rule of conscience. For dealing thus in generalls only, (*Dolosus versatur in generalibus,* you know who said it) you have presented to the people a most excellent ground, not only to dispute, but to disobey the King's commands.

Now Sir I pray you what are you, or by what spirit are you guided, that you should finde yourselfe agreeved at unlimited power, which some of better understanding than yourselfe have given to Kings: or thinke it any innovation in point of doctrine, in case the doctrine of obedience to our superiours bee pressed more home of late than it hath beene formerly. Surely you have lately studied *Buchannan de jure regni*, or the *vindiciae* writ by *Beza* under the name of *Junius Brutus:* or else perhaps you went no further than *Paraus*, where the inferiour magistrates, or *Calvin*, where the three estates have an authority to controule, and correct the King. And should the King be limited within those narrow bounds which you would prescribe him, had you power; he would in little time be like the antient Kings of *Sparta*, in which the *Ephori*, or the now Duke of *Venice*, in which the Senate beare the greatest stroke: himselfe meanetime, being a bare sound, and an emptie name, *Stet magni nominis umbra*, in the Poet's language. Already you have laid such grounds, by which each private man may not alone dispute but disobey the King's commandements. For if the subject shall conceive that the King's command is contrary to God's word, though indeede it be not; or to the fundamentall lawes of state, although hee cannot tell which be fundamentall; or if he finde no precedent of the like commands in holy Scripture, which you have made to be the only rule of *conscience:* in all these cases it is lawfull not to yeeld *obedience.* Yourselfe have given us one case in your Margin, pag. 77. We will put the other. Your reprehension is of those, that so advance man's "ordinances and commandements, as though they be contrary to God's Law, and the fundamentall lawes of state, yet presse men to obedience to them," your instance is of one which was shrewdly threatened (how true that is we meane to tell the world hereafter) for refusing to doe that which "was not agreeable to the word of God, *viz.* for refusing to read the booke of sports, as you declare it in the Margin, pag 26.[1] whether you referre us. So then the case is this. The King permits his people honest recreations on the *Lord's day*, according as had beene accustomed, till you and your accomplices had cryed it down: with order to the Bishops to see *his declaration published in the Churches of their severall dioceses, respectively.*

---

1. The *Book of Sports*, issued in 1618 by James I and reissued in 1633 by Charles I, provoked outrage among Puritans by permitting a variety of recreations on the Sabbath.

This *publication* you conceive to bee repugnant to God's word, (though none but a few factious spirits ever so conceived it, and that your doctrine of the *Sabbath* be contrary to all antiquity and moderne Churches): and therefore by your rule they doe very well that refuse to publish it. It's true indeed, in things that are directly contrary to the law of God, and such as carry in them a plaine and manifest impietie; there is no question to be made, but it is *better to obey God than man.* But when the matter chiefly resteth either in misapplying, or misunderstanding the word of God, (a fault too incident to ignorant & unstable men, & to none more than to your disciples and their teachers too) or that the word of God be made a *property* like the *Pharisees' Corban,* to justifie your disobedience unto Kings and Princes: your rule is then as false, as your action faulty. So for your second limitation, that's but little better; and leaves a starting hole to malicious persons, from whence to worke on the affections of the common people. For put the case, the King in necessary and emergent causes, touching the safety of the kingdome, demand the present aid of all his subjects; and any *Tribunitian* spirit should informe them, that this demand is contrary unto the *fundamentall lawes of state:* according to your rule, the subject is not bound to obey the King, nay he might refuse it, although the businesse doth concern especially his owne preservation. But your third limitation, that of *conscience,* is the worst of it all. For where you make the word of God to bee the only rule of *conscience,* you doe thereby conclude expressly that neither Ecclesiasticall or Civill ordinances doe bind the conscience: and therein overthrow the Apostle's doctrine, who would have *Every soule be subject to the higher powers. Not for wrath only, but for conscience sake.* So that in case the King command us any thing, for which wee finde not some plaine precept or particular warrant in the word of God; as if the King command all *Lecturers* to read the Service of the Church in their *hoods and surplices,* before their *Lectures:* such his command is plainly against *conscience,* at least the lec-

turers are not bound in *conscience* to submit unto it, because there is
no speciall precept for it in holy Scripture. And certainly this plea of
Conscience, is the most dangerous buckler against authority, which
in these later ages hath been taken up. So dangerous that were the
plea allowed, and all the judgments of the king *in banco*, permitted
to bee scanned and traversed in this *Court of conscience;* there were a
present end of all obedience. *Si ubi jubeantur, quaerere singulis liceat,
pereunte obsequio imperium etiam intercedit,* as he in *Tacitus.* If every
man had leave to cast in his *scruple,* the *ballast* of authority would be
soon weighted down.

Yet since you are so much greived at the unlimited power as you
please to call it, which some give to Kings; will you be pleased to
know, that Kings do hold their Crownes by no other *Tenure,* than *Dei
gratia:* and that whatever power they have, they have from God, by
whom Kings reigne, and Princes decrees justice. So say the Constitutions ascribed to *Clements* [...]. So *Irenaeus* also an antient father,
Cuius iussu homines nascuntur, eius iussu reges constituuntur.[2] And *Por-
phirie* remembreth it amongst the Tenets of the *Essenes* a *Jewish* sect,
[...], that no man ever did beare rule but by God's appointment.
Holding then what they have from God, whose deputies they are,
and of whose power they are partakers, how and by whom doe you
conceive they should be limited? Doubtlesse you meane to say by
the lawes of the Land. But then if question be demanded who first
made those Lawes, you must needes answere, They were made by the
King's authoritie. So that in case the kings, in some particulars, had
not prescribed limits unto themselves, and bound their owne hands,
as it were, to enlarge the peoples, neither the people, nor any lawes by
them enacted, without the King's consent, could have ever done it.
Besides the law of *Monarchie* is founded on the law of *nature,* not on
positive lawes: and *positive lawes* I trow are of no such efficacie, as to

---

2. By whose command men are born, by his command kings are established.

annihilate anything, which hath its being and originall, in the *law* of *nature.* Hence is it, that all soveraigne Princes in themselves are above the lawes, as Princes are considered in *abstracto,* and extent of power; and how farre that extent will reach, you may see in the first of *Sam.* and 8 *chap.* though in *concreto* a just Prince will not breake those lawes, which he hath promised to observe. Princes are debtors to their subjects, as God to man; *non aliquid a nobis accipiendo, sed omnia nobis promittendo,*[3] as St. *Austine* hath it. And we may say of them in S. *Bernard's* words, *Promissum quidem ex misericordia, sed ex justitia persolvendum:*[4] That they have promised to observe the lawes, was of speciall grace; and it's agreeable to their justice to observe their promise. Otherwise we may say of kings, as the apostle of the just; *Iusto lex non est posita,*[5] saith the Apostle, and *Principi lex non est posita,*[6] saith the law of nature. Doe you expect more proofe than you use to give? *Plutarch* affirmes it of some kings, οὐ κατὰ τοὺς νόμους μόνον, ἀλλὰ καὶ τῶν νόμων ἄρχειν, that they did not governe only by the law, but were above it. The like saith *Dion* of *Augustus Caesar,* αὐτοτελὴς καὶ αὐτοκράτωρ καὶ ἑαυτοῦ καὶ τῶν νόμων, that he was sure and had an absolute authoritie, as well upon his lawes as upon himselfe. Besides in case the power of kings were restrained by law, after the manner, that you would have it; yet should the king neglect those lawes, whereby you apprehend that his power is limited; how would you helpe yourselfe by this limited power? I hope you would not call a *Consistorie* and convent him there; or arme the people to assert their pretended liberties: though as before I said, the *Puritan tenet* is, that you may doe both. Your learned Councell[7] might have told you out of *Bracton,* an ancient lawyer of this kingdome, *omnem*

---

3. Not receiving anything from us, but promising all things to us.
4. The promise (exists) out of mercy, but it is to be executed out of justice.
5. The law is not imposed by one who is just.
6. The law is not imposed by a prince.
7. In the preface Heylyn refers to William Prynne, barrister of Lincoln's Inn and an outspoken Puritan, as Burton's learned counsel.

esse sub Rege & ipsum sub nullo, sed tantum sub Deo.[8] And *Horace* could have told you, that kings are under none but God. *Reges in ipsos imperium est Jovis,* as he there hath it. You may moreover please to know, what *Gregorie* of *Tours* said once to a king of *France; Si quis e nobis, O Rex, justitiae tramites transcendere voluerit, a te corripi potest; si vero tu excesseris quis te corripiet? &c.* If any of us, O king, offend against the rules of justice, thou has power, "to punish him, but if thou breake those rules, who hath power to doe it? We tell you of it, and when you list, you please to heare us, but when you will not, who shall judge you, but he that tells us of himselfe, that he is justice."

This was you see the ancient doctrine, touching the power and right of kings, not only amongst *Jewes* and *Christians* but in heathen states: whatever new opinion of a limited power, you have pleased to raise.

But you goe further yet, and tell us of some things the king cannot do, and that there is a power which the king hath not; what is it, say you, that the king cannot doe? Marry you say he cannot "institute new rites and ceremonies, with the advise of his Commissioners Ecclesiasticall, or the Metropolitan, according as some pleade from the Act of Parliament before the Communion booke," pag. 65. Why so? *Because,* according to your law, *this clause of the Act is limited to* Queene *Elizabeth, and not extended to her successours of the Crowne.* This you affirme indeede, but you bring no proofe: only it seems you heard so from your *learned councell.* You are I see of *Calvin's* minde, who tells us in his Commentarie on the 7 of *Amos,* what had beene said by Doctor *Gardiner,* after Bishop of *Winchester,* and then Ambassadour in *Germany,* touching the *headship* or *Supremacie* of the king his master: and closeth up the storie with this short note, *inconsiderati homines sunt, qui faciunt eos nimis spirituales,* that it was unadvisedly done, to give kings such authority in spirituall matters. But

8. Everything is under the King, and he under no one, but under God alone.

sir I hope you may afford the king that power, which you take yourselves, or which your brethren at the least have tooke before you: who
in Queene *Elizabeth's* time had their *Classicall* meetings[9] without
leave or licence, and therein did ordeine new rites, new Canons, and
new formes of service. This you may doe, it seemes, though the king's
hands are bound that he may not doe it. And there's a power too, as
you tell us, that the king neither hath nor may give to others. Not
give to others certainely, if he have it not; for *nemo dat quod non habet,*
as the saying is. But what is this? You first suppose and take for
granted, that the *Bishops make foule havocke in the Church of God,* and
persecute his faithfull servants: and *then suppose, which yet you say is not
to be supposed, that they have procured a grant from the king to doe all
those things which of late they have done, tending to the utter overthrow
of religion by law established.* And on these suppositions you doe thus
proceede. Yet

> whatsoever colour, pretext or shew they make for this, the king
> (to speake with all humble reverence) cannot give that power to
> others, which hee hath not himselfe. For the power that is in the
> king is given him by God, and confirmed by the lawes of the
> kingdome. Now neither God in his law, nor the lawes of the
> land, doe allow the king a power to alter the state of religion, or
> to oppresse and suppresse the faithfull ministers of the *Gospell,*
> against both law and conscience. For kings are the ministers of
> God for the good of his people, as wee shewed before. p. 72, 73.

So you, and it was bravely said, like a valiant man. The *Brethren* now
may follow after their owne inventions, with a full securitie: for since
you have proclaimed them to be *faithfull ministers,* no king nor *Keisar*
dares suppresse them; or if he should, the lawes of God, and the law
of the land to boote, would rise in judgement to condemne him, for
usurpation of a power which they have not given him. But take me

9. The author is referring here to the *classis,* a gathering of elders or pastors of Presbyterian church government.

with you brother *B.* and I perhaps may tell you somewhat that is worth your knowledge. And I will tell you sir if you please to hearken, that whatsoever power is in the king, is from God alone, and founded on the law of nature. The *positive lawes* of the land as they conferre none on him, so they confirme none to him. Rather the kings of *England* have parted with their native royalties for the people's good: which being by their owne consent, established for a *positive law,* are now become the greatest part of the subjects' liberties. So that the liberties, possessions, and estates of the king's leige people, are, if you will, confirmed by the lawes of the land; not the *king's authoritie.* As for the power of kings which is given by God, and founded on the law of nature, how farre it may extend in the true latitude thereof, we have said already. Whether to alter the state of religion, none but a most seditious spirit, such as yours would put unto the question: his majestie's pietie and zeale, being too well knowne to give occasion to such *quaeres.* Only I needes must tell you, that you tie up the king's hands too much, in case he may not meddle with a company of *Schismatickes,* and refractarie persons to all power and order, only because you have pronounced them to be *faithfull ministers of the Gospell.* Such faithfull ministers of the *Gospell* as you and yours, must bee suppressed, or else there never will be peace and unitie in the Citie of God. And yet I see you have some scripture for it, more than I supposed: king's being, as you tell us from S. *Paul,* the *ministers of God for the good of their people,* and no more than so? I thought S. *Paul* had also told us, that the *King is a minister of God, an avenger to execute wrath upon him that doth evill:* yea more than so too brother *B.* and it may concerne you, *viz. if thou doe that which is evill be afraid, for he beareth not the sword in vaine. Aut undequaque pietatem tolle, aut undequaque conserva;*[10] Take the whole text along good sir, or take none at all: and if you take all *be afraid,* as you are advised, *verbum sapienti.*

10. Either eliminate piety everywhere, or preserve it everywhere.

I must goe forwards with you yet from the *authoritie* of the *king,* to the *obedience* of the *subject;* which you doe presse indeede, but on such false grounds, as in conclusion overthrow the whole frame of government. The *absolute obedience* of the subject you have dashed alreadie, and reckon it amongst those *innovations* in point of doctrine, which you have charged upon the *Prelates:* and in the place thereof bring in a limited or conditionall obedience, of your owne devising. Your first condition or limitation rather, is, *viz.* that our *subjection unto the King, is to be regulated as by God's law, the rule of universall obedience to God and man, so by the good laws of the king.* p. 38. The king as you informe us p. 42. *having entered into solemne and sacred covenant with all his people, to demand of them no other obedience, but what the good lawes of the kingdome prescribe & require:* as on the other side, *the people swearing no other obedience to the king than according to his just lawes, pag.* 39. and 40. In which restraint, there are two things to be observed, first that wee are to obey the king no farther than there is law for it, and secondly no farther than that law seemes good. So that in case the king commands his people any thing for which he hath no positive law to warrant his command; and of this sort are many *Proclamations, orders, decrees, injunctions,* set out from time to time by the king's authoritie, and *Prerogative* royall, by brother *Burton's* rule the people are at liberty to obey or not. And on the other side, in case the said command bee grounded on some *positive law* which they like not of, whether it be a penall statute, or some old Act of *Parliament* almost out of use, by the reviving of the which they may be prejudiced in *purse* or otherwise: this is no good law in their judgement, and so no more to be obeyed than if the king's command were founded on no law at all. But your next limitation is farre worse than this, though this bad enough. For in the next place you have

grounded all obedience on the people's part, upon that *mutuall stipulation* which the king and his subjects make at his Coronation. Where the king takes an *explicite solemne oath* to mainteine

the antient lawes and liberties of the kingdome, and so to rule
and governe all his people according to those lawes established;
consequently and implicitely all the people of the land doe sweare
fealtie, allegiance, subjection and obedience to their king, and
that according to his just lawes, *pag. 39.* Your inference from
hence is this, that if the king so solemnely by sacred oath, rati-
fied againe in Parliament under his royall hand, doe bind himselfe to maintaine the lawes of his kingdome, and therein the
rights and liberties of his subjects, then how much are the people bound to yeeld all subjection and obedience to the king, according to his just lawes, p. 40.

So that according to your doctrine, the people is no longer to obey
the king, than the king keepes promise with the people. Nay of the
two the people have the better bargaine; the king being sworne *explicitely* and *solemnely* to maintaine their liberties; the people only
consequently and *implicitely* to yeeld him subjection. Is not this excellent doctrine think you? Or could the most *seditious person* in a state
have thought upon a shorter cut to bring all to *Anarchie;* for if the
subject please to misinterpret the king's proceedings, and thinke
though falsely, that he hath not kept his promise with them: they are
released *ipso facto* from all obedience and subjection, and that by a
more easie way, than suing out a *dispensation* in the *Court* of *Rome.*
You tell us, p. 129. of the king's *free subjects;* and here you have found
out a way to make them so: a way to make the *subject free,* and the
king a *subject;* and hard it is to say whether of the two be the greater
Contradiction in *adjecto.* I have before heard of a *free people,* and of
free states, but never till of late a *free subject:* nor know I any way to
create *free subjects,* but by releasing them of all obedience to their
Princes. And I have read too of *Eleuthero Cilices,* which were those
people of *Cilicia* that were not under the command of any king: but
never reade of an *Eleuthero Britannus,* nor I hope never shall. I will
but aske you one question, and so end this point. You presse the

king's oath very much about maintaining of the lawes of the Kingdom, as pag. 39. 40. and 42. before recited, as also, pag. 72. againe and
againe, and finally in your addresse to my Lords the Judges. Is it by
way of *Commemoration* or of *Exprobration?* If of *Commemoration,* you
forget the Rule; *memorem immemorem facit, qui monet quae memor
meminit.*[11] But if of *Exprobration,* what meant you, when you needed
not to tell us, that in a point of Civill Government, it is a dangerous
thing to change a Kingdom setled on good lawes into a tyranny; and
presently thereon to adde a certaine speech of *Heraclitus, viz.* That
citizens ought to fight no lesse for their lawes, than for their walls. I only
aske the question, take you time to answere it.

11. Whoever warns the one remembering to remember, makes the one who is to remember
forgetful.

Battle Joined
1640–1648

[Henry Parker, 1604–1652]

The Case of
SHIPMONY
briefly discoursed,

ACCORDING TO THE
Grounds of Law, Policy,
and Conscience.

AND

MOST HVMBLY
PRESENTED TO THE
Censure and Correction of the
High Court of Parliament,
Nov. 3. 1640.

Printed Anno Dom. 1640.

*H*enry Parker, one of the most prolific writers in the cause of Parliament in the civil war era, has also been dubbed the clearest and most realistic. A graduate of St. Edmund Hall, Oxford, he was called to the bar at Lincoln's Inn in 1637. Parker quickly put his talents to work in support of the Presbyterian, and later the Independent, opponents of the Crown. During the civil war and Interregnum Parker held a series of important posts for Parliament. He served as secretary to Parliament's army under the Earl of Essex, then in 1645 as secretary to the House of Commons where he prepared various declarations, and finally as secretary to Cromwell's army in Ireland. He died in Ireland late in 1652, aged forty-eight.

Parker was renowned among his contemporaries and is recognized *among modern historians as one of Parliament's most important theorists. His first published tract, the anonymous "The Case of Shipmony Briefly Discoursed" reprinted here, was prepared for presentation to the Long Parliament on the day it convened. Three editions appeared. It is not only a vigorous denunciation of a levy widely condemned as an abuse of the royal prerogative but underlines for us the grave constitutional threat contemporaries saw in shipmoney itself and, even more, in the legal reasoning with which the royal judges had upheld it. With crystal clarity Parker forges the link between political grievance and constitutional menace. The Long Parliament went on to outlaw shipmoney.*

The Case of Ship-Money Briefly Discoursed.

Great Fires happening in Townes or Cities, are sometimes the cause that other contiguous houses are spoiled and demolisht, besides those which the flame itselfe seizes. So now, in the case of Ship-money, not only the judgement itselfe which hath been given against the subject, doth make a great gap and breach in the rights and Franchises of England, but the arguments and pleadings also, which conduced to that judgement, have extended the mischiefe further, and scarce left anything unviolated. Such strange contradiction there hath been amongst the pleaders, and dissent amongst the Judges, even in those Lawes which are most fundamentall, that we are left in a more confused uncertainty of our highest priviledges, and those customes which are most essentiall to Freedome, than we were before. To introduce the legality of the Ship-scot,[1] such a prerogative hath been maintained, as destroyes altogether Law, and is incompatible with popular liberty: and such Art hath been used to deny, traverse, avoid, or frustrate the true force, or meaning of all our Lawes and Charters, that if wee grant Ship-money upon these grounds, with Ship-money wee grant all besides. To remove therefore this uncertainty, which is the mother of all injustice, confusion, and publicke dissention, it is most requisite that this grand Councell and Treshault Court[2] (of which none ought to thinke dishonourably) would take these *Arduis Regni,* these weighty and dangerous difficulties, into serious debate, and solemnly end that strife, which no other place of Judicature can so effectually extinguish.

That the King ought to have aid of his subjects in times of danger, and common aid in case of common danger, is laid downe for a ground, and agreed upon by all sides. But about this aid there remaines much variety and contrariety of opinion amongst the great-

1. "Ship-scot" refers to ship levy or so-called ship money.
2. "Treshault court" is a very high court.

est Sages of our Law; and the principall points therein controverted, are these foure: First, by what Law the King may compell aid. Secondly, when it is to bee levied. Thirdly, how it is to bee levied. Fourthly, what kinde of aid it must be.

1. Some of the Judges argue from the Law of Nature, that since the King is head, and bound to protect, therefore he must have wherewithall to protect: but this proves only that which no man denies. The next Law insisted upon, is Prerogative; but it is not punctually explained what Prerogative, whether the Prerogative naturall of all Kings, or the Prerogative legall of the Kings of England. Some of the Judges urge, that by Law there is naturall allegeance due to the King from the subject, and it doth not stand with that allegeance that our Princes cannot compell aid, but must require the common consent therein. Others presse, that the Law hath setled a property of goods in the subject, and it doth not stand with that property, that the King may demand them without consent. Some take it for granted, that by Royall prerogative, as it is part of the Lawes of England, the King may charge the Nation without publick consent; and therefore it being part of the Law, it is no invasion upon Law. Others take it for granted, that to levie money without consent, is unjust, and that the King's prerogative cannot extend to any unjust thing. So many contrary points of warre doe our Trumpets sound at once, and in such confusion doe our Judges leave us, whilest either side takes that for granted, which by the other is utterly denied. By these grounds Royall prerogative, and popular liberty may seeme things irreconcileable, though indeed they are not; neither doth either side in words affirme so much, though their proofes bee so contradictory. King *Charles* his Maxime is, that the people's liberty strengthen the King's prerogative, and the King's prerogative is to maintaine the people's liberty; and by this it seemes that both are compatible, and that prerogative is the more subordinate of the two. The King's words also since have been upon another occasion, That he ever intended

his people should enjoy property of goods, and liberty of persons, holding no King so great, as he that was King of a rich and free people: and if they had not property of goods, and liberty of persons, they could bee neither rich nor free. Here we see, that the liberty of the subject is a thing which makes a King great; and that the King's prerogative hath only for its ends to maintaine the people's liberty. Wherefore it is manifest, that in nature there is more favour due to the liberty of the subject, than to the Prerogative of the King, since the one is ordained only for the preservation of the other; and then to solve these knots, our dispute must be, what prerogative the people's good and profit will beare, not what liberty the King's absolutenes or prerogative may admit: and in this dispute it is more just that wee appeale to written lawes, than to the breasts of Kings themselves. For we know Nationall lawes are made by consent of Prince and people both, and so cannot bee conceived to be prejudiciall to either side; but where the meere will of the Prince is law, or where some few Ministers of his, may alledge what they will for law in his behalfe, no mediocrity or justice is to be expected. We all know that no slave or villaine, can be subjected to more miserable bondage than to be left meerly to his Lord's absolute discretion: and wee all see that the thraldome of such is most grievous, which have no bounds set to their Lord's discretion. Let us then see what *Fortescue* writes, not regard what Court dependents doe interpret, and his words are for *84. Cap. 36. Rex Anglia nec per se nec per suos Ministros Tollagia subsidia aut quavis onera alta imponit legis suis, aut leges corum mutat, aut nova condit sine concessione vel assensu totius regni sui in Parliamento sui expresso.*[3] These words are full, and generall, and plaine, and in direct affirmance of the ancient Law and usage of England, and it is not sufficient for the King's Counsell to say that these words extend not

---

3. The king of England neither by himself nor by his ministers imposes tax subsidies or any other duties or changes their laws, or establishes novelties without the concession or the assent of his entire kingdom expressed in his Parliament.

to Ship-money: for if there were any doubt, the interpretation ought rather to favour liberty, than prerogative.

It is not sufficient for Judge *Jones* to say that it is *proprium quarto modo*[4] to a King, and an inseparable naturall prerogative of the Crowne to raise monies without assent, unlesse he first prove that such prerogative bee good and profitable for the people, and such as the people cannot subsist at all without it: nay such as no Nation can subsist without it. This word Prerogative has divers acceptions: sometimes it is taken for the altitude of Honour, sometimes for the latitude of Power. So wee say the prerogative of an Emperour is greater, than that of a King and that of a King, greater than that of a Duke, or petty Potentate: and yet of Kings we say that the King of Denmarke has not so great a Prerogative as the King of England, nor the King of England, as the King of France, &c. For here though their honor and title be the same, yet their power is not. Sometimes Prerogative signifies as much as Soveraignty, and in this generall consideration, wee say, that all supreame commanders are equall, and that they all have this essentiall inseparable Prerogative, that their power ought to be ample enough for the perfection, and good of the people, and no ampler: because the supreame of all human lawes is *salus populi*. To this law all lawes almost stoope, God dispences with many of his lawes, rather than *salus populi* shall bee endangered, and that iron law which wee call necessity itselfe, is but subservient to this law: for rather than a Nation shall perish, any thing shall be held necessary, and legal by necessity. But to come to the Prerogative of England, and to speake of it in generall, and comparatively; wee say it is a harmonious composure of policy, scarce to be parralled in all the world, it is neither so boundlesse as to oppresse the people in unjust things, nor so straite as to disable the King in just thinges. By the true fundamentall constitutions of England, the beame hangs even

4. Proper in the fourth way.

between the King and the Subject: the King's power doth not tread under foot the people's liberty, nor the people's liberty the King's power. All other Countries almost in Christendome, differ from us in this module of policy: some, but very few, allow a greater sphere of Soveraignty to their Princes; but for the most part now adays the world is given to republists, or to conditionate and restrained forms of government. Howsoever wee ought not to condemne any Nation as unjust herein, though differing from us; for though they seem perhaps very unpolitick, yet it is hard to bee affirmed that God and Nature ever ordained the same method of rule, or scope of royalty to all States whatsoever. Besides what dislike soever wee take at other regiments, yet except it bee in very great excesses or defects, wee must not thinke change always necessary, since custome in those great and generall points obtaines the force of another nature & nature is not to be changed. Divines of late have been much to blame here in preaching one universall forme of government as necessary to all Nations, and that not the moderate, & equall neither, but such as ascribes all to Soveraignty, nothing at all to popular libertie. Some Lawyers also and Statesmen have deserved as ill of late, partly by suggesting that our English lawes are too injurious to our King; and partly by informing, that this King is more limited by law than his Progenitors were, & that till hee be as the King of France is *Rex Asinorum*,[5] hee is but a subject to his subjects, and as a Minor under the command of guardians: but what hath ensued out of the King's jealousy of his subjects, and overstraining his prerogative? Nothing but irreparable losse, and mischiefe both to King and Commonwealth. And indeed the often and great defections, and insurrections, which have happened of late, almost all over Europe,[6] may suffice to warne

    5. King of the jackasses.
    6. Parker probably has in mind not only the so-called Bishops' Wars with Scotland but insurrections such as the revolt of the Netherlands and the devastating Thirty Years War in Europe. Moreover, during 1640 the Spanish empire was shaken by revolt in Catalonia and Portugal.

all wise Princes, not to overstrain their Prerogatives too high; nor to give care to such Counsellors as some of our Judges are, who affirme our King's Prerogative to be in all points unalterable, and by consequence not depending upon law at all. By an other exception of this word Prerogative in England, we mean such law here establisht as gives the King such and such preeminences, and priviledges: before any subject, such as are not essentiall to royalty, but may be annulled by the same power, by which they were created. That a King shall defend and maintaine his subjects, is a duty belonging to the Office, not a priviledge belonging to the Crowne of a King; this obligation nature lays upon him, and no other power can dissolve it. Also that subjects shall afforde aide, and joine with their Princes in common defence, is a duty arising from the allegiance of the people, and not an honor redounding only to the Prince; nature's law hath made this a tie not to be changed, or infringed: for that which is annexed by an eternall superiour power cannot be made severable, by a temporall human power. But that such an Emperour, King or Potentate, shall have such or such aid, and compell it by such or such meanes, at such or such times, as to the particular modes and circumstances of his aid, particular municipall Lawes must direct; and these it would be as dangerous to alter, as it is absurd to hold unalterable. In a Parliament held by *King James*, it was debated, whether or no Tenures *in Capite*,[7] and allowance of Perveyors[8] might bee repealed and divided from the Crowne; and it was held that by no Act or Statute they could bee taken away, because they were naturally inherent to the Crowne.

This resolution seemes very strange to me, since the Law of Tenures and Purveyors is not so naturall and essentiall to Monarchy, that it cannot or may not subsist without it. For if in other Countries it bee held a meere politicall way, perhaps an inconvenient thing, then

7. Tenure *in Capite* refers to land held immediately of the king.
8. Purveyance refers to provision to be furnished to the Crown. In 1604 the Commons claimed this prerogative had been abused.

why may not the Prince's Royalty, and the people's safety bee preserved intire without it in England? And if so, then why shall not the
same authority have vigor to repeale it, which wanted not vigor to
inforce it? I cannot conceive that the Parliament herein reflected
upon what was formall in Law to bee done, but rather upon what was
convenient. Such *insignia suprema Majestatis* as these, I doe not hold
it fit to bee dismembred from the Crowne in policie; I only hold it a
thing possible in Law, nay though the King enjoy divers such like
prerogatives more, as *J. Jones* thinkes, than any Prince in Christendome, yet should not I desire or advise to plucke away one the least
Flower out of the Regal Garland, nor would it be (perhaps) profitable
for the State, to suffer the least diminution thereof. Wee know also,
that in England the prerogative hath been bound in many cases, by
Statute-Law, and restrained of divers such priviledges as were not
essentiall, but meerly politicall. *Nullum tempus occurrit Regi:*[9] This
was one of the English Royalties, and very beneficiall many wayes;
yet wee know this is in divers cases limited by Act of Parliament, and
that very justly, as *J. Hutton* argues. The great and ancient Tax of
Dangelt, it was a Subsidie taken by the Kings of England, for the
common defence of the Kingdome; yet this was first released by King
Stephen, and after abolished for ever by the Statutes of *Edward* the
first: and there is no reason why an Act of Parliament should not bee
as valid in our case, as it was in that. Wherefore it is to bee admired,
that J. *Jones* should account this way of aid by Ship-money, or any
other, without publicke consent, to bee *Proprium quarto modo*[10] to
the Kings of England, and so unrepealeable, since our Kings have in
all ages, done such noble acts without it; and not only defended, but
also enlarged their dominions. The last kinde of acception of this
word Prerogative, is improper. Thus to pardon malefactors, to dispence with penall Lawes, to grant *Non obstantes,* to bee free from at-

9. Time does not run against the King.
10. Proper in the fourth way.

tainders, to call or discontinue, to prorogue or dissolve Parliaments, &c. are not truely and properly called Prerogatives: these all in some sense may bee called Munities, or indemnities, belonging to the sacred person of the King, as hee is inviolable, and subject to no force and compulsion of any other. And as he is the soule of Law, in whose power alone it is to execute Law, and yet not to bee constrained thereto. To grant a pardon to some malefactors for some crimes, may perhaps bee as heinous as to commit them; and that which drawes a guilt upon the King, cannot bee said to bee his priviledge. If it might bee tearmed a Royalty, that the King is not questionable, or punishable, or to bee forced in such acts as tend to the obstruction of justice, it might as well be so tearmed in acts tending to the transgression of Law: for in both hee is alike free from any coercive, or vindicative force. For it is out of necessity, not honour, or benefit, that the King hath a freedome from constraint, or restraint in these cases; and that this freedome is inseparable, because no force can be used but by superiours, or equals, and hee which hath either superiors or equals, is no King. If a King should shut up the Courts or ordinary Justice, and prohibit all pleadings and proceedings betwixt man and man, and refuse to authorise Judges for the determining of suits, hee would bee held to doe a most unkingly thing: and yet this may be as truly called a Prerogative, as to disuse and dissolve Parliaments. But it may bee objected, that the King besides such negative priviledge and freedome from force, hath also a positive of seizing subjects' lands, &c. in divers cases, as in making Bulwarkes upon any man's land for common defence &c. To this it may be answered, That to such power the King is not intitled by his Prerogative, nor is it any benefite to him, necessitie herein is his only warrant: for either this private inconvenience must happen, or a publick ruine follow and in nature the lesse and private evill is to bee chosen: and here the party trespassed, enjoyes safety by it, and shall after receive satisfaction for his detriment. Were there such apparant unavoidable necessity in the Ship-scot, that either that course must bee taken, or the community inevitably perish, or were the King wholly disinterested in point of profit, or were there hope of restitution, it could not bee without consent, and so not against Law. So then, for ought that is yet alledged, Prerogative, except that which is essentiall to all Kings, without which they cannot bee Kings, is alterable, and it ought to be deduced out of the written and knowne Lawes of the Kingdome, and Law is not to be inferred out of that; wee ought not to presume a Prerogative, and thence conclude it to be Law, but we ought to cite the Law, and thence prove it to be Prerogative. To descend then to our owne Lawes, yet there our Judges vary too. What the Common Law was in this point is doubted by some, and some say if the Common Law did allow the King such a prerogative to lay a generall charge without consent, then Statutes cannot alter it.

Some doe not except against the force of Statute Law, but avoid our particular Statutes by divers several evasive answers. Some say our Great Charter was but a grant of the King, extorted by force; some except against the 25. of *Ed.* I. because there is a *salvo* in it; some against the 34. of *Ed.* I. as made in the King's absence; some object against the 14. of *Ed.* 3. as if it were temporary, and because it is not particularly recited in the Petition of Right. And the common evasion of all beneficiall Statutes, and of the Petition of right, is, that they binde the King from imposing pecuniary charges for the replenishing of his owne coffers, but not from imposing such personall services, as this Ship-scot is, in time of danger and necessity. J. *Crawly* maintains this Ship-scot to bee good by Prerogative at the Common Law, and not to be altered by Statute. What the Common Law was, this Court can best determine; but it is obvious to all men, that no Prerogative can be at the Common Law, but it had some beginning, and that must bee from either King or Subject, or both: and in this, it is not superiour to our Statute Law, and by consequence not unalterable. The Medes and Persians had a Law, that no Law once past, should ever bee repealed; but doubtlesse this Law being repealed first, all others might after suffer the same alteration, and it is most absurd to think that this Law might not bee repealed by the same authority by which it was at first enacted. J. *Jones* sayes, our Statutes restraine tollages in generall termes, and cites divers cases, that a speciall interest shall not passe from the King, but in special termes. But his cases are put of private grantees, over whom the King ought to retaine a great preheminence: but the Law is, that where the whole state is grantee, that grant shall have the force of a Statute, because it is *pro bono publico,* and because the whole state is in value and dignity as much to be preferred before the King, as the King is before any private grantee. But J. *Jones* sayes further, if generall words shall extend to these extraordinary publick levies, then they may as well extend to his ordinary private rights, and intradoes, & so cut off *Aide pur faire filz Chivaleir, &c.* The contrary hereof is manifest, for the intent of all our Statutes is to defend the subject against such publick tollages and impositions, as every man is equally liable to, and as are not due in Law otherwise, or recoverable by ordinary action. Now these aides, &c. and the King's ordinary revenues and services, are not such as are due from every man, but recoverable by ordinary action. Howsoever in all these doubts the Law would now bee made cleare, and not only the vertue of Statutes in generall, but also the true meaning of our particular Charters would be vindicated from all these exceptions.

2. I come now to our second difficulty, when a publicke charge may bee laid. Here the favourers of Ship-money yet agree, that the King may not charge the subject meerly to fill his owne coffers, or annually, or when he will invade a forraigne enemy, or when Pirates rob, or burn Townes and Burroughs, for these ordinary defence is sufficient: and when there is imminent and eminent danger of publick invasion, we agree that the subject may be charged.

The Quaere then is, whether the King bee sole Judge of the dan-

ger, and of the remedy, or rather whether he be so sole Judge, that his
meere affirmation and notification of a danger foreseene by him at a
distance, or pretended only to be foreseene, shall be so unquestionable, that he may charge the Kingdome thereupon at his discretion,
though they assent not, nor apprehend the danger as it is forewarned.
J. *Crooke* proves the contrary thus: If danger, sayes he, be far distant,
if it be in report only of French armadoes, and Spanish preparations,
&c. though it bee certaine, and not pretensive, yet Parliamentary Aid
may be speedy enough: and if it be imminent, then this way of Ship-
scot will not bee speedy enough; for either the designe is really to
have new Ships built, and that will require longer time than a Parliament; or else money only is aimed at, whereby to arme other Ships,
and for this the Law hath provided a more expedite way than by
Ship-scot, in case of imminent danger.

If then the King have power to presse all men's persons and ships,
and all are bound *exponere se, & sua*,[11] and to serve *propriis sumptibus*,[12] when imminent danger is, and this defence hath always beene
held effectuall enough, it is consequent that if hee be not destitute of
competent Aid in present distresses, he cannot pretend a greater necessity in dangers more remote, when they are but suspected or perhaps pretended only.

My Lord *Bramston* sayes here, that there is a necessity of preventing a necessity: and that the Sea is part of the Kingdome, and therefore of necessity to bee guarded as the kingdome. The answer is, That
the safety of the Kingdome does not necessarily depend upon the
Ship-scot, and so this necessity being removed, the necessity
grounded upon this, falls off of itselfe. For if the Kingdome may escape ruine at hand when it is a storme, without Ship-money, it may
much more escape it afar off, being but a cloud. But grant the Sea to
be a part of the Kingdome to some purposes, yet how is it a part es-

11. To risk himself and his belongings.
12. By their own expenses; at their own expense.

sentiall, or equally valuable, or how does it appeare that the fate of the Land depends wholly upon the dominion of the Sea? France subsists now without the regiment of the Sea, and why may not we as well want the same? If England quite spend itselfe, and poure out all its treasure to preserve the Seigniory of the Seas, it is not certaine to exceed the Navall force of France, Spaine, Holland, &c. And if it content itselfe with its ancient strength of shipping, it may remaine as safe as it hath formerly done. Nay I cannot see that either necessity of ruine, or necessity of dishonour can bee truly pretended out of this, that France, Spaine, Holland, &c. are too potent at Sea for us.

The dominion of the seas may be considered as a meer right, or as an honour, or as a profit to us. As a right it is a theme fitter for schollers to whet their wits upon, than for Christians to fight and spill bloud about: and since it doth not manifestly appeare, how or when it was first purchased, or by what law conveyed to us, wee take notice of it only as matter of wit and disputation. As it is an honour to bee masters of the sea, and to make others strike saile to us as they passe; it's a glory fitter for women and children to wonder at; than for Statesmen to contend about. It may bee compared to a chaplet of flowers, not to a diadem of gold: but as it is a profit to us to fence and inclose the sea, that our neighbours shall not surprise us unawares, it's matter of moment, yet it concernes us but as it doth other Nations. By too insolent contestations hereupon, wee may provoke God, and dishonour ourselves; we may more probably incense our friends, than quell our enemies, wee may make the land a slave to the sea, rather than the sea a servant to the land. But I pray Master *Selden* to pardon me for this transition, and I returne my matter. If the Kingdome could not possibly subsist without Ship-money in such a danger, yet there is no necessity that the King should be so sole Judge of that danger, as that he may judge therein contrary to the opinion, and perhaps knowledge of other men. I allow the King to be supreame, and consequently sole Judge in all cases whatsoever, as to the right, and as to the diffusion of Judgement; but as to the exercise, and restraint of judgment, he is not, nor ought not to be accounted sole Judge. In matters of Law the King must create Judges, and swear them to judge uprightly, and impartially, and for the subject against himself, if law so require; yea though hee bee of contrary judgement himselfe, and by his Letters sollicite the contrary. The King's power is as the disgestive faculty in nature, all parts of the body contribute heat to it for their owne benefit, that they may receive backe againe from it a better concocted and prepared supply of nourishment, as it is their office to contribute, so it is the stomacke's to distribute.

And questionlesse sole judgement in matters of State, does no otherwise belong to the King, than in matters of Law, or points of Theology. Besides, as sole judgement is here ascribed to the King, hee may affirme dangers to be foreseene when he will, and of what nature he will: if he say only, *Datum est nobis intelligi*,[13] as he does in this Writ, &c. To his sole indisputable judgement it is left to lay charges as often and as great as he pleases. And by this meanes, if he regard not his word more than his profit, hee may in one yeare draine all the Kingdome of all its treasure, and leave us the most despicable slaves in the whole world.

It is ridiculous also to alledge, as J. *Jones* does, that it is contrary to presumption of Law to suspect falsity in the King: for if Law presume that the King will not falsly pretend danger to vexe his subjects, of his owne meere motion, yet no Law nor reason nor policy will presume, that the King may not be induced by misinformation to grieve the people without cause. The Sunne is not more visible than this truth, our best Kings, King *Charles*, King *James*, Queene *Elizabeth*, and all the whole ascending line, have done undue illegall things at some times, contrary to the rights and Franchises of England, being

13. It is given us to be understood.

misinformed, but having consulted with the Judges, or States in Parliament, they have all retracted, and confessed their error. Nay there is nothing more knowne, or universally assented to than this, that Kings may be bad; and it is more probable and naturall that evill may bee expected from good Princes, than good from bad. Wherefore since it is all one to the State, whether evill proceed from the King mediately or immediately, out of malice, or ignorance. And since wee know that of all kindes of government Monarchicall is the worst, when the Scepter is weilded by an unjust or unskilfull Prince, though it bee the best, when such Princes as are not seduceable (a thing most rare) reigne, it will bee great discretion in us not to desert our right in those Lawes which regulate and confine Monarchy, meerly out of Law-presumption, if wee must presume well of our Princes, to what purpose are Lawes made? and if Lawes are frustrate and absurd, wherein doe we differ in condition from the most abject of all bond-slaves?

There is no Tyranny more abhorred than that which hath a controlling power over all Law, and knowes no bounds but its owne will: if this be not the utmost of Tyranny, the Turkes are not more servile than we are and if this be Tyranny, this invention of ship-money makes us as servile as the Turkes. We must of necessity admit, that our Princes are not to be misse-led, and then our Lawes are needlesse; or that they may be misse-led, and then our Lawes are useless. For if they will listen to ill counsell, they may be moved to pretend danger causlesly; and by this pretence defeat all our lawes and liberties, and those being defeated, what doth the English hold, but at the King's meere discretion, wherein doth he excell the Captive's condition? If we shall examine why the Mohametan slaves are more miserably treated, than the Germans, or why the French Pesants are so beggarly, wretched, and beastially used more than the Hollanders, or why the people of Milan, Naples, Sicily are more oppressed, trampled upon, and inthralled than the Natives of Spaine? there is no other reason will appeare but that they are subject to more immoderate power, and have lesse benefit of law to releeve them.

In nature there is no reason, why the meanest wretches should not enjoy freedome, and demand justice in as ample measure, as those whom law hath provided for: or why Lords which are above law should bee more cruell than those which are more conditionate. Yet we see it is a fatall kind of necessity only incident to immoderate power, that it must be immoderately used: and certainly this was well known to our ancestors, or else they would not have purchased their charters of freedome with so great an expence of bloud as they did, and have endured so much so many yeares, rather than to bee betrayed to immoderate power, and prerogative. Let us therefore not bee too carelesse of that, which they were so jealous of, but let us look narrowly into the true consequence of this ship-scot, whatsoever the face of it appeare to be. It is vaine to stop twenty leakes in a ship, and then to leave one open, or to make lawes for the restraint of royalty all other ways, that it may not overflow the estates of the Commonalty at pleasure, and yet to leave one great breach for its irruption.

All our Kings hitherto have been so circumscribed by law, that they could not command the goods of their subjects at pleasure without common consent. But now if the King bee but perswaded to pretend danger, hee is uncontroleable Master of all we have, one *datum est intelligi,* shall make our English Statutes like the politick hedge of Goteham, and no better. I doe not say that this King will falsifie, it is enough that we all, and all that we have are at his discretion if he will falsifie, though vast power be not abused, yet it is a great mischiefe that it may, and therefore vast power itselfe is justly odious, for divers reasons. First, because it may fall into the hands of ill disposed Princes, such as were King *John, Henry* the third, *Edward* the second, *Richard* the second. These all in their times made England miserable, and certainly had their power beene more unconfineable, they

had made it more miserable. The alterations of times doe not depend
upon the alteration of the people, but of Princes: when Princes are
good it fares well with the people, when bad ill. Princes often vary,
but the people is always the same in all ages, and capable of small, or
no variations. If Princes would endure to heare this truth it would
bee profitable for them, for flatterers always raise jealousies against
the people; but the truth is, the people as the sea have no turbulent
motion of their owne, if Princes like the windes doe not raise them
into rage. Secondly, vast power if it finde not bad Princes it often
made Princes bad. It hath often changed Princes, as it did *Nero* from
good to bad, from bad to worse: but *Vespasian* is the only noted man
which by the Empire was in *melius mutatus:* daily experience teaches
this. Dangelt in England within twenty yeares increased to a foure-
fold proportion.

Subsidies were in former times seldome granted, and few at a time,
now Parliaments are held by some to bee of no other use than to
grant them. The Fox in Aesop observed that of all the beasts which
had gone to visit the Lion, few of their footesteps were to be seene
retrorsum: they were all printed *Adversum.* And we finde at this day
that it is farre more easie for a King to gaine undue things from the
people, than it is for the people to regaine its due from the King. This
King hath larger dominions, and hath raigned yet fewer yeares and
enjoyed quieter times than Queen *Elizabeth;* and yet his taxations
have been farre greater, and his exploits lesse honorable, and the people is still held in more jealousy. To deny ship-money which sweeps
all, is held a rejection of naturall allegiance. I speake not this to render odious the King's blessed government, I hold him one of the
mildest, and most gracious of our Kings; and I instance in him the
rather, that wee may see, what a bewitching thing flattery is, when it
touches upon this string of unlimitable power. If this ambition and
desire of vast power were not the most naturall and forcible of all
sinnes, Angels in heaven, and man in Paradise had not fallen by it;

but since it is, Princes themselves ought to be more cautious of it. Thirdly, vast power if it neither finde nor make bad Princes, yet it makes the good government of good Princes the lesse pleasing, and the lesse effectuall, for publick good: and therefore it is a rule both in law and policy, and nature, *Non recurrendum est ad extraordinaria, in iis quae fieri possunt per ordinaria.*[14] All extraordinary aides are horrid to the people, but most especially such as the ship-scot is, whereby all liberty is overthrowne, and all law subjected to the King's meer discretion.

Queen *Elizabeth* in 88. was victorious without this taxation, and I am perswaded she was therefore victorious the rather, because shee used it not. Her art was to account her subjects' hearts as her unfailing Exchequer, and to purchase them by doing legall just things, and this art never deceived her, and in that dismall gust of danger it was good for her and the State, both that she did not rely upon forced aides of money, or the words of grieved souldiers; for this Ship money nothing can bee pretended but necessity, and certainly necessity is ill pretended, when the meer doing of the thing, is as dangerous as that for which it is done. Did not this Ship-scot over-throw all popular liberty, and so threaten as great a mischife as any conquest can? and were not the people justly averse from it? Yet meerly for the people's disaffection to it, it is dangerous to bee relied upon in case of great danger.

We know Nature teacheth us all, of two evils to chuse that which wee thinke the least, though it bee not so; therefore if the people apprehend this remedy as a thing worse than the disease, though they be mistaken therein, yet that very mistake may prove fatall. The Roman Army being harshly treated by the Senators, and their proud Generall, did refuse to charge upon the enemy, or to resist the charge of the enemie, they chose rather to bee slaughtered by strangers, than

14. One is not to have recourse to the extraordinary things in those matters in which it can be done by the ordinary things.

enthralled by their countreymen. The English also in the late Scotch invasion, by reason of this and many other causes of discontent, made so faint resistance, that they did in a manner confesse, that they held themselves as miserable already as the Scots could make them. Thus we see there is no necessity of levying Ship-money, there is rather necessity of repealing it: and wee see that presumption of Law doth not abet this necessity, but rather crosse it. And whereas J. *Jones* further saith, That the King hath no benefite by Ship-money, and therefore presumption is the stronger, that the King will not take it causelesly; wee may answer: The Ship-money is a very great benefite to the King for if not immediatly, yet mediatly it is become a revenue, inasmuch as by this addition all other revenues of the Crowne, nay and Tunnage and Poundage, which were not designed only for ordinary expences, but for extraordinary imployments, and publicke charges also, are now become discharged of that tie, & the Common-wealth hath lost all its interest and property in them. In point of benefit therefore it is all one to the King, and in point of burthen it is all one to the subject, whether Ship-money bee accounted of as part of the King's annuall rents, or no, since by it his rents are enlarged: and as to the subject there is no obligation, that this levie shall not hereafter incorporate with the rest of the King's In-traders and be swallowed up as Tunnage and Poundage now are. Thus we see what the necessitie is, and presumption of Law, which was so much insisted upon; and yet for a further confutation of both, Time, the mother of Truth, hath now given us more light. Now that great danger which was pretended so many years together for the necessity of raising so great supplies of treasure, is as a small cloud blown over, making it apparant that Kings may bee mis-informed; and by mis-information take Molehils for Mountaines, and cast heavie burthens upon their subjects.

3. But I come now to my 3ᵈ Difficultie, How a publick charge is to be laid upon the kingdome. The Law runs generally, that in En-

gland no Tollage or pecuniary charge may bee imposed *Fors que per common assent de tout la Realme*, or, *Sinon per common consent de Parliament*. Some presidents, or matters of fact appeare, wherein some Kings have divers times invaded this right of the subject, but upon conference had with the Judges, or petition in Parliament, redresse was ever made, and the subject's right re-established. All the colour which can be brought to answer the Law in our case, is, that the words of the law are general of Taxes & Tollages, but do not by special mention restrain extraordinary danger. But wee know the Petition of Right, *3. Car.* is grounded upon former Statutes, and recites divers of them, and is a cleare affirmance of the common right of England; and yet by that the commissions for Loanes were damned. And it is evident that those Loanes were demanded for the generall defence of the Kingdome in time of imminent danger; and by the same Statute, not only Loanes, but all other levies of money upon what pretence of danger soever, *Si non per common consent*, are condemned as illegall, and contrary to the Lawes and Rights of England. Two things therefore are objected against Parliaments: First, that they are of slow motion, and so most of the Judges alledge. Secondly, that they may be perverse, and refuse due aid to the King, and so J. *Crawly* boldly suggests. For answer we say in generall: First, that it is the wisdome of the Kings to be always vigilant, and to have their eyes so open upon forraigne Princes, and to maintaine such intelligence that no preparation from abroad may surprize them before recourse had to Parliament; and this is very easie to Insular Princes, who have a competent strength of shipping, Secondly, to have alwayes in readinesse against all sudden surprizes, a sufficient store of amunition and arms both for sea and land-service: and the revenues of the Crowne of England are sufficient for this purpose, and have been held more than sufficient in former times, when hostility was greater, and the Kingdome smaller. Thirdly, to seek advice and assistance from Parliaments, frequently in times of quiet, as well as of danger, as well when war is but smoking, or kindling, as when it is blowne into a flame. Before the conquest this was held policie, and since in *Edward* the third's time, a statute past to this purpose; and if Parliaments of late be growne into dislike, it is not because their vertue is decayed, it is because the corruption of the times cannot endure such sharp remedies. Fourthly, to speak particularly of this case of ship-mony, we say that it is a course more slow than by Parliament: there was more expedition used in Parliament to supply King *Charles*, since he came to the Crowne, than can this way. And we say moreover, that as the extremity of the Kingdom was when Ship-money was demanded, whatsoever was pretended to the contrary, a Parliament might have beene timely enough called, and seasonably enough supplied the King. As to the second objection of J. *Crawly*, too unfit to come out of any honest wise man's mouth, but much more for a Judge's, Judge *Crooke* replies, that as there is *nullum iniquum in Lege*, so neither *in Parliamento*.[15] The three noted factions which are adverse to Parliaments, are the Papists, the Prelates, and Court Parasites; and these may be therefore supposed to hate Parliaments, because they know themselves hatefull to Parliaments. It is scarce possible for the King to finde out any other that thinkes ill of Parliaments or is ill thought of by Parliaments. Of Papists little need to bee said, their enmity is confest, they have little to pretend for themselves, but that Parliaments are grown Puritanicall. The Prelates thinke themselves not to have jurisdiction and power enough; and they know that Parliaments think they have too much, and abuse that which they have much more: therefore to uphold themselves, and to crush their ill-willers, they not only tax Parliaments of Puritanisme, but all Puritans of sedition. As much as in them lies, they wed the King to their quarrell, perswading him that Parliaments out of Puritanisme, doe not so much aime at the fall of Episcopacie, as

15. There is nothing unfair in the law, so neither in Parliament.

Monarchy: and that Episcopacie is the support of Monarchy, so that
both must stand and fall together. Howbeit because they cannot up-
braid Parliaments of attempting anything against Monarchy further
than to maintaine due liberty, therefore they preach an unlimitable
prerogative, and condemne all law of liberty as injurious to Kings,
and incompatible with Monarchy. *Manwarring* denies Parliamentary power and honour, *Cowel*[16] denies propriety of goods, further
than at the King's discretion, and *Harrison*[17] accuses Judge *Hutton* of
delivering law against God's Law, in the case of Ship-money. And
the common Court doctrine is that Kings are boundlesse in authority, and that they only are *Cesar's* friends which justifie that doctrine;
and from this doctrine hath grown all the jealousies of late betweene
the King and his best Subjects; and this is that venemous matter
which hath lain burning, and ulcerating inwardly in the bowels of the
common-wealth so long. The other enemies of Parliaments, are
Court dependants, and projectors, which have taken advantage of
this unnaturall dissention betwixt the King and his Subjects; and
have found out meanes to live upon the spoile of both, by siding with
the King, and being instruments to extend his Prerogative to the pur-
chasing of preferment to themselves, disaffection to the King, and
vexation to the common-wealth. These three factions excepted, and
some few Courtiers which are carried with the current of example,
or are left to speake unpleasing truths, there is scarce any man in all
the King's dominions, which doth not wish for Parliaments, as the
State's best physick, nay almost as its naturall necessary food: but I
will instance in three thinges wherein Parliaments excell all other
Counsells whatsoever.

　　1. For wisdome, no advice can be given so prudent, so profound,

16. See John Cowell, *The Interpreter: Or Book Containing the Signification of Words . . .* (Cambridge, 1607), a provocative dictionary containing definitions that seemed to enhance royal
power. Two further editions appeared in 1637. See STC 5900, 5901, 5902.

17. Thomas Harrison upbraided Judge Hutton for his decision in the case of ship-money.

so universally comprehending, from any other author; it is truly said by Sir *Robert Cotton*, that all private single persons may deceive and bee deceived; but all cannot deceive one, nor one all.

That an inconsiderable number of Privadoes should see or know more than whole Kingdomes, is incredible: *vox populi* was ever reverenced as *vox Dei*, and Parliaments are infallible, and their acts indisputable to all but Parliaments. It is a just law, that no private man must bee wiser than Law publickly made. Our wisest Kings in England, have ever most relied upon the wisdome of Parliaments.

Secondly, no advice can bee so faithfull, so loyall, so religious and sincere, as that which proceeds from Parliaments, where so many are gathered together for God's service in such a devout manner, we cannot but expect that God should bee amongst them: and as they have a more especiall blessing promised them; so their ends cannot be so sinister. Private men may thrive by alterations: and common calamities, but the common body can affect nothing but the common good, because nothing else can be commodious for them. Sir *Robert Cotton* in the life of *Hen.* 3. according to the Court Doctrine at this present, sayes, that in Parliament Kings are ever lesse than they should be, and the people more. If this bee spoken of irregular Kings, which will endure to heare of nothing but Prerogative government, it may carry some semblance of truth: but sure it is, good and wise Kings are ever greatest when they sit immured, as it were, in that honorable assembly: as the History of Queen *Elizabeth* and many of her Progenitors testifies. 'Tis true, *Hen.* the third, met with divers oppositions in Parliament. He was there upbraided, and called *dilapidator regni;*[18] it was true that he was so, and the most unworthy of rule, that ever sate in this Throne; yet those words became not subjects. I doe not justifie, but in some part extenuate such misdemeanours; for the chiefe blame of those times is not to bee throwne upon the Peeres and Commons,

18. Dismantler of the kingdom.

but upon the King and his outlandish Parasites. It is without all question also that in those bloudy unjust times, had it not been for frequent Parliaments, and that soveraigne remedy which thereby was applied to the bleeding wounds of the Kingdome, no other helpe could have stanched them.

Even then, when Parliaments were most prevalent, and when they had so much provocation from so variable and uncapable a Prince, they did not seeke to conditionate prerogative, or to depresse Monarchy for the future, though they were a little too injurious to him in person for the present.

Since that time also many Parliaments have had to struggle for due liberty with insolent Princes, and have had power to clip the wings of Royalty; and the custome of all Europe almost besides hath seemed to give some countenance to such attempts; but the deepe wisdome, and inviolable loyalty of Parliaments to this composure of government hath beene such, that they never made any invasion upon it. As it was in all former ages, so it now remaines intire with all its glorious ensignes of honour, and all the complements of power; and may he be as odious which seekes to alter or diminish Monarchicall government for the future, as he which seekes to make it infinite, and slanders Parliaments as enemies to it, or indeavours to blow such jealousies into the King's eares.

3. No advice can be so fit, so forcible, so effectuall for the publicke welfare, as that which is given in Parliament: if any Cabinet Counsellors could give as wise and sincere advice as Parliaments, yet it could not be so profitable, because the hearts of the people doe not goe along with any other, as with that.

That King which is potent in Parliament, as any good King may, is as it were so insconsed in the hearts of his subjects, that he is almost beyond the traines or aimes of treason and rebellion at home, nay forraigne hostility cannot pierce him, but through the sides of all his people.

It ought to be noted also, that as the English have ever beene the most devoted servants of equall, sweetly-moderate Soveraignty; so in our English Parliaments, where the Nobility is not too prevalent, as in Denmark, nor the Comminalty, as in the Netherlands, nor the King, as in France, Justice and Policie kisse and embrace more lovingly than elsewhere. And as all the three States have always more harmoniously borne their just proportionable parts in England than elsewhere, so now in these times, in these learned, knowing, religious times, we may expect more blessed counsell from Parliaments than ever, wee received heretofore. May it therefore sinke into the heart of our King to adhere to Parliaments, and to abhorre the grosse delusive suggestions of such as disparage that kinde of Councell. May he rather confide in that Community which can have no other end but their owne happinesse in his greatnesse, than in Papists, Prelates, and Projectors, to whom the publick disunion is advantagious. May hee affect that gentle Prerogative which stands with the happinesse, freedome, and riches of his people; and not that terrible Scepter which does as much avert the hearts, as it does debilitate the hands, and exhaust the purses of his Subjects. May he at last learne by experience, that the grievance of all grievances, that that mischiefe which makes all mischiefes irremediable, and almost hopelesse in England at this day, is that Parliaments are clouded, and disused, and suffered to be calumniated by the ill boding incendiaries of our State. May it lastly enter into his beleefe, that it is impossible for any Kingdome to deny publicke assent for their Prince's aid, either in Parliament or out, when publicke danger is truly imminent, and when it is fairely required, and not by projects extorted: that no Nation can unnaturally seeke its owne ruine, but that all Kings, like *Constantine*, may make their Subjects' purses their owne private coffers, if they will demand due things, at due times, and by due meanes.

4. I come now to the last difficulty about the condition and nature of such aides as are due by Law from the Subject to the King.

Though much hath beene argued both at the barre and on the
Bench, for the King, that he may raise monies from his Subjects,
without consent by law, prerogative, and necessity. Yet at last, because the Petition of Right absolutely crosses this tenet, it is restored
to us backe againe, and yeelded, that the King may not impose a pecuniary charge by way of Tollage, but only a personall one by way of
service. And now all our controversie ends in this, that we must contest, whether the Ship-scot be a pecuniary, or a personall charge. For
though the intent of the Writ, and the office of the Sheriffe be to raise
monies only, yet the words of the Writ, and the pretence of State, is
to build and prepare Ships of warre. The Kingdome generally takes
this to bee a meere delusion and imposture, and doubtlesse it is but a
picklock tricke, to overthrow all liberty and propriety of goods, and it
is a great shame that so many Judges should be abetters to such
fraudulent practice contrived against the State. It is not lawfull for
the King to demand monies as monies, but it is lawfull to demand
monies under another wrong name, and under this wrong name all
former Lawes and Liberties shall be as absolutely cancelled, as if they
had beene meere cobwebs, or enacted only out of meere derision. If
former laws made to guard propriety of goods were just, and
grounded upon good reason, why are they by this grosse fallacy, or
childish abuse defeated. If they were not just, or reasonable, what
needs such a fond subtiltie as this? Why should not they bee fairely
avoided by Law? Why were they made at all? But be this invention
what it will, yet wee see it is new; if it be quashed, the State is but
where it was, we are still as our Ancestors left us; and since our pre-
ceeding Kings never heretofore put it in use in the most necessitous
calamitous times, we may from hence infer, that the plea of State necessitie falls off of itselfe; if we admit not of this innovation, then the
State suffers not; but if wee admit it, no necessity being of it, wee can
frame no other reason for our so doing, but that our former franchises and priviledges were unjust, and therefore this way they must

bee annulled. Some of our Judges doe prove, that if this were a personall service, yet it were void; and they cite the case of Barges, and Ballingers vessells, built truly for warre in time of imminent danger, and yet these charges upon complaint made by the Subject, were revoked, and disclaimed. But here in this case many other enormities and defects in Law are, for if ships bee intended to be built in Inland Countries, a thing impossible is injoined; and if monies be aimed at, that very aime is against Law: and if the Kingdome were to be disfranchised, it were not to bee done by an illegall way.

Besides, in the Writ, in the Assessement, in the Sheriffe's remedie against recusants of it, in the execution of Law, by, or after Judgement, many inconveniences, errors, and mischiefes arise many wayes: and sure take the whole case as it is, and since the Creation no whole Kingdome was ever cast in such a cause before.

Besides, though the Judges ought wholly to have bent themselves upon this, to have proved this a personall service, and no pecuniary charge, they have roved after necessity, presumption of Law, and Prerogative, and scarce said anything at all hereof.

My Lord *Bramston* argues very eagerly, that personall services by Sea and Land are due to the King in cases of extremity, and all their records, cases, and precedents prove no more, and that men may be arrayed, and ships pressed, and that *sumptibus populi*;[19] but there is nothing proved that the meere raising of monies in this case, is a personall service. J. *Jones* indeed argues to this purpose: If the Law intrust the King with so great a power over men's persons, why not over their estates? There is cleare reason for the contrary: because the King, if he should abuse men's personall aides, could not inrich or profit himselfe thereby, and we know it is gaine and profit, it is *Auri sacra fames*[20] which hath power over the breasts of men. It is not ordinary for Tyrants to imbattaile hoasts of men, and make them

19. At the expense of the people.
20. Sacred hunger for gold.

charge upon the Sea-billowes, and then to gather up Cockles and Pi-winckle shells in lieu of spoile, as one did once. But the world abounds with stories of such Princes, as have offended in abusing their power over men's estates, and have violated all right divine and human, to attaine to such a boundless power.

Good Kings are sometimes weake in coveting boundlesse power; some affect rivality with God himselfe in power, and yet places that power in doing evill, not good: for few Kings want power to doe good, and therefore it misbecomes not sometimes good Subjects to be jealous in some things of good Kings. But J. *Jones* farther sayes, that Ships must be built, and without money that cannot be done: *ergo*. This necessity hath beene answered, and disproved already: and I now adde, that for the good of the Kingdome there is more neces-sity that Ship-money bee damned than maintained. Such unnaturall slavery seems to mee to bee attendant upon this all-devouring proj-ect, and such infamy to our Ancestors, our Lawes, and ourselves, nay and such danger to the King and his posterity, that I cannot imagine how any forraigne conquest should induce anything more to be de-tested and abhorred.

Those Kings which have beene most covetous of unconfined im-moderate power, have beene the weakest in judgement, and com-monly their lives have beene poore and toilsome, and their ends miserable, and violent: so that if Kings did rightly understand their owne good, none would more shunne uncontrollable absolutenesse than themselves.

How is the King of France happy in his great Prerogative? or in that terrible style of the King of Asses? Wee see that his immoderate power makes him oppresse his poore Pesants, for their condition is most deplorable, and yet set his power aside, and there is no reason why he should not be as a father to cherish them, as a God to comfort them, not as an enemy to impoverish them, as a tormentor to afflict them.

2. His oppression makes him culpable before God: he must one

day render a sad account for all the evill which hee hath imposed, for all the good which he hath not procured to them. That the Vicegerent of God should doe the office of a tyrant, will be no light thing one day.

3. His sinne makes him poore: for were his Pesants suffered to get wealth and enjoy it, the whole land would be his treasury, and that treasury would containe twice as much as now it doth.

4. His poverty makes him impotent, for money being the sinewes of warre, how strong would his joints be, if all his subjects were abounding in money, as doubtlesse they would, if they wanted not liberty, and propriety? Besides, poverty depresses the spirit of a Nation: and were the King of France, King of an Infantery, as he is only of a Cavalry, were he a King of men, as he is only of beasts, had he a power over hearts as he hath over hands, that Country would be twice as puissant as it is.

5. His impotence, together with all other irregularities, and abuses is like to make his Monarchy the lesse durable. Civill wars have ever hitherto infected and macerated that goodly Country, and many times it hath been near its ruine. It now enjoys inward peace, but it doth no great exploits abroad, nor is ever likely to doe, unlesse by practising upon the distemper of other Nations. Should some other Prince practise in the like manner upon that, and propose liberty to the grieved people, much advantage might be taken: but these avisoes would better proceed from that most heroick, most terrible, most armipotent Churchman, which effects such great wonders here. Wee see hence that Princes by some gaine lose, as the whole body pines by the swelling of the spleene. We see that *Rehoboam* catcht at immoderate power, as the dog in the fable at a shadow, but instead of an uncertain nothing, he let fall and lost a certaine substance; and yet flatterers have scarce any other baite than this shadow of immoderate power, whereby to poison the phantasies of weake humours, undiscerning rash Princes.

My humble motion therefore is: First, that the judgement given in the Chequer Chamber for Ship-money, may bee reversed, and damned, as contrary to the right of the Subject.

Secondly, that those Judges which adhered to equity and integrity in this case, might have some honourable guerdon[21] designed them.

Thirdly, that some dishonourable penalty may bee imposed upon those Judges which ill advised the King herein, and then argued as Pleaders, not as Judges; especially if any shall appeare to have solicited the betraying of the Kingdome.

Fourthly, that the meaning of our Lawes & Charters, may bee fully and expresly declared, and the force and vertue of Statutes and publicke Grants, may be vindicated from all such exceptions and objections as have beene particularly or generally made against them.

Fifthly, that a clearer solution may bee given in the foure maine points stirred, how farre prerogative is arbitrary and above Law; and how farre naturall allegeance bindes to yeeld to all demands not of Parliament: next, how the King is sole Judge of danger, as that his meere cognizance thereof shall be sufficient, though there be no appearance or probability thereof. Next, how a necessity of publicke ruine must bee concluded now, if Ship-money be not levied, when no such ruine hath been formerly, when this new plot was not devised. Lastly, how this Ship-scot pretending ships, but intending money, and really raising the same, can bee said to bee no pecuniary tollage within our Statutes, but a meere personall service.

Sixthly, that any Officers, or Ministers of State, which shall attempt to lay the like taxes hereafter upon the Subject, by vertue of the like void warrants, may be held and taken as Felons, or Traitors, or forcible Intruders.

Seventhly, that something may be inacted against forraigne or domesticall Forces also, if they shall be congregated for the like purposes; and that the subject may bee inabled by some fit and timely remedy to bee given against a military kinde of government.

21. Reward.

Eighthly, that the due way of publicke defence, in case of imminent and eminent danger, or actuall necessary warre, for the pressing of men, and other charges of warre, such as Cote and Conduct money,[22] and all doubts thereabouts, may be made more certaine, and settled for the time to come.

Ninthly, that if the King's ordinary Revenues now taken for the Crowne, be not sufficient to maintaine him, as our great Master, some legall order may be taken therefore, and that he may be sensible of his Subjects' loyalty, and his Subjects live safe under him, that his enemies may finde him considerable, and his true friends usefull.

FINIS.

22. "Coat and Conduct money" was a special military tax to provide men pressed into the royal army with any necessary clothing and for appointed conductors who were paid for delivering them to their rendezvous.

John Pym, 1584–1643

THE

SPEECH

OR

DECLARATION

OF

J OH N P Y M, Esquire:

After the Recapitulation or summing
up of the Charge of *High-Treason*,

AGAINST

THOMAS,

EARLE OF STRAFFORD,
12. APRIL, 1641.

Published by Order of the
COMMONS HOUSE.

LONDON,
Printed for JOHN BARTLET. 1641.

*T*he renowned parliamentary leader and politician John Pym was an outspoken critic of the Court. He opposed Arminianism and Catholic influences in the Church of England, and he staunchly upheld what he saw as England's ancient constitution. Pym was educated at Oxford and entered the Middle Temple, although he was never called to the bar. His long parliamentary career began in 1614 in the reign of James I. Pym actively supported the Petition of Right in the Parliament of 1628 and later in that session conducted the Commons' case against Roger Maynwaring. He was a leading member of the Commons in the Short Parliament and, even more important, in the Long Parliament.

Pym was convinced there was a plot to destroy parliamentary institutions and the Protestant religion. When the Long Parliament convened he demanded that those guilty of this conspiracy be punished. Prominent among those he believed culpable was Charles's leading councillor and loyal minister, Thomas Wentworth, Earl of Strafford. Strafford's willingness to resort to extraordinary means on behalf of his master and his high-handed administration as president of the Council of the North and lord-deputy of Ireland had made him notorious. Beyond this Strafford was believed to have urged the king to use an Irish army against the English parliament and was preparing to charge parliamentary leaders with treasonous conspiracy with the Scots.

Pym played the leading role in Strafford's fall. He moved that a subcommittee investigate Strafford's conduct in Ireland and later that he be impeached on a charge of high treason. This meant a trial before the House of Lords. Pym led the attack at every stage, from the collection of evidence and preparation of charges to the presentation of the *case. Strafford's trial began on 22 March 1641. The chief difficulty was that despite his overbearing tactics and possible transgressing of the royal prerogative on behalf of Charles, Strafford had not committed any act of treason against the king. Pym attempted to get around this by arguing that to endeavour the subversion of the laws of the kingdom was treason; that to come between the king and his people was treason; that the culmination of many small, perfidious acts, none of which was in itself treasonous, could constitute treason.*

Strafford defended himself so ably that on 10 April with the Lords reluctant to convict, a bill of attainder was introduced into the Commons. This would simply declare Strafford guilty without the necessity of a trial. As the bill of attainder moved through the legislative process the original impeachment continued with Pym chosen by the Commons to deliver its reply to Strafford's defense. Pym's speech to the Lords on that occasion, published as a tract and reprinted here, sets out the Commons' constitutional position succinctly and eloquently. He explains their notion of treason as a subversion of the laws, an introduction of an arbitrary and tyrannical government. This speech has been acclaimed as the best of Pym's career. At least nine editions of it were printed in 1641.

Despite Pym's efforts the impeachment was dropped. The bill of attainder, however, passed, and on 12 May Strafford was executed. Despite Charles's promise to Strafford that he would pardon him, the king made no move to save his loyal minister. It would be one of his lasting regrets. With the onset of civil war Pym served as a leader of the parliamentary party. He would never live to see its outcome. He died in December 1643.

The Speech or Declaration of *John Pym,* Esq: &c.

My Lords,

Many dayes have been spent in maintenance of the Impeachment of the *Earle* of *Strafford,* by the *House* of *Commons,* whereby he stands charged with *High Treason.* And your *Lordships* have heard his *Defence* with *Patience,* and with as much favour as *Justice* would allow. We have passed through our *Evidence,* and the *Result* of all this is, that it remaines clearly proved, *That the Earle of Strafford hath indeavoured by his words, actions, and counsels, to subvert the Fundamentall Lawes of England and Ireland, and to introduce an Arbitrary and Tyrannicall Government.*

This is the *envenomed Arrow* for which he inquired in the beginning of his *Replication* this day, which hath infected all his *Bloud.* This is that *Intoxicating Cup,* (to use his owne Metaphor) which hath tainted his *Judgement,* and poisoned his *Heart.* From hence was infused that *Specificall Difference* which turned his *Speeches,* his *Actions,* his *Counsels* into *Treason; Not Cumulative,* as he exprest it, as if many *Misdemeanours* could make one *Treason;* but *Formally* and *Essentially.* It is the *End* that doth informe *Actions,* and doth *specificate* the *nature* of them, making not only *criminall,* but even *indifferent words* and *actions* to be *Treason,* being done and spoken with a *Treasonable intention.*

That which is given me in *charge,* is, to shew the *quality* of the *offence,* how *hainous* it is in the *nature,* how *mischievous* in the *effect* of it; which will best appear if it be examined by that *Law,* to which he himselfe appealed, that *universall,* that *Supreme Law, Salus populi.* This is the *Element* of all Laws, out of which they are derived; the *End* of all Laws, to which they are designed, and in which they are perfected. How far it stands in opposition to this *Law,* I shall endeavour to shew in some *Considerations* which I shall present to your Lordships, all arising out of the *Evidence* which hath been opened.

The first is this: It is an offence *comprehending* all other offences; here you shall finde severall *Treasons, Murders, Rapines, Oppressions, Perjuries.*

The *Earth* hath a *Seminarie vertue*, whereby it doth produce all *Hearbs*, and *Plants*, and other *Vegetables*. There is in this *Crime*, a *Seminarie* of all *evils* hurtfull to a *State;* and if you consider the *reasons* of it, it must needs be so. The *Law* is that which puts a *difference* betwixt *good* and *evill*, betwixt *just* and *unjust*. If you take away the *Law*, all things will fall into a *confusion, every man* will become a *Law* to *himselfe*, which in the *depraved condition* of *human nature*, must needs *produce* many great *enormities. Lust* will become a *Law*, and *Envie* will become a *Law, Covetousnesse* and *Ambition* will become *Lawes;* and what *dictates*, what *decisions* such *Laws* will produce, may easily be discerned in the late *Government* of *Ireland.*[1] The *Law* hath a *power* to *prevent*, to *restraine*, to *repaire evils;* without this all kind of *mischiefs* and *distempers* will *break in upon a State.*

It is the *Law* that doth *intitle* the *King* to the *Allegeance* and *service* of his *people;* it *intitles* the *people* to the *protection* and *justice* of the *King. It is God alone who subsists by himselfe*, all other things *subsist* in a *mutuall dependence* and *relation*. He was a wise man that said, that the King *subsisted* by the field that is *tilled*. It is the *labour* of the *people* that supports the *Crowne*. If you take away the *protection* of the *King*, the *vigour* and *cheerfulness* of *Allegeance* will be taken away, though the *Obligation* remaine.

The *Law* is the *Boundarie*, the *Measure* betwixt the *King's Prerogative*, and the *People's Liberty*. Whiles these move in their owne *Orbe*, they are a *support* and *security* to one another; The *Prerogative* a *cover*

1. The Earl of Strafford governed Ireland as lord deputy, a post to which he was appointed in 1632.

and *defence* to the *Liberty* of the *people*, and the *people* by their *liberty* are enabled to be a *foundation* to the *Prerogative;* but if these *bounds* be so removed, that they enter into *contestation* and *conflict*, one of these *mischiefes* must needs ensue. If the *Prerogative* of the *King* over-whelm the *liberty* of the *people*, it will be turned into *Tyrannie;* if *liberty undermine* the *Prerogative*, it will grow into *Anarchie.*

The *Law* is the *safeguard*, the *custody* of all *private interest.* Your *Honours*, your *Lives*, your *Liberties* and *Estates* are all in the *keeping* of the *Law;* without this, every man hath a like *right* to anything, and this is the *condition* into which the *Irish* were brought by the *E.* of *Strafford.* And the *reason* which he gave for it, hath more *mischiefe* in it than the thing itselfe, *They were a Conquered Nation.* There cannot be a word more *pregnant*, and *fruitfull* in *Treason*, than that word is. There are few *Nations* in the world that have not been *conquered;* and no doubt but the *Conquerour* may give what *Lawes* he please to those that are *conquered.* But if the *succeeding Pacts* and *Agreements* doe not limit and restraine that *Right*, what people can be secure? *England* hath been *conquered*, and *Wales* hath been *conquered*, and by this reason will be in little better *case* than *Ireland.* If the *King* by the *Right* of a *Conquerour* gives *Lawes* to his *People*, shall not the people by the same *reason* be restored to the *Right* of the *conquered*, to recover their *liberty* if they can? What can be more *hurtfull*, more *pernicious* to both, than such *Propositions* as these? And in these particulars is determined the *first Consideration.*

The *second Consideration* is this: This *Arbitrary power* is *dangerous* to the *King's Person*, and *dangerous* to his *Crown.* It is apt to cherish *Ambition*, *usurpation*, and *oppression* in great men, and to beget *sedition* and *discontent* in the *People;* and both these have beene, and in reason must ever be *causes* of great *trouble* and *alteration* to *Princes* and *States.*

If the *Histories* of those *Easterne Countries* be perused, where *Princes* order their *affaires* according to the *mischievous principles* of the *E.* of *Strafford, loose and absolved from all Rules of Government,* they will be found to be *frequent* in *combustions,* full of *Massacres,* and of the *tragicall ends* of *Princes.* If any man shall look into our *owne stories,* in the times when the *Laws* were most neglected, he shall find them full of *Commotions,* of *Civill distempers;* whereby the *Kings* that then reigned, were alwayes kept in *want* and *distresse;* the people con-sumed with *Civill wars:* and by such wicked *counsels* as these, some of our *Princes* have beene brought to such miserable *ends,* as no *honest* heart can remember without *horrour,* and *earnest Prayer,* that it may never be so againe.

The third *Consideration* is this, The *subversion* of the *Lawes.* And this *Arbitrary power,* as it is *dangerous* to the *King's Person* and to his *Crowne,* so is it in other respects very *prejudiciall* to his *Majesty* in his *Honour, Profit,* and *Greatnesse;* and yet these are the *gildings* and *paintings* that are put upon such *counsels.* These are for your *Honour,* for your *service;* whereas in truth they are contrary to both. But if I shall take off this *varnish,* I hope they shall then appeare in their owne *native deformity,* and therefore I desire to consider them by these *Rules.*

It cannot be for the *Honour* of a *King,* that his *sacred Authority* should be used in the practice of *injustice* and *oppression;* that his *Name* should be applied to *patronize* such *horrid crimes,* as have beene represented in *Evidence* against the *Earle of Strafford;* and yet how frequently, how presumptuously his *Commands,* his *Letters* have beene vouched throughout the course of this *Defence,* your Lordships have heard. When the *Judges* doe *justice,* it is the *King's justice,* and this is for his *honour,* because he is the *Fountaine* of *justice;* but when they doe *injustice,* the offence is their owne. But those *Officers* and *Ministers* of the King, who are most officious in the exercise of this *Arbitrarie power,* they doe it commonly for their advantage; and when they are questioned for it, then they fly to the *King's interest;* to his *Direction.* And truly my Lords, this is a very unequall *distribution* for the King, that the *dishonour* of evill *courses* should be cast upon him, and they to have the advantage.

The *prejudice* which it brings to him in regard of his *profit*, is no lesse apparent. It deprives him of the most beneficiall, and most certaine *Revenue* of his *Crowne*, that is, the *voluntary aids* and *supplies* of his *people;* his other *Revenues*, consisting of goodly *Demeanes*, and great *Manors*, have by *Grants* been alienated from the *Crowne*, and are now exceedingly *diminished* and *impaired*. But this *Revenue* it cannot be *sold*, it cannot be *burdened* with any *Pensions* or *Annuities*, but comes intirely to the *Crowne*. It is now almost fifteene years since his Majesty had any assistance from his *people;*[2] and these illegall wayes of supplying the King were never prest with more *violence*, and *art*, than they have been in this time; and yet I may upon very good *grounds* affirm, that in the last fifteene years of Queen *Elizabeth*, she received more by the *Bounty* and *Affection* of her *Subjects*, than hath come to His *Majestie's Coffers* by all the *inordinate* and *rigorous courses* which have beene taken. And as those *Supplies* were more beneficiall in the *Receipt* of them, so were they like in the *use* and *imployment* of them.

Another way of *prejudice* to his *Majestie's profit*, is this: Such *Arbitrary courses* exhaust the people, and disable them, when there shall be occasion, to give such plentifull *supplies*, as otherwise they would doe. I shall need no other proofe of this, than the *Irish Government* under my E. of *Strafford*, where the *wealth* of the *Kingdome* is so *consumed* by those horrible *exactions*, and *burdens*, that it is thought the *Subsidies* lately granted will amount to little more than halfe the *proportion* of the last *Subsidies*. The two former wayes are hurtfull to the *King's profit*, in that respect which they call *Lucrum Cessans*,[3] by diminishing his receipts. But there is a third, fuller of *mischiefe*, and it is in that

2. Charles had agreed to the Petition of Right in 1628 in order to convince Parliament to grant him a subsidy. He got his subsidy although he found the amount disappointing.
3. The ceasing of gain or profit.

respect which they call *Damnum emergens*,[4] by increasing his *Disbursements*. Such *irregular* and *exorbitant attempts* upon the *Libertie* of the *people*, are apt to produce such miserable *distractions* and *distempers*, as will put the *King* and *Kingdome* to such vast *expences* and *losses* in a short time, as will not be recovered in many yeares. Wee need not goe farre to seeke a proofe of this, these two last yeares will be a sufficient evidence, within which time I assure myselfe, it may be proved, that more *Treasure* hath beene wasted, more losse sustained by his *Majesty* and his *Subjects*, than was spent by Queene *Elizabeth* in all the War of *Tyrone*,[5] and in those many brave *Attempts* against the King of *Spaine*, and the royall *assistance* which she gave to *France*, and the *Low-Countries*, during all her *Reigne*.

As for *Greatnesse*, this *Arbitrary power* is apt to hinder and impaire it, not only at home, but abroad. A *Kingdome* is a *society* of men conjoyned under one Government, for the *common good*. The *world* is a society of *Kingdomes* and *States*. The *King's greatnesse* consists not only in his *Dominion* over his *Subjects* at home, but in the *influence* which he hath upon *States* abroad; That he should be great even among *Kings*, and by his *wisdome* and *authority* so to incline and dispose the affaires of other *States* and *Nations*, and those great *events* which fall out in the *world*, as shall be for the good of *Mankind*, and for the peculiar *advantage* of his owne people. This is the most *glorious*, and *magnificent greatness*, to be able to relieve *distressed Princes*, to support his owne *friends* and *Allies*, to prevent the *ambitious designes* of other *Kings*; and how much this Kingdome hath been impaired in this kinde, by the late *mischievous counsels* your Lordships best know, who at a neerer distance, and with a more cleare sight, doe apprehend these publique and great affaires, than I can doe. Yet thus

4. The rising loss.
5. Hugh O'Neill, Earl of Tyrone, led an Irish rebellion against the English in 1595. He was vanquished, but after three years of negotiations, hostilities broke out again in 1598. Tyrone suffered a serious defeat in 1601 and finally surrendered on 30 March 1603.

much I dare boldly say, that if his *Majestie* had not with great *wisdome* and *goodness* forsaken that way wherein the *Earle* of *Strafford* had put him, we should within a short time have been brought into that *miserable condition*, as to have been uselesse to our *friends*, contemptible to our *enemies*, and uncapable of undertaking any great *designe* either at home or abroad.

A fourth Consideration is, That this Arbitrary, and Tyrannicall Power, which the *E.* of *Strafford* did excercise in his own person, and to which he did advise his Majesty, is inconsistent with the Peace, the Wealth, the Prosperity of a Nation. It is destructive to Justice, the Mother of Peace; to Industry, the spring of Wealth; to Valour, which is the active vertue whereby the prosperity of a Nation can only be procured, confirmed, and inlarged.

It is not only apt to take away Peace, and so intangle the Nation with Warres, but doth corrupt Peace, and puts such a malignity into it, as produceth the Effects of warre. We need seek no other proofe of this, but the *E.* of *Strafford's* Government, where the *Irish*, both *Nobility* and others, had as little *security* of their *Persons* or *Estates* in this peaceable *time*, as if the *Kingdome* had been under the *rage* and *fury* of *warre*.

And as for *Industrie*, and *Valour*, who will take pains for that, which when he hath gotten, is not his own? Or who fight for that wherein he hath no other *interest*, but such as is subject to the will of another? The *Ancient encouragement* to men that were to defend their *Countries* was this, That they were to hazard their *Persons, pro Aris & Focis*, for their *Religion*, and for their *Houses*. But by this *Arbitrary* way which was practiced in *Ireland*, and counselled here, no man had any *certainty*, either of *Religion*, or of his *House*, or anything else to be his own. But besides this, such *Arbitrary* courses have an ill operation upon the *courage* of a Nation, by embasing the *hearts* of the *people*. *A servile condition doth for the most part beget in men a slavish temper and disposition*. *Those* that live so much under the *Whip* and the *Pillory*, and such *servile Engines*, as were frequently *used* by the *E*. of *Strafford*, they may have the *dregges* of *valour, sullennesse, & stubbornesse*, which may make them *prone* to *Mutinies*, and *discontents;* but those *Noble* and *gallant affections*, which put men on *brave Designes* and *Attempts* for the *preservation* or *inlargement* of a *Kingdome*, they are hardly *capable* of. Shall it be *Treason* to *embase* the *King's Coine*, though but a *piece* of *twelve-pence*, or *sixe-pence*, and must it not needs be the *effect* of a greater *Treason*, to *embase* the *spirits* of his *Subjects*, and to set a *stamp* and *Character* of *Servitude* upon them, whereby they shall be *disabled* to doe anything for the service of the *King* or *Commonwealth?*

The fifth *Consideration* is this, That the *exercise* of this *Arbitrary Government*, in times of *sudden danger*, by the *invasion* of an *enemy*, will *disable* his *Majesty* to *preserve himselfe* and *his Subjects* from that *danger*. This is the only *pretence* by which the *E*. of *Strafford*, and such other *mischievous Counsellors* would *induce* his *Majesty* to make *use* of it; and if it be *unfit* for such an *occasion*, I know nothing that can be *alledged* in *maintenance* of it.

When *warre threatens* a *Kingdome* by the *comming* of a *forrain Enemy*, it is *no time* then to *discontent* the *people*, to make them *weary* of the *present Government*, and more *inclinable* to a *Change*. The *supplies* which are to come in this *way*, will be *unready, uncertain;* there can be no *assurance* of them, no *dependence* upon them, either for *time* or *proportion*. And if some money be gotten in such a way, the *Distractions, Divisions, Distempers*, which this *course* is apt to *produce*, will be more *prejudiciall* to the *publique safety*, than the *supply* can be *advantagious* to it; and of this we have had *sufficient experience* the *last Summer*.

The sixth, That this *crime* of *subverting* the *Laws*, and *introducing* an *Arbitrary* and *Tyrannicall Government*, is *contrary* to the *Pact* and *Covenant* betwixt the *King* and his *people*. That which was spoken of before, was the *legall union* of *Allegeance* and *Protection;* this is a *per-*

sonall union by *mutuall agreement* and *stipulation, confirmed* by *oath*
on both *sides.* The *King* and his *people* are *obliged* to one another in
the *nearest relations;* He is a *Father,* and a *childe* is called in *Law, Pars
Patris.*[6] Hee is the *Husband* of the *Commonwealth,* they have the *same
interests,* they are *inseparable* in their *condition,* be it *good* or *evill.* He
is the *Head,* they are the *Body;* there is such an *incorporation* as cannot
be dissolved without the *destruction* of both.

When *Justice Thorpe,* in *Edward* the *third's time,* was by the *Parliament condemned* to *death* for *Bribery,* the *reason* of that Judgement
is given, because he had *broken* the *King's Oath,* not that he had broken his own *oath,* but that he had broken the *King's oath,* that *solemne*
and *great obligation,* which is the *security* of the *whole Kingdome.* If
for a Judge to take a small *summe* in a private cause, was adjudged
Capitall, how much greater was this *offence,* whereby the *E.* of *Strafford* hath broken the *King's Oath* in the whole *course* of his *Government* in *Ireland,* to the *prejudice* of so many of his *Majestie's Subjects,*
in their *Lives, Liberties,* and *Estates,* and to the danger of all the rest?

The *Doctrine* of the *Papists, Fides non est servanda cum Haereticis,*[7]
is an *abominable Doctrine:* yet that other Tenet more *peculiar* to the
Jesuites is more *pernicious,* whereby *Subjects* are *discharged* from their
Oath of *Allegeance* to their *Prince* whensoever the *Pope* pleaseth. This
may be added to make the *third* no lesse *mischievous* and *destructive* to
human society, than either of the rest: That the King is not bound by
that *Oath* which he hath taken to *observe* the *Laws* of the *Kingdome,*
but may when he sees *cause,* lay *Taxes* and *burdens* upon them without
their *consent,* contrary to the *Laws* and *Liberties* of the *Kingdome.*
This hath been *preached* and *published* by divers; And this is that
which hath been *practised* in *Ireland* by the *E.* of *Strafford,* in his *Government there,* and indeavoured to be brought into *England,* by his
Counsell here.

6. The part or portion of the father.
7. One is not to be loyal or faithful when it comes to heretics.

The seventh is this; It is an *offence* that is contrary to the *end* of *Government*. The *end* of *Government* was to prevent *oppressions*, to limit and restrain the excessive power and violence of *great men*, to *open* the passages of *Justice* with *indifferency* towards all. This *Arbitrary* power is apt to *induce* and incourage all kind of *insolencies*.

Another *end* of *Government* is to *preserve* men in their *estates*, to *secure* them in their Lives and Liberties; but if this Designe had taken effect, and could have been *setled* in *England*, as it was *practiced* in *Ireland*, no man would have had more certainty in his own, than power would have allowed him. But these two have beene spoken of before, there are two behind more *important*, which have not yet been touched.

It is the *end* of *Government*, that *vertue* should be *cherisht, vice supprest;* but where this *Arbitrary* and *unlimited power* is set up, a way is open not only for the *security*, but for the *advancement* and *incouragement* of evill. Such men as are aptest for the execution and maintenance of this Power, are only capable of preferment; and others who will not be *instruments* of any *unjust commands*, who make a *conscience* to doe nothing against the *Laws* of the *Kingdome*, and *Liberties* of the *Subject*, are not only not *passable* for *imployment*, but *subject* to much *jealousie* and *danger*.

It is the *end* of *Government*, that all *accidents* and *events*, all *Counsels* and *Designes* should be improved to the *publique good*. But this *Arbitrary Power* is apt to *dispose* all to the *maintenance* of itselfe. The *wisdome* of the *Councell-Table*, the *Authority* of the *Courts* of Justice, the *industry* of all the *Officers* of the *Crown* have been most carefully *exercised* in this; the *Learning* of our *Divines*, the *Jurisdiction* of our *Bishops* have been moulded and disposed to the same *effect*, which though it were begun before the *E.* of *Strafford's Imployment*, yet it hath beene exceedingly *furthered* and *advanced by him*.

Under this *colour* and *pretence* of *maintaining* the *King's Power* and *Prerogative* many *dangerous practices* against the *peace* and *safety* of this *Kingdome* have been undertaken and promoted. The *increase* of *Popery*, and the favours and incouragement of *Papists* have been, and still are a great grievance and danger to the *Kingdome*. The *Innovations* in *matters* of *Religion*, the *usurpations* of the *Clergie*, the manifold burdens and taxations upon the people, have been a great cause of our present *distempers* and *disorders;* and yet those who have been chiefe *Furtherers* and *Actors* of such Mischiefes, have had their Credit and Authority from this, That they were forward to *maintain* this Power. The E. of *Strafford* had the first rise of his greatnesse from this, and in his *Apologie* and *Defence*, as your *Lordships* have heard, this hath had a maine part.

The *Royall Power*, and *Majesty* of *Kings*, is most glorious in the *prosperity* and *happinesse* of the people. The perfection of all things consists in the *end* for which they were ordained, *God* only is his own *end*, all other *things* have a further *end* beyond *themselves*, in attaining whereof their own happinesse consists. If the *means* and the *end* be set in *opposition* to one another, it must needs *cause* an *impotency* and *defect* of *both*.

The eighth *Consideration* is, The *vanity* and *absurdity* of those *excuses* and *justifications* which he made for himself, whereof divers *particulars* have been mentioned in the *course* of his *Defence*.

1. That he is a *Counsellor*, and might not be *questioned* for anything which he advised according to his *conscience*. The *ground* is *true*, there is a *liberty* belongs to *Counsellors*, and nothing corrupts Counsels more than *fear*. *He* that will have the priviledge of a *Counsellor*, must keep within the just bounds of a *Counsellor;* those *matters* are the proper *subjects* of *Counsell*, which in their times and occasions, may be good or beneficiall to the *King* or *Common-wealth*. But such *Treasons* as these, the *subversion* of the *Laws*, *violation* of *Liberties*, they can never be good, or justifiable by any *circumstance*, or *occasion;* and therefore his being a *Counsellor*, makes his fault much more hainous,

as being committed against a greater *Trust,* and in a way of much
mischiefe and danger, lest his Majestie's conscience and judgment
(upon which the whole course and frame of his *Government* do much
depend) should be poisoned and infected with such wicked principles and designes. And this he hath endeavoured to doe, which by all
Lawes, and in all *times* hath in this *Kingdome* beene reckoned a *Crime*
of an *high Nature.*

2. He labours to *interest* your Lordships in his *cause,* by alledging,
It may be *dangerous* to yourselves, and your *Posterity,* who by your
birth are fittest to be near his Majesty, in places of *Trust* and *Authority,* if you should be subject to be *questioned* for *matters* delivered in
Counsell. To this was answered, that it was *hoped* their Lordships
would rather *labour* to secure themselves, and their posterity, in the
exercise of their *vertues,* than of their *vices,* that so they might together with their own *honour* and *greatnesse,* preserve the *honour* and
greatnesse, both of the *King* and *Kingdome.*

3. Another *excuse* was this, that whatsoever he hath *spoken* was out
of a *good intention.* Sometimes *good* and *evill, truth* and *falshood* lie so
near together, that they are hardly to be *distinguished.* Matters *hurtfull* and *dangerous* may be accompanied with such *circumstances* as
may make it appeare usefull and convenient, and in all such *cases, good
intentions* will justifie *evill Counsell.* But where the matters propounded are *evill* in their own *nature,* such as the *matters* are wherewith the *E.* of *Strafford* is charged, to *break a publique faith,* to *subvert
Laws* and *Government,* they can never be justified by any intentions,
how specious, or good soever they be pretended.

4. He *alledgeth* it was a time of great *necessity* and *danger,* when
such counsels were *necessary* for preservation of the *State. Necessity*
hath been spoken of before, as it relates to the Cause; now it is considered as it relates to the Person; if there were any necessity, it was of
his own making; he by his *evil* counsell had brought the *King* into a

necessity, and by no Rules of *Justice,* can be *allowed* to gain this advantage by his own fault, as to make that a *ground* of his justification, which is a great part of his offence.

5. He hath often *insinuated* this, That it was for his Majestie's service in *maintenance* of the Soveraign *Power* with which he is *intrusted* by *God* for the *good* of his people. The Answer is this, No doubt but that Soveraign Power wherewith his Majesty is *intrusted* for the publique good, hath many glorious *effects,* the better to inable him thereunto. But without doubt this is none of them, That by his own will he may lay any *Taxe* or *Imposition* upon his people without their consent in *Parliament.* This hath now been five times adjudged by both *Houses.* In the Case of the *Loanes,* In condemning the *Commission* of *Excise,* In the Resolution upon the *Saving*[8] offered to be added to the *Petition* of *Right,* In the sentence against *Manwaring,* and now lately, In condemning the *Shipmoney.* And if the Soveraigne Power of the King can produce no such *effect* as this, the *Allegation* of it is an Aggravation, and no Diminution of his offence, because thereby he doth labour to interest the King against the just grievance and complaint of the People.

6. This *Counsell* was propounded with divers *limitations,* and *Provisions;* for securing and repairing the *liberty* of the *people.* This implies a *contradiction* to maintain an *Arbitrary* & absolute Power, and yet to restrain it with *limitations,* and *provisions;* for even those *limitations* and *provisions* will be subject to the same absolute *Power,* and to be dispensed in such manner, and at such time, as itself shall determine; let the *grievances* and *oppressions* be never so heavy, the *Subject* is left without all remedy, but at his Majestie's own pleasure.

7. He alledgeth, they were but *words,* and no *effect* followed. This needs no answer, but that the *miserable distempers* into which he hath

---

8. The "Resolution upon the Saving" refers to the proposal of the Lords, rejected by the Commons, to add to the Petition of Right the phrase "to leave entire that sovereign Power, wherewith your Majesty is trusted for the protection, safety, and happiness of your people."

brought all the three Kingdomes, will be evidence sufficient that his wicked *Counsels* have had such *mischievous* effects within these two or three last years, that many years' peace will hardly repaire those losses, and other great mischiefes which the *Common-wealth* hath sustained.

These excuses have been collected out of the severall parts of his *Defence;* perchance some others are omitted, which I doubt not have been answered by some of my Colleagues, and are of no importance, either to perplex or to hinder your Lordships' judgement, touching the hainousnesse of this Crime.

The ninth *Consideration* is this, That if this be *Treason,* in the nature of it, it doth exceed all other *Treasons* in this, That in the Design, and endeavour of the Author, it was to be a *constant* and a *permanent Treason;* other Treasons are transient, as being confined within those particular *actions* and *proportions* wherein they did consist, and those being past, the *Treason* ceaseth.

The *Powder Treason*[9] was full of horror and malignity, yet it is past many years since. The *murder* of that *Magnanimous* and *glorious King, Henry the fourth* of *France,* was a great and horrid *Treason.* And so were those manifold attempts against Queen *Elizabeth* of blessed memory; but they are long since past, the *Detestation* of them only remains in *Histories,* and in the *minds* of men; and will ever remain. But this *Treason,* if it had taken effect, was to be a standing, perpetuall *Treason,* which would have been in *continuall act,* not *determined* within one *time* or *age,* but *transmitted* to *Posterity,* even from *generation* to *generation.*

The tenth *Consideration* is this, That as it is a Crime odious in the nature of it, so it is odious in the judgement and estimation of the *Law.* To alter the setled *frame* and *constitution* of *Government,* is

---

9. The reference is to the "gunpowder plot" of 1605 in which a group of Catholic conspirators attempted to blow up the king and members of Parliament in order to overthrow the Protestant government.

Treason in any *estate*. The *Laws* whereby all other parts of a King-dome are preserved, should be very vain and defective, if they had not a *power* to secure and preserve *themselves*.

The *forfeitures* inflicted for *Treason* by our Law, are of *Life, Honour,* and *Estate*, even all that can be *forfeited*, and this Prisoner having committed so many Treasons, although he should pay all these *for-feitures*, will be still a Debtor to the *Common-wealth*. Nothing can be more equall than that he should perish by the Justice of that Law which he would have subverted. Neither will this be a new way of bloud. There are marks enough to trace this Law to the very originall of this Kingdome. And if it hath not been put in execution, as he alledgeth, this 240 years, it was not for want of Law, but that all that time hath not bred a man bold enough to commit such Crimes as these; which is a *circumstance* much aggravating his offence, and mak-ing him no whit lesse liable to punishment, because he is the only man that in so long a time hath ventured upon such a *Treason* as this.

It belongs to the charge of another to make it appear to your Lord-ships, that the Crimes and Offences proved against the *Earle* of *Strafford*, are *High Treason* by the Lawes and Statutes of this Realm, whose learning and other abilities are much better for that service. But for the time and manner of performing this, we are to resort to the *Direction* of the *House of Commons*, having in this which is already done, dispatched all those instructions which wee have received; and concerning further proceedings, for clearing all Questions and Ob-jections in Law, your Lordships will hear from the *House* of *Commons* in convenient time.

FINIS.

Charles I, 1600–1649

XIX.
PROPOSITIONS
Made
By both Houses of Parliament,
to the Kings most Excellent
Majestie:

With His Majesties Answer
thereunto.

¶ By the King.
Our expresse pleasure is, That this Our
Answer be read and published throughout
all Churches and Chappels of the
Kingdom of England and
Dominion of Wales,

By the severall Parsons, Vicars, or
Curats of the same.

YORK:
Printed by ROBERT BARKER, Printer
to the Kings most Excellent Majestie: And
by the Assignes of JOHN BILL.
1642.

After Charles abandoned London in January *1642* for what he hoped would be the more loyal North, the two houses of Parliament at Westminster attempted to negotiate with him through a series of published declarations, remonstrances, answers, and open letters. These reached a constitutional climax in June with Parliament's publication on *1* June of the Nineteen Propositions, proposals that would have sharply and permanently circumscribed the king's powers, and Charles's response on *18* June.

Charles's "Answer to the Nineteen Propositions" has become even more famous than the propositions themselves. This answer has been heralded for its endorsement of England's mixed and balanced constitution and for its reliance upon law for support. Of chief significance, however, is the king's acceptance of the concept that he is not above the three estates assembled in Parliament but in fact is one of the three estates. The Answer was written for Charles by two of his moderate advisers, Sir John Colepeper and Lucius Cary, Viscount Falkland—men who had worked in the Long Parliament the previous year to rein in the expanded royal prerogative. The passage in which the king endorses the idea of being one of three estates in Parliament—thus excluding the bishops from membership and reducing the position of the Crown to coordinate membership—was penned by Colepeper. It is unclear whether Falkland fully endorsed the Answer's concession that the king was one of the three estates. He later pleaded inadvertence, claimed Colepeper had been misled by some lawyers, and that clergymen had misunderstood. Sir Edward Hyde, the best known of Charles's moderate advisers, was unhappy with the concession and tried to delay publication. It is even unclear whether the king actually read the crucial passage, although he assuredly glanced at, and gave his approval to, the lengthy reply. In important respects it does not reflect views Charles espoused before or afterward.

Whatever confusion reigned among the king's advisers, however willingly, reluctantly, or unknowingly the king complied, the Answer publicly altered the basis of royal defense and argument.

There is much of interest in the entire reply. Because historians have focused almost exclusively upon its crucial constitutional concessions, however, the answer has seldom been reprinted in its entirety. As a result its tone has been misread. The reply reprinted here was published by royal order at York and is unusual in providing the text of both the Nineteen Propositions and the king's Answer. In earnest of the king's desire that the Answer be widely published and read in churches throughout England and Wales, six further editions were printed in 1642. It is notable that two editions published in 1643 either omitted the reference to the three estates of Parliament or the entire section on the English constitution.

XIX. Propositions made by both Houses of Parliament, to the Kings most excellent Majestie, touching the differences between His Majestie and the said Houses.

Your Majestie's most humble and faithfull Subjects, the Lords and Commons in Parliament, having nothing in their thoughts and desires more precious and of higher esteem (next to the Honour and immediate Service of God) than the just and faithfull performance of their Dutie to your Majestie and this Kingdom, and being very sensible of the great distractions and distempers, and of the imminent Dangers and Calamities which those Distractions and Distempers are like to bring upon your Majestie and your Subjects: All which have proceeded from the subtill Insinuations, mischievous Practises, and evill Counsels of Men disaffected to God's true Religion, your Majestie's Honor and Safetie, and the publike Peace and Prosperitie of your people: After a serious observation of the Causes of those Mischiefs, do in all Humilitie and Sinceritie present to your Majestie their most dutifull Petition and Advice; That out of your Princely Wisdom, for the establishing your own Honour and Safetie, and gracious tendernesse of the welfare and securitie of your Subjects and Dominions, You will be pleased to Grant and Accept these their humble Desires and Propositions, as the most necessarie effectuall means, through God's blessing, of removing those Jealousies and Differences which have unhappily fallen betwixt You and your People, and procuring both your Majestie and them a constant course of Honour, Peace, and Happinesse.

I. That the Lords, and others of your Majestie's Privie Councell, and such great Officers and Ministers of State, either at home or beyond the Seas, may be put from your Privie Councell, and from those Offices and Imployments, excepting such as shall be approved of by both Houses of Parliament; And that the Persons put into the Places

148

and Imployments of those that are removed, may be approved of by both Houses of Parliament; And that all Privie Councellors shall take an Oath for the due execution of their Places, in such forme as shall be agreed upon by both Houses of Parliament.

II. That the great Affairs of the Kingdom may not be Concluded or Transacted by the Advise of private men, or by any unknown or unsworn Councellors; but that such Matters as concern the Publike, and are proper for the high Court of Parliament, which is your Majestie's great and supreme Councell, may be Debated, Resolved, and Transacted only in Parliament, and not elsewhere. And such as shall presume to do anything to the contrary, shall be reserved to the Censure and Judgement of Parliament: And such other matters of State as are proper for your Majestie's Privie Councell, shall be debated and concluded by such of the Nobility and Others, as shall from time to time be chosen for that place by approbation of both Houses of Parliament. That no publicke Act concerning the Affairs of the Kingdom, which are proper for your Privie Councell, may be esteemed of any validity, as proceeding from the Royall Authority, unlesse it be done by the advice and consent of the major part of your Councell, attested under their hands. And that your Councell may be limited to a certain number, not exceeding five and twenty, nor under fifteen; and if any Councellor's place happen to be void in the Intervals of Parliament, it shall not be supplied without the Assent of the major part of the Councell; which choice shall be confirmed at the next sitting of the Parliament, or else to be void.

III. That the Lord high Steward of *England,* Lord high Constable, Lord Chancellour, or Lord Keeper of the great Seal, Lord Treasurer, Lord Privie Seal, the Earle Marshall, Lord Admirall, Warden of the Cinque-Ports, chief Governour of Ireland, Chancellour of the Exchequer, Master of the Wards, Secretaries of State, two chief Justices, and chief Baron, may be alwayes chosen with the approbation of both

Houses of Parliament: And in the Intervals of Parliaments by assent of the major part of the Councell, in such manner as is before expressed in the choice of Councellors.

IV. That he or they unto whom the Government and education of the King's Children shall be committed, shall be approved of by both Houses of Parliament; and in the Intervals of Parliaments, by the assent of the major part of the Councell, in such manner as is before exprest in the choice of Councellors: And that all such Servants as are now about them, against whom both Houses shall have any just exception, shall be removed.

V. That no Marriage shall be Concluded, or Treated for any of the King's Children, with any Forraign Prince, or other Person whatsoever abroad, or at home, without the consent of Parliament, under the penalty of a Premunire unto such as shall so Conclude or Treate any Marriage as aforesaid. And that the said Penalty shall not be pardoned or dispensed with, but by the consent of both Houses of Parliament.

VI. That the Laws in force against *Jesuites, Priests*, and *Popish Recusants*, be strictly put in execution, without any Toleration or Dispensation to the contrary; and that some more effectuall Course may be Enacted, by Authoritie of Parliament, to disable them from making any disturbance in the State, or eluding the Law by Trusts, or otherwise.

VII. That the Votes of Popish Lords in the House of Peers, may be taken away, so long as they continue Papists; and that His Majestie would consent to such a Bill as shall be drawn for the Education of the Children of Papists by Protestants in the Protestant Religion.

VIII. That your Majestie will be pleased to Consent, That such a Reformation be made of the Church-Government, and Liturgie as both Houses of Parliament shall advise, wherein they intend to have Consultations with Divines, as is expressed in the Declaration to that purpose; and that your Majestie will contribute your best Assistance to them for the raising of a sufficient Maintenance for Preaching Ministers thorowout the Kingdom: And that your Majestie will be pleased to give your consent to Laws for the taking away of Innovations and Superstition, and of Pluralities, and against Scandalous Ministers.

IX. That your Majestie will be pleased to rest satisfied with that Course that the Lords and Commons have appointed for Ordering the *Militia*,[1] untill the same shall be further setled by a Bill: And that you will recall your Declarations and Proclamations against the Ordinance made by the Lords and Commons concerning it.

X. That such Members of either House of Parliament, as have, during this present Parliament, been put out of any Place and Office,[2] may either be restored to that Place and Office, or otherwise have satisfaction for the same, upon the Petition of that House, whereof he or they are Members.

XI. That all Privie Councellors and Judges may take an Oath, the form whereof to be agreed on, and setled by Act of Parliament, for the maintaining of the Petition of Right, and of certain Statutes made by this Parliament, which shall be mentioned by both Houses of Parliament: And that an enquiry of the Breaches and Violations of those Laws may be given in charge by the Justices of the King's-Bench every Tearm, and by the Judges of Assize in their Circuits, and Justices of Peace at the Sessions, to be presented and punished according to Law.

XII. That all the Judges and all Officers placed by approbation of

1. Unable to obtain Charles's agreement to transfer the command of the kingdom's militia to Parliament, on 5 March 1642, that body passed the Militia Ordinance assuming such authority without the king's consent.
2. It is unclear which members were put out of "any Place and Office," but the Grand Remonstrance, clause 38, charges that "judges have been put out of their places for refusing to go against their oaths and consciences."

both Houses of Parliament, may hold their Places, *Quam diu bene se gesserint.*[3]

XIII. That the justice of Parliament may passe upon all Delinquents, whether they be within the Kingdom, or fled out of it; And that all Persons cited by either House of Parliament, may appear and abide the censure of Parliament.

XIIII. That the Generall Pardon offered by your Majestie, may be granted with such Exceptions, as shall be advised by both Houses of Parliament.

XV. That the Forts and Castles of this Kingdom, may be put under the Command and Custody of such Persons as your Majestie shall appoint, with the approbation of your Parliaments: and in the intervals of Parliament, with the approbation of the major part of the Councell, in such manner as is before expressed in the choice of Councellors.

XVI. That the extraordinary Guards, and Millitary Forces,[4] now attending your Majestie, may be removed and discharged; and that for the future you will raise no such Guards or extraordinary Forces, but according to the Law, in case of actuall Rebellion or Invasion.

XVII. That your Majestie will be pleased to enter into a more strict Alliance with the States of the United Provinces, and other neighbour Princes and States of the Protestant Religion, for the defence and maintenance thereof against all Designes and Attempts of the *Pope* and his Adherents, to subvert and suppresse it, whereby your Majestie will obtain a great accesse of Strength and Reputation, and your Subjects be much encouraged and enabled in a Parliamentary way, for your aid and assistance in restoring your Royall Sister and her Princely Issue to those Dignities and Dominions which belong

---

3. During good behavior.
4. Charles carefully avoided referring to his growing military force as soldiers, and preferred to call them guards.

unto them,[5] and relieving the other distressed Protestant Princes who have suffered in the same Cause.

XVIII. That your Majestie will be pleased, by Act of Parliament, to cleer the Lord *Kimbolton,* and the five Members of the House of Commons,[6] in such manner that future Parliaments may be secured from the consequence of that evill precedent.

XIX. That your Majestie will be graciously pleased to passe a Bill for restraining Peers made hereafter from Sitting or Voting in Parliament; unlesse they be admitted thereunto with the consent of both Houses of Parliament.

And these our humble desires being granted by your Majestie, we shall forthwith apply ourselves to regulate your present Revenue, in such sort, as may be for your best advantage; and likewise to settle such an ordinary and constant increase of it as shall be sufficient to support your Royall Dignitie in Honour and plenty, beyond the proportion of any former Grants of the Subjects of this Kingdom to your Majestie's Royall Predecessors. We shall likewise put the Town of *Hull* into such hands as your Majestie shall appoint,[7] with the Consent and Approbation of Parliament; and deliver up a just accompt of all the Magazine; and cheerfully imploy the uttermost of our Power and Endeavour in the reall expression and performance of our most

5. Charles's sister Elizabeth had married the Protestant, Frederick V, the Elector Palatine. Frederick's election as King of Bohemia upon the deposition of the Catholic Ferdinand immersed them both in the bitter Thirty Years' War. Frederick became known as the winter king from the brevity of his reign. Elizabeth's sons, princes Rupert and Maurice, were both to fight on Charles's behalf during the civil war.

6. Lord Kimbolton here referred to was Edward Montagu, Earl of Manchester, one of those accused of treason by the king on 3 January 1642. The others were John Pym, John Hampden, William Strode, Denzil Holles, and Sir Arthur Haslerigg.

7. On 23 April 1642, the new parliamentary governor of Hull, Sir John Hotham, arrived just in time to refuse the king entry to the town that housed the major arsenal in the northern part of the kingdom.

dutifull and loyall affections to the preserving and maintaining the Royall Honour, Greatnesse, and Safetie of your Majestie and your Posterity.

His Majesties Answer to the Nineteen Propositions of Both Houses of Parliament.

Before we shall give you Our Answer to your Petition and Propositions, we shall tell you, That we are now cleerly satisfied, why the Method, which we traced out to you by Our Message of the twentieth of January,[8] and have since so often pressed upon you, as the proper way to compose the Distractions of this Kingdom, and render it truly happy, hath been hitherto declined, and is at length thought fit to be lookt upon. We now see plainly (and desire that you, and all other Our good Subjects, should do so too) that the Caballists of this Businesse, have, with great prudence, reserved themselves untill due preparations should be made for their designe.

If they had unseasonably vented such Propositions, as the wisdom and modesty of your Predecessors never thought fit to offer to any of Our Progenitors, nor We in honour or regard to Our Regall Authoritie (which God hath intrusted Us with for the good of Our people) could receive without just indignation, (and such many of your present Propositions are) their hopes would soon have been blasted, and those persons to whom Offices, Honours, Power and Commands were designed, by such ill-timing of their Businesse, would have failed of their expectation, not without a brand upon the attempt. Therefore, before any of this nature should appear, they have (certainly with great wisdom in the conduct of it) thought fit to remove a troublesome rub in their way, the Law. To this end (that they

8. "His Majesties Message to both Houses of Parliament, January 20" (London, 1642), Wing C2450.

might undermine the very foundations of it) a new Power hath been assumed to interpret and declare Laws without Us, by extemporary Votes, without any case judicially before either house, (which is in effect the same thing as to make Laws without Us) Orders and Ordinances made only by both houses (tending to a pure Arbitrary power) were pressed upon the people, as Laws, and their obedience required to them.

Their next step was to erect an upstart Authority without Us (in whom, and only in whom, the Laws of this Realm have placed that power) to command the *Militia;* (very considerable to this their designe). In further Order to it, they have wrested from Us Our Magazine and Town of *Hull,* and bestird Sir *John Hotham* in his bold-faced Treason.[9] They have prepared and directed to the people, unprecedented Invectives against Our Government, thereby (as much as lay in their power) to weaken Our just Authoritie and due esteem amongst them. They have as injuriously, as presumptuously (though we conceive by this time Impudence itself is ashamed of it) attempted to cast upon Us Aspersions of an unheard of nature, as if We had favoured a Rebellion in Our own bowels. They have likewise broached new Doctrine, That we are obliged to passe all Laws that shall be offered to Us by both Houses (howsoever Our own Judgement and Conscience shall be unsatisfied with them) a point of policie, as proper for their present businesse, as destructive to all Our Rights of Parliament. And so with strange shamelesnesse will forget a clause in a Law still in force, made in the second yeer of King *Henry* the fifth, wherein both Houses of Parliament do acknowledge, That it is of the King's Regalitie to grant or deny such of their Petitions as pleaseth himself. They have interpreted Our necessary Guard, legally assembled for the defence of Us and Our Children's Persons, against a Traitor in open Rebellion against Us, to be with intent to levie war

9. For information on the incident involving Sir John Hotham and Hull, see note 7, above.

against Our Parliament (the thought whereof Our very soul abhorreth) thereby to render Us odious to Our people. They have so awed
Our good Subjects with Pursuivants,[10] long chargeable Attendance,
heavie Censures, & illegal Imprisonments, that few of them durst
offer to present their tendernesse of Our sufferings, their own just
grievances, and their sense of those violations of the Law (the birthright of every Subject of this Kingdom) though in an humble Petition directed to both Houses; and if any did, it was stifled in the birth,
called Sedition, and burnt by the common Hangman. They have restrained the attendance of Our ordinary and necessary houshold servants, and seized upon those small sums of Money which Our credit
had provided to buy Us Bread; with Injunctions, That none shall be
suffered to be conveyed or returned to Us to *York,* or any of Our Peers
or Servants with Us; so that (in effect) they have blocked Us up in
that County. They have filled the ears of the people with the noise of
Fears and Jealousies (though taken up upon trust) tales of Skippers,
Salt Fleets, and such like, by which alarms they might prepare them
to receive such impressions as might best advance this Designe, when
it should be ripe. And now, it seems, they think We are sufficiently
prepared for these bitter Pills. We are in a handsome posture to receive these humble desires (which probably are intended to make way
for a superfetation or a (yet) higher nature (if we had not made this
discovery to you) for they doe not tell Us this is all). In them We must
observe, That these Contrivers (the better to advance their true ends)
disguised, as much as they could their intents, with a mixture of some
things really to be approved by every honest man; others, specious
and popular and some which are already granted by Us. All which
are cunningly twisted and mixed with those other things of their
main designe of ambition and private Interest, in hope that at the

10. State messengers with power to execute warrants.

first view, every eye may not so cleerly discern them in their proper colours.

We would not be understood, That We intend to fix this Designe upon both, or either House of Parliament, We utterly professe against it, being most confidenct of the Loyaltie, good Affections, and Integritie of the Intentions of that great Bodie; and knowing well, That very many of both Houses were absent, and many dissented from all those particulars We complain of. But we do beleeve, and accordingly professe to all the world, That the malignity of this Designe (as dangerous to the Laws of this Kingdom, the Peace of the same, and Liberties of all Our good Subjects, as to Ourself and Our just Prerogative) hath proceeded from the subtill Informations, mischievous Practises, and evill Counsels, of ambitious, turbulent Spirits, disaffected to God's true Religion, and the unity of the Professors thereof, Our Honour and Safety, and the publike Peace and Prosperitie of Our people, not without a strong Influence upon the very Actions of both Houses. But how faultie soever others are, We shall (with God's assistance) endeavour to discharge Our dutie with uprightnesse of heart. And therefore since these Propositions come to Us in the name of both Houses of Parliament, We shall take a more particular notice of every of them.

If the 1. 2. 3. 4. 5. 9. 10. 15. 16. 19. Demands had been writ and printed in a tongue unknown to Us and Our people, it might have been possible We and they might have charitably beleeved the Propositions to be such, as might have been in Order to the ends pretended in the Petition, (to wit) The establishing of Our Honour and Safetie, the welfare and securitie of Our Subjects and Dominions, & the removing those Jealousies and Differences, which are said to have unhappily fallen betwixt Us and Our people, and procuring both Us and them a constant course of Honour, Peace, and Happinesse. But being read and understood by all, We cannot but assure Ourself, that this Profession joined to these Propositions, will rather appear a Mockery and a Scorn. The Demands being such, as we were unworthy of the trust reposed in Us by the Law, and of Our dessent, from so many great and famous Ancestors, if We could be brought to abandon that power which only can inable Us to perform what We are sworn to, in protecting Our people and the Laws, and so assume others into it, as to devest Ourself of it; although not only Our present condition (which it can hardly be) were more necessitous than it is, and We were both vanquisht, and a Prisoner, and in a worse condition than ever the most unfortunate of Our Predecessors have been reduced to, by the most criminall of their Subjects. And though the Bait laid to draw Us to it, and to keep Our Subjects from Indignation at the mention of it, The promises of a plentifull and unparalleled Revenue, were reduced from generalls (which signifie nothing) to clear and certain particulars, since such a Bargain would have but too great a resemblance of that of *Esau's*, if we should part with such Flowers of Our Crown as are worth all the rest of the Garland, and have been transmitted to Us from so many Ancestors, and have been found so usefull and necessary for the welfare and security of Our Subjects, for any present necessitie, or for any low and sordid considerations of wealth and gain. And therefore all Men knowing that those accommodations are most easily made and most exactly observed, that are grounded upon reasonable and equall Conditions; We have great cause to beleeve, That the Contrivers of these had no intention of setling any firm Accommodation; but to increase those Jealousies, and widen that division, which (not by Our fault) is now unhappily fallen between Us and both Houses.

It is asked, That all the Lords, and others of Our Privy Councell, and such (We know now what you mean by such, but We have cause to think you mean all) great Officers and Ministers of State, either at home, or beyond the Seas, (for Care is taken to leave out no person or place, that Our dishonour may be sure not to be bounded within this Kingdom, though no subtill Insinuations at such a distance can probably be beleeved to have been the cause of Our distractions and Dangers) should be put from Our Privie Councell, and from those Offices and Imployments, unlesse they be approved by both Houses of Parliament, how faithfull soever We have found them to Us and the Publike, and how far soever they have been from offending against any Law, the only Rule they had, or any others ought to have to walk by. We therefore, to this part of this Demand, return you this Answer, That We are willing to grant that they shall take a larger Oath than you yourselves desire in your eleventh Demand, for maintaining not of any part but of the whole Law; and We have and do assure you, that We will be carefull to make election of such persons in those places of Trust, as shall have given good Testimonies of their abilities and integreities, and against whom there can be no just cause of exception, whereon reasonably to ground a diffidence, that if We have, or shall be mistaken in Our election, We have, and do assure you, That there is no man so neer to Us in place or affection, whom We will not leave to the Justice of the Law, if you shall bring a particular Charge and sufficient Proofs against him; and that We have given you (the best pledge of the effects of such a promise on Our part, and the best securitie for the performance of their duty on theirs) a Trienniall Parliament,[11] the apprehension of whose Justice will, in all probability, make them wary how they provoke it, and Us wary how We chuse such, as by the discoverie of their faults may in any degree seem to discredit Our election. But that, without any shadow of a fault objected, only perhaps because they follow their conscience, and preserve the established Laws, and agree not in such Votes, or assent not to such Bills, as some persons, who have now too great an Influence even upon both Houses, judge or seem to judge, to be for the Publique good, and as are agreeable to that new *Utopia* of

---

11. Despite his original objections to it, on 16 February 1641 Charles I had consented to the Triennial Bill mandating the summoning of a parliament at least every three years.

Religion and Government, into which they endevour to transform this Kingdom; (for We remember what Names, and for what Reasons you left out in the Bill offered Us concerning the *Militia,* which you had yourselves recommended in the Ordinance). We will never consent to the displacing of any, whom for their former merits from, and affection to Us and the publike, We have intrusted, since We conceive, That to do so, would take away both from the affection of Our Servants, the care of Our Service, and the honour of Our Justice. And We the more wonder, that it should be askt by you of Us, since it appears by the twelfth Demand, That yourselves count it reasonable, after the present turn is served, That the Judges and Officers, who are then placed, may hold their places *quam diu se bene gesserint;* and We are resolved to be as carefull of those We have chosen, as you are of those you would chuse, and to remove none, till they appear to Us to have otherwise behaved themselves, or shall be evicted by legall proceedings to have done so.

But this Demand (as unreasonable as it is) is but one link of a great Chain, and but the first round of that Ladder, by which Our Just, Ancient, Regall Power is endeavoured to be fetched down to the ground: For it appears plainly, That it is not with the persons now chosen, but with Our chusing, that you are displeased: For you demand, That the persons put into the places and imployments of those, who shall be removed, may be approved by both Houses; which is so far (as to some it may at first sight appear) from being lesse than the power of nomination, that of two things (of which We will never grant either). We would sooner be content, That you should nominate, and We approve, then you approve, and We nominate; the meer nomination being so far from being anything, That if We could do no more, We would never take the pains to do that, when We should only hazard those, whom We esteemed, to the scorn of a refusall, if they happened not to be agreeable, not only to the Judgement, but to the Passion, Interest, or Humour of the present major part of either House: Not to speak now of the great Factions, Animosities, and Divisions which this Power would introduce in both Houses, between both Houses, and in the severall Countreys, for the choice of persons to be sent to that place where that power was, and between the persons that were so chosen. Neither is this strange Potion prescribed to Us only for once, for the cure of a present, pressing, desperate Disease, but for a Diet to Us and Our Posteritie. It is demanded, *That Our Councellors, all chief Officers both of Law and State, Commanders of Forts and Castles, and all Peers hereafter made* (as to Voting, without which how little is the rest) *be approved of* (that is, chosen) *by them from time to time;* and rather than it should ever be left to the Crown (to whom it only doth and shall belong) *if any place fall void in the intermission of Parliament; the major part of the approved Councell is to approve them.* Neither is it only demanded, That We should quit the power and right Our Predecessors have had of appointing Persons in these places, but for Councellors, We are to be restrained as well in the number as in the persons, and a power must be annext to these places, which their Predecessors had not; and indeed if this power were past to them, it were not fit We should be trusted to chuse those who were to be trusted as much as We.

It is demanded, *That such matters as concern the publike, and are proper for the high Court of Parliament* (which is Our great and supream Councell) *may be debated, resolved and transacted only in Parliament, and not elsewhere, and such as presume to do anything to the contrary shall be reserved to the Censure and Judgement of Parliament, and such other matters of State, as are proper of Our Privie Councell, shall be debated and concluded by such of Our Nobility* (though indeed, if being made by Us, they may not Vote without the consent of both Houses, We are rather to call them Your Nobility) *and others, as shall be from time to time chosen for that place, by approbation of both Houses of Parliament; and that no publike Act concerning the affairs of the King-*

dom, which are proper for Our Privie Councell, may be esteemed of any validitie, as proceeding from the Royall Authority, unlesse it be done by the Advice and Consent of the major part of Our Councell, attested under their hands: Which Demands are of that Nature, that to grant them were in effect at once to depose both Ourself and Our Posteritie.

These being past, we may be waited on bare-headed; we may have Our hand kissed; The Stile of Majestie continued to Us; And the King's Authoritie, declared by both Houses of Parliament, may be still the Stile of your Commands. We may have Swords and Maces carried before Us, and please Ourself with the sight of a Crown and Scepter, (and yet even these Twigs would not long flourish, when the Stock upon which they grew were dead) but as to true and reall Power We should remain but the outside, but the Picture, but the signe of a King. We were ever willing that Our Parliament should Debate, Resolve, & Transact such matters as are proper for them, as far as they are proper for them. And We heartily wish, that they would be as carefull not to extend their Debates and Resolutions beyond what is proper to them, that multitudes of things punishable, and causes determinable by the Ordinarie Judicatures, may not be entertained in Parliament, and to cause a long, chargeable, fruitlesse attendance of Our people, and (by degrees) draw to you as well all the causes, as all the faults of *Westminster-Hall,* and divert your proper businesse. That the course of Law be no wayes diverted, much lesse disturbed, as was actually done by the stop of the proceedings against a Riot in *Southwark,*[12] by Order of the House of Commons, in a time so riotous and tumultuous, as much increased the danger of popular Insolencies, by such a countenance to Riots, and discountenance of Law. That you descend not to the leasure of recommending Lecturers to Churches,

12. A meeting in Southwark in December 1641 for the purpose of drawing up a petition against the bishops became violent when a constable was attacked and beaten. Complaint was made and the sheriff ordered to impanel a jury to examine witnesses. The House of Commons intervened and ordered the undersheriff of Surrey to stop the proceedings.

nor ascend to the Legislative power, by commanding (the Law not having yet commanded it) that they whom you recommend be received, although neither the Parson nor Bishop do approve of them; And that the Refusers (according to the course so much formerly complained of to have been used at the Councell Table) be not sent for to attend to shew cause. At least, that you would consider Conveniencie, if not Law, and recommend none, but who are well known to you to be Orthodox, Learned, and Moderate, or at least such as have taken Orders, and are not notorious depravers of the Book of Common Prayer; A care which appeareth by the Discourses, Sermons and persons of some recommended by you, not to have been hitherto taken, and it highly concerns both you in dutie, and the Common-wealth in the consequences, that it should have been taken; That neither one estate transact what is proper for two, nor two what is proper for three, and consequently, that (contrary to Our declared will) Our Forts may not be seized; Our Arms may not be removed; Our Moneys may not be stopt; Our legall Directions may not be countermanded by you, nor We desired to countermand them Ourself, nor such entrances made upon a Reall War against Us, upon pretence of all imaginarie War against you, and a *Chimaera* of necessitie. So far do you passe beyond your limits, whilest you seem by your Demand to be strangely straitened within them. At least We could have wisht you would have expressed, what matters you meant as *fit to be transacted only in Parliament,* and what you meant by *only in Parliament.* You have (of late) been perswaded by the new doctrines of some few, to think that proper for your debates, which hath not used to be at all debated within those walls, but been trusted wholly with Our Predecessors and Us, and to transact those things which without the Regall Authority, since there were Kings of this Kingdom, were never transacted. It therefore concerns Us the more that you speak out, and that both We and Our people may either know the bottom of your Demands, or know them to be bottomlesse. What concerns

more the Publike, and is more (indeed) proper for the high Court of
Parliament, than the making of Laws, which not only ought there to
be transacted, but can be transacted no where else; but then you must
admit Us to be a part of the Parliament, you must not (as the sence is
of this part of this Demand, if it have any) deny the freedom of Our
Answer, when We have as much right to reject what We think unreasonable, as you have to propose what you think convenient or necessary; nor is it possible Our Answers either to Bills, or any other
Propositions should be wholly free, if We may not use the Libertie of
every one of you, and of every Subject, and receive advice (without
their danger who shall give it) from any person known or unknown,
sworn or unsworn, in these matters in which the Manage of Our Vote
is trusted by the Law, to Our own Judgement and Conscience, which
how best to inform, is (and ever shall be) left likewise to Us; and most
unreasonable it were that two Estates, proposing something to the
Third, that Third should be bound to take no advice, whether it were
fit to passe, but from those two that did propose it. We shall ever in
these things which are trusted wholly to Us by the Law, not decline to
hearken to the Advice of Our great Councell, and shall use to hear
willingly the free debates of Our Privie Councell (whensoever We
may be suffered to have them for sending for) and they shall not be
terrified from that freedom, by Votes (and Brands of Malignants, and
Enemies to the State, for advising what no Law forbids to advise) but
We will retain Our Power of admitting no more to any Councell than
the Nature of the businesse requires, and of discoursing with whom
We please, of what We please, and informing Our Understanding
by debate with any Persons, who may be well able to Inform and Advise Us in some particular, though their Qualities, Education or other
Abilities may not make them so fit to be of Our sworn Councell, and
not tie Ourself up not to hear anymore than twenty five (and those
not chosen absolutely by Us) out of a Kingdom so replenished with
Judicious and Experienced Persons in severall kindes. And though

we shall (with the proportionable Consideration due to them) alwayes weigh the Advices both of Our Great and Privie Councell, yet
We shall also look upon their Advices, as Advices, not as Commands
or Impositions; upon them as Our Councellors, not as Our Tutors
and Guardians, and upon Ourself as their King, not as their Pupill,
or Ward. For whatsoever of Regality were by the Modesty of Interpretation left in Us in the first part of the second Demand, as to the
Parliament, is taken from Us in the second part of the same, and
placed in this new fangled kinde of Councellors, whose power is
such, and so expressed by it, that in all publike Acts concerning the
Affairs of this Kingdom, which are proper for Our Privy Councell
(for whose Advice all publike Acts are sometimes proper, though
never necessary) they are desired to be admitted joint Patentees
with Us in the Regalitie, and it is not plainly expressed whether they
mean Us so much as a single Vote in these Affairs. But it is plain they
mean Us no more at most than a single Vote in them, and no more
power than every one of the rest of Our Fellow Councellors; only
leave to Us, out of their respect and duty, (and that only is left of all
Our ancient Power) a Choice, whether these that are thus to be
joined with (or rather set over) Us, shall be fifteen; or twenty five; and
great care is taken that the Oath which these Men shall take, shall
be such, in the framing the form of which (though sure We are not
wholly unconcerned in it) We may be wholly excluded, and that
wholly reserved to be agreed upon by both Houses of Parliament.

And to shew that no more Care is taken of Our safetie, than of
Our Power, after so great indignities offered to Us, and countenanced
by those who were most obliged to resent them: After Our Town and
Fort[13] kept from Us (from which, if it were no otherwise Ours than
the whole Kingdom is, We can no more legally be kept out, than out
of Our whole Kingdom, which sure yourselves will not deny to be

---

13. The King is referring here to Hull.

Treason). Our Arms, Our Goods sent away, and Our Money stopt from Us, Our Guards (in which We have no other Intention than to hinder the end of these things from being proportionable to their beginnings) are not only desired to be dismissed before satisfaction for the Injurie, punishments of the Injurers, and care taken for Our future Securitie from the like. But it is likewise desired (and for this Law is pretended, and might as well have been for the rest, which yet with some ingenuitie are it seems acknowledged to be but Desires of Grace) that We shall not for the future raise any Guards or extraordinarie Forces, but in case of actuall Rebellion or Invasion, which if it had been Law, and so observed in the time of Our famous Predecessors, few of those Victories which have made this Nation famous in other parts, could have been legally atchieved, nor could Our blessed Predecessor Queen *Elizabeth* have so defended Herself in 88. And if no Forces must be levied till Rebellions and Invasions (which will not stay for the calling of Parliaments, and their consent for raising Forces) be actuall, they must undoubtedly (at least most probably) be effectuall and prevalent.

And as neither care is taken for Our Rights, Honour, nor safetie as a Prince, so Our Rights as a private Person are endeavoured to be had from Us, it being asked, that it may be unlawfull and unpunishable, not only to *conclude,* but even to *treat of any Marriage with any Person for Our own Children, or to place Governours about them, without consent of Parliament, and in the intermission of those, without the consent of Our good Lords of the Councell,* that We may not only be in a more despicable state than any of Our Predecessors, but in a meaner and viler condition than the lowest of Our Subjects, who value no libertie they have more, than that of the free Education and Marriage of their Children, from which We are asked to debar Ourself, and have the more reason to take it ill, that We are so, because for Our choice of a Governour for Our Son, and of a Husband for Our Daughter (in which the Protestant Religion was Our principall

Consideration) We conceived We had reason to expect your present thanks, and the increase of your future trusts.

We suppose these Demands by this time to appear such as the Demanders cannot be supposed to have any such reall fear of Us as hath been long pretended, they are too much in the style, not only of equals, but of Conquerors, and as little to be intended for removing of Jealousies (for which end they are said to be asked, and that is not as Merchants ask at first much more than they will take, but as most necessary to effect it, which (if they be) God help this poor Kingdom, and those who are in the hands of such Persons, whose Jealousies nothing else will remove) which indeed is such a way, as if there being differences and suits between two persons, whereof one would have from the other serverall parcells of his ancient Land, he should propose to him by way of Accommodation, that he would quit to him all those in question, with the rest of his Estate, as the most necessary and effectuall means to remove all those suits and differences. But we call God to witnesse, that as for Our Subjects' sake these Rights are vested in Us, so for their sakes, as well as for Our own, We are resolved not to quit them, nor to subvert (though in a Parliamentary way) the ancient, equall, happy, well-poised, and never-enough commended Constitution of the Government of this Kingdom, nor to make Ourself of a King of *England* a Duke of *Venice*, and this of a Kingdom a Republique.

There being three kindes of Government amongst men, Absolute Monarchy, Aristocracy and Democracy, and all these having their particular conveniencies and inconveniencies. The experience and wisdom of your Ancestors hath so moulded this out of a mixture of these, as to give to this Kingdom (as far as human prudence can provide) the conveniencies of all three, without the inconveniencies of any one, as long as the Balance hangs even between the three Estates, and they run jointly on in their proper Chanell (begetting Verdure and Fertilitie in the Meadows on both sides) and the overflowing of either on either side raise no deluge or Inundation. The ill of absolute Monarchy is Tyrannie, the ill of Aristocracy is Faction and Division, the ills of Democracy are Tumults, Violence and Licentiousnesse. The good of Monarchy is the uniting a Nation under one Head to resist Invasion from abroad, and Insurrection at home. The good of Aristocracie is the Conjuncion of Counsell in the ablest Persons of a State for the publike benefit. The good of Democracy is Liberty, and the Courage and Industrie which Libertie begets.

In this Kingdom the Laws are jointly made by a King, by a House of Peers, and by a House of Commons chosen by the People, all having free Votes and particular Priviledges. The Government according to these Laws is trusted to the King, Power of Treaties of War and Peace, of making Peers, of chusing Officers and Councellors for State, Judges for Law, Commanders for Forts and Castles, giving Commissions for raising men to make War abroad, or to prevent or provide against Invasions or Insurrections at home, benefit of Confiscations, power of pardoning, and some more of the like kinde are placed in the King. And this kinde of regulated Monarchie having this power to preserve that Authoritie, without which it would be disabled to preserve the Laws in their Force, and the Subjects in their Liberties and Proprieties, is intended to draw to him such a Respect and Relation from the great Ones, as may hinder the ills of Division and Faction, and such a Fear and Reverence from the people, as may hinder Tumults, Violence, and Licenciousnesse. Again, that the Prince may not make use of this high and perpetuall power to the hurt of those for whose good he hath it, and make use of the name of Publike Necessitie for the gain of his private Favourites and Followers, to the detriment of his People, the House of Commons (an excellent Conserver of Libertie, but never intended for any share in Government, or the chusing of them that should govern) is solely intrusted with the first Propositions concerning the Levies of Moneys (which is the sinews as well of Peace, as War) and the Impeaching of those, who for their own ends, though countenanced by any surreptitiously gotten Command of the King, have violated that Law, which he is bound (when he knows it) to protect, and to the protection of which they were bound to advise him, at least not to serve him in the Contrary. And the Lords being trusted with a Judicatory power, are an excellent Screen and Bank between the Prince and People, to assist each against any Incroachments of the other, and by just Judgements to preserve that Law, which ought to be the Rule of every one of the three. For the better enabling them in this, beyond the Examples of any of Our Ancestors, We were willingly contented to Oblige Ourself, both to call a Parliament every three yeers, and not to dissolve it in fiftie dayes, and for the present exigent, the better to raise Money, and avoid the pressure (no lesse grievous to Us than them) Our people must have suffered by a longer continuance of so vast a charge as two great Armies, and for their greater certaintie of having sufficient time to remedie the inconveniencies arisen during so long an absence of Parliaments, and for the punishment of the Causers and Ministers of them, We yeelded up Our Right of dissolving this Parliament, expecting an extraordinarie moderation from it in gratitude for so unexampled a Grace, and little looking that any *Malignant Partie* should have been encouraged or enabled to have perswaded them, first to countenance the Injustices and Indignities We have endured, and then by a new way of satisfaction for what was taken from Us, to demand of Us at once to Confirm what was so taken, and to give up almost all the rest.

Since therefore the Power Legally placed in both Houses is more than sufficient to prevent and restrain the power of Tyrannie, and without the power which is now asked from Us, we shall not be able to discharge that Trust which is the end of Monarchie, since this would be a totall Subversion of the Fundamentall Laws, and that excellent Constitution of this Kingdom, which hath made this Nation so many yeers both famous and happie to a great degree of Envie;

since to the power of punishing (which is alreadie in your hands according to Law) if the power of Preferring be added, We shall have
nothing left for Us, but to look on; since the incroaching of one of
these Estates upon the power of the other, is unhappie in the effects
both to them and all the rest; since this power of at most a joint Government in Us with Our Councellors (or rather Our Guardians) will
return Us to the worst kinde of Minoritie, and make Us despicable
both at home and abroad, and beget eternall Factions and Dis-
sentions (as destructive to publike Happinesse as War) both in the
chosen, and the Houses that chuse them, and the people who chuse
the Chusers; since so new a power will undoubtedly intoxicate persons who were not born to it, & beget not only Divisions among
them as equals, but in them contempt of Us as become an equall to
them, and Insolence and Injustice towards Our people, as now so
much their inferiors, which will be the more grievous unto them, as
suffering from those who were so lately of a neerer degree to themselves, and being to have redresse only from those that placed them,
and fearing they may be inclined to preserve what they have made,
both out of kindnesse and policie; since all great changes are extreamly inconvenient, and almost infallibly beget yet greater changes,
which beget yet greater Inconveniencies.

Since as great an one in the Church must follow this of the Kingdom; Since the second Estate would in all probabilitie follow the Fate
of the first, and by some of the same turbulent spirits Jealousies
would be soon raised against them, and the like Propositions for reconciliation of Differences would be then sent to them, as they now
have joined to send to Us, till (all power being vested in the House of
Commons, and their number making them incapable of transacting
Affairs of State with the necessary Secrecie and Expedition; those
being retrusted to some close Committee) at last the Common people (who in the meantime must be flattered, and to whom Licence
must be given in all their wilde humours, how contrary soever to es-

tablished Law, or their own reall Good) discover this *Arcanum Imperii*, That all this was done by them, but not for them, grow weary of Journey-work, and set up for themselves, call Parity and Independence, Liberty; devour that Estate which had devoured the rest; Destroy all Rights and Proprieties, all distinctions of Families and Merit; And by this meanes this splendid and excellently distinguished form of Government, end in a dark equall *Chaos* of Confusion, and the long Line of Our many noble Ancestors in a *Jack Cade*, or a *Wat Tyler*.[14]

For all these Reasons to all these Demands Our Answer is, *Nolumus Leges Angliae mutari*.[15] But this We promise, that We will be as carefull of preserving the Laws in what is supposed to concern wholly Our Subjects, as in what most concerns Ourself. For indeed We professe to beleeve, that the preservation of every Law concerns Us, those of Obedience being not secure, when those of Protection are violated. And We being most of any injured in the least violation of that, by which We enjoy the highest Rights and greatest Benefits, and are therefore obliged to defend no lesse by Our Interest, than by Our Duty, and hope that no Jealousies to the contrary shall be any longer nourished in any of Our good people, by the subtill insinuations, and secret practices of men, who for private ends are disaffected to Our Honour and Safety, and the Peace and Prosperity of Our People. And to shew you, that no just indignation at so reproachfull offers shall make Us refuse to grant what is probable to conduce to the good of Our good People, because of the ill company it comes in, We will search carefully in this heap of unreasonable Demands, for so much as We may (complying with Our Conscience, and the duty of Our Trust) assent unto, and shall accordingly agree to it.

In pursuance of which Search, in the fourth Proposition, under a

14. Jack Cade led the Kentish rebellion of 1450, and Wat Tyler led the Great Peasant Rebellion of 1381. Both men were commoners.
15. We do not wish the Laws of England to be changed.

Demand which would take from Us that trust which God, Nature, and the Laws of the Land have placed in Us, and of which none of you could endure to be deprived, We find something to which We give this Answer, That We have committed the principall places about Our Children to persons of Qualitie, Integritie and Pietie, with speciall regard that their tender yeers might be so seasoned with the Principles of the true Protestant Religion, as (by the blessing of God upon this Our care) this whole Kingdom may in due time reap the fruit thereof. And as We have been likewise very carefull in the choice of Servants about them, that none of them may be such, as by ill Principles, or by ill Examples to crosse Our endeavours for their Pious and Vertuous Education, so if there shall be found (for all Our care to prevent it) any person about Our Children (or about Us, which is more than you ask) *against whom both Houses* shall make appear to Us *any just exception,* We shall not only *remove* them, but thank you for the Information. Only We shall expect, that you shall be likewise carefull that there be no underhand dealing by any to seek faults, to make room for others to succeed in their places.

For the fifth Demand, as We will not suffer any to share with Us in Our power of Treaties, which are most improper for Parliaments, and least in those Treaties in which We are neerliest concerned, not only as a King but as a Father, yet We do (such is Our desire to give all reasonable satisfaction) assure you by the word of a King, that We shall never propose or entertain any Treaty whatsoever for the marriage of any of Our Children, without due regard to the true Protestant Profession, the good of Our Kingdoms, and the Honour of Our Family.

For the sixth Demand, concerning *the Laws in force against Jesuites, Priests, and Popish Recusants,* We have by many of Our Messages to you, by Our voluntarie promise to you so solemnly made never to pardon any Popish Priest, by Our strict Proclamations lately published in this point, and by the publike Examples which We have made in that case since Our Residence at *York,* and before at *London,* sufficiently expressed Our Zeal herein. Why do you then ask that in which Our own Inclination hath prevented you? And if you can yet finde any more effectuall Course to disable them from Disturbing the State or eluding the Law by trusts or otherwise, We shall willingly give Our Consent to it.

For the seventh, concerning *the Votes of Popish Lords,* We understand that they in discretion have withdrawn themselves from the Service of the House of Peers, (and had done so when use was publikely made of their names to asperse the Votes of that House, which was then counted as Malignant as those (who are called *Our Unknown and Unsworn Councellors*) are now) neither do We conceive that such a positive Law against the Votes of any whose blood give them that right, is so proper in regard of the Priviledge of Parliament, but are content, that so long as they shall not be conformable to the Doctrine and Discipline of the Church of *England,* they shall not be admitted to sit in the House of Peers, but only to give their Proxies to such Protestant Lords as they shall chuse, who are to dispose of them as they themselves shall think fit, without any Reference at all to the Giver.

As to the desires for *a Bill for the Education of the Children of Papists by Protestants in the Protestant Profession,* many about Us can witnesse with Us, That We have often delivered Our Opinion, That such a Course (with God's blessing upon it) would be the most effectuall for the rooting out of Popery out of this Kingdom. We shall therefore thank you for it, and encourage you in it, and, when it comes unto Us, do Our Dutie; and We heartily wish, for the publike good, that the time you have spent in making Ordinances without Us, had been imployed in preparing this and other good Bills for Us.

For the eighth, touching *The Reformation to be made of the Church-Government and Liturgie,* We had hoped, that what We had formerly declared concerning the same, had been so sufficiently understood by you and all good Subjects, that We should not need to have expressed Ourself further in it. We told you in Our Answers to your Petition presented to Us at *Hampton-Court* the first of December, *That for any illegall Innovations which may have crept in, We should willingly concur in the removall of them. That if Our Parliament should advise Us to call a Nationall Synode, which may duely examine such Ceremonies as give just cause of Offence to any, We should take it into Consideration, and apply Ourself to give due satisfaction therein. That We were perswaded in our Conscience, That no Church could be found upon the Earth, that professeth the true Religion with more puritie of Doctrine, than the Church of* England *doth, nor where the Government and Discipline are jointly more beautified, and free from Superstition, than as they are here established by Law;* which (by the grace of God) We will with Constancie maintain (while We live) in their Puritie and Glorie, not only against all Invasions of Poperie, but also from the Irreverence of those many Schismaticks and Separatists, wherewith of late this Kingdom and Our City of *London* abounds, to the great dishonour and hazard both of Church and State; For the suppression of whom We required your timely and active assistance. We told you in Our first Declaration,[16] printed by the advice of Our Privie Councell, *That for differences amongst ourselves for matters indifferent in their own nature concerning Religion, We should in tendernesse to any number of our loving Subjects very willingly comply with the advice of our Parliament, that some Law might be made for the exemption of tender Consciences from punishment, or Prosecution for such Ceremonies, and in such Cases, which by the judgement of most men are held to be matters indifferent, and of some to be absolutely unlawfull; Provided, that this case should be attempted and pursued with that modestie, temper, and submission, that in the meantime the peace and quiet of the Kingdom be not disturbed, the Decencie and Comelinesse of God's Service disconte-*

---

16. "His Majesties Message to both Houses of Parliament: February 14, 1641" (London, 14 February 1641/2), Wing C2451.

nanced, nor the Pious, Sober, Devout actions of those Reverend Persons who were the first Labourers in the blessed Reformation, or of that time, be scandalled and defamed. And We heartily wish, that others, whom it concerned, had been as ready (as their duty bound them, though they had not received it from Us) to have pursued this Caution, as We were, and still are willing and ready to make good every particular of that Promise. Nor did We only appear willing to join in so good a Work, when it should be brought Us, but prest and urged you to it by Our Message of the fourteenth of February, in these words, *And because His Majestie observes great and different troubles to arise in the hearts of His People, concerning the Government and Liturgie of the Church, His Majestie is willing to declare, That He will refer the whole consideration to the wisdom of his Parliament, which He desires them to enter into speedily, that the present distractions about the same may be composed: but desires not to be pressed to any single Act on His part, till the whole be so digested and setled by both Houses, that His Majesty may cleerly see what is fit to be left, as well as what is fit to be taken away.* Of which We the more hoped of a good sucesse to the generall satisfaction of Our people, because you seem in this Proposition to desire but a *Reformation,* and not (as is daily preached for as necessary in those many Conventicles which have within these nineteene months begun to swarm; and which, though their Leaders differ from you in this opinion, yet appear to many as countenanced by you, by not being punished by you, (few else, by reason of the Order of the House of Commons of the ninth of September, daring to do it) a destruction of the present Discipline and Liturgie. And We shall most cheerfully *give Our best assistance for raising a sufficient maintenance for preaching Ministers,* in such course as shall be most for the encouragement and advancement of Pietie and Learning.

For the Bills you mention, and the Consultation you intimate, knowing nothing of the particular matters of the one (though We like the Titles well) nor of the manner of the other, but from an Informer (to whom We give little credit, and We wish no man did more) common Fame, We can say nothing till We see them.

For the eleventh, We would not have the *Oath of all Privie Councellors and Judges* straitened to particular Statutes of one or two particular Parliaments, but extend to all Statutes of all Parliaments, and the whole Law of the Land, and shall willingly consent *that an enquirie of all the breaches and violations of the Law may be given in charge by the Justices of the King's Bench every Terme, and by the Judges of Assize in their Circuits, and Justices of Peace at the Sessions to be presented and punished according to Law.*

For the seventeenth, we shall ever be most ready, (and we are sorry it should be thought needfull to move us to it) not only to joine with any (particularly *with the States of the united Provinces,* of which We have given a late proofe in the Match of Our Daughter) *for the defence and maintenance of Protestant Religion, against all designes and attempts of the Pope and his Adherents,* but singly (if need were) to oppose with Our life and fortune *all such Designes* in all other Nations, were they joined: And that for Considerations of Conscience, far more than any temporall end *of obtaining accesse of strength & reputation,* or any naturall end *of restoring our Royall Sister and her Princely Issue to their dignities and Dominions* though these be likewise much considered by us.

For the eighteenth, It was not Our fault, that an Act was not passed *to cleere the Lord* Kimbolton, *and the five Members of the House of Commons,* but yours, who inserted such Clauses into both the Preamble and Act (perhaps perswaded to it by some who wish not that you should in anything receive satisfaction from Us) as by passing the Preamble we must have wounded Our Honour against Our Conscience, and by another Clause have admitted a Consequence, from which We could never have been secured, by declaring, *That no Member of either House, upon any Accusation of Treason, could have his*

Person seized without the Consent of that House, of which he is a Member, though the known Law be, *That Priviledge of Parliament extends not to Treason,* and if it did, any Member (the House being for a short time adjourned, and so their Consent not being so had) how treasonable soever his Intentions were, how cleerly soever known, and how suddenly soever to be executed, must have fair leave given him to go on and pursue them, no way, how legall soever, after the passing such a Clause, being left to prevent it.

To conclude, We conjure you and all men to rest satisfied with the truth of Our Professions, and the Realitie of Our Intentions, not to ask such things as deny themselves; That you declare against Tumults, and punish the Authors; That you allow Us Our Propriety in Our Towns, Arms and Goods, and Our share in the Legislative Power, which would be counted in Us, not only breach of Priviledge, but Tyrannie and Subversion of Parliaments to deny to you. And when you shall have given Us satisfaction upon those persons who have taken away the One, and recalled those Declarations (particularly that of the six and twentieth of *May*) and those in the point of the *Militia,* (Our just Rights, wherein We will no more part with than with Our Crown, lest We inable others by them to take that from Us) which would take away the other, and declined the beginnings of a War against Us, under pretence of Our Intention of making One against you. As We have never opposed the first part of the thirteenth Demand, so We shall be ready to concur with you in the latter.

And being then confident that the Credit of those Men, who desire a generall Combustion, will be so weakened with you, that they will not be able to do this Kingdom any more harm, We shall be willing to grant Our generall Pardon, with such Exceptions as shall be thought fit, and shall receive much more joy in the hope of a full and constant Happinesse of Our People in the True Religion, and under the Protection of the Law, by a blessed Union betwen Us and Our Parliament (so much desired by Us) than in any such increase of Our Own Revenue (how much soever beyond former Grants) as (when Our Subjects were wealthiest) Our Parliament could have setled upon Us.

FINIS.

Henry Ferne, 1602–1662

THE

RESOLVING

OF

CONSCIENCE,

Upon this Question.

Whether upon such a Supposition or Case, as is now usually made
(The King will not discharge his trust but is bent or seduced to
subvert Religion, Laws, and Liberties) Subjects may take Arms
and resist? and whether that case be now?

RESOLVED,

I. *That no Conscience upon such a Supposition or Case can finde a safe and cleare
ground for such resistance.*

II. *That no man in Conscience can be truly perswaded, that the resistance now made
is such, as they themselves pretend to, that plead for it in such a case.*

III. *That no man in Conscience can be truly perswaded that such a case is now,* that
is, *that the King will not discharge his trust but is bent to subvert,* &c.

Whence it followeth,

That the resistance now made against the higher Power is unwarrantable, and
according to the Apostle Damnable, *Rom.* 1 3.

Also that the shedding of bloud in the pursuit of this resistance is Murder.

By H. FERN D.D. &c

*Woe unto them that call evil good, and good evill, that put darknesse for light,
and light for darknesse,* Isa. 5. 20.
O my soule come not thou into their secret. Gen. 49. 6.

Printed at *Cambridge,* and re-printed at
LO𝒳DON, 1642.

*H*enry Ferne, an Anglican divine, was born in York and educated at Cambridge University. He first came to Charles's attention when he preached before the king at Leicester in July 1642. Charles was so pleased with Ferne he made him his chaplain extraordinary, no ordinary chaplaincy then being vacant. That autumn Ferne's first pamphlet, "The Resolving of Conscience upon This Question," one of the first tracts openly on the king's side, was published. In it Ferne wrestled with the no longer theoretical dilemma of whether there was a right for a subject to resist a king and "whether that case be now?" The tract was published at Cambridge, York, and London in four further printings. It so incensed members of the Commons that Ferne was cited that Christmas Eve to answer for it. Instead he abandoned his living in Medbourne and took refuge with the royal party at Oxford where a "second edition" of the offending tract was published in 1643.

"The Resolving of Conscience" provoked a number of impressive replies. One by Charles Herle is reprinted below. Ferne attempted to address these, and in particular Herle's, on 18 April 1643, with a rebuttal, "Conscience Satisfied," far longer than his original essay. Other works followed earning for their author a reputation as the leading royalist writer of the period. In 1644 Ferne was one of five clergymen sent to defend Anglican church government in a debate with parliamentary clergy. After the surrender of the king in 1646 Ferne retired to Yorkshire. There he remained until summoned to the Isle of Wight in 1648 by Charles, where, on 28 November, he preached the last sermon the king would hear before his trial.

Ferne lived quietly in Yorkshire writing religious treatises until the Restoration when he was rewarded with the mastership of Trinity College, Cambridge. During the eighteen months he held this post he twice served as vice-chancellor of the university. He was created bishop of Chester in 1662 but died five weeks later.

The Resolving of Conscience, Touching the Unlawfulnesse of the Warre and Resistance Now Made Against the King.

Lamentable are the distractions of this Kingdome, and the more, because they gather strength from the name and authority of (that, which as it is of high esteeme with all, so should it be a remedy to all these our distempers) a Parliament: and from the pretended defence of those things that are most deare unto us, Religion, Liberties, Laws. Whereupon so many good people, that have come to a sense of Religion and godlinesse, are miserably carried away by a strange implicite faith to beleeve, that whatsoever is said or done in the name of a Parliament, and in the pretended defence of Religion, Liberties, Lawes, to be infallibly true, and altogether just.

But he that will consider, men are men, and would seeke a surer rule for his conscience than the Traditions or Ordinances of men taken hand over head, shall upon reasonable examination find upon what plausible but groundlesse principles, upon what faire but deceiving pretences, upon what grievous but causelesse imputations laid upon Majestie itself, a poore people are drawn into Arms against the duty and allegiance they owe to their Prince by the Laws of God and man. For directing the Conscience in such an examination this ensuing Discourse is framed as briefly and plainly as the matter will permit.

Sect. I.

Conscience in resolving upon a question, first layes down the Proposition or Principle or Ground on which it goes; then it assumes or applies to the present case; then it concludes and resolves: as in this question, affirmatively for Resistance, thus, Subjects in such a case may arm and resist. But that case is now come. Therefore now they may and doe justly resist.

Or negatively against Resistance, either by denying the Principle: Subjects may not in such a case arm and resist; therefore now they doe not justly resist. Or by admitting the Principle and denying the Case; Subjects in such a case may arm and resist. But that case is not now. Therefore now they do not justly arm and resist.

What it is that Conscience is here to admit or deny, and how it ought to conclude and resolve, this ensuing Treatise will discover: which that it may more clearly appeare, we will premise,

First, that in the Proposition or Principle by the word *Resistance* is meant, not a denying of obedience to the Prince's command, but a rising in arms, a forcible resistance. This though clear enough in the question, yet I thought fit to insinuate, to take off that false imputation laid upon the Divines of this Kingdom & upon all those that appear for the King in this cause, that they endeavoured to defend an absolute power in him, and to raise him to an Arbitrary way of government. This we are as much against on his part, as against Resistance on the subjects' part. For we may & ought to deny obedience to such commands of the Prince, as are unlawfull by the law of God yea, by the established Laws of the Land. For in these we have his will and consent given upon good advice, and to obey him against the Laws, were to obey him against himselfe, his sudden will against his deliberate will; but a far other matter it is to resist by power of arms, as is in the question implied, and as we see at this day to our astonishment, first the power of arms taken from the Prince by setting up the *Militia*,[1] then that power used against him by an army in the field.

Secondly, we must consider that they which plead for Resistance in such a case as is supposed do grant it must be concluded upon, *Omnibus ordinibus regni consentientibus* that is, with the generall and unanimous consent of the Members of the two Houses of the repre-

---

1. Ferne is referring to the Militia Ordinance passed by the two houses of Parliament on 5 March 1642.

sentative body of the whole Kingdom. Also they yeeld it must be only *Legitima defensio*, a meer defensive resistance; and this also Conscience must take notice of.

Thirdly, it is considerable that in the supposition or case it is likewise granted by them, that the Prince must first be so and so disposed, and bent to overthrow Religion, Liberties Laws, and will not discharge his trust for the maintaining of them, before such a Resistance can be pretended to. And although the question is, and must be so put now, as that it seems to streighten the Case, and make it depend upon the supposall of the people; yet it so much the more enlarges the falshood of the Principle, for it plainly speaks thus; If subjects beleeve or verily suppose their Prince will change Religion they may rise in arms; whereas all that have pleaded for Resistance in case of Religion, did suppose another Religion enjoined upon the subject first. We will therefore endeavour to cleare all for the resolving of Conscience in these three generalls:

I. That no Conscience upon such a case as is supposed can find clear ground to rest upon for such resistance as is pretended to but according to the rules of Conscience, *What is not of faith is sin:* and, *In doubtfull things the safer way is to be chosen.* Conscience it will find cause to forbeare and to suffer, rather than resist; *doubtfull,* I say, not that a Conscience truly informed will not clearly see the unlawfulnesse of this Resistance but because no conscience can be truly perswaded of the lawfulnesse of it, and so that Conscience that resolves for it, must needs run doubtingly or blindly upon the worke.

II. That the resistance now used and made against the Prince is not such as they pretend to either for that generall and unanimous consent that should precede it, or that defensive way that should accompany it, according to their owne grants that plead for it and therefore Conscience cannot admit such a resistance as is made now adayes.

III. If Conscience could be perswaded, that it is lawfull in such a case to resist, and that this rising in arms is such a resistance as they say may in such a case be pretended to, yet can it never (if it be willing to know anything) be truly perswaded that such a case is now come, that is, That the King refuses to discharge his trust, is bent to overthrow Religion, &c. and therefore Conscience cannot but resolve, this Opposition and Resistance to be unlawfull, unwarrantable, and (according to the Apostle) damnable; and that people running into arms without sufficient warrant, commit murder if they shed bloud in the pursuit of this Resistance, and perish in their own sinne, if die in the cause.

Sect. II.

First then, that the Principle is untrue upon which they go that resist, and that Conscience cannot find clear ground to rest upon for making resistance: for it heares the Apostle expressely say, *Whosoever resists shall receive to themselves damnation:* and it cannot find any limitation in Scripture that will excuse the Resistance of these dayes.

The exception or limitation that is made, is taken from the Persons resisting, and the Causes of resistance, thus, They that are private persons and doe resist upon any cause receive damnation, but the States or representative body of the whole people may resist upon such or such causes. But how will this satisfie Conscience, when every distinction or limitation made upon any place of Scripture, must have its ground in Scripture; this has only some examples in Scripture that come not home to the cause and some appearances of Reason; which are easily refuted by clearer Scripture and Reason.

The examples alleged, are, I. The people's rescuing of *Jonathan* out of the hands of *Saul. Answ.* Here the people drew not into arms of themselves, but being there at *Saul's* command, did by a loving vio-

lence and importunitie hinder the execution of a particular and passionate unlawfull command.

II. *David's* resisting of *Saul. Answ. 1. David's* guard that hee had
about him was only to secure his person against the cut-throats of
Saul, if sent to take away his life. 2. It was a meer defence without all
violence offered to *Saul;* therefore he still gave place as *Saul* pursued,
and did no act of hostility to him or any of his Army when they were
in his power, *I Sam. 26.* But thirdly, because they gather out of the *I
Sam. 23.12* that *David* would have defended *Keilah* against *Saul,* if the
Inhabitants would have been faithfull to him. Wee say that's only an
uncertaine supposition not fit to ground Conscience in this great
point of resistance; also to this and all other David's demeanours, in
his standing out against Saul, we say his example was extraordinary;
for he was anointed and designed by the Lord to succeed *Saul,* and
therefore he might use an extraordinary way of safeguarding his
person.

These are the chiefe examples. They make use also of the high
Priests resisting the King in the temple, and *Elisha's* shutting the
doore against the King's Messenger that came to take away his head;
and the like; which speake not so much as the two former, having no
appearance of such resistance as is implied in the question. But wee
answer, 1. That of the high Priest is more pertinently applied to the
Pope's power of excommunicating and deposing Kings, than to this
power of resisting now used; but truly to neither. For he did no more
than what every Minister may and ought to doe if a King should attempt the administration of the Sacrament; that is, to reprove him, to
keep the Elements from him. Ambrose Bishop of Milain withstood
the Emperour at the entrance of God's house, not by Excommunication, much lesse by force of arms, but by letting him understand
hee was not fit for that place, there to be made partaker of the holy
things, till he had repented of that outrage and bloodshed at Thessa-
lonica. Upon which the Emperour withdrew.

The Priests here are said to thrust him out of the Temple; but we must note God's hand was first upon him smiting him with leprosie, and by that discharging him of the Kingdome also. It is added in the text, *yea himself also hasted to goe out.* But enough of this.

2. *Elisha's* example speaks very little. But let us thence take occasion to say, That Personall defence is lawfull against the sudden and illegall assaults of such Messengers; yea, of the Prince himself thus far, to ward his blowes, to hold his hands, and the like: not to endanger his person, not to return blows, no; for though it be naturall to defend a man's self, yet the whole Common-wealth is concerned in his person, as we see in the Common-wealth of the creatures, one particular nature will defend itself against another, but yeeld to the universall.

If this be drawn from personal defence to the publick resistance now used, as usually they make the Argument thus; If the body naturall, then the body politick may defend itself, if a private person much more the whole State may; and they doe but shut the way up against the King that comes to destroy his Parliament, and take away their heads.

We answer: As the naturall body defends itself against an outward force, but strives not by a schisme or contention within itself; so may the body politick against an outward power, but not as now by one part of it set against the Head and another part of the same body; for that tends to the dissolution of the whole. Again; Personall defence may be without all offence, and does not strike at the order and power that is over us, as generall resistance by Armes doth, which cannot be without many unjust violences, and does immediately strike at that order which is the life of a Commonwealth. And this makes a large difference betwixt *Elisha's* shutting the doore against this messenger, and their shutting up the way against the King by armed men; nor can they conclude upon such an intention in the King's heart without the Spirit of *Elisha.* He professeth hee intends no violence to

his Parliament, nor has he taken away the head of any of theirs that
have fallen into his power, nor does desire any other punishment inflicted upon any that do oppose him, than what a Legall tryall shall
adjudge them to, which no good Subject ought to decline.

Now let us see how Scripture excludes this and all other exceptions, giving no allowance to resistance, in regard of Persons or
Causes, or other pretences, and this not only by examples, but by precept, conclusions, Resolutions, which are more safe.

First, we have the two hundred and fifty Princes of the Congregation, gathering the people against *Moses* and *Aaron, Numb. 16.3* and
perishing in this sin. If it be replied, the persons indeed were publick, but there was no cause for it; *Moses* and *Aaron* did not deserve it.
I answer, but the other supposed they did, and that is now enough, it
seems, to make people not only say to their Prince, *You take too much
upon you*, but therefore to rise in armes also, which I hope will appeare to be without cause too in the end of this Treatise.

Secondly, see for the cause of Resistance, *I. Sam. 8.1*. there the people are let to understand how they should be oppressed under Kings,
yet all that violence and injustice that should be done unto them is no
just cause of resistance, for they have no remedy left them but crying
to the Lord, *vers. 18*.

Thirdly, we have not only example, but resolution and conclusion
out of Scripture. The people might not be gathered together either
for Civill assemblies, or for warre, but by his command that had the
power of the Trumpet, that is, the supreme as *Moses* was, *Numb. 10*.

Also when *David* had *Saul* and his army in his power, he resolves
the matter thus, *Who can stretch out his hand against the Lord's annointed and be guiltlesse, I Sam. 26.9*. If replied, now they intend not
hurt to the King's person; yet might not they as well have hurt his
person in the day of battell, as any of them that were swept away from
about him by the furie of the Ordnance, which puts no difference betwixt King and common souldiers?

This also I must observe concerning this point of resistance, out of the Old Testament (for from thence have they all their seeming instances). That it is a marvellous thing, that among so many Prophets reprehending the Kings of Israel and Judah for idolatry, cruelty, oppression, none should call upon the Elders of the people for this duty of Resistance.

But lastly, that place of the Apostle, *Rom. 13* at first mentioned does above all give us a clear resolution upon the point, which now I shall free from all exceptions.

First, I may suppose, that the King is the *Supreme*, as S. *Peter* calls him; or *the higher power*, as S. *Paul* here, though it be by some now put to the question, as one absurdity commonly begets another to defend it; but I prove it, S. *Peter's* distinction comprehends all that are in authority, *The King as supreme, and those that are sent by him, 1 Pet. 2.12* in which latter rank are the two Houses of Parliament, being sent by him, or sent for by him, and by his Writ sitting there. Also by the Oath of Supremacy it is acknowledged, that there is no power above him without or within this Realm; and that he is in all Causes and over all persons supreme. Also acknowledged by the Petitions of the two houses addressed unto his Majesty, wherein they style themselves *His loyall Subjects*. But enough of this.

Secondly, in the text of the Apostle, all persons under the higher power are expressely forbidden to resist. For *whosoever*, in the second verse, must be as large as the *every soul* in the first, and the resistance forbidden here concerns all upon whom the subject is injoined there, or else we could not make these universalls good against the Papists, exempting the Pope and Clergy from the subjection.

Thirdly, in those dayes there was a standing and continuall great Senate, which not long before had the supreme power in the Romane State, and might challenge more by the Fundamentalls of that State, than our great Councell (I think) will, or can. But now the Emperour being *Supreme*, S. *Peter* calls him; or the *higher power*, as S. *Paul* here, there is no power of resistance left to any that are under him, by the Apostle. This for the Persons that should resist, all are forbidden. Now considering the Cause.

Fourthly, was there ever more cause of resistance than in those dayes? Were not the Kings then not only conceived to be enclined so and so, but even actually were enemies to Religion, had overthrown Lawes and Liberties? And therefore if any should from the Apostle's reasons that he gives against resistance in the 3, 4, 5, verses, *(For Rulers are not a terrour to good works but evill, and he is the minister of God to thee for good)* reply, That Rulers so long as they are not a terrour to the good, but minister for our good, are not to be resisted. The consideration of those times leaves no place for such exception, because the Powers then (which the Apostle forbids to resist) were nothing so, but subverters of that which was good and just.

If it be replied, That prohibition was temporary and fit for those times, as it is said by some, I answer, 1. This is a new exception never heard of (I think) but in these times. 2. It is groundlesse, and against the Text, for the reasons of the prohibition in the 3, 4, 5, 6, verses, are perpetuall, from that order, that good, for which the powers are ordained of God, which will be of force as long as there is government, and will alwayes be reasons against resistance; because resistance (though it be made against abused powers as then they were) doth tend to the dissolution of that order, for which the power itself is set up of God. By which also that other distinction of theirs is made void, when as they reply, as they think, acutely, That they resist not the power, but the abuse of the power.

It is also answered by some, that the Emperors then were absolute Monarchs, and therefore not to be resisted. I answer: They did indeed rule absolutely and arbitrarily, which should have, according to the principles of these dayes, been a stronger motive to resist. But how did they make themselves of Subjects such absolute Monarchs, was it not by force and change of the government, and was not the right of the people & Senate (according to the Principles of these days) good against them with as much or more reason, than the right of the people of this Land is against the succession of this Crown descending by three Conquests?[2] And this I speak not to win an Arbitrary power or such as Conquerours use, unto this Crown, but only to shew that Resistance can be no more made against the Kings of *England,* than it could against those Emperours. Nay, with lesse reason against them, than these.

Lastly, it is replied, That Christian Religion was then enacted against by Law; but the Religion contended for is established by Law. I answer: But is the Religion established denied to any that now fight for it? Shall the Apostle's prohibition be good against Christians in the behalfe of actuall Tyrants persecuting that Religion, and not against Subjects freely enjoying the Religion established? Or may Protestants upon a jealousie resist a Protestant King professing the same Religion, and promising to conserve it entire to them?

2. The prohibition does not only concern Christians, but all the people under those Emperours, and not only Religion was persecuted, but liberties also lost, the people and Senate were enslaved by Edicts and Lawes then inforced upon them, & they (according to the principles of these dayes) might resist, notwithstanding the Apostles' prohibition, & the Laws then forced upon them; or else the State, as they usually say, had not means to provide for its safety. Thus one fancy of theirs thwarts another, because both are groundless. But more anon of those means of safty they suppose to be in every State, by the power of Resistance.

2. This statement is a reference to the theory that a conquered people have only those rights the conqueror chooses to bestow upon them. The English, according to Ferne's reckoning, having been conquered no less than three times, would have no claim to inherent ancient rights.

Hitherto of Scripture, which is most powerful against Resistance, in the prohibition & the reasons of it, by which Conscience will clearly see, it can have no warrant from Scripture for Resistance. Now let us try what Reason can enforce.

Sect. III.

For proving this Power of resistance, there is much speech used about the Fundamentals of this government, which because they lie low and unseen by vulgar eyes, being not written Lawes, the people are easily made to believe they are such as they (that have power to build new Laws upon them) say they are. And indeed none so fit to judge of them as they. Yet this we know, and every one that can use his reason knows, that the Fundamentalls must needs be such as will bear the settled government of this Land, such as are not contradictory to the written established Laws: but both the government we see used in this Land, and the written Laws which we reade, must have a correspondency and analogie of reason to these, Fundamentalls, and they to these.

Well then, they that plead for power of resistance in the people, lay the first ground work of their Fundamentals thus: Power is originally in and from the people and if when by election they have intrusted a Prince with the power, he will not discharge his trust, then it falls to the people; or, as in this Kingdom, to the two houses of Parliament (the representative body of the people) to see to it; they may reassume the power.

This is the bottom of their Fundamentals as they are now discovered to the people. But here we may take notice by the way, that however the Fundamentals of this Government are much talked of, this is according to them the Fundamentall in all Kingdomes and Governments; for they say power was everywhere from the people at first, and so this will serve no more for the power of resistance in England, than in France or Turkey. But if this must be a Fundamentall, it is such a one as upon it this Government cannot be built, but Confusion and Anarchy may readily be raised; as shall appear by the clearing of these two particulars, Whether the power be so originally and chiefly from the people as they would have it; then, Whether they may upon such causes reassume that power.

First, of the originall of power, which they will have so from the people, that it shall be from God only by a kind of permissive approbation, as we may see by the Observator, and all other that plead for this power of resistance. Wee must here distinguish what the writers of the other side seeme to confound, to wit, *the Power* itselfe, (which is a sufficiency of authority for command and coercion in the governing of a people) from the *designing of the Person* to beare that power, and the *qualification* of that power according to the divers wayes of executing it in severall forms of government; and then we grant that the designing of the person is sometimes from the people by choice, and that the power of the Prince receiving qualification by joint consent of himselfe and the people, is limited by the laws made with such consent; but the power itself is of God originally and chiefly, which we prove by Scripture and Reason.

First, by such places of Scripture as plainly shew an ordaining and appointing, rather than a permission or approbation:

1. The Apostle speaks it expresly, *The powers are of God,* Rom. 13.1 and *the ordinance of God,* v. 2. S. Peter indeed saith, *every ordinance of man,* I Epist. 2. but *of man* there, and *of God* here is much differing; there it is ἀνθρωπίνῃ, of man, *subjective,* that is, every ordinance or power set up amongst men; but here it is ἀπὸ θεοῦ, of God, *causaliter,*[3] that is, from him, his ordinance; and if in that ἀνθρωπίνῃ there be implied any creation or causality, or invention of man, it respects the qualification of the power according to the forms of sever-

---

3. Causally.

all governments and offices in them, which are from the invention of man; it does not make the power itselfe the creation of man, which is the constitution and ordinance of God. And men are not only naturally bent to society, but also are bound, as they are reasonable creatures, to set up and live under government, as under an order of that providence by which the world is governed.

2. He is called the *minister of God,* v. 4. but if so from the people and no otherwise from god than they would have him, he should be *minister populi* rather; he is indeed their minister for their good, which makes the people to be the end of this governing power, not the fountain and originall of it. Therefore the necessity of subjection urged in v. 5. has a double ground *the ordinance of God,* whose ministers Rulers are, there's the fountain and originall of power to govern; then *the people's good,* upon which Rulers ought to attend, that is an end of the governing power.

3. To the same purpose speake those other places, *by me Kings reign:* and, *I have said, ye are Gods,* Psa. 82. in relation to which our Saviour saith, Joh. 10. *they are called Gods to whom the word of God came,* that *dixi,* that *word* is the command, the issuing out as it were the commission for the setting up of a governing power among the people.

These places cannot be satisfied with that poor part, they on the other side leave to God in the setting up of power for the governing of men, that is, to approve it when the people have created or invented it. Indeed if we consider the qualification of this governing power, and the manner of executing it according to the severall formes of government, we granted it before to be the invention of man, and when such a qualification or forme is orderly agreed upon, we say it hath God's permissive approbation.

And therefore the imputation is causeless which the Pleaders on the other side doe heedlessely and ignorantly lay upon us Divines, as if wee cried up Monarchy, and that only government to be *jure di-*

vino. For although Monarchy has this excellency, that the Government God set up over his people in the person of Moses, the Judges, and the Kings, was Monarchicall; yet we confesse that neither that, nor Aristocracy, or any other forme is *jure divino*, but we say the power itself, or that sufficiency of Authority to govern, which is in Monarchy or Aristocracie, abstractly considered from the qualifications of either form, is an efflux or constitution subordinate to that providence, an ordinance of that *Dixi*, that silent *Word* by which the world was at first made, and is still governed under God.

Secondly, as this appeares by the former places of Scripture, so is it also suitable to Reason. Because God doth govern all creatures, Reasonable as well as Unreasonable; the inferiour or lower world he governs by the heavens or superiour bodies, according to those influences and powers he has put into them; and the reasonable creatures, Men, he governs too by others set up in his stead over them: for which they are called *Gods,* because in his stead over the people: and the powers are said to be ὑπὸ θεοῦ τεταγμέναι, *Rom. 13.1.* not only ἀπὸ θεοῦ *from God,* but also as orders ranked under him too, subordinate to that providence by which all creatures are governed.

These his Ministers he sometimes designed immediately by himself, as Moses, the Judges, Saul, David, &c. Now he designes his Vicegerents on earth mediately as by election of the people, by succession or inheritance, by conquest, &c. To conclude, The power itselfe of government is of God, however the person be designed, or that power qualified according to the severall formes or government by those Lawes that are established, or those grants that are procured for the people's security. Thus much of the originall of Power.

Sect. IIII.

Now we come to the Forfeiture, as I may call it, of this power. If the Prince, say they, will not discharge his trust, then it falls to the people or the two Houses (the representative body of the people) to see to it, and to reassume that power, and thereby to resist. This they conceive to follow upon the *derivation of power* from the people by vertue of election, and upon the *stipulation or covenant* of the Prince with the people, as also to be necessary in regard of those *meanes of safety*, which every State should have within itself. We will examine them in order, and shall find the arguments inconsequent.

Concerning the derivation of power, we answer, First, if it be not from the people, as they will have it, and as before it was cleared, then can there be no reassuming of this power by the people; that's plaine by their own argument.

Secondly, if the people should give the power so absolutely as they would have it, leaving nothing to God in it but approbation, yet could they not therefore have right to take that power away. For many things which are altogether in our disposing before we part with them, are not afterward in our power to recall; especially such in which there redounds to God an interest by the donation as in things devoted, though afterward they come to be abused. So although it were, as they would have it, that they give the power and God approves; yet because the Lord's hand also and his oile is upon the person elected to the Crown, & then he is the Lord's anointed, & the minister of God, whose hands of the people which were used in lifting him up to the Crown, may not again be lifted up against him, either to take the Crown from his head, or the sword out of his hand. This will not a true informed Conscience dare to doe.

Thirdly, how shall the Conscience be satisfied that this their argument, grounded upon election and the derivation of power from the people, can have place in this kingdom, when as the Crown not only descends by inheritance, but also has so often been setled by Conquest in the lines of Saxons, Danes, and Normans? In answering to this they look beyond all these, and say, the right is still good to the people by reason of their first election. I answer, So then that first election must be supposed here, & supposed good against all other titles, or else this power of resistance falls to the ground. It is probable indeed that Kings at first were by choice here as elswhere; but can Conscience rest upon such remote probabilities for resistance, or think that first election will give it power against Princes that do not claim by it. We tell them the Roman Emperours were not to be resisted, Rom. 13.2. They reply, as we had it above, that they were absolute Monarchs. But how came they of subjects to be absolute Monarchs? Was it any otherwise than by force and arms? The way that the Saxons, Danes, and Normans made themselves masters of this people, & was not the right of the people as good against them for the power of resistance by virtue of the first election, as well as of the people of this Land, against their Kings after so many conquests? This I speak, not as if the Kings of this Land might rule as conquerors, God forbid. But to shew this slender plea of the first election can no more take place against the Kings of this Land, than it could against the Roman Monarchs, especially according to their argument, that hold all power originally from the people, & that (as we observed above) to be the fundamentall of all government. Therefore whether Kings were in this Land at first by election or no, we acknowledge what belongs to the duty of a Prince in doing justice and equity. What Grants also, Lawes, Priviledges have since those conquests beene procured or restored to the people, unto all those the King is bound. But yet not bound under forfeiture of this power to the people, which now comes to be examined in that capitulation or convenant he is said to enter with the people.

In the next place therefore, That capitulation or covenant, and the oath which the Prince takes to confirme what he promiseth, are so alledged, as if the breach or non-performance on the Prince's part were a forfeiture of his power. But we answer, the words *capitulation* or *covenant* are now much used to make men believe the King's admittance to the Crown is altogether conditionall, as in the meerly elective kingdoms of Polonia, Swedeland, &c. whereas our King is King before he comes to the Coronation, which is sooner or later at his pleasure, but always to be in due time in regard of that security his people receive by his taking the oath, and he again mutually from them, in which performance there is something like a covenant, all but the forfeiture. The King there promises and binds himself by oath to performance. Could they in this covenant shew us such an agreement between the King and his people, that in case he will not discharge his trust, then it shall be lawfull for the States of the kingdome by armes to resist, and provide for the safety thereof, it were something.

If it be said, that so much is implied in the first election; we answer, we examined that slender plea of the first election above, as it was thought to be a derivation of power. Now as it is thought to have a covenant in it, we say, that usually in all Empires the higher we arise, the freer we find the Kings, & still downwards the people have gained upon them. For at first when people chose their Rulers, they did as Justine in the beginning of his history observes, resign themselves to be governed by such, of whose prudence and moderation they had experience, and then, *arbitria Principum pro legibus erant,* the will and discretion of the Prince was law unto the people; but men were men though in God's place, and therefore for the restraint of that power, with consent of the Prince, such Lawes have beene still procured by the people, as might make for their security.

Now from a promise the king makes for doing justice (the duty of every Prince) for the continuing those priviledges, immunities, that have been granted or restored to the people, and for the observing of those laws that have been established with the Prince's consent, & from that oath (by which for the greater security of the people he binds himself to the performance of the premises) to infer a great obligation lieth upon him, is right, but to gather thence a forfeiture of his power upon the not performance, is a plain but dangerous inconsequent argument.

And though such argument may seem to have some force in States meerly elective and pactionall, yet can it never be made to appear to any indifferent understanding, that the like must obtain in this kingdom. And to this purpose Phil. *Pareus* excuseth what his father had written more harshly upon Rom. 13. in the point of resistance, that it was to be understood of elective and pactionall government, not to the prejudice of England, or such Monarchies. For where the King, as it is said, never dies, where he is King before oath or coronation, where he is not admitted upon any such capitulation as gives any power to the people, or their representative body, as is pretended to; Nay, where that body cannot meet but by the will of the Prince, and is dissoluble at his pleasure; that there in such a State, such a power should bee pretended to, and used against the Prince, as at this day; and that according to the Fundamentalls of such a State, can never appeare reasonable to any indifferent judgement, much lesse satisfie Conscience in the resistance that is now made by such a pretended power.

What then shall we say? Is the King not bound to perform? Yes, by all means. Or has he not a limited power according to the Laws? Yes, What then if he will take to himself more power, or not perform what he is bound to? Suppose that (though thanks be to God we are not come to that) then may the Subjects use all fair means as are fit to use, cryes to God, Petitions to the Prince, denialls of obedience to his unlawfull commands, denialls of subsidy, aid, &c. But are they left without all means to compell by force and resistance? This however it may at first sight seem unreasonable to the people, and very impolitick to the Statesman, yet has Scripture forbidden it, as before

was plainly shewed, and so doth Reason too, as will appear in the examination of their last proof they make for reassuming this power
and resisting, from that necessity of means of safety, which every
State is to have within itself: Of which now.

Sect. V.

In the last place it is thus reasoned, Were it not so that the two
Houses might take and use this power, the State should not have
means to provide for its own safety, when the King shall please to
desert his Parliament, deny his consent to their bills, abuse His
power, &c. So they.

When right and just will not defend a thing then Necessity is usually pleaded; as if, because *Salus populi* in a good sense is *Suprema lex*,
everything must be honest which is *Sparta Utile*, imagined to conduce to the proposed end. We answer therefore.

1. They have many weapons sharpened for this resistance at the
Philistines' forge, arguments borrowed from the Roman Schools,
among them this is one, the very reason that is made for the Pope's
power of curbing or deposing Kings in case of Heresie. For if there be
not that power in the Church, say they, then in case the Civill Magistrate will not discharge his trust, the Church has not means for the
maintenance of the Catholike faith and its own safety. Well, as we
reply to them, the Church has means of preserving the faith, such as
God has appointed, though not that of one visible head, which
though at first seems plausible for preserving the Unity of faith, yet
has experience shown it, to be indeed the means to bring much mischief upon the Church. So to the other we say, The State has means
of preservation such as the Law has prescribed, though not such as
are here pretended to in this power of resistance; which though seemingly plausible, yet true reason will conclude them dangerous, and at

this day, God knows, we see it. Of this in the 4. answer more particularly.

2. If every State has such means to provide for its safety, what means of safety had the Christian Religion under the Roman Emperours in and after the Apostles' times? Or the people then enslaved, what means had they for their Liberties? Had they this of resistance? *Tertullian* in his Apology sayes, the Christians had number and force sufficient to withstand, but they had no warrant; and the Apostle expressely forbids them, and all other under the higher power, to resist.

If it be replied, as it was above touched, That things being so enacted by Law, it was not lawfull for them to resist. I answer, But it is known that not only those Edicts which concerned Christian Religion, but also all other that proceeded from those Emperours and enslaved the people, were meerly arbitrary and enforced upon the Senate, and that the Senate did not discharge their trust in consenting to them, and therefore according to the former position the people might resist, notwithstanding the Apostle's prohibition, or else no means of safety left in that State.

So would it be in this State, if at any time a King that would rule arbitrarily, as those Emperours did, should by some means or other work out of two Houses the better affected, and by the Consent of the Major part of them that remain, compasse his desires; might the people then resist? The Apostle forbids it to them as well as to the *Romans* in such a case: if so, where are these means of safety by this Power of resistance? Or are these means of safety extinct in the Consent of the Senate, or the two Houses? No, the people will tell them they discharge not their trust, they chose them not to betray them, enslave them; but according to the principles now taught them, they might lay hold upon this power of resistance, for their representative body claims it by them.

Thirdly we answer, We cannot expect absolute means of safety and
security in a State, but such as are reasonable; and such are provided,
especially in the fundamentalls of this Government, by that excellent temper of the three Estates in Parliament, there being a power of
denying in each of them, and no power of enacting in one or two of
them without the third; which as it is for the security of the Commonwealth (for what might follow if the King and Lords without the
Commons, or these and the Lords without the King, might determine, the evils of these dayes do shew) so is this power of denying, for
the security of each State against other, of the Commons against the
King and Lords, of the Lords against them: and must the King trust
only, and not be trusted? Must not he also have his security against
the other, which he cannot have but by Power of denying? This is
that Temper of the three Estates in Parliament, the due observing
whereof, in the moderate use of this Power of denying, is the reasonable means of this State's safety. But now not only the name of Parliament, which implies the three Estates, is restrained usually to the
two Houses, but also that Temper is dissolved. I need not speak it,
the distractions and convulsions of the whole Commonwealth, as the
distempers in a naturall body, do sufficiently shew such a dissolution,
and what's the cause of it.

If it be replied, as it is, for the reasonablenesse of these means of
safety, through that Power of resistance, and the finall trust reposed
in the representative body of the people, That many see more than
one, and more safety in the judgement of many than of one. *Answ.*
True. But 1. Conscience might here demand for its satisfaction, Why
should an hundred in the House of Commons see more than three
hundred; or twenty in the Lords House, more than sixty that are of
different judgement and withdrawn?

2. Reason doth suppose, That the Prince, though one, sees with
the eyes of many, yea with their eyes who are of different judgement
from him, for which his Houses of Parliament are his great Coun-

cell to present to his eyes the differences of things with the reasons of them; and albeit he sometimes dissents from the Major or prevailing part, because he is convinced in his own judgement they seek themselves not his or the publike good, or for other reasons that may perswade him against their Vote, yet have all times thought good to have Kings, and to reduce the judgement of many unto one. The Government which God made choice of to set up among his people was Monarchicall still, first in *Moses,* then in the Judges, then in the Kings; yea generally all Authors yield, and experience has taught it, That Monarchy is a better government than Aristocracy, because the Tyranny and Miscarriage of one, sometime happening in a Monarch, is nothing so dangerous as Oligarchy, Faction, and Division usually incident to Aristocracy or the Government by many equals. Again, as all times have thought it reasonable to have Monarchy, which settles the chief power and finall judgement in One; so will there be always sufficient reason to withhold the King from a willfull deniall of his Consent to the free and unanimous Vote of his Houses. He cannot but see there will alwayes be some necessary good accrewing to him by his Parliament, that will keep him in all reason from doing so, and no cases can be put or inconveniences feared upon his power of denying, but greater and more eminent will appear upon his not having it, as has been insinuated, and now do follow.

Fourthly therefore and lastly we answer. Such power of resistance would be no fit means of safety to a State, but prove a remedy worse than the disease. This is very plain by the drift of the Apostle's reasons which he gave against resistance, in the 3, 4, 5, 6, *Vers.* of the 13. to the *Romans,* in which we may consider, that, although the Powers then were altogether unjust, tyrannicall, subverters of true Religion, nothing answerable to the end for which the Governing power is ordained, yet doth the Apostle draw his reasons against the resisting of them, from that good, that justice, that order for which God hath set up the higher powers; to insinuate, that the resisting of the higher

powers, even when they are so, does tend to the overthrow of that
order which is the life of a Commonwealth; and this not only because
there is still order under tyranny, but chiefly because, if it were good
and lawfull, to resist the power, when abused, it would open a way to
the people upon the like pretences to resist and overthrow even Powers duely administered for the executing of wrath upon them that do
evill.

I enter this discourse, not to cast the least blemish upon Parliaments (which are an only remedy for distempers of the Kingdom)
not to reflect upon the intentions of those that are yet resident in that
high Court, (unto God, the judge of all, they stand or fall) not to raise
jealousies, but to settle Conscience, and in the way of reasoning to
shew according to the Apostle's reasons what dangers and evils may
ensue upon this power of resistance.

For first of all, This power of resistance, if admitted and pursued
may proceed to a change of Government, the Principles that now are
gone upon, and have carried it so farre as we see at this day, may also
lead it on to that greatest of evils. And I have heard and seen it defended by the example of the Low-countreys; how they excuse it,
thoroughly I examine not, but this I am sure they can say, That their
Prince, succeeding in the right of the Duke of *Burgundy* was admitted upon other conditions than the Kings of *England* are. Also that a
contrary Religion was enforced upon them by a terrible Inquisition,
whereas they that do resist the higher Powers here, do freely enjoy
their Religion, and have the Prince's promise and Protestation for it.

Secondly, This power of resistance when used, and pursued, is accompanied with the evils of Civill warre. Former times shew it, and
how little was gained by it beside the expence of bloud; as when all
was referred to the rule and disposing of the 12 Peers, how long lasted
it? What security had the State by it? And at this day we feel and
groan under the evils brought upon us through this power of resistance, the Law silenced, the Property and Liberty of the Subject

every where invaded: and the Lord knows when or how we shall be restored to them, or better secured in them by this way. Thirdly, We see the danger, if (as it is now said, for the justifying of this power of resistance, The King will not discharge His trust, and therefore it falls to the representative body of the people to see to it, so) the People being discontented, and having gotten power shall say, The Members of the two houses do not discharge the trust committed to them, they do not that for which they were chosen and sent for, then may the multitude by this rule and principle now taught them take the Power to themselves, it being claimed by them and say to them as *Numb. 16. Ye take too much upon you*, or, as Cade and Tylar,[4] boast themselves Reformers of the Commonwealth, overthrow King and Parliament, fill all with rapine and confusion, draw all to a Folkmoot, and make every Shire a severall Government. These are Dangers and Evils not conceived in the fancy, but such as reason tells us may follow, and experience hath often, and this day doth shew us, do arise upon this Power of resistance, and for the preventing of which, the Apostle gave his reasons against resisting even of abused Powers, as we heard above. Lastly therefore, Seeing some must be trusted in every State, 'tis reason the highest and finall trust should be in the higher or supreme Power with whom next to himself God hath intrusted the whole Kingdom, all other that have power and trust, having it under him as sent by him; Good reason I say that the supreme Power (which is worth 10,000 of the Subjects) should have the best security on its side, for as much as Order, the life of a Commonwealth, is so best preserved, and not so endangered by Tyranny as by factions, division, tumults, power of resistance on the Subject's part, and this is according to the drift of the Apostle's reasons against resistance, as before they were laid down.

Well now unto all that hath hitherto been said from Scripture and

4. For information on Cade and Tyler, see note 14, above.

Reason let Conscience adde the Oath of Supremacy and Allegeance, also the late Protestation,[5] and consider what duty lies upon every Subject by the former to defend the King's Person and right against what power soever, and how by the latter he hath protested and undertaken before Almighty God, in the first place to defend the same; and then what can Conscience conclude from the Premises? That the Prince hath his power for the good of his people? True, but that power cannot be prevalent for the good and protection of his people, unlesse it be preserved to him intire, unlesse he hath the power of Deniall, and the chiefe command of Arms; or that the Prince hath a limited power, according to the Laws established? True, but if Conscience be perswaded he does not hold himselfe within those bounds so fixed, can it be perswaded also that the people may re-assume that power they never had? Or take that sword out of his hand that God hath put into it? No, Conscience will look at that Power as the Ordinance of God, and the abuse of that Power as a judgment and scourge of God upon the people, and will use not Arms to resist the Ordinance under pretence of resisting the abuse, but cries and prayers to God, petitions to the Prince, denials of obedience to his unjust commands, denialls of Subsidies, aids, and all fair means that are fit for Subjects to use, and when done all, if not succeed, will rather suffer than resist: so would a truly informed Conscience resolve, were the Prince indeed what he is supposed to be, and did he do indeed as the people are made to fear and believe he will do.

Hitherto we have been in the examination of the principle upon which they go that plead for resistance, and we have found both

5. The "late Protestation" is probably that drawn up by the Commons in May 1641, which read: "I, A. B. in the presence of Almighty God, promise, vow, and protest to maintain and defend, as far as lawfully I may, with my life, power, and estate, the true Reformed Protestant Religion, expressed in the doctrine of the Church of England, against all Popery and Popish innovations within this realm contrary to the same doctrine, and according to the duty of my allegiance, his Majesty's Royal person, honour, and estate, as also the power and privileges of Parliament, the lawful rights and liberties of the subjects. . . ." The Protestation went on to include a vow to oppose and bring to punishment all who plot or do anything contrary to it.

Scripture and Reason speak plainly against the resisting even of abused Powers, professed enemies to Religion, actuall subverters of the people's liberties, how much more against the resisting of a Prince that professeth the same Religion which we freely enjoy, promiseth the maintaining of that and our liberties, only upon a supposall he will not stand to his word, will overthrow all.

This however it may seem lesse reasonable to the Statist in the way of policy, permitting as little as he can to the goodnesse of the Prince or the providence of God for the safety of the State; yet ought it to satisfie a Christian in the way of Conscience, which when it comes to a desire of being safe, will not rest till it have a sure ground, which here it hath against resistance laid down by Scripture and Reason, even the Apostle's reasons so powerfull against resistance.

The summe of all is this, Conscience hears the Apostle expressely forbid all under the higher power to resist, findes no other clear Scripture to limit it, findes that the limitations given will not consist with it, for the reasons of them (that are drawn from the Election of the people, and the Covenant supposed therein, from the necessity of means of safety in every State to provide for itselfe) were as strong in the Romane State as any, nay, are supposed by those that urge them, to be the fundamentalls of every State: and so resistance is forbidden as well here, as there in the Romane State, which is also cleared by the Apostle's reasons, shewing the power of resistance cannot be the means of safety, but strikes at Order and power itselfe, though made against tyrannicall and abused powers, as before often insinuated. Therefore Conscience will not dare to go against the Apostle's expresse prohibition, lest it fall into the judgement denounced by him.

But if there shall be any Conscience as strongly carried away with the name of Parliament, as the Papists are with the name of the Church, and thinking Religion may be defended any way, and that upon supposall that their Prince is minded to change it, (which is another humor of Popery) will not be perswaded that the resistance made upon the present supposall is unlawfull, against God's word, and Reason. I am sure such a Conscience cannot be truly perswaded it is lawfull, but must want that clear ground it ought to have, especially in a matter so expresly against the Apostle, and of such high concernment as damnation: must needs run blindly, and headlong by a strange implicit faith upon so great a hazard.

Sect. VI.

Now we come to the application of their principle to the present, where we must enquire according to the second and third Generalls, whether the resistance now made be such as is pretended to by them in such a case as they supposed, and then whether Conscience can be truly perswaded the King is such, and so minded as in the case he is supposed to be.

The chief considerations of these two Generalls, are matters of fact. The principle was examined by Scripture and Reason, these admit the judgment of sense, and are cleared by what we hear and see: which judgment of sense is not so easily captivated by an implicit faith as that of reason is, insomuch as Conscience here cannot be so blinded but it may see that (were the principle good on which they rest, yet) this resistance which they make, is not such as in the case they supposed him to be, not such as ought to be resisted according to their own grants.

The second Generall was, That the Resistance now made, is not such as is pretended to by them that plead for it, and therefore Conscience cannot be truly perswaded it may lawfully bear part in it, or assist them that in the pursuit of it pretend one thing and do another.

It was premised at the beginning, that such a resistance should be *omnibus ordinibus regni conscientibus*, agreed upon and undertaken by the generall and unanimous consent of the whole State, and that it should be only *Legitima defensio*, a mere resistance, and these laid down, not that I admit resistance however conditioned (for all that I have said before, doth altogether condemne it) but according to their own grants that plead for it. To this purpose it is that they say the King is *Universis minor*, lesse than the whole State, and every body naturally defends itself. Therefore if a contention be between the Head and the Body, it must in all reason be the whole Body that is set against it, and if there be such an appearing against the supreme Power, as tends to resistance, the consent and judgment of the whole Kingdom just be against him, or else every prevailing faction might indanger the State, by causing such changes and evils as now it's threatened with. This is the reason of this unreasonable power of resistance in the people.

Well then, how shall Conscience be perswaded that this resistance was agreed upon by an unanimous and free consent of the States assembled in the two Houses, such as in this case may be called the judgment of the whole Kingdom.

He that knows how the Militia (in which this resistance chiefly began) was brought in,[6] with what opposition, especially in the Lords House, and by what number there at length was voted; also how the like proceedings of resistance, that have been voted since, are declared against, by a greater number of each House than do remain in either, such as have been cast out, or withdrawn themselves upon dislike of these proceedings: can he, I say, that knows this (and who knows it not, that hath eyes and ears?) be in Conscience perswaded, that this is such an unanimous, free and generall consent, the judgment of the whole kingdom?

For though a Vote passed by a few upon the place has the power and condition of a Vote for the formality of Law, yet, if the question be, Was this passed in full assemblies? Did they all unanimously as

6. This is a reference to the months of wrangling between Charles and Parliament over control of the militia of the kingdom, with the two Houses eventually passing the Militia Ordinance without royal approval.

one man consent unto it? Conscience cannot be convinced there is such efficacie in the place, as to make a few, the whole, or their agreement to be that judgment of the whole Kingdom, that unanimous consent, which must be in the case of resistance, by their acknowledgment that plead for it. For were it in this case to be held for the judgement of the whole, which is passed by a few, then would the State be unreasonably exposed to that danger (above mentioned) which every prevailing faction might bring upon it under the pretence of the judgment of the whole Kingdome.

Again, as Conscience cannot be truely perswaded that this resistance is agreed upon with such a generall and unanimous consent, as they themselves pretend to, which plead for this resistance, so can it not truly be perswaded that this resistance is such for the mere defensive way of it, as it ought to be according to their grants and pretences that appear for it.

Conscience here will see how to resolve upon the triall of these two particulars, whether the King or they be upon the defensive part? Then, whether the managing of this war, or resistance on their parts, be so void of hostile acts, as the defensive way, which they pretend to, ought to be?

Conscience will discern whether part is upon the defensive, by inquiring, First, Who were first in Arms? He that can number the succession of weeks, and months in his Almanack may decide this. He shall find that armed men were thrust into *Hull*, the King's Arms seized against his will, the Militia set up, and by that, the King's Subjects drawn into Arms, before the King had anything to oppose but Proclamations. That subscriptions for Plate, Money, Horse, That listing of Souldiers for the field, and appointing of Officers of the Armie were begun upon their part, before His MAJESTIE did the like. Now resistance doth in the word itselfe and in their pretence, presuppose a power and force first made against them, whereas it is plain, they were still upon the preventing and forehand with the King, still shewed him example for what he has done since in the way of War: yet must the people believe he raises the War, and they are upon defence; but conscience will not be so forced.

Secondly, by enquiring what is the cause of these Arms? What do they contend for? And though it be clear, That if Subjects be first in Arms, they cannot be upon the defensive, yet the consideration of the cause will more apparently convince it, when Conscience shall see it is not for what is pretended, but for something the King has right to deny, that this resistance is made. The preservation of Religion and Liberties is pretended, but can it be for either? The King denies them not. Their Religion they freely enjoy; and was it ever known that Subjects should rise in Arms against their Prince for a Religion which he promises to maintain? Or does Religion stand in need of a defence, which itself condemns, a defence which would be a perpetuall scandall to it? If therefore Religion be the pretence, but no cause of War than is the War raised on their part, the King is upon the defensive. Or can it be for ancient Rights and undoubted Priviledges that they contend? The King denies them not, promiseth all security, so he may enjoy his own; and God forbid that either he or they should suffer in their just Rights. But would any man ever have defended the revolt of the ten Tribes, if *Rehoboam* had promised to conserve their Liberties? What shall we then think of this generall revolt from Allegiance that has possessed well-neer ten Tribes of twelve? They suppose he will not make good his promises, and therefore they will make all sure, seize his Arms and Forts, strip him of all, and if he begin to stir for his own Right and Dignity, then the people must be made to believe he makes War against his Parliament, intends to destroy their Liberties. But can any man in Conscience think his Majesty since the beginning of this breach was ever in such a condition of strength as might threaten the Liberty of the

Subject, or destroy Parliaments, when as it was long ere he could with much ado attain to any reasonable means of subsistence, or to such a strength whereby he might seem to be able to defend himself.

To speak truth, Religion and Liberties can be no other than the pretences of this Warre, the King has fortified them so with many Acts of Grace passed this Parliament, that they cannot be in that danger which is pretended for the raising of this Warre. It must be something that his Majesty does indeed deny for which the contention is raised. That we shall finde to be his power of Arms and ordering the *Militia* of the Kingdom, his power of denying in Parliament, his disposing of the Offices of State, and such like; Also the Government of the Church, and the Revenue of it. In the three former he challenges his Right, as his Predecessors had: the other he is bound by Oath to maintain as by Law they are established. Well, if these be attempted, and His MAJESTIE will not be forced from them, cannot yeeld them up, but it comes to Arms, then will Conscience easily be convinced the King is upon the defensive, for the maintaining of what he justly holds his right, or is bound by Oath to defend.

And if we hearken to the people's voice, for that commonly speaks the mind of their leaders, we shall hear them usually call this Warre, as they did that with the *Scots*, the Bishops' Warre. His Majesty has indeed alwayes declared against the altering of the Government of the Church by Bishops, being such as it alwayes had since the first receiving of the Christian faith in this land, and of all other Governments simply the best, if reformed from abuses and corruptions that have grown upon it, to the purging out of which his Majesty is alwayes ready to agree. But be it the Bishops' Warre (though the abolishing of that Government be but one of the many inconveniences which this power of resistance doth threaten this Land with, and which the King has reason by power of Arms to divert) whether is it so just in Subjects by Arms to force a change of Government which was alwayes in the Church, and by Law established, as it is in the King to defend the same as he is bound by Oath? It is clear which of the two are upon the defensive.

The second particular by which the defensive way of this resistance is to be examined, was the managing of this Warre on their parts, whether in void of acts of Hostility as that defensive way should be which they pretend to. *David's* resistance made against *Saul* is frequently alledged by them, which example, though it will not countenance their cause (as was shewed before) yet might it tell them their demeanour should be answerable. He offered no act of violence to *Saul,* but still gave place and withdrew from him. The Spear indeed and the Cruse *David* took away from the King's head, but it was only to shew *Abner's* neglect who had the Command of *Saul's* Militia, and to testifie his own integriety, therefore he restored them before they were demanded, I. *Sam.* 26.

But now the King's Spear and his Cruse, his Ammunition and his necessary Provisions are taken away, intercepted, not restored though often demanded, used against him with all advantage; nay he is stript of the very power and command of Arms, his Officers and Ministers thrust out, and other substituted, and by them his people drawn into Arms against him.

Also by these that are in resistance against the King, his Loyale and peaceable Subjects are assauled, despoiled of their Arms, Goods, Estates; their persons imprisoned, because they would according to their Allegeance assist him in this extemity, or would not, contrary to their Conscience, join with them against him. What Conscience that will not follow this way with a stupid implicit faith can be perswaded that this warre is the defence of the Subject's Liberties, and not rather an oppugnation of them? Or that it is a mere resistance or withstanding of a force first made against them, and not rather a violent illation or bringing in of force upon those that were disposed to peace. Therefore no conscience that has a sense of Religion, or of that which is just and right between man and man, can bear a part in this resistance, for fear of that sentence of damnation which the Apostle has laid upon it.

Sect. VII.

But in the last place, if Conscience could be perswaded, that it is lawfull upon such a case as they make, to take Arms and resist, and that this rising in Arms is such a defensive resistance, as in such a case they seem to pretend to, yet how will it be perswaded that the Case is now, that is, That the King is such as the people must be made to believe he is, unlesse it will as desperately offend against the rule of Charitie, in so concluding upon the King, as it does against the rule of Faith and perswasion, in admitting so ungrounded a principle as is now rested on for resistance. So that such a Conscience shall have in its perswasion neither certainty of Rule; for the principle it goes on is false, nor certainty of the Case, for it knows not the heart of the King, to conclude for resistance upon supposals of his intentions, and in its judgement it will be altogether void of Charitie.

Indeed it concerns all such as will resist upon the principles now taught to render their Prince odious to his people under the hatefull notions of Tyrant, Subverter of Religion, and Laws, a Person not to be trusted, or at least as one seduced to such evill designes, by wicked Counsell. But what? Hath this King forbid the exercise of the Religion established, or left off to professe it himself? hath he disclaimed his trust, or not upon all occasions promised Justice and libertie to his Subjects?

Yea! But they have cause to fear Popery will prevail, and that he will not stand to his promises. It seems they are men that would be loath to suffer for their Religion, they are so ready to fly to Arms to secure themselves. But shall subjects rise in Arms against their Prince upon such remote fears and jealousies as these will appear to be?

When can such be wanting in turbulent minds? When shall the Prince be assured of safety? This was the way that *David* himself was shaken out of his throne, and driven from *Jerusalem* by *Absalom*. This cunning Rebell steales away their hearts by rising jealousies in them and an evill opinion of *David's* government, 2. *Sam.* 15.3. Some ground, it seems, he had for his treacherous plea, through the negligence of those that were under *David*, but it was his villanie to make use of it to the alienating of the people from their King. Accordingly let us now consider what slender grounds our people have for their fears and jealousies, then what securitie they have and might have against them, that it may appear how causelesse those jealousies are in themselves; how unjust causes of this resistance.

If we examine the fears and jealousies that have possessed the people we shall find them to be raised upon these or the like grounds, Reports of foreign Power to be brought in, The Queen's Religion, The resort of *Papists* to his Majesty, His intercepting of means sent for the relief of *Ireland*, from whence the people by their good teachers are made to believe, that he means to enslave this people, reestablish Popery, and does comply with the Rebells.

I answer to all which I needed not to say more than what *Michael* Archangel to the devill that arch-accuser, *The Lord rebuke thee, Jude 9.* but in particular; For such reports of invasions from abroad, as were, before the setting up of the Militia, given out to keep the people amused, the easier to draw them into a posture of defence as was pretended, all such are discovered by time to have been vain; if there be now any foreign aids towards the King (as all Christian Kings cannot but think themselves concerned in the cause) it will be as just for him to use them against subjects now in Arms, as it was unjust in the *Barons* to call in the *French* against their naturall King.

For the Queen's Majestie; Her Religion is no new cause, if it be a sufficient cause of Jealousie to them, they have had it from her first entrance; I would to God it were otherwise with her, that it would please the Lord to open her eyes that she may see the truth and light of the Protestant Religion: only this I must say, this is not the way to draw her to it, if she look at it in the doctrines and practices of these times she is not like to fall in love with it.

For the resort of Papists, and the King's entertaining them; He hath often declared what caution he desired to use therein, till necessitie hath driven him to admit of some few into his Army, which also he answered lately. Let me adde this concerning the justnesse of it, If he hath entertained any into this service, he may justly make use of them. We see what manner of men were gathered to *David* in his distresse, *I. Sam. 22.2.* and how false *Ziba* bringing provision to the King when he fled from *Absalom*, was entertained and rewarded, insomuch that the King (when afterward he knew how *Ziba* had abused him to gain his own ends) would not reverse the sentence pronounced in his favour. If therefore in this distresse after much forberrance our King hath admitted the help of some Recusants, it cannot be alledged as a cause of the resistance was a cause of it; and if the *Papist* will shew himselfe a good Subject, it is just and reasonable that the King when he is put to it, may admitt of his help, and the more shame it is for them that professe the Protestant Religion to force him to it; a scandall that would not easily be wiped off from our Religion, were it to stand or fall, by the doctrines of this giddie *Age*.

Lastly, His Majestie hath written enough for the clearing himselfe from those false and odious imputations laid upon him in relation to the *Irish* businesse. I have only thus much to say, concerning anything intended for the relief of *Ireland;* It was great pitie they should want it there, but it is more pitiefull, the King should be forced to make use of it here.

It is not long since our neighbour Nation brought an Army into the Northern parts of this kingdome to the great detriment of the inhabitants there, and it was excused by invincible necessitie, which drove them hither. The necessitie his Majesty was driven to is sufficiently known, and might excuse him, in taking his own where he meets with it, and drawing it from his service abroad to that which more nearly concerned him at home. And when his Arms, Moneys, and Provisions are seized on wherever they be found intended for him, and imployed against him in Warre, the Lord knows how unnecessary, shall it not be lawfull for to take some part of them where he finds it for his necessary defence?

Indeed the distresse of *Ireland* by the help of wicked Pamphlets hath been used as a great engine to weaken the King's reputation with his people; but upon whose account the heavie rekoning of that neglected Cause will be laid, together with the disturbance of this kingdome, any man in conscience may easily discern, that sees what sufficient and reasonable means might have been had for the security of Religion and Liberties, and for the redresse of all just grievances before this time. Which is the next thing considerable: What his Majesty hath done and profered to exempt these scruples of fears and jealousies out of this people's minds.

For Religion, if it be a new frame they contend for, I must acknowledge hee declares against all such; but if they desire the continuance of that true Protestant Religion, which hath been professed without interruption from the beginning of the Queen's dayes, and established by the Lawes of this land, that he undertakes to maintaine, that he hath protested in the head of his Army to defend. For matter of Church-government and discipline he hath offered any just reformation, even with a respect to tender consciences in point of ceremony, hath often called His two Houses to the worke in drawing up the grievances to some head. For privileges of *Parliaments* and Liberty of Subjects hee hath given them the like promises with the deepest Protestations, and by an excellent moderation, amidst the presurres and necessities of Warre, hath showen what respect he hath to the property and liberty of the Subject. Lastly, For his choise of Officers of State, he hath promised to admit any just exception, and thereupon to relinquish the person and as an assurance of all this, hath so far condescended as to take away Star-Chamber, High Commission, Bishops' votes, &c. and the Continuance of this parliament, & the constant returne of a Trieniall. And now after all these promises and protestations and so many expressions of grace, can any man in conscience think there was yet place left for Propositions of such necessary concernment, that except they be granted this kingdome must be imbroiled in a Civill War, & the reliefe of *Ireland* neglected? I speake not this to cast any blemish upon the wisdome of the great Councell, or upon their desires and endeavours to gaine a great security to the publicke: but I would to God, the King were once thought worthy to bee trusted a little, and that the Consciences of his Subjects were more respected, which cannot so easily be commanded into a resistance, being very tender in the points of damnation, and taught out of God's Word, *Not to raise so much as an evill thought against the King, Eccl. 10.* much lesse to lift up an armed hand.

Every man's Conscience now is solicited to adhere either to the King in this great cause, or to joine with Subjects in making resistance. To draw it from Allegiance, tongues are set on fire of hell, which blast His Majestie's Actions and Declarations, and books written by hellish spirits, enemies to peace and quietnesse, are suffered to issue forth into every corner of the Land to possesse the people, that his promises are but words, his Acts of grace were forced, he will not stand to them. It seemes then he must by force of Armes be compelled to be willing. But let us see whether a conscience that desires to be safe can be so perswaded in judging the actions and intentions of him (to whom it owes the highest duty under God) as first to conclude he intends not as he promises, and thereupon to resolve for resistance? No, it will direct itselfe by the rule of Charity, which is, not rashly to conclude upon the heart which it knoweth not, or to think any evill; and if the difference be betwixt two, as in cause, it will hold the rule of indifferency, impartially to consider the actions of both. Conscience therefore that it may be informed of his Majestie's intentions, will it look upon him at such a distance as *London* and read him only in those horrid relations that issue thence, and conceive of him as they report him to the people? Or will it consider some failings that necessity has inforced, or other accidentall occurrences have occasioned, and from these conclude intentions to him, contrary to all his promises and Protestations? This would be too partiall, too uncharitable. Conscience ought alwayes to be tender in judging upon other men's intentions, especially those of the Prince, and those to be concluded as evill, and to be made a ground for resistance, which runs the hazard of Damnation. In the *2 Chr. c. 21.10.* Libuah is said to revolt from the King of Judah because hee had forsaken the Lord; a Text that is objected to us, and should have been answered in the first part: but it is impertinent as all the rest are, for it neither proves the principle, That it is lawfull for the people to revolt when the King forsakes Religion, but shewes that such revolt is a punishment from God upon such a King, though a sinne in the people. Nor doth it come home to the Case; for there the King had forsaken; here is only supposall that he will, and that groundlesse and unconscionable too. For as there was enough in *David* to clear these Jealousies upon which that rebellion of the people following *Absalom* was grounded, so is there on the King's part, to direct conscience against this desperate uncharitable judgment, if it look at those many Acts of grace as new additions to that security, by which this State has so long stood, and from them conclude, He would not in a faire way deny anything reasonable. If it consider those many promises strengthened with the deepest protestations, enforced with desires of successe from God according to his just intentions, and all these, as proceeding from a King, under such affliction, in such danger, after such successe and experience of God's protection, approving thereby the reality and sincerity of his heart. What conscience can here conclude contrary intentions in him, and not think it blasphemeth God and the King?

Furthermore, as conscience will not be uncharitable when it judgeth upon the intentions of another man's heart, so neither will it be partiall when it judgeth between two, unto which of them it should incline: and therefore he that is abused to believe amisse of his King and solicited to enter this way of resistance, is highly concerned first to consider, whether they also that are the main directours of it, and to whom he would adhere, doe discharge their trust they are called to, I say such an one, unlesse he will resigne up his faith to men, and receive their dictates as the immediate rule of his conscience, must consider whether all be just and honest that is done in that way? Whether to divest the King of the power of Armes and to use them against him, be to defend his person, Rights, and dignity? Whether the forcing of the Subjects' property, to the advancing of this resistance, and the imprisoning of their persons for deniall, be the maintaining of the right and liberty of the Subject? Whether the suffering of so many Sects to vent their doctrines with such liberty, and to commit unsufferable outrages upon the worship of God, with such licentiousness, be a defending of Religion and the established worship of this Church? All these duties every Subject respectively is bound to discharge, and the neglect of them His Majesty has chiefly charged upon those that he conceives the chiefe directours and Actours in this resistance made against him, and every man in conscience ought seriously to consider it.

The necessity of the Common-wealth is pretended to defend the not defending of the premises; when as no necessity may excuse any failings on the King's part, as if his promises, by which he stands obliged to his Subjects, did not suppose they for their parts also should performe. I know not how some particular men may be engaged and contract a necessity of resisting, or seeking safety by

Armes; but I am perswaded, no man in Conscience can thinke it a necessity of the Common-wealth to have all confounded, or of a Christian to run the hazard of damnation by resisting. My conscience tells me, and will theirs one day tell them, how much they have to answer for not improving that grace and willingnesse, they had experience of in His Majestie and might still have found in him, to the speedy and happy Reformation of this Church and State. I pray God to give them Consciences truely inlightned, and bowels truly compassionate, that they may speedily and feelingly be sensible of the miseries this Land grones under, and faithfully examine how far they are answerable for them by rejecting such reasonable meanes of security, as they might have had for the safety of this State. *Amen.*

And now if there be any one that will run the hazard of this resistance, I desire he would first set his Conscience before the Tribunall of God, where it must appear, and consider whether it will excuse him there, when he has shed the bloud of others, and expended his owne, to say, I verily supposed and believed my Prince would change Religion, overthrow our Liberties. I must tell him it will not be safe for him to present such a Conscience at that barre, a Conscience that wanted the rule of Faith to warrant and perswade the lawfulnesse of resistance on such a supposall, a Conscience that wanted the certainty of perswasion that the Prince's heart (which God only knowes) was so inclined, a Conscience that wanted the judgement of charity, in concluding such intentions in the King notwithstanding all his promises and deepest protestations made in the time of his trouble, without which Charity all is nothing though he layes downe (as he thinkes) his life for Religion. Such a Conscience I must needs conclude sinfull, and liable to that which the Apostle threatens unto Resistance, Damnation.

FINIS.

[Charles Herle, 1598–1659]

A
FVLLER ANSWER
TO
A TREATISE

Written by Doctor *F E R N E* ,

ENTITVLED,

The Resolving of Conscience upon this Question,

Whether upon this Supposition, or Case (The *King* will not defend, but is bent to subvert *Religion, Lawes* and *Liberties*) Subjects may with good Conscience make resistance.

Wherein the Originall frame, and Fundamentalls of this Government of *England,* Together with those two Texts of Scripture are sufficiently cleered. *viz.*

ROM. 13.1.

Let every soule be subject unto the higher powers: for there is no power but of God, The powers that be, are ordained of God.

1 PET. 2.13.

Submit your selves unto every Ordinance of man for the Lords sake, whether it be to the King as Supreame.

Done by another Authour.

And by him revised and enlarged by occasion of some late Pamphlets Complaining in the Name of the City against the Parliament.

LONDON,

Printed for *Iohn Bartlet,* and are to be sold at the Signe of the Gilt-Cup in *Paul's* Church-yard, neare to *Austins Gate,* 1642.

*C*harles Herle, a Presbyterian divine from Cornwall, was educated at Oxford. He was closely linked to James Stanley, later
seventh earl of Derby, and his family. It was through the good offices
of these future royalist stalwarts that he became rector of the rich
rectory of Winwick in Lancashire. In the 1640s Herle preached frequently before the Long Parliament. He was also active in the Westminster Assembly of Divines. In his numerous pamphlets on behalf of
Parliament he stressed the coordinate nature of the English government, which he saw as based upon an original contract. His views
have been seen as prefiguring those of the Whigs at the Glorious Revolution. In the matter of resistance he followed Calvin's advice that
the privilege belonged not to individual subjects but to the magistrates and courts of a kingdom.

Herle was one of several parliamentarian pamphleteers who
crossed literary swords with Henry Ferne after the publication of
Ferne's "Resolving of Conscience." His first effort, "An Answer to misled Dr. Ferne..." was followed by "A Fuller Answer to a Treatise

Written by Doctor Ferne," which was published on 29 December 1642, only days after Ferne had failed to appear before Parliament to answer for his tract. The "Fuller Answer" appeared in two virtually identical editions, the second of which is reprinted here. Ferne replied to his critics on 18 April 1643 with "Conscience Satisfied...," which Herle attacked the following month in "An Answer to Dr. Fernes Reply." Ferne attempted to have the last word on 1 November 1643 with "Reply unto severall Treatises...." This paper war, intended to provide constitutional guidance to Englishmen perplexed by the unfolding civil war, clarifies the theoretical differences as well as the shared notions of the antagonists.

Although his side emerged victorious, Herle did not approve of the execution of Charles I and was summoned by the government in 1651 on a charge of aiding royalists. It was not until September 1653 that he was freed from restraint. Thereafter he retired to Winwick where, in September 1659, he died. He is buried in the chancel of his church.

An Answer to a Treatise Entituled
The Resolving of Conscience upon this Question, Whether upon such
a supposition, or Case as is now usually made (The King will not
discharge His trust, &c.)

Blowing aside the *Magistery* of the *Title, Author, Style* of this *Treatise,* as but the *pin-dust* of it, that *gilds* but *intercepts* the *Letter:* I find
the substance of it to be a groundlesse *supposition* of the Parliament's
taking up Armes, upon a bare *supposition* of the King's meere *intention* to subvert Lawes and Liberties; for so we see the question itselfe
is proposed: *Whether upon such a supposition? The King will not, &c.*
Here I confesse we have much of the *Chaire* upon the *resolving* part,
but as much beside the *Cushion* on the *supposing* part; for whoever
maintained that the Parliament might upon such a bare *supposition* of
such a meere *intention* of the King's, take up Armes, the actuall *invasion* of Liberties, *invitation* and *detention* of Delinquents from triall by Law, to be a party in Armes against the Parliament, thereby to
dissolve, or at least to *remove* it without the *Houses'* consent, flatly
against a *Law* of this very Parliament, *Importation of forraigne Armes
and Souldiers, illegall Commissions to imploy them,* &c. all voted in Parliament to have been done, amount to more than *suppositions* of
meere *intentions.* But to passe by this, (as the property of the *Ferne,*
which uses to have a broad *top,* but a narrow *roote*) the thing that he
prosecutes, though not proposes, is that 1. *No supposition, or case can
authorize Subjects to take up Armes against their King;* and then 2. *That
such a case as the present Parliament pretends to have, it hath not;* and 3.
Therefore no Subject can take up Armes with good conscience.

The best way therefore of Answer, will be to cleare these three
Propositions.

1. *A Parliament of England* may with good *conscience,* in *defence of
King, Lawes* and *Government* establisht, when *imminently endan-*

gered, especially when *actually invaded,* take up Armes without, and against the *Kings personall* Commands, if he *refuse.*

2. The finall and *casting result* of the State's *judgement* concerning what those *Laws, dangers,* and *meanes* of prevention are, resides in the *two Houses* of Parliament.

3. In this finall *Resolution* of the *States Judgement* the *People* are to rest, and in *obedience* thereto may with good *conscience,* in *defence* of the *King, Laws* and *Government, beare* and *use Armes.*

These made good, the answer to his severall Sections will be very easie.

If anyone thinke much I doe not answer the Doctor in his three proposed *Resolves* upon his *Question,* I answer I am enforced to answer what he *would* say, for (to say truth) *resolving,* as he doth, upon a *Question* that never came in *Question;* That no *conscience* upon such a *supposition* as was never made, can have safe *ground* for such a *resistance* as was never *undertaken,* he sayes (upon the matter) *nothing* at all. Only sets up an *Army* ingaged in a *quarrell* of his owne *fancy,* a *Mawmet* of his own *dressing,* which he cudgels into the *Clouts* he himselfe hath *put it* in. He *disputes* with his owne corner *Cap,* and is his owne *John a Nokes,* and *John a Style* both: much what as *Mountebankes* use to doe, who make *wounds* only, the better to sell their *plasters.* And to answer him word by word, as he goes along in the *Treatise* (wherein for the more *gravity* and (it may be) the more to *amuse* and loose the *Reader,* he makes the *Nominative* case in every sentence, to give the *Verbe twelve-score* at *starting*) would swell the *Answer* into too great an affliction upon these dispatchfull and urgent times. How many *weekes* soever the *Doctor* hath been about the *Treatise,* it is well known to many, the answer cost not many *houres* the doing.

Propos. 1. A *Parliament* of *England* may with good *conscience* in *defence* of *King, Laws* and *Government* established, when *imminently endangered*, especially when *actually invaded*, take up *Armes* without, and against the *King's personall Commands*, if he *refuse*.

Before we judge of what a *Parliament* can doe in *England*, it will be needfull to know what kind of *Government* this of *England's* is. We are therefore to know, that *England's* is not a simply *subordinative*, and *absolute*, but a *Coordinative*, and *mixt Monarchy*. This *mixture*, or *Coordination* is in the very *Supremacy* of power itselfe, otherwise the *Monarchy* were not *mixt:* all *Monarchies* have a *mixture*, or composition of *subordinate*, and under-officers in them, but here the *Monarchy*, or *highest* power is itselfe *compounded* of 3 *Coordinate* Estates, a *King*, and two *Houses* of Parliament; unto this *mixt* power no *subordinate* authority may in any case make *resistance*. The rule holds still, *Subordinata non pugnant, subordinates* may not strive; but in this our mixt highest power, there is no *subordination*, but a *Coordination:* and here the other rule holds as true, *Coordinata invicem supplent, Coordinates* supply each other. This *mixture* the *King's* Majesty himselfe is often pleased in his *Declarations* to applaud, as by a *mutuall counterpoise* each to other, sweetening and alaying whatever is harsh in either. The *Treatiser* himselfe doth no lesse, calling it, *That excellent temper of the three Estates in Parliament*, confessing them *(there)* to be *the Fundamentals of this Government*, and if *Fundamentals*, what *subordinations* (I pray) can there be in them? *Fundamentals* admit not of *higher* and *lower*, all foundations are principall alike. And I cannot but wonder that that position of the *Observator*, the *King* is *Universis minor*, should be by this *Resolver* and others so much exploded, for if the *temper* (as he speakes) of this *Government* be of *three Estates*, he need not *buy* the *Almanack* (he speakes of) to *reckon by, that one is lesse than three*.

But you say, what? Is not the *Parliament subordinate* to the *King?* Are they not all *Subjects?* I answer; the *Parliament* cannot be said properly to be a *Subject*, because the *King* is a part, and so hee should be *subject* to himselfe: no, nor are the *two Houses* without him *Subjects;*

every member *seorsim*, taken *severally*, is a *Subject*, but all *collectim* in their *Houses* are not, nay, *Bracton* the great Lawyer is so bold, as to say, *The King hath above him, besides God, the Law, whereby he is made King, likewise his Court of Earles and Barons, &c.* But we need not goe so high, it will serve our turne, if the *Houses* be in this *mixture* or *temper* of *Government*, not *subordinate* or *subject*, then, if they do as *Coordinates* should, *supply* each other's failings, no *highest* power is resisted.

But you'll say, how can they which are every one apart *Subjects*, not be all *Subjects* in their *Houses?* Doth the *King's Writ unsubject* them? No, it was the *consent* of both *King* and *people*, in the first *coalition* or *constitution* of the *Government*, that makes them in their severall *Houses coordinate* with his *Majesty*, not *subordinate* to him, how else were the *Monarchy mixt* more than that of *Turkie?* But doth not the *King's Writ* make them a *Parliament?* It doth ordinarily, *in actu exercito*,[1] but *in actu signato*,[2] it is the *Constitution* of the *Governement designes* them to it, and accordingly provides for it in an *annuall*, or now *triennuall* vicissitude; where note by the way, that whereas it is often urged, that they are but *his Councell*, to be *called by him*; it is true, that office is *ordinarily betrusted* to him, but they are by the first *constitution* not to be *elected* by him, but *assigned* to him, not *assumed* (as *Moses* his under-officers, of *Jethro's* advice) not only the *King's*, but the *Kingdome's Councell, elected* by *it*, not *him*, and have not only a power of *consulting*, but of *consenting*. The *Writ* for the House of Commons is *ad faciendum, & consentiendum*,[3] however, we know they must *consent* before it can be a *Law*, whereby it sufficiently appeares, they are a *coordinative part* in the *Monarchy*, or *highest* principle of power, in as much as they beare a *consenting* share in the *highest office* of it, the *making* of *Lawes*.

---

1. In the act as performed (i.e., without explicit awareness).
2. In the act as made reflectively explicit (i.e., done while one is adverting to it expressly).
3. To be done and consented to.

But you'll say, can there be more than one *highest?* No, there is but *one*, but that *one* is a *mixt one*, else the *Monarchy* were not *mixt*.

But you'll say, how doth it appeare that the *constitution* of this governement is such? I answer (besides his Majestie's above mentioned confession, and the Houses' share in the highest office of governement, that of *making Lawes*) by the mutuall *Oathes* the King and people are to take to maintaine the *Lawes* that have so *constituted* it. *Fortescue* is herein full and home, (i) *The King is to governe his people by no other than that kind of power which flowes to him from their consent, and that is a polliticall not regall power.* Now he that knowes anything of Greek, knowes the word *Polliticall* implies a *mixt Principal*, specially when opposed to *regall*.

But you'll say (with the *Treatiser*) the *King* is *King* before he takes his *Oath.* 'Tis true, but he is *King* but upon the same *trust* which his *Predecessours* (in whose right he followes) *swore* to; and the *Oath* which the *Law* provides for the *King* and his *Predecessours* to take, *virtually* binds him even before he take it, while he holds the *Kingdome*, but in the right of *succession*, for the same *Law* that conveys upon him the *Crown* in right of *succession*, charges upon him the taking of the same *Oath* his *Predecessours* have done, from whom by *that Law* he claimes the *Crowne;* in that respect it is, that the *King* is said in *Law* not to *die*, but *demise*, because they *all* still live in him.

But you'll say, 'Tis hard to apprehend how the same men that are all *Subjects* severally, should in their houses not be *subject*, but *coordinate* with the King? It may appeare easily thus: a *Father* and a *Sonne* are by a deed of *enfoement* jointly entrusted with *certaine Lands* to uses, the *Sonne* is still *subordinate* to the Father as *Sonne;* but as *Feofee*, in the *trust*, he is not *subject* but *coordinate* and joint with him. And therefore it is not a little to be wondered at, that so many especially of the *Lords*, who are *Conciliarii nati, borne Councellours to the State*, in whom their shares both of *trust* and *interest* in this *Supremacy* of power in Parliament, the very *constitution* itself of the government hath *invested* their very *blood* with, should be so much wanting to *themselves*, their *posterities* and *it*, as upon a bare *whistle* to desert *that trust* and *interest* in the governement, which their *Fathers* with so much of their care conveyed upon them, and so much of their *bloud* preserved for them. Their very style *Comites* and *Peeres* imply in *Parliament* a *coordinative Society* with his *Majesty* in the *government;* they are in *Parliament* his *Comites*, his *Peers*. I know 'tis strongly alleadged that they could not stay with *safety* for *routs* and *tumults*. I must confesse 'tis much to be wished there had been none; but the *Houses* alleadge againe, they hindered them what they could, and there was no *Law* to punish them, specially comming but as *Petitioners,* and that his Majestie's feare was so little from them, that the morrow after the greatest of them, he went into *London* with an ordinary retinue; and that most of the *Lords* departed not, till long after all was quiet; what had become of *Israel,* if *Moses* had left his *charge* upon every *tumult?* But of this but by the way.

The world hath been long abused by *Court-Preachers* (such may be as this Doctor) first crying up the *sole Divinity* of *Monarchy* in generall, and then (what must follow) the *absolutenesse* of this in the *King's sole Person*. No marvell,—*id sibi negoti*—by *this craft they got their living*. Now they doe (with this *Resolver*) begin to fore-see and acknowledge, that if *Monarchy* were of *morall* and *speciall institution* from God, it would at once condemne all other formes of government of rejecting a divinely *morall,* and therefore *universall institution,* and make this *Monarchy* as *unlimited* as any other; for what *limits* or *afterbounds* can man set to God's speciall *institution?* That there be in all *Societies* of men, a *governement* (capable of it's *end, safety*) is out of question *God's institution* and *morall;* but that this governement be so, or so moulded, qualified and limited, is as questionlesse from the *paction* or *consent* of the *Society* to be governed, *Hanc potestatem à populo effluxam Rex habet* (as *Fortescue* before) the qualification of the power is an *efflux* of the people's *consent,* as the power itselfe (as the Doctor tells us) an *eflux* of God's *Providence;* and to say truth, he himselfe acknowledges as much, confessing, *That no particular forme of government* is, *jure divino*, it must be then *humano* sure, from the people's *consent.*

It was but a while since good *Pulpit stuff* with *Court-Doctors, That* safety *being the* end *of government, and the* King *only by God solely* entrusted *with it, he was not bound by or to any* human Lawes *in the managing it to that it's end; he was to use whatever the* result *of his owne* judgement *concluded fit and conducing thereunto, nay he was not bound to keepe any* Oath *he tooke to the people to be ruled therein by* Law; *there could be no* commutative justice *betweene him and them, only* distributive *from him to them, so that all they had was his, to the very* parings of their nails, *his* Oath *was but a peece of his* Coronation show, *he might take it today and breake it tomorrow without perjury, because he was under a former and higher* obligation *to God (by whom only he was* trusted, *and to whom only* accountable) *to use whatever meanes he should thinke conducing to the* end *for which he had it only from God: that the* Salus populi *committed* only *by God, and* solely *to* Him, *was a Law between God and him* only, *before all other Laws, and therefore these must not hinder him in the discharge of that to God by any means, which he should find in his owne judgment conducing therunto, the* Oathe's *fault (not* his) *was in being* taken, *not broken.* And to this purpose the whole body of the *Cannon Law* was mercilesly *racked* and *raked* into, for rules miserably mis-applied, as *A turpi voto muta decretum, Quod incautè vovisti ne feceris,*[4] and *Non perficienda promissio sed paenitenda praesumptio,*[5] &c. yea and some seeming *Scriptures* shamefully suborned too, as that of *David's* confession, *against thee only have I sinned,* spoken, *only* in respect of the secrecy of his sinne, and therefore 'tis added, *and done this evill in thy sight,* or because sinne is properly against no one but God, being a *transgression of his*

4. By a shameful vow change the decree, Do not do what you have carelessly vowed to do.
5. The promise is not to be performed, but presumption is to be regretted.

Law. As if the King tho' he be, *custos utriusque tabulae, Keeper* of both
Tables, yet were bound to *keep* only the first, he owes no duty to man
at all? And againe, *that other* of David's *praise, My Lord the King is as
an Angell of light; now Angels are accountable to God only, not men; and
therefore the* Oath *the King takes, is (forsooth) not to men but God;*
(whereas *Divinity* tells us the formall difference betweene an *Oath*
and a *Vow,* is, that a *Vow* is *to* God, an *Oath* is *by* God, wherein there
are 3 parties still, *who,* by *whom* and *to whom;* belike then, if he sweare
to God, the people are the party *by whom* he sweares. Nay, our owne
Dialect will tell us, That the King is our *liege* Lord, as well as we his
liege people, that is (as the word signifies) *mutually bounden* each to
other). All this and much more of this *Demetrian* divinity was ordinarily preached by these *Court Earewiggs,* and all upon this errour
that the Doctor *resolves* on, that the *sole Supremacy* of power was in
the *King's Person,* and that *his* judgement was the *sole* supreame *rule*
of that power. But we go on.

Now the *end* or purpose of this *mixture* of the 3 *Estates* in this government, 'tis the *safety* of its *safety,* as all governement aimes at *safety,*
so this temper in it at the making this *safety* more *safe* or sure. The
common interest of the whole body of the Kingdome in Parliament,
thus twisted with the Kings, makes the *Cable* of its *Anker* of *safety*
stronger. So then, the government by *Law* its *rule,* unto *safety* its *end,*
is ordinarily betrusted to the King, wherein, if he faile and refuse, either to follow the *rule* Law, or to its *end* safety, his *coordinates* in this
mixture of the supreame power must according to their trust *supply.*
But you'll say, there is no *written* or *fundamentall* Law for this. I answer (to speake properly) if it be *written* it is *superstructive* and not
fundamentall, written Lawes, that were not Lawes before *written,* are
repealeable and alterable, even while the government remaines the
same, *fundamentals* cannot: a foundation must not be stirred while
the building stands. That of *Magna Charta,* where most of these *fundamentals* are (at least) implied was *Law* before 'twas *written;* and but

there, and then, collected for easier conservation and use; but if we would know what is meant by those *fundamentall Lawes* of this Kingdom, so much jeered at in this and other *Pamphlets;* it is the originall *frame* of this *coordinate* government of the 3 *Estates* in Parliament *consented* to, and *contrived* by the people in its first *constitution,* and since in every severall raigne confirmed both by mutuall *Oathes* between King and people, and constant *custome time* (as we say) *out of mind,* which with us amounts to a *Law,* wherein the *rule* is, *Quod non disprobatur praesumitur,*[6] it cannot be disproved from taking place upon all occasions, therefore it is to be presumed to have continued from the beginning, even in the Parliament Summons of *Edward* I. This Law is called, *Lex stabilita, & notissima,*[7] even before it was a *record.*

Now as this *mixture,* the mean unto this fuller *safety,* dies not, 'tis not *personall* but *incorporate,* and *Corporations* (the Law sayes) *die not,* so, that *Reason* or *Wisdome* of *State* that first *contrived* it dies not neither, it lives still in that which the law calls the *Reason* of the *Kingdome,* the *Votes* and *Ordinances* of *Parliament,* which being the same (in the construction of the Law) with that which first *contrived the government,* must needs have still power to *apply* this *coordination* of the *government* to its end *safety,* as well as it had at first to *introduce* it; otherwise it should not still continue in the *office* of a *meane* to its *end.*

Here, in our present case the necessity of applying this *coordination* or *mixture* of the *government* is *imminence of danger,* which (if any man will make himselfe so very a stranger at home and to all the world besides) as to deny it, the matter is not great, 'tis *coram non judice,*[8] it has another competent and entrusted *judge,* the *two Houses* (wherein the *Law* makes the *Reason* of the *Kingdom* to reside) who have by *Vote* concluded it. Nay the *King's Majesty* himselfe acknowl-

---

6. Whatever is not disproven is presumed.
7. An established and well-known law.
8. In the presence of one who is not a judge.

edges *imminence of danger* in his *Writ of Summons, Mandamus quod consideratis dictorum regotiorum arduitate, & periculis imminentibus,*[9] imminent *dangers:* where, (by the way) we may take notice, that his Majesty is by the above-mentioned fundamentall *Law* to call a *Parliament* when there shall be any *imminent danger.*

Well, in this *imminent danger* of the State, the meane thought fit by this the Kingdome's *reason* to this end its *safety,* is, the securing of its *Militia:* (the *seeds* of Reformation are to be sowne, and no man but makes his *fence* before he sowes his *seed;* the State is in its unsound and rotten parts to be *lanced,* it may be *dismembered,* and who will goe about such a cure, but he will first bind the *patient*). In this, the ordinary way is taken, by a *Bill* offered the *King,* he refuses to passe it; I know 'twill be said, he never refused to passe it. It cannot be denied but that he refused to passe it according to the *advice of the Houses,* which is (sayes the Law) the same *ever-living reason* of the State that first *advised* the government, and must still *advise* the way of *applying* it. But doth not this you'll say deny the King his *negative* voice in making Law? No. This *Vote* or *Ordinance* of the two Houses, 'tis not an *Act* of Parliament, or Law; 'tis but an occasionall supply of this *coordination* of the government (in case of one part's refusall) least the whole should ruine, and to continue but untill a *Law* may be had.

But you'll say, how, and where doth this *Reason* of the State thus residing in the *Votes* of Parliament, live in the *intervals* of Parliament. I answer, *virtually* it lives to the needs of the State, in the present *Laws,* the births of those *Votes, potentially* in Parliaments to be called when there is need, it being but *occasionall,* needs no continued actuall existence.

Well, hereupon the ordinary way of *Bill* failing, the Houses must not desert their trust, but apply it that way which by the first *consti-*

9. We command that the arduousness and the imminent dangers pertaining to the business stated be taken into consideration.

tution of the government in such case is left them, that is, by their *Votes* and *Ordinances,* wherein (as before) the same *Reason* of the State still lives to pursue its *safety.* The King still persists in his refusall, and insteed of passing a *Bill* for this secured *Militia,* raises an *Army* against their *Ordinance* for it, claiming *trust* thereof to belong to him; they deny it not, so he discharge it by this entrusted *Reason* of the Kingdom, the advice of Parliament. He will doe it, but it shall be by the advice of them against whom it is to be secured, whom the Parliament has voted enemies of the State, and against whom especially it was first *called.* Now 'tis a rule in Law, *Interest reipublicae ne sua re quis malè utatur,* No man may use his own right to the *Commonwealth's* wrong or damage; the *Law* provides, that a man *burne not his own Corne, drowne not his own Land;* nay, that a man *bind not himselfe from Marriage, or the manurance or tillage of his own Land,* because against the good of the *Common-wealth.*

Well, the *King* insteed of applying this trust of the *Militia* (ordinarily his) against these *voted* enemies of the *Common-wealth's,* gathers those very enemies into an *Army* against the *Parliament,* that had *voted* them such, or which is all one, the *over-voting* party therein; 'tis certaine the *Law* allowes not the *King* without consent of *Parliament* to raise an *Army,* 'tis as certaine these men thus in Armes, tho' raised by his *Personall command,* are enemies to him in his *politicke capacity* as *King,* because they are in Armes against *Law,* and so against the *Kingdom,* and so against *him as King;* who (tho' in place he be) cannot in *Law* be divided from his *Kingdom* or *Parliament,* no more than the *head* can from the *body;* nay, they are not only in Armes against *Law (i)* without its authority, but against the very being of it which depends on *Parliament.* What shall the two other *Estates doe?* Nothing but an *Army* is left whereby to represse these enemies of *King* and *Kingdome;* the third *Estate,* the *King,* is so farre from joining to raise an *Army* to that purpose, as he invites and detaines these enemies of the *Kingdome* from its justice. What, but use that *power* in

Armes, which the *government* in such case of the *King's* refusall hath *entrusted* them with to its *preservation*, especially when 'tis but for the apprehending of such enemies to it, as (besides their *voted delinquency* by the *State's* judgement) are sufficiently convinced by their own *flight* from its *justice*; *qui fuget Legem fatetur facinus*, flight argues guilt alwayes. Every *Court* in its *capacity*, has power to apprehend and bring *Delinquents* to the justice of it, and that by force, and if need be, by arming the *posse comitatus* to enforce it, and why not the *Parliament* the *regall Court*, the *posse Regni?* An *attempt* to kill a *Judge* on the *Bench*, the *Law* makes *treason*, and why? But because 'tis in his *Laws* and *Courts* that the *King* specially raignes, 'tis in them his *Crowne* and *dignity* is more specially *impeached*. But you'll say, 'tis the *King* makes it a *Parliament*, and he is not there.

To which I answer, in a *coordinate* and *mixt government*, one part's refusall exempts not the other from its *duty*, nor must it *defraud* the whole of its *safety;* so, it should *frustrate* the very *end* of that its *coordination*, which is (as we have seene) *supply*, for the more *security* of its *safety*.

Next, at all times the *Houses* are *a part* in the supremacy of power, and in case of the other part's absence and refusall both, *virtually* the *whole*, but more specially at this time, now the *King* hath bound himselfe by *Law* not to *dissolve* them without their *consent:* for however many style them now in the *King's* absence no *Parliament* at all, and his Majestie's own *Papers* have some expresses tending that way, yet I would faine know, whether there be now actually in *England* a *Parliament* or no? If there be not, how came it *dissolved?* The *King* hath bound himself from being able to *dissolve* it without their *consent*, they cannot without *his*, neither *consent* hath been obtained. *Legally* dissolve it he cannot by his *removall*, for, then he should be able to *keepe* and *breake* his *Law* at once, for the *Act* is against *removall* without *consent* as well as *dissolution*. And illegally *dissolve* it he cannot, if so *dissolved*, it would remaine a *legall Parliament* still, an *injury* cannot take away a *right*. Well then, a *Parliament* it still remaines in his absence, and if a *Parliament*, why should it not have the *power* of a *Parliament?* A *Parliamentary power* is the *inseparable adjunct* of a *Parliament:* why not able then, in *order* to the *end* of a *Parliament* his and its *preservation*, and therein of the *whole*, to apply the power of that *whole* wherewith it is *entrusted?* Why should the *whole* be frustrated of its *safety*, the *end* it first *coordinated*, and thereby fitted the *government* to, by one part of that *government's* refusall, when the other part is willing? Specially when that one part hath bound itselfe out from hindering the other's willingnesse, willingnesse to preserve the *whole*, and in the *whole* that unwilling part too. However this *Resolver* slight the *Observator's* Argument drawn from the highest *end* of *government*, the people's *safety*, he cannot deny but that the *rule* holds alwayes, *finis quo ultimatior eo influxu potentior*, the *highest end* hath the *strongest influence*, to that *end* still all other *subordinate ends* stand but in the *office* of *meanes*, and this that very Text the *Resolver* so much clings to, evinces, where the *higher power is called a Minister for thy good*. The people's *good* is the *highest end* of the *highest power*, and therefore that which gives *essence* and *denomination* to that *power* according to those *rules* in nature, *Finis habet rationem formae in moralibus*, the *end* hath the *office* of the *forme* in *moralls*, and *Forma dat nomen & esse*, the *forme* gives *denomination* and *essence* both, the *end* then being tho' last in the *execution* yet first in the *intention* of the *efficient*, must needs qualifie and regulate the *worke*.

Yes, a fine way you'll say of preserving the *King* by fighting against him; no such matter, the *King* hath a double *capacity, politick* and *naturall*, in his *politick capacity* as *King*, in fighting for the preservation of the *Land* and *Kingdome* they fight for him, what *King* could he be without a *Kingdome* to governe, and *Law* to governe it by? In that therefore the *Law* tells us, he cannot be severed from his *Kingdom*, or *Parliament* its representative body (tho' never so farre in Person distant from it). And in his *naturall capacity*, as a man, they fight not against him in that neither, they humbly begge his safer presence with them, at least his withdrawing from his, and their enemies; nay, they fight for him this way too, we never reade of a *King* once *unkinged* but he is quickly *unmanned* too, they fight to disingage and unthrall his Person from that unsafe and unworthy imployment those enemies to *him* and his *Kingdom* put it to, in making it a *shelter*, a *breast worke*, but a *mudd wall* to their *own dangers*, which they feare from his *own Laws:* for however his Majesty may be perswaded by them, 'tis his *cause* has engaged them, (most of them) 'tis their own *guilt* and danger that hath *engaged them*, and *engaged* them to *engage* him. And although in their mutuall *engagements*, they may think either's turne served, it may be neither sufficiently knows who *steers* their course, what depth of water they *draw;* certainly, he that looks on the *conjunctures* of the late affaires of this and the neighbour *States*, cannot but beleeve (tho' unknown to his Majesty, and it may be many about him) that those *long-spoones* to feed with the *Devill* with, (as one calls them) the *Jesuites*, both at home and abroad throughout most parts of Christendome have (tho' at a distance) the *first* and *highest* and therefore *strongest influence* into his *Majestie's present councels*, baiting their unseen *hooks* with his and his Armie's *interests*, making them but to *pull* at the *Oare* while those *sit* at the *stern.* His Majestie's aime (may be) is to bring his *Crown out of wardship*, (as *Lewis II* of *France* bragged of his) his Army's (may be) many of them but at keeping their necks out of the *haltar*, but those *Basilisks* (that kill with their *eyes* at distance) look further, and have their *ends mingled* with, and *lapt* up in these, upon *Religion* and the *State* both.

2. *The finall and casting result of this State's judgement, concerning what those Proposed Laws, dangers, and means of prevention are, resides in the two Houses of Parliament.*

Well, in this *mixture* of the *Monarchy* or *supreame power* and *trust* of Government, the two *Houses* of *Parliament* making a *coordinate* part, what is their share? You'll say, they are the King's *great Councell*,

but what, only to *consult?* (Then questionlesse; he, and not we were to
elect them, who chuses not his own *Counsell* that he is but to consult
with? No, but to *consent* with him in the making of Lawes the highest office of *Government;* but how a Councell voluntarily *assumed* by
him (as *Moses* his *substitutes* in the *Wildernesse*) no, but *assigned* to
him by the first *constitution* of the Government from the very same
consent of the people that first made the *King,* and by succession him
that King, in whom the first *King* still lives as in a *Corporation* (as the
Law calls him) which *dies* not; For the Doctor dares not *speak out,*
when he talkes of the *King's right* by conquest to the Kingdome. *Conquests* (I confesse) may give such a right as *plunderers* use to take in
houses they can master, a *jus in re,* not a *jus ad rem,* (as the Law
speaks) a *jus tenoris,* not a *tenorem juris,* a right of tenure, but no
tenour of right; how, not only undoctorall, but how unchristian, inhumane a *barbarisme is it,* to talke of a right of *Conquest* in a *civill,* a
Christian State? Were a Land inhabited by *Wolves* and *Tigers* only
conquest might give a right because none could claime any other; but
among *men* capable of, and invested in a *right,* there was never more
than two wayes of *alienation* of a *right, forfeiture* and *consent,* and even
in *that* of *forfeiture* there is a *consent* too implied, the condition is
(therein) consented to, on both sides, and what *forfeiture* can there
be where there was never any *covenant?* If *Conquest* may create a *Title*
where there was none before, certainly it may make *that Title* as *absolute* and *arbitrary* as the Conquerour pleases, for what should *let,*
where there needs no *consent* or *covenant,* and then, why might not
such sooner a King in a *limited Monarchy* (as this is) make himselfe as
Arbitrary as he pleased by *Conquest?* 'Tis easier to *augment* than to
create: no conquest may *restore* a right, forfeiture may *loose* a right, 'tis
consent only that can *transact* or *give* a right. And I cannot let passe
how many ways this *Resolver* abuses his Majesty herein. A *Title* he
has (he sayes) by conquest; but he must not *rule by it;* a *King* as *Conquerour,* and yet he must not *rule* as *Conquerour;* what a strange *Title*

is this that makes him a *King*, but gives him not any *Rule?* And how *injurious* doth he (herein) labour to make the King to his *posterity*, as well as *rulelesse* in *himselfe?* How much doth he wrong his *inheritance* that subscribes and *sweares* to a *limited Title*, and has a *free* one the while to hold by?

Well a power of *consenting* is of all hands agreed on to be in the *two Houses*, the faculty of *Legem dare*[10] is not in difference, the question is about the *Declarative* that of *Legem dicere*,[11] the Law is the *rule*, and cannot be framed without all the *three Estates*, but who must *apply* this *rule* by giving it the finall and casting *resolution* of its sence? without which the *Record* is but the *Sheath*, 'tis the sence is the *Sword* of the Law; such a *power* or *faculty* there must be in every legall *government*, after all *debatement* to give Lawes their sence, beyond all *further debatement*, otherwise, there would be a *Processus in infinitum*, *debatement* still upon *debatement*, and as *nature* avoids *infinitudes*, so the Law *inconveniences*, even above *mischiefs*: and it were a defect of no lesse than infinite inconvenience to the *end* of the Law, Government. If this *decisive faculty* after the *debative* hath passed upon the sence of the Law, were not some where resident in the governement, *Perfectum est cui nihil quod convenit deest*, and 'tis a monster in Nature, *quod deficit necessariis, That is perfect which wants not what is convenient, that a monster in Nature which is defective in what is necessary.* And where should this faculty reside, but in the *two Houses?* in whose *Votes* the Law itselfe places that very same specifick *reason* of the kingdome, that at first *contrived* and still *animates* the Government; and which ever since contrives the very Laws themselves to be declared, (*every one abounding most in his owne sence*); which thus we prove.

This *Principle* which all *debates* about the sence of the Law are to be *resolved* into *without further debatement*, must be either the *Records*

10. To give the law.
11. To utter the law.

themselves, or the *Judges*, or the *King*, or *Houses of Parliament:* Not 1.
The *Records*, for that's the peculiar Priviledg of God's word to be *au-
tocriticall*, its own last Judge, and even therein too, 'tis he who was the
first *contriver*, that is, the last *Interpreter*. God only could fore-see
from the beginning, what doubts may arise about the meaning of any
part of his *Records*, and therefore he only can *supply* & fit those with
some other part thereof to *interpret them;* Man's Laws are therefore
still liable to *repeales & dispensations*, because the makers could not
for-see how unfit they might prove for after times, & even then those
repeals & dispensations given them are (in construction of Law) no
other than *interpretative* still; it is *interpreted* that had their first makers of them lived to see their unfitnes, they would have consented to
those their *repeals* and *dispensations;* the *Records* then may be helps to
their *Interpreters*, not the *Interpreters*, because 'tis they that are to bee
interpreted, they are the *rule*, they cannot be the *hand* too, to apply it;
though penned with never so much care, time will weare them into a
capacity (at least) of different sences to different understandings, and
a *different* or *double* sence cannot be this highest *principle* of *resolution*, there can be but *one highest.*

Why not the Judges then? They take *solemne Oathes to interpret
Law aright;* true, yet we see *their interpretations* and *Oathes* to fall
under *further debatement* still, witnesse (besides many other) the late
case of *Ship-money*, the *Oath* they take 'tis to the *State*, and therefore
that by its *reason* residing in *the Votes* of *Parliament*, is to judge how
truely they have *kept it.* It comes then to fall betweene the King and
Parliament, which shall have *it?* Both cannot, if devided, as now they
are (at least *personally*) and the principle of *ultimat resolution* cannot
be a *divided one*, for then it cannot *resolve.*

But you'll say the *principle* of making Law is *King* and *Parliament
jointly.* True, *jointly*, a *joint principle* it may be, but not a *divided* one.
But you'll say, If *Lawes* cannot when the principle is *divided* be made,
nor must they in such a case be *declared?* I answer there is more need

of *declaring* old Lawes than of *making new,* a *State* may be governed by *the old ones without new;* but not by the *old* ones without this finall *resolution* of their sense, they are of no use *without it,* the making of Law, is a standing *permanent* Act *in facto,* done at *once,* the applying them by their *interpretations,* a transient one, *in fieri* alwayes a *doing.* But you'll say then, if this *declarative* power be so necessary, and so necessarily in the Houses, how shall we doe in *the intervals of Parliaments?* I answer the *judgements* of inferiour *Courts* must stay further debates untill a *Parliament* be had to try those *judgements* by, which therefore should (by Law) be once a *yeare* (at least). Well then, if this last casting principle be so necessary, and cannot be a *divided* one, why not the King? He cannot in himselfe be *divided,* the *Parliament* may? I answer, first, though the Members be devided, the *major part* that carry the *Vote* cannot be. Next, this *principle* as it is thus *necessary,* so it must be a *competent* one too, and that requires two things, *ability* and *fidelity; ability* to know what he is to judge, and *fidelity* to judge but what he knowes aright; for matter of *ability* to take cognizance of the cause by. His Majesty often professes himselfe no *Lawyer;* therefore, in Law he judges not but by his *Courts,* in the meanest of which the *sentence* past stands good in Law, though the King by *Proclamation* or in *Person* should oppose it: whereas there is nothing more frequent or proper to *Parliaments* than to *reverse* any of their *judgements.* But the King (you'll say) has *promises* of assistance from *God* himselfe to enable him herein, A *divine sentence is in the mouth of the King, and his lips shall not transgresse in judgement;* and againe, *my Lord the King is as an Angell of God to discerne betweene good and evill.* True, such Scriptures I know have been taught to speake what Kings *can doe* instead of what Kings *should doe,* but *these* are no *promises* but *precepts,* at least but particular *praises* of one, no generall *claimes* of all Kings, nay one of the wisest Kings (and ours too) experimentally confesses, *That with Kings 'tis so much the more hard to doe right, by how much 'tis so easie to doe wrong;* and indeed what would such a power be lesse than *arbitrary*, if what he *please* to declare to be so, must be *Law*, so, what *vaine things* would *Parliaments* be, what *wild things Kings*, and what *miserable things* Subjects? But in point of *fidelity*, why not the King rather than the *Parliament?* Why may there not be a factious, packt or enslaved *Parliament*, as well as a willfull, flattered, abused King? Yes I confesse 'tis possible, but nothing so likely, and it behoves the wisdome of a Government, where nothing can be *contrived* against *possibility* of miscarriage, to secure what may be against *probability*. So much the *Resolver* acknowledges, *Wee cannot* (he says) *expect absolute meanes of safety in a State, but such as are most reasonable.* Now experience shews that most men's actions are swayed (most what) by their *ends* and *interests;* those of Kings (for the most part) *as absolutenesse of rule, enlargement of Revenue by Monopolies, Patents,* &c. are altogether incompatible and *cross centered* to those of Subjects, as *Property, Priviledge,* &c. with which the *Parliament's* either *ends* or *interests* cannot thus dash and *interfer,* the Members are all Subjects themselves, not only *entrusted with,* but selfe *interested* in those very *priviledges* and *properties;* besides they are *many,* and so they not only *see* more, but are lesse *swayable; as* not easily reducible to *one* head of *private interest;* but by a neer *equality* of *Votes* (you'll say) in *Parliament* it may come to an odde man to cast by, and then the whole *trust* and *interest* both, lies in him wholy.

I answer, no such matter, *ultimum Stilricidium non exhaurit Clepsydram* the last odde sand doth not make the houreglasse *empty* more than any of the rest it doth but tell us when 'tis *empty* suppose 200, of one side and 201 of the other, the *odds* is carried by the one but the *vote* by the whole 201. The *odde* one tells us 'tis the *major part* but 'tis *all* the rest that *make* it so: so that we have (however) the *judgement, trust* and *interest* of 201 chosen men engaged in the equity and fitnesse of the *Vote*. This is it that great Father of the Law, so much magnifies the wisdom of this government in, *Dum non unius aut centum solum consultorum virorum, sed plus quam trecentorum electo-*

rum hominum, quali numero olim Senatus Romanorum regebatur, ipsa sunt edita, and neer upon that number of 300 the major part of both Houses falls to be.

But you'll say, how if one or both Houses be devided, and that into equall *Votes*, how then is the principle either one, or able to *resolve?* I answer, *de impossibilibus non est deliberandum*, impossibles are not to be consulted on, it cannot be; for in such a case of either House's, equality of Votes their severall Speakers have then, and not till then *Votes* to *cast by*.

But how yet doth it appeare, but that (at least) this power of last Resolution, is as *Arbitrary* in the Houses, as it would be in the King. I answer, it cannot be denied nor avoided, but that as the Government (in the forme or qualification of it) was at first an act of the *will*, and so Arbitrary; so it still remaining the *same* it must remaine somewhere *arbitrary* still, else our forefathers should not convey that same government to us which they began, but should bind us in that wherein they were themselves free. It is the priviledg of God's Laws only to bind unalterablie, now where should the *arbitrariness* of this facultie reside for the *State's* use, but where it was at first in the *consent* and *reason* of the *State?* which as (we have seen) the Law places in the *Votes* of Parliament, where this arbitrariness allaied and ballanced by *number, trust, self interest,* 'tis best secured from doing hurt; in the naturall bodie the *will* followes always the last dictate or resolution of the *understanding,* and that, (in this politick bodie) being the wisdom of its great Councell, what so fit as it to give dictate to what necessarilie remains of will or *arbitrariness* in this faculty? The *Resolver* himself acknowledges no lesse, when he sayes *the King is to see with their eyes that are of different judgment from him.* But yet further if *ability* and *fidelity* make up the competency of a *faculty* to give Law, its finall *resolution* by; why not then the Judges in the *Checquer-chamber* rather than the Members in *Parliament?* They for matter of *ability* are *skilled,* and for matter of *fidelity sworn,* have more *dexterity* to

judge and lesse *liberty* to erre. I answer, for their *skills* and *oath*, the
Houses may make use of both if they please. It was the wisdom of
this government, considering men's aptness rather to warpe after
their *interests* and *ends*, than to be kept upright by their *skills* and
oaths, to trust it rather to many independent men's *interests*, than a
few dependent men's *oaths*, every daye's experience tells us that *interests* are better state security than oaths, specially when those *interests* have (as here) the command of those *oaths*, to bind all that *skill*
too to their service. Besides, as their *interests* with us tie them more to
do a *right*, so our *elections* of them tie us more to suffer what they do
if not a *right:* because, what *they* do, *we* do in them, and self *wrong* is
seldom self *revenged*. Lastly, if theirs be the finall judgment what is
Law, then (*à fortiori*) much more when it is *endangered*, and the state
in it? And what fitting *meanes* of prevention are to be used.

PROP. 3
*In this finall Resolution of the State's judgment the people are to rest, and
in obedience thereto, may with good conscience, in defence of the King,
Laws, and Government bear and use armes.*

This last and casting *resolution* of judgment then (we see) resides in
the two *Houses* of Parliament, which are therefore called the great
Councell, not of the King only, but of the kingdom, and therefore by
it *elected* and *entrusted*, but how resides it in them? *Infallibly?* (As this
Resolver imposes on their *Idolizers* (as he speaks) no. They are not
therein in themselves *infallible*, but to us *inevitable*. Our judgments
are not *enthralled*, 'tis our interests are *entrusted* and so, subjected to
their decisions. Our judgments are not *infallibly* guided from either
erring with them or differing from them, but bound up in, and *superseded* by theirs from gaine-saying or *resistance;* here then (we see)
is no *Parliament Papacy* at all (as the Doctor pleases to descant) he
himself well knowes, that though the *Pope* claim an *infallibility*, and

we deny it *him*, or a generall *Councell* either, yet we ascribe to a rightlie constituted generall Councell; a power of binding all under it, from all manner of disturbance to its decisions; and why should a civill *generall Councell* of *England* have lesse power in it? Yea further, why should we not, (as we have bound ourselves by our choice and trust, externally to submit to their determinations, so) be enduced too, to believe their joint judgments better than our single opinions? There intelligence and assistance is, (in all likeliehood) *much* better, I must confesse in the *Militia Ordinance*, my opinion (possibly) and another's, of this, or that Lord's *fidelity*, may incline us to think they might have been as well continued in their *trusts*. But why should we not beleeve, we may sooner erre therein than they? We know our own, we know not their *informations, discoveries, reasons;* the Law is called *mens sine appetitu*, a mind without passions, and the Law-makers should be (as neer as may be) so too, the *Parliament* a speaking *Law*, as the *Law* a silent *Parliament*. Law-makers should be (as *Aristotle* speaks) but λόγοι than ἄνθρωποι rather *reason* than *men*, and (as he speaks) but [. . .] at most, but peeces of quick and walking *reason;* every Member of Parliament, ('tis like) is not such, yet certainly if some neighbour Members might personally hate this or that *Lord,* upon particular entercourse of wrongs, yet, no one Lord hath in all likeliehood provoked the greater number of the Commons *House,* and 'tis that must go to the displacing him; or if he should, 'tis very much if the other *House* should jumpe with all them in such a *personall* hatred.

Well then, wee see what power the *Law*, through our trust, gives the two *Houses*, and all, in order to the safety of the *King, Law* and *State*. They judge by the *reason* of this *State*, and *rule* of this *Law* (both residing in them) that all three, *King, Law,* and *kingdom*, (in *Law*, as we have heard before not separable), are not only *imminently endangered*, but *actually invaded* by an Army, *engaged* by the adjudged *forfeiture* of their own lives. There remaines no way in the highest *re-*

sult of the State's *reason* to preserve these, and prevent those from apparent mischief, but an *army* to withstand this other *army* ready to *advance,* nay in actuall attempts of hostility; of whom should this *army* of the *state* consist, but those who are *endangered,* nay *assaulted,* yes assaulted, and *plundered* too, nay *murdered,* before in any Parliament army there was so much as man *listed,* all before were but *Musters,* and *manning* of *Forts,* for the kingdome's better defence against Forraign dangers.

Well the case thus standing, this great *Centurion* of the kingdom the Parliament (for the King refusing, we may now (better than our forefathers) give that name to the Houses) sayes unto one of this now necessarily yet voluntarily listed army too, *go and he goes, to another come and he comes, to a third do this and he doth it;* and wherein lies now the unconscionablenesse of this obedience? It is *naturall* all the faculties and members in the naturall body are to the defence of the whole commanded to their offices by the understanding's last *result* or *dictat.* It is *politick, prevention* is the *right* eye of policie, *recovery* is but the *left,* the *after game.* What other authoritie hath a Sheriff or executioner to put a malefactor to death? But you'll say conscience must have some higher footing, 'tis God's *Accomptant,* and must have his *warrant:* and it has that fully to. First, a *warrant* of *Charity,* in the sixth commandement, which not only forbids *murder* but commands the *preservation* of our own & our neighbour's lives. Secondly, of *justice: Render to all what is due,* and we have seen, that in case of the King's refusall (already *voted* by the kingdom's *Reason*) the command of the kingdom's *power* (in order to its *safety*) 'tis its *Councell's due.*

Lastlie, of *obedience, submit yourselves to every ordinance of man, and that for the Lord's sake.* Says *S. Peter,* we have seen it was the *ordinance* of man, the first men that introduced the government of this State, and now of the men that are *ordained* to administer that government. *Let every soule be subject to the higher powers* (saith S. *Paul*)

and that not *for wrath but conscience' sake,* (which place I shall sufficiently cleer anon) besides *David* in his own defence used an army, &
(though against the King) yet is said to *fight the Lord's Battells.* Now
we have seen the Coordination of this highest power in this kingdom
for its better safety, & therein the entirenesse still of its efficacy to its
end, though one part withdraw; if the King (especially now he has
bound himself by Law not to dissolve this present *Coordination*) he
should be able legally to break the *Law,* then his government were
utterly *absolute,* or rather absolutely *impossible,* and *illegally* he cannot, for the Law hath provided that as King *he can do no wrong,* (I)
nothing against Law, because he cannot, (in that capacity) be severed from his Parliament, and what they enact together is *Law.* So
then the *houses'* commands are in this our case acts of the *highest
power* to which the Apostle bids us to be *subject.*

I do not say if any Souldier in this Army of the King and Parliament's (for we see legally severed they cannot be) do fight not satisfied in his own conscience, but that he sins, and that (as the Doctor
urges so often) *Damnably:* I say only, that he hath warrant enough
for his conscience if he apply it, & if he do, the Doctor's *Damnation*
is not that of the *Apostles,* but much what of the nature of that of the
Dammees[12] of these times. And now these three Propositions being
cleered, the Answer to the severall Sections of his Treatise will be
both very short and easie. To answer that all his arguments and instances against resistance are *mis-scaened* in absolute Monarchies,
whereas this of ours is *mixt* would serve the turne; however particularly thus.

The first Section contains little else than the laying down of the
manner of consciences, discourse, by *assuming* to the *Proposition*
granted, and so *concluding:* saving that he there tells us, that all his
fellow *Divines deny to the King an arbitrary Government,* and yet, in

12. "Dammees" was a nickname given to royalist soldiers because of their reputation for
blasphemy.

his fifth Section he tells us too that *the chief power and finall judgment is in one, and he that one:* which what (I pray) amounts it lesse to, than an *Arbitrary* Government? And he denies that again too almost the next word, in his *omnibus ordinibus regni consentientibus,* for what consent of all needs there if the *finall Judgement be in one?* Now that (though the King in Person withdraw) there are *virtualy, omnes ordines regni consentientes,*[13] it hath sufficiently appeared; and for his *person,* if that were with them to consent or dissent either, doubtlesse there would be no resistance made at all.

The 2ᵈ. Section begins with certaine instances of resistance, as that of the people in behalfe of *Jonathan, David's* resistance, and *Elisha's,* but wee make no use of them, need them not, and therefore need not answer the Doctor's refutation of them, only (by the way) *David's* resistance was by an Army, and what use of an Army unlesse it may fight against, as well as avoid the danger, besides 'tis said that (though against the King) *he fought the battels of the Lord* (as before). Other instances hee there hath against resistance, but in all *simple* and *absolute Monarchies,* those of the *Jewes and Romans:* nothing to our case. Only take notice by the way, that those *Monarchies* were *absolute* and *arbitrary* not by *conquest,* but by consent of the people, the *Jewes* desired of God a *King,* to be governed by, *after the manner of the Nations* (sayes the Text) which was *arbitrarily* (as the Doctor observes out of *Justin*) and thereupon is it that God by *Samuel* tells them what such a King *would doe to them,* not what he *might* do (as the Doctor seemes to inferre from the place). And for the *Roman Empire,* its *arbitrarinesse* was not introduced by conquest, but by consent of the Senate, (however it may be awed thereto by Armes). And for that Title of *succession* (he there speakes of) it no way excludes *consent,* for it begins first in the election and *consent* of the people, and *virtually* continues so still in the mutuall bonds of oathes betweene *King* and

13. All consenting orders of the kingdom (probably referring to the orders or estates of Parliament, the king, lords, and commons).

people, to governe and bee governed by Lawes by them *jointly* to be made.

But the maine substance of this Section is a couple of Texts, that of *Rom. 13.* and *I Peter 2.* To the first we easily answer (if not written particularly to the *Romans,* who were under an absolute *Monarchy,* and so no more to concerne us than the Judiciall Law doth (*i.e.*) only in the generall equity of obedience) yet suppose it referre to all government in generall it makes (as 'tis often alledged) altogether for us, it requires obedience to *ordained* powers, (*i.e.*) *legall* commands not *willfull* pleasures of Governour. Now ours is *ordained* to be *coordinate* and *mixt,* and resides in that part of it from which the other though withdrawing in person cannot take it, and to which the Law in such a case cleerely gives it, including (as we have seene) in it *virtually* the other part too, who in his politicke *relation* cannot be thence (as *King*) divided. The meaning of the place then must be this; *The power that be (i.e.) so* or *so* established by *consent* of man, are *ordained* of God to be obeyed; or it is God's *ordinance* that men should live under some government, and *submit* without *resistance* to that kinde of government they have by *consent established,* just (as Saint *Peter* followes him) *to the ordinance of man for the Lord's sake.* When the Papists pressed with this Text, aske us why wee, that are so much for obedience to higher powers, doe not submit to the Church's highest *highest power* in the *Pope?* we answer, 'tis a *usurpt,* not an *ordained* power, *ulcus protestatis,* a *tumor* or wen, no part of the body, a power never either *consented* to by the body of the whole Church, or substituted by its Head CHRIST JESUS. There are two kindes (wee use to say of tyranny, *regiminis* and *usurpationis,* that which is only of *Governement,* though never so heavie yet must be endured, *not only to the good* (sayes the Apostle) *but the froward too,* and therefore I know no man that defends the tenne Tribes' revolt from *Rehoboam* as the Doctor insinuats. That other kind of *usurpation* it hath no right, no *ordination* at all, and so no subjection due to it. In all power of government

Divinity tells us there are foure things; the *institution,* the *constitu-tion,* the *acquisition,* and the *use:* the two latter *acquisition* and *use* are confessed to be often times rather from the Devil by bribery, blood, rapine and the like: the *constitution* alwayes from man's *consent,* the *institution* alwayes from *God,* so that here is more than God's bare *permission or approbation* either (as the Doctor charges us to hold). Here is in every *ordained* power as well God's *institution* of it, and *in-junction* of obedience to it, as man's *constitution* of it. *That* there *be* a Government, 'tis of God, *what* this government shall *be,* whether *Monarchy* or *Aristocracy:* or if *Monarchy,* whether simple and meerely *subordinate,* or mixt and *coordinate* 'tis of man, so then, *Let every soule be subject to the higher powers, for the powers that be, are ordained of God, (i.e.) therefore* let every soule be subject to *powers* (not *wills*) be-cause God's providence hath *instituted* them and *so* subject as man's consent hath *constituted* them. Now we have sufficiently seene by the *constitution* of the power of government of this kingdom, the Law (as the *rule*) is put into the hands of the two *Houses* of Parliament by their *Votes,* (as its *reason*) wherein we must rest to be applied to its *end,* the *safty* of K. & State.

I wonder therefore the Doctor should so much insist on this Text, for if he cannot prove (what he indeed denies) the government to be *absolute,* and soly in the King, he cannot hence enforce obedience to his *personall* commands.

The next text is that of *I Pet. 2. Submit to every ordinance of man,* wherein the Dr. hath espied a double *advantage,* one from the Greeke word ἀνθρωπίνῃ which rather signifies *human* than of *man,* so that it is called *human* (*i.e.*) in or on man (as he would have it) as only the *subject* of it, not any way the *cause.* 'Tis strange a Doctor of Divinity should trifle thus with Scripture, and as *Shoomakers* doe with their Leather, with his teeth stretch it thus to his *Last,* doth he not a few lines after acknowledge (to use his owne words) *that the forme, whether Monarchy, or Aristocracy and qualifications of either forme (i.e.)*

if Monarchy, whether absolute or tempered, are not *jure divino,* what then? Not *jure diabolico* sure, it must be *humano* then, and in *jus humanum,* as 'tis opposed to *divinum,* man sure is the cause and Author, and not the subject only, nay why should the word *human* be there at all, but as contradistinct to what followes, for *God's sake?* Why unlesse to make the sence this? that although the *ordinance* or government, in the manner of its *constitution* be from *man,* yet because in the necessity of its *institution* 'tis from God, submit to it though of *man* for the *Lord's* sake.

His other advantage is in the words *supreme* and *sent,* the King as *supreme, and such as are sent (i.e.)* (sayes hee) the *Parliament:* but the Parliament is *called,* not sent, a difference (at least) as great as betweene *too* and *from;* but wee have already seene how the King is supreame, not (as those of S. *Peter's* times) *absolutely* so, but in his *mixture* and *coordination* with his Parliament, in which every subject is a subject still (as the Doctor urges) but the whole *accordinate* part with him in the *supreame* otherwise they could not hinder him from *making* Lawes, *nor* finally *declare* Law without him, the two highest acts of *Supreame* power.

The third Section especially contains two other texts of Scripture, the first of *Prov. 8.15. By me Kings Reigne.* I answer, 'tis spoken of and by *Wisdome,* and doth shee not as well say (as followes) *by mee Nobles and Senators decree Judgment?* What is here said more of Kings' *Reignes,* than of Parliament's *Decrees,* they should both be guided by *Wisdome,* that is all the place will beare.

The second place is that *Psal. 82.6. I have said yee are God's;* and doth hee not there too (when he speakes it) *stand in the Congregation of the Judges* (as the text speakes) *reproving such as judge unjustly, and accept the persons of the wicked, all* Rulers are *God's* alike, (i.e.) God's *substitutes* and *representatives* towards men, upon whom hee derives some of his power and authority; doth not the word of God come to them all alike (i.e.) as it followes in the Doctor's own words, *a com-*

mission for the setting up of a governing power, whereof the manner of its constitution, hee himselfe before confesses to be from the *people,* not *God;* did not this word come to *Pilat,* as well as to *Caesar. Pilat* had not his power but from above, (as our Saviour tells him), as well as them the Doctor speakes of I wonder *touch not mine Anointed* comes not in among the rest? (as usually it doth) a Text plainely spoken to *Kings* of God's people, not to the people of KINGS; they were (sayes the very Text) *Kings whom he reproved for their sakes, saying touch not mine Anointed.*

What remaines in this Section, 'tis nothing else but a jeering the fundamentall Lawes of this kingdome, so often mentioned by the Parliament, which what they are I have before shewed, not as the Doctor would have it the same with those of *France, Turkie* and all other kingdomes, but proper to *coordinate* and mixt ones, and especially this.

The fourth Section is spent upon a confutation of any power in the people to *reassume* the power they first betrusted to the *King,* the which no man (for ought I know) maintaines, what need the people *reassume* that which in the first *Coalition* of the Governement they reserved (as hath appeared before).

The fifth Section. Here, wee have nothing but strange involutions of the matter, and intanglings of the Reader, most what inconsistent as well as impertinent, one while *the state hath meanes of preservation such as the Law prescribes,* and yet not twentie lines after, *wee cannot expect absolute meanes of safety in a state,* meanes of preservation, but not absolute safety; if it bee preserved, questionlesse 'tis absolutely preserved, *dubiam salutem qui dat afflictis, negat,* he that gives not absolute safety gives none, againe this chiefe power and finall judgement (he sayes) *must be in one,* scarce twelve lines after but *Parliaments* (hee sayes) *are the only remedy for the distempers of the Kingdome,* Parliament is the only remedy and yet the *only* judgement is in the *King.*

And yet againe he tells us in the same Section, that that only judgement too of the *Kings is to see with their eyes that are of different judgment from him.* What remaines in this Section is a plaine *begging* of three *questions* hee would faine have us to maintaine.

First, that every state whether *reserving* it or no, hath this meanes of *safety* by *resistance,* and to this purpose that of the *Church* is objected: a *State* indeed, but neither *civill* nor of its own *constitution,* this state Christ the head did not only *institute* but *constitute* it too, and that without any concurrence of its own consent. Then the Christians in *Tertullian's* time are objected, as if they were a *civill* distinct state from the *Romans,* in which they lived, or the *Roman* other than an *absolute* Monarchie by *consent* of the Senat (as before).

A second question begged is, that *in case the King* and *Parliaments should neither discharge their trust, the people might rise and make resistance against both* a position which no man (I know) maintaines the Parliament's, is the people's *owne consent,* which once passed they cannot revoke; hee still pursues his owne dreame of the people's *reassuming* power, whereas wee acknowledge no power can be imployed but what is *reserved,* and the people have reserved no power in themselves from themselves in Parliament.

This groundlesse preassuming aspertion of the people *reassuming* power I wonder the Doctor so much insists on it.[14] There is indeed a late sawcie Scurrilous pasquill that hath broken prison out of the Gate-house from a company of Delinquents there (and no marvaile if such would reassume all Parliamentary power) by the *resolving* title it should bee a Journyman of the same Trade to this of the Doctor's: where after many stale malitious slanders on the Parliament's proceedings, disproved long since by almost every man's experience, as well as severall Declarations, all to disable the Parliament from the

14. This paragraph was added to the second edition, probably in order to respond to the "late sawcie Scurrilous pasquill" mentioned in the next sentence. This tract was "A complaint to the House of Commons, and resolution taken up," Oxford [London], 1642, Wing C5620. There were two subsequent editions, both printed in Oxford.

kingdome's urgent preservation by any way that the written Lawes
prescribe not, (as if the Circumstances and exigences of publike actions of this sort did not (above written laws) warrant and even element their justnesse) this raving *Bedlam* (I say) broke loose without
a *Keeper*, (deserving (as it professes to desire) no answer, one of *Vul-
can's* forge I confesse were best, *fire* or *fetters);* threatens *the People's
reassuming the entrusted power of Parliament,* and with *Salomon's*
foole, *Pro. 26.18. throwing about him arrowes and fire-brands and death;
complaining* and *threatening* both (according to its Title) concludes
at length with this Resolution, *to lay hold of what is next at hand,* to
the *reassuming* this power: otherwise for ought I know this *reassumption* of power is like that *Popish reassumption* of the House of *Loretto,*
a meere Castle in the air of the Doctor's brain.[15]

The 3d. question in this *Section* begged is; that we hold the *cause*
may warrant a *resistance,* and here we are told what the *Primitive
Christians* suffered without *resistance:* and that the *Netherlands* had
greater *cause* than we to make *resistance,* a contrary *Religion* was urged
on them, whereas we have *ours* still offered us. No, we hold not whatever *cruelty* can be suffered *cause* enough to make *resistance,* 'tis not
the *cause,* 'tis the *constitution* of the governement, *reserving* in its *coordination* a power of *resistance,* in order to its *preservation:* otherwise
were this an *absolute Monarchy,* should the King alone, or (as it is)
should King and Parliament enjoin us all to deny Christ and worship
the *Sun,* we were (though never so able) not to make any *resistance*
but by suffering; the *cause* cannot alter the case here, 'tis the *constitution* must doe it: and yet, if his Majesty might (in case of *Religion*)
helpe the *Rochellers* to resist their King in an *absolute Monarchy,* why
much more might not the Parliament in this.

---

15. The so-called "House of Loretto" in Italy was believed to be the original house at
Nazareth in which the Virgin Mary was born and brought up and had received the annuncia-
tion. Legend had it that this stone house had been brought to successive sites and eventually to
Loretto by angels.

The sixth *Section* containes in substance three bitter invectives, sharpened I believe at the *Philistine's forge* (the Doctor speaks of) *for they defie the host of* Israel.

The first calls the *Parliament,* a *prevailing faction of a few.* Is the *representative Body* of the Kingdome become but a *prevailing faction?* And how a *Faction,* if *prevailing,* though never so *few,* 'tis the *major part prevailes,* and so *prevailing* is the *body,* and can the *Body* make a *Faction* or *Schisme* from *itselfe;* if many of the Members withdraw, the more fault theirs, and shame too, to desert their trust. The Law and reason both tells us, *That no man can take advantage by his owne default;* so, all Parliaments and their Acts too, how easily might they be eluded? Certainly what is *punishable* is not *pleadable,* and *Crompton* (we see) cites the Bishop of *Winton's* case herein, who was *arraigned* in the King's *Bench,* for that he came to the Parliament and departed without its licence.

The second invective is against the Parliament's hostile manner of proceeding in this their warre. *His Majesty hath alwayes been* (he sayes) *upon the defensive part,* questionlesse he is upon the *offensive part* by whom the *offence* comes, and that is that part in this *coordinate government* (that in case of such danger) refuses to doe his part, and resists the other from making supply. Surely the Doctor's *Almanacke* (he speaks of) is an *Erra Pater,* for untill his Majesty had hostilely entered the *Commons House,* with the attendance of his listed Souldiery; they had scarce so much as a *voluntary guard,* and when they had one, 'twas not a guard on the *Members' safeties,* 'twas rather on the *safety* of their late *Act* against *dissolution,* for if at any time that House should have been by force but kept one halfe day out of the place, where they had the day before appointed their next meeting, it had been utterly *dissolved.* Since then, the manning of *Hull,* and (after his Majesty had in the name of a guard, raised an Army to take it from the *Parliament's trust*) Sir *John Hotham's* humble declining His Majestie's entrance, but untill he should acquaint the Parliament in discharge of his *trust;* what *Hostilities were these?* The *setling the Militia by Ordinance* (His Majesty having refused it) in order to his and his Kingdome's *defence* (where note that the *Statute* of II *Henry 7.c.I.* which charges all the King's Subjects with his and the Land's *defence,* makes the rule of *that defence* to be according *to the duty of their Allegiance,* and that binds them to doe their duty whether accepted or no, and what *hostility* in all this? Since then, look down through the sieges of *Warwick, Coventry, Banbury, Wells, Manchester,* &c. even to *Keynton,* and what other resistance than *defensive* has the *Parliament* made? And even there too his Majesty was but followed with a *Petition* (as *Scotland* had successefully done before) untill he was pleased to turn back upon them and give fire.

The third invective in this Section, is against its distrust of the reality of his Majestie's *Protestations, to continue Religion, Lawes* and *Liberties,* &c. To this, all that I have to say is, that be his *Majestie's Protestations* never so reall and hearty, yet if there be in the *Parliament's* power a surer *bottome* to set these on, than the most reall *purposes* and *protestations* of a *mortall man* they discharge not their *trust* if they do it not. I know his Majesty (besides his constant and fixed goodness of disposition) hath more and stronger ties upon him of *honour, hazard, trust,* than any else whoever; but all men must follow their principles, which in morals will and must vary with the last *results* of their judgements, and even those in creatures that know not by *intelligence* as Angels, but discourse as men, are things that upon further light must vary too; the Law as we observed before is *mens sine appetitu* a *better bottome* for government to stand on, than the most *constant Resolution* or *Protestation* that ever meer man made, besides his Majesty dispences but by his Ministers, and then his *Protestations* rise to no more than this, *That he will governe us by such Lawes and Cannons as his Judges and Bishops will by their interpretations fit us with.*

The 7 *Section* containes little more than a setting on the same charges with more *bitternesse,* calling the *Parliament's Declarations wicked Pamphlets, false, odious, scandalous imputations of this giddy age,* &c. wherein both his virulence and impotence at once appears; in that (he sayes) he *will with* Michael *use no railing accusations on the Parliament,* and yet uses the most railing and accusing one of all other, in likening them as he doth (therein) to the *Devill* the *Archrailer* and *accuser* both; if he looke but a little further than the place he above urged in the Apostle *Peter,* he will tell them who they be that are thus *presumptuous* and do *speake evill of Dignities,* and *that Michael did not so.*

For those empty feares and jealousies (as hee calls them) grounded on *reports of forraigne power and preparations, the Queene's Religion, the great resort of Papists to his Majesty, His intercepting* Ireland's *re- liefe, &c.* I have no more to say to these, then, than for the first; *abun- dans cautela non nocet,*[16] State jealousie it has no right-hand error, none on the *excesse* side, its *extention intends* it, the more the better, an *Enemy* is met anywhere better than within our owne doores. Besides, if forraigne *States* have (possibly) with their engagements altered their designes, may we condemne the *vigilancy* of *ours* that (may be) was it that diverted those designes from us; nor are those *clouds* yet so farre blowne over us (as the Doctor would have it) for ought I see they grow *blacker* still.

2. For the *Queen's Religion* it was as *well knowne* (as he speaks) be- fore as now, but (may be) not so justly *feared,* as since we heare of so many *Priests* and *Jesuites* let out of prisons at back doors, of Pope's *Nuncios* and orders of *Friers* in *England,* especially now, when we see a Popish *Army* raised in their *defence,* when the enemies of our *State* have armed the enemies of our Church against both.

3. For the resort of *Papists* to his *Majesty,* whom the Doctor calls such *good Subjects,* so much *better* than the *Parliament:* all that I will

16. A lot of warning does no harm.

say is, that if such are become the *King's better Subjects,* God help him, he hath but a few *good* ones left; what? such as professe to owe a greater *subjection to a forraine State,* and a *State,* not only utterly crosse centered in its interest of *State,* but meritoriously malicious by its very *Articles of Faith* to this of his Majestie's, these *better Subjects* than those of his *great Councell?* How will *Rome* ring of this suffrage from the *mouth* of a *Protestant Doctor?* And yet why not the best *Subjects,* if we may judge by their usage? for of all sorts of men we heare not one of them by his Majestie's Army *plundered* yet. Sure there is some *Covenant,* these *Aegyptians'* doors are *sprinkled* with somewhat questionlesse, they enjoy this *Passeover* so solemnly.

Lastly, for *the interception of Ireland's reliefe,* if all the rest that was taken, was the King's, because the *Kingdom's,* at least the poor *Carrier's horses* were his own *proper goods. Necessity* is the excuse of all, but if in a man's *choice,* it is no *necessity* at all, the *definition* of it is, *quod aliter se habere non potest, (i.)* that can no otherwise be; well, *necessity* is pleaded yet, but on both *sides,* I pray God it be not shortly on *backs* and *bellies* too. I shall only add this short *Prayer,* and with my very soule I speak it, *God blesse the King and send us peace,* and if it must not be untill *one side* have prevailed, I pray God it may be that *side* that loves the *King* best.

Anonymous

Touching the

Fundamentall Lawes,

Or Politique Constitution of this King-
dome, The K I N G S Negative
Voice, and The Power of
P A R L I A M E N T S.

To which is annexed,
The priviledge and power of the Parliament touching The M I L I T I A.

LONDON
Printed for *Thomas Underhill*, and are to be
sold at the signe of the Bible in Woodstreet.
M.DC.XLIII.

*A*lthough the author of this short, but powerful, essay has yet to be identified, the tract has earned him a reputation as one of the clearest and most profound thinkers of the era. The piece was published in London about 24 February 1643, a time when some ardent supporters of Parliament felt a pressing need to shore up the constitutional bases of their cause.

The winter of 1642–43 was an anxious time for more radical adherents of Parliament. They feared that the negotiations with the Crown that had begun in December 1642 after the indecisive campaign season would end in Parliament's submission on the king's terms. With everything seemingly at stake, a series of parliamentary tracts appeared that were more radical than earlier works in their *thrust. These probed the extent of Parliament's powers to depose a king and even to change the constitution. The present tract is in this vein. Its nameless author attributes to Parliament sweeping powers to override laws or remove the king, all in the name of a fundamental law superior to particular laws. He even denies the king's right to veto legislation. But he places final authority in the people themselves, not in the Parliament. With the collapse of peace negotiations in April 1643 fears of a parliamentary surrender faded and with them, for the time being, the reliance upon radical arguments.*

Only one edition of "Touching the Fundamentall Lawes...." appeared. It was printed in blackletter, a typeface customarily reserved for the text of laws or royal proclamations.

Touching Fundamentall Laws, and the Kings Negative Voice.

Fundamentall Laws are not (or at least need not be) any written agreement like Meare-stones between King and People, the King himselfe being a part (not party) in those Laws, and the Commonwealth not being like a Corporation treated by Charter, but treating itselfe. But the fundamentall Law or Laws is a setling of the laws of nature and common equity (by common consent) in such a forme of Polity and Government, as that they may be administered amongst us with honour and safety. For the first of which therefore, we are governed by a King: and for the second, by a Parliament, to oversee and take order that that honourable trust that is put into the hands of the King for the dignity of the Kingdome, be rightly executed, and not abused to the alteration of the Politique Constitution taken up and approved, or to the destruction of that, for whose preservation it was ordered and intended. A principall part of which honour, is that royall assent he is to give for the enacting of such good Laws as the people shall choose, for they are first to consult their own safety and welfare, and then he who is to be intrusted with it, is to give an honourable confirmation to it, and so to put an Impresse of Majesty and Royall authority upon it.

Fundamentall Laws then are not things of capitulation between King and people, as if they were Foreigners and Strangers one to another, (nor ought they or any other Laws so to be, for then the King should governe for himselfe, not for his people) but they are things of constitution, treating such a relation, and giving such an existence and being by an externall polity to King and Subjects, as Head and Members, which constitution in the very being of it is a Law held forth with more evidence, and written in the very heart of the Republique, farre firmlier than can be by pen and paper, and in which sense we owe our Allegiance to the King as Head, (not only by power, but influence) and so part of the constitution, not as a party capitulating for a prerogative against or contrary to it, which whosoever seeks to set up, or side with, doe break their Allegiance, and rebell against the State, going about to deprive the King of his juridicall and lawfull authority, conferred upon him by the constitution of this State, under the pretence of investing him with an illegall and un-constitutive power, whereupon may follow this grand inconvenience, The withdrawment of His people's Allegiance, which, as a Body con-nected with the Head by the constitution of this Kingdome, is owing to him; his person in relation to the body, as the enlivening and quickening head thereof, being sacred and taken notice of by the laws in that capacity, and under that notion is made inviolate.

And if it be conceived that Fundamentall Laws must needs be only extant in writing, this is the next way to bring all to confusion, for then by the same rule the King bids the Parliament produce those laws that fundamentally give them their being, priviledges & power, *(Which by the way is not like the power of inferiour Courts, that are springs of the Parliament, dealing betweene party and party, but is an-swerable to their trust, this Court being itselfe Fundamentall and Para-mount, comprehending Law and Equity, and being intrusted by the whole for the whole, is not therefore to be circumscribed by any other Laws which have their being from it, not it from them, but only by that Law which at first gave it its being, to wit,* Salus populi). By the same rule I say the Parliament may also intreat the King to produce those Laws that Fundamentally give him his being, power and honour. Both which must therefore be determined, not by laws, for they themselves are laws, yea the most supreame and fundamentall law, giving law to laws themselves, but by the received constitution or polity, which they themselves are; and the end of their constitution is the law or rule of their power, to wit, An honourable and safe Regiment of the Common-wealth, which two whosoever goeth about to divide the one of them from the other, breaks the fundamentall constitutive law or laws and polity of this kingdome, that ordinance of man which we

are to submit unto; nor can or ought any statute or written law whatsoever, which is of later Edition and inferiour Condition, being but
an off-spring of this root, be interpreted or brought in Plea, against
this primary and radicall constitution, without guilt of the highest
Treason and destructive enmity to the Publique weale and polity, because by the very constitution of this Kingdome, all laws or interpretation of laws tending to confusion or dissolution, are *ipso facto* void.
In this case we may allude and say, That the Covenant which was
400. yeers before the Law, an after-Act cannot disanull it.

Ob. It may be objected, that this discourse seems to make our Government to be founded in Equity, not in Law, or upon that common
rule of *Salus populi,* which is alike common to all Nations, as well as
any: and so what difference.

Ans. The Fundamentall laws of England are nothing but the Common laws of Equity and Nature reduced into a particular way of policy, which policy is the ground of our title to them, and interest in
them. For though it is true, that Nature hath invested all Nations in
an equall right to the laws of Nature and Equity by a common
bounty, without respect of persons, yet the severall models or externall Government and Policie renders them more or lesse capable of
this their common right. For though they have an equall right in Nature to all the Laws of Nature and Equity, yet having fundamentally
subjected themselves by their politique Constitutions unto a Regal
servitude, by Barbarisme or the like they have thereby much disabled
and disvested themselves of that common benefit. But on the contrary, where the outward constitution or polity of a Republick is purposely framed for the confirming and better conferring this common
right of Nature and Equity, (as in ours) there is not only a common
right, but also a particular and lawfull power joined with this right
for its maintenance and supportation. For whereas other people are
without all supreame power, either of making laws or raising monies,
both these bodies of supremacie being in the arbitrary hands only of

the Soveraigne Magistrate amongst many Nations, these with us are in the hands of the supreame Government, (not Governour) or Court of Judicature, to wit, the King and Parliament. Here the people (like free-men) give money to the King, he doth not take it; and offers Laws to be enacted, doth not receive them so. Now in such a constituted Kingdome, where the very Constitution itselfe is the fundamentall law of its owne preservation, as is this mixt Regiment of ours, consisting of King and Parliament, as Head and Body, comprehending Monarchie, Aristocracie, and Democracie; there the fundamentall laws are like fundamentall truths in these two properties. First, they are comprehended in a very little room, to wit, honour and safety; and secondly, they have their influence unto all other inferiour Laws which are to be subjected to them, and correspondent with them, as lawful children and naturall branches.

Ob. But in processe of time there are many written Laws which seem at least to contradict this Fundamentall Constitution, and are not they binding notwithstanding it?

Ans. The Constitution of this Kingdome which gave it its being, and which is the radicall and fundamentall law thereof, ought therefore to command in chiefe, for that it never yeelds up its authority to those inferiour laws, which have their being from it, nor ought they which spring from it tend to the destruction of it, but on the contrary, it is to derive its radicall virtue, and influence into all succeeding laws, and they like branches are to make the root flourish, from whence they spring, with exhibiting the lively and fructifying virtue thereof, according to the nature and seasons of succeeding times; things incident in after-ages not being able to be foreseen, and particularly provided for at the beginning, saving in the fundamentall law of *Salus populi*, politiquely established. Nor can any laws growing out of that root, bear any other fruit, than such as the nature thereof dictates; for, for a particular branch to ruine the whole foundation by a seeming sense contrary to it, or differing from it, is very absurd; for

then how can it be said, Thou bearest not the root, but the root thee?
Laws must always relish of, and drink in the constitution or polity
where they are made; and therefore with us, the laws wherein the
King is nominated, and so seems to put all absolute authority into
his hands, must never so be construed, for that were with a breath to
blow downe all the building at once, but the King is there comprehended and meant under a two-fold notion. First, as trusted, being
the Head, with that power the Law confered upon him, for a Legall,
and not an absolute purpose, tending to an honourable preservation,
not an unnaturall dissolution. Secondly, as meaning him juridically,
not abstractly or personally, for so only the Law takes notice of the
King as a juridicall person; for till the Legislative power be absolutely
in the King, so that laws come down from him to his people, and goe
not up from them to him, they must ever be so interpreted: for as
they have a juridicall being and beginning, to wit, in Parliament, so
must they have a suitable execution and administration, to wit, by
the Courts, and legall Ministers, under the King's authority, which
according to the constitution of this Kingdome, he can no more suspend for the good of his people, than the Courts can theirs; or if he
doe, to the publique hazard, then have the Courts this advantage,
that for publique preservation they may and must provide upon that
principle, *The King can doe no wrong, neither in withholding justice,
nor protection from his people.* So that then *Salus populi* being so principally respected and provided for, according to the nature of our
constitution and polity, so being *Lex legum,* or the rule of all laws
branching thence. Then if any law doe by variation of times, violence
of tryrannie, or misprison of Interpreters, vary therefrom, it is a bastard, and not a son, and is by the lawful parents either to be reduced
or cast out, as gendering unto bondage and ruine of the inheritance,
by attempting to erect an absolute and arbitrary Government. Nor
can this equitable exposition of particular Statutes taken from the
scope of the politique constitution be denied without overthrow of

just and legal Monarchy, (which ever tends to publique good and preservation) and the setting up of an unjust and illegall tyrannie, ruling, if not without law, yet by abused laws, turning them as conquered ordnance upon the people. The very Scripture itselfe must borrow from its scope and principles for explanation of particular places, else it will be abused (as it is through that default) unto Heresies. See we not how falsely Satan quoted true Scripture to Christ when he tempted him, only by urging the letter without the equity, or true intention and meaning? We are to know and doe things *verum vere, justum juste*, else we neither judge with righteous judgement, nor obey with just obedience.

Ob. But is not the Parliament guilty of excercising an arbitrary power, if their proceedings be not regulated by written laws, but by *Salus populi?*

Ans. For the Parliament to be bound up by written laws, is both destructive and absurd.

First, it is destructive, it being the Fundamental Court and Law, or the very *Salus populi* of England, and ordained, as to make laws, and for them executed so to supply their deficiencie according to the present exigencie of things for publique preservation by the prerogative of *Salus populi*, which is universally in them, and but particularly in particular laws and statures, which cannot provide against all future exigents, which the law of Parliaments doth, and therefore are not they to be limits to this. And it would yet be further destructive, by cutting the Parliament short of half its power at once, for it being a Court both of Law and Equity (as appears by the power of making laws, which is nothing but Equity reduced by common consent into Polity) whenever it is circumscribed by written laws, (which only is the property of inferiour Courts) it ceaseth to be supreame, and divests itselfe of that inherent and uncircumscribed power which *Salus populi* comprehends.

Secondly, as it is destructive, so also it is absurd; for the Legislative power which gives laws, is not to receive laws, saving from the nature and end of its owne constitution, which as they give it a being, so they endow it with laws of preservation both of itselfe & the whole, which it represents.

I would not herein be misunderstood, as if the Parliament, when as it only doth the office of inferiour Courts, judging between party & party, were not limited by written lawes. There I grant it is, because therein it only deales between *meum & tuum*, which particular written lawes can and ought to determin. So that its superlative and uncircumscribed power I intend only as relating to the Universe and the affaires thereof, wherein it is to walke by its fundamentall principles, not by particular precepts or Statutes, which are made by the Parliament, between King and people, not between people and Parliament. They are ordained to be rules of Government to the King, agreeing with the liberty and property of the people, and rules of Obedience to the people without detainment of their freedome by the exercise of an illegall, usurped, and unconsented power, whereunto Kings (especially in hereditary Monarchies) are very prone, which cannot be supposed by a Parliament, which is representatively the Publike, intrusted for it, which is like to partake and share with the Publick, being but so many private men put into authority *pro tempore*, by common consent, for common good.

Nor is the Parliament hereby guilty of an Arbitrary Government, or is it destructive to the Petition of Right, when as in providing for publick weale, it observes not the letter of the law, first, because as aforesaid, that law was not made between Parliament and people, but by the people in Parliament betweene the King and them, as appears by the whole tenour of it, both in the complaining and praying parts, which wholly relate to the King. Secondly, because of the common consent, that in the representative Body (the Parliament) is given thereunto, wherein England in her Polity imitates Nature in her Instinct, who is wont to violate particular principles for publique preservation, as when light things descend, and heavy ascend, to prevent a vacuum; and thirdly, because of the equitable power which is inherent in a Parliament, and for publique good is to be acted above and against any particular Statute, or all of them. And fourthly, because the end of making that Law, to wit, the publique preservation, is fulfiled in the breaking of it, which is lawfull in a Parliament that is chosen by the whole for the whole, and are themselves also of the body, though not in a king, for therein the Law saith, Better a mischeife than an inconvenience. But it may be objected, though it be not Arbitrary for the Parliament to goe against written law, yet is it not so when they go against the King's consent, which the law, even the fundamentall law, supposeth in Parliamentary proceedings. This hath beene answered, that the King is juridically and according to the intention of the law in his Courts, so that what the Parliament consults for the publick good, That by oath, and the duty of his office, and nature of this polity he is to consent unto, and in case he do deny it, yet in the construction of the fundamentall law and constitution of this Kingdom, he is conceived to grant it, supposing the head not be so unnaturall to the body that hath chosen it for good and not for evill.

But it will be answered, where is the King's Negative Voice if the Parliament may proceed without his consent? I answer, That there is no known nor written law that gives him any; and things of that nature are willingly beleeved till they be abused, or with too much violence claimed. That his Majesty hath fundamentally a right of consent to the enacting of laws is true, which (as aforesaid) is part of that honourable trust constituted in him. And that this royall ascent is an act of honour and not of absolute and negative power or prerogative, appears by these following reasons.

First, by his oath at the Coronation mentioned in one of the Parliament's Declarations where he doth or should sweare to confirme and grant all such good lawes as his people *shall choose* to be observed, not *hath chosen*, for first, The word *concedes* in that oath were then unnecessary, the lawes formerly enacted being allready granted by foregoing Kings, and so they need no more *concession* or confirmation, else we must run upon this shelfe that all our laws die with the old king, and receive their being a new, by the new King's consent. Secondly, Hereby the first and second clause in that interrogatory, *viz. Concedes iustas leges & permittas protegendas*, are confounded and doe but *idem repetere*. Thirdly, *Quas vulgus elegerit* implies only the act of the people in a distinctive sence from the act or consent of the King, but laws allready made have more than *quas vulgus elegerit*, they have also the royall consent too, so that that phrase cannot meane them wherein the act or consent of the King is allready involved.

Secondly, by the practise of requiring the royall ascent even unto those very acts of subsidies which are granted to himselfe and for his owne use, which it is supposed he will accept of, and yet *Honoria gratia* is his royall ascent craved and contributed thereunto.

Thirdly, by the King's not sitting in Parliament to debate and consult lawes, nor are they at all offered him by the Parliament to consider of, but to consent to, which yet are transmitted from one house to another, as well to consult as consent to, shewing thereby he hath no part in the consultory part of them (for that it belongs only to the people in Parliament to discerne and consult their own good), but he comes only at the time of enacting, bringing his Royall Authority with him, as it were to set the seale thereof to the Indenture allready prepared by the people, for the King is head of the Parliament in regard of his authority, not in regard of his reason or judgment, as if it were to be opposed to the reason or judgment of both houses (which is the reason both of King and Kingdome) and therefore do they as consult so also interpret lawes without him, supposing him to be a person replenished with honour and royall authority not skilled in lawes, nor to receive information either of law or councell in Parliamentary affaires from any, saving from that supreame court and

highest councell of the King and Kingdome, which admits no coun-
terpoize, being intrusted both as the wisest Councell and justest judicature.

Fourthly, either the choise of the people in Parliament is to be the
ground and rule of the King's assent, or nothing but his pleasure, and
so all Bills though never so necessary for publique good and preservation, and after never so much paines and consultation of both
houses may be rejected, and so they made meere cyphers, and we
brought to that passe, as either to have no lawes, or such only as come
immediately from the King (who oft is a man of pleasure, and little
seene in publicke affaires, to be able to judge) and so the Kingdome's
great councell must be subordinated either to his meere will, and then
what difference between a free Monarchy, and an absolute, saving
that the one rules without Councell, and the other against it, or at
the best but to a cabinet councell consisting commonly of men of private interests, but certainly of no publicke trust.

Ob. But if the King must consent to such laws as the Parliament
shall chuse *eo nomin*, they may then propound unreasonable things to
him, as to consent to his own deposing, or to the lessening his own
revenue, &c.

Ans. So that the issue is, whether it be fitter to trust the wisdome
and integrity of our Parliament, or the will and pleasure of the King
in this case of so great and publicke concernment. In a word, the
King being made the fountaine of justice and protection to his people by the fundamentall lawes or constitution of this Kingdome, he is
therefore to give life to such acts and things as tend thereunto, which
acts depend not upon his pleasure, but though they are to receive
their greater vigour from him, yet are they not to be suspended at
pleasure by him, for that which at first was intended by the kingdome: for an honourable way of subsistence and administration must
not be wrested contrary to the nature of this Polity, (which is a free
and mixt Monarchy and not an absolute) to its destruction and con-

fusion, so that in case the King in his person should decline his duty, and the King in his courts are bound to performe it, where his authority properly resides, for if he refuse that honour which the republicke by its fundamentall constitution hath conferred upon him, and will not put forth the acts of it, for the end it was give him. *viz.* for the justice and safety of his people, this hinders not but that they who have as fundamentally reserved a power of being & well being in their own handes by the concurrence of Parliamentary authority to the royall dignity, may thereby provide for their own subsistence, wherein is acted the King's juridicall authority though his personall pleasure be withheld, for his legall and juridicall power is included and supposed in the very being, and consequently in the acts of Courts of justice, whose being he may as well suspend as their power of acting, for that without this is but a cypher, and therefore neither their being nor their acting so depend upon him, as not to be able to act and execute common justice and protection without him, in case he deny to act with them, and yet both so depend upon him, as that he is bound both in duty and honour, by the constitution of this polity to act in them and they from him, so that (according to that axiome in law) *the King can doe no wrong,* because his juridicall power and authority is allwayes to controle his personall miscarriages.

Se Defendendo.[1]

God and nature hath ordained Government for the preservation of the governed. This is a truth so undeniable, as that none will gainsay it, saving in practice, which therefore being taken for granted, it must needs follow that to what end Government was ordained, it must bee maintained, for that it is not in the power of particular persons or communities of men to depart with selfe preservation by any covenant

---

1. In or when defending oneself, or self-defense.

whatsoever, nor ought it to bee exacted by any superiours from their inferiours, either by oath or edict, because neither oathes nor statutes are obligatory further than they agree with the righteous Laws of God and nature; further than so they ought neither to be made nor kept.

Let it be supposed then for argument sake, that the *Militia* of the Kingdom, is in the power of the King, yet now as the case stands it is lawfull for the Parliament to reassume it; because though they passed it into his hands, for the people's preservation, yet it was never intended that by it he might compasse their destruction, contrary to the Law of nature; whereby every man, yea everything is bound to preserve itselfe. And thus much in effect is confessed at unawares, by the Author of the Reply to the Answer of the London Petition:[2] who affirmeth, saying, *The King is invested with the sole power of Training, Arraying, and Mustering,* and then gives the reason, *because it is most consonant to reason, as well as grounded on Law, That he which is bound to protect, should be able to compasse that end.* Which reason overthrows both his position and intention. 1. His position, for this is no reason why the sole power of the *Militia* should be in the hands of the King; *because he is bound to protect,* except he were bound solely to protect, that is, without the counsel and advice of Paliament: but it hath beene resolved that He is not sole judge of necessity, and therefore not sole protector against it, but together with His Parliament, who consequently shares in the power of the *Militia.* 2. It overthrows His intention, which is so to put the power of the *Militia* into the hands of the King, as to enable him to do what he will with it, when as yet he himselfe cannot but affirm, it is his to protect withall, so that when he

---

2. Wing STC attributes authorship of the reply to the answer of the London petition to William Chillingsworth, a royalist theologian and godson of William Laud. The reply appears in "The Petition of the most substantiall Inhabitants of the citie of London, to the Lords and Commons for peace. Together with the answer to the same. And the reply of the Petitioners" (Oxford, [5 December] 1642), Wing C3880.

ceaseth to use it to its end, it ceaseth to be in his power, or else let the man speake plain, and say, it is His to destroy as well as to protect.

Ob. But the *Militia* is passed to the King, absolutely without any condition of revocation expressed, or of limitation to circumscribe the use whereunto it ought to be imployed.

1. *Ans.* Laws of God and nature, neither are nor need to be expressed in contracts or edicts, for they are ever supposed to be supreme to human ordinances, and to chalenge obedience in the first place, and other Laws so far only as they are consonant to them, though these Laws be further backed with Oathes and Protestations. As for instance, I give a man a sword, and sweare I will never take it from him; yet if he actually assault me, or it manifestly appeare he intends to cut my throat, or take my purse with it, I may lawfully possesse myselfe of it again if opportunity serve, because in such agreements betwixt man & man, the laws of nature neither are nor can be exempted, but are necessarily implied, still to be of force, because no bonds can lawfully invalid them, and *id solum possumus quod jure possumus*.[3] But it may be asked how it appears that the King intends to imploy the *Militia* to the destruction of this people. Why first because He hath refused to hearken to the wholsome counsel of his Parliament, the representative body, and the highest Court and Counsel of the Kingdom. 2. Because, *è contrario*, he hearkens to the councels of notorious Papists and Malignants, men engaged against the publike good and welfare of this Kingdome, in a diametrall opposition, so that if they perish it prospereth, and if it prosper they perish. 3. Because hee hath had a deepe hand in contriving and plotting the ruine and extirpation of the Parliament, by secret and open violence, and in them of the whole Kingdome of whom they are the Epitome, and as the King is the head, so they are the heart. But further it may be replied, that the King hath promised to maintain Par-

---

3. We can only do what we can do legally.

liaments and governe by Law. *Ans.* That is so far as he knowes his own heart, and as he can be master of himselfe. He sware the same at His Coronation, and promised as much when he granted the Petition of Right, but how they have beene kept God knowes, and we are not ignorant. It may be His Majesty may meane as he speakes, but 1. Temptations may change his minde, as it hath done too often, and as it did his that said to the Prophet, Is thy servant a dog that he should do such things? and yet did them. The welfare of Kingdomes is not to be founded upon bare spontaneous promises, but reall contracts. 2. He himselfe sayes, he himselfe is not skilled in the Laws, and we have found it true, so that he must take information of them from somebody from his Parliament (that is his people that made them) he will not, and are any fitter to be Judges of the Law, than the highest Court; if they may be Judges that are delinquents to the Law, and Malignants against it, and have beene grievous oppressors of the People, even against the known Laws (so much cried up) we are like to have just Judges and righteous Lawyers.

2. *Ans.* If the *Militia* be so absolutely the King's, as that all power of defence and preservation of ourselves and our rights be taken from us, to what purpose do we strive for liberty & property and laws to confirm them? These are but imaginary things, if they have no hedge to fence them. If the *Militia* be for the King, let us burne the Statutes we have already, and save a labour of making more. No man would thinke it a good purchase to buy land, and when he hath paid his money to have it in the power of the seller, to take it from him by his sword.

Ob. It is true that Kings are tied by oath, and legall contracts, to governe by *Laws*, and to maintain liberty and property to their people, which puts them under an obligation of conscience to God, so that they are responsible to him for the breach of fidelity and duty, but not to the people who may minde them of their duty, but not compell them to it.

Ans. This Objection hath two parts, First, That Kings are only responsible to God. 2. That Subjects must suffer wrong, but not by force maintain their right. To the first I answer. That if Kings be solely answerable to God, then contracts are in vaine, for they shall answer for all their arbitrary and unjust tyrannie over their people, though there were no contracts. That which makes us happier than other Nations, sure is not this, that the King for the breach of his duty hath more to answer at the day of judgement than other Kings have, if that bee all wee have small cause to joy in our priviledges, they are neither worth the blood that hath been shed for them, nor the money that hath beene paid for them. Secondly, Government must be considered under a twofold notion, divine and human. The *Genus* which is government itselfe is divine, so that people are absolutely bound to have government, but not bound to have an absolute government for the *species* or the *modus gubernandi* is human, and therefore the Apostle sayes, *Be subject to every ordinance of man,* that is, to every such kinde of Government as your lot falls to be under, by the constitution of the Common-wealth you live in. Now Government being thus of a mixt nature, the Ordinance both of God and man, it is not only subject to God but also to men, to be regulated, amended, and maintained by the people: for as it is God's Ordinance for their good, so doth he give them liberty to provide it bee not abused to their hurt, so that when God shall put an opportunity into other hands, they ought to improve it to the setting of government up right, or the keeping of it so from apparent violations. There was a time when both Government and the manner of governing belonged to God, to wit, amongst the Israelites, for to that people he was both a God of moralls and politiks, and therefore he tooke it so ill for them to usurpe upon his right, as to desire to change their government from Judges to Kings, but this was a peculiar right he assumed over that particular people only. To the second I answer thus. Every Subject taken *divisim,* and apart from the whole, is to suffer under abused authority, and to obey passively, rather than to breake union or cause confusion, but no Subject is bound to suffer by that which is not authority, as is the will of the Magistrate. If a Court of Justice should unjustly condemne a man, he is patiently to undergoe it, but if a Judge or the King himselfe should violently set upon him to kill him, he may defend himselfe; for the Ordinance of God and man both, is affixed to the office, and not unto the person, to the authority and not unto the will, so that the person acting out of office, and by his will may be resisted, though the ordinance may not. But the representative body of the Common-wealth, (which is all men conjunctim) they may not only oppose the person and his will, but even the office and authority itselfe when abused, and are bound to it both in conscience to God when he gives them opportunity, and in discharging of their trust to them that imployed them. For first God calls to have the wicked removed from the Throne, and whom doth he call upon to doe it but upon the people (in case the King will not) or their trustees, for as he hath originally founded all authority in the people, so he expects a discharge of it from them for his glory, & the publike weale, which are the ends of Government, from which God and nature hath ordained it. Secondly, In discharge of their trust for the whole, for order sake, making them their representative actors, and putting that universall and popular authority that is in the body of the people, and which (for the publike good, and preservation) is above every man and all Laws, into their hands, they may expect and chalenge them by vertue of their stewardship, to provide for their safety and well being, against whomsoever shall oppose it, no one being above all, and therefore ought not that universall power, which by way of trust is conveyed over to the Parliament be betrayed into the hands of any by admitting or allowing any authority to be superiour, by tollerating abuses and usurpations, as if they had not power to regulate them.

FINIS.

William Ball

Constitutio Liberi Populi.

O R ,

THE RULE

OF A

Free-born People.

BY

WILLIAM BALL

O f

BARKHAM, ESQVIRE.

In Deum Omnia.

Printed, *Anno Dom.* 1 6 4 6 .

*L*ittle information has survived about William Ball of Barkham, esquire. He and his friend Sir Francis Pile, baronet, to whom he dedicated "Constitutio Liberi Populi...," were both from Berkshire. Ball was probably the William Ball, attorney of the Exchequer Court's Office of Pleas. If so he started out writing as a royalist pamphleteer but apparently had a change of heart by 1645 when he stood for, and was elected to, the Long Parliament for Abingdon. Certainly the views expressed in this tract published the following year would have placed him among the radicals.

The preface of the present tract is dated 12 May 1646, the month Charles I surrendered. The probable publication date was 18 June 1646. The collapse of the royal cause with the surrender of the king had provoked urgent discussion about the appropriate shape of a future government. Concerns that had arisen during the first winter of civil war, when Parliament was negotiating with the king, reemerged with greater force. Again there was the danger, as radical supporters of Parliament saw it, that members of the Commons eager for a settlement might betray the cause.

Ball's tract makes it clear, however, that he was a champion of popular, not parliamentary, sovereignty. He insists that if a people are free-born as the English are, ultimate power resides in them, not in their government. That being so if either the king or Parliament attempted to deprive them of their rights, the people were entitled to resist. In this he differs from the Levellers who looked to representative government to protect the people. When Levellers referred to appeals to the people, they meant new elections. Their goal was to make parliaments more truly representative.

"Constitutio Liberi Populi" appeared in a single edition. Other tracts by Ball would follow. In 1648 he engaged in a lively published exchange with the imprisoned royalist judge, David Jenkins, over the power of kings and the role of the people. There is uncertainty over Ball's activities after 1648. Although he was not purged from the Long Parliament by Colonel Pride in December of that year, he did not serve in the Rump Parliament that succeeded it. Ball's friend Pile had been elected to Parliament about the same time as Ball and, like Ball, was not excluded during Pride's Purge but does not seem to have sat in Parliament after that event. Both men may have been so distressed by the army's purge of Parliament that they chose to abandon their seats. Such behavior would have accorded with Ball's views about sovereignty residing with the people. In any event Ball continued to publish during the 1650s.

Constitutio Populi Liberi. Or, the Rule of a Free-Born People.

First, Reason is Queen-Regent of Human Affaires; by the sight whereof men discern to walke in the prudent paths of Morality and Policy, even as by the Light of the Day they discerne to tread the paths of the Earth. And albeit that this interior light of understanding is in Divine things darkened, by the fall of our first Parent, yet doth the Eternall Light ever communicate to Mankind sufficiency of Reason (I intend for worldly things) thereby to direct his goings out, and comings in (according to the unnecessitating determination of God) as it were by a cloudy Daylight, though not a cleare Sunshine, whereby the Actions of men may severally be discerned.

2. Not long since I wrote a small Treatise, intituled, *Tractatus de jure Regnandi, et Regni,* or the Sphear of Government,[1] the which albeit I conceived that I had squared it according to the Rule of Reason; yet some conceive, that it wants its true proportion, or line, and that I have too much extended the *Innate liberty of the Free-born People of England:* to satisfie (or otherwise convince) such, I have published this Epitome of State-Rule, or Government, desiring all men to weigh, and consider what I have written, not with the Prejudicating Eye of Affectation (which many times misleadeth apprehensive judgments) but with the Ballance of Reason to ponder every Graine, and if the weight be just, and levell to approve, and accept of it; if somewhat too light, to adde of their own understandings what is deficient.

3. It is certain, that had Man never fell from his state of Innocence, there had been a superiority, or rather *priority* in Nature (*viz.* That the Parent should have been known and reverenced as the Instrumentall cause of the Child, &c.) but there had been no sover-

1. William Ball, "Tractatus de Jure Regnandi & Regni: or, the Sphere of Government," (25 October) 1645. Wing B597.

aignty, and consequently no subjection; for had there been no sinne there had been no need of a justiciating Power, nor a Subject to which that Power could have determinated, or *terminated* itself; every man's Actions would have been regulated by the *Eternall Law,* written in the hearts of men; So that there had been no need of Additionall, or Nationall Lawes. Wherefore (by the way) I cannot assent to the Opinion of that Gentleman (*Fortescue*) who said, that *all Mankind should have been governed by the Lawes of* England, *if* Adam *had not sinned in* Paradise; for by his favour if *Adam* had never sinned [in School-Reason, or Divinity] he had either always lived in Paradice, or else finished a compleat thousand years (which the Apostle *Peter* calls a Day with God, *2 Pet. 3.8.*) and then had he either been assumed into Heaven alive, or else (if God had decreed a separation between his Soul and Body) he had yeelded himself into the hands of his Creator, *sine dolore mortis, sine timore paenae,* without pain of death, or fear of punishment, and had left his Earthly habitation to his posterity, who should have possessed and enjoyed the same, without any the least contention, or controversie, regulated only by the *Eternal Law* aforesaid. But (to return) no sooner sinne, but with it *subjection* entered as a curse, and therefore God said to woman, that she should not only bring forth in pain (which God would have dispenced withall if she had not sinned) but also that *her desire should be subject to her Husband, and he should reign over her, Gen. 3.16.* It is very probable that if she had not sinned, she should notwithstanding have tendered a reverence to her Husband as more noble in Sex and created before her in time but she should not have rendered *a subjective Obedience,* if disobedience had not made her subject.

4. And albeit that subjection is a scourge of sinne, yet it hath pleased the Almighty according to his divine will, to cause some Persons, and Nations, to be more subject than other some; many times enthralling, and enslaving them by Tyrannicall, or Imperious In-

struments for their sinnes (as the sacred Bookes of the Judges, Kings, and Chronicles sufficiently declare) and upon their Humiliation, or for other secret causes known to his Divine wisdome, he hath mercifully released, or mitigated their yoak, as the sacred Writ yea and human Records testifie at large. And sometimes God hath done this by speciall, or miraculous meanes, as he did to the people of Israel; sometimes by ordinary wayes, as the Florentines (albeit of late enslaved) purchased their liberty of the Emperour for money, and so also did other Cities of *Italy,* and elsewhere in *Europe,* others by plain defiance and Arms, have regained their Freedome (*that is, to dispose of themselves*) as did the Cantons of *Switzerland,* the Provinces of *Holland, Zeland,* &c. and either of these wayes may be said to be just; for *Id Iuris est, quod Nationis est,* that is lawfull, or *Law which a Nation generall approveth, or admitteth of;* and there need no speciall Warrant from God for anything that they shall do agreeable to their Naturall, or Human Reason, anymore than it needed to the petty Kings and people of *Sodom,* and *Gomorrah* (instanced in my former Treatise) or to the Nation of the Jewes in the time of the Machebees. And albeit that a *Nation in generall* should approve, and admit an erroneous Law (as I know not any Nation, State, or Parliament that is infallible) yet such Law ought to be kept, and observed as *a Law,* because men have power to tie and oblige themselves to inconveniences (if God prevent not and prudent Reason dictate not the contrary) as to conveniences, and their Errour being Nationally generall, must either be *admitted* of all persons (comprehended within their Rule) as *legall just,* or else *permitted,* because it is constituted by the highest Power human, from which there is no appeale but to God, who in his good time will either *mercifully* illuminate their understandings or reform their Errour, or *justly* chastise them for their perseverance in Errour.

5. And the Rule of a *Free-born People,* or a People *free to dispose themselves* consists in that, wherein the People in generall constitute

or determine themselves, not in that wherein they are constituted; or determined, *tanquam ab alio agente,* by some other instrumentall cause, for then are they not free. So that it is destructive to the very Essence of their Freedome not to be able to determine themselves to that which they conceive to be *Bonum commune,* that being their adaequate, and proper object. And this they must not be able to do sometimes only, and *originally,* but *perpetually,* otherwise, *deficiunt a libertate proprie loquendo, & sunt tantum liberi secundum quid, vel denominative;* they cease to speak truly, to be free, and are only free in Denomination or a kind of Titulary Freedome; for naturall Reason dictates, that everything ceases to continue, when the Form thereof, or the Originall Form ceases to be; so that if a people can *Originally* dispose or determine themselves, and cannot afterwards *Actually* do it, their Original power, or form of disposing or determining themselves ceases to be—But it is to be noted, that no People in the world (intending to be free) *subditi potius quam subjecti,* and who have either conserved their Originall Freedome, or Actually regained it, do, or did ever grant a Power to one, or more or constitute a Power in one, or more that should be destructive to their intended Originall Freedome; For as *John Cook* of Gray's Inne Barrester, in his Epistle Dedicatory, in a Booke entituled the *Vindication of the Professours, and Profession of the Law,*[2] hath ingeniously said; *All Power and Authority is given for preservation, and edification, nothing for destruction and desolation;* so that albeit a People, or Nation, to avoid disorder, do constitute a Ruler, or Rulers to conserve Order and do generally consent to direct their human Affaires according to *such Rules* as shall be by him, or them, or both given or prescribed; yet they ever intend that *such Rules* must not be directly opposite, or against the Law of Nature, or their Naturall Liberty. If they be, they may chuse whether,

2. John Cook, "The Vindication of the Professors and Profession of the Law. By way of Answer to a printed Sheet intituled Advertisements of the New Election of Members for the House of Commons," [6 February] 1646. Thomason Tracts E320 (17).

or no they will admit, or receive them; they constitute, or institute
their Ruler or Rulers their power *extensive,* but not primitive, or *intensive,* that is to say, their innate and inseperable Freedome ever intended to dispose, or determine themselvs, *In bonum commune prout omnibus visum erit,* this they never part, or parted withall; for at what time soever they should do it, they cease to be *Populus liber, or liberi subdita,* a free People, or a People which are freely under a Law by common consent as aforesaid—And of this I shall instance a similitude in Nature: The Element of Water is not of itselfe *extensively* coloured, but is apt or applicable to receive any colour; yet it is *intensively* white (it being Nature's Innocent Originall colour) as is sufficently discerned, when it is converted into Snow, or congealed into Ice, or praecipitated Torrent-like, by an extraordinary fall. So People or Nations are not of themselvs *extensively* regulated but apt or applicable to receive any Rule, which they, whom they institute, or intrust, shall apply unto them; howsoever they are *intensively free to dispose themselves* (it being their Natural-Innocent-Originall Rule) as is sufficiently discerned by the severall Alterations of Government in Athens, Rome, Geneva, Switzerland, Holland, and many other places, where the people's affections have been either congealed by their over-domineering Lords (as it were creatures of the second Region of the Aire) or (Torrent-like) have been praecipitated by an extraordinary fall, occasioned by some violent disturbers of their common Liberty (τὸ ἀνθρόπινον ἀγαθὸν) the generall benefit of Mankind. For my part, Anathema be to such, who desire to deprive a King of His just Prerogative; Anathema be to such, who desire to deprive a Parliament of their just Priviledge: but Anathema Maranatha[3] be to such who should any way desire to deprive a Free-born People of their just Liberty, or Propriety.

3. This expression means a thing accursed.

6. Nor can I conceive, but that the English Nation, or People are (if rightly considered) one of the most freest Nations in the World; for they cause, or require their Kings to take their Oaths *to conserve their Lawes and Liberties,* before the Crown actually invest their Temples; thereby shewing that they reserve, and *intend their generall Liberty and Propriety.* And albeit, that a King of England have his *Ius Regnandi,* or Right of Reigning by Inheritance as I have instanced in my former Treatise; yet *illud jus quamvis sit quoad potentiam, sive officium potestatis derivativum, est tamen quoad exercitium potestatis Relativum,* that Right of Reigning, although it be derivative in respect of the King's personall Authority, or rather Office for Authority, yet is it relative in respect of his Exercising, or performing that Authority; for though the people obey the King as their chiefe Ruler, or Magistrate before his Oath taken, yet it is ever with reference, or relation, that He should take His Oath for their preservation, and good in generall, and performe the same; otherwise they have recourse to their primitive, or *intensive power,* as in the case of *Edward* the second, from whom Sir *William Trussell,* Speaker of the Parliament, *in the name of all men, or people of England,* constrained, or took his Royall Office, or Authority; or to speak more truly, deprived him of it, without any former precedent, exercising the *intensive power* of the people; for *Trussell* said not to EDWARD the second, in the Name of the Lords and Commons assembled in Parliament, or in the Names of the Commons assembled in Parliament, but in the Name of all men or people of England, &c. thereby expressing, or manifesting the People's *Primitive, or intensive Power,* more than the Parliament's *secundary or extensive Authority.*

7. And as the English Nation, or People cause their Kings formally to swear, or take their Oaths to conserve their Lawes, and Liberties; so they cause the Parliament (I meane the Body collective, or representative of the People, *viz.* the Knights, Citizens, and

Burgesses) to take their Oaths (if not formally) yet at the least *virtually*, to conserve their generall Liberty, and Propriety, to do all good they may for the places that intrust them; all which they faithfully promise at their Elections. So that the English Nation, or People never gave, or voluntarily assented, that their Kings, or Parliaments, or Both, should have an absolute Domineering, or Arbitrary power over them, but only a *Discretive*, or Legall *Authority intended ever for their good in generall; their ever reserved*, and as it were *Essentiall Propriety*.

8. Wherefore I cannot but marvell at such (whether Kingly Royalists, or Parliamentary Realists, in this case it makes no matter) as by a kind of Idolizing King, or Parliament, or King and Parliament, would suppose, or perswade the People that *their Lives, Liberties, and Proprieties are disposable by King, and Parliament, ad Placitum;* one *John Cook* of Graye's Inne Barrister,[4] by me already cited, hath in his Vindication of the Professours, and Profession of the Law inserted, that I have in my former Book, intituled, *The Spheer of Government*,[5] introduced a dangerous Opinion, by putting, or stating a supposition, or rather a Praesuppositive case, that *if King, and Parliament, or King, or Parliament, should make an Act that they would, and might dispose of all Subjects' Estates in England (he should have added* ad Placitum, *for those are my words) that in such case the Counties, Cities, and Townes corporate might if not remedied declare, and protest against such an Act, if violated, then they might defend themselves by Armes*. And to convince this my Assertion, in the next Page, he sayes, *if the supream Court be not supream to all intents, it is not supream to any intent, because there is an higher above it*. This is no good consequence; for a Power (and consequently a Court of Power) may bee supream to some things, yet not to all. The King of Polande, for life, is supreame

4. See reference on p. 287.
5. See Ball, "Tractatus," 13.

to appoint what place he thinks fit within the Precincts of the Do-minions of Poland for the convening or assembling the Diets, or Courts of the Peers Spirituall and Temporall of that Kingdome; and the King of Poland is also supreame to censure, or punish any of his owne Tenants, and Vassals, or Slaves; yet is he not supreame to cen-sure, or punish any of the chiefe Nobility, but by consent of his As-sembly, or Court of Peers; nor can hee meddle with any of their Tenants, Vassals, or Slaves; or determine absolutely of Peace or Warre, &c. In the Common-Wealth of Geneva (which he calls a pure Democracy) the People in generall are supreame to nominate, or elect Two Hundred which are the Grand-Councell; and those Two Hundred are supreame to nominate, or elect the Twenty five, and yet not supreame to elect the foure Syndiques, or Annuall Governours, or rather Rulers, &c. So that it is no good consequence (as afore-said) to affirme that, *if the Supreame Court be not supreame to all intents, it is not supreame to any intent, because there is another above it.* For in Geneva it is evident, that the Two Hundred or *Grand-Councell,* is the supreame Court, and yet not supream to all Intents; the People indeed, or Common-Wealth in generall, (which are the supreame Power, though not Court) are supreame to all Intents; but of that hereafter.

9. But the Gentleman sayes, that *there are in the Kingdome so many thousand Acres of Land, either the Parliament may settle, and determine the Right of all their Acres* (hee meant surely those Acres) *or not of any one of them, for there is no medium,* &c. But what is this to the pur-pose, of the Parliament having a power to dispose of all Subjects' Estates *ad placitum?* Who knowes not, but that the Parliament can determine the Right of all Acres in England, *in foro judicii,* as v. g. the Parliament can determine whether White Acre belong to Right to Oakes, or Stiles, let the Title of either of them be never so difficult, or obscure, and the Parliament can determine whether or no, Oakes

or Stiles have forfeited their Propriety of, or to White Acre for Delinquency, &c. Moreover the Parliament can (which no other Court can
doe) *applicare in necessitatem Regni,* apply to, or for the necessity of
the Kingdome so much of the profits of White Acre, as to them shall
seeme convenient; provided that the cause, or causes thereof be made
manifest, that Oakes, Stiles, and all men may (if they will) take notice
thereof; and provided also, that an Accompt be given how and which
way the profits of White Acre have beene for such cause, or causes
applied, and disposed of; for no Free-born Englishman (much lesse
the Nation in generall) ought to be deprived of any his Right, or propriety without good cause. Notwithstanding the Parliament of England cannot *disponere ad Placitum,* dispose at their will and pleasure
barely of White Acre (no, nor of one Acre of waste in England) v. g.
that whereas White Acre belongs of Right to Oakes, Stiles shall
notwithstanding have it because it is their will and pleasure; this they
cannot doe; for at what time they should do it (albeit I suppose it almost impossible that they should do it, as I have formerly instanced)
they faile, or fall from the Protection of the People, and usurpe to
themselves an absolute Arbitrary and irregular Power, destructive to
the generall good of the People and consequently cease to be a Parliament, and become Tyrants and Oppressors.

    10. I cannot therefore but somewhat admire, that a Lawyer, and
one that seemeth unto me to have understood Logic, should be (having been as it seemes to me sometimes seasoned with Intellectuals) so
unsound in his Intellectuals, as not to distinguish between *Disposing
at Pleasure, and Determining of Right, or setling according to Right,*
being things of a different *species,* and not *magis,* or *minus,* in the
same *species.* But it is not amisse to take a little notice how the Gentleman opposes himself; in his Book Page 4. he sayes, *it is resolved in
the Earl of Leicester's Case, that an Act of Parliament against the Law of
God and Nature is void; but this must be cautiously understood* (sayes

he) *that I speak not of secundary, or lesse principalls of Nature*, &c. Pray let him tell me, whether to dispose of Oakes', or Stiles' white Acre *ad Placitum*, be not directly against the Law of God and Nature; the Decalogue sayes, *Thou shalt not steale; Thou shalt not desire thy Neighbour's house, &c.* And Nature dictates, *doe, as thou wouldst be done unto.* Now he, or they that dispose at their owne pleasure, of their Neighbour's Acre, or Acres, *do steale*, for that he, or they deprive their Neighbour, or Neighbours of their Right, and Propriety; they covet also, for that they desire, and acquire to themselves a power of disposing at pleasure; they oppose also directly the Law of Nature, for they would not have anyone to dispose of their Propriety *ad Placitum*, or at their own wills, and therefore ought not to doe it to another; so that if the King and Parliament should make an Act, or King, or Parliament make an Ordinance, that *they might dispose of all Subjects' Estates, ad Placitum*, &c. they oppose *the Law of God and Nature*, and even by his own citation, and assertion, it is void. And I am sure it is also directly opposite to the Rule, frame, and constitution of a free Nation (such as are the English, being no Turkish, or Muscovian slaves) where the Rulers and Governours are but intrusted (as I in my former Treatise have instanced) for the generall good of the Nation. And the Gentleman, albeit he hath cavelled at me in the latter end of his Book, yet hath he confessed, and acknowledged as much in his Epistle Dedicatory in two severall places. The first is by me already cited, notwithstanding I will mention the words again; which are, *all Power and Authority is given for Preservation, and Edification, nothing for destruction, and desolation;* the others in the same page are, *for by the fundamental constitutions of this Kingdom, and the very frame and series of Government, the Power is intrusted into their hands to superintend and supervise all other Courts of Justice.* Now surely if Power be intrusted to the Parliament (as truly it is) then can they not go beyond their Trust to dispose of the Free People of England their Estates, *ad Placitum*, but only to determine of them, *ad Rectum*, or *Ius*, or to apply them *ad necessitatem Regni*, to or for the necessity of the Kingdome, of which necessity they are the Judges. The Gentleman sayes, that *many a man marries a widow that would be gladly rid of her children*. For my part, I know not whether, or no, the Gentleman be married; or whether he have married a Maid, or Widow, but I am sure (if he rightly consider it) he may be glad to be rid of his sick-brain begotten Childe [his Asserveration that the Parliament is un-limited, and consequently may dispose of all the Subjects', or Peoples' Estates, *ad Placitum*] for I verily believe, that no man found in his Intellectuals will harbour it, or give it entertainment, nor can himself sustain it.

11. I grant him that the Parliament is the highest *Court extensive* (*viz.* to conserve the Rule, Order, &c.) but the People in generall (*viz.* the Counties, Cities, and Towns corporate) are the highest, or greatest *Power Intensive*, in that they are the efficient, and finall cause under God, of the Parliament. Now the efficient and finall causes are the most noble of causes, nor are they, or can they be subject, or sub-ordinate to their owne effects, so farre forth as they are causes of such effects; so that the Parliament can never deprive the Counties, Cities, and Towns Corporate, by an Act, or Ordinance whatsoever, of their innate, and inseparable Right and Power of Electing, or creating Knights, Citizens, and Burgesses, *de futuro*, or for time to come, whereby a Parliament might be instituted, or assembled by any other way, than by way of *free Election*. No more can the Parliament de-prive the free People, or Nation of *England*, of their *Generall Liberty, and propriety*, for in these things the Sphear of the Parliament's Ac-tivity is circumscribed by the Nation's large Bulke of *Primitive, or in-tensive Power*. Wherefore the Gentleman mistakes when he sayes page 89. *It is impossible that the supreame Court in any Kingdome should be limited*, &c. In these Precedents, amongst free Nations all supreame Courts are *de facto*, limited; as in Aragon, Geneva &c.

And for my part, I cannot find that the Parliament Practiceth an unlimited or absolute Power, for amongst other things they have instituted Committees, and Sub-Committees of Accompts, not only to vindicate themselves from the scandall imputed by some, (viz. that *the Parliament should exact more from the people than the necessity of the Kingdome required*, &c.) but also to give the people a generall satisfaction, how, and which way their Estates are applied, and imployed *for the Necessity of the Kingdome.*

12. And now I think good further to satisfie the Gentleman and such as adhere or incline to his opinion aforesaid, concerning the *Primitive or Intensive power* of a free People. I have already said that a free People are ever free to dispose, and determine themselves *in Bonum commune, prout omnibus vissum erit*, to a generall common good, as it shall seeme good to themselves: and that they never part, or parted with this power, for that at what time soever they should doe it they cease to be *Populus liber*, or *liberi subditi*, a free People &c. And to make this Assertion more conspicuous, and plaine, I instance this *simile*; Joint Free-holders, or Free-holders jointly, let a Lease for one thousand, or two thousand yeares, if the World endure so long, *with reservation notwithstanding of a continuall acknowledgment to themselves*, or otherwise the said Lease shall determine, and cease to be, and it shall be lawful for the said Free-holders, their Heires, or Successours to reenter into the said Free-hold, or Free-holds, and to dispose and settle them, at their pleasure. Even so a free Nation, or People let a Lease of their power for one thousand, two thousand, ten thousand yeares if the World so long endure, (no matter what time) to their Rulers (whom they institute and intrust) in which they give and grant power to them of Determining conserving, and applying their Liberties, Rights, and Proprieties justly, *So to the particular good of every man, as may not repugne the generall good of all; so to the generall good of all men, as may not annihilate the particular good of one unjustly, or indirectly;* with reservation notwithstanding *of a con-*

tinuall acknowledgment to, or for themselves, that they (viz. the Nation, or People) *are the efficient cause of their power, by electing, and creating them; and that they are not to domineer over, or dispose of their Liberties, and Proprieties, ad placitum,* but only to determine of them *ad Rectum,* and apply them to the generall good of the Kingdome, according to the necessity of the Kingdome, Nation, or People, as aforesaid; if otherwise their Power determines, and ceases to be; and it may be lawfull for the Nation or People to re-enter *viz.* to make use of their first primitive power, and to dispose and settle themselves at their pleasure, or as they shall think good. And even as the Freeholders cease not to be Free-holders, notwithstanding their long Lease, for that there is a Reservation of a continuall acknowledgment due unto them, and a power of Re-entry in case of Breach of Covenants, and the like; even so a free Nation, or people, cease not at any time to be free, notwithstanding their *long Lease of Trust,* for that there is a Reservation of a continuall acknowledgment belonging unto them (*viz.* that they are the efficient cause, *de saeculo in saeculum,* from Age to Age) and they have likewise a power of using their *power primitive, and intensive, or power alwayes intended and reserved,* in cases aforesaid. Notwithstanding, as the Free-holders cannot re-enter, but only in case of Breach of Covenant aforesaid; for if otherwise they do it, they are meere usurpers, and Oppressours; so the free Nations, or people cannot use their primitive, or intensive power, but only when the fundamental frame of their Efficient Power and their Liberties, and Proprietie are destroyed or violated *ad placitum,* as aforesaid, if otherwise they doe it they are meer Rebels and Anarchists, for they have intrusted all their other Judiciall Power concerning Determination, Conservation, and Application to their Rulers.

13. The Gentleman whom I have formerly cited hath said in his Book, that he never heard or read of anything more prejudiciall to

the Parliament's Authority, than my Assertion in my last Book, and in this, (*viz.* that *the Parliament cannot dispose of the Free-people, or Subjects' Estates here in England, ad placitum;* but I must tell him that I never read of a more prejudicious, or pernicious to the Parliament, than to say that they may doe it; for what say many of the vulgar; if the Parliament may dispose of our Estates at their pleasure, how shall wee know that they will not? If any man tell them, that it is very unlikely, that so many will never consent to doe such a thing, for that they might by that means enslave their own Posterities. What say they, if they can dispose of all the Subjects' Estates *ad placitum,* for ought we know they might exempt themselves, their Heires, and Successours; and likewise for ought we know they might make a Law that they will no more be Elected, or created by the Counties, Cities, and Townes Corporate, but by a perpetuall Denomination by, or from themselves. And what can be of more dangerous consequence, than that such an Opinion, or Opinions as these should once take root in the mindes of the Common People? And what can sooner cause them to take root than that they finde and reade a printed Booke allowed of to that purpose? But if one tell the vulgar, that the Parliament cannot dispose of the Subjects' Estates *ad placitum,* or meerly at their pleasure, but that they can only apply in an equall way the Estates of the People to, or for the necessity of the Kingdome, of which Necessity they are the Judges; and likewise that the PARLIAMENT cannot make a Law, or Ordinance, that the Knights, Citizens, and Burgesses, shall, or may be appointed, or denominated by themselves (thereby to alter the frame and constitution of this NATION) but that they must perpetually from Age to Age be Elected, or created by the Counties, Cities and Towns Corporate; then they begin to harbour a better Opinion, and are more inclinable to undergoe their Ordinances. And I believe that the intent why the HONOURABLE HOUSE OF COMMONS published lately a Declaration the Seventeenth of April, 1646.[6] Ordered to be read in Churches, was to undeceive the People that they never had any thought to dispose of their Estates *ad placitum*, and so forth; for they expresly say, and Declare, *To maintain the Ancient and Fundamentall Government of this Kingdome, to preserve the Rights and Liberties of the Subject*, &c. Wherefore I would not have the Gentleman, or any other to run beyond the marke; I like not *Quid nimis*, it hath been the cause of many Enormities in Church and Common-wealth. For my part I wish, as I have ever wished, and formerly expressed my-selfe, that the King might enjoy his just Prerogative (as some call it) or Right of Reigning; and I wish, and desire as much as any other, that the Parliament might sustain their Priviledges, and Judicatory Power. But I could never suffer, nor would I if it were in my power any way to prevent it, endure that my Nation, or Fellow-Subjects should be enslaved by any Exorbitant Power (Potentate or Potencies) Forrain or Domestic; And I doubt not, but that the Ruler of Heaven and Earth will by his Divine Providence establish such Rulers and Rules in this KINGDOME, as may be a meanes to conserve this Nation from slavery and thraldome, AMEN.

Furthermore, having in my former Treatise and in this affirmed that the Parliament is the supreame Power Judicatory to censure and de-termine all matters doubtful, and disputable (for such hath been the constitution of this Kingdom for many Ages) I conceive therefore that the Parliament may, and have only Power to settle what form of Religion they shall think good; and albeit they should erre therein (as Parliaments may erre, and some *de facto* have erred) yet their Or-

---

6. "A Declaration of the Commons of their true Intentions concerning the Government of the Kingdom, the Government of the Church, the present Peace, etc." (London), April 17, 1646. Wing E2562. Note by George Thomason states that four thousand copies were ordered to be printed, distributed throughout the "county," and set up in every parish church.

dinances oblige *Iure humano;* that is, men ought either to obey such Ordinances, or if otherwise their Consciences dictate such Ordinances to be erroneous, they ought to undergoe such penalties as should be by them inflicted if they should impose or ordain any such. And as it is in the power of the Parliament to inflict penalties, so is it in their power to mitigate penalties, or inflict none at all for matter of Religion; wherefore for my part I greatly honour and reverence the care that the Parliament seemeth to take, and which the Honourable House of Commons have published in their Declaration 17. *April* 1646. already mentioned, *That they have not as yet resolved how tender Consciences, such as differ not in Fundamentals may be provided for, so as may stand with the peace of their soules, and peace of the Kingdome;* thereby intimating that they intend not to use severity, for matters of Religion meerly (a course though practiced by Pagans, befitting no men, much lesse Christians) but rather by clemency to induce men to embrace, or follow such Orders, or Ordinances touching Religion, as they shall institute. Moreover, I cannot but greatly blame such as would save men's Consciences wrackt and enforced in disputable matters, or *Tenets* of Religion; such as blame Domineering in others, and yet would exercise it themselvs not considering what the Apostle Pet. hath written, I. Pet. 5.3 μηδ' ὡς κατακυριεύοντες τῶν κλήρων ἀλλὰ τύποι γινόμενοι τοῦ ποιμνίου that Rulers should not be as over-domineering Lords or Christ's Flock, but as Types, or examples to the flock; nor do such consideratly weigh the Apostles' words, Gal. 6.1 *Brethren, if a man be overtaken in a fault, ye which are spirituall, restore such a one in the spirit of meeknesse, considering thy selfe, least thou also be tempted.* He bids them not menace, much lesse persecute for errour, nay the Apostle directly forbids it, Gal. 5.15. *But if ye bite, and devour one another take heed ye be not consumed one of another,* as if he had said, if ye break the Bond of Christian Charity, take heed least God give you not over to your malicious intentions and

practices, by which ye may become Instruments one to destroy another. The holy Apostle likewise Rom. 14.10. forbiddeth men directly
not so much as to judge a Brother for things indifferent, or for things
which Christian Liberty in Christ giveth leave unto; for saith he, *We
shall all stand before the Judgement Seat of Christ:* but it may be some
will say, these, and such like Councels, or Precepts of the Apostle
were spoken, or delivered by him concerning meeknesse, to be used
in admonishing our Brethren, in errours meerly of Practice not of
Doctrine, or in things not cleerly expressed in Scripture, not in things
evident and plain in Scripture. To such I answer; what are the great
matters in debate and controversie, or rather small matters in great
strife, and contention now adayes agitated, but either matters meerly
Practicall or exteriour Formes of Worship and Ceremonies, whether
tollerable, or intollerable; or else matters obscure, or but by probable
Arguments deducible out of Scripture, as Lay-Elders (a Businesse
now of dayes, of no small consequence) whether they be not sufficiently warranted by this Text I Tim. 5.17. *Let the Elders that rule well,
be counted worthy of double honour, especially they who labour in the
Word and Doctrine;* the Greek hath it, οἱ κοπιῶντες ἐν λόγῳ καὶ
διδασκαλίᾳ "labouring in Word and Doctrine," and from hence it
must be deduced forsooth, that there were some Elders that did not
labour in the Word and Doctrine, and consequently that such were
Laymen. Truly others that are as sound in their judgments (it may
be) as those that make this Deduction, will say that the meaning of
that Text is this *viz.* Presbyters (or Elders) that rule well be ac-
compted worthy of double honour in respect of the younger or inferiour; but chiefly such as beside their care, and ordinary performance
of their charge labour extraordinarily in Preaching, and exhorting or
edifying; even as one might say, let Civill Magistrates that govern
well be counted worthy of double honour, in respect of other ordinary, and inferiour Persons; but chiefly such as beside their care, and

ordinary performance of their Offices, according to their Oathes, and
Duties, labour extraordinarily for the Publique good, by advising,
and consulting. I doe not finde that it could be deduced from this last
inference, that Clergiemen were, or ought to be Civill Magistrates;
nor can I finde that it can well be deduced from the Apostle's words,
that Laymen ought to be Presbyters, or Church-Elders: and yet a
great deale of stirre is kept about this businesse, and such like; And
some would faine have their but probable Deductions, if so much, to
be Orthodoxal Expositions, and so to be held *de jure Divino*, that's no
presumption. But by the favor of such, I would fain know whether
they are infallible, or no; if no, why would they then impose their Expositions *de Jure Divino;* if they are infallible, I would gladly know
how they now come by such an extraordinary gift of Infallibility, and
that the World (by their own acknowledgment) hath wanted it for so
many Ages, as they say, in all Ages since the Apostles' time; as I have
said, that in Civill Affaires there should not be *Quid nimis;* so I say in
Church-Affaires and wish that men (for alas what are we all but men)
would not take upon them *Quid nimis,* especially in matters either
indifferent, or else obscure, and difficult or such as may admit of severall interpretations, and Constructions. I will instance for Example
sake one Text of Scripture; *viz.* ἐν ἀρχῇ ἦν ὁ λόγος &c. *In the beginning was the word,* &c. All Divinity tells us that Eternity is *Identicum
nunc,* the selfe-same now, and that it hath neither *Prius* or *Postivius,*
beginning, or ending; what beginning then can the *Eternall Word* (or
Sonne of God) have? No beginning in time, because *Eternall,* nor in
Nature because *Increate.* What beginning then? Or what may the
word *Beginning* in that place signifie? Some will have the meaning
of that Text to be this; In the beginning when the World was created,
the word (*verbum mentis*) of the Father's understanding was, and so
if that were in the Beginning, that was before all Beginning; but this
is no good consequence, sayes an Arrian, for the word might bee be-

fore the World, and yet be *a patre tanquam effectus a causa*, be as an effect caused by God the Father, and so have some beginning (as every effect hath) though before the World and to hold this is Heresie, for that the Father is not *causa filii*, but only *Principium filii*, not the cause, but naturall beginning of the Sonne. Others will have the meaning to be thus; in that beginning, or instant (which was, and is ever, or Eternall) wherein the Father knew formally his Essence, and Attributes, he spake, or begot the word of his mind, or understanding, being a *Terme* of his infinite Knowledge, not produced by necessity, or will, but emanating, or flowing as it were by naturall faecundity. Others will have the meaning to be thus; in that beginning or instant aforesaid, wherein the Father knew not only formally his Essence, and attributes, but also all creatures possible and existent he spake or begot the word of his mind or understanding; for say they, the word which is the *Terme* of the Father's infinite Knowledg, is *a perfectissima, & plenissima cognitione ejus*, from his most perfect, and fullest knowledge; and from hence arise divers Arguments *pro & contra*, not only between the Thomists, Scotists, and other School-men, but also amongst other sorts, or Sects of Christians; but must men for these or the like disputable differences cut one another's throats, or persecute one another? God forbid, there is not the least warrant in the New Testament for it. In the time of our blessed Saviour's passing his humanity on the Earth, some there were casting out Devils in his Name, whom his Disciples forbad because they followed not Christ as they did; but our Saviour rebuked them, and bade them suffer them, and let them alone, saying he, or they that are not against us, are with us, adding moreover that it was not likely that any one should doe a miracle in his Name and speak ill of him. Our Saviour said not, that such as workt miracles in his Name *should confesse, and speake all that ought to be confessed, and spoken of, or to his honour;* but that such as spake not ill of him should (if they confessed his Name) be permitted, or suffered in this World. And shall not we then suffer one another in matters of Religion? Shall we ambitiously compasse our Neighbour's goods, or meanes, under pretence of Religion, thereby scandalizing Christianity. No! Let all self-ends be abolished, and Peace and Union be embraced that we of this Nation may become an *Elisium* of comfort of Christian Charity, and mutuall Amity, one to another, and a Precedent of them all to other Nations.

William Ball

FINIS.

Uncharted Waters

John Goodwin, 1594?–1665

Right and might
Well mett.

*J*ohn Goodwin, a staunch Puritan and an Independent, was one of the most radical of the republican divines. He was not only a frequent contributor to the paper wars on constitutional and religious subjects before and during the civil war but also an instigator of them.

Goodwin was born in Norfolk about 1594 and educated at Queen's College, Cambridge. In 1633 he was instituted to the vicarage of St. Stephen's in London where he became a popular preacher. Alderman Isaac Pennington, later lord mayor and member of the Short and Long Parliaments, was one of Goodwin's parishioners. Goodwin's combative nature led him into one controversy after another. He helped draft the London clerical petition against Archbishop Laud's infamous canons of 1640 which had upheld the divine right of kings and proclaimed the unlawfulness of resistance to authority. Goodwin was one of the first clergymen to support the resort to war. Despite his adherence to Parliament, however, his emphasis on a gathered church of followers convinced the parliamentary Committee for Plundered Ministers to eject him from his living in 1645. This action presumably soured Goodwin on some members of Parliament. His ejection did not keep him from his calling; Goodwin managed to continue serving as pastor of his independent congregation, which met in the vicinity of his old church. In 1649 he was finally restored to his living.

Unabashed by tough measures, Goodwin rushed to defend the actions of the New Model Army after its purge of the moderate members of Parliament on 6 December 1648. His astonishing tract, "Right and Might Well Mett," has been described as the most striking document *in the development of the Independent party's political theory. Its ironic dedication to General Thomas Fairfax, a man who had hoped to preserve constitutional forms, was dated 1 January 1649, the day the Rump Parliament voted to bring Charles I to trial for treason. The first of the tract's two issues, reprinted here, appeared the following day. In it Goodwin maintains that the New Model Army was a truer representative of the English people than the Parliament it had purged. As the representative of the people the army had acted to save the nation. It was justified, he argued, by "a Law of greater authority, than the Lawes of the Land," the law of necessity. Goodwin even suggested that many of the laws of God, "thinke it no disparagement . . . to give place to their elder Sister," the law of necessity.*

Not surprisingly this tract provoked a reply within the week. Sir Francis Nethersole, former secretary to the king's sister, the Electress Elizabeth, had taken no part in the civil war but felt compelled to rebut Goodwin. A second response, this time by a Puritan divine John Geree, appeared on 18 January. By 25 January when Nethersole released a further reply the king's trial for treason had already begun. Goodwin has been referred to as the first Protestant minister to have approved regicide.

Goodwin continued to publish throughout the Interregnum. He was taken into custody at the time of the Restoration but treated with amazing lenience, merely being banned from holding any public trust. He returned to his London congregation but not to the income from it and died in the plague year of 1665.

That the children of prey, and men lately under hope of dividing the spoile of this miserable Kingdome, when it should be reduced under the iron rod of enslaving tyranny and oppression (betweene which sad condition, and it, there was now but a step) should rise up with passionate outcries, and be ready to curse the Armie and their late proceedings, with bell, booke, and candle, is no matter of wonder, or much observation. But if the body of the people of the Land, or such who have no minde to be gratified with the sorrows or sighings of innocent men, should professe any dissatisfaction, or stand in conscience about the lawfulnesse or justnesse of such their engagements; it would argue, either first, that they alwayes lived not only free from oppression, but from the fear of it also, & so never had occasion to enquire, either upon what grounds, and by what means, oppression imminent may lawfully be prevented, or incumbent, be shaken off and suppressed; or else, in case they have suffered under oppression, that they never saw any visible or probable meanes of deliverance, and so wanted an inviting opportunity to consider, whether these meanes might lawfully be improved in order to such an end, or no. For certainely the grounds and principles upon which the said proceedings of the Army stand cleare and justifiable, are no parables, no darke, or disputable notions, or conceptions, but such, wherein even *he that runneth, may read* equity and truth; and which have been asserted for such, by grave, learned, and judicious men, who *neither lent, nor tooke upon usury;* I meane, who were no wayes interested in any such concernment, or case, as that now upon triall.

Though some other things have been of late acted by the Armie, wherein many pretendingly complaine of want of conscience and justice; yet I suppose they have done nothing, either more obnoxious to the clamorous tongues and pens of their adversaries, or more questionable in the judgements and consciences of their friends, than that late garbling of the Parliament, wherein they sifted out much of the drosse and soile of that heap, intending to reduce this body, upon the regular motion whereof, the well-being, indeed, the (civill) life of the whole Kingdome depends, to such members, who had not manifestly turned head upon their trust, nor given the right hand of fellowship to that most barbarous, inhumane, and bloody faction amongst us, who for many yeares last past have with restlesse endeavours procured the deepe trouble, and attempted the absolute enslaving, (which is, being interpreted, the utter undoing) of the Nation. So that if this action of theirs shall approve itselfe, and appear to be regular and conformable to such lawes, and rules of justice, which all considering and disingaged men conclude ought to be followed and observed in such cases, as that which lay before them; especially if it shall appeare to have been the legitimate issue of true worth and Christianity; I presume all their other actions of like tenor and import, will partake of the same justification, and honour, with it.

Let us first take into consideration the substance of such exceptions, which can with any pretence of reason, or colour of conscience be levied against the lawfulnesse of it. Afterwards if it be needful, we will consider further, whether those that be with it, be not more, or at least more weighty and considerable, than those that are against it.

The first born of the strength of those, who condemn the said act of the Armie, as unlawful, lieth in this; that the Actors had no sufficient authority to doe what they did therein, but acted out of their sphere, and so became transgressors of that Law, which commandeth every man to keepe order, and within the compasse of his calling.

To this I answer 1. as our Saviour saith, *that the Sabbath was made for man* (i. for the benefit of man) *and not man for the Sabbath;* so certain it is, that callings were made for men, and not men for callings. Therefore as the law of the *Sabbath,* though enacted by God, was of right, and according to the intention of the great Law-giver himselfe, to give place to the necessary accommodations of men, and ought not to be pleaded in bar hereunto; in like manner, if the law of callings at any time opposeth, or lieth crosse to the necessary conve-

niences of men, during the time of this opposition, it suffereth a totall eclipse of the binding power of it. It is a common saying among
the Jewish Doctors, *that perill of life drives away the Sabboth;* yea
Master *Ainsworth* citeth this saying out of the *Hebrew Canons: Circumcision in the time thereof driveth away the Sabboth;* and afterwards,
that perill of life driveth away all. So that as there were severall cases,
wherein (as our Saviour's expression is) they *who polluted the Sabboth
were blamelesse;* In like manner, there are very many cases, wherein
men may transgresse the ordinary law of Callings, and yet be no
transgressors. Therefore unlesse it can be proved, that the Armie had
no necessity lying upon them to garble the Parliament as they did;
their going beyond their ordinary callings to doe it, will no wayes impaire the credit or legitimatenesse of the action.

2. Nor did they stretch themselves beyond the line of their callings, to act therein as they did. Their calling and commission was, to
act in the capacity of Souldiers for the peace, liberties, and safety of
the Kingdome. What doth this import, but a calling to prevent, or
suppresse by force, all such persons and designes, whose faces were
set to disturb, or destroy them? Nor did their Commission (I presume) limit or conclude their judgements to any particular kind of
enemies, as if they had only power, or a calling thereby, to oppose or
suppresse, either such, who should confesse themselves enemies, or
such, who by the interpretation or vote of any one party, or faction of
men in the Kingdome, should be reputed and deemed enemies: but
all such, without exception, whom they, upon competent grounds,
and such, as upon which discreet men in ordinary cases are wont to
frame acts of judgment, and to proceed to action accordingly, should
judge and conclude to be enemies. Or if it shall be supposed, that by
their Commission they were limited to judge only those enemies to
the Kingdome, with their abbettors and supporters, who were in
Armes with the King, or on the King's behalfe against the Kingdome,
in their Representatives; those Parliament-men, whom they have ex-

cluded from sitting in that house, having notoriously discovered themselves to be men of this engagement, friends and abettors of those, who very lately were, and yet in part are, in armes against the peace and safety of the Kingdome, in this consideration fall directly and clearly under their commission; and consequently, by warrant hereof, they have, and had a *calling,* to proceed against them as they did.

3. If the calling which the Parliament itselfe had to levy Forces against the King and his Party, to suppresse them, and their proceedings, as destructive to the peace, liberties, and safety of the Kingdome, was warrantable and good, then was the calling of the Armie to act as they did in the business under debate, warrantable and good also. But the antecedent is true, therefore the consequent also. The minor proposition, *viz.* that the calling of the Parliament, to levy Forces against the King and his Party, in order to the ends mentioned, was every wayes warrantable and good, I presume will not be denied by the Parliament-men themselves. Or if they should deny it, they would but deny the Sunne to be up at noone-day, inasmuch as the truth thereof hath beene brought forth into a cleare and perfect light, by many pennes, yea and by their owne (in many of their Declarations) yea, and Mr. *Prynne* himselfe hath set it up in a great Volume as *upon a mountaine, that it cannot be hid;* though by the fervency of his late Devotion to the King's interest and cause, he hath attempted the melting downe of that mountaine.[1]

The connexion in the major proposition is valid upon this consideration. The Parliament (or at least the Parliament men who did the thing) had no other calling, to oppose the King and his, by force, but only the generall call of the major part of the people, by which they

---

1. William Prynne, "The Soveraign Power of Parliaments and Kingdomes: divided into foure parts" (London, 1643), Wing P4088; William Prynne, "The Soveraigne Power of Parliaments and Kingdoms, or, Second Part ... wherein the Parliaments and Kingdomes Right and Interest in, and Power over the Militia ...," Wing P4088.

were inabled to act in a Parliamentary capacity, [i. more effectually, and upon more advantagious termes, than singly, or out of such a capacity, they could] for their good. By this call by the major part of the people, they were enabled only in a generall, implicit, and indefinite manner, to raise forces against the King and his complices, for the safetie, and behoofe of the Kingdome. So that the particularity of this action was not warranted simply by the nature, or tenore of their call, but by the regular and due proportion which it had to the accomplishing of the end, for which they were chosen or called, *viz.* the people's good. From whence it followes, that whether they had beene in a Parliamentary capacity, or no, yet if they had been in a sufficient capacity of strength, or power for matter of execution, their call to doe it, for substance, had been the same, though not for forme. And suppose there had beene no Parliament sitting, or in being, when the King and his party rose up in armes against the Peace, Liberties, and safety of the Kingdome; doubtlesse if any one man had been able to have secured the Kingdome in all these against them, his action had not been censurable for want of a calling to it; in as much as every member, as well in a body politique, as naturall, hath a sufficient call, yea an ingagement lying by way of duty upon it, to act at any time, and in all cases, according to its best and utmost capacity, or ability, for the preservation and benefit of the whole. Now then, supposing the same proportion to the peace, benefit, and safety of the Kingdome, in what the Army did in purging the Parliament, and in what the Parliament itselfe did, in opposing the King by force (which is a point of easie demonstration, and is *ex super abundanti*, proved in the large Remonstrance of the Army lately published)[2] let us consider, whether the call of the Army, to act for the Kingdome as

2. "A new Remonstrance and Declaration from the Army; and their Message for the conducting of His Majestie's Royall person from the Isle of Wight to his Palace of Westminster" (London, 18 November 1648), Wing N740.

they did, be not as authentique, cleare, and full, as that of the Parliament to act as they did, in reference to the same end.

First, the authority and power of the people [or rather the present exercise and execution of this power] to act for their owne preservation and well being in every kind, was as well formally, and according to the ceremonie of the Law, as really, and according to the true intentions and desires of the people, vested in the Parliament. So that the Parliament by vertue of this investiture, and during the same, had the same right of power to raise an Armie, and to give unto it what Commission they judged meet, in order to the benefit of the people, or to act any other thing of like tendency, which the people themselves had, to chuse for themselves a Parliament. Therefore whatsoever lieth within the verge of the Armie's Commission derived from the Parliament, relating to the Kingdome's good, they have as full and formall a call, or warrant, to act, and put in execution, as the Parliament itselfe had, either to raise an Army, or to doe any other act whatsoever. If then first, the tenor of their Commission stood towards any such point as this, (which I presume is no way questionable) *viz.* to suppresse by strong hand, all such persons, whom upon rationall grounds they should judge enemies to the peace and welfare of the Kingdome; and secondly, that those Parliament Members, whom now they have cut off from that body, were upon such grounds judged such by them, (of the truth whereof they have given a super-sufficient account in their said late Remonstrance); it is as cleare as the Sun that their calling to act as they did in cutting off these Members, is every whit as legitimate and formall, as that of the Parliament itselfe is to act anything whatsoever, as a Parliament.

Nor is it of any value to pretend here, and say, that it is not to be beleeved, that a Parliament should give any Commission unto men, to act against themselves, or in a destructive way to their priviledges, or honours. For to this I answer.

First, that Law-givers, whilst they are sober, and in their right
mindes, may very probably make such Lawes, for the ordering and
restraint of persons distracted and madd, which in case they afterwards become distracted, may, and ought to bee put in execution,
upon themselves. And in case any of those Parliament men, who
joined in granting that Commission unto the Army, by which they
were inabled to fight, slay and destroy all those that were in armes
against the Parliament, should afterwards have turned Cavaliers
themselves, and been found in armes against the Parliament (as some
of them, if my memory faileth me not, were) they might very lawfully have beene encountered and destroyed by the Army, by vertue of
that Commission which was granted by themselves.

Secondly, what only one Emperour explicitely spake to an inferiour Officer created by him, when hee delivered him the Sword; *If
I doe justly, use this for me; if unjustly, use it against me;* the same implicitely, and according to the exigency of the trust committed by
Office, doth every superiour Magistrate say unto him, whom he
chuseth and admitteth into a place of subordinate office, or power
under him. For *the punishment of evill doers,* and so the procurement
of the publique good, doth not lie by way of Office, or duty, upon the
chiefe Magistrate only, but upon all subordinate Magistrates also,
and Officers whatsoever. This is evident from this passage in *Peter:
Submit yourselves to every ordinance of man for the Lord's sake, whether
it be to the King, as supreame; Or unto Governours.* [i. inferiour Magistrates or Officers] *as to them that are sent by him for the punishment of
evill doers, and for the praise of them that do well.* So then, *the punishment of evill doers,* and this simply, without all partiality, or distinction
of persons, (which are things sinfull in all Magistrates whatsoever, as
well subordinate, as supreame) and likewise the protection and incouragement of *those that doe well,* lying by way of Office and duty,
upon all those, who by the *King,* or supreme Officer, are invested
with any power of authority, though subordinate; evident it is, that

whensoever a *King,* or other Supreame authoritie, creates an inferiour, they invest it with a legitimacy of magistraticall power to *punish* themselves also, in case they prove *evill doers;* yea and to act any
other thing requisite for *the praise* or incouragement of the good. Nor
is there any pretence here for such an exception, as the Apostle *Paul*
findes, in the grand Commission of Christ. *But when hee saith all
things are put under him, it is manifest that he is excepted, which did put
all things under him.* God the Father being uncapable of sin, is not
capable of losing that soveraigne dignity, which is native and essentiall to him; and consequently, not capable of comming into subjection under any creature, as *Christ* Mediator, in respect of his human
nature, is. But Kings and Magistrates of the highest, being very capable even of such sins, which are destructive to the peace and welfare of the people under them, and repugnant to the incouragement
of those *that doe well,* and consequently, which appertaine to the cognizance of every Magistrate, to whom the care of such things is intrusted, are very capable also of forfeiting that dignity, which is
naturall and essentiall to them, as Kings, or Supreame, and of ren-
dering themselves obnoxious to those authorities and powers, which
out of such cases, are under them, but upon such miscariages, are
above them; as *Reuben* forfeited that *excellency of dignity,* which ap-
pertained to him, as *the first borne* of his Father, by *going up unto his
Father's bed.* Upon this very ground *Calvin* himselfe, *Zwinglius,* and
other reformed Divines, and the *Scottish* Ministers themselves (more
generally) and Master *Prynne* more voluminously than they all, determine and adjudge it, not only lawfull, but matter of duty and
charge lying upon the subordinate Magistrates, to curb and bridle
the tyrannous extravagancies and incursions of Kings and Princes
against their people. But

Secondly,[3] suppose the Armie had not a call to act as they did, in

3. This is the third, not the second point.

the case under debate, every waye's as full of formality, as the call of
the Parliament to act as they did, in opposition to the King, yet might
their call be (and indeed was) as materiall, as weighty, as considerable, and as justifiable in the sight of God, and of all unprejudiced
intelligent men, as the other. The call of the Parliament we spake of,
was from the *persons* of the people, expressed by formality of words,
or other ordinary gestures, testifying such a call from them: and this
call they (or most of them) received from the people, whilst as yet
they (the people) were in no visible, at least in no imminent or present danger of being swallowed up in slavery and tyranny. But the *call*
of the Armie, to deny the opportunity of the house, to those Members of Parliament, whom they sequestered, was from the strong and
importunate cries of the people's *Liberties,* yea and of many of their
lives, being now laid upon the Altar, ready to be offered up in sacrifice upon the service of the lust and revenge of a most inhumane generation of men, who (it seemes) thirsted after them with that
furiousnesse of thirst, that they made no spare of their owne deare
lives themselves to make the purchase, and were now under a great
additionall enragement, as having been for a long time chafed up and
downe in their owne blood, and by a strong hand kept falling from
their desires. Now the calls of the miseries and extremities of men
for reliefe, are more authorizing, more urging, pressing, and binding
upon the consciences of men, who have wherewithall to afford reliefe
unto them, than the formall requests or elections of men to places of
trust or interest, when the electors have no such present or pressing
necessity upon them, for the interposall of the elected on their behalfe. The necessities of men *call* more effectually, than men themselves; yea, the truth is, that the calls of men, calling others there to
helpe or assist them, being in a tolerable condition of subsisting,
without receiving the helpe they call for, are but dallyings, or sport-
ings, and shadowes of calls, in comparison of the loud, vehement,

and importunate cries of the exigencies and extremities of men, though the men themselves should hold their peace.

Fourthly, (and lastly to the first objection) the common saying, that *in case of extreame necessity all things are common*, extends unto *callings* also. In cases of necessity, all *callings* are common, in order to the supply of the present necessity. *David* and his men being hungry, were all *Priests*, in reference to the satisfaction of their hunger, and did, and that lawfully, eate that *bread, which* (as our Saviour himselfe affirmeth) *was lawfull only for the Priests to eate. Polanus* a reformed Divine of good note, granteth, that *when Bishops and Ecclesiastiques are defective either in will, or skill, for the reformation of Religion, and the Church; laicks,* or private men "may lawfully supply their defect herein," and act the part of Bishops or Ecclesiastical persons, in such reformations.

When the Pilot, or Master of a Ship at Sea, be either so farre overcome and distempered with drinke, or otherwise disabled, as through a freneticall passion, or sicknesse in any kinde, so that he is uncapable of acting the exigencies of his place; for the preservation of the Ship, being now in present danger, either of running upon a quick sand, or splitting against a rock, &c. any one, or more of the inferiour Mariners, having skill, may, in order to the saving of the Ship, and of the lives of all that are in it, very lawfully assume, and act according to the interest of a Pilot, or Master, and give orders and directions to those with them in the Ship accordingly, who stand bound at the perill of their lives in this case to obey them. By such a comparison as this, Master *Prynne* himselfe demonstrates how regular and lawfull it is for *Parliaments*, yea and for particular men, to turne Kings, I meane, to assume that Interest and power, which the Law appropriates to the Office, and vesteth only in the person of the King, when the King steereth a course in manifest opposition to the peace and safety of the Kingdome.

The passage in Master *Prynne*, though it be somewhat large, yet being thorough and home to the point in hand, I shall present Verbatim. *Go too now* (saith this *Anti Protyrannicall* Spirit) *in this our Politique Ship, the Master gluts himselfe with Wine; most of his Assistants either asleepe, or drunke with mutuall cups, sportingly behold an imminent rock. The Ship in the meane time, either holds not that course, which is expedient for the owner, or seemes speedily to be wracked. What thinkest thou is here to be done under the Master, by one who is vigilant and solicitous? Shall he pull those by the eares, who are asleepe, or only jogge them by the sides? But in the meane time, lest he should seeme to doe ought without their command, shall hee not afford his helpe and assistance to the indangered Ship? Truly what madnes, or rather impietie, will this be? Seeing then (as Plato saith) TYRANNY IS A CERTAIN FRENZY and drunkenness, the Prince may utterly subvert the Republique, the most of the Nobles may collude, connive, or at least are fast asleepe; the people, who are Lords of the Republique, by the fraude and negligence of their Ministers, which is their fault, are reduced into greatest streights. In the meane time, there is one of the Nobles, which considers the incroaching tyranny, and detests it from his soule: what think'st thou is now to bee done against him by this man? Shall he only admonish his Colleagues of their duty, who themselves doe as much hurt as they may? But besides, as it is perillous to admonish, and in that state of things it may be deemed a capitall crime. Shall hee doe like those, who contemning other helpes, casting away their armes, shall cite Lawes, and make an Oration concerning Justice, among theeves, in the midst of a wood? But this truly is that which is commonly said, to be mad with reason. What then? Shall he grow deafe at the people's groans? Shall hee be silent at the entrance of theeves? Or shall he finally grow lazie, and put his hands into his bosome? But if the Lawes appoint the punishment of a Traitor against one wearing buskins on his legges, who counterfeits sicknesse for feare of the enemies, what punishment at least shall we decree against him, who either through malice, or slothfulnesse, shall betray those whom he hath undertaken to protect? But rather he shall command those things that are needfull to such as are wary, by a Mariner's shout: he shall take care lest the Common-wealth receive any detriment, and shall preserve the King-dome even against the King's will and resistance, by WHICH HE HIM-SELF BECOMES A KING and shall cure the King himselfe as a frantique man, by BINDING HIS HANDS AND FEET, if he may not otherwise doe it.* Thus farre Mr. *Prynne;* and full far enough to justifie whatsoever is said in these papers for the justification of the Army in their *binding the hands and feet* of some *frantique* Parliament men (as himself in a Platonick strain phraseth those, who *either through mal-ice, or slothfulnesse, shall betray those, whom they have undertaken to protect*).

It were easie to multiply instances of like import. But by what hath been argued, the nullitie of that argument against the proceedings of the Army, drawne from the defect of a calling to act as they did, fully appeareth.

A second Objection is this: They *resisted* Authority, or the powers lawfully set over them; and therein, the *ordinance of God:* therefore their fact is to be condemned and cannot be justified. I answer,

First, To *resist* Authority, imports either a detracting or deniall of obedience to the just commands of Authority, or else the ingaging of a man's selfe to dissolve, and take away Authority. Now certaine it is that the Army, in that act of theirs now in question, neither did the one, or the other. First, the authority of Parliament, had made no such Act, passed no such Vote, that none of their Members, though voting, or acting never so palpably, or with never so high an hand against the Interest, peace, and liberties of the Kingdome, should be debarred sitting in their house. In which respect, the Army debar-ring those Members, which had thus voted and acted, from sitting in that House, did not *resist Authority* in the former sence. Or in case it should be supposed, that the authority of Parliament, had made such an act, or passed such a Vote, as that mentioned, unlesse the eq-

uity and justnesse of it could be sufficiently cleared, the crime of resisting authority could not upon any sufficient ground be imputed to
those, who should decline obedience to it.

Secondly, neither did the Army in the aforesaid act, resist authority in the latter sence; because what they did, no way imported any
dislike of Parliament authority, nor had any tendency towards the
abolition, or taking of it away; but only implied a disapprovement of
the factious carriage of things in this present Parliament, as evidently
bent against the safety, liberties, and well-being of the Nation; and
tended withall towards a prevention of the like, or worse, for the future. But as for their approbation of, and resolutions to maintaine
Parliaments, and Parliamentary authority (stated and formed in a
regular and due proportion to the behoofe and benefit of the Kingdome) they stand abundantly declared to all the World in their late
Remonstrance.[4]

If it be here yet further said; yea but though it should bee granted,
that they did not *resist* Authority, in either of the two considerations
specified, yet they did that, which was worse, or every whit as bad, as
either of them. For they offered violence to persons in authority, and
would not suffer them to act in that authoritative capacity, which was
lawfully vested in them. To this also I answer;

First, it is lawfull for any man, even by violence, to wrest a Sword
out of the hand of a mad man, though it be never so legally his, from
whom it is wrested. The reason is, because in case a man that is mad,
should be let alone with a Sword in his hand, either untill he be willing of himselfe to part with it, or untill it can be recovered from him
by a due processe and course in Law, there is a probability in reason,
and according to the frequent experience of the workings of such a
distemper, that he will doe much mischiefe with it in the meane time:
and the lives and limbs of men, are to be preferred before the exorbi-

---

4. "A new Remonstrance and Declaration from the Army."

tant wills, or humours of men under distemper. This is the very case
in hand. The Members of Parliament dis-housed by the Army, were
strangely struck with a politicall frenzy (as *Plato* tearmeth it); they
acted as men bereaved of their senses, that had quite forgotten the
businesse committed unto them, and that knew, or understood nothing of matters relating to the peace or well being of the Kingdome, or
of those who had intrusted them with their power: their counsels and
votes of late still smiled upon their owne enemies, and the grand and
most inveterate enemies of the Kingdome, but frowned and looked
gastly upon their friends, and those that had constantly guarded
them with their lives and estates.

> *Hic furor haud dubius; haec est manifesta phrenesis. i.*
> This madnesse is without all doubt,
> And phrensie manifest throughout.

Now then Parliamentary power being in the hands of these men,
but as a sword or speare in the hand of a man distraught in his wits
and senses, wherewith hee is like to doe little or no good but in continuall danger of doing much harme, it might very lawfully, and with
the full consent of all principles of reason, equity, and conscience, be
seized upon, and taken from them by a strong hand, for the prevention of such mischiefes and miseries, which, remaining in their hand,
it daily and hourly threatened to bring upon the whole Nation and
Kingdome.

Secondly, The King had as legall and formall an investiture into
the power of the Militia, of sitting in Parliament, &c. as these men
had into their Parliamentary places and trusts: yet did not the Parliament unjustly, or contrary to rules of equity, upon a plenary discovery of a bent in his will and counsels to suppresse the liberties of
the Nation, to deprive him, and that by force, of the injoyment and
exercise of those interests and priviledges, notwithstanding the legality of their investiture in him. Therefore upon a like discovery of
the same bent in the wills and counsels of these Parliament men, the

lawfulnesse of their elections into their places of trust, cannot reflect any unlawfulnesse upon that act, by which they were removed from, or debarred of them.

Thirdly, (and lastly) there is no Client that hath enterteined a Lawyer, or Advocate to plead his cause, but upon discovery, yea or jealousie, of prevarication, and false-heartednesse to him in his cause, may lawfully discharge him, his entertainement notwithstanding. There is the same liberty in a Pupill, or person in his minority, to disentrust his Guardian, how lawfully soever chosen, upon suspicion of male-administration, or unfaithfulnesse. And why should the like liberty be denied unto a people or Nation, for the removing of such persons, whom they have chosen for Guardians to their Estates and Liberties, from these places of trust, when they evidently discerne a direct tendency in their proceedings, to betray them, both in the one and the other, unto their enemies?

But two things (it is like) will bee here objected. First, that the Parliament were Judges lawfully constituted, of the King's delinquency against the Kingdome; but the Army were no Judges of such a constitution, of the miscarriages of the Parliament. Therefore there is not the same consideration, in point of lawfulnesse, in the proceedings of the Army against the Parliament, which is of the Parliament's proceeding against the King. There is the same difference likewise betweene the act of a Client and Pupill, wherein the one dischargeth his Advocate, and the other his Guardian; and the act of the Army, in dethroning the Parliament men. To this I answer,

First, That whether we place the lawfulnesse of a Parliamentary Judicature in respect of the King's Delinquency, either in their Election by the people, or in the conformity of this their Election unto the Lawes of the Land, certaine it is that the Army were Judges of every whit as competent, and lawfull a constitution of their delinquencies in the same kinde. For,

First, If we measure the lawfulnesse of Parliamentary Judicature by the call of the people thereunto, the Army (as was formerly proved) hath every whit as lawfull a constitution to judge who are enemies to the peace and safety of the Kingdome, as the Parliament itselfe hath. Nor doth it at all argue any illegality in their judgements about the Parliament men, that they had not the explicit and expresse consent of the people therein, or that they had no call by them so to judge; no more than it proveth an illegallity in many Votes and Or-dinances of Parliament, that they were both made and published, not only without the particular and expresse consent, but even contrary to the minds and desires of the people, or at least of the major part of them. Besides it is a ridiculous thing to pretend a want of a call from the people, against the lawfulnesse of such an act, which is of that soveraign necessity for their benefit and good, which the actings of the Army were; especially at such a time, when there is no possibility of obtaining, or receiving a formall call from the people, without run-ning an eminent hazard of losing the opportunity for doing that ex-cellent service unto them, which the providence of God in a peculiar juncture of circumstances, exhibits for the present unto us. Men's consents unto all acts manifestly tending to their reliefe, are suffi-ciently expressed in their wants and necessities.

If it be yet said, "But the people doe not judge the proceedings of the Army against the Parliament men, as tending to their reliefe, or welfare in any kinde, but as contrary unto both, nor doe they give so much as their subsequent consents thereunto"; I answer (besides what was lately said to the nullifying of this pretence) that Physitians called to the care and cure of persons under distempers, need not much stand upon the consents of such patients, either subsequent, or antecedent, about what they administer unto them. If the people be uncapable in themselves of the things of their peace, it is an act of so much the more goodnesse and mercy in those, who being fully ca-pable of them, will ingage themselves accordingly to make provision for them. It is a deed of Charity and Christianity, to save the life of a

lunatique or distracted person even against his will. Besides it is a
ruled case amongst wise men, that *if a people be depraved and corrupt,
so as to conferre places of power and trust upon wicked and undeserving
men, they forfeit their power in this behalfe unto those that are good,
though but a few.* So that nothing pretended from a non-concurrence
of the people with the Army, will hold water. Or,

Secondly, If wee estimate the lawfulnesse of that Judicature, by the
conformity of their elections thereunto, to the Lawes of the Land,
the investiture of the Army into that Judicature, which they have exercised in the case in question, is conforme unto a Law of farre
greater authority, than any one, yea than all the Lawes of the Land
put together; I meane, the Law of nature, necessity, and of love to
their Country and Nation: which being the Law of God himselfe
written in the fleshly tables of men's hearts, hath an authoritative jurisdiction over all human Lawes and constitutions whatsoever; a prerogative right of power to overrule them, and to suspend their
obliging influences, in all cases appropriate to itselfe. Yea many of
the Lawes of God themselves, thinke it no disparagement unto them,
to give place to their elder Sister, the Law of necessity, and to surrender their authority into her hand, when shee speaketh. So that
whatsoever is necessary, is somewhat more than lawfull; more (I
meane) in point of warrantablenesse. If then the Army stood bound
by the Law of nature and necessity, to judge the Parliament men as
they did, *viz.* as men worthy to be secluded from their fellowes in
Parliamentary interest, this judiciary power was vested in them by a
Law of greater authority, than the Lawes of the Land; and consequently the legality, or lawfulnesse of it was greater, than of that in
the Parliament, which derives its legality only from a conformity to
the established Lawes of the Land. Yea the truth is, that that Law of
necessity, by which the Army were constituted Judges of those Parliamentary Delinquents we speake of, cannot (in propriety of speech)
be denied to be *one of the lawes of the Land,* being the law of nature,

and consequently the law of all Lands, and Nations whatsoever, established in this, and in all the rest, by a better, and more indubitable legislative Authority, than resides in any Parliament, or community of men whatsoever.

If it be here further objected; yea but what necessity was there lying upon the Army, to assume that judicative power unto themselves, which they exercised upon the Members of Parliament? It is an easie matter to pretend a necessity (almost) for every unjust, and unrighteous thing; but not so easie to judge what such a necessity is, which is authorized by God with a suspensive power over human lawes. To this I answer,

First, That they cannot (at least in the ordinary signification of the word) be said to *assume* a power of judicature unto themselves, who only judge either of persons, or of things, in respect of themselves, and with relation to what concernes themselves by way of duty, either to doe, or to forbeare. The exercise of such a judging, or judicative power, as this, is imposed by God by way of duty upon all men: and woe unto them, who doe not judge, both persons and things, in such a consideration, as this. The neglect, or non-exercise of that judging faculty or power, which is planted in the soules and consciences of men by God, upon such termes, and with reference to such ends as these, draweth along with it that sin, which the Wise man calleth, the *despising of a man's wayes*, & threateneth with death. *But he that despiseth his wayes shall die.* Now certain it is, that the Army did exercise no other judiciary power than this, about, or upon those Parliament men, nor in any other respect, nor with any other consideration, than to their own duty concerning them; which every other person in the Kingdom, either did, or ought to have done, as well as they. Every man is bound to consider, judge, and determine, what is meet, and necessary for him to doe, either to, with, for, or against, all other men; or at least all such, to whom he stands in any relation, either spirituall, naturall, or civill. That judgment then

which the Army passed in their own brests and consciences upon
those Parliament-men, as *viz.* that they were such, whom they stood
bound in duty, having an opportunity in their hand to doe it, to cut
off as unsound members from their body, was nothing else but the
issue, fruit, and effect of that consideration of them and of their
wayes, which they stood bound to levy, raise, and engage themselves
in, about the one and the other. If the judgement which they passed
in this kinde was erroneous, it was not erroneous through an usurpation of an unlawfull power to judge, but either through a defect and
weaknesse of those discerning, or judging abilities, which they stood
bound (however) to use; or else through an oscitancy, carelesnesse,
or sloath, in not improving or acting these abilities, as they might,
and ought, to the discerning of the truth. Certainly they who judge
these Parliament-men worthy Patriots or Members of their House,
or meet to have beene let alone without disturbance in their way, doe
assume the same power of judicature concerning them, yea and concerning the greatest and weightiest matters of State, which the Army
did, when they judged them meet to be sequestered. Yea they who
judge, and condemne the Armie as evill-doers, for what they acted
about these men; and not only so, but smite them also with the sword
of the tongue, reviling them without any just warrant or ground, doe
they not every whit as much usurp, and assume to themselves a power
of judging, without any authority at all, as the Armie did in that very
act of judgement, at which they make themselves so highly agrieved?
Insomuch that to all such, that of the Apostle may be justly applied.
Therefore thou art inexcusable O man, whosoever thou art that judgest.
For wherein thou judgest another, thou condemnest thyselfe: for thou that
judgest, dost the same things. Nay, If we speak of an authoritative power
to judge, they who presume to justifie and absolve the Parliament-
men from the crime charged upon them, and to condemn the Army
for charging them, are farre deeper in the usurpation of such a power,
than the Armie. For the Army (as hath been said) had a legall com-

mission from the Parliament itselfe, to oppose, slay, and destroy the enemies of the Kingdome, and therein a kind of authority derived unto them, to judge of these enemies, when they should meete with them (for a Commission or warrant to apprehend, or destroy such and such persons, without a liberty, or power, either granted, or supposed, to judge them such, when they are found, were a ridiculous nullity) whereas they, who being private men, shall undertake not only to censure, judge, and sentence the Armie as Malefactors in what they have done, but to proceed likewise to the execution of this their sentence by inflicting the penalty of stigmaticall and opprobrious terms upon them; by casting them out of the affections of their friends, by firing the spirits, and strengthening the hands of their enemies against them, doe all this without the least colour, shadow, or pretence of any lawfull authority whatsoever. But

2. That the judgement or sentence which the Armie passed upon those men, as meet to be dispossessed of their Parliamentary interest, was not erroneous in either of the considerations mentioned, or in any other, but every wayes just, and according to the truth, stands cleer upon this ground, *viz.* that they were become Renegadoes from their Trust, and acted by their counsels, debates, votes, and interests, in a diametrall opposition to the peace and safety of the Kingdome, and to publique good. Yea the tenour of their Parliamentary actings before their removall from the House, in the known dialect of politicall prophesie, presaged nothing but ruine and destruction to the liberties of the free-borne Subjects of the Kingdom in generall, and to the lives and estates of many thousands in the Kingdome, whom they stood bound in conscience, in a speciall manner to protect. For what could that grand encouragement, which they administered by their Votes to a potent party of men in the Kingdome who had so lately, and with so high an hand, acted hostility against the peace and liberties of the people, and against the lives of those who stood up to protect them, not having given the least overture of any relenting in

their olde principles, but were now through that extreamity of paine which they lie under, having beene so often, and so deeply bitten, and stung by the fidelity and valour of the Army, more enraged in their spirits, than ever. What could (I say) such an encouragement, given by such hands, unto such men, but portend, either a re-imbroiling of this already miserably-wasted Nation, in Wars and blood, or else the necessity of a patient and quiet subjection of the Nation to the iron yoke of perpetuall tyranny and bondage, together with the certaine ruine of the lives and estates of those, who had shewed most faithfulnesse and courage in the defence of the Parliament and the Kingdome's liberties, in opposing the King and his party, if the Army had not preventingly interposed, as they did? The by-past actions of men, especially such, which they have for any considerable space of time inured themselves unto, are propheticall of what their future actions are like to be, if opportunity paralleleth. The civill Law saith, that *he that hath injured one, hath threatened many:* and by the rule of proportion, he that hath injured many, hath threatened all. It is the saying of that late great Scholar and Statesman, Sir *Francis Bacon;* that *men's thoughts are much according to their inclination: their discourse and speeches according to their learning, and infused opinions: but their deeds are after as they have beene accustomed.* Insomuch as afterwards he saith, *as a man would wonder to heare men professe, protest, engage, give great words, and then doe just as they have done before.* Yea the Scripture itselfe giveth testimony to this maxime, that what men have been by custome, they are like to be by continuance. *Can the Ethiopian* (saith God himselfe to the Jews) *change his skinne, or the Leopard his spots? Then may ye also doe good that are accustomed* [or, taught] *to doe evill.* And elsewhere (speaking of the same people) *they hold fast deceit, they refuse to returne—no man repented him of his wickednesse, saying, what have I done? Every one turned to his course* [or race] *as the horse rusheth into the battle,* meaning, that as the warlike horse, having been for a while curbed and held in by his Rider with a sharp bit, &

strong hand, rusheth with so much the more violence and fury into the battle, when he feeles his liberty. In like manner these men, (and it is the case generally of all men) when they had been at any time restrained for a while, whether by my word, or my judgments upon them, from these vile practices; still upon the first opportunity that they found themselves loose, they re-practiced their former wickednesse with so much the more eagernesse and keenenesse of spirit.

It were easie to bring Authorities in great numbers, both divine and human, and these attended with a like traine of examples, both ancient and modern, for the further confirmation and credit of this axiome, that men generally are much more like to practice on their owne vices, than to fall off to the exercise of other men's vertues. But by what hath been delivered in already upon this account, most evident it is, that the men deparliamented by the Army, were in their full career to the utter undoing of the Kingdome, when they were dismounted: and consequently, that the judgment of the Army looking upon them, as persons meet to be discharged from that great Trust, wherein they so prevaricated, was according to righteousnesse and truth. Therefore

3. (And lastly as to the objection last propounded) it is no such great matter of difficulty, clearly to discern, and judge of such emerging necessities (at least of many of them) which are authorized by God with a prerogative interest of suspending human laws. Hunger is by the holy Ghost himselfe enrolled amongst those necessities, which are invested by God with a faculty and right of suspending his owne lawes, so farre and in such cases, as they oppose the reliefe of it. *Have yee not read,* saith our Saviour to the *Pharisees, what* David *did when he was an* HUNGRY, *and they that were with him, how he entered into the house of God, and did eate the shew-bread, which was not lawfull for him to eate* (viz. in ordinary cases) *neither for them that were with him, but for the Priests only?* meaning, and yet were innocent and unreprovable, notwithstanding the transgression of a divine law (as

touching the plain & expresse letter of it). Now if God hath asserted such a priviledge unto the necessity of *hunger*, whereby to supersede the conscientious obligation of his own law, in order to its present satisfaction, much more hath hee authorized it to the superseding of any constitution or law, meerly human, in reference to such an end; unlesse wee shall thinke, that hee is more jealous for the observation of the lawes of men, than of his owne. So then if it be no great matter of difficulty for a man to judge when he is *an hungry*, evident it is, that there are some cases of necessity obvious enough, whereunto the lawes of men ought to give place, and to be content to be, as if they were not. For the reason why *hunger* is invested with such a priviledge from God, as we speak of, is not simply, as, or because, it is *hunger*, i. such a peculiar and determinate πάθος, which in a way proper to it-selfe, threateneth and endangereth the life of man; but in respect of the generall nature of it, and as it simply threateneth and endangereth this life, if it be not timely healed by the application of food, or nourishment. It was the preciousnesse of the lives of men in God's sight, not any respect he bare to any particular way, or meanes of endangering them, which obtained from him the grant of such a priviledge unto *hunger*, that in order to its necessary satisfaction, it should overrule his owne law. So that whatsoever else it be, as well as *hunger*, which so apparently menaceth, or portendeth ruine and destruction to the lives of men, partakes of the same indulgence and grant of priviledge from God, with *hunger*, and is facultated by him, in order to the prevention of the mischiefe menaced, to transgresse a Law without guilt of sinne. By the cleare warrant of this consideration and deduction, the Jewes extended that grant of priviledge, which God (as we have heard) made, or indulged explicitly unto *hunger* only, unto all manner of things and cases whatsoever, whereby, and wherein life was exposed to imminent hazard and danger. Their common maximes were (as they were formerly mentioned, *Sect. 4*) that *danger of life drives away the Sabbath: Perill of life drives away all, &c.*

Now if the perill of the life of one man, or of a small parcell of men (as *David*, and *those that were with him*, were no great party) was priviledged from heaven with a sinlesse transgression of a speciall law of God; certainly, the imminent danger of bloody combustions in the middest of a great Nation, wherein the lives of many thousands were like to be sacrificed, besides the hazard of bringing many other most deplorable and sad calamities upon the whole Land, which (as hath beene proved) wrought effectually in the counsels and actings of the disseated Parliament-men, is a broad and unquestionable ground of equity and right, for the Armie to build a prevention or diversion of them upon, though it be with a temporary disobedience to such lawes of men, which were never (doubtlesse) intended by the Law-makers themselves, for the binding, either of men's consciences, or their hands, in such cases.

Only, lest the truth we assert, should possibly suffer through any man's mistake, I shall adde one thing by way of caution, or explication about the premises. When wee seeme to approve of that principle of the *Jewes*, wherein they say, that *Peril of life drives away all*, and speak many things concerning the priviledges of necessity, we doe not suppose, nor intend to say, that men may lawfully transgresse every law or precept of God whatsoever, for the saving of their lives, being in danger, as for (example) that they may lawfully lie, forswear themselves, deny *Christ*, or the like, in such cases; for men (doubtless) ought rather to accept of death, than *deliverance*, upon such tearmes as these. But that which we suppose upon the account specified, is only this; that hunger, or any parallell exigence or necessity, have such an indulgencie of priviledge from God, which extendeth to the suspension of all such Lawes, as well Divine, as human, in order to the safety of men lying under them, which the light of nature, and that sence of equity and of what is reasonable, planted in men by God, may well judge to have beene intended by the respective Law-makers, not for Lawes of an absolute and universall obligement, without all manner of exception, but only for the regulating of men in ordinary cases, and such as are of more frequent and usuall occurrence. Now certaine it is, that as there are some Divine Lawes which fall under this consideration (as we have seene) so there are scarce any (if any at all) of human constitution, but are subject unto it; I meane, which may not, according to the regular intentions of the Lawmakers themselves, lose their binding force and authority for a time, as cases may be; it being a true Rule, subscribed as well by Lawyers as Divines, that *Every Law binds only according to the regular and due intention of the Law-maker.*

The reason why no human Law, can reasonably be judged to bee of universall obligation (no, not according to the intention of the Lawmakers themselves) is, first, because the adequate end and scope of Law-makers in their Lawes, is presumed to be, the publique and common benefit and good of the community of men, who are to obey them. Now, as *Aquinas* the Schooleman well observeth, *it often falls out, that that, which ordinarily, and in most cases is much conducing to common good, in some particular case would bee most repugnant and destructive to it,* whereof hee gives an instance; unto which many others might readily be added. Therefore in such cases, wherein the observation of a Law, cannot but be of dangerous consequence, and prejudiciall to the publique, it is to be presumed, that it was no part of the intention of the Law-givers that it should be observed, or bind any man.

Secondly, it being out of the Sphere of all earthly Law-makers, to foresee, or comprehend all particular cases, that may possibly happen, they generally content themselves with framing such Lawes, the keeping whereof ordinarily, and in cases of a more frequent occurrence, is conducing to publique benefit and safety, not intending by any of these Lawes to obstruct or prejudice the publique, in any anomalous or unthought of case, but to leave persons of all Interests and qualities at full liberty, to provide for the publique in such cases, though with a practicall contradiction to any, or all of their Lawes.

Thirdly (and lastly, for this) If it could, or should be supposed, that human Lawgivers are able to comprehend and make provision for all possible emergencies and cases, yet were it not expedient (saith my Author) for the Common-wealth, that they should multiply Lawes to such a number, as the particular stating and regulating of all such cases would necessarily require. Confusion in Lawes ought to bee avoided, which yet could not be avoided, if particular and expresse provision should be made in them, for the regulation of all persons, of what different capacities, or conditions soever, under all possible occurrences, in a due proportion to the common interest and benefit of men.

These things considered, evident it is, that there was never yet any Lawgiver amongst men, who, understanding himselfe, ever intended to impose any Law of a politique constitution upon men, without a reserve for those, on whom it was imposed, to provide for themselves, or for the publique good in cases of necessity, besides, yea and against, the literall import of such a Law. Therefore perill of life, which is the most confessed case of necessity of all others, though it cannot claime exemption from under some of the Lawes of God (such as were lately intimated) yet may it challenge this priviledge in respect of the Lawes of men. The reason of the difference hath been already in part signified, but more compleatly is this: *viz.* because those Lawes of God, which we now speake of, prohibiting such actions, which are intrinsically, and in their proper natures, as being contrary to the essentiall purity and holinesse of God, and not only because they are prohibited, matter of defilement unto men, must needs bee of universall obligation, in as much as no necessity whatsoever can be greater than, nor indeed equall to, this, that a man refraines all such actions, which are morally, essentially, and intrin-

secally corrupting and defiling: whereas the civill or politique Lawes
of men restraine only such actions, the forbearance whereof, as in ordinary cases, it is commodious for the publique Interest, so in many
others, possibly incident, would be detrimentous and destructive to
it. In which respect all the necessity of obeying such Lawes as these,
may for the time, not only be ballanced, but even swallowed up and
quite abolished by a greater necessity of disobeying them. And concerning such Lawes of God himselfe, which we call typicall, or ceremoniall, because they restraine only such actions, which are not
intrinsecally, or essentially sinfull, or defiling, as not being in themselves repugnant to the holinesse of God, but had the consideration
of sinne put upon them by a Law, in reference to a particular end;
hence it commeth to passe, that God was graciously pleased, and
judged it meet, to subject such Lawes as these to the pressing necessities of the outward man; or rather (indeed) to those other Lawes of
his, by which he commanded reliefe for them; as it is written; *I will
have mercy, and not sacrifice.* This by way of caution. But

Secondly, Another thing, that (its like) will be objected, upon, and
against what hath been answered to the second maine objection, is
this: That the Parliament men disturbed in their way by the Army, at
least many of them, were Religious and conscientious men; voted,
and acted as they did, conscientiously, really judging the course they
steered, to be the safest and most direct for bringing the great Ship of
the Common-wealth into the harbour of rest and peace. And is it not
contrary, as well to principles of reason, as Religion, that such men
upon so *faire* an account as this, should be so *fouly* handled? To this
I answer;

First (not to question that, which I make no question but will be
sufficiently proved in due time, I meane, the *Religiousnesse* of the
Gentlemen spoken of) Religious men, are as well men, as religious:
and consequently, are not yet baptized into the spirit of that divine
prerogative, which should make them (in the Apostle *James* his

phrase) ἀπείραστος κακῶν, persons *untemptable by* things that are *evill.* They that are capable of *receiving* gifts, or of any inordinacy in their desires after earthly accomodations, how wise, or just soever they be otherwise, are subject both to have their eyes blinded, and their words perverted. *A guift,* saith God himselfe, *doth blinde the eyes of the wise* [i. of those that are religiously wise, as well as others; the Scripture not often tearming any men wise, but upon that account] *and pervert the words of the righteous.* A *guift,* or anything equivalent to a *guift,* and that not only after it is received, but much more whilst it is yet desired, and expected, is apt to have both these sad operations even upon the best of men. For who can be better than those whom *wisedome* and *righteousnesse* joine hand in hand to make excellent?

Secondly, When men are religious only to a mediocrity, and withall servile in their judgments to some principles, which are commonly and with great confidence and importunity obtruded upon the consciences of professors, for sacred Truths, and yet are extreamly discouraging, and full of enmity to a thorough, stable, and quiet dependence upon God, by being religious upon such tearmes as these, they become twofold more the children of feare, than otherwise they were like to be, and consequently, so much the more capable and receptive of sad and dismall impressions from the World upon all occasions. And it is not more commonly than truely said; that *Feare is a bad Counsellor.*

Thirdly, When religious men sinne against the common Interest and liberties of a free borne Nation, and make one purse with the knowne and thrice declared enemies of their Land and people, whether they doe it, with, or against, their judgments and consciences, the Law of nature and necessity, cannot (for the present) stand to make, either a scrupulous inquiry after such a difference, or a regular assignement of favour to the qualifying circumstances of demerit; but calls, yea and cries out immediatly, and commands all men without exception, that have a prize in their hand, to give it for the redemption of their Nation out of the hand of Oppression and Tyranny. And when this Law hath been obeyed to the securing of the Nation, she presently resigneth, and this freely and willingly, all her authority and command, into the hand of positive and standing Lawes, calculated for the ordinary posture and state of things, untill there be another cry of like danger in her eares. When these standing Lawes come to resume their authority and power; there will be an opportunity to inquire, if it shall be thought convenient, who sinned, with, and who against, their consciences: and their assesments, which were we uniformly rated by the Law of necessity, may be reduced to tearmes of more equity by those other lawes. But

Fourthly, According to the Notion of that maxime in naturall Philosophy, that *The corruption of the best, is worst*, so are the miscarriages and errours of the best men, of worst consequence (in many cases). The *digressions* of men religious, are many times worse, than the thorough *discourses* of other men. When conscience and concupiscence meet (as oft they doe in religious men) the conjunction is very fiery. It was the saying of *Gregory* long since, *When men conceive of sinne under the notion of a duty, there it is committed with an high hand and without feare.* Nor ever was (nor is ever like to bee) the persecution of the Saints more grievous, than when those that shall persecute them, and *put them to death, shall thinke that* [therein] *they doe God service.* So that whereas the objection in hand pleads, on the behalfe of those Parliament men, who were religious, that they followed the light and dictate of their judgements and consciences, in complying with the King and his complices; the truth is, that though it may reasonably be thought so much the lesse sinful in them, if they did it upon such tearms; yet was it a ground so much the more justifiable for the Army to proceed upon to the dis-interesting of them, as they did. For when religious men breake out of the way of righteousnesse and truth, with the renitency and obmurmuration of their judgements and consciences, it is a signe that their judgements and consciences are yet at liberty, and in a condition to reduce them. But when these are confederate with their lust, there is little hope of their repentance. But

Fifthly (and lastly, for this) whereas the objection intimates some hard measure offered unto them, being men of conscience, and acting according to their judgements, the truth is, that I know not how the Army could walke towards them with a softer foot, to secure the liberties of the Kingdome, together with their owne lives and estates, against the menaces of their judgements and consciences, than they did.

A third grand Objection, wherewith some encounter that action of the Army, hitherto justified, is this: they therein (say these men) made themselves Covenant-breakers, and sinned against the Solemne Vow and Oath which they, or at least some of them, sware unto God *with hands lifted up to Heaven,* (if not with hearts also). In this Covenant they promised and sware, that they would *endeavour with their estates and lives mutually to preserve the rights and priviledges of Parliaments,* whereas by that violent dismembering of the Parliament, they brake and trampled upon them. To this we answer (more briefly).

First, That most certaine it is, that it is no right or priviledge of Parliament to Vote or Act in opposition to the benefit and good of the Kingdome, and those who have intrusted them. It is unpossible that anything that is sinfull, should be the right or priviledge of any person, or society of men under Heaven. Therefore if the Army did nothing more, but only restraine from acting in such a way, they did not herein violate a Right or priviledge of Parliament.

If it be replied, that though it be no *right or priviledge of Parliament* to Vote or Act contrary to their trust; yet it is a *right and priviledge* belonging to this house, that, in case any of the Members shall at any time so act, or vote, they should not bee questioned, or suffer for so doing; at least not by any other power, but by that of the House itselfe only; To this also I answer.

1. By concession, that this is indeed a *right and priviledge of Parliament,* taking the word *Parliament* in a due and proper signification; *viz.* for a Parliament consisting of a competent number of men not dead to their trust, who are in a capacity of faithfulnesse and integrity to discharge the office and duty of a Parliament, in endeavouring at least to relieve the pressures and grievances of the people, to protect their liberties, &c. It is the manner of the holy Ghost himselfe in the Scripture, frequently to deny the common Name of things, to such particulars in every kinde, which are defective in those properties for use and service, which should be found in them, and which are found in other particulars of the same kind. Thus *Paul* expressely, *Hee is not a Jew which is one outwardly, neither is that circumcision which is outward in the flesh: But hee is a Jew which is one inwardly; and circumcision is that of the heart in the Spirit, not in the letter, &c.* So elsewhere: *when yee come together into one place, this is not to eate the Lord's Supper. This* is not, &c. meaning, that as they went to worke, that which they did, deserved not the Name, of an *eating of the Lord's Supper.* Therefore

2. By way of exception, I answer further, that if by *Parliament,* be meant any number of men whatsoever, chosen by the people into Parliamentary trusts, and sitting in that House, where Parliaments (truly and properly so called) use to assemble about the great affaires of the Kingdome, whether these men, or the major part of them, love the interest of the Kingdome, and be cordially affected to the liberties of the people, or no, I know no such *right or priviledge of Parliament,* as that specified. A *Parliament* that is unusefull and unserviceable for Parliamentary ends, is no more a *Parliament,* than a dead man, is a man, or a Virgin defloured, a Virgin. And as a dead man hath no right or priviledge of a man (truly so called) belonging to him, unlesse it be to be so ordered & dealt with, that he may not be an an-

noyance or offence unto others: so neither doe I know any right or priviledge of a *Parliament* indeed appertaining to a *Parliament* politically dead, and which is not animated with a spirit of faithfulnesse to the publique, unlesse it be to be so entreated and handled, that it may not destroy the publique Interest, or endammage their Trustees (the people) in their liberties. It is a rule in Logicke; that an argument drawn from termes of diminution, is of no validity, or force. As for example, when a man is dead, it doth not follow; that because he is a dead man, therefore he is a man, or hath the properties of a man, as that hee is rationall, risible, or the like. By the reason which rules in this principle or maxime, our Saviour denies that inference of the Jewes, who argued themselves to be the children or seed of *Abraham*, because they were his carnall seede, or came from him according to the flesh. *If yee were Abraham's children*, saith hee to them, *yee would doe the works of Abraham:* implying, that because they did not the workes of *Abraham*, they were not his children (*viz.* in that proper and emphaticall sence, wherein the Scripture is ordinarily to be understood, when it speaketh of *Abraham's children*, and of the great promises and priviledges belonging to them). In like manner the Apostle *Paul*, when hee speaks of the priviledges and blessednesse setled by promise upon *Abraham* and his seed, still understands the word, seed, not in that diminutive or equivocall sense, wherein it comprehendeth as well his *carnall* or wicked seede, as that of a more noble descent, but in that emphaticall, weighty, and appropriate sence, wherein it only signifieth the *children of Abraham* indeed, *i.* spiritually such, and who resemble him in his faith and holinesse. After the same manner, when either the lawes or people of the Land, in their accustomed discourse, (and consequently the Solemn League and Covenant) speake of *rights and priviledges of Parliament*, they (doubtlesse) doe not take the word, *Parliament* in an equivocall and comprehensive sence, wherein it may be extended to anything, which in any sence or consideration may be called a *Parliament*, but in an emphatical & restrained sence, *viz.* as it signifieth a politicall body, consistory, or court of men, chosen by the people into Parliamentary Trust, faithfully prosecuting and discharging the import of the Trust committed to them. If this property be wanting in them, they are but a *Parliament* so called, not having the worth or consideration, where-unto *such Rights and Priviledges* which are called, *Parliamentary,* either according to principles of reason and equity, or according to the intention of the first Donors or founders of them, doe belong or appertaine. The premisses considered, evident it is, that the Army did not violate or breake any the *rights and priviledges of Parliament,* properly, or *Covenantly* so called, when they reduced the *Parliament* to the true nature, dignity, and honour of a *Parliament,* by secluding such Members from it, who altered the property, and turned the glory of it into a lie.

2. Be it granted, that the Army stood bound by their *Covenant and Oath,* to *preserve the rights and priviledges even of such Parliaments* as that was, which they divided, yet they stood bound also by the same *Covenant and Oath,* to such a duty or engagement, the faithfull application of themselves whereunto, in the case in hand, did fairely both in the sight of God, and men, discharge them from that other obligation: even as the duties of circumcising, and of sacrificing, when the seasons appointed for them by the law, fell on the Sabboth, priviledged those from guilt in breaking the law of the Sabboth, who performed them on that day. It is a common rule avouched by the best of our Divines, and by the light of nature and reason itselfe, *that when two duties or commands meete in such a streight or exigent of time, that they cannot both receive that honour of observance, which belongs unto them, that which in the judgement of the Law-giver is the greater, ought to be observed, and the lesser to give place, for the time.* Now in that *Covenant and Oath* which the objection speaketh of, there are these two duties or engagements (amongst others) imposed upon those, who take it. 1. An *endeavour to preserve the rights and priv-*

iledges of Parliament. 2. The like *endeavour to preserve THE LIBER-*
TIES OF THE KINGDOME. The Covenant in both these, as in all
other particulars contained in it, the takers of it stand bound by the
expresse tenour thereof (in the sixth Article) to *promote according to*
their power against all lets and impediments whatsoever: and what they
are not able THEMSELVES TO SUPPRESSE or overcome, they shall
reveal and make knowne, that it may be timely prevented or removed:
all this they shall doe as in the sight of God. Which last words (compared with the words mentioned from the third Article) cleerely import, that the Covenanters stand bound, to *promote the liberties of the*
Kingdome against all lets and impediments even in *Parliaments* themselves, if any be found there: yea and further suppose, that they may
THEMSELVES SUPPRESSE and overcome what they *are able (viz.*
of whatsoever opposeth the intent & end of the *Covenant,* which
doubtlesse, was the benefit and good of the Kingdomes) especially
when they know not where, or to whom *to reveale* or *make knowne*
the obstructions they meete with, in order to any probable or likely
prevention, or removall of them, in due *time.* Therefore if the duty of
preserving or *promoting the peace and liberties of the Kingdome,* be
greater, than that of *preserving the rights and priviledges of the Parlia-*
ment; and the Armie could not performe the former, without making
such a breach as they did, upon the latter; evident it is, that in making this breach they are innocent and blamelesse. For the latter of
these, it is cleare as the Sun from what was laid downe *Sect. 21.* that
had not the Army interposed to such a breach of rights and priviledges, as is charged upon them, the peace of the Kingdome, had (in
all human likelihood) been swallowed up in blood, and the liberties in
oppression and tyranny. Concerning the former, there is full as little, or rather lesse, question. That common maxime, which rules especially in politicall affaires, *Bonum quo communius, eò melius,* the
more common or extensive a good is, the greater or better it is, doth
sufficiently confirme it. The *preservation* of the *liberties of the* whole

Kingdome, is without peradventure a greater duty, than the maintenance or *preservation* of the *liberties* or priviledges only of a part of
it; especially of such a part, which, for numbers, is inconsiderable.
Besides, that which gives a kinde of sacred inviolablenesse unto *the
rights and priviledges of Parliament,* is that typicall relation which they
beare to the *rights, priviledges,* and liberties, of the Kingdome, and
Common-wealth. New types are alwayes inferiour to the things imported, and represented by them, as servants are unto their Masters;
and when they occasion, or threaten any damage, to their anti-types,
they may and ought so far to suffer a defacement, as the brasen ser-
pent was beaten to powder by *Hezechiah,* when it occasioned Idolatry against him, whom it represented.

Thirdly (and lastly) suppose there had beene no expresse clause in
the Covenant, injoining the *preservation of the liberties of the Kingdome,* as well as of *the rights and priviledges of Parliament,* yet had the
Army a more than warrant sufficient to have stood up for the *preservation* of them, as they did, and that without any breach of *Covenant.*
Men by the tenure of their very lives and beings, which they hold of
the God of nature, their great Creator, stand bound to obey the
Lawes of nature, and that against all other obligations or bonds
whatsoever: yea, the truth is, that all other obligations cease in the
presence of this, all Lawes, Covenants, and engagements besides,
being homagers unto it. Now there is no Law of nature that speakes
more plainely, or distinctly, than this; that the strong ought to stand
by the weake in cases of extremity, and danger imminent, especially
when reliefe cannot reasonably be expected from other hands. Nor
is it credible that either the Covenant-makers, or the Covenant-
takers, did thereby intend, either in the generall, any disobligation
from the Lawes of nature, or from duties, otherwise than by the said
Covenant, lying upon men: nor in particular, any such *preservation of
the rights and priviledges of parliament,* which should be inconsistent
with *the liberties of the Kingdomes.* And it is a common rule amongst

Lawyers, for regulating the interpretation of Lawes, as likewise of all other Declarations of men by words, whatsoever; that *the mind or intent of the speaker, is to be preferred before, and is more potent* [and consequently rather to be obeyed] *than his words.*

Nor doth the Act of the Army in that dissociation of the Parliament under debate, colour, or shadow (in the least) with the act of the King, breaking into their House, and demanding which, and how many of their Members he pleased, to be sacrificed upon the service of his will. For

First, It was more civility in the Army, to deny admission, or entrance into the House, unto those Members, whose sitting there they judged of desperate consequence unto the Kingdome, than it would have been, by force and violence to have pulled them out from thence; which was the King's act, *in actu signato* (as the Schoole men distinguish) though not *in actu exercito,* the providence of God and men comporting to prevent this. And we know the old saying,

> *Turpius eiicitur, quàm non admittitur, hospes. i.*
> A guest we like not, 'tis more commendable
> To keep, than cast, out from our doores and table.

Secondly, The Members which the King fought to lay hold of, and to disparliament, were such, who THEN were (or at least were so looked upon by him) as the greatest Patrons and Protectors of the Kingdome's Interest, and who, like the *cloudy and fiery pillar* of old, kept the *Egyptian* prerogative from comming at the *Israelitish* liberty, to destroy it. Whereas the Members, who were denied the House by the Army, were turned Proselytes to prerogative, and had renounced the Law and Doctrine of the people's liberties. Therefore

Thirdly (and lastly) the cleare tendency of the Act of the King, was the violation of the Law of nature, by seeking to advance the will and power of one, or of some few, above, and against, the peace and comforts of many, whereas the act of the Army held a *loyall* conformity with the *royall* Law, the face of it being manifestly set to subject the power, interest and will of one, unto their lawfull Superiour, the just Interest or comfort of many. Therefore to goe about either to justifie the King's act, by the act of the Army, or to condemne the act of the Army, by the King's, is as if I should undertake to prove, that the night is lightsome, because the day is so, or that the day is darke, because the night is so.

A fourth objection in the mouthes of some, against which they conceive the Army cannot be justified in the businesse in question, is, that all such actions are contrary unto, and condemned by the Lawes of the Land. But to this objection, at least to the weight and substance of it, we have already answered over and over; and particularly have asserted and proved, First, that all human Laws and constitutions, are but of a like structure and frame, with the Ceremoniall Lawes of old made by God himselfe, which were all made with knees, to bend to the Law of nature, and necessity. Secondly, That it is to be presumed, that the intent of all Law-givers amongst men, is, notwithstanding any, or all their Lawes seemingly commanding the contrary, to leave an effectuall doore alwayes open for the common good, and in cases of necessity, to be provided for by any person, or persons, whatsoever. Thirdly, that all Lawes binde only according to the regular and due intentions of the Law-makers. Fourthly, that the Lawes of nature, and necessity, are as well the Lawes of the Land, as those commonly so called. Fifthly, that when any two Lawes encounter one the other in any such exigent, or straite of time, that both of them cannot be obeyed, the Law of inferiour consequence ought to give place to that of superior, and the duty injoined in this, to be done, though that required in the other, be left undone. We now adde,

First, That we charitably suppose, that there is no such Law of the Land, which prohibiteth or restraineth any man, or sort of men, from being Benefactors to the publique; especially from preserving the publique liberties in cases of necessity, when they stand *in extremâ tegulâ*, and are in imminent danger of being oppressed forever, there being no likelihood of reliefe from any other hand. And if there be no such Law as this, there is none that reacheth the case of the Army, no not in the criticall or characteristicall circumstance of it.

Secondly, That in case there be any such Law as this, that it is a meere nullity, and the matter of it no more capable of the forme of a Law, i. of an obliging power, than timber or stone is capable of information by a reasonable soule, which according to vulgar Philosophie, rather than the truth is, the proper forme of a man. The Lawes of nature and of common equity, are the foundation of all Lawes (truly and properly so called) and whatsoever venditateth itself under the name or notion of a Law, being built besides this foundation, wanteth the essence and true nature of a Law, and so can bee put equivocally such.

Thirdly, If there be a Law, which maketh force, offered to Magistrates, or persons in Authority, in any kinde, or any interrupting or disturbing them in their way, punishable; yet neither doth this evince the act of the Army, we so much speake of, to have been contrary to the Lawes. The reason is, because it is the constant genius and manner of Law-givers and of Lawes, to lay down only the general rule, and to conceal the exceptions; which they still suppose, are, or may be. Now the exception doth not breake the Rule, nor is it properly contrary to the rule, I meane, so as to evince a nullity, or crookednesse in, only it is not comprehended within the verge or compasse of the rule. *All cases*, saith the Roman Oratour and Statesman, *are not provided for by written Lawes, but only those which are plaine, the exceptions being left out,* or omitted. Consonant hereunto is that of *Grotius: In Lawes prohibitorie,* saith he, *the words are commonly larger, than the minde or intent of the Law.* Upon which occasion, that vertue, which the *Grecians* call ἐπιείκεια, we, *Equitie*, appeares to be most necessary in a Judge, or any other, to whom it shall appertaine to expound Lawes; the property hereof being as *Aristotle* long since observed, *to rectifie* [or right state] *the Law, where it is defective, thorow the generality of it. By rectifying the Law,* he meanes nothing else, but a limiting and restraining the binding force of it to cases intended by the Law-makers; together with an exemption of such cases from it, which upon grounds of reason and equity it may be conceived never were intended by them to be concluded in it. So that in some cases to presse and urge the rigorous extent of the letter of the Law, is to turne the waters of the Law into blood, and to overturne the true intent and meaning both of the Law, and Lawgiver, at once. Such urgings and pressings of Laws without due limitation, gave occasion to that Proverbiall saying in *Tullie;* that *the Highest justice, is the Highest injustice.* And the Imperiall Law itself makes him no better, than a transgressor of the Law, *who fraudulently abuseth the sterne prerogative of the words contrary to the sense and meaning of the Law.* And elsewhere: *no reason of Law, or fairnesse of equity will indure it, that through hard constructions* [of words] *we should turne those things against the benefit of men, which were wholesomely brought in* [amongst them] *for their profit and good.* Doubtlesse they stumble at this stone, who pretend to finde any such Law amongst the Lawes of the Land, by which the Army should be denied a liberty, or lawfulnesse of power to secure the peace and liberties of the Nation, by such a method and course, as they steered, necessity lifting up her voice, and crying unto them with such importunity, to doe it. For (as the aforementioned *Grotius* well observeth) *amongst all the exceptions, which are tacitly included in Lawes, there is none, either more usually, or more justly admitted, than that which ariseth from necessity.* By what we have argued, and related from learned and judicious men in this point, evident it is, both by the light of reason, as also from the testimony of very competent witnesses, that whatsoever *the Lawes of the Land* be, the Army could be no transgressors of any of them in standing up, and interposing as they did, to vindicate the publique liberties of their Nation, in such a case of necessity, as that before them.

A fifth Objection, wherewith some strengthen and comfort themselves against the deportment of the Army, hitherto justified, is this. The example of the fact must needs be of very dangerous consequence to the Kingdome. For by the same reason, and upon the same account, that the Army opposed the present Magistracy, and proceedings of the publique affaires amongst us, any other party of men, making, and finding themselves strong enough for the undertaking, may at any time attempt the like disturbance, and confusion: and so the Kingdome shall be alwayes in danger of the like combustions and broiles. I answer,

First, That the lawfulnesse or goodnesse of an action is not to be measured or judged, but by what *may* follow upon it, by way of sequell or event, by what is *like* to follow upon it, and this not by accident, or by misconstruction, but according to the native tendency, proper ducture, and inclination of it. It is wittily said by one, that *he that goeth about to read the badnesse, or goodnesse of an action by the event, holds the wrong end of the booke upward. Christ* did not amisse in giving a sop to *Judas*, though presently upon the receiving of it, the *Devill* entered into him, and prevailed with him to betray him very suddenly. Nor would it argue anything amisse in what the Army did, though never so many troubles, and tumultuous risings of people should breake out upon pretence of it. The reason is, because, as the grace of God itselfe, though a thing of most incomparable sweetnesse and worth, may neverthelesse be (yea, and daily is) *turned into wantonnesse,* and much sin and wickednesse occasioned by it in the World; so, and much more, may the most worthy actions and services of men, bee compelled to pretence the worst and vilest deedes that lightly can bee perpetrated. Therefore,

Secondly, Suppose the Army should have apprehended, not only a possibility, but even a probability, that that fact of theirs we speak of, would beget out of its owne likenesse, and occasion disturbances of quite another genius and spirit from itselfe; yet might it have been sinfull and unworthy in them notwithstanding, to stand still, and not to have acted as they did. The reason is, because when seed time is come, men must not *observe the windes;* nor *regard the clouds*, when it is time to *reape.* As men must *not doe evill, that good may come of it*, so neither must they forbeare the doing of good, *because* evill *may* come of it. Men are bound to sow the seed of good actions, though they had some cause to feare that an increase of Dragons would spring from it. But,

Thirdly, That no action of any bad consequence to the Kingdome, can truly plead legitimacy of descent from this of the Army, is evident thus. Where there is not a concurrence of the same circumstance (I meane, either formally, or equivalently the same) there can be no place for exemplarinesse, or likenesse of action. And when there is, or shall be, the like politicall constellation with that, under which the Army acted, the like action cannot in the direct and native tendency of it, be of any ill consequence to the Kingdome. The killing of a man by *Titius* being assaulted, and in his owne defence, is no ground, so much as in colour or pretence for *Sempronius* to slay a man travelling peaceably by him on the way.

Fourthly, Nor is it like, that the action of the Army wee speake of, should by any back doore of misconstruction whatsoever, let in mischiefe or disturbance into the Kingdome; considering that it was performed and done, in due order to such a provisionall settlement of affaires in the Kingdome, that as far as is possible, there may, neither occasion be given, on the one hand, nor opportunity left, on the other, to any party or number of men, to attempt any interrupture, distraction, or disturbance therein. Therefore, to pretend or plead, that the said action of the Army, is like to cause future trouble or disturbance in the Nation, is as if a man should say, that to build an house strong, walls, doores, and windows, were of dangerous consequence to invite theeves to asault, and break into it.

Fifthly (and lastly) The action of the Army is not disparageable by any possibility or likelihood of evill, that it may occasionally bring upon the Kingdome afterwards, more than the preservation of a man from imminent death is reproveable, because by it he is occasionally exposed to die another time. They who conceive that it had been better for the Kingdome, and more conducing to the peace of it in after times, that the Army should have sat still, and not interpose, as they did, argue at no better rate of reason, than I should doe, in case I should perswade my friend being dangerously sick, not to use the helpe of a Physitian for his recovery, because in case he did recover, his recovery might prove a probable occasion of more sicknesse unto him afterwards.

—*Quis furor est, ne moriare, mori? i.*

What madnesse is't, through feare of future death,

To wish myselfe deprived of present breath?

If the Army had not applied that plaister of steele to the boile, or plague sore of the Kingdome, which they did, there had been little, or no hope of the recovery thereof, from that politicall death, the symptomes whereof, had so strongly seized the vitall parts of it. So that though the cure, in processe of time should prove an occasion of a relapse, or bring the like distemper againe upon it; yet, as *Hezechiah* was not without cause thankfull unto God, who made an addition of fifteene yeares unto his life, after his sicknesse unto death, though this addition did not excuse him from dying afterwards. So shall the people of the Nation have just cause of thankfulnesse unto the Army for those dayes of freedome and peace, be they fewer, or be they more, which they shall enjoy, though slavery and oppression should returne upon them afterwards like *clouds after the raine.*

Another Objection, deemed by some impregnable, and above answer, is framed by way of inference from *Rom.* 13.1,2. *Let every soule be subject to the higher powers—Whosoever therefore resisteth the power, resisteth the Ordinance of God: and they that resist, shall receive to themselves damnation.* From hence the Army are concluded Transgressors, and liable to condemnation, because they *resisted the higher powers;* and therein, *the Ordinance of God.* But with this Objection we are not behinde hand, having given a sufficient answer unto it already, the substance of it being nothing but what the second Objection offered. Notwithstanding because we desire to give heaped measure of satisfaction, especially to such arguments, which pretend to the Scriptures; we thought it not amisse to lay the words themselves before you, out of which the objection is framed, and so to give in the surplussage of a further answer unto it. Therefore

1. We answer, by distinguishing (with the Ministers of *Scotland,* in their briefe *Theses de Majestatis jure*) betweene the *power* of Magistrates, and the *abuse* of this power. *The power* (say they) *is from God,* and so his *ordinance,* but not the *abuse* of it. *Yea, hee no whit more allowes the abuse of a lawfull power in one Tyrant, than* [the use of] *an unlawfull power in another.* So that if it were the *abuse* only of a lawfull *power,* which the Army *resisted,* they *resisted no Ordinance of God,* nor are they, for such an act, made liable to any *condemnation* by the Scripture mentioned. Now that it was not any *power,* but the *abuse of power,* which the Army *resisted,* hath been more than once, clearly enough evicted in this Apologie; and is further evidenced from hence; no other *power,* but that which is Parliamentary, can be pretended to have been *resisted* by them, in that act so often mentioned. But that they did not *resist* this *power,* but the *abuse* of it only, appeares; 1. Because this *power* remaines at this day quiet and undisturbed, in the midst of them. Yea 2. Their great care and desire is, to settle this *power* upon better terms for the due government of the Nation, than those, on which it hath been continued hitherto.

If it be said, that the Parliamentary *power* now in being, is no lawfull *power,* because it is under force; I answer, 1. that it is no more under force, than it was, whilst all the Members now secluded, had free liberty to sit and vote in that House. The same Army, which is now pretended to overawe, or keep under force the present Parliament, was as neer, and did as much to the Parliament then, in matter of force or awe, as now it is, or doth. Therefore if it were a lawfull *power* then, it is no lesse lawfull now. 2. Nor is the Parliament at this day under any more force, by reason of the Army, than it was for the space of about two years together before, by reason of the continuall tumultuous engagements and practices, both in City and Countrey. Nay 3. I verily believe, that if the Members of Parliament now sitting, would please to declare themselves upon the point, they would acknowledg and confesse, that they are as free from force, or feare (at least in respect of the Army) now, as they have beene at any time since their first meeting in their House. But to the maine objection in hand, I answer.

2. The *ordinance of God* in Magistraticall power, being the adequate foundation, upon which that *subjection,* or obedience, which he requireth of men unto it by his command, is, and ought to be built; evident it is, that this *subjection* is not commanded or required to this *power,* beyond the *ordinance of God* in it; i. unto any act, or injunction of men invested with this *power,* which swerveth from, especially which opposeth, this *ordinance of God* (in the end and intent of it). Now the end and intent of the *ordinance of God* in magistraticall *power,* being (as the Apostle cleerly asserteth, *vers. 4.*) the *good* of those that are subject to it [*For he is the Minister of God to thee, for good*] it is evident yet further, that there is no *subjection* commanded by God unto any *higher power,* further, or otherwise, than they act and quit themselves in a due order and proportion to the *good* of men. And where *subjection* is not commanded, *resistance* is not prohibited; and consequently, is not unlawfull. *For where there is no law, there is no transgression.* Therefore if those *higher powers,* the *resistance* whereof the objection chargeth upon the Army, were found acting, and apparantly bent to act on, in a way of manifest prejudice and opposition to the *good* of those from whom they expected subjection (which I presume, is little questionable to him; that hath read and weighed

the premisses) and consequently, quite besides the end and purport of the *ordinance of God,* the Army, in that *resistance* which they made against them, transgressed no law, or precept of God.

Nor doth it follow from anything that had been said, that a Magistrate for every errour in the administration of his power, may be deposed from his place of Magistracy by any party of men: but this is that, which only followes, that, when the supreame Magistracy of a Kingdome shall be so farre, whether blinded in judgement, or corrupted in affection, that such counsels and actings put forth themselves in them from time to time, which are apparantly detrimentous and destructive to the generall and great interest of the due liberties of the people, reasonable security may be taken of them by any party of this people, having the opportunity, and all others wanting it, that they shall proceed and act no further in such a way.

3. (And lastly) that *resisting the ordinance of God* in the *Higher Powers,* which the Apostle (in the Scripture in hand) *condemneth,* Is not a detaining of men in Authority, though with a strong hand, from doing mischiefe in their places; but either (as was formerly said) a refusing obedience unto their lawful commands, or awards: or rather a complotting or attempt-making to shake off the yoke of all obedience unto civill Magistracy. *Calvin* upon the place seemes to incline to the latter; *Paraeus,* unto the former, whose words are these: *Yet every disobedience is not to be termed rebellion, or resistance; but only that, which out of malice is practised, or admitted, contrary to the lawes, by those, who refuse to satisfie the law, by suffering such punishment, as they have deserved.* If either of these interpretations of the place be admitted, certain it is, that it reflects no bad colour at all upon the action of the Army; who neither refused obedience in what they did to any command (much lesse to any lawfull command) of their Superiours, nor yet declined the giving of satisfaction unto the lawes, by refusing to suffer any punishment, which they had deserved. *Paraeus* layes downe this position upon the place, and maintaines it by argu-

ment; viz. *That it is lawfull for subjects, though meere private men, in case a Tyrant shall assault or set upon them, as Thieves use to doe, and offer them violence, in case they want opportunity to implore the ordinary power for their reliefe, and can by no other means escape the danger, to defend themselves and theirs, in the case of present danger, against this Tyrant, as against a private robber upon the highway.*

But concerning the true sence of the place, *Calvin's* apprehensions are of best comportance with the words; which properly and primarily speake of magistraticall power or Authority in the abstract, and this under such a circumscription and consideration only as it proceeds from, and is authorized by God, and not of the persons of Magistrates at all, otherwise than they administer this power in a regular and due order to the end intended by God in it, which is (as hath beene shewed from *vers. 4.*) the *good* of those, that live under it. First, he doth not say, *let every soule be subject to the higher Magistrates,* but, *to the higher powers.* 2. Nor doth he say, *There is no* Magistrate, *but of* God; but, *there is no power but of God.* Nor 3. doth he say, *the Magistrates that are,* but, *the powers that are, are ordained of God.* Nor 4. *Whosoever resisteth the Magistrate,* but, *whosoever resisteth the power, resisteth the ordinance of God: and they that resist* [viz. *the power,* not the person] *shall receive to themselves damnation.* 5. He demands, *Wilt thou then not be affraid of the power?* not, of the Ruler or Magistrate. *Chrysostome* takes speciall notice of these expressions, and thereupon commentarieth the place, thus: *What sayest thou* [Paul] *Is then every Ruler ordained by God? No,* saith he, *I say not so: nor doe I now speake of particular Rulers, or Magistrates, but of the thing* [or, matter] *itself* [i. of the order, or power of ruling]. *For that there should be powers* [or Magistracy] *and that some should rule, and some be ruled, and that all things should not runne loosely and hand over head, or the people bee like the waves* [of the Sea] *carried hither and thither, I affirme it to be the worke of the wisedome of God.* *Pareus* himselfe likewise carrieth the words directly to the same point. Hee *names powers,* (saith hee), *rather than Kings, Princes, &c. because he would bee understood to speake, not so much of the persons, as of the order.* [or ordinance itselfe of ruling] *For in the persons* [of Rulers] *vice oft times, and causes of not obeying, are found: therefore he would have the powers, to be differenced from the persons.*

It is true, the Apostle names *Rulers,* ver. 3. where he saith, *Rulers are not a terrour to good workes, but to the evill.* And *ver. 4.* of the Magistrate or Ruler he saith, that *hee is the Minister of God to thee for Good;* and afterwards, that *he is a revenger to execute wrath upon him that doth evill.* But evident it is, that in these passages, hee speakes of Rulers and Magistrates not simply, or at large, but under the precise consideration of persons exercising the power, which they have received, in a due subordination unto God, and with a single eye to the procurement of that *good,* which God intended unto those, who are to obey, in his *ordination* of such *powers.* So that nothing can be more cleere, than that the adequate scope of the Apostle, in the Scripture before us, was to perswade *Christians* to owne, and to subject themselves unto, civill Authority, as the ordinance of God, so farre, and in such cases, as it should be administered by the persons invested in it, in a regular and due proportion to the benefit and good of those. *i.* of those communities of men respectively, who live under them; and from whom obedience and subjection are, upon such an account, due unto them. This supposed, we may safely, and without the least occasion of scruple, conclude, that there is nothing appliable in the Scripture in hand, to the case of the Army hitherto argued; unlesse (haply) it should be supposed (and the supposition will not be altogether without ground) that the Apostle inforcing subjection unto civill Authority, meerely as, or because, *the ordinance* of God, and as administered according to the gracious intentions of the founder and ordainer of it, tacitly, and in a consequentiall way, implieth a liberty in men to decline this subjection, when the administrations of it are irregular, and the gracious intentions of God violated in them. For in many cases, when an action is pressed in the nature of a duty, upon a speciall consideration or ground, the consideration failing, the action loseth the nature and relation of a duty. Now if this supposition be admitted, it is a cleare case, that the Scripture under debate, is altogether with, and not at all against, the Army.

I know nothing of moment, that can be opposed against the lawfulnesse of the action, hitherto apologised and justified in these papers, beyond what hath been already bought and sold (I meane, urged, and answered) at sufficient rates. The lawfullnesse of the action we speake of, being supposed, the honour and worth of it are of much more easie demonstration. For what better favour can a Christianly-heroique Spirit spread abroad of itselfe, than when men shall put their lives in their hand, and in this posture stand up to take Lions by the beards, when they are ready to teare in peeces, and devoure the Sheepe of the fold? To attempt the wresting of an Iron Sceptre out of those hands, which were now lifting it up to breake a poore Nation in peeces *like a potter's vessell?* What the Army hath done in this behalfe, calleth to minde the unparallelable example of the Lord *Jesus Christ,* blessed forever, who *descended into the lower parts of the Earth,* went downe into the chambers of death, from thence to bring up with him a lost World. It was the saying of *Plato,* that *to doe good to as many as we can, is to be like unto God.* But to doe good to as many as we can, as well enemies, as friends, by an exposall of our owne lives unto death for the accomplishment of it, is a lineament of that face of divine goodnesse, which *Plato* (it is like) never saw. It was the manner of almost all Nations (as the *Roman* Orator observeth) to place the Assertors of their Countries' liberties, next to the immortall Gods themselves, at the Table of honour. And I make no question, but when the Inhabitants of this Nation shall have dranke a while of the sweet waters of that Well of liberty, which the Army have digged and opened with their Swords, after it had been for a long time stopped and filled up with earth by the *Philistines,*

they will generally recover that Malignant feaver, which now dis-
tempereth many of them, and be in a good posture of sobriety and
strength to *rise up early*, and call their Benefactors, *Blessed*. However,
the *good will of him that dwelt in the Bush*, be upon the head of such
Warriors, who pursue that blessed victory of *overcomming evill*, by
doing *good*; and according to the method of the warfare of Heaven,
seeke to *reconcile* a Nation *unto themselves*, by *not imputing* their un-
thankfulnesse, or other their evill intreaties unto them, but in the
midst of their owne sufferings from them, set themselves with heart
and soule to set them at liberty from their Oppressors.

FINIS.

Anonymous

THE
PEOPLES
RIGHT

BRIEFLY

ASSERTED.

LONDON,
Printed for the Information of the Commonality of *England*,
France, and all other neighbor Nations, that groan under
the oppression of Tyrannical Government. 1649.

*O*n 1 January 1649 the Rump House of Commons passed an act creating a High Court of Justice to try Charles I for treason. There was, of course, no established mechanism for holding a king personally accountable, let alone putting him on trial. When the House of Lords rejected the ordinance, the Commons responded with a proclamation announcing that the ultimate constitutional power lay with the people, and the people had delegated it to them, their elected representatives. The Commons then passed an act setting up a High Court of Justice.

Almost immediately a series of pamphlets appeared debating the legality and necessity of putting the king on trial. Some parliamentary stalwarts, such as William Prynne and Colonel Edward Massey, *who had been excluded at Pride's Purge, published tracts that vehemently objected to the proceedings.*

"The Peoples Right Briefly Asserted" appeared on 15 January in the midst of preparations for Charles's trial. Its anonymous author fully endorsed the right of Parliament to try the king. He bases this conclusion on the theory that the law "is more powerful than the King. . . . But the whole Body of the people are more powerful than the Law, as being the parent of it. For the People make the Law." Unlike William Ball, however, he insists that the people's power had been transferred to their representatives. The people were above the law, but practically speaking, sovereignty belonged to Parliament.

The tract appeared in a single edition.

The Peoples Right Briefly Asserted.

It is the Judgment of Ancient, and the best of Modern Writers, That the Body of a People, represented in a Convention of elected Estates, have a true and lawful power to despose of things at pleasure, for their own Safety and Security; and in order to that, to despose of the King or Prince, if he neglect his Duty, or act contrary to that end for which he was at first ordained; for that Kings are constituted for the People's good, not the People made for a King's pleasure, is a thing granted by all rational men.

That therefore Kings have been, and justly may bee laid aside, or otherwise censured, when they fail of that Duty, Historians will give Examples in all Kingdoms; and Political Writers sufficient Reasons for such Examples. Of which multitude it is not needful to grasp all; but such as have happened in those Kingdoms which are neerest to *England*, both in Situation and Constitution of Government. Nor is it probable that such Examples had been so frequent, had it not been generally thought a thing consonant to the Laws of Nature and Reason.

The Kingdom of *France* hath heretofore, not only in the boast of her own Writers, but consent of others, been esteemed a Government of the best Constitution, (though of late years it hath lost, in a high degree, the just Liberty of the Nation), and hath abounded with Examples of this kinde. It is not therefore incident only to those Kingdoms, where the King is apparently Elective, but Hereditary also, as *France* is accounted. For the People never lost, nor gave away their supream Power of making Election, when need required, even in such Kingdoms. For though inheritance in the Crown were tolerated, to avoid ambitious Contentions, Divisions, Interegnums, and other inconveniences of Elections; yet when greater mischiefs happened, as Tyranny in Government, the people did still retain to themselves a power of curing that Malady; namely, of expelling those Tyrants, and choosing good Kings in their room.

The Parliaments of *France* (saith *Aimonius*) had so supream an Authority,[1] that not only all Laws were by them made and established, Peace and War decreed, Tributes imposed, and Offices conferred; but *Kings* also were by the same Authority, for Riot, Sloth, or Tyranny, laid aside, thrust into Monasteries, or otherwise punished; and sometimes, by that Power, whole Royal Families were deprived of Succession to the Crown, even as they were at first advanced by the People. So that (saith he) *By whose approbation they were at first preferred, by their dislike they were again rejected. But before we come to particular Instances, let us consider the Reasons.*

Whosoever considereth that Kings and all Governors were instituted for the people's happiness, and made by their consent, must needs acknowledg that end to be first and especially looked into. And because Kings, as men, may stray from their right way, and fail of their Duty; therefore Laws were made for a Bridle to them: which were indeed no Bridle, if there were no power to apply them, and see the Execution done: Which hath made divers of the learned political Writers (for it is not the voice of one) to wonder, that in Legitimate kingdoms (for we speak not of barbarous Tyrannies) any man should be so sottish, as to think or say, that private men should be enabled by the Law to sue the *Prince* for a small quantity of Land or Goods: and yet that the Representative Body of the whole *People* have not power to lay the Law against him for *Parricide, massacering of the People,* and Treason (for that is their word) against his whole Country, and the Being of the Laws themselves: that the Law should use any severity

---

1. Floriacensis Aimoin was a French chronicler of the tenth and eleventh centuries. His chief work was *Historia Francorum,* or *Libri V. de gestis Francorum,* which deals with the history of the Franks from the earliest times to 653; it was continued by other writers until the middle of the twelfth century and was printed at Paris in 1567. François Hotman, A Huguenot humanist, in *Francogallia* (published in 1573) made these points, citing Aimoin as his source.

in small things: and give impunity, with absolute license, in the greatest and most heinous offences. And upon that point of a *King's* offending against his *People* and Country, it is that *Bartolus* speaks,[2] when he proveth the whole *People* to be superior to the *King*, and Proprietary Lord of the kingdom: whereas the *King* is but as Steward and Administrator of it.

Therefore (saith he) *A King may commit Treason against the People, and be a Traitor and Rebel to his Country: and may justly be deposed, and further punished, by that Lord against whom he hath offended, which is the People, and those who represent them. And if the King (saith he) go so far as to Arms and Force, those Representers are to call the People to Arms, and proceed against him, in all points, as against a publique enemy.*

Hence came that old saying of wise men, That in the Nature of Man there are two Monsters, Anger and Lust: and that it is the Office of the Law to bridle these two, and subject them to the rule of Reason. *He therefore that would* (saith *Buchanan*)[3] *let loose a King, or any other Man, from the curb of the Law, doth not let loose one Man, but two Monsters, to affront Reason.* To the same purpose *Aristotle* concludeth, *that he, which obeyeth the Law, obeyeth God and the Law: but he that absolutely obeyeth a King's will, obeyeth a Man, and a Beast.*

The *Law* is more powerful than the *King*, as being the Governor and Moderator of his lusts and actions. But the whole Body of the people are more powerful than the *Law*, as being the parent of it. For the *People* make the Law, and have power when they see cause, to abrogate or establish it. Therefore seeing that the *Law* is above the *King*, and the *People* above the *Law*: it is concluded as a thing out of

---

2. Bartolus was a fourteenth-century Italian jurist and professor of civil law. While I was unable to find the exact source of this passage, it is most likely from his *Commentary on the Code of Justinian.*

3. The reference is to the Scottish humanist George Buchanan, author of *De Jure Regni apud Scotos Dialogus*, first published in Edinburgh, 1579. This is presumably a translation from one of the Latin editions because Wing's *Short Title Catalogue* notes no English translation of this work until 1680. The quotation cited can be found in the 1689 translation printed for Richard Baldwin, London, 58, Wing B5276.

question, by *Buchanan, Junius,*[4] and many others, that the *People* of right have power to call in question, and punish a *King* for transgressing the *Law.*

If you look after examples, you may find many in almost all the legitimate *Kingdoms* that are known. Certain it is that the *French,* by authority of their publike Convention or *Parliament,* deposed *Childerike* the first, *Sigibert, Theodorike,* and *Childerike* the third for their Tyranny and unworthiness, and set up some of another Family in their rooms; some of them for being too much governed by wanton and wicked Favourites, esteeming it all one, whether himself were extream vicious, or ruled by them that were so. By the same Representative authority, in conventions of the whole people (which were not much unlike the *French* or *English Parliaments*) were two *Emperors* of *Germany* deposed, *Adolphus* and *Wenceslaus,* though not so much bad *Princes,* as not good enough. The like hath been done in *Denmark,* and in *Sweden,* with divers other *Kingdoms* in *Europe,* as *Hungary, Spain, Portugal, Bohemia,* testified by good and authentick Historians.

But in the *Kingdom of Scotland* their own Historian *George Buchanan* expresseth in plain terms,[5] that he could name above a dozen *Kings of Scotland,* who, for their bad Reigns, were either condemned to perpetual imprisonment: or else by banishment, or voluntary death, (which some of them chose) escaped the just punishment of their offences.

But least (saith he) *any man should think I produce only old and obsolete examples of Kings long ago, such as were* Culeous, Evenus, Ferchardus, *and the like, I will instance one in the memory of our Fathers.* James *the third was by the General Consent of Parliament declared to be justly slain for his cruelty, and wicked Raign; and it was ordered for the*

4. Junius is the pseudonym used by the author of *Vindiciae contra Tyrannos* (Defence of Liberty against Tyrants), first published at Basel in 1579.

5. See note 3, above.

future, That none of those who had any hand, or gave assistance in his death, should ever be questioned, or tainted with any ignominy. That thing therefore (saith he) *which being already done, was judged by the State to be well, and justly done, was doubtlesly proposed as exemplary for the future.* This *James* the third was slain in *Chase,* after a Battel, in which he was vanquished; where *Buchanan* expresseth, That the State made one War against him to destroy his wicked Councel; but the second War was to destroy the King himself, as being incorrigible.

This Restraint of Regal License the same Author confidently praiseth in his Nation, as a thing not only good and wholesome for the People, but profitable for the Kings themselves, and advantagious to their Posterities, alledging that for a main Reason, Why the Crown of *Scotland* hath continued the longest of any Crown in one Family, whereas other Crowns in *Europe* have been often changed from one race to another.

England hath not wanted examples in this kind, though they have not been so frequent as in *Scotland;* two of the greatest note were *Edward* the second, and *Richard* the second, whose unfortunate Raigns are so generally known, and have so often upon this sad occasion in present been produced as instances, that it were needless to dwell upon the particulars of them; therefore I only name them, and forbear also particularly to relate how far from other deviating Princes, as *King John,* and *Henry* the third, have been restrained by Parliaments; and how much the best of *England's* Princes, such as *Edward* the first, *Edward* the third, and *Henry* the fifth, have freely yeelded to the Controul of that high Court, and thought it no dishonor to them.

Examples also of this kind have happened, and are averred by good Authors, concerning the Popes themselves; namely, that the Cardinals, upon some special occasions, may, without the consent of the Pope, call a Councel, and judg him by it, if by any great and notorious sin he become a scandal to the Universal Church, and be incorrigible, since Reformation is as necessary in the Head, as in the

Members; if contrary to his Oath he refuse to call a General Councel, &c. But certain it is, that some of them have been deposed by authority of a Councel. This is (saith *Baldus*)[6] *in case the Pope be very obstinate. For first, Exhortations must be used; secondly, more severe remedies; and last of all, plain force; and where no wisdom can prevail by Councel, force of arms must be the remedy to cure him.* If therefore by consent of almost all the learned men, and many examples in fact, it appear, that a Councel may justly depose a Pope, who calleth himself *King of Kings,* and challengeth as great a superiority above the Emperor, as the Sun is above the Moon, and more than that, an authority to depose *Kings* and *Emperors* when he sees cause: Who may not as well grant, that the publike Councel of a *Kingdom* may lawfully put down, and punish their *King* for extremity of misgovernment?

Concerning this power of the people in restraining wicked Princes, *Junius,*[7] in his book *Contra Tyrannos,* makes a notable inference upon a place in the Prophet *Jeremiah,* where the Prophet in the eleventh *Chapter,* and fourth *verse,* expressly declareth to the *Kingdom* of *Judah,* that for the impiety and cruelty of *King Manasses,* the people were carried away captive by the *Assiyrians;* upon which place (saith he) very learned Expositors suppose (for we must not think that they were unjustly punished) the people were guilty for not resisting the impiety and cruelty of their *King.*

But where this power of resisting a *King,* within the Realm of *Judah,* lay, whether in the seventy *Princes,* or more General Assemblies of State, (being a Government far different from ours), I make no Judgment. For the *Kings* of *Judah* raigned in a very absolute way, as far as we can perceive, and exercised a very Tyranny, being that Government which God gave them in his displeasure, for not being

6. This reference is to Petrus Baldus de Ubaldis, a fourteenth-century Italian jurist and author of *Commentary on the Liber Feudorum.*

7. See note 4, above.

content to be honored with God's immediate Government, administered by his inspired *Prophets;* but desiring a *King* as the Heathen had. But the Limitation of Monarchy is better understood now by people in their own Countries, and by their own Laws, and therefore by English men in *England,* whose just Liberties cannot be altogether unknown to those that are wise in their neighbor Nations, who also have title to the same (or very like) Liberties. Neither can it be denied (in this late sad and bloody trial), but that the *Parliament* of *England,* if they had a lawful power to proceed in this War, have also a just power to despose of that Victory which God hath put into their hands, as they shall think best for the future security of the whole people, whom they represent. Nor is that security, by the Laws of Reason and Nature, to be made slightly, which hath cost the lives of so many thousands, and so vast an expence of Treasure for the purchase of it. And though they long suffered with patience the pressure of Tyranny heretofore, and moved more slowly to a Vindication than sharp necessity seemed to require, (as being not more afflicted with the sence of their wounds, than grieved to discover the hand that made them), yet wise men will so censure of their past sufferings, and present actions, as neither to think the just Rights of English Freedom lessened by any length of patience, nor the *King* made more excusable by any continuance and increase of his offences.

FINIS.

A

DECLARATION

OF THE

PARLIAMENT

OF

ENGLAND,

Expressing the Grounds of their late

PROCEEDINGS,

And of Setling the present

GOVERNMENT

In the way of

A Free State.

LONDON:
Printed for *Edward Husband,* Printer to the Honorable House of
Commons, and are to be sold at his Shop in Fleetstreet, at
the Sign of the Golden-Dragon, near the
Inner-Temple. *March* 22, 1648.

*C*harles Stuart, king of England, was executed on 30 January 1649. The kingdom was left without a ruler. Members of the House of Commons turned to the urgent task of remodeling the government. The House of Lords had opposed bringing the king to trial. When the Lords now offered to assist with the rebuilding, a majority of the Commons turned their wrath on them. On 6 February a resolution stating that the House of Lords was "useless and dangerous and ought to be abolished" passed the Commons without a division. The following day, 7 February, the Commons, now calling itself the Parliament of England, passed a resolution that "the office of a king in this nation, and to have the power thereof in any single person, is unnecessary, burdensome, and dangerous to the liberty, safety and public interests of the people of this nation, and therefore ought to be abolished." This too was carried without a division.

Bold decisions. Yet it was not until 17 March and 19 March that these resolutions that abolished the House of Lords and monarchy were transformed into acts. Executive authority was entrusted to a Council of State of some forty-one members. Two days later, on 22 March, the Parliament published a declaration that publicly justified their "late proceedings." These proceedings included the trial and execution of the king as well as the abolition of the House of Lords and the monarchy.

This short but crucial constitutional document has been strangely neglected by constitutional scholars and historians. The text printed below was taken from the single English edition published. The declaration was also published in Latin as "Parliamenti Anglia Declaratio" and, presumably looking to good foreign relations, in other languages as well. Three months later a protest from the Scots Parliament was published objecting to the trial and execution of the late king. And a little more than a year later, on 31 May 1650, an anonymous tract appeared that directly attacked Parliament's declaration.

A Declaration of the Parliament of *England*, Expressing the Grounds of Their Late Proceedings, and of Setling the Present Government in the Way of *a Free State.*

The *Parliament* of *England,* Elected by the *People* whom they Represent, and by them Trusted and Authorized for the *Common good,* having long contended against *Tyranny;* and to procure the *wellbeing* of those whom they serve, and to remove *Oppression, Arbitrary power,* and all *Opposition* to the *Peace* and *Freedom* of the *Nation,* Do humbly and thankfully acknowledge the Blessing of Almighty God upon their weak endeavors, and the hearty Assistance of the wellaffected in this Work, whereby the Enemies thereunto, both publique and secret, are become unable for the present, to hinder the perfecting thereof.

And to prevent their power to revive *Tyranny, Injustice, War,* and all our former Evils, the *Parliament* have been necessitated to the late *Alterations* in the Government, and to that *Settlement* which they judge most conducible to the honor of God, and the good of the *Nation,* the only end and duty of all their Labors.

And that this may appear the more clearly and generally, to the satisfaction of all who are concerned in it, they have thought fit to Declare and publish the *Grounds* of their *Proceedings.*

They suppose it will not be denied, That the first *Institution* of the *Office* of *King* in this Nation, was by *Agreement* of the *People,* who chose one to that Office for the *protection* and *good* of them who chose him, and for their better *Government,* according to such *Laws* as they did consent unto.

And let those who have observed our Stories, recollect how very few have performed the *Trust* of that *Office* with Righteousness, and due care of their *Subjects'* good.

And how many have made it their study and labor, to satisfie their particular *Ambition* and *Power,* with high Pressures and Miseries upon their *Subjects;* and with what horrid prodigality of *Christian blood,* upon Punctilio's of their own Honor, Personal Titles, and Distastes.

And in the whole Line of them, how far hath the late *King* exceeded all his *Predecessors,* in the destruction of those whom they were bound to preserve; and instead of spreading his Protection to all, scarce permitting any to escape the violence of his fury.

To manifest this *Truth,* it will not be improper to take a short view of some passages in his Reign; wherein he much further out-went all his *Forefathers* in evil, than any Example can be found of punishment.

In the dissolution of the *Parliament* the second year of his Reign, and afterwards he shewed an unnatural forgetfulness, to have the *violent Death* of his *Father* examined.[1] The sad business of *Rochell* and the *Isle of Ree,*[2] the poor Protestants of *France* do yet lament. The *Loans,* unlawful *Imprisonments,* and other Oppressions, which produced that excellent Law of the *Petition* of *Right,* were most of them again acted, presently after the Law made against them; which was most palpably broken by him almost in every part of it, very soon after his *Solemn Consent* given unto it. His *Imprisoning* and prosecution of *Members* of *Parliament,* for opposing his unlawful Will; and of divers worthy *Merchants,* for refusing to pay *Tunnage* and *Poundage,* because not granted by *Parliament,* yet exacted by him expresly against Law; and punishment of many good *Patriots,* for not submitting to whatsoever he pleased to demand, though never so much in breach of the known Law. The *multitude* of *Projects* and *Monopolies,* established by him; His Design and Charge to bring in *German*

---

1. Among the charges presented to the House of Commons against the Duke of Buckingham was the allegation he had hastened the death of James I. There was even some hint that Charles himself may have been implicated in this deed.

2. English military expeditions in 1627 and 1628 led by Charles's favorite, the Duke of Buckingham, to help the Protestants of La Rochelle and the Isle of Rhé ended in disaster and humiliation.

Horse to awe us into *Slavery;*[3] and his hopes of compleating all by his Grand Project of *Ship-Money,* to subject every man's Estate to whatsoever proportion he only pleased to impose upon them. The private *Solicitations,* promises of *Reward,* and *Threats* from him unto the *Judges* of Law, to cause them to do his Will, rather than equal Right, and to break his and their own Oathes. The Oppressions of the *Councel-Table, Star-Chamber, High-Commission, Court-Marshal;* of *Wardships, Purveyances, Knighthood, Afforrestations,* and many others of the like nature, need no large repetition, remaining yet in most of our Memories.

The exact *Slavery* forced upon those in *Ireland,* with the *Army* of *Papists* to maintain it, and the position of being loose and absolved from all *Rules* of *Government,* was but a patern for the intended Model here.[4]

The long *intermission* of our *Parliaments,* and the *determination* to be troubled with no more, and the great *mistake* in first sending the *new Service-Book* into *Scotland,* raised their opposition against him, and gave no encouragement to the *English* to engage against them; which with the doubtfulness of success, produced the last short *Parliament,* which was only considered as to serve the *King's pleasure,* to cloak his *breach* of the *pacification* with *Scotland;* and with *twelve Subsidies* demanded by him to buy out his unlawful and unjust *exaction* of *Ship-money.* But failing in his expectation therein, he suddenly and wilfully, to the terror of most men, dissolved it. The *Scots* upon the

3. In 1628 Charles allocated scarce funds to levy a thousand mercenary cavalrymen in Germany and the Low Countries to be brought to England for his service. He later explained that these men were intended to be sent to help the King of Denmark. The troops were never raised but there were grave suspicions about his real aim in planning to bring the mercenaries to England.

4. This apparently refers to the administration of Thomas Wentworth, Earl of Strafford, which, according to S. R. Gardiner, "seemed liable to no rule, and broke in upon the ancient traditions and the fixed if disorderly habits of the population with all the caprice and violence of the powers of nature." S. R. Gardiner, *The First Two Stuarts and the Puritan Revolution* (rpt., New York, 1970), 105.

King's breach of his *faith* with them, and perceiving the discontents amongst *us*, came with an *Army* into *England.* The *King* by many unjust and unlawful means, raised and brought a great force into the *North* to oppose them, where being moved by worthy *Petitions* from several parts, and by the honorable Endeavors of many Noble Persons, but principally by perceiving the backwardness of his *Subjects* of both *Kingdoms*, at that time to engage in the *destruction* of one another; for which end, such numbers of gallant men were prepared by *him*, whose *Office* was to be the preserver of them. And seeing no other way, he did at last condescend to do that part of his *duty* to call this *Parliament.* Vast *sums* of *money* were required and raised of the *people* of *England,* to gratifie those by whom they had been highly damnified; and both *Armies* paid by *them*, who neither occasioned nor consented to the raising of either. But above all, the *English Army* was labored by the *King,* to be engaged against the *English Parliament:* A thing of that strange impiety and unnaturalness, for the *King* of *England* to solicite his *Subjects* of *England*, to sheath their *Swords* in one another's bowels, that nothing can answer it, but *his own,* being born a *forreigner;* nor could it easily have purchased beliefe, but by his succeeding visible *Actions* in full pursuance of the same.

The first Execution of this design of *Misery,* fell upon our poor Brethren in *Ireland,* where so many stores of thousands of them were with such wonderful *cruelty* murthered, that scarce any bowels but are fill with *compassion* at it;[5] and yet some of the *Murtherers* themselves have not forborn to affirm, They had the *King's Commission* for their Actions.

His *late* and *slender* proclaiming of them *Rebels;* his *Consent* to a *Cessation* when the *Rebels* gained all *advantages,* and the *Protestants* were destroyed by it; his intercepting and taking away *provisions* and

---

5. This is a reference to the Irish rebellion that began in October 1641 with the massacre, it was then believed, of some 40,000 Protestants living in Ireland.

supplies going unto them, are no good *testimonies* of his clearnesse from that *blood* which cried loud for *vengeance*.

But to return to *England*, where appeared matter enough of mourning. Upon the *King's* coming in *Person* to the *House* of Commons to seize the *five Members*, whither he was followed with some hundreds of unworthy *debauched* persons, armed with *Swords* and *Pistols*, and other *Arms*; and they attending at the *door* of the *House*, ready to execute whatsoever their *Leader* should command them.

And upon some other Grounds (whereby doubts being raised in the people, that their grievances would not be redressed, they grew into some *Disorders*) the *King* took occasion from thence to remove from *London*, where presently Forces appeared for him of his own *Company* at *Kingston*.

From thence, he travelled to the *North*, endeavoring to raise Forces there, inticed many *Members* of both Houses to desert the *Parliament* and *Trust* reposed in them by their Countrey, and to join with him in bringing destruction upon their *Brethren*, and upon themselves. Instead of doing *Justice*, he protected *Delinquents* from it. At *Nottingham* he set up his *Standard*; from *Wales* and the *Marches*, he got together a powerful Army, and gave the first *Onset* of *Battel* at *Edgehill*.

He possest and fortified *Oxford* his Head-quarter, and many other *Towns* and *places* of *strength*, and prosecuted a fierce and bloody War against the *Body* of all his own *Subjects* represented, and then sitting in *Parliament*; a thing never before attempted by any *King* in this *Nation*, and which all men have too sad cause with much grief to remember.

Their *Towns* and *Habitations* burnt, and demolished; their pleasant *Seats* wasted; their *Inheritances* given away to *those* that were most *active* in doing *mischief*; their *Servants*, *Brothers*, *Friends*, and *Children* murthered. Thus his own people, whom by the duty of his *Office* he was bound to protect from all injury, were by himself in person, pursued with *fire* and *sword, imprisonments, tortures, death,* and all the *Calamities* of *War* and *Desolation.*

Notwithstanding all this, and in the heat of it, many *Addresses* were made by the *Parliament* unto the *King* for *Peace;* but in none of them could an Agreement be obtained from him; when the least word of his *consent,* would have stopped that issue of *blood,* and torrent of *misery,* which himself had opened in all the parts of his *Kingdom.*

When the great *God* of *Battel* had determined very much in favor of the *Parliament,* and the *King's* strength was almost fallen away; so that he thought it unsafe to trust himself any longer with his owne Forces, yet would he not then vouchsafe to come in unto the *English,* but rendered himself to his *Countrey-men* the *Scots,* giving unto them the honor both of *receiving* him, and *parting with him* again upon their own terms.

After his *Restraint,* yet further *Addresses* were made unto him by the *Parliaments* of *both Kingdoms* for *Peace,* with *Propositions,* not heightened by success. But these would not be granted, there being *new* and *hopeful designs* of *his* in hand, for bringing new miseries upon his people, which an Agreement upon those *Propositions* might easily have prevented. After this passed the *Votes* for no further *Addresses* to be made unto him.

The last Summer the effect of those designs, even whilest he was under restraint, began to break forth; a *new* vein of *blood* was opened in the *King's* name; a *plot* laid (as the Terms of their own boasting were) as *deep* as *Hell;* the Army divided into several bodies; the *fire* brake forth in many parts of the *Kingdom* at once; and for fear lest the numbers of their *English* should be too small, or their Compassion to their Countrymen too great, a *Malignant party* in *Scotland* is easily *invited* hither. And although at first they understood the *Covenant* in that Sence, and prosecuted the ends thereof, in joining with the *Parliament* of *England,* and fighting against the *King's party;* yet now their judgements are rectified to prosecute the same ends by *joining* with the *King's party*, and fighting against their *fellow-Covenanters*, The *Parliament* of *England*. But God will not be mocked; and though this Cloud of fresh Calamities, both here and from the *North*, threatened the poor Nation, and in all human probability was pouring utter ruine upon us; yet the visible hand of *God*, as many times formerly, so now *mightily* and *miraculously* appeared for us, and led the Army (whom he was pleased to make his Instruments) with that Courage, Wisdom, and Fidelity, as amazed and subdued our enemies, and preserved (under him) all that can be dear unto us.

During these distractions (and by what means is sufficiently known, and related more fully in a late *Declaration*)[6] and eighth Address must be made unto the *King*, *contrived* by his *party*, the *Votes* of *Parliament* to the contrary *revoked*, and *Commissioners* sent to the *Isle* of *Wight*.

Where, instead of yielding to their *just desires*, whilest they were treating with *him* for *peace*, even then was *he* plotting to raise a *new War* against them, and to draw more blood of his people. To this end his *two* elder *Sons* were in hostility, and armed with power of granting *Commissions* further to *destroy* the people committed to his charge.

Upon all these and many other *unparalleled offences*, upon his *breach* of *Faith*, of *Oaths* and *Protestations*, upon the *cry* of the blood of *Ireland* and of *England*, upon the tears of *Widows* and *Orphanes*, and *Childelesse parents*, and millions of *persons* undone by him, Let all the world of indifferent men judge, whether the *Parliament* had not sufficient cause to bring the *King* to *Justice*.

But it was objected (and it was the late King's own Assertion) That those in his high place are accountable for their Actions to none but

6. This is probably a reference to "A Declaration of the Commons in Parliament expressing their Reasons for the Adnulling of these ensuing Votes [i.e. the Ordinances of the 8th and 30 June 1648, abandoning the proceedings against the eleven impeached Members, and of the 17 August, ordering the negotiations for the Newport Treaty]" (London, January 1648–49), Wing E 2560.

God, whose Anointed they are. From whence it must follow, That all the men of this Land were only made for the sake of that *one* man the *King,* for him to do with them what he pleaseth; as if they had been all created for no other purpose, but to satisfie the lusts, and to be a sacrifice to the perverse will of a Tyrant.

This will not easily be believed to be so ordained by *God,* who *punisheth,* but never establisheth *injustice* and *oppression;* whom we finde offended when the people *demanded* a *King,* but no expression of his displeasure at any time, because they had no King. Such an *unaccountable Officer* were a strange *Monster* to be permitted by mankinde. But this doctrine is better understood by the present age, than in former times, and requireth the less to be said in *confutation* of it, being enough to *confute* itself.

For the phrase of *Anointed,* no learned Divine will affirm it to be applicable to the *Kings* of *England,* as to those of *Judah* and *Israel,* or more to a *King* than to every other *Magistrate,* or *Servant* of *God;* or that the words *Touch not mine anointed,* were spoken of *Kings,* but unto *Kings,* who were reproved, and enjoined to do no harm to the *Prophets* and *Saints* of *God,* there understood to be his Anointed.

Another Objection was, That to bring a *King* to *trial* and *capital punishment,* is without precedent.

So were the *Crimes* of the late *King;* and certainly, the children of *Israel* had no known Law or Precedent to punish the *Benjamites* for their odious abuse of the *Levite's* Wife; yet God owned the Action.

There wants not *precedent* of some of his *Predecessors,* who have been *deposed* by *Parliaments,* but were afterwards in darkness, and in corners basely murthered. This *Parliament* held it more agreeable to Honor and Justice, to give the *King* a *fair* and *open trial,* by above an hundred Gentlemen, in the most publike place of *Justice,* free (if he had so pleased) to make his own defence; that part of his Crime being then only objected against him, of which the *Parliaments* of *both* his *Kingdoms* had by their *joint Declaration* formerly declared him *guilty.*

With his *Offences*, were joined all along a strange *obstinacy* and *implacableness*, and incessant *labour* for the *destruction* of his People; which (with the *unerring Truth* (wherein is no dispensation for Kings) that *No satisfaction shall be taken for the life of a Murtherer, but he shall surely be put to death*; and, *That the Land cannot be cleansed of the Blood that is shed therein, but by the Blood of him that shed it*) brought on and effected the work of *Justice* upon him.

The *King* being dead, The next consideration fell upon his *Children*; from these *Branches* could be expected no other, than the same *bitter Fruit* which fell in the Reign of the *Father*, who had engaged *Them* in his own ways and quarrel; and the *two Eldest* so early appearing in actual *Arms* and *Hostility* against the *Parliament*, No more *Safety* or *Security* could be hoped for from *Them*, than from their *Predecessor*; nor in human probability, as Affairs then stood, any safe way for a *sure Peace*, and prevention of future *Troubles*, and to avoid a *Succession* of *Misery*; but by *taking away* the Succession of *that*, from whence it hath always *risen*, and would certainly spring again, if permitted to take new Root, the *Designs* and *practices* of Kings, their flatterers and evil Councellors.

The Objection is obvious of Injustice, to disherit those who have a Right and Title to the *Crown*. Surely, the *elder* Right is the *People's*, whom they claim to Govern. If any Right or Title were in the *eldest Son*, the same is forfeited by the *Father's* act, in other cases; even of Offices of *Inheritance*, which being forfeit for *breach* of *Trust*, (a Condition annexed to every Office) none will deny, but that the same excludeth the Children as well as the Officer. But here the *elder Sons* Leavied *War* against the *Parliament*; and it cannot be alledged, That the yonger Children were born to anything.

But the same *Power* and *Authority* which first erected a *King*, and made him a *publique Officer* for the common good, finding them perverted, to their common Calamity, it may justly be admitted at the pleasure of *those* whose Officer he is, whether they will continue that

Officer any longer, or *change* that Government for a *better*, and instead of *restoring Tyranny*, to *resolve* into *A Free State*.

Herein the *Parliament* received encouragement, by their observation of the *Blessing* of *God* upon other States; The *Romans*, after their *Regifugium* of many hundred years together, *prospered* far more than under any of their *Kings* or *Emperors*. The State of *Venice* hath flourished for One thousand three hundred years. How much do the Commons in *Switzerland,* and other *Free States,* exceed those who are not so, in *Riches, Freedom, Peace,* and all *Happiness?* Our *Neighbors* in the *United-Provinces,* since their *change* of Government, have wonderfully increased in *Wealth, Freedom, Trade,* and *Strength,* both by Sea and Land.

In *Commonwealths,* they finde *Justice* duly administered, the great Ones not able to oppress the poorer, and the Poor sufficiently provided for; the seeds of *Civil War* and Dissention, by particular *Ambition,* Claims of *Succession,* and the like (wherein this Nation hath been in many Ages grievously embroiled) wholly removed, and a just *Freedome* of their *Consciences,* Persons and Estates, enjoined by all sorts of men. On the other side, looking Generally into the Times of our *Monarchs,* what *Injustice, Oppression* and *Slavery* were the *Common People* kept under? Some great *Lords* scarce affording to some of their Servants, Tenants or Peasants, so good meat, or so much rest, as to their *Dogs* and *Horses.* It was long since warned in Parliament by a *Privy Councellor* to the late *King,* That *we should take heed, lest by losing our Parliaments, it would be with us, as with the Common people in a Monarchy, where they are contented with Canvas clothing, and Wooden shoes, and look more like Ghosts than Men.* This was intended for the *fate* of *England,* had our *Monarch* prevailed over us. To bring this to pass, their Beasts of Forrests must grow fat, by devouring the poor man's Corn; for want of which, he, and his Wife and Children must make many a hungry Meal. A *Tradesman* furnishing a *great man* with most part of his *Stock;* or a *Creditor* with *Money,* and expecting due satisfaction and payment, is answered with *ill words*, or *blows*, and the dear-bought Learning, That *Lords' and Kings' servants are priviledged from Arrests and Process of Law*. Thus many poor *Creditors* and their *Families*, have perished in the *Injustice* and *prodigality* of their *lawless* Creditors.

A poor *Waterman*, with his *Boat* or *Barge*; a poor *Countreyman* with his *Teem* and *Horses*, and others of other *callings*, must *serve* the *King* for the *King's pay*; which (if they can get) is not enough to finde themselves *bread*, when their *wives* and *children* have nothing, but the *husbands'* labor to provide for them also.

For that one *Exaction* of the *Court*, called *Purveyance* (about which our *Ancestors* made so many good and *sharp* Laws; yet none of them could be kept) it hath been lately *computed* to cost the Countrey more in *one year*, than their *Assessments* to the Army.

These are *some* of those generally observed, and more publike *exactions*, which were obvious not to the *understanding* only, but to the sence of the many grieved sufferers; but if the *vast expence* of the *Court* in ways of *luxury* and *prodigality* be considered; As on the one side by a standing ill ordered *diet:* for a number of *drones* and unprofitable *burthens* of the Earth, by chargeable *Feasts;* and *vainglorious Masques* and *Plays* (their Sabbath days' exercise or preparations) together with the other (less sinful, but no less) *chargeable provisions* for *Sports* and *Recreations;* for which *thousands* of *Acres*, *scores* of *Miles*, and great parts of whole *Counties* have been separated from a much better and publike improvement.

On the other side, by those *profuse donations* of yearly *sallaries* and *pensions* granted to such as were *found*, or might be *made* fit *instruments* and *promoters* of *Tyranny;* or else such as had *relation* to the *King* in *native* or *personal respects*. In which latter kind may be shewed accompts of above fifty thousand pounds *per an.* that was paid out of the *Exchequer* to *Favorites* of the *Scotish Nation;* besides the secret supplies from the privy purse & otherwise, best known to the *Receivers* (which may perhaps be one reason why *they* are so zealous to uphold the *Kingly power* in this *Nation*, whereof the *King* was their *Countreyman).*

He that observes so many *hundreds* of *thousands communibus annis* expended in those ways, and shall know that the *legal* justifiable *Revenue* of the *Crown* (besides the *customs* and some other *perquisites* charged with the maintenance of the *Navy* and *Forts*) fell short of *One hundred thousand pounds,* might justly wonder what *secret* underground *supplies* fed those *streams* of *vanity* and *mischief;* were it not as *notorious,* that the *Projects, Monopolies, sales* of *Offices, Bribes, Compositions* for *breach* of *penal Laws,* and the like ways of draining the *people's purses* as wickedly got, so were only fit thus to be imployed. By occasion whereof, the *Court* arrived at that unhappy height, as to be the great *nursery* of *luxury* and *intemperance,* the *corrupters* of the *maners* and *dispositions* of many otherwise hopeful *Branches,* sprung from the *noblest Families,* and an *universal perverter* of *Religion* and *goodness* therein, making good the Proverb, *Ex eat Aula qui vult esse pius.*

In a *Free State,* these, and multitude of the like *grievances* and *mischiefs* will be *prevented;* the *scituation* and *advantages* of this *Land,* both for *Trade* abroad, and *Manufactures* at home, will be better understood, when the dangers of *Projects, Monopolies,* and *obstructions* thereof, are together with the *Court,* the *Fountain of them* removed, and a *Free Trade,* with *incouragement of Manufacturies,* and *provision* for *poor* be setled by the *Common-wealth,* whereunto the same is most agreeable; and which the *former Government* had never yet leasure effectually to do.

Upon all *these* before mentioned, and many other *weighty considerations,* The *Representatives* of the *People* now Assembled in *Parliament,* have judged it *necessary* to change the *Government* of this

Nation from the former *Monarchy*, (unto which by many injurious incroachments it had arrived) into a *Republique*, and not to have any more a *King* to *tyrannize* over them.

In *Order* hereunto, and for the *better settlement* of this *Commonwealth*, it being found of great inconvenience, That the *House* of *Lords* (sitting in a *Body* by themselves, and called by *Writ* to treat and advise, yet) in the making of *Laws*, and other great Affairs, should any longer exercise a *Negative Vote* over the people, whom they did not at all represent; And likewise, a *Judicial* power over the *Persons* and *Estates* of all the *Commons*, whereof they are not *competent Judges;* and that *their power* and *greatness* did chiefly *depend* upon the power and absoluteness of a *King*, whereunto they had lately expressed a sufficient inclination.

And it being most *evident*, That (especially in these times of Exigency) neither the Government of *Republique*, nor the *common safety* could bear the *Delays* and *Negatives* of a *House* of *Lords*, It was therefore thought *necessary*, wholly to *Abolish* and take the same away.

Leaving *nevertheless* unto those *Lords*, who have been, and shall be *faithful* to the *Commonwealth*, the same *priviledge* of *choosing*, and being *chosen* Representative of the People, as other persons of Interest and good affections to the *Publique* have Right unto; and which is not improbable to have been the *way* of our *Ancestors*, when *both* Lords and Commons formerly *sat* together.

But an *Objection* is frequently made, concerning the *Declaration* of the Houses, of *April*, 1646, for Governing the Kingdom by *King*, *Lords and Commons*, and other Declarations for *making* him a *great* and *happy* Prince.

It was fully then their *intent*, being at that time confident, That the *King's ill Councel* once removed from him, *he* would have conformed himself to the *desires* of his *People* in *Parliament*, and the *Peers* who remained with the *Parliament*, would have been a great *cause* of his so doing. But finding, after *seven* fruitless *Addresses* made unto him, that he yet both lived and died in the obstinate maintenance of his usurped *Tyranny,* and refused to accept of what the *Parliament* had declared. And to the upholding of this *Tyranny,* the *Lords* were all obliged, in regard of their own Interest in Peerage; whereby they *assumed* to themselves an *exorbitant* Power, of *Exemption* from paying of their just *Debts,* and answering Suits in *Law;* besides an Hereditary *Judicatory* over the People, tending to their *Slavery* and *Oppression,* The *Commons* were constrained to *change* their former *Resolutions,* finding themselves thus frustrated in their Hopes and Intentions so declared. Which *change* being for the *good* of the *Commonwealth,* no *Commoner* of *England* can justly repine at. Neither could the *King* or *Lords* take any advantage thereof, because they never consented thereto; and where no *Contract* is *made,* there none can be said to be *broken.* And no Contract is truly *made,* but where there is a *Stipulation* on both sides, and *one* thing to be rendered for another; which not being in this case, but refused, the *Commons* were no ways tied to maintain that *Declaration;* to the performance of which, they were not bound by any *Compact* or acceptance of the other part, and to the *alteration* whereof, so many Reasons for the *preservation* of the People's *Liberties* did so necessarily and fully oblige them.

Another *Objection* is, That these *great* Matters ought (if at all) to be determined in a *full* House, and not when many *Members* of Parliament are by *force* excluded, and the *Priviledge* so highly broken, and those who are permitted to sit in *Parliament,* do but *Act* under a *force,* and upon their *good* behavior.

To this is answered, That every *Parliament* ought to Act upon their good behavior; and few have *Acted,* but some *kinde* of *force* hath at one time or other been upon them; and most of them under the *force* of *Tyrannical Will,* and *fear* of ruine by displeasure thereof; some under the force of several *Factions* or *Titles* to the *Crown.* Yet the *Laws* made, even by such Parliaments, have *continued,* and been *re-*

ceived and *beneficial* to succeeding Ages. *All which*, and *whatsoever* hath been done by this *Parliament*, since some of their *Members* deserted them, and the late King raised *Forces* against them, and several *Disorders* and *Affronts* formerly offered to them (if this Objection take place) are wholly *vacated*.

For any *breach* of *Priviledge* of Parliament, it will not be charged upon the *remaining* part, or to have been within their power of *prevention* or *reparation;* or that they have not enjoyed the *freedom* of their own *persons* and *Votes*, and are *undoubtedly* by the Law of Parliaments, far exceeding that *number* which makes a *House*, authorized for the dispatch of any business whatsoever. And that which at present is *called* a *Force* upon them, is *some* of their best *Friends*, called and appointed by the Parliament for their *safety*, and for the *guard* of them against their *Enemies;* who by this means being disappointed of their Hopes to *destroy* the Parliament, would nevertheless scandalize their Actions, as done under a *force*, who, in truth, are no other, than their own *Guards* of their own *Army*, by themselves appointed. And when it fell into Consideration, Whether the *Priviledge* of Parliament, or the *Safety* of the Kingdom, should be preferred, it is not hard to judge which ought to *sway* the Ballance; And that the Parliament should pass by the *breach* of *Priviledge* (as had been formerly often done upon much smaller grounds) rather than by a sullen declining their *Duty* and *Trust*, to resign up all to the apparent hazard of *Ruine* and *Confusion* to the Nation.

There remains yet this last and weighty Objection to be fully answered, That the *Courts* of *Justice*, and the good *old Laws* and *Customs* of *England*, the *Badges* of our *Freedom* (the benefit whereof our Ancestors enjoyed long before the Conquest, and spent much of their blood, to have confirmed by the *Great Charter* of the *Liberties*, and other excellent *Laws* which have continued in all former changes, and being duly executed, are the most just, free, and equal of any other *Laws* in the world, will by the present *alteration* of *Government* be taken away, and lost to us and our posterities.

To this, they hope some satisfaction is already given by the *shorter Declaration* lately published;[7] and by the *Real Demonstrations* to the contrary of this Objection by the earnest care of the *Parliament,* That the *Courts* of *Justice* at *Westminster* should be supplied the last *Term;* and all the *Circuits* of *England* this *vacation,* with learned and worthy *Judges;* that the *known Laws* of the *Land,* and the *Administration* of them, might appear to be continued.

They are very sensible of the *excellency* and *equality* of the *Laws* of *England* being duly executed; of their great *Antiquity,* even from before the time of the *Norman slavery* forced upon us; of the *Liberty,* and *property,* and *peace* of the *Subject,* so fully preserved by them; and (which falls out happily, and as an increase of *God's* mercy to us) of the clear *Consistency* of them, with the present *Government* of a *Republique,* upon some easie alterations of *Form* only, leaving intire the *Substance;* the *name* of *King* being used in them for *Form* only, but no *power* of *personal Administration* or *Judgement* allowed to him in the *smallest matter* contended for.

They know their *own Authority* to be by the *Law,* to which the people have assented; and besides their particular *Interests,* (which are not inconsiderable) they more intend the *Common Interest* of those whom they serve, and clearly understand the same, not possible to be preserved without the *Laws* and *Government* of the *Nation;* and that if those should be taken away, all *industry* must cease, all *misery, blood,* and *confusion* would follow, and greater *calamities,* if possible, than fell upon us by the late *King's misgovernment,* would certainly involve all persons, under which they must *inevitably* perish.

---

7. The declaration referred to is probably "A Declaration of the Parliament of England, in Answer to the Late Letters" (London, 22 February 1648/49), Wing E1501.

These *Arguments* are sufficient to perswade all men to be well contented to submit their lives and fortunes, to those just and long approved *Rules* of *Law*, with which they are already so fully acquainted, and not to believe, That the *Parliament* intends the *abrogation* of them.

But to continue and maintain the *Laws* and *Government* of the *Nation*, with the present *alterations;* and with such further *alterations* as the *Parliament* shall judge *fit* to be made, for the due *Reformation* thereof, for the taking away of *corruptions*, and *abuses, delays, vexations, unnecessary travel* and *expences*, and whatsoever shall be found really *burthensome* and *grievous* to the people.

The *sum* of all the *Parliament's* design and endeavor in the present change of *Government*, from *Tyranny* to a *Free State;* and which they intend not only to declare in words, but *really* and *speedily* endeavor to bring to effect, is this;

To *prevent* a new *War*, and further expence and effusion of the *Treasure* and *Blood* of *England;* and to *establish* a firm and safe *peace*, and an *oblivion* of all *Rancor*, and ill will occasioned by the late troubles; to provide for the due *Worship* of *God*, according to his *Word*, the *advancement* of the true *Protestant Religion*, and for the liberal and certain *maintenance* of *Godly* Ministers; to procure a just Liberty for the Consciences, Persons, and Estates, of all Men, conformable to God's Glory and their own Peace; to endeavour vigorously the Punishment of the cruel Murderers in *Ireland*, and the restoring of the honest Protestants, and this Commonwealth, to their Rights there, and the full Satisfaction of all Engagements for this Work; to provide for the settling and just observing of Treaties and Alliances with foreign Princes and States, for the Encouragement of Manufactures, for the Increase and Flourishing of Trades at home, and the Maintenance of the Poor in all Places of the Land; to take Care for the due Reformation and Administration of the Law and public Justice, that the Evil may be punished, and the Good rewarded; to order the Revenue in such a Way, that the public Charges may be defrayed, the Soldiers' Pay justly and duly settled, that Free-quarter may be wholly taken away, the People be eased in their Burdens and Taxes, and the Debts of the Commonwealth be justly satisfied; to remove all Grievances and Oppressions of the People, and to establish Peace and Righteousness in the Land.

These being their only Ends, they cannot doubt of, and humbly pray to the Almighty Power for, his Assistance and Blessing upon their mean Endeavours; wherein as they have not envied or intermedled, nor do intend at all to intermedled, with the Affairs of Government of any other Kingdom or State, or to give any Offence or just Provocation to their Neighbours, with whom they desire intirely to preserve all fair Correspondence and Amity, if they please; and confine themselves to the proper Work, the managing of the Affairs, and ordering the Government of this Commonwealth, and Matters in order thereunto, with which they are intrusted and authorized by the Consent of all the People thereof, whose Representatives, by Elections, they are. So they do presume upon the like fair and equal Dealing from abroad; and that they, who are not concerned, will not interpose in the Affairs of *England*, who doth not interpose in theirs. And in case of any Injury, they doubt not but, by the Courage and Power of the *English* Nation, and the good Blessing of God, (who hath hitherto miraculously owned the Justness of their Cause, and, they hope, will continue to do the same) they shall be sufficiently enabled to make their full Defence, and to maintain their own Rights.

And they do expect from all true-hearted *Englishmen*, not only a Forbearance of any public or secret Plots or Endeavours, in Opposition to the present Settlement, and thereby to kindle new Flames of War and Misery amongst us, whereof themselves must have a Share; but a chearful Concurrence and acting for the Establishment of the great Work now in Hand, in such a Way, that the Name of God may be honoured, the true Protestant Religion advanced, and the People of this Land enjoy the Blessings of Peace, Freedom, and Justice to them and their Posterities.

END

Law and Conscience During the Confusions and Revolutions of Government

[Francis Rous, the Elder, 1579–1659]

THE
LAWFULNES
Of obeying the
Present Government

Proposed
By one that loves all Presbyterian
lovers of Truth and Peace, and is
of their Communion.

JOHN 7.24

*Judge not according to the appearance, but judge righteous
judgement.*

Printed at *London* for *John Wright*, at the Kings
Head in the Old Bailey. 1649.

*I*f the attribution is correct it was at the age of seventy, after an already long career as a prominent Puritan divine, a member of Parliament, and a pamphleteer that Francis Rous wrote "The Lawfulnes of Obeying the Present Government" in defense of the new-modeled English government. He had set to work within a month of the publication of Parliament's "Declaration," and the tract appeared on 25 April 1649.

Rous was born in Devonshire, was educated at Oxford, and was step-brother to John Pym. In both religion and politics he was a vociferous member of the Presbyterian party. He already had published numerous religious tracts by the outbreak of the civil war. Shortly before the king's execution he switched from the Presbyterian to the triumphant independent party.

Rous's parliamentary career began with the first parliament of Charles I. He was to sit in every subsequent Parliament, including those of the Interregnum, until his death in 1659. In the Parliament of 1628 he was notable for his violent attack on Roger Maynwaring and "popery." In the Long Parliament it was he who began the debate on the legality of Archbishop Laud's new canons of 1640. He was speaker of the parliament of 1653. And in 1656 Rous was one of those selected to urge Cromwell to accept the crown.

The arguments Rous relied upon to urge obedience to the new regime were a break with the past. Rather than defending the legality of the Rump's assumption of power, he argued that even an unlawful government could and should be obeyed. "It must not be looked at what he is that exercises the power," he maintained, or "by what manner he does dispense it, but only if he have power." Why? Because all power came of God. Moreover, not to obey those in power would cause chaos. In short, Rous turned to the arguments many royalists had used to insist upon obedience to the king. It was the most pragmatic sort of appeal, one Thomas Hobbes would endorse in Leviathan. *"The Lawfulnes of Obeying the Present Government" was designed to win over the war-weary enemies of the regime. But despite its moderate tone, its arguments provoked a furor. Three replies were published within weeks, one of which is reprinted below. Within four months Rous brought out a second edition of the tract with additions, while a third edition was published in 1650. An expert on the pamphlets of the period judges that Rous's was the one tract we can assume all his successors had read. The reasonable tone he adopted was one of his bequests to them. The first edition is reprinted below.*

The Lawfulnesse of Obeying the Present Government.

A Declaration hath been lately published,[1] wherein the grounds are exprest of setling the present Government, with which if any be not so far satisfied as to think that Settlement lawfull, yet even to such is this Discourse directed, which proposeth Proofes, that though the change of a Government were beleeved not to be lawfull, yet it may lawfully be obeyed.

The Apostle intreating of purpose upon the duty of submission and obedience to Authority, layes down this precept; *Let every soul be subject to the higher powers, for there is no power but of God; the powers that are, are ordained of God;* and hereupon infers, *Wherefore ye must needs be subject not only for wrath, but for conscience' sake.* And that he speakes not in this place meerly of power or authority abstracted from persons, but of persons cloathed with that authority, appeares in that he saith; *For, rulers are not a terrour to good workes.* So that he speakes of persons ruling, as well as of the power by which they rule. And againe, *He is the Minister of God,* and they are God's Ministers; & accordingly he directs *Timothy,* to pray for a blessing upon those that are in authority. Now if the Powers, Rulers, and those that were in authority in that time were ordained of God, and were to be obeyed for conscience' sake, let us consider how lawfully they came into that power, rule, and authority. This Epistle most probably, if not certainly, was written in the time of *Claudius Caesar,* or *Nero,* the former of which banished the Jews out of *Rome,* upon which occasion *Aquila* and *Priscilla* came out to meet with *Paul* at *Corinth:* and by the sentence of the latter, *Paul* having made his appeale to *Caesar* finished his course, and passed unto a crowne of righteousnesse. And now, behold the lawfulnesse by which these two persons came to be invested in their power and authority.

1. The declaration referred to is the Declaration of Parliament of March 1648/49 reprinted above.

Of *Claudius Caesar* the Story tells us this; After the death of *Gaius Caligula,* the Consuls and Senate of *Rome* entered into a consultation, how they might restore the Common-wealth to her ancient freedom, which by the *Caesars* had been taken from them. So that the taking in of an Emperour, and consequently of *Claudius* for Emperour, was directly against the wills and resolution of the Counsuls and Senate; yet these anciently for many hundred yeares had the chiefe power of Government. But see the way of *Claudius* his coming to the Empire; during the *Interregnum, Claudius* being frighted with the newes of *Caligula's* death, and fearing himselfe might be enquired for upon suspicion withdrew, and hid himselfe behind the Hangings, or covering of a doore; where a Souldier seeing his feet, and desirous to know what he was drew him forth, and upon knowledge of him saluted him Emperour, though even then for feare falling downe low before him. This one Souldier brought him forth to his fellow Souldiers, who lifted him up as Emperour; and thus while the Senate was slow in executing their purposes, and differences grew among them, *Claudius,* who was sent for by the Senate to give in his councell concerning the common freedome, undertooke the Empire. Thus in one Souldier at first, and then in more, was the foundation of *Claudius* his Emperiall power, against the will, consultations, and endeavours of Consuls and Senate. And for *Nero* (his Successor) *Britannicus,* who was nearer of kin to *Claudius,* being his Son, was kept in by the cunning of *Nero's* mother, and by the same craft *Nero* being brought forth to the Souldiery, was first saluted Emperour by them. This sentence of the Souldiers was followed with the consent of the Senate, and then it was not scrupled in the Provinces; so that the Souldiery was also the foundation of *Nero's* Empire. Thus we see Rulers put by Souldiers into that power which is said by the Scripture to be ordained of God; and even to these Rulers men must be subject for conscience.

But passing from the Romane state to our owne; sure we are that in this Nation many persons have beene setled in supreame power and authority by meere force without title of inheritance, or just conquest. And it hath been observed by some that accurately have looked into our story, that not any three immediately succeeding each other, came to the Crowne by true lineall succession and order of blood. Neither is there any great difficulty in finding it, untill we come to Queene *Mary*, whose title being by an incestuous marriage,[2] these observers say that Queene *Elizabeth* should have raigned in her stead. However, we are cleerly told by story, that five Kings on a row (of which the Conquer was the first) had no title at all by lineall descent and proximity of blood. The first came in by force; The second and third had an elder Brother living when they came to the Crowne; The fourth raigned when his Predecessor had a Daughter, and Heire living which was *Mawd* the Empresse; The fifth being the Son of that Empresse, raigned while his Mother was alive, by whom his Title came. But leaving these, and *Edward* the third who raigned in his Father's lifetime, and the three *Henries;* fourth, fifth, and sixth, who raigned upon the *Lancastrian* (that is a younger Brother's) Title, Let us more particularly consider *Henry* the seventh. This *Henry* came in with an Army, and by meere power was made King in the Army, and by the Army; so that in the very field where he got the Victory, the Crowne was set upon his head, and there he gave Knighthood to divers. And upon this foundation of military power, he got himselfe afterwards to be solemnely Crowned at *Westminster.* And soone after upon authority thus gotten, he called a Parliament, and in that Parliament was the Crowne entailed upon him and his Heires. Thus both his Crowne and his Parliament were founded upon power. As for any right Title, he could have none; for he came from a Bastard of *John* of *Gaunt*, which though legitimated by Par-

2. This reference is, of course, to the assertion that the marriage of Henry VIII and Catherine of Aragon, Mary's parents, was incestuous because Catherine had been previously married to Henry's brother Arthur.

liament for common Inheritances, yet expressely was excluded from right to the Crowne. And for his wive's Title, that came in after his Kingship, and his Parliament, which before had setled the Crowne upon him and his Heirs. And he was so farre from exercising authority in her right, that her name is not used in any Lawes as Queene *Marie's* was, both before and after her marriage with the Spanish King. Now this and the rest who came in by meere power without Title of inheritance, being in their opinion who are now unsatisfied, to be held unlawfull, yet the maine body of this Nation did obey them, whilst they ruled, yea doth yield subjection to their Lawes to this very day. And the learned in the Lawes doe continually plead, judge, justify, and condemne according to these Lawes. So that herein the very voice of the Nation with one consent seemes to speake aloud; That those whose title is held unlawfull, yet being possest of authority may lawfully be obeyed.

And hereunto Divines and Casuists give their concurrence; among them one that is resolute both for Monarchy and lineall Succession, thus expresseth his judgement, both for seeking of right and justice from an usurper (whom he calleth a Tyrant, in regard of an unjust Title, not in respect of Tyranicall oppression) and for obeying his commands. First, that Subjects may lawfully seek justice of him; And secondly, that if his commands be lawfull and just, they must be obeyed. And another well esteemed in the Reformed Churches, is of the same judgement.

Pareus saith, That it matters not by what means or craft *Nimrod, Jeroboam,* got Kingdomes to themselves; For the power is one thing which is of God, and the getting and the use of the power is another.[3] And after: The beginning of *Nimrod's* power was indeed evill, as to the getting and usurping power, because abusing his strength, force, & wealth, he violently subdued others, and compelled them to obey;

3. Paraeus was a celebrated sixteenth-century Calvinist divine. His *Commentary on Romans,* cited here, offended James I by its antimonarchical principles.

but not the power or force wherewith he seemed to be indeed by God, above others: And another more plainely. When a question is made whom we should obey; it must not be lookt at what he is that exerciseth the power, or by what right or wrong he hath invaded the power, or in what manner he doth dispence it, but only if he have power. For if any man doe excell in power, it is now out of doubt, that he received that power of God; wherefore without all exception thou must yield thyselfe up to him, and heartily obey him.

And indeed how can it be otherwise? For when a person or persons have gotten Supreme power, and by the same excluded all other from authority, either that authority which is thus taken by power must be obeyed, or else all authority and government must fall to the ground, & so confusion (which is worse than tituler Tyranny) be admitted into a Common-wealth; And (according to the doctrine of King *James*) the King being for the Common-wealth, and not the Common-wealth for the King, the end should be destroyed for the meanes, the whole for a part. If a Master's mate had throwne the Master over Board, and by power would suffer no other to guide the Ship but himselfe; if the Marriners will not obey him commanding aright for the safe guiding of the Ship, the Ship must needs perish and themselves with it. And whereas some speake of a time for setlement, they indeed do rather speak for a time of unsetlement; for they will have an unsetlement first, and a setlement after. And whereas like doth produce its like; yet they would have an unsetlement to beget a setlement. They would have confusion, distraction, destruction, to bring forth order and safety. But the former Scriptures speake not of the future, but of the present time; not of obeying those that shall be powers, and shall be in authority; but the powers that are, and those that are in authority. Neither doe the Casuists and Divines speake of obedience to those that shall be setled but those that are in actuall possession of authority. Neither did our Ancestors in the former examples defer obedience to the Kings that came in by power without Title; but gave it presently, being presently vested and possessed of authority. Besides, let it be considered whether that may not be called a setlement, how soone soever it is when there is such a way setled that men may have Justice if they will, and may enjoy that maine end of Magistracie, to live a peaceable life in godlinesse and honesty.

And indeed when one is in possession by power, and another pretends a Title, what can the maine body of a Nation, which consists of the Common-people doe in this case? They cannot judge of Titles; but they see who doth visibly and actually exercise power and authority. Yea even Learned men, and Statesmen have been found ignorant of the former observations, of the not succeeding three in order of blood since the Conquest; and then how should the Common people know it? Yet further, even Peeres, chiefe Cities, Parliaments, and all having to one in every three, thus subjected themselves upon termes of power and not of right; what can be expected but that what hath been done, may or should be done hereafter? especially when in this present age obedience is given to the Lawes and Commands of those Princes? But some say that there are Oathes that justifie disobedience to the present Government. Surely Oathes are sacred bonds and reverent obligements, and where they doe not themselves leave or make us free, we are not to cut or breake them in pieces. Yet concerning these there are faults on both hands: On the one side the slighting of an Oath, (and such is the comparing it with an Almanack) which is a light as well as an unproper comparison; except it were such an Oath as was made only for a yeare; But we finde some part of the Vow and Covenant to speake of all the dayes of our lives, which doubtlesse may lie on many of the takers for many years. True it is that the obligation of some things may end, because they can no longer be kept, as that of the King's person; for to impossible things there is no obligation: but will any man that understands, and favours Religion and Piety, say that the clauses which concerne Re-

ligion and Piety are expired? Did we promise to God in our severall
places and callings, to extirpate Profanenesse, Heresie, and Blasphemy, and to endeavour a reformed life in ourselves and ours; only
till our Enemies were overcome, and then to make an end? What
were this but to say unto God, If thou wilt deliver us, we will be
bound to thee till we are delivered and no longer? Would this invite
God to deliver us from our enemies, or rather to keep our Enemies
still in strength against us? Least we being delivered from our Enemies should not serve him in righteousnesse and holinesse all our
lives. Surely this is too like that course of carnall *Israel*, of whom it is
written, *When he slew them, then they sought him, and they enquired*
early after God; but their heart was not right with him, neither were they
stedfast in his Covenant. Much more piously and faithfully a reverend
and truly spirituall Divine; *A well grounded covenant is a sure, a firme*
and an irrevocable Act. When you have such an All This *(and such you*
have) as is here concentered in the Text, to lay into, or for the foundation
of the Covenant; the superstruction (is aeternitati sacrum and) must
stand forever.

But on the other side there are other faults; such are the urging of
an Oath or Covenant against enemies, and not against friends in one
and the same Action; and if not altogether so, yet a slight and diminishing charge of it upon one, and a vehement and aggravating
charge of it upon the other. Another fault may be, a stiffe insisting
on one part, and a neglect, or at least silence in another part; as likewise when by event two parts of it come to be inconsistent, to chuse
and inforce the keeping of the lighter or lesse necessary part, and
to give way to the losse and not keeping of the greater. There is another, in racking an Oath or Covenant, to make it speake that which
it meant not. And here it were good to consider, whether there be
any clause in any Oath or Covenant, which in a faire and common
sence forbids obedience to the commands of the present Govern-

ment and Authority, much lesse when no other can be had, and so the Common-wealth must goe to ruine. And whether it forbids obedience to the present Authority more than to Lawes that have beene formerly enacted, by those which came into Authority meerly by power? If it be said that in the Oath of Allegiance, Allegiance is sworne to the King, his Heires, and Successors, if His Heires be not His Successors, how doth that Oath binde? Either the word Successors must be superfluous, or else it must binde to Successors as well as to Heires; and if it binds not to a Successor, that is not an Heire, how can it binde to an Heire that is not a Successor? And if you will know the common and usuall sence (which should be the meaning of an Oath) of the word Successors, you need not so much aske of Lawyers and learned persons, as of men of ordinary knowledge, and demand of them, Who was the Successor of *William* the Conqueror, and see whether they will not say, *William Rufus;* and who succeeded *Richard* the third, and whether they will not say *Henry* the seventh? And yet (as it appeares before) neither of them was Heire. So it seemes in the ordinary acception, the word Successor is taken for him that actually succeeds in Government, and not for him that is actually excluded. And as in Language the ordinary acception of a word is to be taken for the meaning, so that meaning is to be understood as most proper to have been taken in an Oath.

Yet withall this Quaere may be added; While the Son is in the same posture in which the Father was, how comes this Oath at this time to stand up and plead for disobedience in regard of the Son, that was asleep and silent in regard of the Father?

Thus have I gone towards peace (as I beleeve) in the way of truth; and as farre as it is truth, and no further, I desire it may be received. I also wish that those who read and examine it, may doe it (as I professe sincerely myselfe to have endeavoured) with a calme, cleare, and peaceable spirit, without prejudice or partiship. And I doubt not but to such upright seekers of Truth, Truth will appeare in a true shape; whereas partiall and prejudiced mindes speake unto Truth what they would have her speake unto them, and doe not heare her what she saith of herselfe.

FINIS.

Anonymous

The Grand
CASE OF CONSCIENCE STATED,

about Submission to the new and present Power.

OR,

An impassionate A n s w e r to a modest B o o k concerning the law-fullnesse of submitting to the present Government.

By one that professeth himself a friend to Presbytery, a lover and em-bracer of Truth wheresoever he find's it.

*F*rancis Rous's tract, "The Lawfulnes of Obeying the Present Government," designed to assure a war-weary public of the good sense and logic of obedience to the republican regime, set off a furor. "The Grand Case of Conscience Stated" was one of the first and most compelling essays in the debate that followed. Penned by an unknown author, the tract's single edition appeared on 22 June 1649, about two months after Rous's work, and took great exception to it.

Its author claimed to have adhered to the Parliament during the war but objected to the startling changes in government. He argued against convenience and pragmatism. He insisted that it was immaterial whether a free state was more convenient than a monarchy since England already had an ancient monarchy. Nor were oaths of allegiance only to be kept when convenient. He saw an insupportable contradiction between both the prewar oath of loyalty to Charles I, the Solemn League and Covenant of 1643 with its vow to "preserve and defend the king's Majesty's person and authority," and obedience to a kingless government. Rous was also taken to task for the dangerous implications of his argument that any ruler, no matter how he came into power, must be obeyed. This would, readers were warned, merely open the door to tyranny.

The issues set out in this debate between Rous on behalf of the Rump and his anonymous opponent were to form the basis for the argument over the engagement oath that followed several months later. Indeed the exchange hit upon most of the key issues that would constitute the controversy for the next decade. These tracts mark a sharp break with earlier debates on allegiance and political power that focused upon the ancient constitution and the proper limits of monarchy as revealed in scripture, history, and law. The new questions fixed upon the legitimacy of pragmatism, the needs of the community, and the requirements of oaths of loyalty. These same issues would resurface in the wake of the Glorious Revolution.

Although I love not contention, yet I desire satisfaction: that whilst I live amidst a tumultuous generation, and unquiet times, I may be delivered from a troubled spirit and discalmed minde. *A wounded spirit who can bear?* I was willing to have sat down in silence, resolving to have kept my conscience, as void of offence to others, so free from disturbance in itself, chusing rather quietly to suffer for not doing what was commanded, than knowingly to act what is (at least to me) unlawfull: such a *Liberty of Conscience* I conceive none will deny me. But since that Book came to mine hands, I (although unwillingly) undertook this task, not only out of an earnest desire I had to finde out truth, but for the unusuall modesty of the Tract itself, knowing that the fowlest corn is best winnowed in a gentle gale; a tempestuous winde blowes away chaffe and corne too.[1]

I shall take a brief view of the book, and submit what I shall speak to the Authour's judgement, *A Declaration hath been lately published,* &c.[2] Indeed there was such a Declaration published, which I desired with much earnestnesse, and read with some deliberation, expecting to have found the very quintessence of reason, and strength of argument, whereby judicious men might have been wholly convinced, and abundantly satisfied; but my scruples were not answered by it. For suppose that had been proved, which was there much argued, That the government of a free State were in some respects more convenient than that of Monarchy; that might have been a prevalent argument to an irregulated people, who were (*de novo*) to constitute a Government, not to those, who had before an ancient form suited to the people, established by Law, confirmed by Oath, and engaged to by the severall Declarations of them who are so sollicitous for the altering of it. Surely if convenience or inconvenience only can break a promise, and disingage an Oath, *David* was much mistaken in the

1. The author's reference is to Rous, "The Lawfulnes of Obeying the Present Government." The page references that follow are his references to that tract.
2. See p. 396.

15th *Psalm*, and others may be easily cheated, who expect ready performance of, not needlesse disputing about Oaths, in which men stand bound to them. What is there said concerning Declarations [*That the Lords and Commons were of that minde when they made them*] may serve their turns for the present, but would equally serve others' turns for the future;[3] For by the same reason, when those that penned and published that Declaration, shall borrow money of men, and declare to pay them, imploy Souldiers with an engagement to satisfie them, people may suspect that their mindes may alter, and then (by this rule) their former Declarations will be of no strength.

What is further spoken in the Preface for a lawfull obedience to an unlawfull change of Government, will be touched on in the further prosecution of this discourse. It is said [*The Apostle commands obedience to higher powers, Rom. 13. and thence it is inferred, that he speaks not in that place meerly of power or authority abstracted from persons, but of persons cloathed with that authority*].[4] The Apostle speaks there directly of Authority, of men only in subordination to that Authority; no further than as the executioners of that power, because it is impossible Authority should be exercised, but where men are to manage it. The Apostle in that place requires submission to legall Authority, by whomsoever executed, not to any men commanding by an illegall power.

Higher powers are there expressed indefinitely, not pointing at any particular government. In a Monarchy, an Aristocracy, a Democracy, the people under the severall constitutions may, yea must, by the Apostle's command obey the higher powers, those who by their legall constitution are in Authority, not in power, over them: there is a law of nature, that will make man obey a power if he cannot resist, but the injunction of the Apostle (there) is only to lawfull Authority. I beleeve the Authour of that Book knows, that those only can be the

3. See p. 398 of the Declaration, above.
4. See p. 396.

higher powers, or legall Authority of any Kingdom, which the constitution of that Kingdom makes such, and that only can exact obedience according to the Scripture rule. Now what the Higher powers of *England* are, by the constitution of this Kingdom, is sufficiently known.

The Apostle commands wives to submit to their husbands, *Ephes. 5.22.* surely the injunction is for obedience to husbands, *quà* husbands, not *quà* men, indeed not abstracted from their persons, because it is impossible the authority of an husband should be submitted to, where a man is not to exercise it. But should a stranger come to another's wife, and call himself husband (having before either imprisoned or slain the rightfull husband) and require submission, I scarce think the Authour himself (especially if he be married) would presse for obedience to such an usurped power: such a woman may be forced, and overpowered, but to submit to him as an husband, were a sinne.

What is there urged as the great argument to prove the lawfullnesse of obedience to the present Government, hath been my main deswuasive (*viz.*) the Apostle's command to *obey higher powers for conscience' sake.* Had I been convinced that the King in his person had been the *higher powers* of *England,* and that his personall command had by the Apostle's rule exacted undeniable obedience, although he had been visibly acting what we suspected, and palpably introducing what we feared, I should have submitted for conscience' sake. The great inducement I had to adhere to the Parliament, was (besides the hopes of better reformation) that thorow conviction that lay upon me, both by mine own reason, and Parliamentary practices, that the two Houses of Parliament, in case of the King's absence, weaknesse or refusall, had in them such a part of the *higher powers,* and supream authority, as to defend, and preserve the people without, yea against the King, doing, commanding or exacting anything besides or against the law. And this is that main block, at which I stumble in yeelding obedience to this new power, because I am yet convinced, that they are not the *higher powers* of our Kingdom, to which the Apostle requires obedience.

I acknowledge a government may be altered (although I think it not safe, but upon urgent and evident necessity) to which being altered obedience is required, but it must be done by the *higher powers* still, whom we ought equally to obey in submitting to an altered, as a continued form; but for any party by force to lay low the *higher powers*, and to exact obedience as to the legall Authority, is to me a sinne.

I am not ignorant what pleas there may be from inconvenience in such a doctrine, but according to the light I have, where lawfull or unlawfull are in question, their convenience and inconvenience must keep silence.

It is to be observed what is spoken by the Apostle in the same place, *the powers that are, are ordained by God:*[5] to which in the second page of the book is a little addition, *viz. Rulers and those that were in authority were ordained of God:* the Scripture enjoins obedience to powers, to men only as intitled to those powers: the authority was ordained by God, not the Rulers, they were constituted by men, the power may be God's Ordinance, when the deputing of persons to the exercise of that power may be (at most) but God's permission: nay, that men in Authority (Rulers in the Apostle's expression) are to be obeyed no further than as acting according to that Authority, is the judgement of one much used by the composer of that book. When a Tyrant shall offer violence to his private Subjects, which they can by no other means avoid, they may defend themselves and theirs against that Tyrant as against a thief. When are men properly called tyrants, but when they either usurp or exercise a power contrary to the law and usage of those places where they rule? when a consciencious obedience is required to the Authority, but not to those, who by their

5. See p. 396.

own will, or procured force, either usurp or exercise a power besides that Authority.

Should we grant that men assuming to themselves the place and power of Magistrates, by what right or means soever they came by it, must be obeyed, surely it would be the greatest inlet to tyranny in the world, and the speediest means of destroying states that could be invented: for then should none govern in any Kingdome any longer, than their swords and their strength could bear them up.

Thus much I shall yeeld, That when any shall usurp Authority, by whatsoever title or force he procures it, such may be obeyed in reference to their power, while they command lawfull things, but not in reference to Authority. A man being overpowered may yeeld for his own safety, but to submit to that usurped power, as to the legall Authority of that Kingdome where it is, is to assert that as lawfull, which is but usurped, and in the Scripture language *to make a lie.*

From this I shall take a just occasion to speak to those instances there urged, from obedience to whom, the argument is drawn to prove the lawfullnesse of our submission now.

Concerning *Claudius Caesar* and *Nero* which are mentioned, *pag. 2, 3.*[6] how they came in by force, yet were obeyed by the people, I shall not trouble myself nor the Reader with any tedious search into, or large recitall of the story, but take it as there laid down, and give a brief answer to it.

But before I fall upon a plain answer to what is there fallaciously urged, and shew the insufficiency thereof to prove that for which it is asserted: I conceive there will appear such a disproportion between the quoted instances and our present case, that should we grant all the premises, yet the conclusion would not directly follow to prove the question. The most that can be asserted from those examples is, That people did obey a supream power as exercised by those who had

6. See pp. 396 and 397.

no true (at least but a dubitable) title, when the same form of government was still continued, for so it had been for many years before, during the reign of 4 Emperours, yea, such a government which was the pristine constitution of that place, it being Monarchicall for above 44 years, till *Tarquinius,* about the businesse of his son with *Lucretia,* was rejected. Whether party had or pretended most right, and the best ends in their changing of the government, either *J. Brutius* from, or *Julius Caesar* to Monarchy, I shall not dispute: nor shall I decide, whether God might not justly give them to see the evill of a change, who (it may be) chiefly out of a desire of change, would wholly alter a constituted form. But this is not our case. The insubmission of people now, is not grounded upon a suggested scruple of a dubious title to the same, but upon an apprehended illegality of the new and needlesse establishment of another government. It is one thing, and as in itself more lawfull, so to people lesse scrupulous, upon a pretended title to usurp the exercise of an established Authority: another, and as in itself lesse just, so to people more doubtfull upon pretended apprehensions to eradicate a lawfull Authority, and illegally to lay low those which legally are the higher powers of a Kingdome. In the one, people lesse able to examine titles, submit to the established government of that Kingdom where they are, and this is sufficient to yeeld obedience, that they know not who hath the right. In the other, they must give themselves up to a new-fashioned modell illegall to them, because not the constituted powers of that place, and this is enough to withhold Allegiance, that they know such have not (nor pretend) a Title.

Now to the instances themselves, to see how farre they prove the lawfullnesse of our submission *to a change of government, although the change be beleeved unlawfull.*

After the death of Gaius Caligula, *the Consuls and Senate of* Rome *entered into a consultation, how they might restore the Common-wealth to her ancient freedom,* I think this argument will take in all that is therein spoken: if the people of the Roman Empire did submit to the power of *Claudius* and *Nero,* who by force were put upon them, then the people of *England may lawfully submit to a change of government, though beleeved unlawfull:* but they did submit, therefore these may, I will finde no fault with the Syllogisme, because it is of mine own making, although it be the very summe of what is urged. What aequivocall terms there are whereby a spirituall eye would quickly see four terms (at least) in it I shall discover in mine answer to the severall propositions.

In the first Proposition, it being hypotheticall, I shall deny the consequence. For 1. A People may possibly do what is not in itself lawfull either for themselves or others to do, *a facto ad jus non valet argumentum,*[7] had the author proved their submission legall, it had been more urgent. Indeed it is said at the end of that paragraph, *We see Rulers put by souldiers into that power which is said by the Scripture to be ordained of God, and even to these Rulers men must be subject for conscience' sake.*[8] But the Apostle doth not command obedience to these men, but to the *powers,* nay not to any men, but as commanding according to those *powers* (as was said before) nor is it materiall who put men in, nor what men are put into *powers,* if they are the *powers that are ordained of God:* those that command according to that Authority, must be obeyed: and whatsoever the souldiery of *Rome* did, had the souldiery of *England* (in this tacitely pleaded for) observed that doctrine before, we had not been (I think) disputing this question now. But 2. What might be lawfull for the people in the Roman Empire, may not be lawfull for the people of this Kingdome: I finde not in any History that ever they were sworn to a particular government as we have been. Things in themselves indifferent are made necessary, when by an oath engaged to. But of that more afterward.

To the Minor proposition, I shall say 1. That those mentioned had

7. The argument from what is done to what is right does not prevail.
8. See p. 397.

(at least seeming) titles to the Empire. Indeed it is agreed by all Historians I have met withall, that they were first encouraged by souldiers: but what iniquity is in that, if they might pretend a Title? The very end of power and strength is or should be to conserve and recover just right, we have always acknowledged it lawfull and expedient by force of Arms to acquire a rightfull possession illegally detained; But I could wish that this story had been printed and read by the sword-men in this kingdome five months agoe, that they might but have thought whether it had been greater honour to be recorded as men, that should guard a King of doubtfull title to the Crown, or to be storied as men that should bring a King of an indubitable right to the Scaffold.

I will not here dispute by what title, or according to what law *Julius Caesar*, nor yet his successour *Octavius* assumed the Empire, but when that government and those governours were received, and acknowledged by the Senate, it became lawfull to that people. Although Conquest be no true Title, nor durable tenure any longer than strength can keep it, yet compact upon that Conquest, gives a title to the Conquerour, and engageth submission from the other party to those rules resolved on at, or given out according to that agreement.

Tiberius from whom indeed both *Claudius* and *Nero* had their government, did not only for a great part of his time, do all he did by the advise of the Senate, but would (at least seemingly) be chosen by the Senate, as not contented secretly to step into a government either by the earnest engagement of his mother, or by the fond adoption of *Augustus*, but would have the call and election of the Commonwealth too: now here surely was a lawfull title, if the consent of the people could make it lawfull, although (it may be) not in its first acquisition, yet in its after establishment: and *Claudius* deriving his title from him, why should not people obey it? Yea, me thinks the Authour of that book intimates a title that *Claudius* had, where he saith, *pag. 3. Claudius being frighted with the news of Caligula's death, and fearing himself might be enquired for, upon suspicion withdrew.* Had not he been the heir apparent to the Empire, what ground of fear, or what cause of withdrawing? Nay, if he had not been looked on as the right-full successour, why should the souldier *primo intuitu* salute him by the name of Emperour?

For *Nero* he descended in a direct line on the mother's side, from *Livia, Augustus* his wife, and although *Brittanicus* was the naturall son of *Claudius,* yet *Nero* (by *Agrippina's* means) was his adopted son for the Empire, and brought to the Senate, where it was consented unto, that he should have his *togam virilem,* and be called Prince of youth: it being their usage, as far as I have observed in the story, that an Adoptive title assented to by the Senate, hath commonly been acknowledged, when a lineall succession hath been rejected: yea, the Authour seems to grant a kinde of title to *Nero* too, where it is said, *pag. 3.* that *the sentence of the souldiers was followed by the consent of the Senate.* If the Senate had any share in either constituting or declaring a King, *Nero's* title was hereby established.

But what is this to our case? A rightfull or doubtfull heir was brought by souldiers to the Senate, who among themselves were contriving to alter their government.[9] This heir was received by the Senate, and upon that submitted unto by the people. But doth the Authour think that if the Senate had declared and acknowledged, yea, promised to preserve the Title of a rightfull Prince, and the souldiers by the advice, counsell, or assistance of some party in this Senate, should imprison or slay their Prince, and take away the Major part of the Senate, only because against their actings, and this minor part relict should alter their government, yea, make themselves without the consent of the people their Rulers, that then the people would

9. See p. 397.

or lawfully could have submitted to them as their legall and rightfull governours nay, would not rather have resisted them, as not being those higher powers, whom they ought *for conscience' sake to obey?*

Indeed had the King for some reason hid himself (as *Claudius*) or for other reasons absented himself, and the two Houses of Parliament legally elected, and freely sitting (at such a time esteemed) the *higher powers,* contrived a way for the altering the government, although I should not have proclaimed their wisdome, yea, should have bewailed their sin, in respect of the many ties and bonds of Declarations and Oaths upon them, I think I should have submitted to their power, yet I would not for my Oath's sake (had I liked the thing) have acted in it. In which I think I yeeld more than many Anti-malignant men in *England* will do: yet how far from our case this is, what hath been spoken will testifie.

But 2. Had the instance been of *Julius Caesar,* who by meer force and violence, without the least pretence of Title acquired the government, which had better suited our businesse, yet I should say, that what submission the people yeelded, and what commands he gave, were in relation to a power which he by force had gotten, and did exercise without any pretence to a legall constituted power, till received and acknowledged by the Senate.

I confesse should these Rulers now in our Kingdom command submission to them, as to a conquering party, and acknowledge they did by power exercise, what by force they had gotten, I should in that sense submit to them, because not able to defend myself against them: but they call themselves the legall Authority, and *higher powers* of *England,* under which notion I cannot submit, because positively to obey what is thus commanded, whatsoever secret reservation I may have, I doe and must assert their power as lawful, and their Authority as the legall Authority.

By this I shall fitly descend to those instances of our Nation, to which what hath been already spoken, will give (*me judice*)[10] sufficient answer:[11] For

1. What submission was given to the Conquerour, was yeelded as to a forced power, untill by after-compact it was acknowledged and made legall.

2. What was practised by the successors mentioned (besides the acknowledged force in their unrightfull acquisitions, and violent exercise of power) it was only upon difference of Title, *which people may not be able to judge of,* as the Authour says, pag. 9. But amongst us, here is an alteration of government, where a change only seems to be asserted, no Title at all pretended.

3. What is spoken of *Hen. 7.* may be enough to answer the argument drawn from him and the rest too.[12] Although the Title might be unjust, and the power illegally gotten, yet when the Title was acknowledged, at least, confirmed by Parliament, and the Laws whereby he (or they) should rule, were enacted in a Parliament, that did engage the people to an unquestionable obedience, the constituted *higher powers* then commanding, to whom the Apostle requires obedience: for although a Parliament (such I mean, which by the known law and continued usage of the Kingdom as a Parliament) should acknowledge or do anything civilly evill (I mean in reference to the State) it is lawfull and just in respect of the people, and engageth obedience, which I think will be a sufficient excuse for people's *yeelding obedience to their laws,* not only because then enacted, but since confirmed by *the higher powers of our Nation:*[13] although in the meantime upon the same ground they rest *unsatisfied* in the lawfullnesse of submission to the present power.

I might adde, that what *the whole body of a Nation did, if illegall,*

10. With me as the judge; or, as long as I am the judge.
11. See pp. 397 and 398.
12. See pp. 398 and 399.
13. See p. 399.

doth not engage our practices:[14] for we know Papists (and such they were all who submitted to the forementioned Rulers) make no conscience of denying a rightfull Title, nor yeelding to an illegall power, when they may but probably carry on their own design: but what is spoken already will satisfie, and I had rather give a rationall answer, than question the wisdome or honesty of Ancestors, where it may be avoided.

What is urged from the Casuists and *Paraeus*[15] (although I am not bound *jurare in verba,* being of Dr. *Moulin's* his minde,[16] rather to like one argument than ten Authours) I shall agree to in that sense, in which I conceive they delivered it, to submit to such power as forced, not to their Authority as legall, unlesse it be such an Authority which by constitution and usage are the *higher powers of our Kingdome.*

The Authour after the example of others, proceeds now to give some reason of his own, which I shall also endeavour to examine, and so far as they carry strength and truth (at least to me) shall submit: where otherwise, I shall give mine on the contrary.

Indeed how can it be otherwise? For when a person or persons have gotten supream power, and by the same excluded all other from Authority, either that Authority which is thus taken by power must be obeyed, or else all Authority must fall to the ground.[17] Persons may indeed get themselves the greatest strength, and in that sense may be submitted to, but they cannot illegally get themselves the legall power, nor can they exclude others from their Authority, although by force they may keep them from the exercise of it. A man may be a man, yea a living man, although by the violence of disease, he may be kept from outward

14. See p. 399.

15. See pp. 399 and 400.

16. Probably Peter Moulin, an Anglican divine, who sided with the royalists. Among his twenty written works was an anonymous reply to Milton, "Regii Sanguinis Clamor," written during the Interregnum. His authorship was undetected by the regime, and at the Restoration he was made a chaplain to Charles II.

17. See p. 400.

actings. An husband may be a husband still although imprisoned and thereby kept from the exercise of his duty to his wife. A Parliament may be a Parliament still, although by violence kept from sitting and executing their Authority. I am so far from thinking that *disobedience to such power* will make *all Authority and government fall to the ground,* that I beleeve submission to such will quickly lay all Authority waste: for by the same reason that we obey this altered government and usurped authority now, we must obey any other suddenly, if another party get more strength, and what an unsetled state and unknown Authority we should then have may easily be judged. Nor do I think the Authour himself would be of the same minde, should the Prince with a potent army get the power into their hands. Surely were this doctrine true, those renowned men shall be rased out of the Calendar for Saints, that opposed the King's power in Ship-money: nor must such be sequestered who under the King's power formerly did lend or give whatsoever he required, whether men, money, horse or arms: nor these put out of the Parliament, who obeyed him in sitting at *Oxon:* nay, nor himself neither put to death for doing what was urged against him, if men in power howsoever they come by it are Rulers ordained by God, and to be obeyed for *conscience' sake.*

If Confusion be worse than titular Tyranny,[18] I wish that seeing we had no titular tyranny, we had had no confusion neither: and I should be glad that confusion may befall (if any) only such, who in this Kingdome have been the greater introducers of it, either those who acquire and assert, or those who cannot receive or submit to an usurped government: for although the *end must not be destroyed for the means,*[19] yet he that destroys the means in its tendency to the end, will scarcely preserve the end at last.

If a Master's mate had thrown the Master over-board, and by power

18. See p. 400.
19. See p. 400.

would suffer no other to guide the ship but himself, if the mariners will not obey him commanding aright for the safe guiding of the ship, the ship must needs perish, and themselves with it. I doubt here is a fallacy, and this case will not concern our question, for I suppose, although I am not so well skilled in the discipline of marriners, as to know that a Master's mate hath a kinde of Title to the government of the ship in case of the Master's miscarriage, which suits not our condition. But suppose him to have no title, or state the question somewhat nearer our case, That if a party of the Sea-men should throw the Master overboard, and assume to themselves the government of the Ship. I shall then answer, That if that Mate or this party having the greater strength, should by power enforce and exact obedience of the rest, these ought for the safety of their own lives, although not to obey the Authority, yet to do the commands of the enforcing party, and if ever they come ashoar, to doe what they can to bring such unworthy persons to condigne punishment, who, besides the murder of the Master, would so basely hazard the ship too. But if that mate or party should command the Sea-men to obey them as the rightfull Master, I think (although with submission to better judgements) they ought not, although for the safety of their lives thus to obey them. It is better to lose a naturall life, than a quiet conscience, and a spirituall soul. The greatest advantage will not warrant the least evil. In such a case it would easily be judged both by God and men, to whose fault the losse of the ship should be imputed, either to them that did unjustly require, or those who dared not unwarrantably to do an unlawfull thing. I know not what the sudden fear of unavoidable death might make such men (*de facto*) do, and I can easily think what harsh censures their hazarding or losing their lives upon such refusall, may bear from rash and lesse considerate men, as an empty product of meer peevishnesse: but I am confident that a Synod of religious and intelligent Divines would conclude, that (*de jure*) they ought rather to adventure the loss of all, than call him a lawfull, who is but an usurped master, which they must by yeelding to his or their commands under that notion.

Whereas *some speak of a time for settlement, they indeed do rather speak for a time of unsettlement, for they will have an unsettlement first and a settlement after.*[20] If I mistake not the desires of those who withhold submission to the present power, the Authour of that Book is mistaken in his apprehensions of them. That they desire a settlement (I think) is true, but that they desire an unsettlement first, is besides my thoughts of them; I know it is the grief of their souls, and causeth sad searchings of heart, that ever they were brought into such unsettlements, and thereby put upon such racks of conscience as these are. It is not unsettlement but a deliverance from unsettlement they long for: I scarce see how we can be more unsetled than now we are. Indeed being unsetled, we would use any means for a settlement, although for its procurement our unsettlednesse were more unsettled. If man be at the river's brink, I would advise him to keep out of the water, but if at once he leap into the middle of the river, I should perswade him to come to the bank, although he wade through much water to come thither. I would counsell a man to prevent distempers, but when the disease is already contracted, I should prescribe some Physick for the safety of his life, although for the present it should more disease him.

What is spoken of the former Scriptures and Casuists in the same Page, I shall refer to what was before answered.

But it is asked: *Whether that may not be called a settlement, how soon soever it is, when there is such a way setled, that men may have justice if they will, and may enjoy that main end of Magistracy, to live a peaceable life in godlinesse and honesty?*[21] To speak of what justice some have had at *Westminster,* since the unsettlement of our times, or what to be expected, when Colonels appear as parties with their arguments by

20. Page 400.
21. Page 401.

their sides before Committees, (an argument too often used in the House too, as I beleeve the Gentleman knows), where to engage a bustling daring Colonel is to carry a cause: as also what peaceable lives men live, when the souldiers having put other men in power in the State, put themselves in command in men's houses: and what godlinesse and honesty may be looked for, when blasphemy must be tolerated, wickednesse must not be punished, when in the meantime godly men (if but of a contrary judgment, a liberty of conscience formerly pleaded for) are made offendors for a word, would be too large a field to walk in, and besides the swelling of this tract, but give too wide an occasion to further contests. But this shall suffice, that the gentleman a little begs the question in calling it justice, for although men may have, or might expect, what he calls justice, *viz.* things in themselves just, yet if he grant, as I have proved, that Authority illegall by which they act, what they do or is done by any under that Authority, although in itself just, yet is not properly justice. Judgement (for I conceive the Authour means *justitiam distributivam*[22]) is then only just, when it is exercised by the *higher powers,* the legall Magistracy of that Kingdome where it is acted. The Hebrews expresse justice by that word, which they likewise use for the usage and custome of that people, that are concerned in it.

Another argument the Authour useth is, because *People cannot judge of Titles:* when they cannot judge, then an usurped Title is true to them, and will exact obedience: but if this be an Argument, then (for *contrariorum eadem est ratio*[23]) when Titles are visibly unlawfull, people are disingaged from obedience. This is our case, where there is not any pretence of Title.

But some say, *There are Oaths that justifie disobedience to the present government.*[24] There are indeed severall Oaths that engage us to the

22. Distributive justice.
23. The same reasoning pertains to contraries.
24. Page 401.

continued observance of our formerly established government, and then how far they justifie disobedience to this, let the Authour judge. *That Oaths are sacred bonds and reverend obligaments, and where they do not themselves leave or make us free, we are not to cut or break them in peeces.* I shall equally assert, and could heartily wish it had been as truly practised in the Kingdome as plainly spoken in the book. But seeing there are indeed, as the Authour affirms *concerning these, faults on both hands,*[25] let us a little examine the faults he mentions, and see whether there are not other faults too, that he speaks not of.

On the one side the sleighting of an Oath, &c. This is a fault indeed. Oaths and Covenants are the strongest engagements, whereby we can binde ourselves either to God or man, if these come once to be sleighted and no longer observed, then they may conduce to the palpable advantage of those that made them, I am afraid that may justly be written upon the door-posts of *England,* what was set in the front of *David's* song, *Psa. 12.1, 2.*

I am loth to misjudge any person, whom I finde so modest, else I should fear that this fault was purposely argued, the more secretly to insinuate another, though not under the name of a fault. It is said, *We finde some part of the Covenant to speak of all the days of our lives:*[26] as if some part had been but of a temporary engagement. But if I mistake not, the Covenant did in every part of it oblige us to a continued observance of it: we did not swear constantly to keep this part, or that clause, but all our lives to keep this Covenant, which is known to comprehend every part of it.

True it is, that the obligation of some things end, because they can no longer be kept, as that of the King's person &c.[27] I grant that the obligation of a people to anything ends, when that thing obliged to, nec-

25. Page 401.
26. Page 401.
27. Page 401.

essarily, and in its own nature ends; but if men shall by violence put an end to the thing, that thereby the obligation may end too, I doubt such will be esteemed by God as Covenant-breakers; I do not think, that he breaks his Covenant, that doth not preserve the King's person, when he is dead; but I think he is guilty, that did not endeavour to preserve it while he was living. Had the Covenant, in that part, been observed then, for all that I know, it might have obliged now. A woman promiseth to be faithfull to her husband so long as he lives, but if she, out of love to another man, shall lay violent hands on her husband to end his life, that thereby she might marry another, I beleeve she would scarcely be thought to have performed her promise. A Tenant bargains with his Landlord to pay him rent for his house, so long as he lives in it: but if he through malice shall pull down the house, that he cannot live in it, and thereby to extinguish his bargain, it may be easily thought what determination the Law would make in such a case.

What is spoken here of the King's person, might as well have been spoken of any other part of the Covenant. It is Covenanted to preserve Religion, but if those that made the Covenant should by force extirpate, or by deceit undermine Religion: would the Authour think himself or others disingaged from that part of the Covenant, or rather look upon himself as bound to preserve it, while it hath a being? If this liberty should be given, no man would keep any Oath any longer, than he saw good, if it were in his power to put an end to that thing to which he is obliged. But let's see what faults are found on the other hand.

But on the other side there are other faults: such are the urging of an Oath or Covenant against enemies, and not against friends in one and the same action. In this I am wholly of his judgement, and could wish that he had instanced in some things, whereby I might have guessed what aim he had taken, and against what he had levelled it. As I would not have any unequally excused, who are equally guilty, so I would not have him free from blame, who imputes guilt to one, when another shall be connived at, or incouraged in the same thing.

In that clause of bringing Delinquents to condigne punishment: If the Covenant engage to bring one to punishment, that raised arms against the Parliament in *Kent* and *Essex,* why not another that raised arms against the Parliament in *Oxon* shire and *Berks* shire? If according to our Covenant we should preserve the priviledges of Parliament against a malignant party, that would have taken away but Five Members; why not against an Haereticall party that took away above two Hundred?[28] If one party be charged as guilty in not obeying Orders of, but offering violence to the Parliament; why should another be excused as faultlesse, whose disobedience was more manifest, and whose violence was more palpable? Or if not altogether so, yet (as the Authour)[29] a slight and diminishing charge of it upon one, and a vehement and aggravating charge of it upon the other.

Another fault may be a stiffe insisting on one part, and a neglect or at least silence in another part.[30] This is not always a fault, for when there is no occasion given to speak, silence is no evil. One part may be in more danger to be broken than another, when a more violent asserting, and stiffe contending for that part is more necessary. If I had two children, the one at home in safety, the other in imminent danger, that I were more earnest and industrious for the saving and preserving of this, doth not at all argue lesse love or care to the other. But to take it in the best sense, to pretend much care in the keeping of one part, and in the meantime, to neglect another, I think a fault. As when men are seemingly violent against Popery and Prelacy, yet very

28. The references are to the five members Charles I intended to arrest when he strode into the Commons accompanied by an escort of armed guards in January 1642 and to the 270 members of the Long Parliament permanently removed from that body by Pride's Purge in December 1648.

29. See p. 402.

30. Page 402.

indulgent to Heresie and profanesse. When men shall plead Covenant in the preservation of the subjects' liberties, yet forget their Oath for the safety of the King's person in the preservation of Religion; which in respect of the Covenant are of equall concernment; for although it be pleaded by some, and granted by all that Religion, yea asserted by others, that the subjects' liberties are of greater concernment than the King's person, it must be *ratione materiae*, not *ratione juramenti*,[31] for in that regard, we are equally obliged to one as the other.

As also when by event two parts of it came to be inconsistent, to choose and inforce the keeping of the higher and lesse necessary part, and to give way to the losse and not keeping of the greater.[32] Here is to me a *falsum suppositum;* I think it a sinne in any to enjoin, and wickednesse in any to take a Covenant for the doing of two things that are or may be inconsistent; nor do I know what parts of our Covenant are such; when the Authour makes such appear, I shall bewail my sinne in taking it. If it be by him meant, what is talked by others, (*viz.*) That the safety of the King's person, and the preservation of Religion are inconsistent, I must declare my dissent in this; for I am yet convinced, that both the truth and honour of Religion might have better been preserved by the safety of his person, and the continuance of our Government, than hitherto it hath been, or for all I see, like to be, by the altering of the one, or taking away of the other.

There is another, in racking an Oath or Covenant, to make it speak that which it meant not.[33] I will adde, there is another fault to stop the mouth of a Covenant, and denying it to speak what it would. Nay, there is yet one more, when men shall put what interpretation upon Covenants they please, or reserve to themselves a power to make any other interpretation upon them, than what the common and natu-

---

31. By reason of the subject matter, not by reason of an oath.
32. Page 402.
33. Page 402.

rall sense of the words in which they are taken doe afford. Oathes ought to be their own interpreters; we may deceive men, *but God is not mocked.*

But to come to what I conceive is the main end of what hath been hitherto asserted about Oathes; *To consider whether there be any clause in any Oath or Covenant, which in a fair and common sense forbids obedience to the commands of the present Government and Authority.* There is in the solemne League and Covenant, that which engageth to another Government, and then what forbids obedience to this? In one clause we solemnly Covenant to preserve the Person, and not to diminish the just Rights of the King; had his Person and just Rights been perserved, this Government could never have been attempted; but seeing that cord is broken (*unhappy blow that strook it asunder!*) is there yet no bond will hold us? Yes, we do in the same clause faithfully promise to preserve the Law of the Kingdom, and surely to change the Government is to alter the *fundamentall* Laws of the Kingdom; if we are bound to preserve our Law, then that Government that is established by Law; nay yet further. In the same place, we doe swear, yea and call the world to witnesse it, that we will not diminish the just Rights and greatnesse of the King. Is not a man's right as much concerned in his Heirs inheriting, as in his own enjoying what legally belonged to him? Is it not a man's undoubted right to have his lawfull Heirs succeed him in his lawfull enjoyments? But now by this Government the King's Heirs are wholly divested of any possession, and absolutely debarred of that right, which by the usage of the Kingdom belongs to them.

Much lesse when no other can be had, (as the Authour)[34] I do not yet see impossibility in having another, truly I think, if the Covenant had been strictly observed, we had never had this, and if it were yet carefully performed, we might quietly have another Government, such

34. Page 403.

under which godly people might live with more comfort, and lesse scruple.

If it be said that in the Oath of Allegiance, Allegiance is sworn to the King, his Heirs and Successors. If his Heirs be not his Successours, how doth that Oath binde? Either the word Successours must be superfluous, or else it must bind Successours as well as Heirs, &c.[35] If I should grant that the word *Successours* were superfluous, it would not be the only superfluous word in things of that nature; or that it is an exegeticall expression which is not unusuall in all writings both Divine and profane, the more fully to express the same thing by two words: *His Heirs and Successours are conjunctive,* which must necessarily imply, that his *Heirs* according to the usage of this Kingdom ought to be his *Successours:* so that it can binde to no Successours besides the Heir. Indeed should the Line extinguish, then the legall Successour were to be obeyed by that Oath, and yet that too in the continuance of the Government, for he is not properly a Successour, unless in the same form of Government; for *without asking Lawyers and Learned men,*[36] he is properly a Successor, that succeeds any man in the place where he was. If the Agitators in the Army should depose the Generall, and order the Army according to their wills, would they be justly called his Successours, when the frame of their Discipline were altered? This seems partly to be acknowledged by the Authour in the same page, where he instanceth only in those for Successours, which succeeded in the same Government, and saith *that the word Successour is taken for him that actually succeeds in Government,* I conceive it must be meant, when the same form still is continued, else what he asserts, and the instances he names, would hold no proportion.

But there is one engagement to the former Government yet lies upon us in reference to our Oaths, which is mentioned either in that (before named) or in the Oath of Supremacy, *That no power on earth*

35. Page 403.
36. Page 403.

shall deter or absolve us from the keeping of it. If so, I would but humbly begge the Authour conscienciously to judge, whether the force or fear of any party, were they stronger than they are, should affright a people into a submission to any other Government, than that to which they have thus sworn.

I may take the same liberty to propose a few short, yet considerable Quaeries, *While the Son is in the same posture in which the Father was, how comes this Oath at this time to stand up, and plead for disobedience in regard to the Son, that was asleep and silent in regard of the Father?*[37] I do not know in what one title this Oath is more urged for the Son, than it might have been, and was for the Father; unlesse that now there is more need of pressing it, because in the Son's days the Government is altered; in the Father's, it was (at least) promised to be continued. Those, who were against the irregular actings, the Court-faults, the wicked Counsels of the Father, were for the safety of his person, the preservation of his Rights, and the continuance of his Government. And now the same persons that are for the Rights of the Son, and the continuance of the Government, are as much against the vices and counsels in and about him, as about the Father. Besides it might be said, that the Father was not opposed, untill there was a Parliament, that being the legall means in our Kingdom of resisting Arbitrary and extra-legall power; the King in the intervalls of Parliaments being the chief officer, not to be resisted by private subjects. And certainly I think, were there now a Parliament sitting according to the constitution of *England,* and the Received to the Crown, should act anything against the known Law, and the kingdom's safety, those who are now for the reception of the Son, and for the performance of their Oaths, would as truly and conscienciously (according to their Covenant) join with them against the exorbitancies of the Son, as they did against the evil of the Father: only I

37. Page 403.

beleeve they would expect some security, that his Person and rights (parts of the Covenant) should be better preserved and lesse diminished than his Father's were.

Besides what hath been spoken to the book, I might adde also one finall Quaere about altering the government: Whether in such an alteration there is not necessarily required, either the generall consent of the major part of the people, or at least the major part of their trustees? If so, what right have these men to do, who now act in it, some of them being the Trustees of no people, having no election, others who were legally chosen denied their liberty? May not any number of people (there being no known Law nor constituted rule for this transaction) by the like reason conceive, and (if they have strength) alter it again tomorrow? But if they will (which is but equall) give them liberty of dissenting from their government, whom they deny the liberty of debating or consenting to it, I shall be free.

Whether there be any Scripture example or prudentiall rule unnecessarily to oppresse, and, where it may be avoided, to rack the tender consciences of unquestionably godly men, not only when they are the major part, and most judicious Christians (both of Ministers and People) and most likely to know the truth but when they are the least strong, and most discountenanced, and therefore unlikely to be biassed by any private Interests? Indeed those who side with the strongest party, lie under grounded suspition of having particular ends, who can turn any way, to any party, where they may get the best places, the greatest preferments, and the largest rewards: such many have received, and I beleeve most expect; for it is observable, that for the most part, your only Parliament converts before, are your greatest Parliament Assertors now. But how a poor people despised and opposed by power, who can expect the conferment of nothing but punishment, should design an interest in standing to their principles, when they know (some of them at least being very able and prevalent) they might upon their least turning have as large a share in the rewards of the Kingdom as those who now enjoy the greatest, is to me irrationall and improbable. The Apostle *Paul* would avoid a lawfull thing rather than offend the scrupling consciences of weak brethren: what then is their fault, who do unlawfull things, and thereto engage the dijudicating consciences of weak Christians?

Whether both in human probability, and religious reason, it were not more likely to conduce to God's glory, to Religion's settlement and honour, to Christians' union and satisfaction, to the Kingdom's peace, to the prevention of danger, and the safety of all (who have not wickedly out-acted all hopes of safety, and are conscious to themselves that their bucket must sink, whensoever Authoritie's bucket shall arise) to endeavour ere it be too late, to join Authority and Power, Title and Strength together; that as Power may arm Authority, and render it formidable, so Authority might justifie Power, and make that lawfull? Least when the Title shall be claimed, those who may dislike the vices, and oppose any Tyranny (were they legally authorized) of the claimer, yet should not *for conscience' sake* deny his Right; and those who could like well the pretensions of our new Governours (were they justifiably managed) should not adventure for Religion's sake to assist their usurpation: Whereby, as by our unwise actions, we have too much justified Malignants' actions, and made them our deriders: we may strengthen their hands, and make them our Masters.

I am confident that if the great managers of our new-work, and the violent assertors of this changed Government would but seriously lay these things to heart, it might make them seasonably retract, what they untimely attempted, and rather finde out ways to settle, than further unsettle the Kingdom, rather to satisfie than disturb the peaceable consciences of religious and unbiassed men (*The Lord prevail upon their spirits*).

Thus have I endeavoured to answer that with a meek, which was written with a peaceable spirit, where I shall professe (if I mistake not myself) to side rather with truth than with any party.[38] What I have hastily spoken I shall submit to the deliberate judgements of more intelligent men. I shall be willing to receive a rebuke wherein I have erred, and ready to yeeld wherein I may receive satisfaction. I hope I have not discovered any turbulency of spirit, but a willingnesse to examine truth. As I would keep my conscience from being wounded by doubtfull pressures, so I would keep my tongue and pen from wounding others by imbittered expressions. I would not willingly give offence, I hope none will be taken. If it be lawfull for one man to propose, it must be lawfull for other to answer arguments, in reference to satisfaction. It would be too great a burthen to true English spirits, to see one man permitted to stand with a drawn weapon daring all that passe by, and he only faulty that takes up the weapons to answer him: either prevent such darings, or else excuse the provoked. It will be my comfort to give, it will be my advantage to receive satisfaction: howsoever, I shall commit myself, the safety of our Kingdom, the establishment of such a government that is most conducible to God's honour, to that God, who is able to answer scruples, to preserve a people, and to command settlement according to his own will and way.

ROMANES 3.8.
And not rather as we be slanderously reported, and as some affirm, that we say, Let us do evill that good may come & whose damnation is just.

ROMANES 13.23.
Whatsoever is not of faith is sinne.

38. See p. 403.

[George Lawson, d. 1678]

CONSCIENCE
PUZZEL'D,
ABOUT

Subscribing the *New Engagement;*
in the Solution of this *Quaere:*

Whether a man that hath taken the
Oaths of *Allegiance,* and *Supremacy,* the *Protesta-*
tion and *Covenant,* may, upon the alteration of the
Government from a *Monarchy* into a *Free State,*
subscribe this ensuing *Engagement?*

I *A. B.* declare, and promise to be
true and faithfull to the Common-
wealth of ENGLAND, as it is now
established without *King* and House
of *Lords.*

Zach. 8.17.
Love no false Oath: for this is a thing that I hate, saith the Lord.
Rom. 14.22, 23.
Happy is he that condemneth not himself in that thing which he al-
loweth.
And he that doubteth, is damned if he eat.

Printed in the Yeer, 1650.

*O*ne of the most remarkable tracts published in defense of the Commonwealth and the Engagement is the tract reprinted below. The Engagement, an oath of loyalty to the new government, had been especially crafted to enable individuals to swear to it even if they had reservations about the legitimacy of the regime. Nevertheless it caused great consternation. Until 2 January 1650 the Engagement had only been required of officeholders, barristers, and other specific groups. Thereafter the Engagement was imposed upon the entire male population over the age of eighteen. There is some uncertainty about the date on which this anonymous pamphlet appeared. It is dated 1650, but George Thomason, a contemporary bookseller and preeminent collector of civil war tracts, claimed it appeared on 20 December 1649. In either case, the tract was intended to prepare the public to accept the requirement.

The author of the tract draws upon a whole battery of arguments to persuade his readers that they could take the Engagement without qualms. Among these he includes the notion that all governments are equally lawful. He demonstrates how the language of the Engagement can be interpreted in such a way that any honorable Englishman might take it in good conscience. But what makes the essay so striking is the writer's unblinking use of conquest theory. He accepts the royalist notion that the English are now a conquered people, then concludes that as such they must obey the conquerer. It is a Hobbesian argument presented a year before the publication of Leviathan. Little wonder the tract was anonymous. It appeared in only a single edition.

A case has been made for the authorship of George Lawson, a minister whose works have begun to attract considerable scholarly attention. Lawson was a staunch supporter of Parliament and served as rector of More in Shropshire during the Commonwealth. We know little about him today, despite the interest in his work. He was a correspondent of Richard Baxter, the influential Presbyterian clergyman and author. Baxter seems to point to Lawson's authorship of the present tract when he reports that he had seen a manuscript of Lawson's with arguments in favor of taking the Engagement. Among Lawson's known works are "Examination of the Political Part of Hobbes's Leviathan," published in 1657, and "Politica sacra et civilis," in defense of resistance, published in 1660 and reprinted in 1689.

I A. B. declare and promise, That I will be true and faithfull to the Common-wealth of ENGLAND, *as it is now established without* King *and House of* Lords.

The Question is, *Whether a man that hath taken the Oaths of Allegiance and Supremacy, the Protestation, and Covenant, may upon the alteration of the Government from a Monarchy into a Free State, subscribe this Engagement.*

Premise.

There is no doubt, but unengaged men may: All Governments being of themselves equally lawfull. And, were we upon the point of choosing a Government, we know no reason to compell us to pitch upon a Monarchy more than a Common-wealth. And (whatever may be said in Law for the childe's virtuall obligation to the Oaths of this nature, wherein his father was personally engaged) we see no reason in Divinity, but our children, who never were engaged by the Oaths, Protestation, and Covenant above-mentioned may (when they shall come to yeers of discretion) oblige themselves either by promise, or oath of fealty unto this Government.

But the Question is concerning Engaged men: (as all, but a very few, of those, who are liable to this Subscription, are).

Answer to this may be made in the affirmative, upon two Concessions.

First, if the words of the Engagement import nothing contrary to those Oaths, Protestation and Covenant.

2ly, If (upon supposition that they do import something contrary to those Oaths, &c.) it may be made good unto us, that the obligation of our former Oaths, &c. doth cease upon this new Establishment.

First, If the words of the Engagement import nothing contrary unto those Oaths, &c., As,

First, If by *Common-wealth* be meant the whole company of men and women, both of higher and lower rank, contained within the bounds and territories of these Dominions. So we were wont to call the Common-wealth in the time of Monarchy, unlesse when we took it for the Civill State, as contra-distinct unto the Ecclesiasticall. And, if it have that large signification here, and if the words (*as it is now established*) be to be understood *adversativè*, and not *reduplicativè*, and so binde us to be faithfull to the Common-wealth (in this sense) *Licet stabilitae*, and not *quâ stabilitae absque; Domino Regis, &c.*[1] it will be nothing contrary to our Oaths and Covenants to subscribe thereunto. For unto the Common-wealth (in this sense) we must be faithfull, whatsoever Government it be under. And he that will not be true and faithfull to this Common-wealth, now it is without King and House of Lords, was never (conscientiously) faithfull to it, when it was subject to a King, and House of Lords.

And we are somewhat inclined to think, that this may be the meaning. Because not only all of lower rank, but also all of superior rank (as the Speaker, and the House of Commons, the Lord President, and the Councell of State, the Lord Generall, and Councell of War, &c.) are enjoined to subscribe. If they (or any of them) be the Common-wealth here meant; we somewhat strange at the Injunction. Our Kings were never wont to swear fealty to themselves, or Monarchy. If it may be declared that the words are intended in the sense above specified, we beleeve the Engagement cannot want Subscribers. But,

2ly, If the words (*Common-wealth of England*) be taken for a certain State of Government, as it stands contra-distinct to Monarchy (as it is generally conceived they are) then (without perjury) engaged men cannot subscribe thereunto, unlesse they fetch some help from the exposition of the words, *True and faithfull.*

---

1. Stability is permitted, but without any stability for the Lord and King.

First, If the words (*True and faithfull*) be to be understood only negatively, and oblige a man only, not to be false, or treacherous to, or turbulent in the Common-wealth: we conceive, that a pre-ingaged man may (with a safe conscience) subscribe to this present Engagement. Insomuch as whatsoever we were formerly engaged unto was to be compassed by all lawfull wayes and means, by every man in his vocation and calling. But for any private man by treachery or turbulency, raising tumults and factions to disquiet the present peace (though it be to the attainment of those ends whereunto he was pre-ingaged) is to do evill that good may come thereby, out of his calling and vocation to act for a publick good, which no man (without an immediate call from heaven) hath warrant to do. So that, if it be declared that no more is intended by the words, than what may be comprehended in the negative sense of them, we shall not refuse to subscribe the Engagement, though it be to a Common-wealth, as it stands contra-distinct to Monarchy.

2ly, If the words (*true and faithfull*) be to be understood positively (yet in a strict sense) so as to oblige us to submit and yeeld obedience to this State of government *in licitis, honestis & necessariis,* we may (notwithstanding our former Oaths) subscribe thereunto. For, as for those things that come within the number of *necessaria,* necessarie duties to be performed to God, we are obliged unto them, though we were never enjoined them by men, whose command puts a tie upon us, as subjects, but such as is of inferior nature to the tie which God's command puts upon us, as creatures and Christians. And though we obey not the Command (meerly) for the Civil Sanction's sake; yet we hold ourselves bound to reverence the Civill Sanction so much the more for the Command's sake. And as for those things which come within the number of *licita & honesta,* things lawfull and honest, though not necessary, we count ourselves obliged to the performance of them for the Command's sake (meerly). Uncommanded, we may neglect them, because not necessary: but commanded, we shall not refuse to observe them, because lawfull. "But we trust (in the meanwhile) that none will be so irrationall, as to bring that yoke upon us, which neither we nor our fathers were ever able to bear: *viz.*: to enslave us to the performance of meer indifferent things, as necessary duties, where the performance of them doth not necessarily argue us good subjects, or good Christians." But,

3ly, If the words (*true and faithfull*) be to be understood positively, and in a large sense, so as to oblige us to assist, and defend with our lives and fortunes the present Establishment, against all whatsoever (*though it be the Parliament of England itself*) that shall (hereafter) endeavour by lawfull means to introduce a Monarchy, or any other State of Government in this Nation; we humbly conceive that (without perjurious forcing of our Consciences) we cannot subscribe hereunto. For this is expresly against the words of our former Obligations, wherein we are bound with our lives, power, and estates, to maintain and defend the power and priviledges of Parliament.[2] And this were to pawn our souls to oppose a lawfull Government in doing a lawfull thing.

Secondly, If (upon supposition that the words of the Engagement do import something contrary unto those Oaths, &c.) it may be made good, that the Obligation of our former Oaths and Covenants doth cease upon this new establishment. This is the grand *Quere*.

First, We do acknowledge, that some things, whereunto we formerly have been obliged, are (by the wonderfull providence of our God) rendered infeazible and impossible to us: *viz.*: such as con-

2. The author is referring to the "Protestation of the House of Commons, 3 May 1641," in which the members protested against the supposed designs of priests and Jesuits to undermine the Protestant religion, subvert the fundamental laws of England and Ireland, and cause dissention between king and people and between Parliament and the army. The protest included an oath to defend the Church of England, the power and privileges of Parliament, and rights and liberties of the subjects. In addition the Engagement seemed to contradict the Solemn League and Covenant of September 1643, which pledged subscribers to preserve the rights and privileges of parliaments and to preserve and defend the king's person and authority. See Wing E2211.

cerned the person of our late King, &c. God hath disobliged us from such: and our hands are upon our mouthes, because God hath done it.

2ly, But yet there are other things, that are left by the providence of the same God feazible and possible, as, the exclusion of the Popes and forrain Princes and States' Supremacy, and intermedling with the affairs of this Kingdom, the extirpation of Popery, Prelacy, superstition, heresie, schisme, profanenesse, &c. as may be seen in the particulars of those Oaths, Covenant, and Protestation. Some of which seem to crosse the very intention of this present Engagement, as that particular of our swearing, to bear faith and true allegiance to the King's Heirs, and lawfull Successors, &c. Unto such things as these, we are still bound, if there be not sufficient reason alledged for our disobligation to those Oaths, by virtue of the present Establishment.

Now we conceive there may be three grounds, whereupon a people may hold themselves dis-obliged from their Oaths to former governments, upon the succession.

First, If those Oaths were *vincula iniquitatis, (i.e.)* if they did oblige men unto any Government that is of itself unlawfull, and contrariant to the rule of God's Word. When Monarchy shall be made good to us to be so, we shall not refuse to engage against it.

2ly, In case the alteration be made by such, who, by the fundamentall Laws of the Land, have the power of making such alteration. Which power, by the Statute of 13 *Eliz.* is expresly conferred upon the three Estates in Parliament. If this alteration come to us with such an Authority, we hold ourselves disobliged from our Oaths to all former Establishments, and are ready to subscribe.

3ly, In case of Conquest; when an over-ruling power (by force of Arms, or otherwise) shall conquer a Nation, and render, as well the people unable to maintain their former Government, and Governors, as the Governors to defend and protect their people, in the pursuit of their Oaths, Covenants, and Obligations to them; Then we count it lawfull for a people to make the best conditions they can with the Conquerors, to desire protection from them, and promise subjection to them. And the reason is, because all former Obligations either of the Governors to the Governed, or the Governed to the Governors, did extend no farther than the power of the obliged on both parts. Which power, on both parties, being, by a totall Conquest, over-come by a third party; the obligation to the mutuall exercise of that power must needs cease, because the power itself is ceased.

This Case if it be ours, and it be declared, avowed, and owned that we are a conquered Nation; We are readie to make the best conditions we can for ourselves. And the former power (under the shadow whereof we breathed) being vanished, whilest we cry Quarter, and look for protection from the succeeding Power, we declare, and promise that we will be true and faithfull thereunto in all things, whereby we may not draw upon ourselves the guilt of disobedience unto God.

FINIS.

Isaac Penington Jr., 1616–1679

THE
Right, Liberty and Safety

OF THE

PEOPLE

Briefly Asserted.

*I*saac Penington the younger was the son of Sir Isaac Penington, lord mayor of London and a staunch Puritan. The elder Penington represented London in the Short and Long Parliaments. He served on the council of state in 1648 and sat at the trial of Charles I although he refused to sign the death warrant. Although the younger Penington was well-educated, he did not follow any profession. He seems to have been preoccupied with religion and racked with doubts about his own faith. Most of his published works dealt with religion. He was a Puritan until 1657 when he became a Quaker. During the Interregnum, however, between 1651 and 1653, Isaac junior veered from this religious preoccupation to write several political tracts. "The Right, Liberty and Safety of the People" is one of these.

This intelligent and original piece was published on or about 15 May 1651. The Engagement Controversy was then raging, but Pen-

ington addresses himself instead to a different subject matter. He criticizes long-sitting and unrepresentative parliaments such as the Rump and probes the theory of government itself. He is particularly interested in how government should be structured and representatives chosen to promote the liberty and welfare of the people. He sees the people's well-being as the end of government and supports their right to alter the government as they wish. Anticipating Locke he advocates the separation of powers, a representative legislature, a limited executive, and a separation of church and state. A second edition of Penington's essay appeared in 1657.

At the Restoration the elder Penington was imprisoned in the Tower where he died. Isaac the younger suffered intermittent terms in prison for his Quaker beliefs, which included a refusal to take any oaths—including the oath of allegiance to Charles II.

The *Right, Liberty* and *Safety* of the *People* lieth chiefly in these three things; in *the Choice* of their Government and Governors, in *the Establishment* of that Government and those Governors which they shall chuse, and in *the Alteration* of either as they find cause. This belongs to every people (though few, if any, are in possession of it), and that people, which enjoyeth these, enjoyeth its *Right,* is indeed *free* and *safe* while it so remaineth.

    1. *The Right, Liberty and Safety of the People* consists in *the Choice of their Government and Governors.*

    It is their *Right:* for in *Civil Societies* Nature hath not cut out the *body* into form and shape, but hath left it to be done by the *will and wisdom* of man, having imprinted in him a sense of and desire after the enjoyment of *Justice, Order, Love, Peace* (and whatsoever else is good and profitable for him) both particularly in himself and in common with others; which desire thoroughly kindled in man, and guided by *the true light of Reason,* will lead man to chuse that which is properly good both for himself and others. And though man may possibly or probably abuse this, yet that is no sufficient ground for depriving him of his *right.*

    Their *Liberty* lies in it too. They only are *a free People* who have their *Government* of their own choice. Such upon whom others do intrude, or upon whom other *Laws* or *Regents* are imposed than what themselves judg meet and necessary, and besides that which they themselves voluntarily and by *free consent* submit unto for their good and welfare, are so far under slavery and such a miserable *subjection* as Nature never appointed them unto.

    Their *Safety* likewise lies in it: for to be sure they will chuse nothing but what in probability will conduce to their own *good* and *happiness;* whereas others, making *Laws* for them, or setting *Governors* over them, may respect their own particular benefit and advantage, and not so much the good of the People, which is the main end why

Laws, Governments and Governors are appointed, and to which they should in a direct line be guided.

And upon this ground I conceive it very requisite, that men who are chosen to sit in *Parliament* to make or alter *Laws,* to set up or alter *Governments* or *Governors* for and in behalf of *the People,* should, as soon as any, lie open to the force of all the *Laws* they make, or of anything they do in that kind; that no *Law* they make should take effect till they be dissolved, and come to lie as liable to it as any, otherwise they will not be sensible enough of the People's *condition,* and consequently not fit to stand in their stead, or to act for them in cases that concern them so nearly. The greatest *security* the People have concerning their *Parliaments* is that they chuse persons whose condition will keep them from injuring them, for if they prejudice them they prejudice themselves, if they neglect their good they neglect their own good. This *security* is good while the people chuse them that are of their own *rank,* and while these make no *Laws* for them which shall have any *life* or *vertue* to do *good* or *hurt* till they come also to be exposed to them, but otherwise it is very invalid, if not wholly lost. They who are to govern by *Laws* should have little or no hand in making the *Laws* they are to govern by: for Man respects himself in what he does; (The Governor will respect himself, his own ease, advantage and honour in Government, and lay loads upon the people, but make his own burthen light). Therefore things should be so ordered, in the behalf and for the security of the people, that such as are chosen and appointed to act in this kind should lay no *load* upon the people, but what their own backs may come as soon and as fully, in their degree and station, to bear, as any of the people's.

2. *The Right, Liberty and Safety of the People* consists in *the Establishment of their Government and Governors.* As they have right to chuse, so they have right to confirm what they chuse, to establish that *Government* and such kind of *Governors* as they judg or find most

convenient and necessary for them. Without this the people can be neither *free* nor *safe* no more than without the other, nay without this their *right to chuse* would be to little purpose, the end of choice in things of this nature being for the *duration* of its appointed season.

3. Their *Right, Liberty* and *Safety* lieth also in enjoining and exercising (as need requires) *the Power of altering their Government or Governors:* that when they find either burdensom or inconvenient they may lay it aside, and place what else they shall judg lighter, fitter or better in the stead of it. *Nature* still teacheth everything, as it groweth, to reach further and further towards *perfection*. No man is bound to that which he chuseth or establisheth further than he findeth it suitable to the *end* for which he chose and established it. Now several *states* and *conditions* of things and persons changing, there must of necessity be an answerable change in *Laws, Orders, Governments* or *Governors* also, or man will be instrumental to introduce *slavery, misery and tyranny* upon himself, which Nature teacheth everything both to abhor, and as much as may be to avoid.

It is the desire of most men both in reference to *Church and State* (as men commonly speak) to have *Laws* and *Ordinances,* after the manner of the *Medes and Persians,* which cannot be altered: I cannot but approve the desire, since it is written in man's *nature*. It is natural to man, and a *stamp* of the *divine Image* upon him, to press after *unchangeableness* both in himself and in the things which appertain unto him. But yet it is not suitable to his *present condition* which will in no wise admit of it, because it is continually subject to change and alteration. And as it still changeth, so do his *needs* and *desires,* as also his *experience* and *wisdom,* and so must the *Laws and Orders* which he prescribes to himself and others, or he will be grievously cruel to himself and others. *Ages* have their *growth* as well as particular persons, and must change their *garments,* their *Customs,* their *courses,* &c. for those which are still suitable to their present state and growth. *Laws* are but *temporary;* and as they are founded upon *Reason,* so they are no longer to last than *the Reason* of them lasteth, to which they ought to give place, and admit of such a *succession* as it appoints. Only herein hath *Nature* provided well for *the people,* if they could fairly come to their Right, and had wisdom to use it (which sense and experience is continually instructing them how to do) in that she doth allot them to make and alter their own *clothes,* to shape out their own *burdens,* to form, renew or alter that *yoke of Government* which is most necessary and convenient for their necks.

All this, or any part of this (*either the chusing, establishing or altering Governments, Laws or Governors*) the people cannot do in a Body; an whole *Nation* is too unweildy to act together themselves: therefore *Nature* hath taught them to do it by *Substitutes,* whom they themselves chuse to stand in their stead to do any of these things for them as their present *condition* and *need* requires, which Body of persons is with us called a *Parliament,* who are picked out by the whole to be the *Representative* of the whole, to do that for the whole which they would have to be done, and would do themselves if they were a Body in a *capacity* to act.

And from this first *rise* of things may best be discovered the *nature, ends, proper use and limits of Parliaments,* all which are necessary to be known, both that they may move according to their *nature,* pursue their *ends,* be rightly *used,* keep within their *compass,* and that the people may clearly discern that they so do, whereby they will come to rest satisfied in their *proceedings,* and in their *expectations* of good thereby.

We see here of what kind of *persons* the *Parliament* is to consist, *viz.* of *the common people,* that they may be fit to represent their burdens and desires.

We see here of what *use* and for what *end* they are, *viz. to relieve the people,* to redress any occasion of *grief* or *burden* to them, to make

Laws, alter *Laws*, set *Laws* in a due way of *Administration*, set up or
alter *Governments* and *Governors*, dispose of everything in such a way
as the people may freely enjoy their *Rights* in Peace and Safety.

We see also their *bounds* in general, *viz.* the exercising *the power of
the People* in such ways as were proper for the people to exercise it in
were they capable of joint and orderly acting.

We see likewise their *Nature* or *Constitution*, what they are. They
are *the ELECTIVE POWER, the CONSTITUTIVE POWER, the
ALTERATIVE POWER*. What lies confused and unuseful in the
people is treasured up in them in order, and in a fitting way for use. Is
there a *Government* wanting? The people cannot orderly or wisely
debate or chuse that which is likely to be most commodious and safe.
Are there any *Laws* wanting? The people cannot well set about making Laws. Are there any *Laws, Customs,* or *Encroachments* burdensom? The people cannot rightly scan how far they are so, or proceed
to a regular alteration of them. So that the whole, *Right, Freedom,
Welfare* and *Safety* of the People consists in *Parliaments* rightly and
duly called, constituted and ordered towards acting faithfully in the
discharge of the Trust reposed in them.

Yea lastly, Here we may see in a direct line *the proper course and way
of Parliaments*, which speaks out itself, and would easily be discerned
by us, if our eyes were kept fixed here, and not entangled with other
intermixtures, which are apt to seize upon everything, and inter-
weave with everything, hardly anything keeping its own pure *nature*
or proper *current*. Take it thus, (with a little kind of Circuit for the
better illustration of it, yet very briefly).

All *Governments* (though intended for and directed towards common good) are still declining and contracting private, selfish and corrupt *Interests*, whereby the people come to feel *burdens* under them,
and find want of *fences* to guard them from the *insolencies* and *assaults*
of such as are above them, which are very usual everywhere, for every
man (I think I need not add, almost) though he be unwilling to have

any tyrannize over him, yet he is too prone to tyrannize over such as are under him. Who would not, when he feels *oppression,* if he were able, thrust the *Oppressor* out of his *seat?* And yet who sees how ready he himself would be, so soon as he hath done it, to seat himself in the same *throne of oppression;* and that he will as certainly do the one as the other, if he be not hindered by *outward force,* or (which is better) by an *inward principle?* Indeed man can by no means come to see this concerning himself, but the people still come too soon to feel it.

Now the People, who wear their *Government,* finding by *experience* where it sitteth easie or pincheth, what present *loads* they groan most under, what future *fences* they stand in need of to shelter them from the injurious assaults of *Powers* above them; accordingly chuse *persons,* who lie under the same sense with them, to represent, consult about, and redress these their *grievances,* by *punishing Offenders* for misdemeanors past, by *opening the course of Law* for time to come, as also by *adding* thereto, or *detracting* therefrom, as the condition and need of the people requires, &c.

These persons thus chosen are to come with the sense and desires of the particular *Counties, Cities or Boroughs* for which they serve, mutually to represent these, and to consult together how all *burthens* may be taken off, and all *desires* satisfied in such a way as may stand with the *good* of the whole.

After full *debate* had how these things may be done, to come to an *agreement* of full *setling* them accordingly in the *firmest way* that can be, which having done to *dissolve,* and leave the people experimentally to try and reap the benefit of their *care, pains* and *fidelity,* and to return immediately into their former *condition,* to lie with them sensibly again under the *benefit* or *inconvenience* of what they have done.

And this to be done with as much *speed,* as the motion of such a kind of Body, in Affairs so weighty, can permit; that if they chance to fail in effecting what is desired and expected from them, the people may quiet themselves with the expectation of another *remedy* in its

season approaching. The reason why *Parliaments* should with all possible speed dispatch their work, is for avoiding of that *corruption*
which *standing pools* are subject to, and which is most dangerous in
them; for what shall rectifie *the last remedy,* if that be out of order, and
grow so corrupt, that it hath more need of a *Physician* itself, than to
act the part of a *Physician?* All things by degrees gather *corruption,*
the *governing Power* by degrees declineth from its first purity, and so
also doth the *rectifying* and *reforming Power,* its *deviation* is as easie as
the others, and of far greater consequence; more *destructive,* less *cur-
able.* Therefore better were it for *Parliaments* to leave part of their
work undone, than to sit so long as to contract *corruption.* It is better
to want somewhat of the full *application* of a *remedy,* than to have it
poisoned. But of this more by and by under a distinct head by itself.

Now the whole *Right, Liberty, Welfare and Safety* of the People
consisting in *Parliaments;* the right *Constitution* and orderly *motion* of
them is of the greatest consequence that can be, there being so much
embarqued in this *Vessel,* where, if it miscarry, it is irreparably lost,
unless it can be recovered again out of the *Sea* of *Confusion.*

Wherefore it becometh every one (both in reference to himself and
the whole) to contribute his utmost towards the right steering of *this
Vessel,* towards the preserving of it pure both in its *state* and *motions,*
lest both the *good and welfare* of the *whole* and of every *particular* miscarry, for want of due care and observation.

Towards which work, the further to incite and provoke others, I
cast in this present *offering,* making mention of those *dangers* which
lie open to my eye in reference to *Parliaments,* whereby the *true and
genuine fruit* of them may either be hindered from *growth,* or come to
be *corrupted,* whereby the People at least cannot but miss of the
proper use and benefit, which it ought to reap from them.

There are, in reference to Parliaments, six *Cases* or *Considerations,*
evident to me, whereby the hazard of the people may be very great,
which I shall set down distinctly that they may be the better taken
notice of, weighed and judged.

1. *Want of Parliaments.* Parliaments are the proper *Remedy* to relieve the *grieved People* from their *burdens and oppressions;* from any kind or the several kinds of oppressions that may befall them; from the oppressions of any *Government,* any *Governors,* any *Laws,* any *Incroachments,* &c. (for by several ways, means and instruments the people may be oppressed). Now if *Parliaments* be wanting, that is to say, be not duly called according to the need of the people (it being their *proper engine* whereby alone they can duly, orderly and safely act) their *Right, Liberty* and *Safety* is much hazarded, and they obnoxious to lie under the burden of oppression without remedy. If *diseases* grow, and a due *course of physique* be not to be had, the body cannot but suffer damage and hazard.

There are two things essentially necessary to the health and wellbeing of a *Nation,* as well as of other bodies both *natural* and *politique,* which are, the cutting off of exuberances, and the supplying of defects, both which in the principal and most weighty part of them, are peculiar to *Parliaments;* so that where there is want of them, the *radical life and vertue* of the people must needs be obstructed, languish and decay. This is a very ill disease, however those who never knew or experimented the sweetness of enjoying their *Right* and *Liberty,* may not be considerably sensible of it.

2. *Want of fair Elections,* as thus, If the people be by any means drawn from minding their own good, from bending themselves to chuse persons who may be fit to act for them. How easily may *Parliaments* warp aside from easing and relieving the people unto further burthening and grieving of them, if such persons be chosen to appear in their behalf, who are friends to their Oppressors, and have a particular advantage of sharing with them in the benefit of that which is the burden and cause of grief to the people? And here is a great danger the people are very obnoxious to: Their burdens commonly arise from the miscarriage of the still *present Governors,* and these Governors cannot but have great advantages, by their Power over them, to have an influence upon their choice. Therefore if the

people be not so much the more wary, that which was intended for their greatest *relief* may turn to their greatest *prejudice*. O how miserable is man, whose remedies against multitudes of dangers are so few, and even those few all along so subject to miscarry! A *Parliament* may be prevented, that it may not be to be had when there is most need of it. A *Parliament* may be corrupt before it hath a Being, it may be so ill constituted in respect of the *materials* of it, that it may be a fitter engine of slavery and misery than of freedom and happiness to a poor enthralled people. And yet this is not all the danger that *Parliaments* are exposed unto, as also the people, in relation to that good they hope for by *Parliaments*.

3. *Short continuance of Parliaments.* Suppose the people have *Parliaments*, have a fair and free choice without being overpowered therein, or swayed aside; nay suppose yet more, that they chuse well for themselves; yet *the Power* they are to deal with may overbear them, and (if they cannot bend them aside) enforce their *dissolution*. And hereby the people must needs be deprived of reaping that good they desired and hoped for by their endeavors.

Parliaments are *great Bodies,* and consequently *slow* in motion, which is their proper pace and advantage, for they can hardly do anything well but what they do slowly; for motions that require swiftness *Nature* hath cut out other kind of bodies. Again, *Parliaments* are to act very *warily,* (as the things they are to do, are of great concernment, and require much *circumspection* and *consideration),* and therefore in both these respects must have time convenient to act accurately in the discharge of *so great a Trust,* and in the managing of *so Weighty Affairs,* which if it be not answerably allotted them, they must of necessity be defective in.

4. *Want of Power to Parliaments.* Parliaments have a difficult piece of work, *viz. to chastise the greatest Oppressors, and to strike at the very root and foundation of oppression* in any kind, and unless they have Power answerable they cannot possibly go through with it. *Opposi-*

tions and *interruptions* from *other Powers* they must expect to meet with, which if they be not able to graple with and overcome, they cannot exercise the full Right and Liberty of the People, either in *punishing Offenders against the People,* or in *chusing, establishing or altering Governments, Laws or Governors* for the People. This must necessarily much hinder, if not put a stop to their work: for if any fall short of those means which are proper to an end, they cannot possibly attain that end. If the hand which imposeth and would keep burthens upon the back, be stronger than that which would remove them; If the hand which would supply defects, be weaker than that which stands in its way to stop it in its course, vain and fruitless will all its endeavors be. (The Power that relieveth from oppression must of necessity be greater than the Power that oppresseth.) And this was the condition of this present *Parliament,* there was visibly such a *Power* over them as they could do nothing to purpose for the good of the People. This doubtless they had great reason to strive to get loose from, and the people had great reason to stick to them in it, as also to expect from them their own freedom after they were made free, the freedom of the people being the end (theirs but the means), and therefore most to be eyed. 'Tis to no purpose at all to have never so free a *Parliament,* unless we have also a *People* put into the possession of their freedoms by the *Parliament.*

5. *Over-long duration of Parliaments.* This was glanced at before, but yet it will be requisite to consider of it further, because after those many changes which of late we have been much driven and necessitated into,[1] we may at present lie more open to the *ill influence* of this, than of any of the former: and it should be the especial wisdom and care of man to take most heed of that danger which he lieth most open to. Everything hath its *appointed seasons, bounds* and *proper way of operation,* within which it is very beautiful and profitable, but be-

1. The most significant of those changes were, of course, the trial and execution of Charles I and the abolition of the monarchy and of the House of Lords.

yond it very uncomely and dangerous. *Parliaments*, in their season, may bring forth a most sweet and excellent kind of fruit, which may vigorously refresh the spirits, and recover the decaying Liberties of a dying *Nation;* but continuing longer than its season, the *Root itself,* may easily grow corrupt, and *the fruit* prove soure, harsh, and deadly, yea may tend to a more bitter death than it was ordained to prevent. Many dangers *Parliaments* are exposed to by long continuance, whereby their *nature and constitution* may be depraved, or they induced to act after a different nature, or in other ways than is proper for them, or good for the people. Those dangers which more principally in this respect represent themselves to my eye, I shall here make mention of.

1. *Parliaments,* by long continuance, will be subject to fall into *factions,* which is the foundation of so many breaches and divisions in the whole, upon which they cannot but have an influence to conform them unto themselves, the eye of the people being still upon the *fountainhead.* We have had sufficient experience to evidence the truth of this, for still as the *Parliament* hath been divided, there have also been divisions throughout the whole *Nation.* Persons who act jointly and uniformly at first, (having one and the same *sense* upon their spirits, one and the same *end* in their eye, one and the same *desire* in their hearts) may in process of time lose this *sense,* this *desire,* this *end,* and be drawn aside to another *sense, desire, end,* and differ also in their new choice, which may insensibly creep in upon them; and according to this difference, there will ensue a division among them both in their motions and actions. Now how dangerous this is to have a breach *in the Root,* to have a seed of division *in the heart,* working there, springing forth from thence, and diffusing itself throughout the whole body, I think it will be needless to express.

2. Parliament men, by the long continuance of a *Parliament,* will be exposed to the temptation of *seeking themselves,* of minding and prosecuting their several particular *ends* and *interests.* A Parliament

man, as he is chosen to be, so he should set himself to be *a publique person*, as it were forgetting himself, and giving up himself to be taken up only with the *publique good*, for the season of this work. This a good *Patriot* may find somewhat easie to do for awhile, but if the *Parliament* last long, Self which is very strong in him, and may challenge a right to be looked after, will revive its right, pleading both *reason* and *necessity* in its own behalf. That man, that could be content to lay all aside, and bend himself wholly for the publique for a short time, cannot hold out in doing so, but will be enforced to look after himself, his own affairs, his own profit and thriving in the world, &c. And when he comes to manage these and the other together, it will be very difficult for him to avoid making use of that advantage, which both his power and the long continuance of it affords him, towards his own particular benefit. And Self, having thus crept in, will grow more and more upon him, and will be continually, secretly and subtilly drawing him more and more towards himself, and more and more from the publique: and killing those affections in him (which are too apt of themselves to do) which were very lively at first for the publique, and consequently much unfit him for his work.

3. *Parliaments* by long continuance are in danger of contracting *a particular Interest* (an Interest distinct from that Interest which they have as a part of and in common with the people) in the *publique Government*. Every man hath an allowable *Interest* in common with the whole, so that if it goeth well with the whole, everyone shares in it. This is a good, a profitable Interest, no way prejudicial to any else. But then there is a *particular Interest*, whereby it may go well with some, though ill with the generality; nay the welfare of some may arise out of the incommodity of the generality. That wind which bloweth ill upon the publique, may blow profit to some. This *Interest* all Powers doe readily contract to themselves, partly by their own *strength*, and partly by their advantage to winde into other Powers, the greater still bringing the less into subjection, which must be at

its command and use, or be broken by it. This snare which other Powers by their continuation are still running into, the *Parliament* is to redeem and purge them from; but to take heed lest their own continuance should be so long, as to bring them into the same snare; which may both *unfit them for their proper work*, which is to be Judges on the behalf of the Commonwealth, which how can they truly execute, who have a particular interest and share of their own (besides that which they have in common with the people) in the present Government, whom as it favours, so they must again favour it? As also it may *engage them in an improper work, viz.* in becoming Administrators in the present Government, which is no way proper for such as are appointed to be the Judges of Administrators and Administrations.

A *Parliament* have an interest in the Government with the rest of the people, yea a right and power conferred upon them by the people to *order, settle, amend,* or (if need be) *new-make* the Government for themselves and the people; but not to meddle with the *administration* of it, or to endeavor to bend it aside, in the *administration* of it, for any particular end or advantage of their own, which their Power may easily do, and which their overlong duration may too much intice them to assay to do.

4. *Parliaments*, by long continuance, may incur the danger of interrupting, if not of swallowing up the *ordinary course* of the people's enjoying their *Right* in obtaining *speedy, free and impartial Justice* by the administration and execution of the Laws. The greater doth commonly weaken, if not devour the less. Extraordinary remedies are apt to thrust into the place of the ordinary, especially when by long duration they may seem to challenge to themselves the right of becoming ordinary.

5. (Which is worst of all) *Parliaments*, by over-long duration, may slip into danger of depriving the people of the proper use and benefit of Parliaments. The proper use of Parliaments is to be a *curb* to the

extravagancy of Power, of the *highest standing Power.* But if they themselves become *the standing Power,* how can they be a fit curb for it? A *Parliament* is to be such a Body as may have the sense of the people upon them, that so they may be led by that sense to ease, relieve and safeguard the people. But if once they become *Governors,* they will lose that sense, and have a sense of different nature upon them. They will (like other Governors) have a sense of the *duty* of the people which they owe to their Governors, but lose (by degrees, still more and more) their sense of the *burthens* and *grievances* of the People. So that if Parliaments succeed in the place of the *supream-administering-power,* there will be as much need of somewhat else to stand between the people and them, as there was of them to stand between the people and *Kingly Power:* for they coming into that place and Authority, the people are in as much danger of them, as they were of the Power of Kings: for it is not the person simply, but the power, wherein the danger or benefit lieth. And this doubtless is the *Right* and *Liberty* of the People, and herein lieth their *Safety, viz.* to have an *extraordinary, legislative, alterative, corrective Power* above the *ordinary standing Power;* and this Power, as to consist of *the Body of the People,* so likewise to be kept altogether free from having any particular *hand in Government,* (but to keep within the bounds of their own extraordinary work, which is not so much in as about Government), that so they may both have and retain the sense of the people, being engaged by their state and condition to do nothing which may prejudice the people, because in case they do, they themselves will suddenly feel the smart of it.

6. The last *danger,* which I shall at this time mention in reference to *Parliaments,* is this. *The assuming a Power of a different nature from them, not proper to them; and intermedling with a work which they are not fitted for, entrusted with, or appointed to.*

Powers, like other things (and somewhat more advantagiously than other things, having stronger hands) are still gathering in to themselves. The rich man will be gathering riches, the wise man will be gathering wisdom, and the powerful man will be gathering power. And in attracting to himself (especially where he is the *sole Judg*) it is very difficult for him to be *moderate* or *innocent*. He who hath a right power in some things, it is hard for him to keep there, and not to seek after and lay hold on, if he can, that power which he ought not to have, and in those other kind of things wherein he ought not to have power. That a *Parliament*, as well as other *Powers*, is subject to this temptation, cannot be denied.

This is dangerous everywhere. (To have things endowed with a different, if not contrary nature, to have things employed about a different, if not a contrary work, to neglect their own work for which they are fit, to which they are appointed, and execute another work for which they are not fit, to which they are not appointed; this, let it be never so carefully and faithfully managed, must needs bring *disorder, confusion*, nay greater *inconveniences*). But the greater the power is, the greater is the danger: because as the greatest power may do most good in its own way, so it may do most harm in a wrong way. *Powers* that are great, bring forth great effects either of *Peace* or *Trouble, Order* or *Confusion, Salvation* or *Destruction*. No remedy so sovereign, so restorative as a *Parliament* rightly constituted, rightly applied, and rightly acting. No disease more deadly, more consuming the very *heart-life* of the Rights and Liberties of a Nation, than a *Parliament* misconstituted, misapplied, misacting.

But everyone here will be ready to say, What is *that Power* which is proper to *Parliaments?* What is their *proper work?* What is that Power of a different nature, which will be so dangerous for them to assume? And what is that work, which they are not fitted for, entrusted with, or appointed to?

To satisfie the desire of such as may greedily enquire after this, I shall answer somewhat, according to that insight which is afforded me into the nature of things, shewing (from the *Principles* foregoing) both what their proper *Power* and *Work* is, and then what *Power* and

Work is improper for them. And it is a clearer and far safer way, to search out and discover things from their first rise in Nature, than from succeeding *Principles* or *Practises*, which may easily decline awry and cover the true knowledg and intent of things.

Now concerning their proper *Power* and *Work*, I shall not undertake to define the particular limits of it, it will suffice to my purpose, to express the general nature of it, which to me appeareth thus.

It is a *NATURAL (Human or Civil) EXTRAORDINARY, CONSTITUTIVE, CORRECTIVE, ALTERATIVE POWER.* I shall speak chiefly of their *Power*, which will of itself discover their *Work*, therefore that will not need so particularly to be opened.

First, I say it is *NATURAL:* such a Power as is sown in *man*, in the *nature* of man. Man hath a power over himself, to dispose of himself, according to that wisdom and righteousness which is seated in him, grows up with him (if it be not blasted or kept under), which he further attains to, or is in a further degree bestowed upon him. Of this common kinde is this, with all other earthly Powers.

But this expresseth only the *kinde* of it, we are yet far from the *particular nature, end,* or *use* of it.

Therefore to describe it further, I term it *EXTRAORDINARY,* which it discovers itself to be, being a thing not for common and constant use, but for extraordinary ends and purposes; and the nature of things must be suited to their end, for thither it is to direct them.

Then more particularly there is expressed what kinde of extraordinary Power it is, namely, *CONSTITUTIVE, CORRECTIVE, ALTERATIVE.* It is a Power of seting up or establishing Laws, Governments, Governors; of correcting them, of altering them.

This is the nature of their Power, which pointeth out their work so plainly, as it will not need more particularly to be specified in this place.

Now by this there are two sorts of Power cut off from them, one whole kinde of Power, and one main branch of another kinde.

1. *Spiritual Power,* which claimeth its descent from *Christ as the*

Head of his Church, and is appropriated by its nature, end and use, unto his Body the Church, which is his *City* or *Kingdom,* to be governed by him, even by that power of his *Spirit* which he pleaseth to exercise upon them, whether immediately by himself, or mediately by such as he substituteth under him. This Power, as it is *spiritual,* so it is fit to be managed only by *spiritual* hands: Not by *Men,* but by *Christians;* nor by every Christian, but by such only as can clear the derivacy of it from *Christ* to them, such as are fitted and appointed by him to be under him in his own seat and place of Government. Nor are Christians to exercise this Government over other men, but only over Christians, whom alone it is suited to. Nor are they to govern as men; by outward force; but as Christians, by spiritual vertue and efficacy upon the Conscience, the seat of *Christ* in man, so that it may appear that not they, but *the Spirit of Christ, the Spirit in Christ,* doth rule and govern. O how sweet would this Government be! How pleaseant to a Christian the strictest execution of the sharpest Laws in it! *Christ's yoke is easie, and his burthen is light,* even in the sharpest and weightiest part of it.

But this Power belongeth not to any *Nation* or People under Heaven, there being not any Nation or People which can evidence the fair and clear derivacy of this Power from *Christ* to them: (as it was not intended for any Nation or People, save only *his own Nation, his own People*). Therefore not to any *Parliament,* who are but the People in a representative Body, in a Body contracted into a narrower compass for the use and service of the People; who as they stand in their stead, so they have only their Power. The People being the stock or root from whence their Power and Authority doth spring, it can rise no higher, nor be of any other nature, than that which is in the People.

2. In *Civil Power,* the administrative or governing part of it appeareth from hence not to appertain to them.

In *Civil Societies,* as well as in *natural,* Nature hath cut out the proportion (in general, though not in particular). There is *the Head* and *the Members,* having each their several innate *Properties, Motions, Laws* and *Priviledges,* which cannot be transgressed without violence to Nature, or without danger to that Body or Society which breaketh the bounds limited by Nature. In every Society which is orderly, there is the Head and the Members, part to govern, and part to be governed; to each of which appertain their particular Rights: to the one such as they may be advantaged for and in government by, to the other such as they may be advantaged under government by; that the *yoke* may be gently, orderly, and sweetly managed by the one, and sweetly born by the other.

Now this is most evident, that the People are *the Body,* the People are *to be governed;* not to be *the Head,* not *to govern.* The *Legislative Power* indeed belongs to them, that their yoke might be the more easie. But the *Administrative Power* doth in no wise belong to them, but to those who are to govern. And though the People might be flattered and encouraged, from sense of the misuse of this Power, to take it into their own hands, yet it can never thrive there: and though they should set themselves to rest content, nay to please themselves with it; yet you must needs grow weary of it, and that very quickly, the inconveniences will multiply so fast, and grow so unavoidable.

Parliaments are the Body of the People, chosen by the People to stand for them, to represent them, to act in their stead. Answerably, They have that Power which is proper to the People, the *Legislative,* the *Supremely Judicative;* but not that Power which belongs not to the People, *viz.* the *Administrative.*

In like manner this discovers a double kinde of work improper for them.

The one is, *medling with spiritual affairs.* The *constituting* of these, the *amending* of these, the *altering* of these is only proper to such as are invested with *spiritual Power and Authority.* The *Laws* of *Christ* were never appointed to be set up by the Power of man, but by the

Power of his Spirit in the *Conscience.* It is accounted profane, and much startled at, to touch that which man hath *made holy,* which man hath *separated* and consecrated to *divine use;* and yet how propense are, almost all persons, to be laying hands on that, *which God hath made holy and set a part* for himself! How sad an effect we have seen and felt from undertakings in this kinde, cannot but be fresh in our memories; what a sad *breach* and *disunion* it hath occasioned throughout the whole *Nation,* and particularly in the *Parliament.* Nor can I conceive readily, how it could be otherwise. The closest bond of union mistaken and misapplied must needs become the greatest instrument of division (to let pass God's interest to blast men, when they will be venturing upon that work which he hath not appointed them unto, but reserved for himself). The wound thus made may prove incurable. Men differing in their judgments, and consequently in their desires; differing in the apprehension of their duties; their motions and endevors must needs run cross and become irreconcilable, while the foundation of this difference remains. While a man is strongly perswaded, that this or this is the way and Will of God, that it is his duty to use the utmost of his abilities, opportunities and advantages for the promoting of it, that this is the main end for which power is put into his hands, the chief thing God expects from him, and will call him to a very strict account about the improving of all his power and interest unto the advancing of this; I say while things stand thus, how can he with the quiet of his Conscience neglect acting accordingly? The *Presbyterian* is now engaged indissolubly, to use his utmost strength and endevor towards the advancing of *Presbytery,* which is God's instituted way of Worship in his eye; and so the *Independent* of *Independency,* which is Christ's Institution in his eye. Now having tasted so much of this, and smarted so much by this, men should be very wary of intermedling in things of this nature, further than their ground is clear.

The other is, *The taking upon them the Administration of Govern-*

ment, or intermixing with the administration of Government. This is the most pernicious thing to a *Parliament* that can be, for it both diverteth them from their own work, and out of their own way, into one of another nature; and so thrusteth them into a necessity of doing disservice, and into an incapacity of doing service. This may make useless, nay may make burthensom, the best constituted *Parliament.* Suppose a *Parliament* of never such entire-hearted-honestmen, most studiously bent and applying themselves to publique service; yet if they be over-full of another kind of business than their own, or intermix another kinde of business with their own, they can neither well dispatch that other kinde of business which they are so over-full of, or which they so intermix; nor their own neither. And it is the ready way to turn the hearts of the People from *Parliaments:* for finding things go so grievously amiss (as by this means they needs must), and in the hands too of such men, as they can hardly hope for better, they will begin to look on a *Parliament* no longer as a *remedy,* but as a worse *disease,* than that which they addressed themselves to it for cure of. O consider your snare, ye who are in danger of it! How prone was the *Administrative* Power to intrench upon the bounds of the *Legislative,* and how afflictive did it become thereby! Is not the *Legislative* Power as prone to intrench upon the *Administrative?* And in so doing, is it not likely to prove as afflictive?

Look into *Nature,* See if ever this kinde of Body was cut out, fitted or appointed by it to govern. It hath not a fit form or shape for it; it is unweildy for such a kinde of motion.

Again, Look into *the tenor of your Call and Trust.* Were ye ever entrusted herewith by the People? Is it, or ever was it, the minde of the People? Did they chuse you for this end? Have ye a *Commission* from them, I mean not formally, but so much as vertually, intentionally? They called you to rectifie Government, that is clear enough; but did they call you to govern? O remember, remember, when any such motions arise in you, when any such temptations beset you; Ye are not fitted to it by Nature: your motion is slow, but the work and way of Government requires speed and swiftness. And if ye should from a desire, from an apprehension of advantage, from sense of present need, or any other never so good an intent, alter your own slow pace and strive to act swiftly; it will quickly appear how uncomely it is in you, and how unsafe for the People. Remember also, that ye are not called to it by the People: and if ye will yet be venturing upon it, doubtless ye will run the hazard of ruining both yourselves and the People.

These are some of the *dangers* which *Parliaments* (and through them the People) are obnoxious to. How far *this present Parliament* hath been overtaken with any of them, or how far the People hath suffered thereby, I shall not take upon me to determine. Only thus much I cannot but express, That *the present state of affairs* is (to my eye) much *entangled,* and that *the true foundations of Right and Freedom* (so far as I can discern) are not yet laid; and I could earnestly desire and much entreat those in whose power it is, to do *the main work,* and to do it thoroughly: To let fall all desire of *Power or Supremacy* (whose sweetness will be tempting the best) to strike at the root of all *particular Interests* which stand in the way of *publique good,* and to set upon such ways of publique good, so evidently and directly tending thereto, as might be forcible to convince very *enemies* to them by their clearness in reason, and by the sweet benefit which they should not be able to avoid tasting and reaping from them. Having such advantage of Power in their hands, what is it which might not be done for publique good, if men had hearts, and were in a right way?

It is commonly said, that *a stander by may see more than a gamester:* which if it be true, I may assume unto myself some freedom of speech more than ordinary, my condition interesting me in it. For I have been long taken off from being an *Actor* in any kinde, to become only a *Spectator;* yea and I think I may say safely, not an engaged but a free Spectator. I have not been interested in the designs of any party whatsoever, nor so much as in desire to have any party thrive, further than they have been guided by *Principles* of *Reason* and *Righteousness* unto common good. There is not one sort of men upon the face of the Earth, to whom I bear any enmity in my spirit (though in some respect I must confess myself an enemy to every sort of men) but wish, with all my heart, they might all attain and enjoy as much *Peace, Prosperity,* and *Happiness,* as their state and condition will bear. There are not any to whom I should envy *Government,* but, who ever they are, they should have my vote on their behalf, whom I saw fitted for it and called to it. Indeed I am offended, very much offended with most persons and things, and I have a deep *Charge* against them, which at present I keep secret, not intending to bring it forth till I come upon that stage where I may have fair play. Yet thus much I will say, which toucheth a little upon it. I am offended both with *Light* and *Darkeness,* or rather with that which pretends to be Light, and that which is acknowledged to be Darkness. *I am offended with that which pretends to be Light,* because it doth not more fairly overcome Darkness; but while it blames it for its dark paths of *Tyranny, Cruelty* and *Oppression,* itself seeks (not by the pure vertue and power of Light, but) by the same weapons, *viz.* of *dark violence* to conquer it; and if it ever prevail this way to do it effectually, I shall be much mistaken. *I am* also *offended with Darkness;* because it is not *true* to itself, not *just* to itself, not *at peace* with itself, nor keeps within the *sphere* of its own *dark Principles* (even those which it doth acknowledg) in its own motions, or in its opposing either Light or Darkness *Christians* dishonour themselves and their Principles; They speak indeed of *the Light of God,* of *the Life of God,* of *the Power of God,* of *the great Name of God,* but are fallen short of the true *vertue* and *glory* of all these, both in *Religion,* and in their *course* in the World. *Men* dishonor themselves and their Principles, falling short of that *common love, good will* and *righteousness* which very Nature would teach them to observe, notwithstanding its depravation, were their ears open.

But I delight neither to complain nor accuse, only I cannot but wish that all cause and occasion of complaint and accusation were taken away from him who doth delight in either. All the liberty I shall now make use of, is only freely to express what I conceive necessary, in the present confused state of things, to reduce them into some certain safe and well-grounded order, according to plain Principles of Reason and Righteousness, without aiming either at the throwing down or setting up of any person or thing: Which, what interpretation soever of weakness, folly or disaffection may be put upon it, I finde not myself very prone to value. This *temper* hath long attended my spirit, not much to regard, what account either I myself or any else put upon things, but rather to expect what things will then appear to be, when they shall be made manifest by *that Light*, which doth discover them as they are, and will pass such a *judgment* upon them as they deserve, and shall not be able to gainsay or avoid.

It is a kinde office and a commendable peece of service to help out of the mire, or to offer so to do, yet can hardly be so esteemed by him who observeth not himself to be in the mire, and consequently hath no sense of any need of help. He will rather entertain it with disdain than acceptation, it implying him to be in such a condition as he is unwilling to own or acknowledg. But however, as I have on the one hand expressed my sence (though very sparingly) of our present *entangled condition*, wherein we finde ourselves at a loss in our very *remedy:* so I shall on the other hand offer what help my Reason and Judgment presents to me as proper and necessary to dis-involve us and bring us into a right course.

To come then to what I drive at, first I shall speak a word in general towards setling, and then propound more particularly, what things are needful (considering our present state) towards the setling of affairs in order, justice and safety, both to dis-engage us from fundamental miscarriages and dangers (which it is very easie to slip into, and very hard to wade out of, especially after our so long treading in

such an unusual track, as of late we have been much driven into) and
to set us straight.

Towards setling in general I should say three things.

First, That we should look well to our setling, look well how we
settle.

Secondly, That we should be careful of avoiding *Arbitrariness*
of *Government* in our setling.

Thirdly, That we should have regard to the *Rights of the People,*
and especially to their *rectifying Right,* that it have its free current.

1. *We should look well to our setling.* Shakings generally tend to setling;
and setlings frequently make way for future shakings. Shakings are
sudden and violent most commonly, not flowing so much from deliberation as from force: but setlings require great wariness and circumspection, lest that *corruption* which caused our disturbance (and
should be shaken out) put on *a new guise,* and settle again on our *new
foundation;* whereby there are not only new seed-plots strown of fresh
ensuing miseries, but also preparation made for a new *Earthquake.*
Therefore it behoveth us to look well about us, and to settle warily,
that we may settle surely.

2. *We should be careful to avoid Arbitrariness of Government in our
setling.* If *Arbitrariness* of Power, and a *Government* by *Will,* not *Law,*
was our burthen, and that which we so strongly desired and ende-
vored to throw off from our backs: then surely they to whom it appertaineth, and who have engaged themselves to free us from it,
ought to be exceeding careful and watchful against involving us again
in it. If it hath already miscarried in one hand, it may also do in another. However, in reason we are not to be tied to run the venture. It
is not the change of the hand, but the change of the Rule, which we
expect as our *foundation* of Safety. He that doth us good in an arbitrary way, and by an arbitrary power today, may by the same way and
power do us harm tomorrow.

3. *In our setling regard should be had to the Rights of the People, and especially to their rectifying Right, that it have its free current.* The *Rights* of the People were the main thing presented to view in this great conflict, and therefore in equity should be mainly prosecuted: and most principally those which are their most needful and useful *Rights.* Our *Laws* are our Rights, and we should be loth to be deprived of any of them (whose reason was both good at first, and remaineth still in force). But there are some Rights and Liberties which are the *root* and *foundation* of our Laws, and our *ultimate Refuge* for succour and safety; and therefore much nearer to us, and more essential to our happiness, than others are. These are especially to be regarded. And this so much the rather, because the people are so fit a Body to be subjected and trampled upon, that it is very hard for those which are great in power, to keep their feet from off their necks. Alas, the people have no way to avoid danger but by running upon the *Rocks;* they have no way to shun ruine, but by hasting into ruine. Those they chuse to govern them gently, to defend them, may sit hard upon their backs, yea themselves may make a prize of them. And if they can in length of time, through many difficulties, obtain and appoint Trustees to rectifie these miscarriages, yet how many temptations they have to mismanage it, they think not of, and how they will manage it, they know not. *Experience* doth still shew how difficult it is thoroughly to mind the good of the people. One half of the work is sometimes done (sometimes very often) *viz. the crushing of Oppressors:* but the other half, *viz. the breaking the yoke of oppression,* is very rare and hard even for them to do who have prevailed to shake the Oppressors out of their seats.

Thus much in general. Now more particularly, there are four things appear to me as necessary, unto a fair and firm setling.

1. *A clear distinction between the administrative or executive Power, and the legislative or judicative:* that as they have in themselves, so they may retain in their course, their clear and distinct natures, the

one not intermixing or intermedling with the other. That the *administrative* may not intermingle itself, or meddle with the *legislative*, but leave it to its own free course; not the *legislative* with the *administrative* by any extemporary precepts, directions or injunctions, but only by set and known Laws. Things which are severed in their nature must likewise be severed in their use and application, or else we cannot but fail of reaping those fruits and effects which we desire from them, and which otherwise they might bear, and we enjoy.

2. *A prescription of clear and distinct Rules and Bounds to each.* That the *Trust, Power, Priviledges* and *Duty* of each, which flow from the common light of man, and are intended for the common good of man, may be made evident to that common light; that the people may know hereby what they are to expect from each, what they are to expect from the *Parliament,* what they are to expect from their *Supream Governor* or Governors, and so may be understandingly sensible of good or ill usage. There is nothing (among that nature of things we now treat of) of itself unlimited: and the more clearly the limits of anything are set and known, the greater advantage hath it both to move safely, and to vindicate the integrity and righteousness of its motions. If the limits of Power be not described and made known, it will be left too loose in its actings, and the people also will be left too loose in the interpretation of its actings (neither of them being groundedly able to justifie themselves in either unto the other) neither of which is safe. If the *Parliament* hath one apprehension of its limits, and the people another, they can neither be satisfied in the other; but the people must needs disrelish the actions of the *Parliament,* and the *Parliament* cannot but think themselves injured by the people, which may occasion the laying of a dangerous foundation of discontent and division between them. Yea hereby the Parliament's best friends may be forced to become its enemies, and it may be forced to deal most sharply with its best friends, and so weaken its

best strength, and the best strength of the *Nation*. Those that are friends to *things* are not friends to *persons,* any further than they are subservient to *things.* It is as hateful to *true-bred-spirits* to idolize the name of a *Parliament* any more than of a *King:* it is *righteousness,* rightly administered in its own *proper way* and *channel,* by persons in place and power, which alone can make them lovely to such as love not *men,* but *righteousness.* It was the error of the foregoing governing Power to esteem itself more at liberty, than in right it was; it may also be the error of the present legislative power, yea their condition exposeth them more unto it (their Liberty being larger, or of a larger kind); and therefore they ought the more abundantly to beware of it, and to apply themselves to produce, or cause to be produced, a true and fair discovery of those bounds and limits wherein they are (by the nature of things) circumscribed: for if they do not know them, it will be impossible for them to keep within them; and if the people do not know them, it may be difficult (in many considerable cases) to them to believe that they do keep within them.

3. *An unquestionably free and equal Parliament.* It is not every *cause* which will produce a true and genuine *effect,* but the cause must be rightly tempered to bring forth kindly fruit. It is not every *Parliament* which can heal or settle a *Nation,* or that the people have just cause to rest satisfied in; but a *Parliament* fairly chosen, equally representing the people, and freely acting for the people.

Now every man knoweth *force* to be opposite to *freedom.* That which is *free* is not *forced,* and that which is *forced* is not *free.*

This *Parliament* hath, visibly to every common eye, been more than once forced;[2] and it is not very easie after violence to break forth again into perfect liberty: the sense and remembrance of the former force, together with an inward fear of the like again (if the like occasion shall happen) may be a secret, though not so apparant a *bond*

---

2. Pride's Purge, which took place in December 1648, was an obvious use of such force in this Parliament.

upon their spirits, which may in some particulars incline them both to do what they would not, and to neglect the doing of what they would.

Besides, it may be considered how far that *visible force*, which caused so great an *alteration* in the *Parliament*, and such a change in affairs, did intrench upon the *freedom* of *Parliament*. For though every *detention* of some or many Members may not disanul the freedom of a *Parliament*, yet some kind of detention, so and so qualified, necessarily doth. An *occasional* or *accidental detention* is not of so great force as an *intentional:* yet if such an accidental detention of some of the Members should happen, whereby the *state* and *course* of the *Parliament* should be changed, it might well be disputed, whether the rest (still sitting and acting contrary to what was done before those Members were detained) might be accounted a free *Parliament*, (when such a force was visibly upon some part of it, as changed the whole state of affairs in it). For this were plainly an accidental bending of the *Parliament* from its intended *course*, from its *free current*, and so far as it is bent it is not free. But in the case in hand there was yet more,[3] There was an *intentional* bending of the *Parliament*, (as was expressly declared by them who were the instruments to bend it) there was a culling out of those who stood in the way of what the *Army* thought just, safe and necessary to be done. And this was done purposely that the *Parliament* might be put into another posture, and act other things different from what, as they were then constituted, they could be drawn unto. Now though there should be a violent detention of divers Members of the *Parliament* from doing that service, which they ought and desire to do according to their Judgments and Consciences; yet if the *Parliament* be not bent hereby, but go on in the same path it was walking in before, it hath the greater advantage thereby to argue and to make good its freedome. But if by this force

3. The "case in hand" was Pride's Purge.

it be visibly and apparantly bent, put into another posture, and into contrary ways and motions, the evidencing of its freedom will, in this case, be more difficult.

There might yet be further added the Judgment of the *Army* concerning this action of their own, who were likely to look favourably upon it being their own, but I purposely wave it: for I do not go about to make the most of these things, but desire only the granting of thus much to me, that this *Parliament* is not unquestionably free, and so the people, who are sensible thereof, cannot rest fully satisfied in their spirits, that this present engine is their evidently-genuine and proper engine.

And as this present *Parliament* is not unquestionably free, no more is it an unquestionably equal Representative of the people, neither in respect of the number of the persons, nor in respect of the qualification of the persons.

First, for *the number of the persons*. Every *County, City, Borough*, having their stock going, their right and interest concerned in the whole, their particular advantage or disadvantage while *Parliaments* sit; so they ought to have their proper *Substitutes* or *Representers* to appear for them, to stand in their stead, to have an influence in the managing of their particular cases, and their right in the whole, which, as the case now stands, many do want.

Secondly, for *the qualification of the persons*. For it is not a number of persons (though chosen by the people) simply considered, that do or can represent the people. They are but *shadows*, not the *true Representatives* of the People (though designed by the people to that end) unless they be rightly qualified. How is that? Why thus: by understanding the condition and desires of those they stand for, and by representing those desires seasonably in their stead: for they are chosen to be *common persons*, and therefore ought to have the *common sense* of the *Rights, Liberties, Safeties, Needs, Desires* of those they stand for. If a man undertake to appear for me, and doth not know or care to know what I need or desire, he doth me a double injury; both putting me to the loss of that which I might obtain, and depriving me of the means I might otherwise have attained it by.

Now there is a great exception against these present Representers in this respect, the state of things, and consequently burthens being much changed, since they were chosen to represent them. It is a long while since the first sitting of this *Parliament*, and the change of Power, with other things, may have caused many new burthens, which they, being in power, cannot so fully feel, nor seem so fit to be *Judges* of. The *burthens* of the *People* still arise from the *present Power*, that power from which they did formerly arise is removed, another hath succeeded. Now they who are the greatest in the *succeeding Power* seem no way fit to represent the burthens of the people under that power: but such of the common people as lie most under them, and most feel them, are likely to be most fit to represent the sense of them. These indeed might be fit, when they were chosen, to be Judges of former burthens and oppressions, but they seem not now so fit to be Judges concerning present burthens and oppressions. Not that which manageth the power can so fairly, clearly and sensibly judg whether it be easie or grievous, but that which lieth under it.

And here I may not unfitly add one thing concerning the way of managing affairs in *Parliament* so much in use, *viz.* by *Votes;* the necessity whereof in some cases, and the multitude of transactions, may have been an occasion to draw into more common use than is either fit or safe. My ground of excepting against it is this. The actions of the people (and so of the *Parliament*, who are the collective body of the people) should be very clear and evident to the eye of *common sense*, so as to bear down all opposition or gainsaying. The *people* should desire the removal of nothing but what is evidently burthensom, the addition of no *Law* but what is evidently good, the punishment of none but him who hath evidently been an *offender*. But the putting things to Vote is an argument against this clearness and evidence, and doth seem to whisper, if not to speak out, that things are doubtful, and that the determination is also doubtful, arising not necessarily from the strength of reason, but perhaps from the number of voices. I confess it is impossible for such a body to manage many affairs without this course: but I cannot conceive that ever *Nature* cut out such a *body* for the managing of many affairs. It is a body of the common people, who are not supposed to be skilful in administering *Government*, nor intended to meddle in managing of *affairs*, but only to set them in a right posture, and in a fair way of *administration*. A few, easie, necessary things, such as *common sense, reason* and *experience* instructeth the *common sort* of men in, are the fittest things for them to apply themselves unto. Indeed the people should have no more hand in or rather about *Government*, than necessity requires for their own preservation, safety and welfare; and dispatch quickly what they have to do (as a few plain things may quickly be done) and so return into *subjection* unto *Government* again, whereby alone they will be able to know whether they have done well or ill in what they have done. Again, as it is a Body of the *common people*, so it is of a *great bulk* (it cannot be otherwise formed), and therefore not fited for many motions, but only for such as are slow and sure. Yet their slowness of motion (the right order of *nature* being observed) will be neither burdensom to themselves nor others, being recompenced by the fewness of those things which *Nature* (I mean the nature of their end, call and trust) hath appointed for them to do.

4. *A regular way of Elections:* that the people might be put into a fair, clear, understanding way of managing this: that they might not be urged from favour to the present *administering power* to make their choice according to their desires, but might be left free therein, and might be incited to wariness by being instructed of what concernment their choice is: that if they chuse amiss they contribute towards the laying a foundation of enslaving themselves and the whole

Nation. The people have a sense of their own *good,* as well as a desire to please their *Superiors,* and if that sense were by suitable means quickened in them at the time or season when they chuse, they would be so much the more careful to make choice of such as were fittest to represent that sense. In such a great and extraordinary *Remedy* there should be extraordinary care about every step and degree of the framing and constituting of it that we may be sure (as sure as possibly we can) to have it right and fit for its appointed end and use: for one error here is as it were a *womb* of danger and misery, which hereby it is in a way to bring forth. Now that the people might the better understand the *end, work,* &c. for which they are chosen, and put themselves, or rather be put (for they can hardly do anything themselves orderly) into such a posture as they might chuse most advantagiously to their own good; and that those whom they chuse might the better apply themselves thereto; that both these might be more commodiously done, I shall propound these three things. (And here I desire free scope in the ballance of everyone's Judgment, for I propose not these things from any conceit of them, but meerly from the strength of that *reason* which representeth itself to me in them, having no desire they should take place, so much as in anyone's mind, any further than the *reason* in them makes way there for them, and it will be my delight and joy to see them give place to anything which is better or more solid.)

1. That the *Counties, Cities* or *Boroughs* meet together (as they were wont to do to chuse their *Knights, Citizens* or *Burgesses*) to chuse a convenient number of their Commonalty as a *Committee* to chuse their *Knights, Citizens* or *Burgesses* for them for that one time.

I speak now in general concerning a convenient way of chusing, but if I were to speak concerning a sudden new choice, I should add this. That none should be admitted either to be chosen or to vote in this choice, but such as have been *faithful* to their *Country* in the late great *defection:*[4] for which end, that *exceptions* should be drawn up, and great *penalties* annexed to them, to be inflicted on such as should venture to give their vote, who are excepted from chusing; or such as shall accept of the choice, who are excepted from being chosen. (Only these *exceptions* should be so plain, as there may be no cause of doubt or scruple concerning the interpretation of any of them, lest they prove a *snare* to any to deprive them of the exercise of their just Right and Liberty herein.) It is undeniably just and rational, that the people having fought for their *Rights* and *Liberties*, and purchased them with the expence of their *blood*, should now enjoy them, and not permit such a participation of those among them, who endeavored and fought against them, as may cause a new hazard of the return of that into their hands, which hath been thus difficultly and costily recovered from them.

2. That this *Committee* immediately upon their being chosen (before or at their first sitting) may have an *Oath* administered unto them, to this intent, That without *partiality*, regard to *friendship*, or any other *by-respect*, they shall chuse (either from among themselves or elsewhere) him whom they shall judg most fit, both for ability and fidelity, to serve his *Country* in general, and that *County, City,* or *Borough* in particular.

3. That this *Committee*, immediately after they have finished their choice, consult about and draw up (and that an *Oath* be administered for this end likewise, or a clause for it inserted in the former *Oath*) a Copy of what, according to their Consciences, they conceive them to be entrusted with by the people; with what kind of *power,* in what *sphere,* and to what *end;* which might be before them as a *Light* and *Rule* unto them, though not absolute, yet it might be very helpful: Whereas otherwise (without some such help) persons called to that employment may be ignorant what their work is, and from this ig-

4. The Scots uprising led by Charles II to establish him on the throne of England was still in progress as Penington wrote. This constituted the most recent "defection."

norance (and their own modesty together) may join with others in the way they find them in (if a *Parliament* be sitting) or in the way some, who are most looked upon, may propose; in the meanwhile they themselves not understanding where they are, to what direct *end*, or upon what *ground* they act. And I must confess this hath ever made me unwilling to venture upon that *employment*, not having clear and certain *instruction* how or what to act therein: and I must confess myself somewhat unsatisfied to undertake a *Trust*, the nature whereof is not clearly manifested unto me. I am content to serve my *Country* with all my poor strength, but withall cannot but be shy of such a snare of doing them disservice instead of service, as my own remediless ignorance herein may necessarily expose me to. And perhaps there may be some others who may stand in need of this help as well as I: however, a clear and plain way of knowledg, me thinks, should be burdensom to none.

Such kind of things as these are proper transactions for a *Parliament,* for there may be errors or defects in this kind which the people cannot come together to consult about and heal, yet it is requisite such things, in this kind amiss, should be healed, who therefore fitter to do it than their *Representatives?* And what might not be done in this nature, and entertained thankfully by the people, if it were so managed, upon such plain *grounds* of *Reason* and *principles* of *Justice,* and in such a *plain clear way,* as might carry *conviction,* that it was not done from any *selfish respects,* but for *common good.* It is a jealousie in the people, that their *Substitutes* neglect them, and mind themselves, which makes them interpret their actions so ill, which jealousie by this means would easily be rooted out of the people, nay it would fall of itself.

These are the things which to me seem necessary to set us right. And if it were once thus, that *Powers* were rightly distinguished according to their own *natures,* rightly bounded within their own *spheres, ranks, orders and places;* if there were also a *Parliament* in every respect fairly chosen, set right in its *constitution*, and rightly acting according to its own *nature, end* and *work* within its own *bounds*, there might be some ground of *hope* both towards the well setling of things at present, and the easie further amending of what should be found amiss afterwards. But I dare confidently affirm it, that until the *true way, course* and *end* of Nature be discovered and observed, let there be never so many other advantages; a *Parliament* never so *wise*, never so *industrious*, never so *faithful;* a *People* never so *pliable* and *thankful*, never so *quiet* and *patient,* both in submitting unto the pains of their cure, and in continual renewing of their expectations when it will once be; yet the desired end will never be effected by the *Parliament,* nor enjoyed by the *People.* If a *Parliament* will produce such or such effects, it must become such or such a cause as is proper to produce those effects, (and operate like that cause) otherwise it will be impossible.

There is one thing more I desire to mention, of no small importance, (with the same freedom which I have used hitherto) which hath been acted publiquely in the sight of the world, and will one day be examined more publiquely. That which is well done will endure a review; and that which is ill done doth deserve a review, that it might be amended: yea that which is of very great consequence may in equity require a review.

The thing is this, that there might be a Revisal of this present *Government* (whether by this present Parliament, or an ensuing, or by both, I determine not) wherein it might be taken into full consideration (more full perhaps than that present *exigence* of affairs, when it was first pitched upon, would permit); First, the *necessity* of a change; and secondly, the *commodiousness* of this change, or certainty of *advantage* by this change: for changes are never good but when they are necessary, and when the change is certainly, or at least very probably, for the better. Now as there is at some times *need* of a *change*, so there is at other times an *itching humour* in man after change, when there is no need: yet a man who hath a mind to change, will take it for granted that there is a need of change, and run greedily into it though he suffer loss thereby, changing for that which is ten times worse, even in that very respect, because of which he changeth, only his eye being blinded by his present desire and interest, he cannot discern it.

There ought to be much *circumspection* in all weighty changes: This, being the most weighty and of most concernment to the people, deserves the greater wariness and the more thorow scanning. It doth not become *wise men* to take a prejudice against a thing because they have smarted by it, or to conceive well of another thing because it is *different* from that, or because it appeareth *plausible* at first view, or because they have not yet had experience of the *incommodiousness, evil* or *danger* of it; but narrowly to pierce into the *ground* and *nature* of things, and from a clear sight thereof to bottom their change.

In changing either *Governments* or *Governors*, it is very incident to man to be unjust. Man ordinarily doth that unjustly which is just to be done. Because of his sense of smart, he is become an *enemy* (and so far an unfit Judg) to that and them which he smarted by; and can very hardly afford them a fair hearing of what they can say for themselves. Yet this is the due of everything which is laid aside. And for my part, though I shall not plead for the resettlement of *Kingly Government* (for I am not so far engaged in my affections to it, as it yet hath been) yet I would have a fair and friendly shaking hands with it, and not any blame laid upon it beyond its desert: For doubtless it is both *proper, good* and *useful* in its kinde, and hath its *advantages* above any other *Government* on the one hand, as it hath also its *disadvantages* on the other hand.

Now since I have waded thus far herein, I will proceed a little further, propounding what way I should judg most convenient for myself to take, if I were to have an hand in this particular, so as I might discharge it with most *Justice* in reference to the thing itself, and with most *satisfaction* in reference to my own spirit. (Every man must be master of what he doth in his own Understanding, or he cannot act justly; and his heart is poor and weak, if it can be satisfied in managing things beyond his strength.)

In the first place (supposing I had Power) I would require such *learned Lawyers,* as I should judg most fit, to give me a plain and full description of *Kingly Government;* of the *Duty, Power, Prerogatives* of it, with all the *several bounds* of it, according to the *Laws* of this *Land.*

Secondly, I would consider, whether any of these were *defective;* and particularly since the *Prerogative part* was so encroaching, what *bonds* might be laid upon it for the future, and how far they might be able to bind it fast from intrenching upon the *Rights* and *Liberties* of the People.

Thirdly, I would consider, what *security* or *certainty* might be had of a setled course of *Parliaments* in fitting seasons and with sufficient Power for remedying any grievances which might arise to the People from this *Government,* or from any *Governors* which might be employed in it: for in every *Government* there are (besides the Supreme) *Sub-governors,* who are usually the greatest Oppressors.

Having done this, fully and fairly, to the satisfaction (not of my *will* or *desire,* but) of my *understanding unbiassed;* I would as fairly propound, to my view, the other *Government,* which might seem fit to succeed in the stead of this. I would take a full draught of it; the *Duty, Power, Prerogatives* (for such it ought to have; its work being hard, in equity it should have priviledges to sweeten it) and *several limits* of it. I would consider again and again, how it could be bound faster than the other: How the *Convention* and *Session* of *Parliaments* in season, with full *Power and Freedom,* might be more certain under this. And after full and thorow consideration of everything needful to be considered, if it did indeed appear that *Errors* in the former kind of *Government* could not safely or easily be amended, nor the *dangers* thereof well prevented, but might with much more safety and ease be both amended and prevented in the latter; then would I abolish the former, and settle the latter.

This, in my apprehension, would be a fair and just way, and would not expose me to drink in *prejudices* (which become not a *Judg*) against the *Government* which is to be called into question; or to lay that as a particular *Objection* to it, which other Governments are as liable unto. *Neglecting of Duty, grasping of extraordinary Power, enlarging of Priviledges and Prerogatives, trampling upon them that are low, that are as it were the earth under them, riding in pomp upon the backs of the People, &c.* these are common to every *Government,* and will be growing up under every *Government* further than they are powerfully suppressed. As for that great Objection of the enmity of *Kingly Government* to *Parliaments,* any other Government may be as liable to it. No ordinary supreme Power loveth an extraordinary supreme Power; and what Power soever be set up, it will go neer (if much care be not used to prevent it) to have an influence upon the choice of *Parliament* men, and will be molding the *Parliament* to itself, which if it cannot do, it will hardly look upon it as its friend. I must confess the changing of the form of *Government* is not so considerable in my eye, but the fixing of so strong and safe bounds and limits, as a good Governor or Governors may delight to keep within, and a bad or bad ones may not be able to break through: which may be much helped by the frequent use of *Parliaments,* if they can be kept within their bounds, or else that will be worst of all according to that known Maxim, *Corruptio optimi pessima,* the best thing being corrupted proveth worst.

When this is done (for I do not look upon it as yet done, till all reviews, which in reason and equity can be desired, are first over) and *the supreme Governor* or *Governors* fully agreed upon: then it will be seasonable, just and requisite to restore to them those *Rights* and *Priviledges* which belong unto them, and which it is the minde of the

People they should have: as particularly his or their *consent* in making *Laws*. It is great reason the People should make their own Laws; and it is as agreeable to Reason, that he who is to govern by them should consent unto them. As the People (so far as they understand themselves) cannot but be unwilling to be made slaves by their *Governor*, to be governed by such *Laws* as he should make at his pleasure: so neither should they desire to make him a slave, by putting what *Laws* they please into his hand, requiring him to take care of the observation of them: but a mutual agreement & transaction in things of this nature is fairest and most just. Yea this would be most advantagious to the people, for he who constantly weilds the *Scepter* is in likelihood best able to give advice concerning *Laws*, and may put them into a better way (by vertue of his *experience*) of attaining their *ends* and *desires* than they of themselves can light upon. If *the chief Governor* or *Governors* shall refuse to assent to such *Laws* as are evidently good and necessary, a better remedy may be found out than the depriving of him from this Liberty. The true way of curing is difficult, requiring much *skill, care* and *pains;* the common way of man is by running out of one *extream* into another, which he is apt to please himself much in, because he observeth himself at such a distance from that which he found so inconvenient and perhaps so mischievous before. But this is neither just in itself, nor can prove either easie or safe in the issue.

To draw to a *conclusion;* I shall only mention some few *properties of a good Governor,* to which the people should have respect in their choice, and to which he who is chosen by the People to that degree and honor, should have respect in his acting.

There are two *properties* or *proper ways of motion* (which contain in them several properties) of a good *Governor*, which, if he will be furnished unto, will make him very useful and serviceable in his place.

1. To manage his *Trust* with all *care* and *fidelity*. To neglect him-

self, his own particular *ease, pleasure, advantage;* and apply himself to the *good* of the whole. To minister *Justice* equally, fairly, freely, speedily; and *mercy* tenderly. To punish meerly for necessity sake, but to relieve from his heart.

2. To settle the *Foundations* (so far as lies in his way and within his reach) of the *People's Liberty, Peace* and *Welfare,* that it may be in a thriving condition growing still more and more. For the welfare of the People doth not so much consist in a quiet, prosperous, setled state at present, as in a good seed for future growth, whereby alone the Government can come to yeeld the good fruit of a present good setling. It may cost much at present to manure the ground and plant a good Government, the benefit is to be reaped afterwards, which will lie much in the *Governor,* who may help much to cherish or blast it.

The main thing in a *Governor* (which will fit him unto both these) is to keep within his bounds: Not to think or undertake to do all the good which is needful to be done, but that good which belongs to his place and office: Not to avoid bonds, but to desire to be bound as fast as may be. He who is indeed unwilling to *transgress, to do evil;* is willing to be tied up, as fast and close as can be, from all *temptations* and *advantages* thereunto. Good honest plain-dealing-hearts are too apt to desire scope, thinking only to improve it for good; and others are too apt to trust them, little suspecting that they will do otherwise, till at length on a sudden so evident snares and temptations overtake them, as give too plain a proof of the contrary. This *experience* is so deep, that it may well be questioned, *Whether it were better to have a bad Governor being fast bound, or a good Governor being at liberty;* which would be very difficult to resolve, because on the one hand it is so hard to finde bonds to binde a bad Governor fast enough, and so difficult on the other hand for a good Governor being left at liberty, to act well. He who hath had experience what he is, when he is left *at liberty,* and what others are when they are left *at liberty* (how easily his or their *Judgment, Will* and *Affections* are perverted) will neither desire to be left at liberty himself, nor to have others left at liberty. A good *Governor* might do great service in this respect, namely both by a ready compliance with his bonds (for the good and necessary use of them) which is very rare; as also by seeking further bonds, where he can discover starting holes, which is yet more rare.

Man naturally seeketh *liberty from bonds*, desireth to avoid them: He would binde others, but be without bonds himself. Others need bonds, but he can act well without them, yea he can do more good without them than with them. They may be a fit *curb* for others, but they will be but a *clog* to him in the pursuit of the people's happiness, whereby he shall be hindered from doing that good service which he would and otherwise might. Thus the best men, many times, come to do most hurt, least suspecting themselves, and being least mistrusted by others. (Who would not beleeve his own heart, that if he were in place and Power he would not do thus or thus, but amend this and that and the other thing; and the more scope he had, the better and more swiftly would he do it?) But to seek *bonds*, to desire to be hedged up from everything that is *unlawful* or *unfit*; to seek where one might evade and prepare before-hand *strength* to resist it, *engines* to oppose and keep it back, this is as unusual an undertaking in *Governors*, as needful and profitable for the people.

There would one great *advantage* from this arrive unto *Posterity*, besides that which the People themselves might enjoy under it at present: for it would make the fruit of a good GOVERNOR'S Government extend itself to future *Generations*, in this respect, because by this means there would be bonds prepared to tie up such as should afterwards succeed, who might be more inclinable to break forth into unjust and by-ways, than a present Governor or Governors. There are none who have such advantage to espy starting-holes, as those who are penned up: and if they be careful in espying and faithful in stopping up those holes (by putting the *Parliament* upon setting such fences of Laws so made about them, as may best secure the People in this respect) the *Administration* will soon prove both regular and safe, as also in a thriving condition, in so much as that the *Liberty, Safety,* and *sound Prosperity* of the People will grow more and more upon them.

FINIS.

The "After Game"

[Sir Roger L'Estrange, 1616–1704]

A *Plea* for limited

MONARCHY,

As it was Established in this

NATION,

Before the late W A R .

In an Humble Addresse to his Excellency,

General MONCK.

By a Zealot for the Good Old Laws of his Country, before any
Faction or Caprice, with Additions.

Optima Libertas, ubi Rex, cum Lege, Gubernat.

LONDON,
Printed by *T. Mabb,* for *William Shears* in *Bedford* street, neer *Coven-
Garden,* at the *Blew Bible,* 1660.

*A*uthorship of this tract has been attributed to Roger L'Estrange, an ardent royalist and prolific pamphleteer. In 1639 L'Estrange accompanied Charles I and his army to war in Scotland. With the outbreak of the civil war his father served as royalist governor of Lynn. After that city fell to Parliament Roger moved to Oxford where he became active in the royalist army, serving in Prince Rupert's cavalry troop. He was anxious that Lynn be retaken but a plot he devised to seize the city was betrayed. L'Estrange was captured and sentenced to death. The Commons reprieved him and, if he had agreed to take the Solemn League and Covenant, would even have pardoned him. However, L'Estrange brashly declined the offer of a pardon. He was kept prisoner in Newgate until he managed to escape in the spring of 1648. He fled to Kent where he plunged into planning an uprising in that county. When the plan failed L'Estrange fled to Holland. Seven years later he returned to England to face an act of indemnity and was released upon payment of a substantial fine.

L'Estrange was a busy pamphleteer, writing from his cell in Newgate about his misfortunes and in 1659 publishing a series of anonymous broadsides attacking the leaders of the army. These last were republished after the Restoration under his name.

His "Plea for a Limited Monarchy" appeared on 20 February 1660 little more than two weeks after George Monck and his troops entered London. It was specifically addressed to Monck. In it L'Estrange pleads eloquently for a return to the traditional constitution of England, which he describes in language reminiscent of the early seventeenth century. The tract appeared in two editions and mirrored the sentiments and nostalgia of Englishmen for their old, limited monarchy.

Ironically, the measured government he praises in this tract was at odds with his own intolerance in his official role after the Restoration. L'Estrange was placed in charge of the new regime's censorship which he administered with extreme rigor. He led a great assault on freedom of the press, silencing all opposition while continuing to publish furiously himself. In his tracts he blamed the civil war on the Presbyterians whom he branded as inveterate rebels. He has been described during this period as the greatest of Tory pamphleteers—prolific, unscrupulous, and deaf to ridicule.

A Plea for Limited Monarchy, as It Was Established in This Nation Before the Late War.
In an humble Address to his Excellency, General Monck.

SIR,

Finding, by several Letters, published in Your Name, that you professe a more than ordinary zeal to popular Government; and not knowing anything herein, that can so mislead you, but the glorious pretence of a Free State (a notion, which hath, even, intoxicated many; otherwise, great and worthy Persons); I held it my Duty, first, to acquaint you, how necessary it is to distinguish betwixt the Form and Essence of a Common-wealth, the mistake whereof (each for the other) hath proved so fatall in our times. Next to examine, whether those that surfeited of our Kingly Government, and longed for Novelty have not, indeed (like the Dog in the Fable) lost the substance of Liberty and happinesse, in pursuit of the shadow.

Our fierce Champions of a free State will not, I presume, maintain, that it is subject to no violations, least wofull experience confute, and force them to confesse, either that a Common-wealth may degenerate; or, at least, that this never was a Commonwealth. And, as they must renounce their senses, so they must deny the Faith of Story, which proves, that Republicks have been sometimes invaded with Usurpation, sometimes Debauched, and Embased with Oligarchy; mostly (by reason of their weaknesse, and divisions) subdued, or forced to truckle under their neighbouring Princes, always tormented with faction. Neither, indeed do they, themselves offer any argument but such, as, in effect, beg the question, by presupposing great unity in the Coalition, great probity in the Intention, and great purity in the Exercise; which doubtlesse, being admitted, we should so little need to differ about Forms, that perhaps, we should scarce need any Government at all. The stoutest assertors of Monarchy, likewise, must acknowledg, That it, being but earthen ware, (though the finest and strongest) is subject to divers accidents; For nothing under heaven is perfect. And when we constitute Governments, we must not think to build Babels against the Deluge, but embank against floods and enclose the best we can against Trespassours. This being premised, let us consider these two Governments, not Metaphysically, in notions, abstracted from their subjects, (a pastime, which our Platonicks much delight in) but morally and reasonably, as concrete, & adapted to times, places, and persons, *viz.* our own.

I might, perhaps decide the question, in few words, by alledging the manifest inclination of the whole people, now to Monarchy; For, *As no man can be wronged with his consent, so neither is any to be obliged against his will*, and how should a Government founded upon inequality and force, ever subsist without it? Or a State, which is the meer Adjective of an Army, become a Substantive; beginnings of this kinde being so ominous? As reasonably might I object matter of Title, and foreign pretence; For the same estate, with a flaw in the Conveyance, or clogged with Statutes and Judgements, is not, surely, of like value, as if it had descended clearly from the great Grandfather, and were free both from Claimes and Incumbrances; and one that hath little, yet owes nothing, is likelier to thrive than he, who owing vast sums (which he resolves never to pay) dares not walk the streets for fear of Serjeants. But my intent, is only, to shew, that, our former Government (as it excellently complied with the Laws Genius, & Interest of this Nation) so it comprehended all the benefits of a Common-wealth, in great perfection. And this I shall doe, as briefly, as I can.

To shew how it complied with our Laws and Constitutions, let it suffice that (Monarchy in these Nations, being more ancient than story or record, more Venerable than Tradition itself) our Laws were (as it were) under that Climate, habituated to that air and diet, grafted into that stock; and though they have (God be thanked) forgot their *Norman,* yet they will hardly learn *Greek,* much lesse *Utopian.* That, in the late Protectour's times, our Lawyers with one voice, importuned him, rather to assume the style and power of a King, to which, they found all our Laws were shaped, than retain that of a Protectour, unknown to the Law. That nothing hath rendered our Architects of a Common-wealth more obnoxious, than that their infinite discords in other things, generally, agreed in the necessity of subverting all our Fundamentals, in order to their Designe; which hath likewise obliged all sober men, and true Patriots (even the chiefest Pillars of the Parliament's Cause, in the late War) to unite themselves, with the Royall Interest, as not enduring to hear of those violent and dangerous alterations, which they see a Republick must introduce.

For its compliance with our Genius, consider, that as our English nature is not like the French, supple to oppression, and apt to delight in that pompe and magnificence of their Lords, which they know, is supported with their slavery and hunger; Nor like the Highland *Scots,* where the honour and Interest of the Chief is the glory of the whole *Clan;* so doth it, as little or lesse, agree with the *Dutch* humour, ad-dicted only to Traffick, Navigation, Handy-crafts, and sordid Thrift; and (in defiance of Herauldry) every man fancying his own Scutcheon. Doth not every one amongst us, that hath the name of a Gentleman, aim his utmost to uphold it? Every one that hath not, to raise one? To this end, do not our very Yeomen commonly leave their Lands to the eldest Son, and to the others, nothing but a Flail or Plough? Did not every one, that had anything like an estate, pinch himself in his condition, to purchase a knighthood or small Patent? What need further proof? Our late experience of that glimpse and shadow of Monarchy, (though in persons hated, and scorned, and upon a most scandalous account) yet (for meere resemblance) ad-mitted as tolerable, and in respect of a Common-wealth, Courted, clearly evinces, how gratefull the substance would be to Englishmen.

For our Interest, briefly (to waive tedious and politick discourses), certain it is, that our Republick, (were it like to settle) would alarme all our Neighbours, would make our best Allies, our bitterest enemies, and (upon several accounts) probably draw upon us, the united forces of Christendome to crush the *Embrio*. Which (the Nation being so weakened, and divided, as it is), must evidently endanger our totall oppression, or at least, to bring in the King by Conquest. Besides, by what Title shall we pretend to hold *Scotland* and *Ireland*, since that of Descent is now avoided, and Consent we know there is none, nor, indeed, can any be expected?

I come now to assert, that our former Government, eminently, included all the perfections of a Free-State, and was the Kernel, as it were, of a Common-wealth, in the shell of Monarchy. First I will begin with the essentiall parts of a Common-wealth, which are three, *viz.* The Senate proposing, the People Resolving, the Magistrate Executing. For the Senate or Parliament, if, ever there were a free, and honourable one, it was here; where the Deputies of the whole Nation, most freely chosen, did, with like freedome, meet, propound, debate and vote all matters of common Interest. No danger escaped their Representing; no grievance, their complaint; no publick right, their Claim; or good, their Demand; In all which the least breach of Priviledge was branded as a civil sacriledge. And though there lay no Appeal to the dispersed body of the People (a decision manifestly impracticable in Government, and fitter indeed for Tribunes to move, than Nations to admit) yet (Elections being so popular, and Assemblies frequent) the same end was attained with much more safety and convenience. The Prince had, likewise (in effect) but an executive Power, which he exercised by Ministers and Officers, not only sworn, but severely accomptable. For though both he and the Lords had their Negatives in making Laws; yet (no Tax being impossible, but by Consent of the Commons, nor any Law, (without it) of such validity, that the Ministers of Justice durst enforce it); There was a wise and sweet necessity for the King, and likewise for the Lords (who were but as a grain in the Royall Scale) to confirm all such Bills, as were convenient for the People and not greatly hurtfull to the Prince; and so this Bugbear Negative,[1] was resolved into a meer Target, to shelter and preserve the Government from being altered, at the Will of the Commons, if, at any time they should prove Factious: which (being in reason manifest) hath been also confirmed by great experience: Our Kings having, rarely, obstructed any Bill, which they might safely grant; but on the other side, passed many high Acts of meer Grace, circumscribing their Prerogative, and clipping its Wings; nay, I could wish they had not pierced its bowels. This was that triple Cord, which one would think, could not be broken; nor indeed, was it broken, but cut asunder. This was our Gold, seven times refined; for every Bill, being thrice read, debated and agreed, in either House, was at last, brought to the King, for his Royal Assent, the Mint of our Laws. A triall so exact, that surely, no drosse could escape it; since all Interests must thereto concur (as truly, it was but fit they should, in the establishment of that, which must binde them all). This was that Temperament, which poised our Humours, and at once endued us, with health, vigour and beauty. No Vote was precipitated, no act was huddled up; As by sad events, we have since seen, that, Power being engrossed by one of the Estates, purged and modelled to the Interests of a faction; a consequence natural to such premises: (As in a Ballance consisting but of one scale) nothing hath been weighed, our laws have been Mandrakes of a Night's growths, and our times as fickle as the weather or multitude.

The King indeed, had the Power of making War, but he had not the means; And then, it signified no more, than giving him leave to

1. There was considerable debate in the Long Parliament and the Interregnum parliaments over the issue of an executive veto, the so-called "negative voice." See, for example, Charles's comments on the Militia Ordinance in his "Answer to the Nineteen Propositions," 154–55, above.

flye, if he could get wings; or to go beyond Sea, so he went without
shipping. He had a Sword, but he alone could never draw it; for the
Trained Bands were a Weapon, which he (decently) wore, but the
Nation, only, could use. He chose his Ministers, (as who doth not his
servants?) But alas, he was accomptable for them, to the Trienniall
Parliament, which none but the soundest Integrity could abide. He
could hinder the stroke of Justice with his Pardon (though still, the
jaws not being muzzled, it would bite terribly) but certainly, it was
great wisdom, rather to give way; since (with his own scandall) he
could afford offenders but a lame and scurvy Protection; and since
the Power of relieving his Wants rested in the Commons, to ballance
his Will, and oblige him to a Correspondence with Parliaments.

That his Person should be most Sacred, it was but needfull; to
avoid circulation of accompt; reasonable, since it carries with it, the
Consent of Nations; Just, that he should not be the meer But of Faction and Malice, in worse condition, than the basest of Vassals; Honourable, that the nakednesse of Government might not be daily
uncovered; Wise, in the constitution, not at once, to trust and provoke, by forcing him to shift for his own Indemnity, no danger to the
Publick seeming so extream, as the Outlawry of a Prince; no task by
daily experience so difficult, as the arraigning of any Power, whether
Regall or Popular. And since we make golden Bridges, for flying
enemies, much more may we afford them to relenting Soveraignes;
(upon which account, in our neighbour Kingdome of *France,* even
Princes of the blood are not subjected to capitall Punishments). Finally, very safe, in the consequent, for (being (by the danger, threatening his corrupt Ministers) in all probability, stript of Agents) his
personall impunity might, well, signifie somewhat to himself, but
nothing to the People.

A Revenue he had, for the support of his State and Family, ample;
for the ordinary Protection of his People, sufficient; but for any undertaking, defective; and for publick oppression, so inconsiderable,

that when Prerogative was most Rampant, our greatest Princes (and some doubtlesse, we have had, the most renowned Warriours of their Ages) could never prudently aspire to make themselves sole Legislatours, nor presumed to maintain *Red-coats* in times of Peace.[2] If any object, (as some, concerned, are ready enough) that Kingly Power could here, no longer, subsist, for want of Revenew; It is easily answered, That a King of *France,* indeed, could not, and God forbid, he should; but a King of *England* might, and (for ought I see) still may (the sale of Crown Lands, which exceeded not the value of £.100000 *per annum,* being, methinks, no matter of utter ruine, but rather of easie compensation). For the publick Revenue was proportioned to the maintenance of Courts, not Campes and Fleets. A Gentleman of reasonable estate may live well on his Rents; But then, it is not convenient, he should keep Wenches, or hangers on, nor build, nor study Chimistry. In fine, the Revenue was very competent for ordinary disbursements, as for extraordinary, if he resorted to Parliaments, the wiser he, the safer and happier, we.

I desire all our Projectours of Common-wealths, to contrive greater freedom for their Citizens, than is provided by *Magna Charta,* and the *Petition of Right;* Or shew us, that it is not much easier to violate, than to mend them. For, thereby our Lives, Liberties, and estates were, under Monarchy secured, and established, I think, as well as anything, on this side Heaven. It were no soloecisme to say, the Subject had his Prerogative as well, as the King; And sure I am, he was in as good (if not better) condition to maintain it, the dependance being lesse on his side. Liberty was no lesse sacred than Majesty; *Noli me tangere,*[3] was likewise its Motto. And in case of any, the least infringement (as escapes in Government may happen even in the most perfect); It was resented, as if the Nation had received a

---

2. The redcoats referred to are presumably professional soldiers.

3. Touch me not. *Noli me tangere* is the Vulgate translation of the Risen Lord's words to Mary Magdalene after she found the empty tomb and recognized Jesus risen from the dead.

box on the Ear. If it be, as they say, the glory of a Free-State, to exalt, the scandall of Tyranny, to Embase our Spirits; doubtlesse, this was our only Common-wealth: for, ever since, me thinks, we have learned quietly to take the Bastonade.

I wish we now could, or could ever hope, under our Common-wealth (whatever promises may be made us) so perfectly to distinguish the Legislative from the Ministerial Authority, as once we did; when the House of Commons had not the power of a *Court Leet*[4] to give an Oath, nor of a Justice of the Peace, to make a *Mittimus:*[5] Which distinction, doubtlesse, is the most vitall part of Freedome, and far more considerable to poor Subjects, than the pretended Rotation; As on the contrary, the confusion of them is an accomplishment of servitude; For which the best Republicks, I fear, have more to answer, than any limited Prince can have. Certain it is, that as our King in his personall capacity, made no Laws, so neither did he, by himself, execute or interpret any. No Judge took notice of his single Command, to justifie any Trespass; no, not so much, as the breaking of an Hedge; his Power limited by his Justice, he was (equally with the meanest of his Subjects) concerned in that honest Maxime, *We may do just so much and no more, than we have right to do.* And it was most properly said, *He could do no wrong:* because if it were wrong, he did it not, he could not do it; It was void in the act, punishable in his agent. His Officers, as they were alike liable, so perhaps, they were more obnoxious to Indictments and suits, than any other, by how much their trespasse seemed to be of a higher nature, and gave greater alarm. His private Will could not countermand his Publick; his Privy seal, ever buckled to the great Seal, as being the Nation's, more than his; his Order superseded no Processe, and his displeasure threatened no man with an hour's imprisonment, after the return of

4. A court leet was a court of criminal justice.

5. A mittimus is a writ enclosing a record sent to be tried in a county palatine. It commands the county officer to order the sheriff to summon a jury for the trial of the particular cause.

Habeas Corpus. An Under Sheriff was more terrible, a Constable more sawcy, a Bailiff more troublesome than he. And yet, by his gentle Authority, this Scabbard of Prerogative (as some in derision, have called it) which (if it would) could scarce oppresse an Orphan, Tumult was curbed, Faction moderated, Usurpation forestalled, Intervales prevented, Perpetuities obviated, Equity administered, Clemency exalted, and the people made, only nice and wanton with their happinesse, as appears by their (now so impatient) calling for that Mannah, which they so causelessely loathed.

To Conclude, what shall I add? The Act, enjoining the Keepers of the great Seal, under pain of High Treason, to summon a Triennial Parliament, of course, by virtue of the Act without further Warrant; The Act, forbidding the Privy Councel, under like penalty, to intermeddle with *Meum & Tuum*, the Laws abolished the *Star-chamber, High-commission,* &c. branding all past, and bridling all future enormities; the Statutes limiting the King's Claimes, and relieving his Tenants from exaction of Forfeitures; Besides many other principal immunities, wherewith (by the speciall favour of God, and bounty of our Princes) we were blessed, farr beyond any of our Neighbours. Above all, our assurance, that we might readily, have obtained such further addition and perfection of Liberty (if, yet, any such, there were) as would consist with modesty, or liberty itself to ask. Do they not, aloud, proclaim, that we were then, the mirrour of Governments, envy of Monarchies, and shame of Commonwealths; who could not but blush, to see themselves so ecclipsed and silenced, in all their pretences to Freedome? Do they not more than justifie my Assertion, *That with all the Ornaments of the noblest Kingdome, we had likewise, all the enjoyments of the Freest State.*

FINIS.

J. M. [John Milton, 1608–1674]

THE
READIE & EASIE

WAY

TO

ESTABLISH

A

Free Commonwealth,

AND

The EXCELLENCE therof

Compar'd with

The inconveniences and dangers of
readmitting kingship in this nation.

The author J. M.

LONDON,
Printed by *T. N.* and are to be sold by *Livewell Chapman*
at the Crown in Popes-Head Alley. 1660.

The best-known defender of the Commonwealth government was also one of England's greatest men of letters, the poet and writer John Milton. "The Readie & Easie Way" is his desperate plea for the continuation of republican government in the face of mounting sentiment for the restoration of monarchy. While Milton has been honored for his poetry and for other prose works, this heartfelt piece, probably the boldest and most passionate essay he ever wrote, has been passed over by scholars in favor of the longer, more measured second edition. The splendid first edition is reprinted here for the first time in eighty years.

Milton's career was an odd one for a staunch republican. He became disaffected from the Laudian church as a student of Christ's College, Cambridge. After university he devoted himself to literature and entered the political fray with contributions to the pamphlet debate over episcopacy. When the civil war broke out he shied away from military service and remained in London teaching pupils whom he took into his home. In 1643 he married the daughter of a royalist. He clashed with Presbyterian members of Parliament in 1643 over his controversial tract on divorce and again the following year when he took issue with Parliament's controls on the press in his famous tract, "Areopagitica." Perhaps it is not surprising that Milton sympathized with the New Model Army's purge of the Presbyterian members of Parliament in 1648. After the execution of the king he wrote in defense of the people's right to judge their rulers. The new Council of State invited him to become their Latin secretary. He accepted, and despite his growing blindness he continued to hold this post through the protectorates of Oliver Cromwell and his son Richard. He also continued writing political tracts including, at the request of the government, a response to the Eikon Basilike, the best-selling book supposedly written by Charles I.

Milton's growing disenchantment with the governments of the 1650s and the collapse of Richard Cromwell's regime failed to shake his faith in republican government. Shortly after the arrival in London of General George Monck and his army on 3 February 1660 Milton composed "The Readie & Easie Way." Milton feared that Monck and the Rump might agree to an election with few restrictions on who voted or stood for office. Such an election would almost surely produce a majority of members keen to restore Charles II. "The Readie & Easie Way" was a frantic appeal to Monck, the Rump, and the English people to resist the overwhelming sentiment for a return to monarchy. In it Milton acknowledges past problems with the republican experiments and makes various suggestions for reform.

The tract was published on 3 March 1660, but the essay may have been composed as early as 22 February. Political events overtook the tract, and Milton composed another version, softening his tone and adding additional sections. This second edition appeared in early April. It was all to no avail. On 21 April Monck invited former members of the Long Parliament to resume their seats. With their support a monarchist Council of State was created with authority to invite Charles II to return. Many of Milton's warnings about the repercussions of the reestablishment of the monarchy would come to pass. Milton himself narrowly escaped execution. In his bitterness, pain, and blindness he would create what some consider to be the greatest epic poem in the English language, Paradise Lost.

Although since the writing of this treatise, the face of things hath had some change, writs for new elections have been recalled, and the members at first chosen, readmitted from exclusion, to sit again in Parliament, yet not a little rejoicing to hear declared, the resolutions of all those who are now in power, jointly tending to the establishment of a free Commonwealth, and to remove if it be possible, this unsound humour of returning to old bondage, instilled of late by some cunning deceivers, and nourished from bad principles and false apprehensions among too many of the people, I thought best not to suppress what I had written, hoping it may perhaps (the Parliament now sitting more full and frequent) be now much more useful than before: yet submitting what hath reference to the state of things as they then stood, to present constitutions; and so the same end be persued, not insisting on this or that means to obtain it. The treatise was thus written as follows.

The Parliament of *England* assisted by a great number of the people who appeared and stuck to them faithfullest in the defence of religion and their civil liberties, judging kingship by long experience a government burdensom, expensive, useless and dangerous, justly and magnanimously abolished it; turning regal-bondage into a free Commonwealth, to the admiration and terror of our neighbours, and the stirring up of *France* itself,[1] especially in *Paris* and *Bourdeaux,* to our imitation. Nor were our actions less both at home and abroad than might become the hopes of a glorious rising Commonwealth; nor were the expressions both of the Army and of the People, whether in their publick declarations or several writings, other than such as testified a spirit in this nation no less noble and well fitted to the liberty of a Commonwealth, than in the ancient Greeks or Romans.

1. Milton is referring to the uprising against the French Crown from 1648 to 1653 known as the Fronde.

After our liberty thus succesfully fought for, gained and many years possessed, except in those unhappie interruptions, which God hath removed, and wonderfully now the third time brought together our old Patriots, the first Assertours of our religious and civil rights, now that nothing remains but in all reason the certain hopes of a speedy and immediate settlement to this nation forever in a firm and free Commonwealth, to fall back, or rather to creep back so poorly as it seems the multitude would, to their once abjured and detested thral-dom of kingship, not only argues a strange degenerate corruption suddenly spread among us, fitted and prepared for new slaverie, but will render us a scorn and derision to all our neighbours. And what will they say of us, but scoffingly as of that foolish builder mentioned by our Saviour, who began to build a Tower, and was not able to finish it: where is this goodly tower of a Common-wealth which the *English* boasted they would build, to overshaddow kings and be another *Rome* in the west? The foundation indeed they laid gallantly, but fell into a worse confusion, not of tongues, but of factions, than those at the tower of *Babel;* and have left no memorial of their work behinde them remaining, but in the common laughter of *Europ,* Which must needs redound the more to our shame, if we but look on our neighbours the United Provinces, to us inferiour in all outward advantages: who notwithstanding, in the midst of greater difficulties, coura-giously, wisely, constantly went through with the same work, and are settled in all the happie injoyments of a potent and flourishing Re-publick to this day.

Besides this, if we return to kingship, and soon repent, as un-doubtedly we shall, when we begin to finde the old incroachments coming on by little and little upon our consciences, which must nec-essarily proceed from king and bishop united inseparably in one in-terest, we may be forced perhaps to fight over again all that we have fought, and spend over again all that we have spent, but are never like to attain thus far as we are now advanced, to the recoverie of our freedom, never likely to have it in possession, as we now have it, never to be vouchsafed heerafter the like mercies and signal assistances from heaven in our cause, if by our ingratefull backsliding we make these fruitless to ourselves, all his gratious condescensions and answers to our once importuning prayers against the tyrannie which we then groaned under to become now of no effect, by returning of our own foolish accord, nay running headlong again with full stream wilfully and obstinately into the same bondage: making vain and viler than dirt the blood of so many thousand faithfull and valiant English men, who left us in this libertie, bought with their lives; losing by a strange aftergame of folly, all the battels we have wonne, all the treasure we have spent, not that corruptible treasure only, but that far more precious of all our late miraculous deliverances; and most pittifully depriving ourselves the instant fruition of that free government which we have so dearly purchased, a free Commonwealth, not only held by wisest men in all ages the noblest, the manliest, the equallest, the justest government, the most agreeable to all due libertie and proportioned equalitie, both human, civil and Christian, most cherishing to vertue and true religion, but also (I may say it with greatest probabilitie) planely commended or rather enjoined by our Saviour himself, to all Christians, not without remarkable disallowance and the brand of *Gentilism* upon kingship. God in much displeasure gave a king to the *Israelites*, and imputed it a sin to them that they sought one: but Christ apparently forbids his disciples to admitt of any such heathenish government: *the kings of the gentiles*, saith he, *exercise lordship over them; and they that exercise authoritie upon them, are called benefactors. But ye shall not be so: but he that is greatest among you, let him be as the younger; and he that is chief, as he that serveth.* The occasion of these his words, was the ambitious desire of *Zebede's* two sons to be exalted above their brethren in his kingdom, which they thought was to be ere long upon earth. That he speaks of civil government, is manifest by the former part of the comparison, which inferrs the other part to be always in the same kinde. And what government comes neerer to this precept of Christ, than a free Commonwealth; wherein they who are greatest, are perpetual servants and drudges to the publick at their own cost and charges, neglect their own affairs; yet are not elevated above their brethren, live soberly in their families, walk the streets as other men, may be spoken to freely, familiarly, friendly, without adoration. Whereas a king must be adored like a Demigod, with a dissolute and haughtie court about him, of vast expence and luxurie, masks and revels, to the debaushing of our prime gentry both male and female; nor at his own cost, but on the publick revenue; and all this to do nothing but bestow the eating and drinking of excessive dainties, to set a pompous face upon the superficial actings of State, to pageant himself up and down in progress among the perpetual bowings and cringings of an abject people, on either side deifying and adoring him who for the most part deserves none of this by any good done to the people (for what can he more than another man?) but even in the expression of a late court-Poet, sits only like a great cypher set to no purpose before a long row of other significant figures. Nay it is well and happy for the people if their king be but a cypher, being oft times a mischief, a pest, a scourge of the nation, and which is worse, not to be removed, not to be controuled, much less accused or brought to punishment, without the danger of a common ruin, without the shaking and almost subversion of the whole land. Whereas in a free Commonwealth, any governour or chief counselour offending, may be removed and punished, without the least commotion. Certainly then that people must needs be madd or strangely infatuated, that build the chief hope of their common happiness or safetie on a single person; who if he happen to be good, can do no more than another man, if to be bad, hath in his hands to do more evil without check, than millions of other men. The happiness of a nation must needs be firmest and certainest in a full and free Councel of their own electing, where no single person, but reason only swayes. And what madness is it, for them who might manage nobly their own affairs themselves, sluggishly and weakly to devolve all on a single person; and more like boyes under age than men, to committ all to his patronage and disposal, who neither can perform what he undertakes, and yet for undertaking it, though royally paid, will not be their servant, but their lord? How unmanly must it needs be, to count such a one the breath of our nostrils, to hang all our felicitie on him, all our safety, our well-being, for which if we were aught else but sluggards or babies, we need depend on none but God and our own counsels, our own active vertue and industrie. *Go to the Ant, thou sluggard,* saith Solomon, *consider her ways, and be wise; which having no prince, ruler, or lord, provides her meat in the summer, and gathers her food in the harvest.* Which evidently shews us, that they who think the nation undone without a king, though they swell and look haughtie, have not so much true spirit and understanding in them as a Pismire. It may be well wondered that any nation, styling themselves free, can suffer any man to pretend right over them as their lord; whenas by acknowledging that right, they conclude themselves as his servants and his vassals, and so renounce their own freedom. Which how a people can do, that hath fought so gloriously for libertie, how they can change their noble words and actions heretofore so becoming the majestie of a free people, into the base necessitie of court-flatteries and prostrations, is not only strange and admirable, but lamentable to think on; that a nation should be so valorous and courageous to winne their libertie in the field, and when they have won it, should be so unwise in their counsels, as not to know how to value it, what to do with it, or with themselves; but after ten or twelve years prosperous war and contestation with tyrannie, basely and besottedly to run their necks again into the yoke which they have broken, and prostrate all the fruits of their victorie for nothing at the feet of the vanquished, besides our loss of glorie, will be an ignominie, if it befall us, that never yet befell any nation possessed of their libertie. Worthie indeed themselves, whosoever they be, to be forever slaves; but that part of the nation which consents not with them, as I perswade me of a great number, far worthier than by their means to be brought into the same bondage, and reserved, I trust, by Divine providence to a better end; since God hath yet his remnant, and hath not yet quenched the spirit of libertie among us. Considering these things, so plane, so rational, I cannot but yet further admire on the other side, how any man who hath the true principles of justice and religion in him, can presume or take upon him to be a king and lord over his brethren, whom he cannot but know, whether as men or Christians, to be for the most part every way equal or superiour to himself: how he can display with such vanitie and ostentation his regal splendour so supereminently above other mortal men; or, being a Christian, can assume such extraordinarie honour and worship to himself, while the kingdom of Christ, our common King and Lord, is hid to this world, and such *Gentilish* imitation forbid in express words by himself to all his disciples? All Protestants hold, that Christ in his Church hath left no viceregent of his kingly power, but himself without deputy, is the only head thereof, governing it from heaven. How then can any Christian man derive his kingship from Christ, but with worse usurpation than the Pope his headship over the Church, since Christ not only hath not left the least shadow of a command for any such viceregence from him in the State, as the Pope pretends for his in the Church, but hath expressly declared that such regal dominion is from the gentiles, not from him, and hath strictly charged us, not to imitate them therein?

I doubt not but all ingenuous and knowing men will easily agree with me, that a free Commonwealth without single person or house of lords, is by far the best government, if it can be had; but we have all this while, say they, been expecting it, and cannot yet attain it. I answer, that the cause thereof may be ascribed with most reason to the frequent disturbances, interruptions and dissolutions which the Parliament hath had partly from the impatient or disaffected people, partly from some ambitious leaders in the armie; much contrarie, I believe, to the mind and approbation of the Armie itself and their other Commanders, when they were once undeceived, or in their own power. Neither ought the small number of those remaining in Parliament, be made a by-word of reproach to them, as it is of late by the rable, whenas rather they should be therefor honoured, as the remainder of those faithfull worthies, who at first freed us from tyrannie, and have continued ever since through all changes constant to their trust; which they have declared, as they may most justly and truly, that no other way they can discharge, no other way secure and confirme the people's libertie, but by setling them in a free Commonwealth. And doubtless no Parliament will be ever able under roy-altie to free the people from slavery: and when they go about it, will finde it a laborious task; and when they have done all, they can, be forced to leave the contest endless between prerogative and petition of right, till only dooms-day end it. And now is the opportunitie, now the very season wherein we may obtain a free Commonwealth, and establish it forever in the land, without difficulty or much delay. The Parliament have voted to fill up their number: and if the people, lay-ing aside prejudice and impatience, will seriously and calmly now consider their own good, their own libertie and the only means thereof, as shall be heer laid before them, and will elect their Knights and Burgesses able men; and according to the just and necessarie qualifications decreed in Parliament, men not addicted to a single person or house of lords, the work is done; at least the foundation is firmly laid of a free Commonwealth, and good part also erected of the main structure. For the ground and basis of every just and free government (since men have smarted so oft for committing all to one person) is a general Councel of ablest men, chosen by the people to consult of publick affairs from time to time for the common good. This Grand Councel must have the forces by sea and land in their power, must raise and mannage the Publick revenue, make lawes, as need requires, treat of commerce, peace, or war with forein nations; and for the carrying on some particular affairs of State with more secrecie and expedition, must elect, as they have already out of their own number and others, a Councel of State. And although it may seem strange at first hearing, by reason that men's mindes are prepossessed with the conceit of successive Parliaments, I affirm that the Grand or General Councel being well chosen, should sit perpetual: for so their business is, and they will become thereby skillfullest, best acquainted with the people, and the people with them. The ship of the Commonwealth is always under-sail; they sit at the stern; and if they stear well, what need is there to change them; it being rather dangerous? Adde to this, that the Grand Councel is both foundation and main pillar of the whole State; and to move pillars and foundations, unless they be faultie, cannot be safe for the building. I see not therefore how we can be advantaged by successive Parliaments; but that they are much likelier continually to unsettle rather than to settle a free government, to breed commotions, changes, novelties and uncertainties; and serve only to satisfie the ambition of such men, as think themselves injured, and cannot stay till they be orderly chosen to have their part in the government. If the ambition of such be at all to be regarded, the best expedient will be, and with least danger, that everie two or three years a hundred or some such number may go out by lot or suffrage of the rest, and the like number be chosen in their places; (which hath been already thought on heer, and done in other Commonwealths): but in my opinion better nothing moved, unless by death or just accusation. And I shall make mention of another way to satisfie such as are reasonable, ere I end this discourse. And least this be thought my single opinion, I shall adde sufficient testimonie. Kingship itself is therefore counted the more safe and durable, because the king and for the most part, his Councel, is not changed during life: but a Commonwealth is held immortal; and therein firmest, safest and most above fortune; for that the death of a king, causeth oft-times many dangerous alterations; but the death now and then of a Senator is not felt; the main body of them still continuing unchanged in greatest and noblest Commonwealths, and as it were eternal. Therefore among the Jews, the supream Councel of seaventie, called the *Sanhedrin*, founded by *Moses*, in *Athens* that the *Areopagus*, in *Lacedaemon* that of the Ancients, in *Rome* the Senat, consisted of members chosen for term of life; and by that means remained still the same to generations. In *Venice* they change indeed ofter than everie year some particular councels of State, as that of six, or such others; but the full Senate, which upholds and sustains the government, sits immovable. So in the United Provinces, the States General, which are indeed but a Councel of State delegated by the whole union, are not usually the same persons for above three or six years; but the Provincial States, in whom the true sovrantie is placed, are a standing Senate, without succession, and accounted chiefly in that regard the main prop of their libertie. And why they should be so in everie well ordered Commonwealth, they who write of policie, give these reasons; "That to make the whole Senate successive, not only impairs the dignitie and lustre of the Senate, but weakens the whole Commonwealth, and brings it into manifest danger; while by this means the secrets of State are frequently divulged, and matters of greatest consequence committed to inexpert and novice counselors, utterly to seek in the full and intimate knowledg of affairs past." I know not therefor what should be peculiar in *England* to make successive Parliaments thought safest, or convenient heer more than in all other nations, unlesse it be the fickelness which is attributed to us as we are Islanders. But good education and acquisite wisdom ought to correct the fluxible fault, if any such be, of our watrie situation. I suppose therefor that the people well weighing these things, would have no cause to fear or murmur, though the Parliament, abolishing that name, as originally signifying but the *parlie* of our Commons with their *Norman* king when he pleased to call them, should perpetuate themselves, if their ends be faithfull and for a free Commonwealth, under the name of a Grand or General Councel. Nay till this be done, I am in doubt whether our State will be ever certainlie and throughly settled: and say again therefor, that if the Parliament do this, these nations will have so little cause to fear or suspect them, that they will have cause rather to gratulate and thank them: nay more, if they understand their own good rightly, will sollicit and entreat them not to throw off the great burden from their shoulders which none are abler to bear, and to sit perpetual; never likely till then to see an end of their troubles and continual changes, or at least never the true settlement and assurance of their libertie. And the government being now in so many faithful and experienced hands, next under God, so able, especially filling up their number, as they intend, and abundantly sufficient so happily to govern us, why should the nation so little know their own interest as to seek change, and deliver themselves up to meer titles and vanities, to persons untried, unknown, necessitous, implacable, and every way to be suspected: to whose power when we are once made subject, not all these our Patriots nor all the wisdom or force of the well affected joined with them can deliver us again from most certain miserie and thraldom. To return then to this most easie, most present and only cure of our distempers, the Grand Councel being thus firmly constituted to perpetuitie, and still, upon the death or default of any member, supplied and kept in full number, there can be no cause alleaged why peace, justice, plentiful trade and all prospertie should not thereupon ensue throughout the whole land; with as much assurance as can be of human things, that they shall so continue (if God favour us, and our willfull sins provoke him not) even to the coming of our true and rightfull and only to be expected King, only worthy as he is our only Saviour, the Messiah, the Christ, the only heir of his eternal father, the only by him anointed and ordained, since the worke of our re-

demtion finished, universal Lord of all mankind. The way propounded is plain, easie and open before us; without intricases, without the mixture of inconveniencies, or any considerable object to be
made, as by some friviously, that it is not practicable: and this facili-
tie we shall have above our next neighbouring Commonwealth, (if
we can keep us from the fond conceit of somthing like a duke of
Venice, put lately into many men's heads, by some one or other subtly
driving on under that prettie notion his own ambitious ends to a
crown) that our liberty shall not be hampered or hovered over by any
ingagement to such a potent family as the house of *Nassaw*,[2] of whom
to stand in perpetual doubt and suspicion, but we shall live the cleer-
est and absolutest free nation in the world. On the contrarie, if there
be a king, which the inconsiderate multitude are now so madd upon,
marke how far short we are like to come of all those happinesses,
which in a free State we shall immediately be possessed of. First, the
Grand Councel, which, as I said before, is both the basis and main
pillar in everie government, and should sit perpetually, (unless their
leisure give them now and then some intermissions or vacations eas-
ilie manageable by the Councel of State left sitting) shall be called, by
the king's good will and utmost endeavour, as seldome as may be; and
then for his own ends: for it will soon return to that, let no man hope
otherwise, whatever law or provision be made to the contrarie. For it
is only the king's right, he will say, to call a Parliament; and this he
will do most commonly about his own affairs rather than the kingdom's, as will appear planely so soon as they are called. For what will
their business then be and the chief expence of their time, but an endless tugging between right of subject and royal prerogative, especially
about the negative voice, militia, or subsidies, demanded and oft-
times extorted without reasonable cause appearing to the Commons,
who are the only true representatives of the people; but will be then

---

2. The House of Nassau was a powerful European family with possessions in Germany
and Holland.

mingled with a court-faction; besides which, within their own walls, the sincere part of them who stand faithful to the people, will again have to deal with two troublesome counter-working adversaries from without; meer creatures of the king, temporal and spiritual lords, made up into one house, and nothing concerned with the people's libertie. If these prevail not in what they please, though never so much against the people's interest, the Parliament shall be soon disolved, or sit and do nothing; not suffered to remedie the least greevance, or enact aught advantageous to the people. Next, the Councel of State shall not be chosen by the Parliament, but by the king, still his own creatures, courtiers and favorites; who will be sure in all their counsels to set their maister's grandure and absolute power, in what they are able, far above the people's libertie. I denie not but that there may be such a king, who may regard the common good before his own, may have no vicious favorite, may hearken only to the wisest and incorruptest of his Parliament; but this rarely happens in a monarchie not elective; and it behoves not a wise nation to committ the summ of their well-being, the whole state of their safetie to fortune. And admitt, that monarchy of itself may be convenient to some nations, yet to us who have thrown it out, received back again, it cannot but prove pernicious. For the kings to come, never forgetting their former ejection, will be sure to fortifie and arme themselves sufficiently for the future against all such attempts heerafter from the people: who shall be then so narrowly watched and kept so low, as that besides the loss of all their blood, and treasure spent to no purpose, though they would never so fain and at the same rate, they never shall be able to regain what they now have purchasd and may enjoy, or to free themselves from any yoke imposed upon them. Besides this, a new royal-revenue must be found; which being wholly dissipated or bought by private persons, or assigned for service done, and especially to the Armie, cannot be recovered without a general confusion to men's estates, or a heavy imposition on all men's purses.

Not to speak of revenges and offences that will be remembered and
returned, not only by the chief person, but by all his adherents; accounts and reparations that will be required, suites and inditements,
who knows against whom, or how many, though perhaps neuters, if
not to utmost infliction, yet to imprisonment, fines, banishment; or
if not these, yet disfavour, discountnance, disregard and contempt
on all but the known royalist, or whom he favours, will be plentious;
whatever conditions be contrived or trusted on.

Having thus far shewn with what ease we may now obtain a free
Commonwealth, and by it with as much ease all the freedom, peace,
justice, plentie that we can desire, on the other side, the difficulties,
troubles, uncertainties nay rather impossibilities to enjoy these things
constantly under a monarch, I will now proceed to shew more particularly wherein our freedom and flourishing condition will be more
ample and secure to us under a free Commonwealth than under
kingship.

The whole freedom of man consists either in spiritual or civil libertie. As for spiritual, who can be at rest, who can enjoy any thing in
this world with contentment, who hath not libertie to serve God and
to save his own soul, according to the best light which God hath
planted in him to that purpose, by the reading of his revealed will and
the guidance of his holy spirit? That this is best pleasing to God, and
that the whole Protestant Church allows no supream judge or rule
in matters of religion, but the scriptures, and these to be interpreted
by the scriptures themselves, which necessarily inferrs liberty of conscience, hath been heertofore proved at large in other treatises, and
might yet further by the publick declarations, confessions, and ad-
monitions of whole Churches and States, obvious in all historie, since
the Reformation. He who cannot be content with this libertie to
himself, but seeks violently to impose what he will have to be the only
religion, upon other men's consciences, let him know, bears a minde
not only unchristian and irreligious, but inhuman also and bar-

barous. And in my judgement civil States would do much better, and remove the cause of much hindrance and disturbance in publick affairs, much ambition, much hypocrisie and contention among the people, if they would not meddle at all with Ecclesiastical matters, which are both of a quite different nature from their cognisance, and have their proper laws fully and compleatly with such coercive power as belongs to them, ordained by Christ himself and his apostles. If there were no medling with Church matters in State counsels, there would not be such faction in chusing members of Parliament, while every one strives to chuse him whom he takes to be of his religion; and everie faction hath the plea of God's cause. Ambitious leaders of armies would then have no hypocritical pretences so ready at hand to contest with Parliaments, yea to dissolve them and make way to their own tyrannical designs. In summ, I verily suppose there would be then no more pretending to a fifth monarchie of the saints:[3] but much peace and tranquillitie would follow; as the United Netherlands have found by experience: who while they persecuted the *Arminians*, were in much disquiet among themselves, and in danger to have broke asunder into a civil war; since they have left off persecuting, they have lived in much more concord and prosperitie. And I have heard from *Polanders* themselves, that they never enjoyed more peace, than when religion was most at libertie among them; that then first began their troubles, when that king by instigation of the Jesuites began to force the *Cossaks* in matters of religion. This libertie of conscience, which above all other things ought to be to all men dearest and most precious, no government more inclinable not only to favour but to protect, than a free Commonwealth; as being most magnanimous, most fearless and confident of its own fair proceed-

3. The Fifth Monarchists believed there was to be a fifth universal monarchy on earth under the personal reign of Jesus Christ and thought it their duty to bring this to pass. They plotted unsuccessfully to blow up Oliver Cromwell at Whitehall and later plotted against his son, Richard. In 1661 the Fifth Monarchists were to launch an abortive uprising against Charles II.

ings. Whereas kingship, though looking big, yet indeed most pusill-
lanimous, full of fears, full of jealousies, startled at everie umbrage, as
it hath been observed of old to have ever suspected most and mistrusted them who were in most esteem for vertue and generositie of
minde, so it is now known to have most in doubt and suspicion them
who are most reputed to be religious. Q. *Elizabeth*, though herself
accounted so good a Protestant, so moderate, so confident of her subjects' love, would never give way so much as to Presbyterian reformation in this land, though once and again besought as *Cambden*
relates,[4] but imprisoned and persecuted the verie proposers thereof,
alleaging it as her minde and maxim unalterable, that such reformation would diminish regal authoritie. What libertie of conscience can
we then expect from others far worse principled from the cradle,
trained up and governed by Popish and *Spanish* counsels, and on such
depending hitherto for subsistence.[5] For they hear the Gospel speaking much of libertie, a word which monarchie and her bishops both
fear and hate; but a free Commonwealth both favours and promotes;
and not the word only, but the thing itself.

The other part of our freedom consists in the civil rights and ad-
vancments of every person according to his merit: the enjoyment of
those never more certain, and the access to these never more open,
than in a free Commonwealth. And both in my opinion may be best
and soonest obtained, if every county in the land were made a little
commonwealth, and their chief town a city, if it be not so called alreadie; where the nobilitie and chief gentry may build, houses or
palaces, befitting their qualitie, may bear part in the government,

4. William Camden, *The History of The most Renowned and Victorious Princess Elizabeth,
Late Queen of England,* 3d ed., thus (London, 1675), 107, 191–92, but see p. 421. The Latin edition first appeared in 1615.

5. Elizabeth's predecessor and half-sister Mary Tudor, the daughter of a Spanish princess,
launched a campaign against Protestant heretics when she became queen. Charles II was the
son of a French Catholic and received support during his years in exile from the French court.

make their own judicial lawes, and execute them by their own elected judicatures, without appeal, in all things of civil government between man and man. So they shall have justice in their own hands, and none to blame but themselves, if it be not well administered. In these imployments they may exercise and fit themselves till their lot fall to be chosen into the Grand Councel, according as their worth and merit shall be taken notice of by the people. As for controversies that shall happen between men of several counties, they may repair, as they do now, to the capital citie. They should have heer also schools and academies at their own choice, wherein their children may be bred up in their own sight to all learning and noble education, not in grammar only, but in all liberal arts and exercises. This would soon spread much more knowledge and civilitie, yea religion, through all parts of the land: this would soon make the whole nation more industrious, more ingenuous at home, more potent, more honourable abroad. To this a free Commonwealth will easily assent; (nay the Parliament hath had alreadie some such thing in designe) for of all governments a Commonwealth aim most to make the people flourishing, vertuous, noble and high spirited. Monarchs will never permitt: whose aim is to make the people, wealthy indeed perhaps and well-fleeced for their own shearing, and for the supply of regal prodigalitie; but otherwise softest, basest, viciousest, servilest, easiest to be kept under; and not only in fleece, but in minde also sheepishest; and will have all the benches of judicature annexed to the throne, as a gift of royal grace that we have justice done us; whenas nothing can be more essential to the freedom of a people, than to have the administration of justice and all publick ornaments in their own election and within their own bounds, without long traveling or depending on remote places to obtain their right or any civil accomplishment; so it be not supream, but subordinate to the general power and union of the whole Republick. In which happie firmness as in the particular above mentioned, we shall also far exceed the United Provinces, by having, not many sovranties in one Commonwealth, but many Commonwealths under one sovrantie.

I have no more to say at present: few words will save us, well considered; few and easie things, now seasonable done. But if the people be so affected, as to prostitute religion and libertie to the vain and groundless apprehension, that nothing but kingship can restore trade, not remembering the frequent plagues and pestilences that then wasted this citie, such as through God's mercie, we never have left since, and that trade flourishes no where more, than in the free Commonwealths of *Italie*, *Germanie* and the Low Countreys, before their eyes at this day, yet if trade be grown so craving and importunate through the profuse living of tradesmen that nothing can support it, but the luxurious expences of a nation upon trifles or superfluities, so as if the people generally should betake themselves to frugalitie, it might prove a dangerous matter, least tradesmen should mutinie for want of trading, and that therefor we must forgoe and set to sale religion, libertie, honour, safetie, all concernments divine or human to keep up trading, if lastly, after all this light among us, the same reason shall pass for current to put our necks again under kingship, as was made use of by the *Jews* to return back to *Egypt* and to the worship of their idol queen, because they falsly imagined that they then lived in more plenty and prosperitie, our condition is not sound but rotten, both in religion and all civil prudence; and will bring us soon, the way we are marching, to those calamities which attend always and unavoidably on luxurie, that is to say all national judgments under forein or domestic slaverie: so far we shall be from mending our condition by monarchizing our government; whatever new conceit now possesses us. However with all hazard I have ventured what I thought my dutie, to speak in season, & to forewarn my country in time: wherein I doubt not but there be many wise men in all places and degrees, but am sorrie the effects of wisdom are so little seen among us. Many circumstances and particulars I could have added in those things whereof I have spoken, but a few main matters now put speedily into execution, will suffice to recover us, and set all right: and there will want at no time who are good at circumstances, but men who set their mindes on main matters and sufficiently urge them, in these most difficult times I finde not many. What I have spoken, is the language of the good old cause: if it seem strange to any, it will not seem more strange, I hope, than convincing to backsliders. Thus much I should perhaps have said, though I were sure I should have spoken only to trees and stones, and had none to cry to, but with the Prophet, *O earth, earth, earth:* to tell the verie soil itself what God hath determined of *Coniah* and his seed forever.[6] But I trust, I shall have spoken perswasion to abundance of sensible and ingenuous men: to some perhaps, whom God may raise of these stones, to become children of libertie; and may enable and unite in their noble resolutions to give a stay to these our ruinous proceedings and to this general defection of the misguided and abused multitude.

THE END.

6. Coniah, or Jehoichin, the ill-fated king of Judah, had been appointed to his throne by the Babylonians in 598. His brief three-month reign was ended when the Babylonian king decided to carry him off as a hostage. The prophet Jeremiah prophesied the end of his rule and of his dynasty. His fate is described in II Kings and II Chronicles.